Haynes

Restoration Manual

Classic Car Interiors

Cleaning • Refurbishing • Replacing

Kim Henson

First published in 1995 as Classic Car Interior Restoration Guide
Reprinted in 1997
Reprinted in 1999 as Classic Car Interiors Restoration Manual, with new cover and minor text amendments
Reprinted 2001, 2003, 2004 and 2006

Published by:
Haynes Publishing
Sparkford, Yeovil, Somerset BA22 7JJ, UK
Tel: 01963 442030 Fax: 01963 440001
Int. tel: +44 1963 442030 Int. fax:+44 1963 440001
E-mail: sales@haynes.co.uk
Website: www.haynes.co.uk

A catalogue record for this book is available from the British Library

ISBN 1 85010 932 X

Printed and bound in Great Britain by J.H. Haynes & Co. Ltd, Sparkford

Contents

Using this book

The layout of this book has been designed to be both attractive and easy to follow during practical work. However, to obtain maximum benefit from the book it is important to note the following points:

1. The captions to the illustrations are an integral part of the text, and should be read as such.

2. All references to the left or right of the vehicle are from the point of view of somebody standing behind the car looking forwards.

3. Being a general guide to vehicle interior restoration procedures, the book does not include specific information for individual models, and it is therefore strongly recommended that the appropriate manufacturer's manual and/or Haynes Owners Workshop Manual for your vehicle be used as a reference, in particular for any special procedures needed when removing items of trim, etc.

4. SAFETY FIRST! Boring though it may be considered, especially when you really want to get on with the job, your safety and that of those around you must ALWAYS be your foremost consideration. This can be ensured by the use of correct procedures, and it is essential that you read and understand the SAFETY FIRST information given in this book before undertaking any of the practical tasks described.

Foreword

When my friend and regular *Practical Classics* contributor, Kim Henson, told me he was working on this book, my first reaction was that I would definitely want a copy when it is published! That's because trim work really is a blank area to me. I'm perfectly happy cutting and bending bits of metal, and I take a positive delight in restoring a neglected mechanical component to full health, but show me a sad-looking seat, or a drooping, discoloured headlining, and I'll run a mile! And I know that many other practical enthusiasts are the same.

It's all a question of confidence, really, and that's where I think *Classic Car Interior Restoration Guide* scores. With his clear, easy-to-follow style, Kim explains in simple straightforward terms how to go about the various jobs.

He starts with the basics – cleaning, tidying and preserving what's already there, as not everyone immediately wants to do a complete internal overhaul, and many people actually prefer honest, slightly worn leather to immaculate new stuff. Being encouraged by the good results achieved relatively quickly and easily with these simple jobs, the beginner will soon want to have a go at the more involved tasks.

In the pages that follow, Kim shows you how to do absolutely everything that's likely to need doing. As far as I know, this is the first time that *all* these techniques have been included in one volume. From dismantling and structural rectification (there's no point putting a new, pristine set of carpets in a car with a rusty floor) to repairing seats and seat frames, restoring interior woodwork, making and fitting carpets, and repairing/recolouring vinyl and leather. And, removing and replacing the headlining, the job I always reckon is the hardest of all to do neatly, is made to seem almost like child's play!

All the important background information is included – things like choosing and buying tools and materials, and advice on deciding whether something is worth refurbishing or should really be replaced.

As with almost everything, though, there are one or two aspects of trimming which are better tackled by professionals. Where this is the case, Kim isn't afraid to advise against DIY, but gives plenty of advice on how to minimize the amount of paid-for labour required.

Happy trimming!

Peter Simpson
Associate Editor of *Practical Classics* and *Popular Classics* magazines and Technical Editor of *Classic Car Weekly* magazine

Acknowledgements

During the course of writing this book I have received help, advice and encouragement from many people and organizations, without which there would have been no book. It is only fair now to offer my sincere thanks to them all.

First of all, for valued technical guidance on machinery and products, I must thank John Carpenter, of John Carpenter Sewing Machine Services in Bridgwater; Jim Monaghan, of Dunlop Adhesives in Birmingham; and Oakwood (hardwood suppliers) in Sherborne, Dorset.

For the provision of tools and products for photography, my grateful thanks to Tim Ward, Managing Director of Bradleys Plastic Finishers in Stowmarket, Suffolk (Vinylkote); Dave Edbrooke, Marketing Manager of The Eastwood Company, in Yate, near Bristol (tools and equipment, etc.); Damian Halliwell of Frost Auto Restoration Techniques Ltd, in Rochdale (tools and equipment, etc.); Jay Products, in Cleveland, Ohio, USA ('wood graining' kit); Loctite UK in Welwyn Garden City (Vinyl Bond Adhesive), and both Ian Woolstenholmes and Duncan Allen, of 'Woolies' – I. and C. Woolstenholmes Ltd – in Market Deeping, near Peterborough (leather renovation kit, carpet fasteners and hood fixings).

For a fascinating day at the long-established premises of hide suppliers Connolly Leather, in Wimbledon, I must thank Tony Hussey and Renovation Department Manager, John Humpage.

Thanks also to Peter Simpson, currently Associate Editor of *Practical Classics* and *Popular Classics* magazines and Technical Editor of *Classic Car Weekly* magazine, for having enough faith in me to write the Foreword to this book.

To all the staff of N.R. Green Ltd, of Parkstone, I express my gratitude and apologies for 12 months of constant chasing and worrying over photographic processing.

I am very grateful, also, to classic car dealer Derek James, and his assistant Brett, for allowing me to attend their premises in Sherborne during the retrimming of a vintage Rolls-Royce in the coldest week of the winter 1993/94.

I must also mention my long-time friend David Lovering, who generously and willingly gave his time to help with various photographic shoots. His sense of humour and cheery outlook were a tonic when time was against us – and I shall be eternally thankful for that.

I owe a huge debt of gratitude to my long-suffering friends Simon Frazier and Anne Powys, of Auto Elegance, near Sherborne, Dorset. They have consistently helped me throughout the project, often at short notice and often when (I know) they had other urgent business to attend to. Yet, without fail, they always tried to help. For the many hours spent in their workshops, photographing and making notes on the various techniques, and for their assistance (and for all the coffee) I am extremely grateful.

My thanks, too, to Kevin Baggs, of Kevin Baggs Trimming, Bournemouth, for his kind assistance with some aspects of the 'Soft tops and sun roofs' chapter.

Last, but not least, I must mention all the members of my family, whose support and assistance enabled me to finish the project. These include father-in-law Peter, who kindly devoted many hours of his free time to helping with photographic sessions for the book, and my mother, who also donated to the cause endless evenings, tirelessly double-checking my own proof-reading, photograph numbering and so on.

Finally – for their patience in putting up with a man who has lived with this book for a year, and for having to do without his company for day after day and night after night while he attended to its every need – I must thank my wife and children.

There are a number of others who assisted me in various small but important ways, and I hope they will forgive my not listing all their names. To them all, I say, simply: 'Thanks for your help.'

Kim Henson

Introduction

The purpose of this book is to help you renovate the interior of your car by giving you the confidence to tackle jobs that perhaps you had never before dreamed of attempting. It takes you step-by-step through the stages required, enabling you to achieve and maintain results you will be proud of.

The interior of your car is, after all, a place in which you can spend a great deal of time, and travelling is a much happier experience if your surroundings are clean, tidy, sound and comfortable – as opposed to dirty, tatty-looking, falling apart and uncomfortable! This latter situation often creeps up unawares over a long period.

Traditionally, interior renovation is an area of restoration which has largely been left to the professionals, and frankly there are some aspects of the work which are still best dealt with by people with years of know-how and experience in their trade. Where I feel this to be the case, I have not hesitated to say so.

However, there are many aspects of interior renovation which do lend themselves to a considered DIY approach, and this can give enormous satisfaction when the finished job looks and feels right – particularly when you can reflect that it is all your own work.

Bearing in mind the principle – for most us – that very little in this life can be achieved without effort, I fully appreciate that many aspects of interior renovation require time, practice and large reserves of patience in order to get first-class results. If you are prepared to invest these three elements in the work, the potential rewards in terms of long-term job satisfaction (to say nothing of money saved) can be very great.

Throughout the book I have presumed you have no prior in-depth knowledge of vehicle interiors, and I have attempted to make the text and illustrations as user-friendly and informative as possible, so that you are not left stranded at any point.

I have included a cross-section of types and ages of car, and in the various sections and chapters you will find individual photographs, references and sequences depicting old and more recent vehicles spanning humble saloons, sports cars and luxurious executive flagships. In alphabetical order, models which appear include examples of Alvis, Austin, Bentley, Cadillac, Daimler, Fiat, Ford, Jaguar, MG, Morris, Rolls-Royce, Rover, Saab, Standard, and Triumph. These were chosen as guinea-pig vehicles, and it is important to appreciate that the restoration techniques employed on them apply equally well to other makes.

Indeed, whatever your car, I hope that this book will help to inspire and encourage you to tackle at least some aspects of renovating and maintaining the interior of it, and to achieve satisfaction from such work.

Safety first!

However enthusiastic you may be about getting on with the job in hand, do take time to ensure that your safety – and that of those around you – is not put at risk. A moment's lack of attention can result in an accident, as can failure to observe certain elementary precautions.

There will always be new ways of having accidents, and the following points do not pretend to be a comprehensive list of all dangers. They are intended, rather, to make you aware of the risks, and to encourage a safety-conscious approach to your work at all times.

Always read carefully and observe the operating and health-and-safety instructions relating to any materials and equipment you may use. The suppliers or makers should be contacted in case of doubt.

Essential DOs and DON'Ts

DON'T use ill-fitting spanners or other tools which may slip and cause injury.
DON'T attempt to lift a heavy component or equipment which may be beyond your capability – get assistance.
DON'T rush to finish a job, or take unverified short cuts.
DON'T allow children or animals in or around an unattended vehicle.
DO wear eye protection when using power tools such as drills, sanders, grinders, etc.
DO apply a barrier cream to your hands prior to undertaking dirty jobs – it will protect your skin from infection, as well as making the dirt easier to remove afterwards; but make sure that your hands aren't slippery.
DO keep your work area tidy – it is all too easy to fall over articles left lying around. In addition, dust and accumulated paper, etc., can be a fire hazard. If, during a work session, it gets to the stage where you cannot find anything, stop and have a clear up – for safety as well as for avoiding further frustration!
DO carry out work in a logical sequence and check that everything is correctly assembled and tightened afterwards.
DO take extreme care when working with glues and solvents, in particular ensuring that you do not work in a confined area, and that there is adequate ventilation. Take frequent breaks for fresh air and, when working alone, ensure that someone else checks periodically that all is well.
DO take very great care when working with knives, scissors, needles and other sharp implements. Make very sure that these are properly tidied away after use, and that they are stored out of reach of children, and where they are not likely to be a danger to people or animals.
DO keep a first-aid kit handy – AND ensure that you know how to use it.
IF, in spite of following these precautions, you are unfortunate enough to injure yourself, seek medical attention as soon as possible.

Fire

Remember that many substances (such as glues and solvents) used in renovating vehicle interiors are liable to ignite in the presence of naked flame. NEVER smoke when working with such substances. In addition, and especially if you have to disconnect any of the vehicle's wiring/electrical components, ALWAYS disconnect the battery's earth (ground) terminal BEFORE you start work. This is to avoid an electrical short-circuit which could cause a spark and start a fire. Remember, too, that a spark may also be caused by two metal surfaces striking against each other, or even by static electricity in your body under certain circumstances.

It is recommended that a fire extinguisher of a type suitable for fuel and electrical fires is kept handy at all times in the garage or workplace. Never try to extinguish a fuel or electrical fire with water.

If you should have a fire, DON'T PANIC! Direct your fire extinguisher at the base of the fire. If you still cannot halt the fire, clear all people and animals from the immediate vicinity, and straightaway telephone for the Fire Brigade. Briefly give any helpful details regarding the nature of the fire, especially if gases, petrol, adhesives or solvents (for example) are involved.

Fumes – and other dangers

Certain fumes are highly toxic and can lead to unconsciousness, and even death if inhaled to any extent. Petrol (gasoline) comes into this category, as do the vapours from certain adhesives and solvents, such as trichlorethylene. Any draining or pouring, or indeed general use of such volatile liquids should be done in a well-ventilated area.

When using adhesives, cleaning fluids and solvents, etc., carefully read the instructions. NEVER use any materials from unmarked containers – they may give off poisonous vapours.

Cellulose thinners should be treated with very great respect. Keep the lids on all cans, and keep the cans well away from heat and naked lights – the vapour will readily ignite (again – NO smoking!). Avoid skin contact, and keep away from eyes. The same applies to all adhesives, solvents, etc.

Take care, too, when working with paints/colouring agents. Make sure that the paints you are using do not contain isocyanates, or are otherwise poisonous. If they do (certain 'etching' primers and synthetic finishes are typical examples), you will need special breathing apparatus.

Even when spraying cellulose-based products, you must wear the correct protective mask (usually charcoal) and goggles specified for the product. Again, the spray fumes are highly inflammable.

The suppliers of paints, adhesives and solvents provide printed sheets giving health and safety information about their products. DON'T take chances. If in doubt, ask for such information, or contact the paint manufacturers direct. In all cases, only work in a well-ventilated area.

Never run the engine of a motor vehicle in an enclosed space, such as a garage/workshop. Exhaust fumes contain carbon monoxide, which is extremely poisonous. If you need to run the engine, always do so in the open air; or at least have the rear of the vehicle outside the workplace.

Mains electricity

When using electric power tools, inspection lamps, etc., which work from the mains electricity supply, always ensure that the appliance is correctly connected to its plug, and that, where necessary, it is properly earthed (grounded). DO NOT use such appliances in damp conditions, and in any event beware of creating a spark or applying excessive heat in the vicinity of vapours from fuel, solvents, adhesives, etc.

Make sure, too, that all cables, switches and the tools themselves are sound. Keep cables free from entanglement, and ALWAYS unplug tools immediately after use. After each working session, double check that no power tools are plugged in. Keep such tools under lock and key if children are liable to enter the working area when you are not around.

All this may sound obvious, but accidents happen all the time, and it would be sad if your restoration project turned out to ruin your life, or that of someone else, simply through lack of care.

Chapter 1

First steps

Restoring the interior of any car can be a long and complex operation, but many aspects can be successfully tackled at home, provided that a systematic, commonsense approach is followed. To achieve a high standard of finish, it is vitally important that the work is not rushed, and that meticulous attention is paid to detail.

There are some parts of the job for which it may be desirable/preferable to seek professional assistance, and these are highlighted in the appropriate sections throughout the book.

Also, it has to be accepted that for satisfactory and neat stitching of tough materials such as leather, carpets and the like, a domestic sewing machine is not up to the job. Even if you succeed in joining such materials using a machine designed for lighter duties, it is unlikely that the results will look as good as they should, nor are they likely to be as strong as they should. In truth, a domestic machine is really only suitable for tackling thin materials such as headlinings.

A heavy-duty industrial sewing machine is a necessity for many aspects of upholstery renovation, but they are expensive (1994 prices being within the range of £1,500 to £4,050 in the UK, plus VAT) and it is difficult to justify the outlay for occasional DIY purposes. Good quality used machines are available for about half the cost of new, but be careful if offered so-called 'reconditioned' machines, since many have been found to be old machines which have simply been resprayed to make them look good.

If you are only planning the restoration of one vehicle, an alternative to buying an industrial machine is to hire one (usually about £225 plus VAT for three months), or you could do as much of the preparation work yourself, entrusting the final stitching operations to professional upholsterers.

Most professionals will be only too pleased to help, providing you discuss things with them at the start of your work, so that you are all talking the same language in terms of how far you should go in stripping/preparing assemblies and materials. If you work together, along the same lines, you have a better chance of a result to be proud of.

Incidentally, there is no shame in asking for professional help on such aspects of interior work. If you are at all doubtful about your own abilities in terms of achieving a high standard of final finish, it would be better to admit it, than to struggle on and make a disappointing job of it.

This is particularly important when working with expensive materials such as leather. As already indicated, there are still areas where you can save professional time, and therefore your hard-earned cash, in terms of DIY dismantling, preparation and, of course, refitting to your vehicle.

TOOLS AND EQUIPMENT

It is perhaps surprising that there are very few essential tools required for most aspects of upholstery work. However, a few basic items will help you achieve a better job, and save you time in the process. It is therefore worth considering buying these at the outset. In general – with the notable exception of the industrial-type sewing machine – these are relatively small and inexpensive. Also, once purchased, if looked after properly, they should give many years of service, and consequently can be regarded as a long-term investment.

▲ *1.1. An industrial-type sewing machine really is a must for serious interior renovation work. You will need a well-built machine designed for heavy duty work. This Singer – an old favourite 211 model – is the sort of machine to look for. They can be obtained second-hand, although buying in this way can be something of a lottery. The alternative is to buy new, but prices range from around £1,500 to over £4,000. This is a great deal of money to most people, but taking your upholstery work to a professional is also expensive! You really do need a machine with a 'walking' foot (alternating presser) which actually moves the material being stitched past the needle. A reverse feed facility, for reinforcing the ends of seams, is also invaluable. To complement the machine, you will also need a range of special needles, and various 'feet' to suit different jobs. Trying to manage without these really is a waste of time.*

Most modern vehicle manufacturers employ a mixture of specially designed automatic sewing machines and the more conventional variety. The type of stitch most commonly used to produce good quality stitching on a wide range of textiles, as well as on leather and vinyls, is the lockstitch.

When choosing a machine for DIY use it is imperative to ensure that it is fully capable of carrying out all that you are going to want it to do. Not all industrial sewing machines are suitable for upholstery work. For example, a machine designed to sew shirt seams in quantity may be classed as an industrial machine, but it will not be capable of properly coping with the thicker materials employed in car interiors. It is perhaps obvious, but it is essential to ensure that you are easily able to obtain spares, accessories and service for the machine you are buying. Always enquire about these things before parting with your money. Reputable suppliers will be happy to help you in making the correct choice. Alternatively, and in view of the outlay involved, it is wise to seek the advice of someone fully conversant with the various types of machine and their respective capabilities.

From my conversations with several restorers who daily rely on their industrial sewing machines in the repair and renovation of vehicle upholstery, and with John Carpenter, of John Carpenter Sewing Machine Services, in Bridgwater, Somerset, it is evident that probably the most important – but often least considered – aspect of any sewing machine is its capacity, or the thickness of material that it can handle. This, as well as the variety of material and thread being used, will determine the needle type required. Consideration should also always be given to the finished appearance of the stitches, particularly on leather and heavy vinyls. A machine with an adjustable capacity is extremely useful, particularly when it is needed to tackle a wide range of applications.

Needles come in a variety of forms, each to suit a specific job, and machine suppliers will be able to provide the range of needles for the type of work you are likely to be tackling. The correct choice of needle is vital, not only for the finished appearance of the work, but also to ensure strength. For example, a fabric needle, which has a circular sharp point to separate the fibres in the material, is totally unsuitable for stitching leather, the stitches in which, when closely examined, appear to run diagonally. For working on leather, a cutting point needle should be used, such as a 'Tritip' or 'narrow wedge' type. These incorporate a cutting edge, or sharp cornered section, just behind the tip. This sharp section cuts very slightly into the leather, to leave some clearance for the thread. If a needle designed for fabric is used when stitching leather, the resulting high stress on the thicker material can literally cause it to fall apart at the seams!

The choice of thread is equally important, since each type has different properties. Full details of the ranges available can be obtained from the companies listed in the 'Useful addresses' section at the back of this book. It can be seen that a needle passing quickly through material causes a build-up of heat – the thicker the material, the greater the heat generated – and some threads, particularly nylon types, can literally melt in the eye of the needle. Therefore, for very high speed work, a cooler running polyester thread may be more suitable, depending on the application.

Lubrication of the thread can help to keep it cool, and for many applications a pure silicone lubricant is suitable; very little is required. Many machines have a built-in thread lubricating mechanism, incorporating a reservoir and adjustable feed, via a felt pad, directly on to the thread as it is fed to the workpiece. For some jobs, such as dealing with bindings having smooth surfaces, lubrication is imperative, or the bindings can stick like glue to the machine.

All those I consulted also agreed that by far the best type of sewing machine in terms of 'feed' is the 'walking foot' (alternating presser) variety, which literally steps forward on the work and climbs up different thicknesses of materials as it feeds the work along. As already mentioned, a reverse feed (auto backtacking) facility is also invaluable for reinforcing the ends of seams to prevent the stitching from unravelling at the ends. Useful other options include needle positioning, thread trimming, stitch counting and ply sensing.

Additional attachments are used to achieve special seams where uniformity of the stitching is paramount, and for ease of operation, for example as in piping (welting) around the edges of seats, etc.

All machines require lubrication of their moving components, and on the more expensive machines this is automatically carried out. In all cases, each time the machine is used, a lubrication service is advised comprising the topping up the automatic feed reservoir (where fitted), and/or applying oil to specific moving parts of the machinery.

Always follow the advice given in the machine's handbook. As a general rule, though, it is preferable to over-lubricate than to starve the machine of oil and risk damage or seizure! It is essential that only the correct type of sewing machine oil is used. General purpose light oils are often of too thick a viscosity.It is important also to appreciate that the lubricant for the works of the machine should not be used to lubricate the thread. Although the correct sewing machine oil is stainless, and may well cause no adverse effects if applied to the thread when working with leather, its use on fabrics is totally unsuitable as it wouldn't properly dry out.

In any event, after lubricating the machine it is wise to run a practice piece of sewing on soft rag through it, to soak up any excess oil, before attempting to sew valuable upholstery materials.

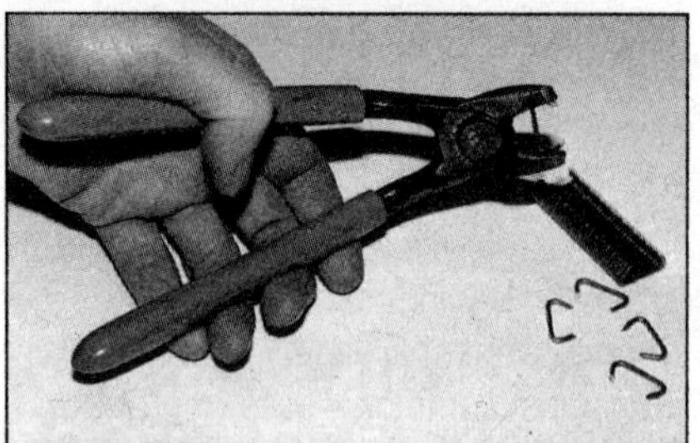

▲ *1.2. Hog ring pliers are essential for installing hog rings – the looped staples which connect seat covers to the frame of the seat, etc. These, supplied by Frost Auto Restoration Techniques Ltd, have grooved jaws to grip the hog ring, and an angled head for easy working. They are spring-loaded to grip the hog ring – useful if you need to stop work mid-way through installation! It is also possible to buy straight pliers, and types which are spring-loaded to remain in the open position.*

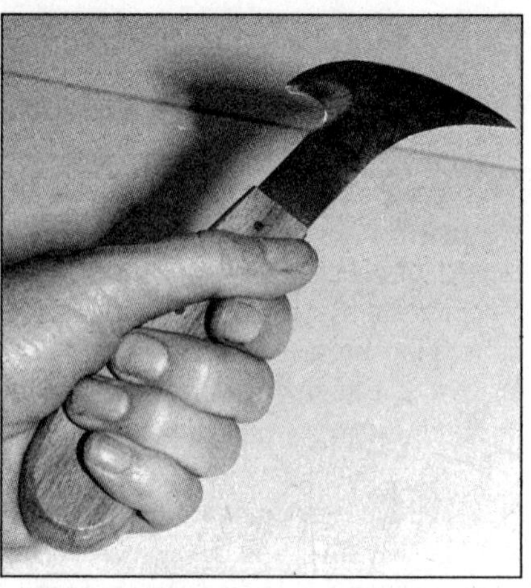

▲ *1.4. Cutting materials is part and parcel of upholstery work, and a trimming knife like this, obtainable from The Eastwood Company, can help to carry out cutting operations quickly and cleanly. TAKE GREAT CARE and NEVER leave such implements – which are extremely sharp – lying around where children or animals might find them.*

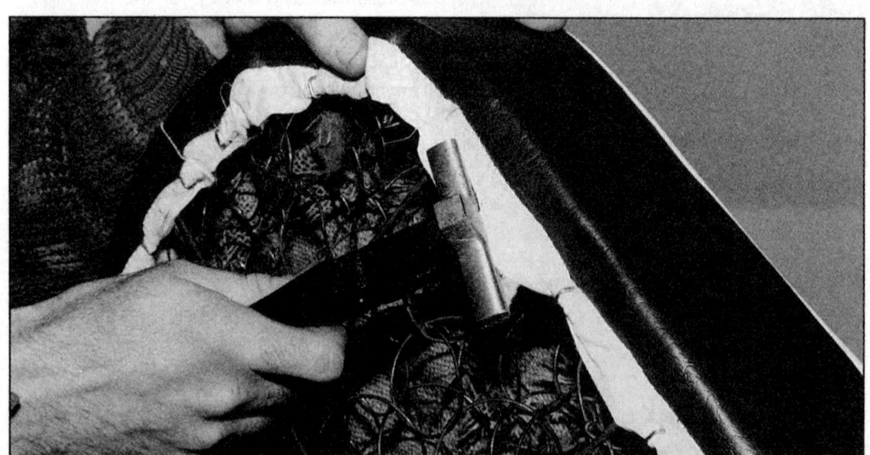

▲ *1.3. Upholsterer's pliers are also invaluable for gripping and stretching material (for example, on to seat frames). These, with 2.5-in wide, smooth, ribbed jaws (designed to stretch material without marking it) are supplied by Frost Auto Restoration Techniques Ltd. The square block forming part of the tool is intended as a fulcrum point for stretching material over edges.*

▼ *1.5. A good quality, sharp pair of scissors, kept only for upholstery work, is also a valuable addition to your tool kit. If you can run to a range of different-sized scissors, so much the better. It is also useful to have types with both straight and offset handles.*

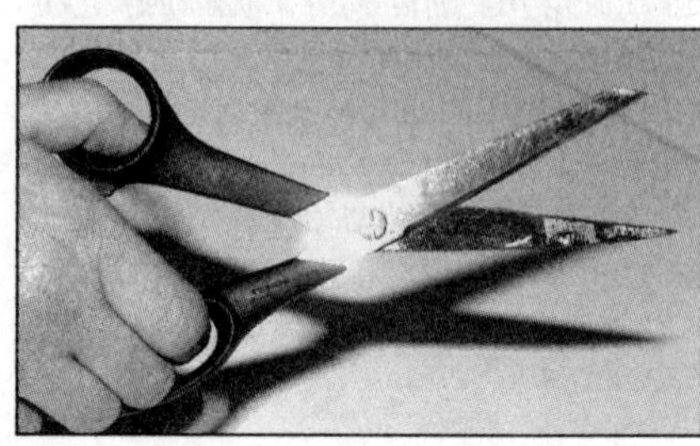

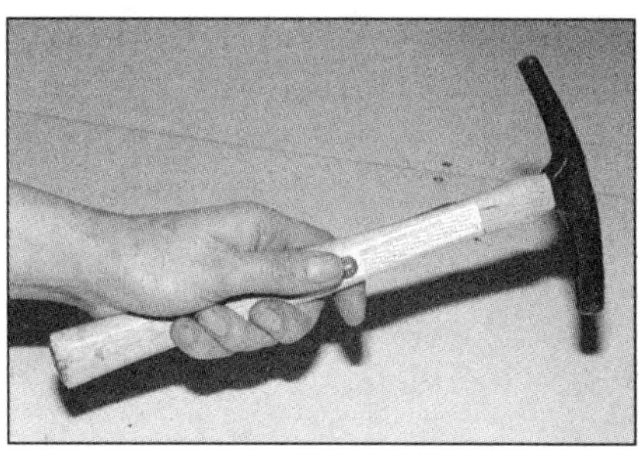

▶ 1.6. A magnetic trim hammer is another essential implement. This one was purchased from Woolies. The head is magnetic on one side, to collect the tack and hold its head during initial tapping in, while the other, non-magnetic, side of the head is used to drive the tack fully home.

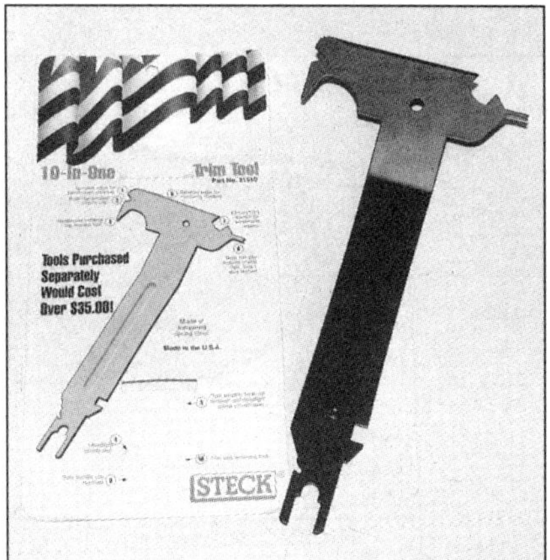

▶ 1.7. Universal trim tools like this – from The Eastwood Company – are available to tackle a range of jobs. This one is designed for cleaning up panel seams, removing door clips, releasing windscreen moulding clips, dealing with headlamp springs, removing door handles, taking off trim pads, tackling weather strip retaining clips, installing door trim clips, removing various mouldings, and incorporates a spanner for releasing screen wiper nuts!

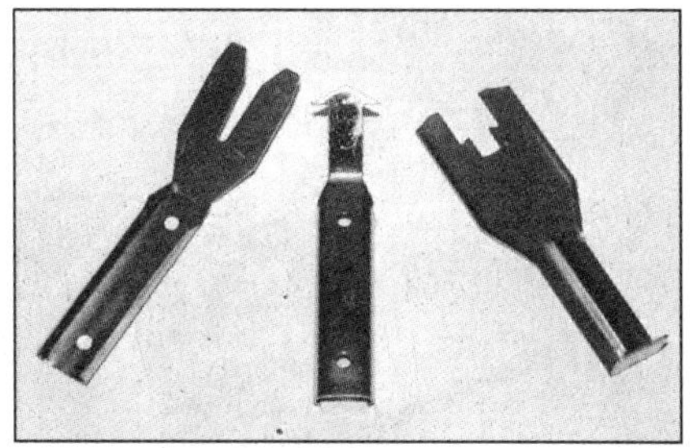

▶ 1.8. Removing trim panels without damaging the panels or breaking the clips can be a difficult business. This set of three tools, from Frost Auto Restoration Techniques Ltd, enables the clips to be removed safely and without damage, so that they can be stored for re-use on reassembly. This is, of course, especially important in cases where the original clips are scarce or unobtainable. From left to right, the tools shown here are designed to (1) enable door panel clips to be removed without damage, (2) safely take out windscreen moulding retainers and (3) allow window winder retainers to be withdrawn easily.

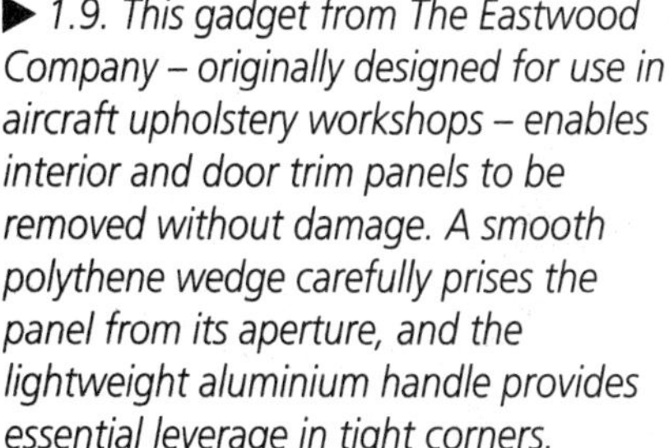

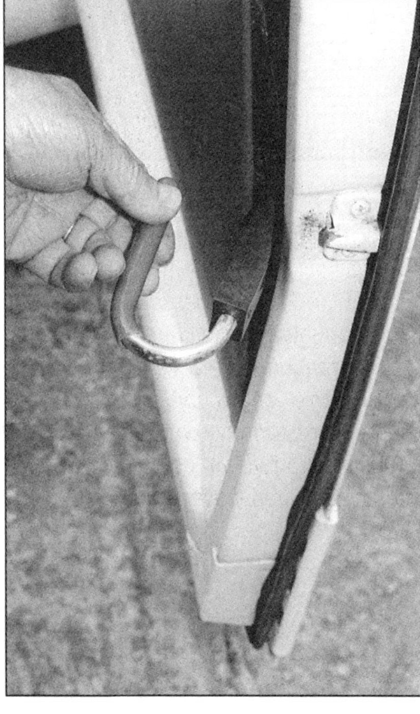

▶ 1.9. This gadget from The Eastwood Company – originally designed for use in aircraft upholstery workshops – enables interior and door trim panels to be removed without damage. A smooth polythene wedge carefully prises the panel from its aperture, and the lightweight aluminium handle provides essential leverage in tight corners.

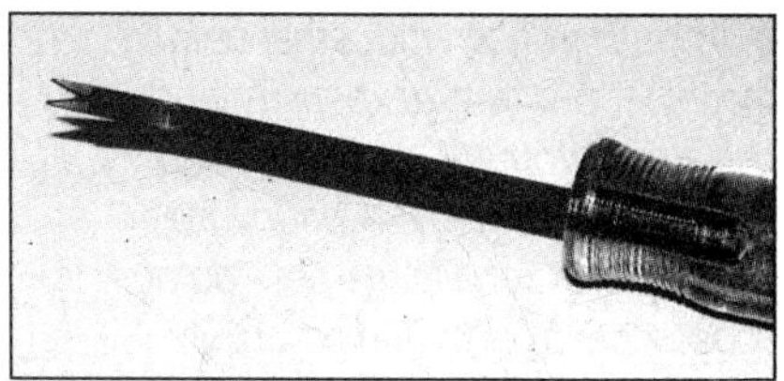

▲ 1.10. Dismantling of original seat assemblies, etc., is made much easier with a staple and tack remover like this one, available from Frost Auto Restoration Techniques Ltd. Most important, the use of such a tool avoids damage being caused to the underlying materials.

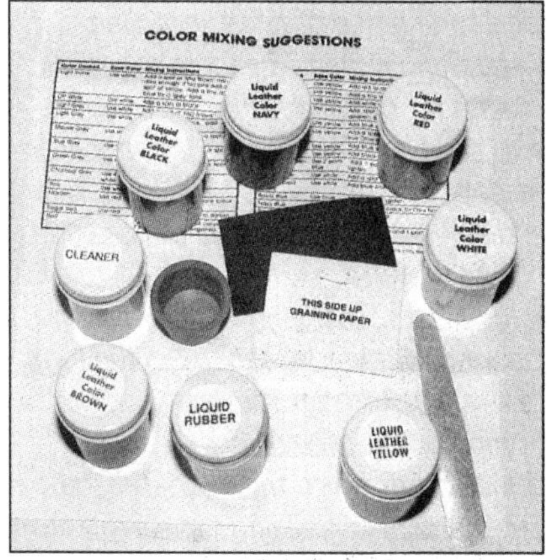

▲ 1.11. If the leather upholstery on your car is generally sound, but suffering from small cracks and tears, a leather repair kit like this one from The Eastwood Company could be the answer. The kit contains 1 oz bottles of cleaner, leather mender and colouring agents.

▲ 1.12. Frost Auto Restoration Techniques Ltd supply two kits; one is for repairing fabric, velour and carpet, and the other, for vinyl and leather. Each kit contains everything needed to apply the adhesives, mix the correct colours and even match the grain pattern to the original.

▶ *1.13. Hardly an industrial sewing machine, but this inexpensive and versatile automatic awl, from The Eastwood Company, is handy for tackling seat repairs, carpet edging, convertible hoods, and so on.*

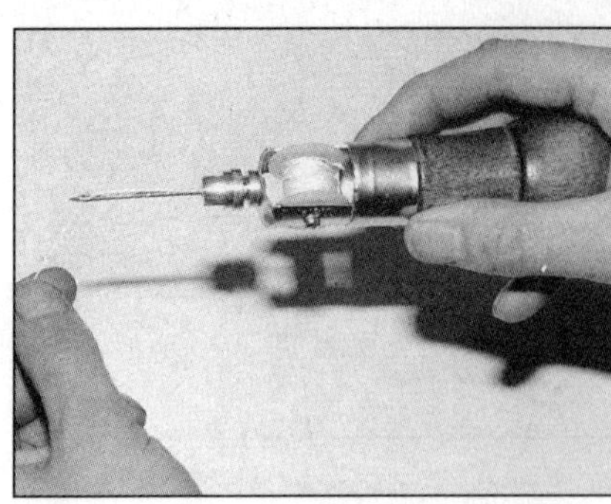

▶ *1.14. Another simple but extremely useful tool from Frost Auto Restoration Techniques Ltd is this Trim Regulator. This is a general purpose implement, ideal for a range of tasks, including distributing material beneath outer coverings, turning pleated covers inside out, and for locating holes in trim panels, carpets, etc. This one is 12 in long, $\frac{5}{64}$ in in diameter and has an eye at one end.*

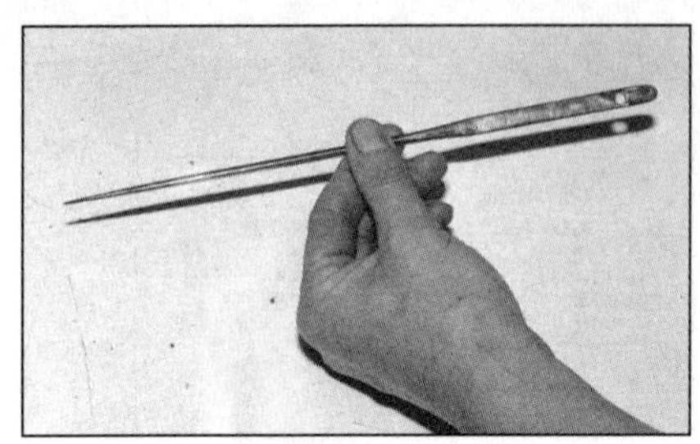

▲ *1.17. An adjustable hole punch, with a range of punch diameters, is useful for making holes in materials for installing eyelets, fasteners and so on. This one, from Frost Auto Restoration Techniques, provides a range of hole diameters from $\frac{5}{64}$ to $\frac{3}{16}$ in.*

▶ *1.15. Dashboards often suffer from cracking, but help is at hand in the form of a repair kit from The Eastwood Company. The kit includes six 'master' colours from which the desired shade can be created, graining papers to enable the original pattern to be duplicated, and full instructions.*

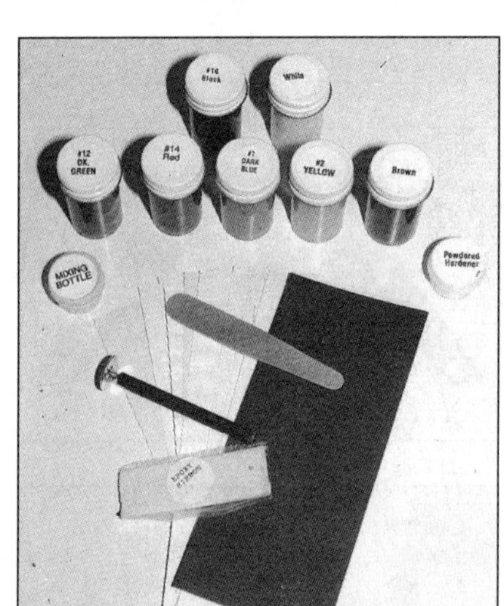

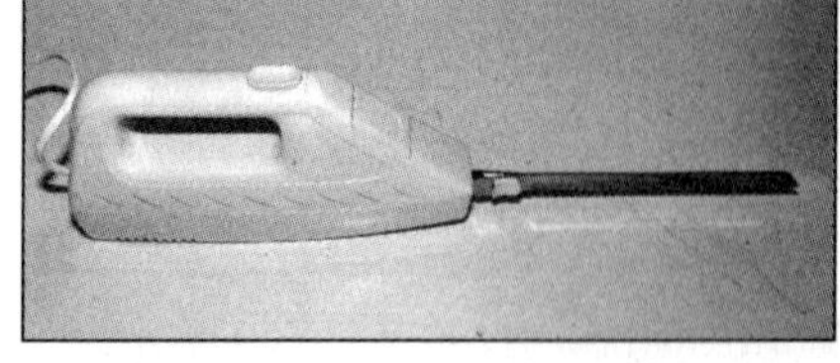

▲ *1.18. Unlikely as it may seem, an electric carving knife can be very helpful if you plan to do a lot of upholstery work. For example, it makes light of trimming foam seat bases to the correct profile and size.*

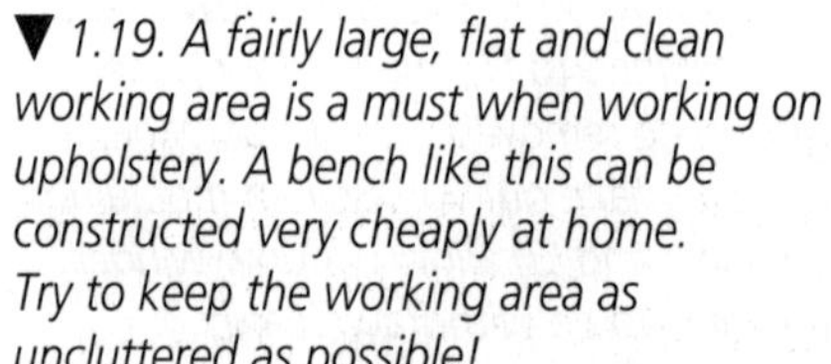

▼ *1.16. A staple gun is a very useful implement. In particular it can help when working single-handed, for initially securing headlining materials, etc., in position, prior to tacking in place. It is also an invaluable aid when securing covering material to trim panels.*

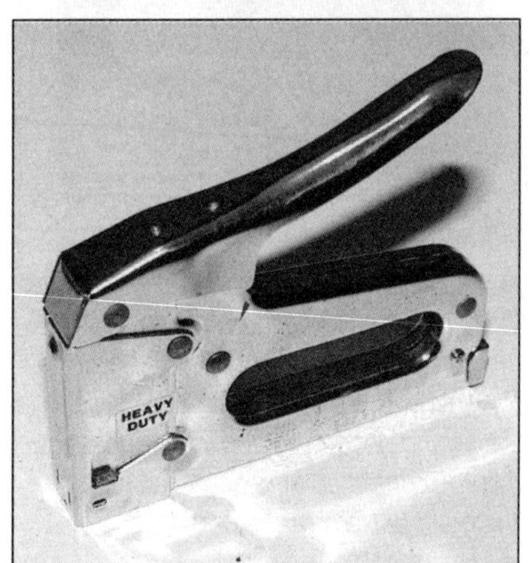

▼ *1.19. A fairly large, flat and clean working area is a must when working on upholstery. A bench like this can be constructed very cheaply at home. Try to keep the working area as uncluttered as possible!*

▶ *1.20. Measuring and marking implements are essential for trim work. A good quality set square and rule are necessary. Depending on the type and application, trimming materials can be marked with tailor's chalk, felt tip markers, artists'/carpenters' or Chinagraph pencils, or even ball point pens. Care should always be taken to ensure that the outer side of the material is not affected by markings made on the reverse.*

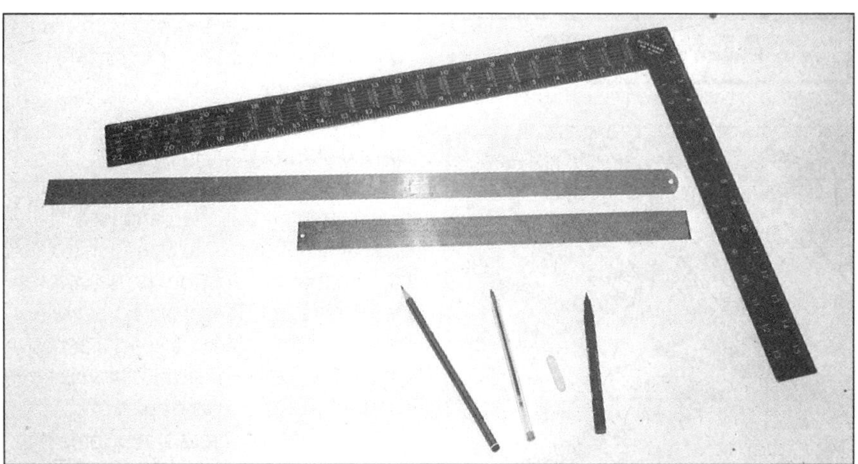

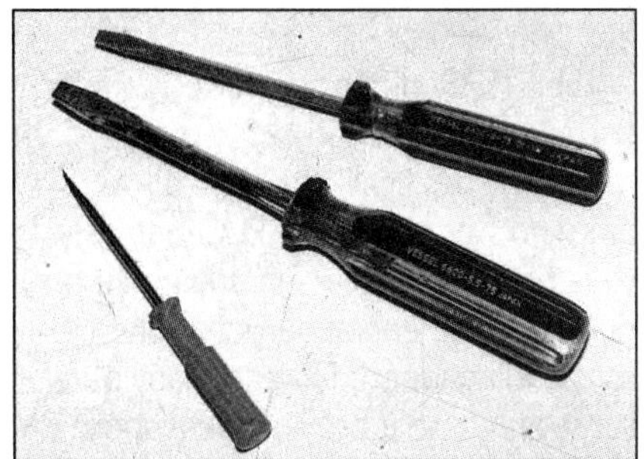

▲ *1.21. A range of screwdrivers is invaluable. In addition to the flat-bladed types shown, a selection of cross-head screwdrivers will help in a wide range of dismantling/refitting operations.*

▲ *1.22. These steel clips are helpful for holding materials together during sewing work, etc. Make sure that you buy only types with rounded corners; those with sharp angles can tear the material.*

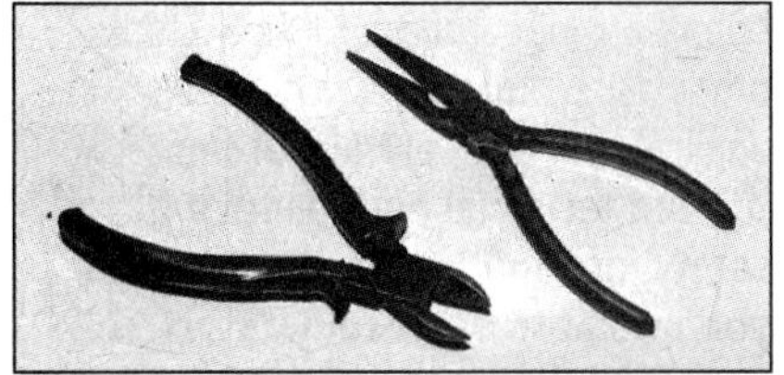

▲ *1.23. Pliers and side cutters are handy implements to have around when working on vehicle upholstery. They can be extremely useful when extricating reluctant fasteners, etc.*

▲ *1.24. Many older cars had mock wood grain effect finishes on dashboards and window surrounds. This kit, from Jay Products, of Cleveland, Ohio, USA, contains all the necessary tools and paint, plus full instructions, to enable wood grain patterns to be recreated.*

In addition to the items shown here, there is a wide range of other implements which can be useful – if not essential. The more interior work you attempt, the more you will appreciate a range of good quality tools to save you time and money. One example is a pair of special pliers, designed for the easy removal of J-clips (which often secure trim panels, dashboard trims, and so on) without causing damage to the clip or the panel.

Another useful implement is a tucking tool, to make installation of headlinings quicker and easier. Among other items which may be worth considering are a printer's roller – for eliminating air bubbles from materials glued to backing boards, etc.; dashboard crack repair foam; a set of hollow hole punches (plus a lead block to place on the workbench, beneath the material being holed); pins for holding material in place prior to final stitching; special needles for 'hidden' stitching in leather and other tough materials; vinyl and leather colouring agents; vinyl 'fusion' repair liquid; rubber moulding kits for forming new pedal rubbers and other rubber trim items, where these cannot be purchased ready-made.

Valuable, too, are the various cleaning agents (of which more later), Velcro (for holding carpets, etc., in place), and other kits for specific restoration tasks – for example, the various steering wheel restoration kits which are available.

ADHESIVES

▲ *1.25. Car upholstery renovation is not possible without the use of suitable adhesives. Traditional brush-on types are available in tins, while aerosol sprays are handy for smaller areas and for instant results. For high quality, lasting results, always ensure that the glue you buy is suitable for the purpose intended.* ***It is absolutely vital that adhesives are only applied in well ventilated areas. In any event, take frequent breaks in fresh air when working with glues.***

I am including adhesives under the general heading of 'Tools and equipment', since it really is not possible to tackle upholstery work without employing them. There is a very wide range of adhesives available, each with a specific purpose, and designed to cope with particular materials and operating conditions.

To give some idea of the potential complexity of choice, the Dunlop range alone comprises some 300 different adhesives! Among the many potential adverse factors which are relevant to the choice of adhesive are high temperatures and migration of the plasticizer within PVC materials.

Even in temperate climates such as the UK's, the temperatures immediately beneath a car roof panel – can, in high summer, reach 80° to 90° Celsius, and in parts of the United States and southern Europe (for example) temperatures can easily be 10° or more higher. Therefore the adhesives used (in both vehicle manufacture and any subsequent upholstery repair/restoration work) must be capable of maintaining their grip in such conditions.

In addition, where adhesives are applied directly to plain PVC, the plasticizer in the PVC can migrate to the glue, causing it to soften and lose its grip. Unless a closely woven fabric backing (normally cotton) is used on the PVC (to prevent direct contact between the PVC and the glue), a special adhesive which resists plasticizer migration is required. These two examples of potential problem areas show some of the considerations necessary.

In most cases, contact adhesives are suitable for upholstery work. Specific operating instructions vary in detail (always read them!), but in general, when using contact type adhesives, the two materials to be joined are separately pre-coated with the glue (typically sprayed or brushed on, or spread with a special applicator), which is then allowed to dry until tacky, usually after a few minutes. The surfaces to be joined are then brought together in the correct position, forming an immediate and strong bond between the two.

Fortunately, manufacturers such as Dunlop can provide specification sheets and printed health and safety information on all their products, which gives full details on their use and suitability for specific applications, as well as the all-important precautions which need to be applied in using them. To illustrate some of the differences between the various types of adhesives, it is worth looking at four popular products from the Dunlop range.

Dunlop's L107 is a natural rubber, multi-purpose upholstery solution which will cope with a wide variety of materials (including latex foam, polyether, polyester foam, rep cloth, upholstery fabrics, felt, scrim and leather), which may also be bonded to wood, hardboard and foam-rubber laminations. It is widely used in the motor industry for bonding headlining and sound deadening materials, and in seat manufacture as a pre-stitching adhesive, etc. Its resistance to temperature is classed by Dunlop as 'fair'.

The commonly used general purpose S1358 adhesive is a neoprene-based product, providing 'excellent' heat resistance, and suitable for joining rigid PVC sheet, good quality supported (i.e. closely woven cloth backed) PVC leathercloth, polyurethane foams of polyester and polyether types, leather, rubber sheet and extrusions, painted and unpainted metal, as well as rigid plastics. Its high temperature resistance makes it ideal for attaching vinyl roof coverings etc., to vehicles.

The S1588 nitrile adhesive is safe for use even in direct contact with PVC, and has been specifically developed for bonding soft plasticized PVC materials together, or to metals. In addition it can be used as a general purpose adhesive for bonding wood, felt and many other substrates, and it provides very good resistance to oil and grease.

Although not a DIY product, since it requires special spraying equipment, another product worth mentioning, as it has different characteristics and is widely used by car manufacturers, is S1762 polyurethane adhesive, a low viscosity sprayable product, which successfully bonds plasticized PVC and many other substrates where migration of the plasticizer is a problem.

A widely available product from the Dunlop Motorcare range is 'Formula 1' general purpose contact adhesive. Available in one litre tins, this is a non-drip, high strength product, providing a resilient bond across a wide range of materials, and providing good resistance to environmental extremes.

From the foregoing it will be seen that the choice of adhesives can be a bewildering one. Talk to the supplier before buying, and ask for advice on products recommended for specific applications. Also, **always obtain printed technical and health and safety information on the products you intend to use. Study this closely, and obey the instructions to the letter, for effective, long-lasting results and to avoid any potential dangers in working with the products.**

GENERAL UPHOLSTERY SUPPLIES

In order to carry out any vehicle interior renovation you will need some basic supplies, including, for example, covering materials for seats and trim panels, headlining fabric, carpet and a wide range of fixing materials, plus, where available, replacements for broken trim clips, etc.

It is worth noting that the covering materials you buy these days *should* be fire-retardant types, but always ask the supplier just to be sure. There may still be unused stocks of older, less safe materials on offer, at autojumbles for instance.

Most of these items you will acquire as you go along, and to start with, at least, you will be able to achieve a great deal using only a few types of fastener. In addition to the adhesives already described, it is useful to purchase a supply of tacks (the traditional, 'blue cut' variety are available in 1.5 oz packets), staples and gimp pins. By contrast with normal tacks, gimp pins have parallel shafts and smaller heads.

The smaller heads of the gimp pins make them less noticeable when used to secure visible areas of trim, and also, for example, enable them to easily fit into the necessarily narrow confines of a length of 'hidem' banding (more of which in Chapter 6 on Seats).

Fortunately, these days there are a number of specialist suppliers of upholstery materials and fasteners (the Appendix gives details), and most offer speedy mail order services as well as counter service.

Just one example is the long-established firm of Woolies (I. and C. Woolstenholmes Ltd) of Market Deeping, near Peterborough. Their wide range of products is listed in an illustrated catalogue which also gives helpful hints and tips on using the various items.

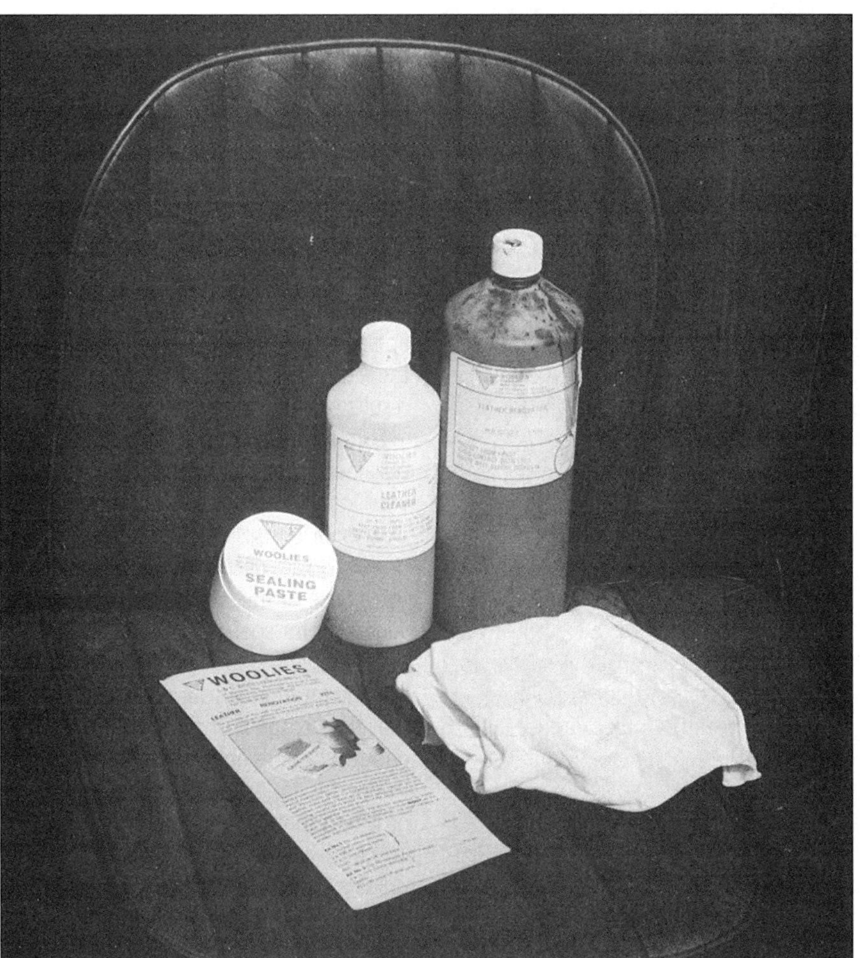

◀ *1.26. One of the products supplied by Woolies, to make life easier for DIY enthusiasts tackling vehicle interior restoration, is their leather renovation kit. It is easy to use and gives good results.*

CONCLUSIONS

With the exception of the industrial sewing machine, it is not necessary to spend a great deal of money on tools and equipment in order to achieve good results in restoring vehicle upholstery. A fairly modest initial tool kit can gradually be expanded as and when the need arises, to enable more complex jobs to be tackled.

At least as important as the range of implements available is enthusiasm and commitment to do the job right, combined with practice – on test pieces of work – of the various techniques required. The expression 'practice makes perfect' is especially true of upholstery work! With these attributes, anything is possible, and the satisfaction of having properly restored the interior of your car by yourself is reward in itself.

Chapter 2

Cleaning and tidying

The interior of any car past its first flush of youth can be improved with a little physical effort and, in most cases, without the need to spend a fortune. A basically sound interior can be restored to 'as new' condition in a few hours, and even those verging on the tatty can be brought up to an acceptable, usable standard by careful application of a little elbow grease.

Often it is only when the trim materials are properly cleaned that minor imperfections come to light. So, unless it is obvious that all the upholstery is so far gone as to need replacement, cleaning the interior can be regarded as the first essential step in restoration.

These days there is a wide choice of cleaning products – some multi-purpose and some more specific to their purpose. The most important point to note is that all work better if the manufacturer's application instructions are followed to the letter! In many cases the cause of poor results can be traced to incorrect use.

Suitable cleaning agents can be obtained from mail order firms, or from your local motor accessory shop. It is always wise to use products specifically designed for vehicle interiors, and to ask the advice of the supplier about suitability for specific jobs and materials before buying.

If the interior of your car is so dirty that the prospect of cleaning it is daunting, remember that once clean it will be far easier to keep that way, provided that routine attention is given in the future.

For a car in everyday use, a thorough clean-up of the interior every three to four months, with occasional vacuum-cleaning in between, will help to keep it looking good and feeling fresh. In addition, a clean interior is likely to survive far longer than a dirty one.

▶ *2.1. A useful first move is to remove all unwanted items from the car (it's amazing how they accumulate!) and to vacuum-clean all surfaces. Start by using a soft brush on the seats and dash, and any other easily marked surfaces.*

▲ *2.2. When vacuum-cleaning the carpets/rubber mats, ensure that all engrained grit is removed. It is tiny particles of grit like this which will eventually wreck a carpet, the sharp edges having a cutting effect on the fibres of the carpet.*

▲ *2.3. If the carpets are particularly grimy, a carpet shampoo can be applied to lift the dirt. Try to avoid getting the carpets over-wet in the process, and allow them to dry out thoroughly after cleaning. It may pay to have them professionally cleaned in situ, using a wet cleaning/suction process. Alternatively, machinery to do this job can be hired. This job alone can start to transform your car.*

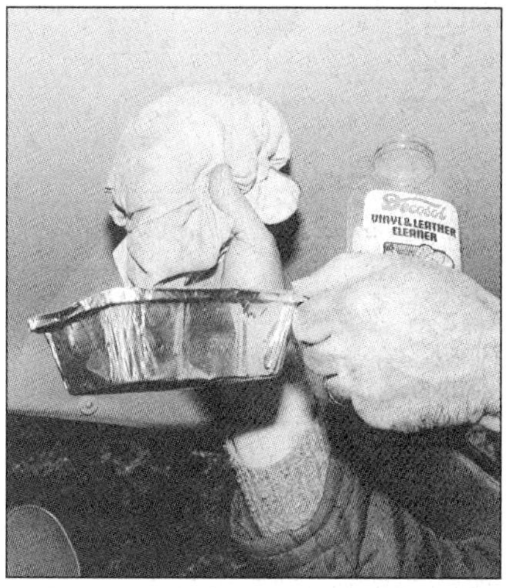

▲ *2.4. Headlinings (headliners) gradually become dirty as they age, and the process is hastened considerably if the occupants of the car are smokers. Proprietary cleaning solutions are available to 'melt away' the dirt. These vary from the brush-on/wipe off type shown here, to those applied by aerosol spray or hand pump. Be especially careful when cleaning cloth linings which have seen more than a few summers' service – they tend to get brittle and great care is needed if they are to survive the cleaning process. On the other hand, you may have little to lose, for if a lining is really badly stained, cleaning may have little effect, and replacement of the material may be the only sensible option. Plastic linings tend to survive better, and are more easily cleaned.*

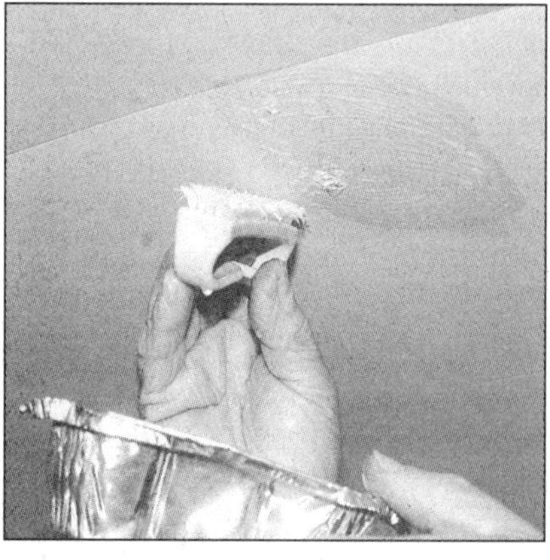

▲ *2.5. In cases where dirt is really engrained in the material, agitation with a nail brush can help to shift the grime. It may take several applications to remove the accumulated dirt of many years!*

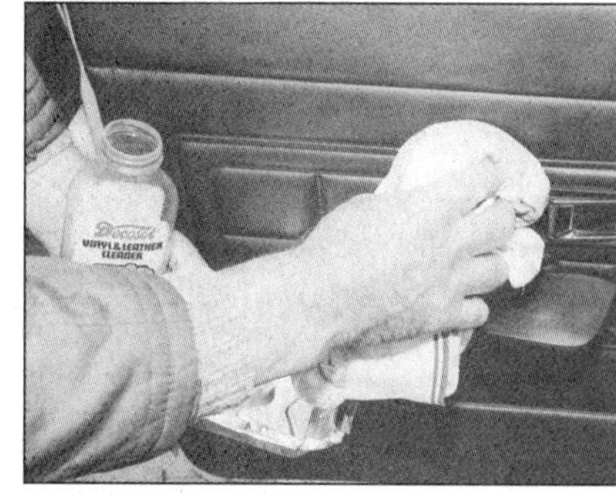

▲ *2.6. Trim panels are often darker in colour than headlinings (headliners), yet still get dirty and lose their original lustre. Cleaning processes are similar to those used on the headlining. Again, several applications may be necessary in order to remove years of accumulated dirt.*

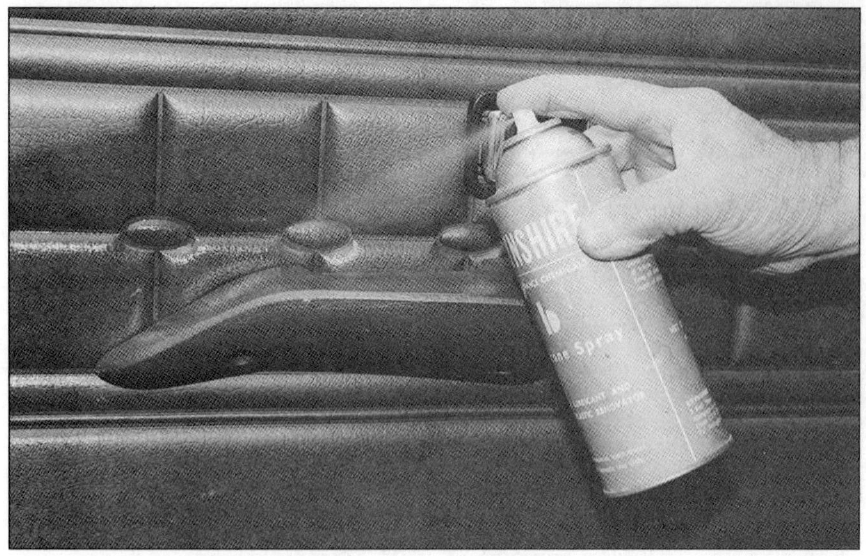

▲ 2.7. *Often, the cleaning process will temporarily dull the surface of, for example, vinyl trim panels. The original lustre can be restored by the use of a silicone spray, once the panel has fully dried.*

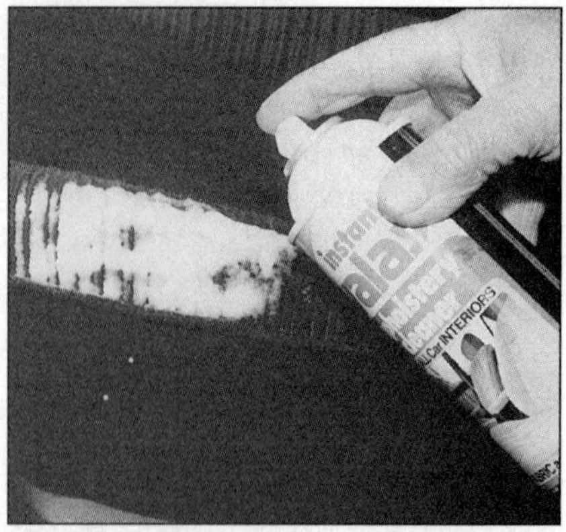

▲ 2.10. *Cloth-faced seats present their own problems when it comes to properly cleaning them. It can be difficult to purge all the dirt without soaking the material. However, one alternative is to use a special foam cleaning spray designed for fabric seat coverings. Another option is to have the seats professionally cleaned, using a machine which sprays cleaning agent on to the seat, then sucks it out again, complete with all the dirt. Such machines can also be hired for DIY cleaning.*

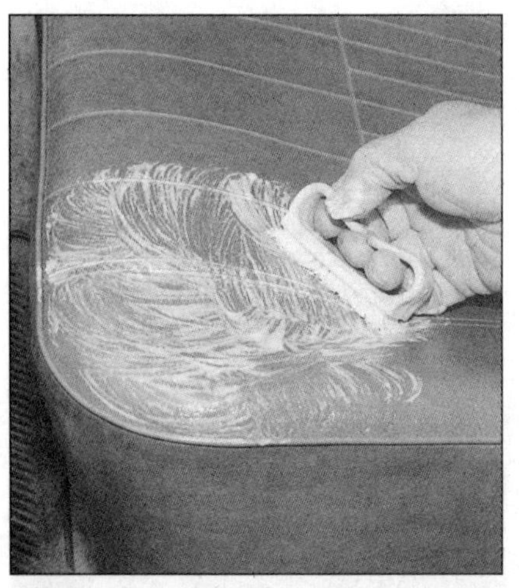

◀ 2.8. *Vinyl covered seats are normally quite easy to clean, using a brush-on/wipe-off solvent, or a spray-on type. If the seats haven't been cleaned for many years (or even decades!), several applications may be required. However, perseverance pays off, and eventually the surface will come clean.*

▲ 2.11. *The method of cleaning the facia will depend on the material from which it is made. Most cars built during the last 20 years or so employ fairly large areas of plastic, for which special cleaners are available. Many of these are also claimed to have a beneficial effect in terms of reducing the effect of ultra violet rays in sunlight. When cleaning/polishing a facia, avoid areas which could cause stray reflections, and therefore distractions, when driving. NEVER polish a steering wheel rim. If slippery, control of the car could be lost, with lethal consequences.*

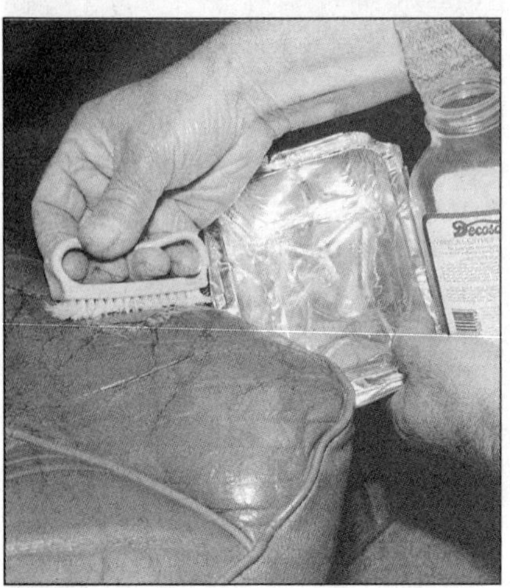

◀ 2.9. *As shown later in this book, leather upholstery requires special care to keep it supple and in good condition. However, some proprietary cleaning solutions are very effective in removing surface grime from hide upholstery. Before application, ensure that the product is suitable for use on leather, and always try it on a small unobtrusive area before setting to work on the whole of a seat – just to be on the safe side!*

▶ *2.12. Wood finish dashboards and door cappings, etc., which are in good condition, will benefit from periodic polishing, just as with any piece of furniture. Old fashioned wax polish can work wonders in providing protection and maintaining shine.*

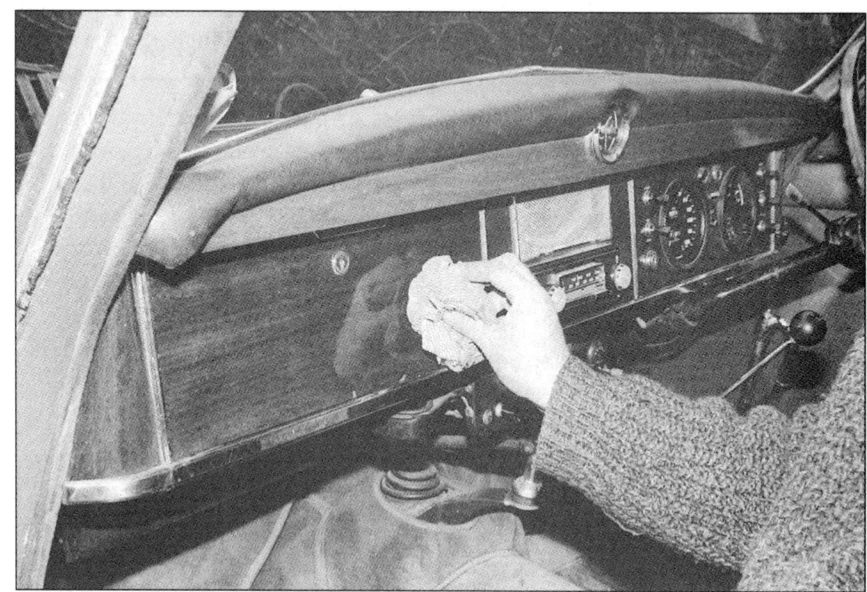

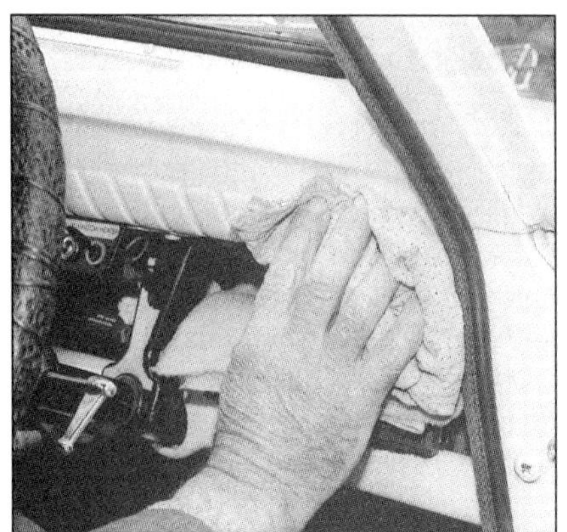

▲ *2.13. Many cars of the 1940s and 50s have large areas of painted metal on display. This can be maintained in a similar manner to exterior paintwork. Start by washing with a little warm water containing car shampoo, then rinse using a sponge and clean water, and finally dry the surface using a chamois or artificial leather.*

▲ *2.14. If the paintwork is dull, use a little fine liquid cutting agent to remove the oxidized top surfaces of the paint. Take it very easy in the vicinity of sharp edges, and never use coarse paste compounds in such areas, or the undercoat (where applied – it seldom was at the factory!) or bare metal can quickly show through. Wipe off the residue, then ...*

▲ *2.15. ... apply a wax polish, and buff up to give the surface a brilliant shine.*

▼ *2.16. Seat belts require special care and should not, under any circumstances, be subjected to harsh cleaning substances or processes. Use a mild solution of warm, soapy water only, and ensure that moisture doesn't enter the catches of inertia reel mechanisms, where fitted. Now is a good time to make a thorough examination of the entire length of the webbing on each belt. If the belts are at all frayed or otherwise damaged, replace them at once. Your life, or someone else's, may depend on it.*

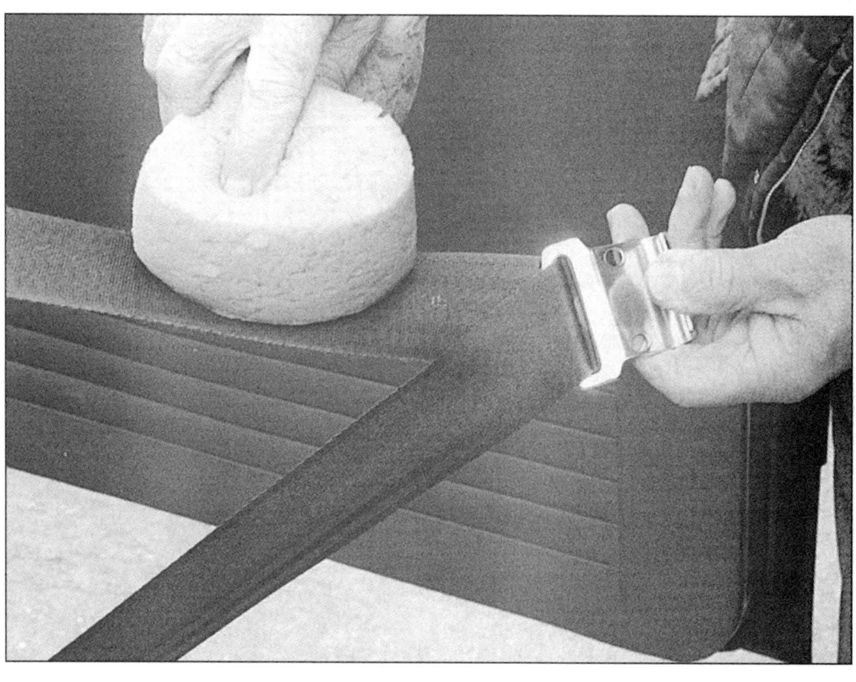

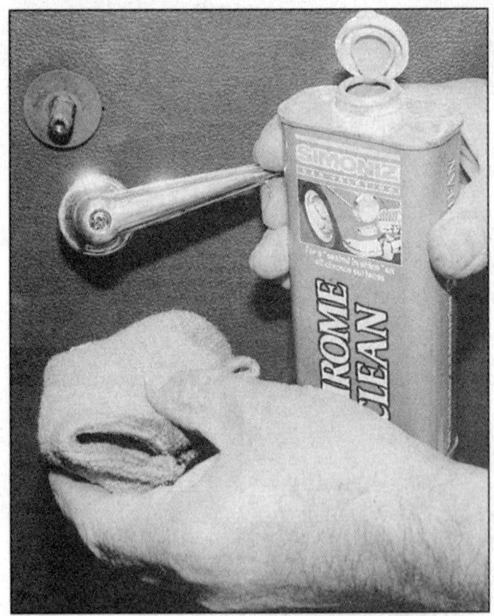

▲ *2.17. Many older cars have chrome-plated fittings adorning the interiors. If in good condition, these can be treated with a coat of wax polish, as for interior paintwork. However, if the surface has suffered from oxidation, it is best, where possible to remove the fittings and apply a little chrome cleaner. Such items are far easier to clean when out of the vehicle. Always use as mild a chrome cleaner as you can get away with, and avoid excessively abrasive types, or the chrome finish will disappear along with the dirt! Always apply a wax polish to seal in the shine after cleaning.*

▼ *2.18. Items such as sun visors are best removed from the car for proper cleaning. Attention to over-stiff mechanisms, etc., can be attended to at the same time.*

TIDYING

There are many jobs which come under the general heading of tidying, many of which will become apparent as the cleaning process takes place! Once the interior is clean, closely scrutinize every square inch of it, looking for imperfections and items requiring attention. Often, a little time spent now can avoid the necessity for more major remedial action at a later date.

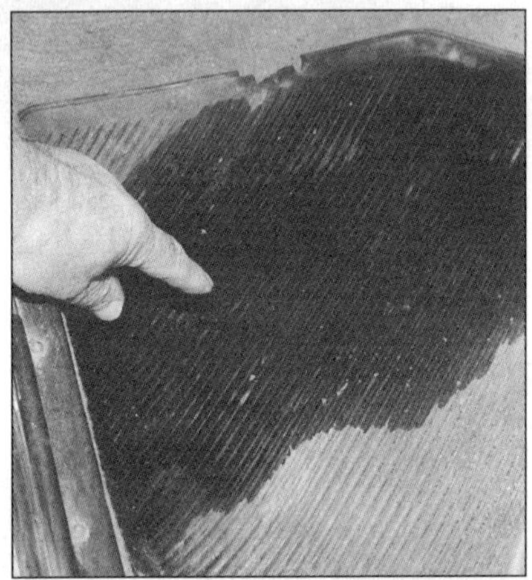

▲ *2.19. If, during the cleaning operations already described, you discover that the carpets/floor coverings are already damp, find out where the water is coming from, or the floor will eventually rust away unseen. Often the problem is a leaking screen seal or door aperture sealing rubber. Renew any suspect items.*

▲ *2.20. It is imperative to dry out any sections of the floor coverings which are wet, especially where absorbent underlay is present. An electrical fan heater is ideal for this, but always make sure that nothing can fall on top of the heater and block its air inlet and outlet vents, and that it is not placed too close to items of plastic trim which may distort in the heat.*

▲ *2.21. Having first dried them, always lift the floor coverings (if necessary, first releasing the securing screws along their edges), and examine the condition of the metalwork beneath. If any holes are found, obviously removal of the floor coverings and rectification of the damage by welding in new sections of metal will be necessary. If only surface rust is present, first use a wire brush and/or medium grit (220) silicon carbide wet or dry paper, used dry, to remove this.*

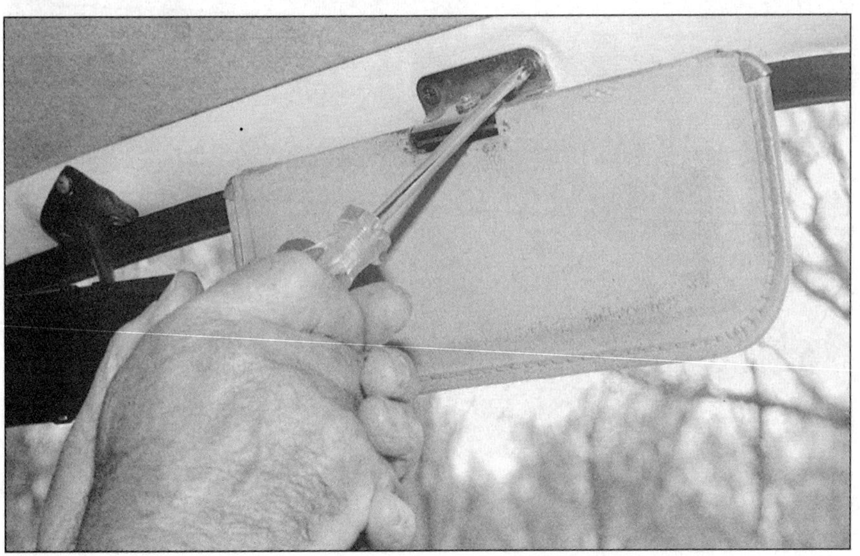

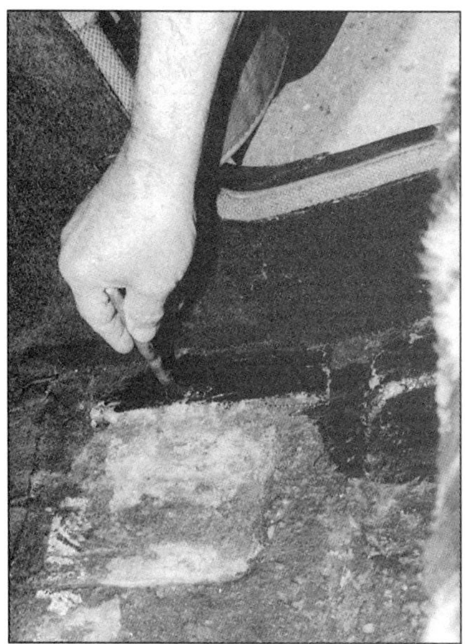

▲ 2.22. Use a vacuum cleaner and a tacky cloth to remove all dust and debris from the vicinity, then apply two or more coats of anti-rust paint, having first double-checked that the surface of the floor is completely dry. If you are aiming for complete originality, apply two coats of an anti-rust primer, followed by suitable top coats. If only small areas of the floor are affected, rectification can often be made merely by lifting and pulling back the relevant floor coverings. For more extensive work, the carpet and underlay are best removed completely from the car.

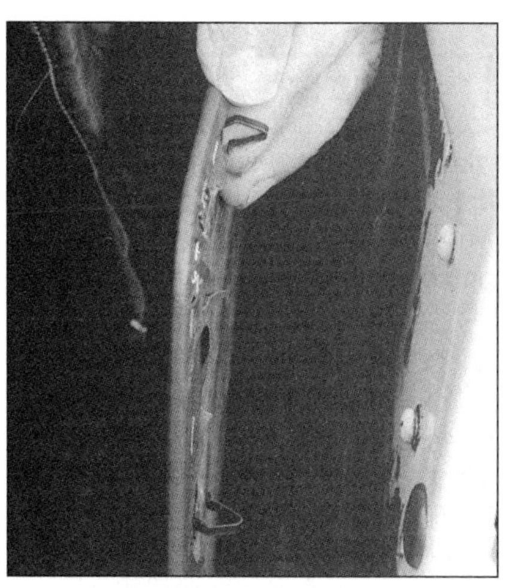

▲ 2.23. Often on your tour of inspection you will come across broken or missing trim panel retaining clips. Replace these at once to avoid placing undue strain on the remaining clips.

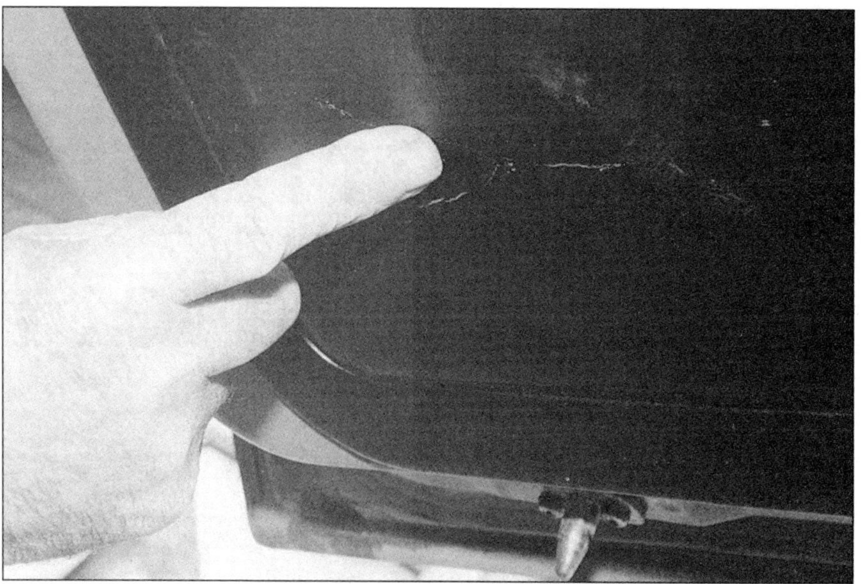

▲ 2.24. Sometimes minor damage may be discovered, such as slightly torn panel coverings, which is not serious enough to warrant re-covering of the entire panel. Prompt action to carefully glue such offending 'flaps' back in position (using an upholstery adhesive) will prevent the damage from becoming more serious, and restore the original look of the panel, as far as all but the most critical of observers is concerned!

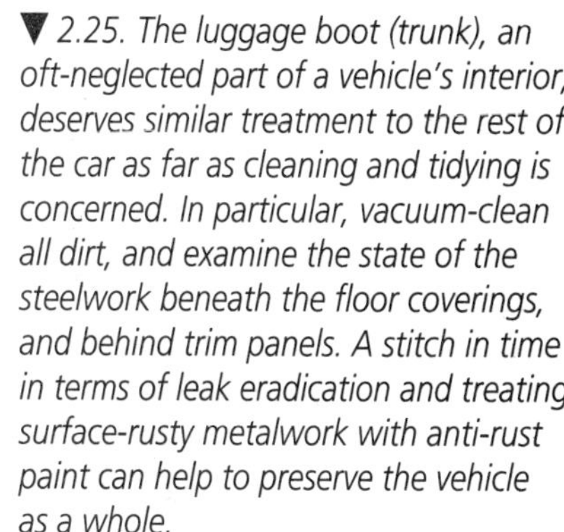

▼ 2.25. The luggage boot (trunk), an oft-neglected part of a vehicle's interior, deserves similar treatment to the rest of the car as far as cleaning and tidying is concerned. In particular, vacuum-clean all dirt, and examine the state of the steelwork beneath the floor coverings, and behind trim panels. A stitch in time in terms of leak eradication and treating surface-rusty metalwork with anti-rust paint can help to preserve the vehicle as a whole.

Chapter 3

Stripping an interior

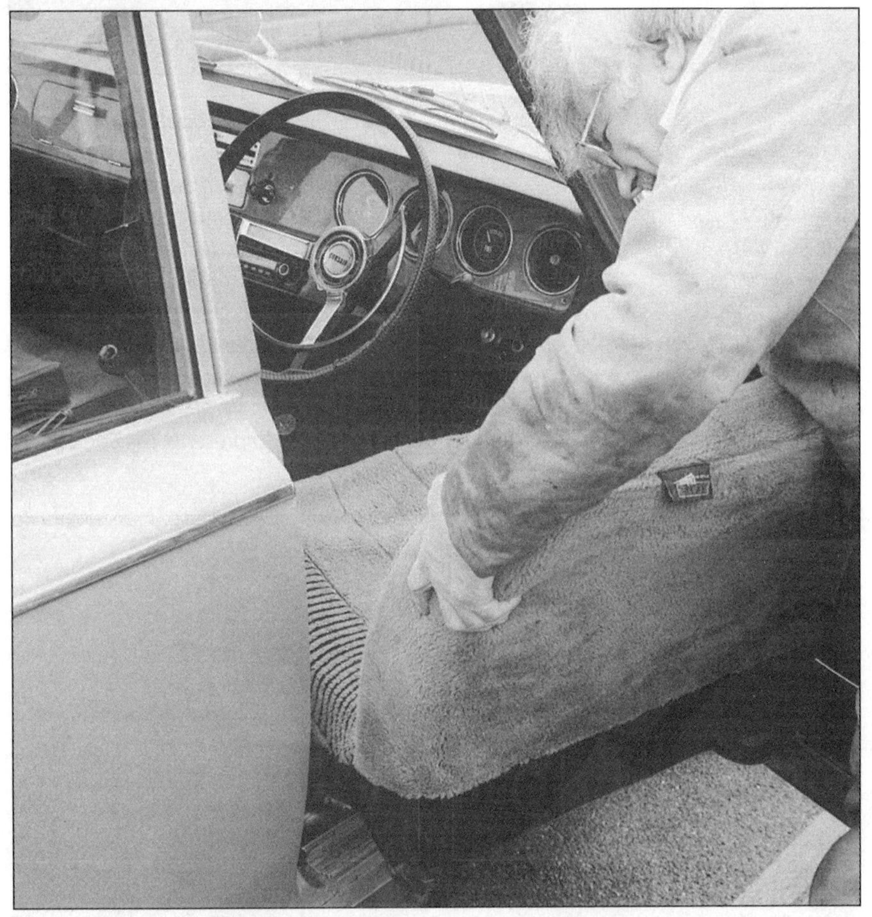

When tackling renovation work on any vehicle's upholstery, there is always need for a degree of dismantling, if only to free a single item of trim needing attention. For a full restoration, more often than not the whole of the interior will have to be removed.

In every case, though, it is vital to carefully assess things before wading in, or unnecessary damage will be caused, the rectification of which may prove difficult, time consuming and expensive!

So, start by deciding in which order you are going to dismantle the interior. This is usually dictated by the sequence in which the car was assembled at the factory, and it is important to establish the correct order of things before you start. Often the most logical sequence is: door trim panels, seats, carpets, headlinings (headliners), dashboard and the general items, including remaining interior trim panels. However, there are many possible variations on this general theme.

Always consult your car's workshop manual (if available), for this can give vital information on the correct manner of removing the various items of interior trim and fittings. Also, where possible, talk to others who have tackled similar vehicles – their first-hand experience may help you avoid making mistakes.

Close study of each trim component will usually give an indication of how it is removed. However, sometimes there are hidden fixings which need to be discovered and dealt with, or damage will be caused.

TAKE CARE

Always take the greatest care when dismantling, and work with precision rather than haste. It is worth taking photographs and/or making sketches of difficult areas. Better still, If you have a camcorder, make a video tape of the interior in its original complete form, and at appropriate stages during the dismantling process. Written or tape-recorded notes, are also useful. All this can be invaluable when the time eventually comes for reassembly – which might be months (or even years!) after you first started taking things to pieces, and the memory can play tricks!

It is surprising just how useful a few minutes worth of film can be in showing how things originally fitted together.

As each item is removed, label it in unmistakable fashion (noting, for example, left-hand or right-hand side, front or rear, top or bottom, etc.) and store it in a safe place, together with any associated fixings and small components. I have found that the plastic containers in which 35mm films are purchased are ideal for storing screws, etc., and their smooth tops are easily marked with indelible felt tip pens. For larger items, baby food tins with flexible plastic lids are ideal and, again, are easily labelled. Always make a separate, written master list of what is in each container – a quick scan of the list can save hours of fruitless searching later on!

In all cases – and especially where it is unlikely that things will be put back together for some time – keep all the interior components together in a dry place. Even if many components are only suitable for use as patterns, they should be preserved in as good a condition as possible until replacements have been made and fitted.

Many recent cars (and a few older ones) have a multitude of electrically operated gadgets – such as side windows, sunshine roofs, seat belt alerts, heated rear windows and audio systems – and it is essential for safety that the vehicle's battery is disconnected, and the relevant wiring labelled and then disconnected, before any items of trim in the vicinity are removed. Often switches are built in to door trim panels, centre consoles, etc., and the wiring must be disconnected before these items can be taken out of the vehicle.

The following photographs show some of the methods of fixing interior components which you are likely to encounter on a wide range of vehicles. However, you may also come across variations on the themes shown, and even different methods of construction. Motor manufacturers often employed clever systems and devices of their own when assembling the interiors of their cars. In every case it *will* be possible to dismantle the interior, although close study of the vehicle may be needed to establish precisely how this can be done!

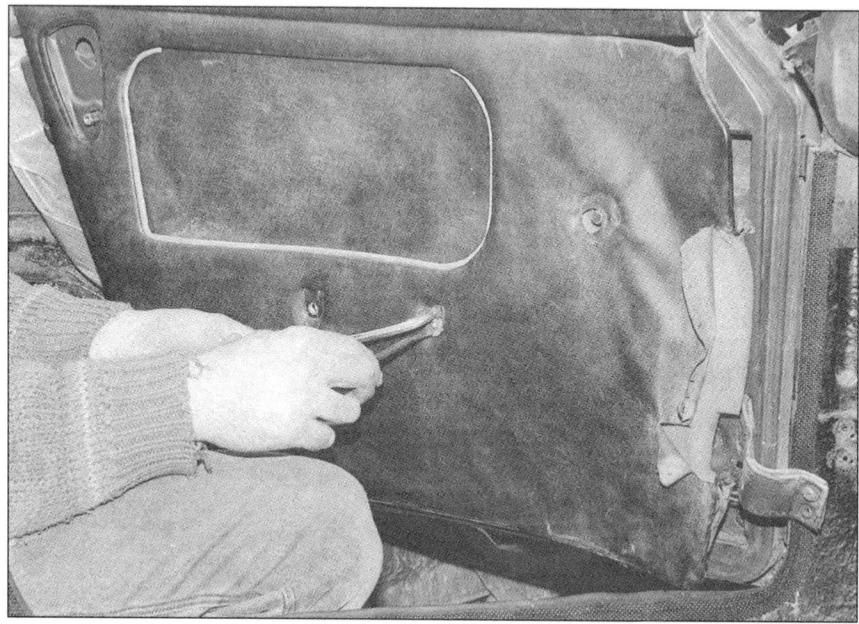

▲ *3.1. Before a door trim panel can be removed, ancillary items (including arm rests) must come off. These are usually secured by screws which pass through holes in the panel into the frame of the door. Look underneath the arm rest to find the screws!*

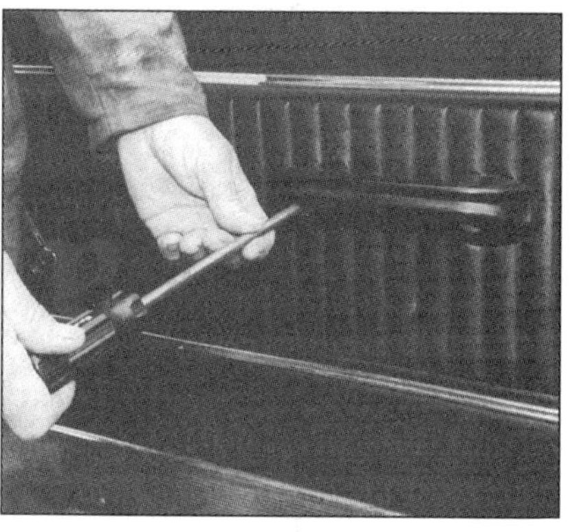

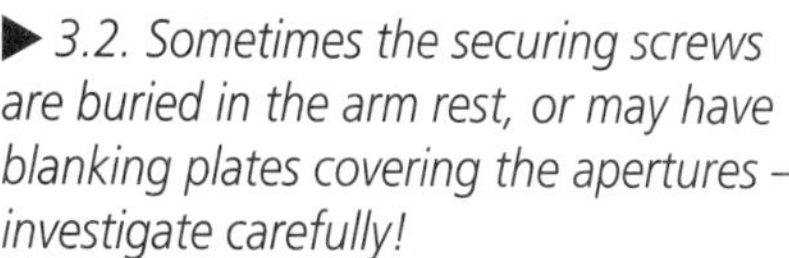

▶ *3.2. Sometimes the securing screws are buried in the arm rest, or may have blanking plates covering the apertures – investigate carefully!*

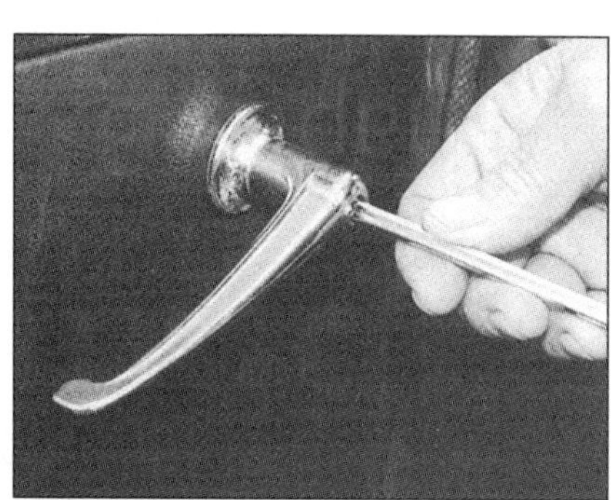

▲ *3.3. The handles controlling the remote control door lock mechanisms and the window winders are often retained by a single screw passing through the centre of the boss. If the handle hasn't been removed for a few years it may be very tight on the shaft, in which case sparingly apply penetrating oil around the shaft. Take care to salvage any fibre and steel washers that may be fitted between the handle and the trim panel.*

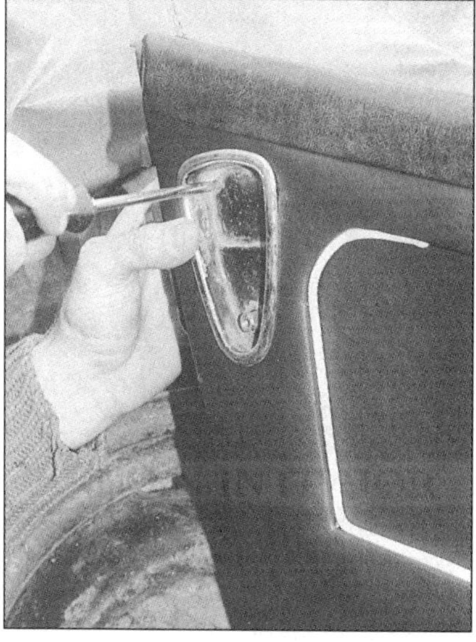

▲ *3.4. There are often recessed housings around door handles, etc. These are usually secured by screws 'hiding' in the corners, as on this MG.*

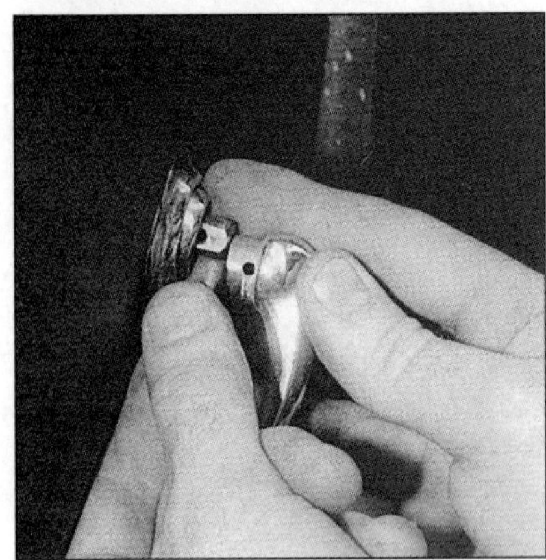

▲ 3.5. Some door handles are secured by a circlip sitting in a groove in the operating shaft, or by a pin which passes through holes in the handle and in the square shaft on which it sits. The handle is held in tension against the pin by a spring-loaded ring assembly which pushes outwards from the door trim panel, and holds the pin in place. Removal can be effected by compressing the spring-loaded ring and gently driving out the pin, using a small, parallel punch. Although – usually – the pins are parallel sided, occasionally tapered types are fitted which will only come out in one direction! As the pin emerges it can be withdrawn by hand. Keep all components together (noting the sequence in which they were fitted) and don't lose the pin!

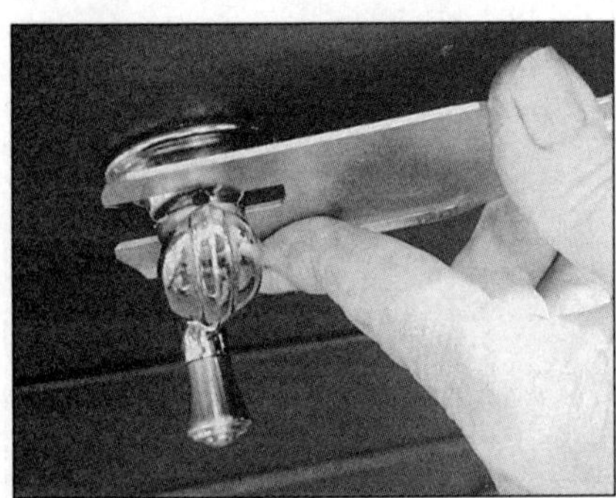

▲ 3.6. If difficulty is experienced in evenly compressing the spring-loaded ring covering the retaining pin on a door handle or window winder shaft, a pair of screwdrivers (one on either side of the shaft) can be employed. An extra pair of hands can be invaluable during this operation. Better still, use one of the special tools purpose-designed for the job.

▼ 3.7. When refitting a door handle or window winder retaining pin it can be pushed home by gently using a screwdriver blade. To aid movement, and to prevent seizure in the future, apply a little copper-based anti-seize compound to the pin as it is slid into position.

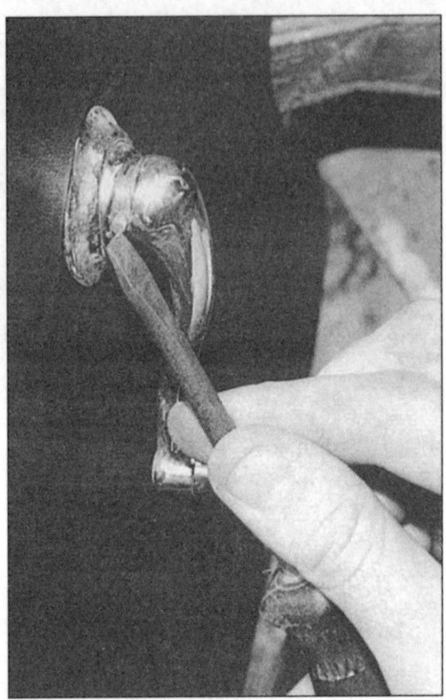

▼ 3.8. The easiest trim panels to remove are those secured by screws around their perimeter. Usually, chrome-plated cup washers are used under the heads of the screws.

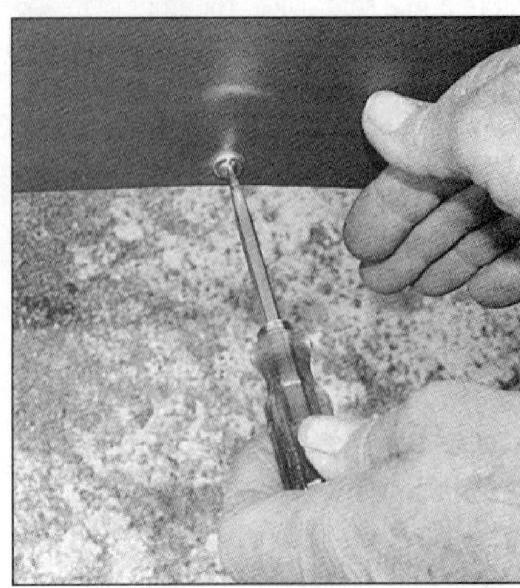

▼ 3.9. Panels which are secured by spring clips (either metal or plastic) can be safely prised from the door by using this special wedge-shaped tool from Eastwood. In all cases, before levering, first check carefully to ensure that there are no additional retaining screws (for example, passing through the sides of the door frame). Even if not fitted by the vehicle manufacturer, such screws may have been added by a previous owner of the car.

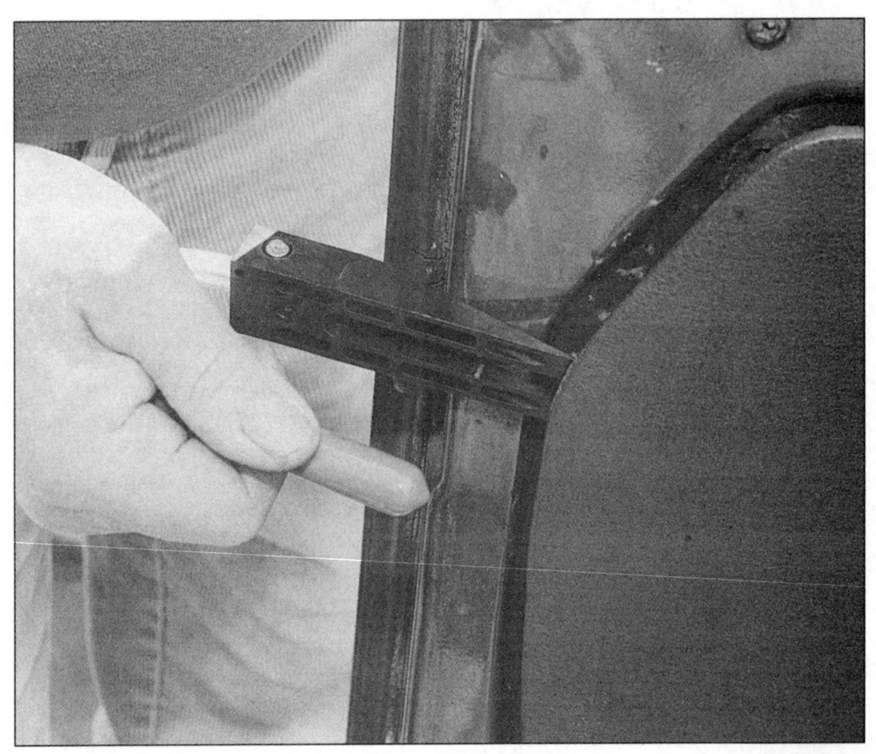

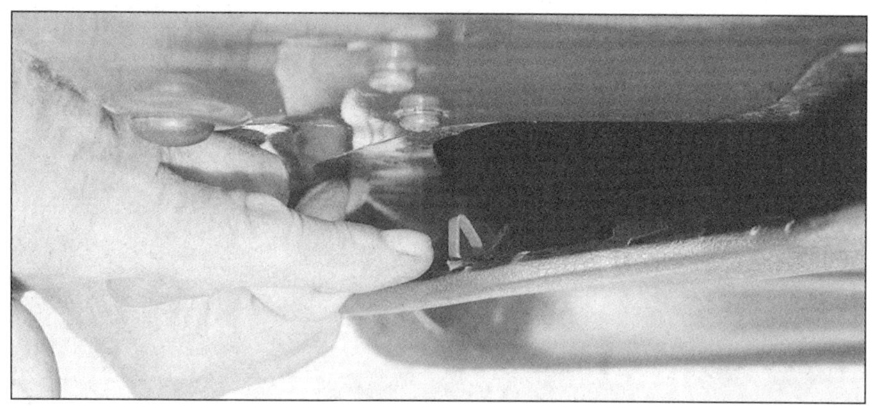

▲ *3.10. A wide variety of steel retaining clips have been used by motor manufacturers. This type is found on many small BMC cars, but other types are generally similar. The clips are simply pushed into place within apertures in the backing board of the trim panel, with the sprung section of each clip being pushed into a corresponding hole in the frame of the door. Once it has squeezed through, the clip opens out again on the inside of the door to hold the panel in place. As they age these clips tend to lose their grip. By slightly spreading the 'legs', using a screwdriver blade, matters can usually be improved.*

▼ *3.12. Seats are retained by a number of methods. The simplest is by spring clips like this which are unhooked from the retaining lugs to release the seat.*

▲ *3.11. On almost all relatively recent cars plastic clips will have been used to retain trim panels. These are prone to break when you try to remove the panel, or the panel can break up around the clip. To avoid such problems, use a special tool like this one from Frost Auto Restoration Techniques Ltd. The gadget is slid around the clip, between the trim panel and the door frame, protecting the clip and the panel as they are removed.*

Other types of panel retainers commonly encountered include the 'keyhole' variety, in which a keyhole slot in the door trim panel's backing board engages on a screw/stud projecting from the frame of the door. This type is shown in detail in Chapter 8 in the 'More complex panels' section.

Panel retainers can also take the form of a clip which rotates about a screw (fixed to the panel) to lock the panel in place.

Complications can arise with door trim panels which have hidden retainers. For example, these can be screws hidden beneath sealing rubbers, or 'finisher' panels – often fitted just beneath the windows. Such finisher panels – of wood or fabric-covered steel – need to be released before access can be gained to the main trim panel fixings beneath.

While the door trim panels are off, it is a good idea to clean and lubricate (with waterproof grease) the window winder mechanisms and the remote control door handle linkages within each door.

▼ *3.13. Sometimes the seats are screwed to the floor by means of brackets which secure each seat's cross-runners. Often the screws locate in captive nuts beneath the car floor. Check before attempting to wrench off the captive nut!*

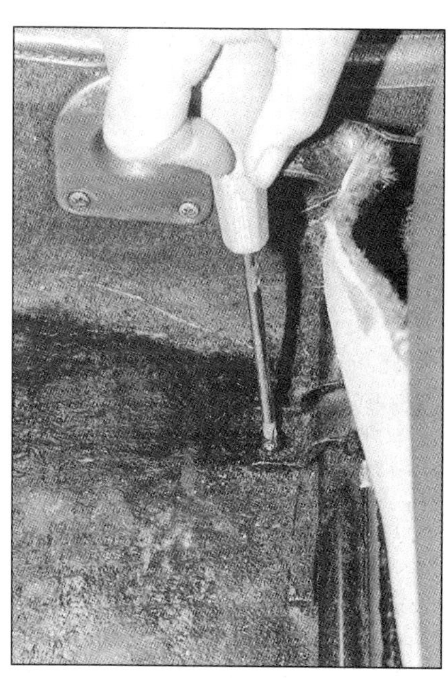

▶ *3.14. Many car seats sit on runners/ slides which are screwed to the floor. Some modern vehicles employ recessed head screws which require the correct type of screwdriver in order to release them.*

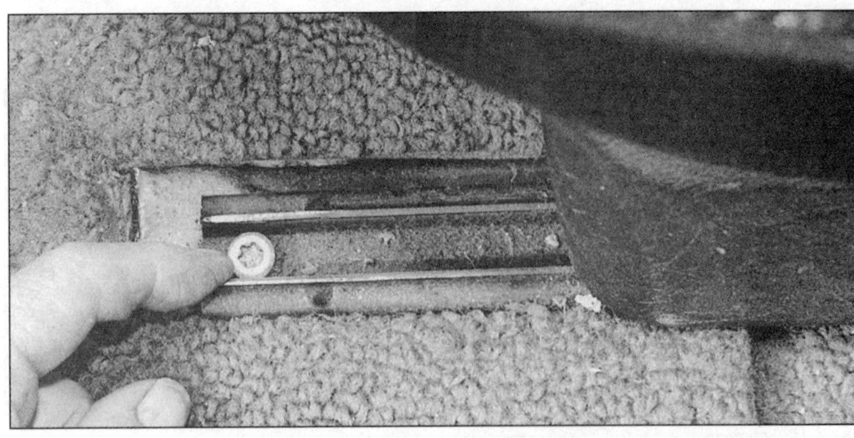

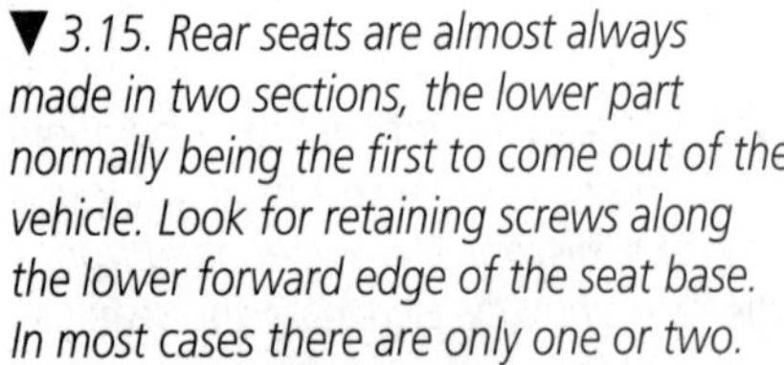

▼ *3.15. Rear seats are almost always made in two sections, the lower part normally being the first to come out of the vehicle. Look for retaining screws along the lower forward edge of the seat base. In most cases there are only one or two.*

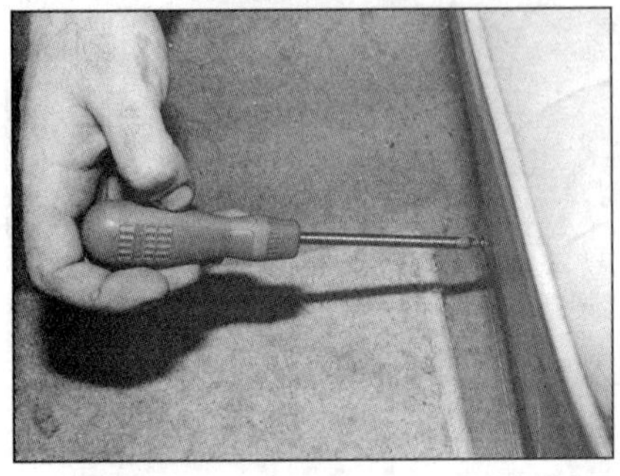

▼ *3.16. Once the retaining screws have been released, the seat base should easily lift forwards and upwards to freedom, as in this Daimler Sovereign.*

▲ *3.17. On many cars, removing the floor coverings is simply a matter of unclipping them and lifting them out.*

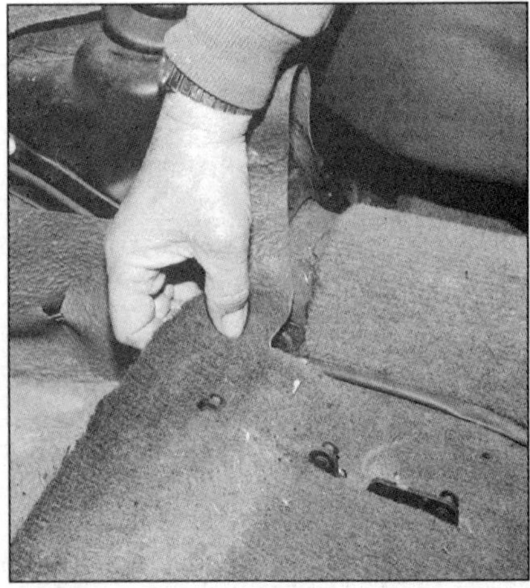

▲ *3.18. On some vehicles the seats need to be removed to enable the carpets to be extricated – a glance at the manner in which the carpet was originally fitted will confirm this.*

▲ *3.19. A high proportion of relatively recent models have carpets which are secured to the top of the sill (rocker) panels by means of plastic, stainless steel or aluminium cover panels, which are screwed in place. These areas are often damp, with the result that the screws frequently rust in position. Penetrating oil and an impact screwdriver are useful aids in their removal! On reassembly, preferably with new screws, apply a little copper-based anti-seize compound to the threads to help prevent the same thing happening again.*

▲ *3.20. There are many ways in which dashboards (and parcel shelves) are secured. Usually they are screwed/bolted to the vehicle structure, and often a separate dash top assembly is screwed in place from underneath. A visual examination with an inspection lamp or torch (flashlight) will help determine how to tackle the one on your vehicle. Note that some makers use slotted fixing apertures to avoid the need for completely removing screws positioned in awkward places. If this is the case, it is necessary only to slacken rather than remove them.*

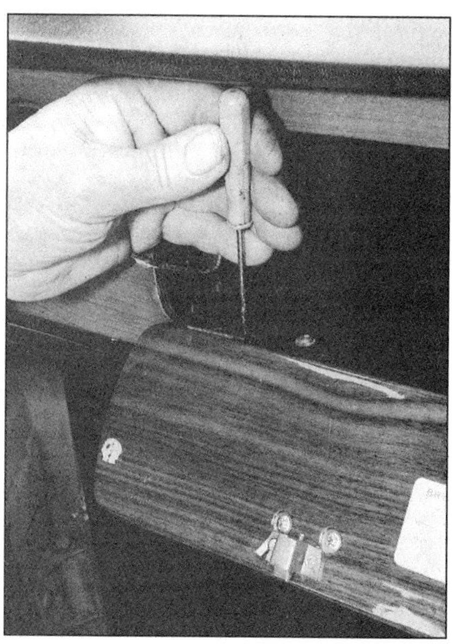

▲ *3.21. The glovebox lid is usually easy to remove as a separate item. Normally, the lid is bolted or screwed to its hinges. Bear in mind that on many cars a courtesy lamp is activated as soon as the lid is opened. In such cases, disconnect the battery before removing the lid.*

◀ *3.22. It is often necessary to take out seat belts in order to free carpets, trim panels and so on. Always use a socket or ring spanner on the large securing nuts/bolts. While the belts are out of the car, inspect them very carefully and only refit if in perfect condition. If frays, cuts or other damage are visible, replace the belts with new items.*

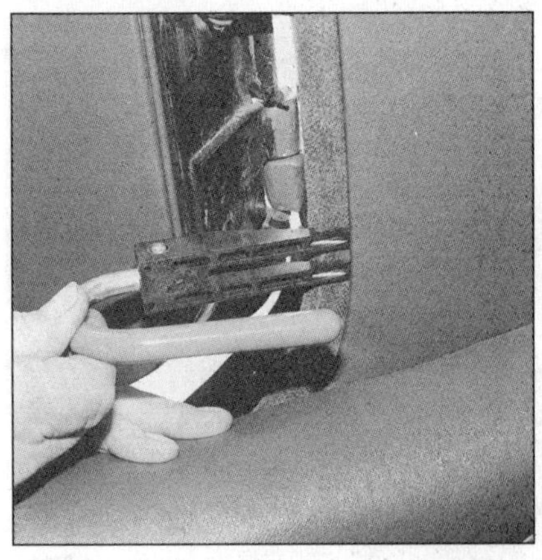

▲ 3.23. Trim panels fitted to the rear quarters of many cars are often secured in the same manner as door trim panels, and removal is therefore effected in the same way. However, these panels are not normally as accessible as those on the doors, so patience is advised when attempting removal and refitting!

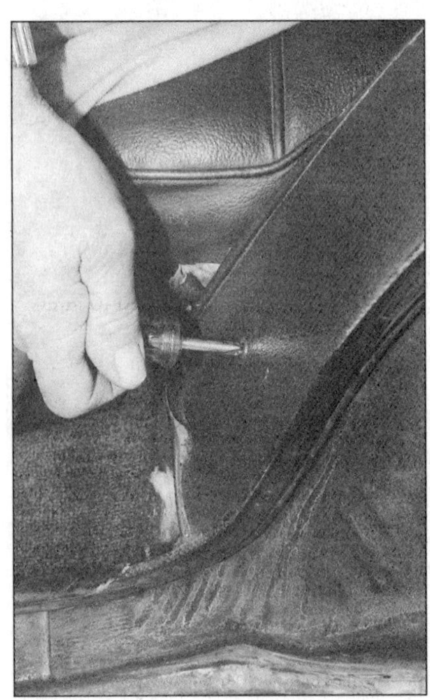

▲ 3.24. On many older cars, small trim panels covering door pillars, rear wheel arches, etc., are secured in place by means of screws and chrome plated cup washers. Remove carefully, and apply copper-based anti-seize compound on reassembly.

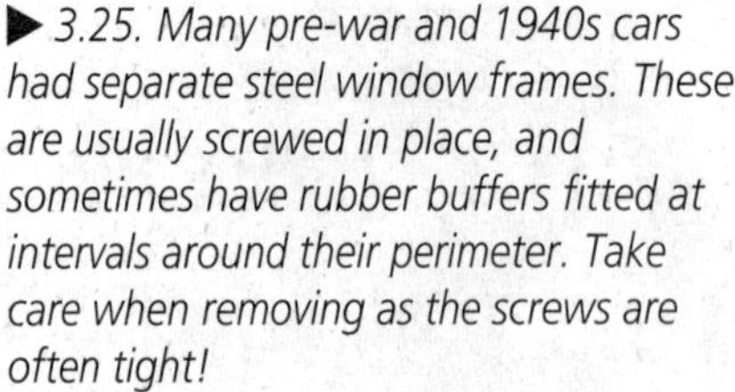

▶ 3.25. Many pre-war and 1940s cars had separate steel window frames. These are usually screwed in place, and sometimes have rubber buffers fitted at intervals around their perimeter. Take care when removing as the screws are often tight!

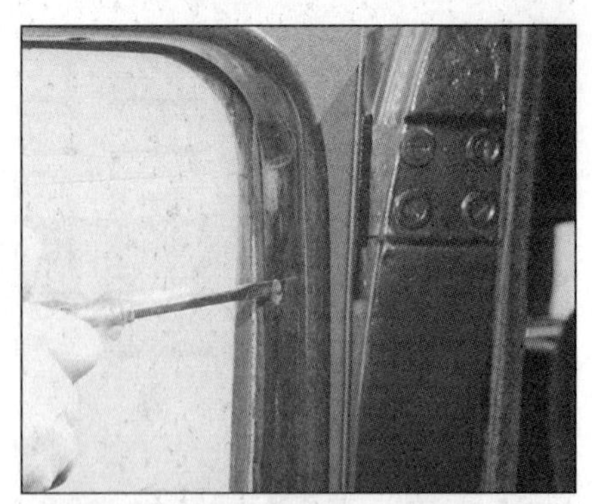

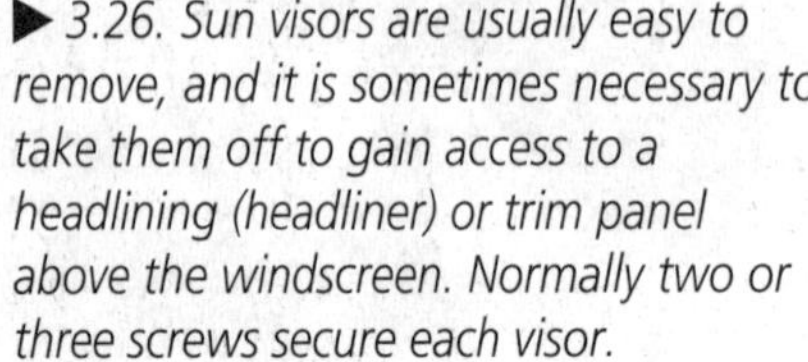

▶ 3.26. Sun visors are usually easy to remove, and it is sometimes necessary to take them off to gain access to a headlining (headliner) or trim panel above the windscreen. Normally two or three screws secure each visor.

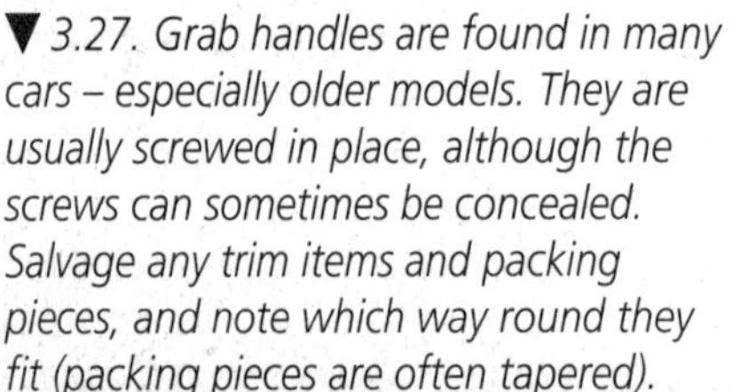

▼ 3.27. Grab handles are found in many cars – especially older models. They are usually screwed in place, although the screws can sometimes be concealed. Salvage any trim items and packing pieces, and note which way round they fit (packing pieces are often tapered).

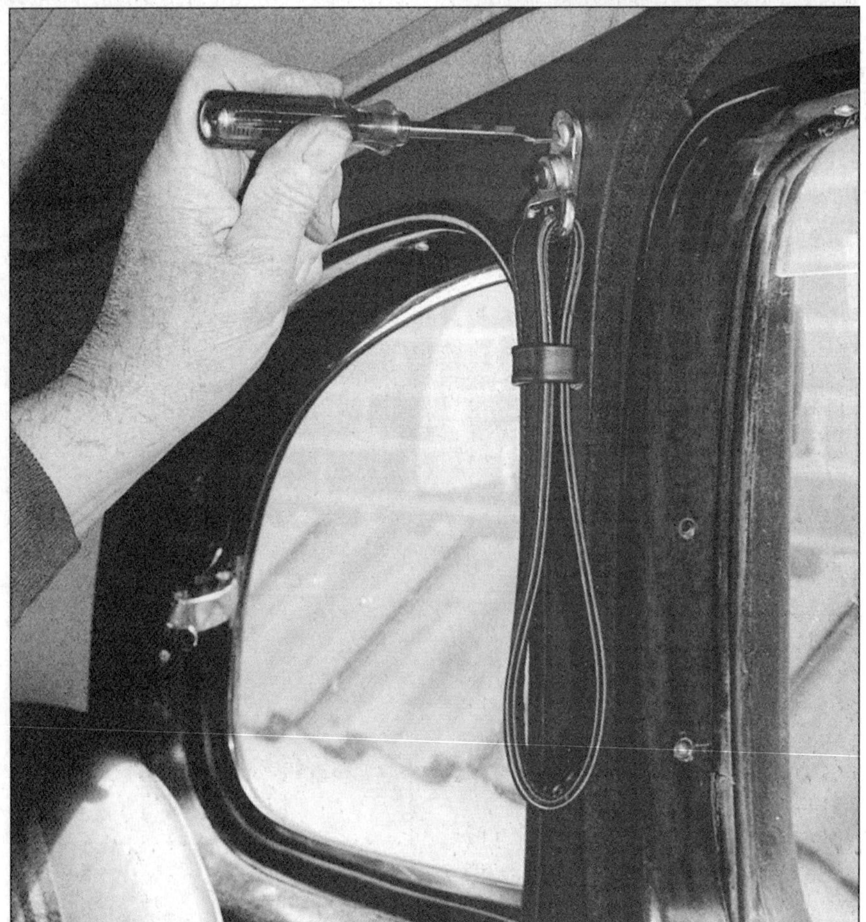

Chapter 4

Maintaining leather

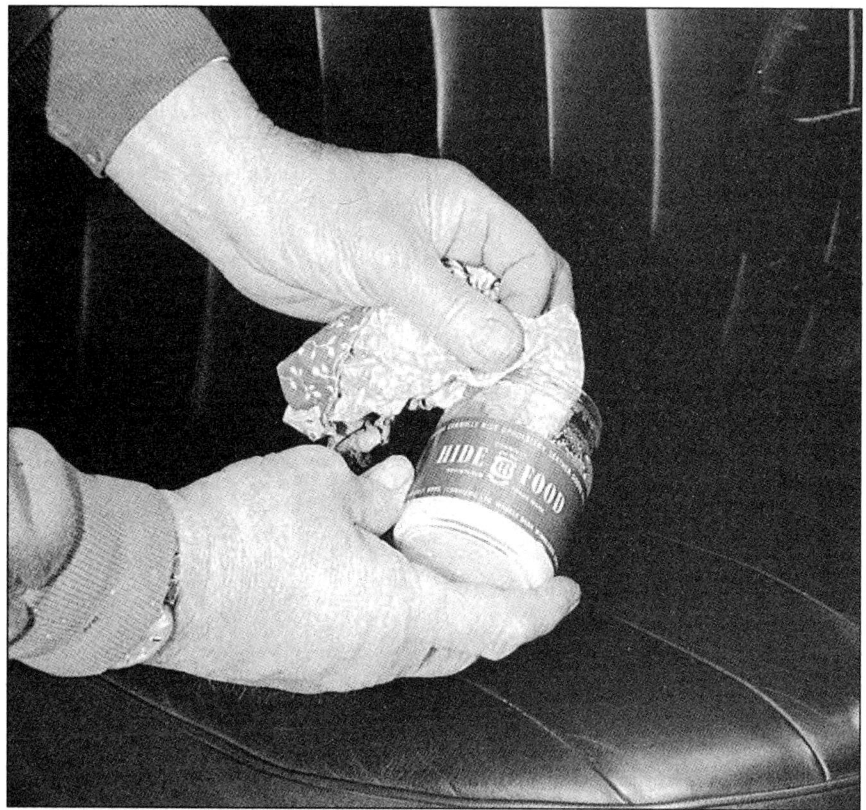

There is nothing to match the soft feel, warmth and opulent smell of leather upholstery when in good condition but, although it has durable qualities, if left to its own devices it eventually becomes brittle and starts to disintegrate. When this stage is reached, a once attractive and comfortable interior looks shabby and feels even worse!

Fortunately, it needn't be like this; for a little regular care and preventive attention, plus – where necessary – revival, will ensure that the leather in your car will last and look good for many decades.

Taking care of leather not only helps retain its suppleness and good looks, but will also save you money in the long run, as renewing leather upholstery is not cheap.

CLEAN IT AND FEED IT

Proper cleaning and feeding of leather should be carried out on a regular basis – ideally every 6 months to a year. In every case, the leather should be cleaned before it is fed, or the food products will not be able to properly penetrate into the hide. For routine cleaning use warm water (but don't flood the surface) and a good quality leather or toilet soap – never use detergents. Leather which has been neglected will require the use of specialist cleaning products.

Care is needed when using cleaning agents. Only ever use products which are specifically stated to be suitable for leather, and even then take care, especially on older hides which were 'surface coloured', as opposed to later types which will have been 'soak coloured' (i.e. throughout the fibres of the leather). If too harsh a solvent is applied to surface-coloured leather, the colour may be lifted from it.

For leather in sound condition, hide food (available as a soft paste) is appropriate. Alternatively, saddle soap, which is of a much firmer consistency, can be used. This imparts a longer-lasting finish, but requires a lot more effort to apply. Even new leather can be treated with saddle soap – up to perhaps three times in the first year, and then once a year.

If the leather is already showing signs of brittleness, first apply a liquid leather dressing (several applications may be needed), which will help to restore its natural softness. Only then should hide food be used, having allowed several weeks to elapse after the liquid dressing treatment.

THE CONNOLLY TRADITION

To see how the experts tackle renovation and care of leather, I first visited world famous Connolly Leather Ltd at their Wandle Bank, Wimbledon premises. Connolly – the most widely known curriers in the world – have been in the leather business since 1878, and their highly respected products have been used in vehicle upholstery since the dawn of motoring.

Connolly's business grew with the development of the motor car, and they have consistently supplied quality manufacturers such as Rolls-Royce (since 1904!), Jaguar, Aston Martin and Bristol. In the boom years of the British car industry, sports and family models such as those from Austin, MG, Morris, Rootes, Rover and Standard also sported Connolly leather.

These days, Audi, Nissan, Peugeot, Renault and Volvo – and still, of course, Rolls-Royce/Bentley – are among the companies which fit Connolly leather trim to their products, aware that buyers of their upmarket models appreciate the comfort and other special qualities of leather.

As well as supplying leather for new vehicles, the Wimbledon based firm – through its Renovation Department, which has existed for more than 60 years – is able to help owners of old models with Connolly trim by sympathetically restoring interiors to their original state. This process makes the leather look and feel better, and also helps to slow down further deterioration. The firm is also able to pre-age (by distressing the material) and colour leather to match existing trim.

The two-day Connollising process can either be carried out in the firm's Wimbledon workshops, or – sometimes – on site. The company also supplies leather, hide food and complete renovation kits to the trade, and to the general public for DIY application.

According to John Humpage, Manager of Connolly's Renovation Department (who has, himself, worked for Connolly Leather for over 30 years), the critical factor in deciding whether the leather in a car can be revived is the condition of the grain layer – which is, essentially, the structure of the leather.

There comes a point when the fibres of neglected leather are literally falling apart. Such deterioration can be hastened by the application of products totally unsuitable for it – for example, cellulose paint! John has seen many examples of leather in poor condition brought about by such misguided 'restoration' efforts. In most of these cases the answer is replacement rather than renovation!

It is worth noting that if the leather *does* have to be replaced, the original grain patterns and colours can be precisely matched at Connolly by reference to their unique and extensive library of grain and colour samples, which dates back many years.

CONNOLLY CLASSIC

By using today's methods, Connolly can simulate the look and feel of old leather. It does, though, have a slightly different character to it, and some enthusiasts prefer leather produced by traditional processes for the ultimate in originality. In response to this need, largely from the restorers of classic vehicles, Connolly have re-introduced a traditionally produced leather under the Connolly Classic label.

This had been discontinued on the introduction of the soft hides used in today's luxury cars. Rather harder in texture than such leather, Connolly Classic – originally produced for over 50 years – is manufactured using the traditional, old-fashioned tanning and finishing processes, to give the aroma and durability associated with the original product.

Connolly Classic is available in plain and Luxan (hand antiqued) finishes in a range of standard colours, and the company provides a colour matching service for special requirements.

THE CONNOLLY SYSTEM

Assuming that the leather is essentially sound, if shabby, the first step in the Connolly renovation system is to establish the original colour of the upholstery. By releasing the hessian covering, etc., at the base of a seat, sections of the leather unaffected by years of exposure to sunlight, and heavy use, are revealed. This is then checked against the samples in Connolly's library, and matched so that lacquer of precisely the right shade can be mixed for application to sympathetically bring the trim back to its original condition.

The sequence of photographs that follows shows the stages in the restoration process, as carried out in the Renovation Department at Connolly's Wimbledon premises, on a seat taken from a Bentley. The same stages apply if using a Renovation Kit purchased from the company for home application.

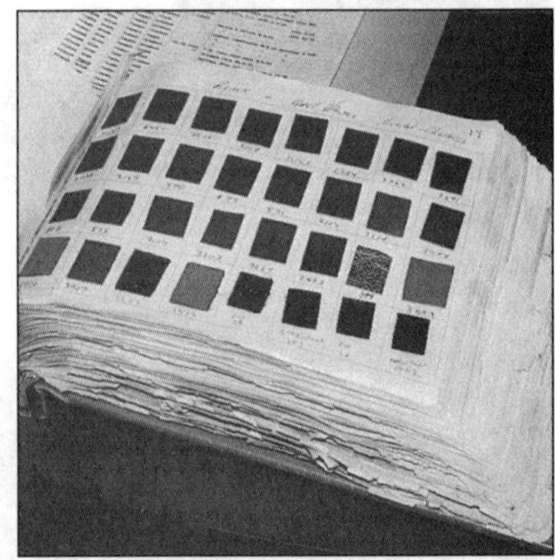

▲ *4.1. An extensive library of samples, dating back to the earliest years of motoring, enables Connolly staff to identify precisely the colour and texture of the Connolly leather as originally installed in the vehicle – perhaps many decades ago! A small sample of original leather from the vehicle – best taken from an out-of-the-way area, such as under a seat – is required for matching purposes, so that lacquer of exactly the right shade can be made up for the customer.*

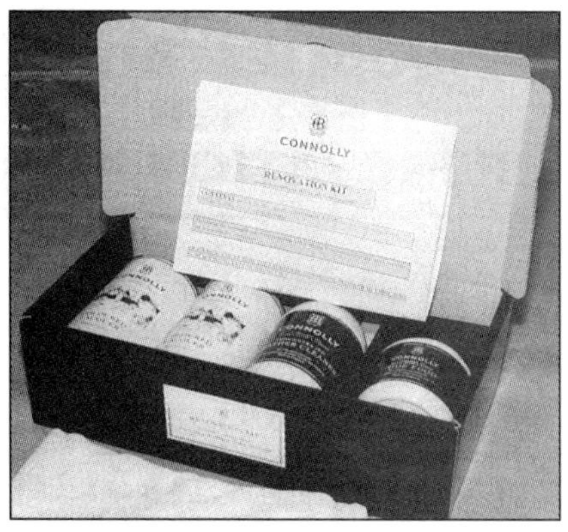

▲ 4.2. Renovation kits from Connolly Leather each contain 500ml of concentrated cleaner, two 500ml containers of specially prepared lacquer (to match the sample), a jar of hide food, stockinette for application of the products, and written directions on how to use them. The products used by Connolly restoration staff are the same as provided in the kits available for sale.

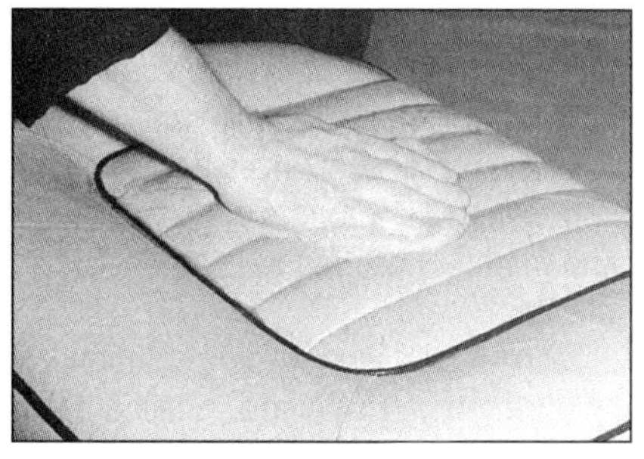

▲ 4.3. Having removed the seats from the vehicle, the first step is to dilute (with water) the concentrated cleaning solution, as directed, and apply to the surface of the leather using stockinette cloth.

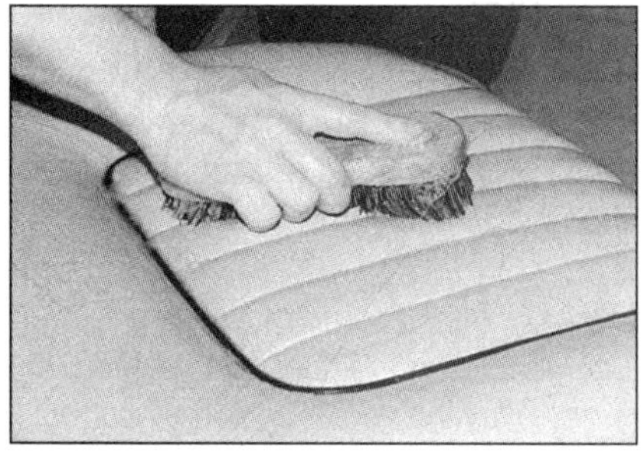

▲ 4.4. In cases where the dirt is deeply ingrained into the leather, encouragement with a scrubbing brush is necessary.

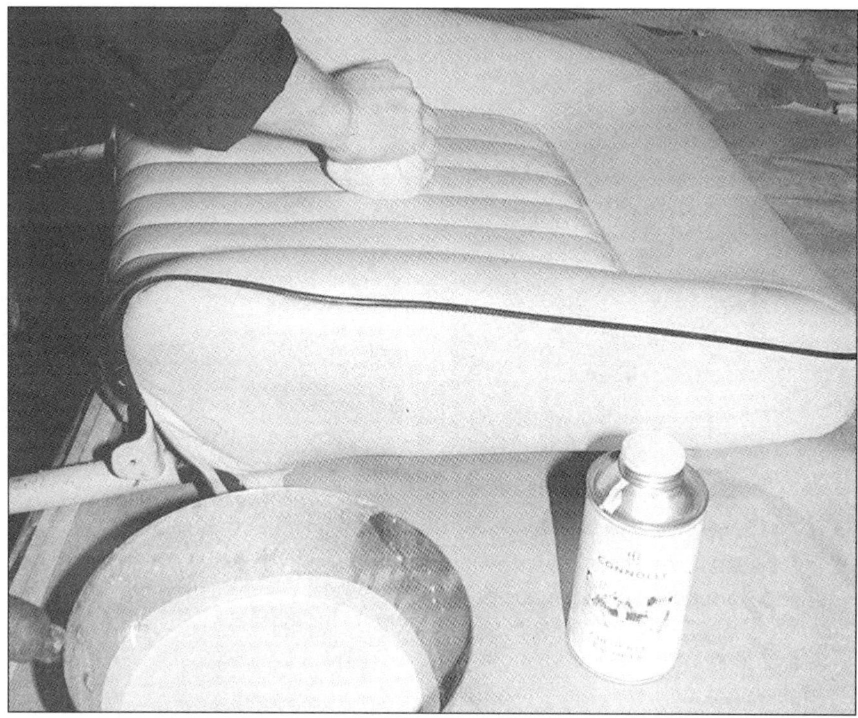

▲ 4.5. The coloured lacquer is poured into an appropriate receptacle, and having first masked off any piping to be finished in a contrasting colour (in this case the seat was to be coloured uniformly) it is applied to the leather. Stockinette, formed into a pad, is used in circular movements to spread the lacquer. The lacquer is allowed to turn tacky before a second coat is applied. Note that it is imperative that the lacquer does not come into contact with plastic. This is important to bear in mind where the sides of the seat are made from plastic, with only the seat facings being of leather.

▼ 4.6. Preferably, subsequent coats of lacquer should be sprayed on to the leather, building up the coats gradually (although application by stockinette also works very well). Several applications may be required to achieve perfect results, but the kits contain plenty of lacquer. For dealing with seat piping, etc., of a contrasting colour, a small brush can be used to apply the product by hand. Try to avoid getting the lacquer on your hands – it can be difficult to remove, although hand cleaners available at car accessory shops can be effective.

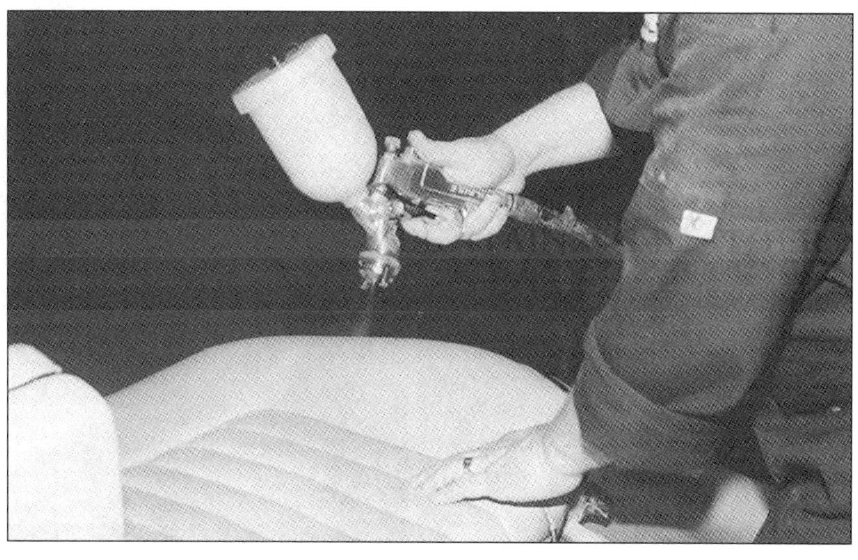

▲4.7. *When the lacquer has fully dried, hide food should be applied, to maintain the leather's suppleness. Applications should be repeated on a regular basis – a little and often is the maxim to apply here! Connolly can supply a Leather Care Kit, comprising a bottle of their concentrated leather cleaner and a jar of hide food, for maintaining the upholstery in first-class condition in the future. Hide food is also available separately.*

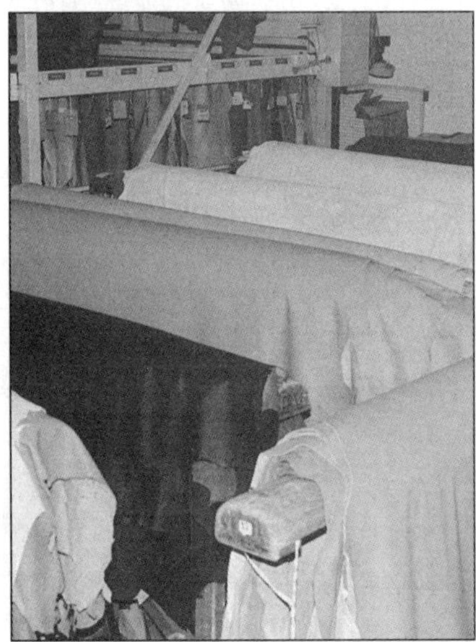

▲4.8. *If the leather trim in your car has deteriorated beyond the stage of renovation, Connolly can provide new hides from which new seat coverings can be made, as described in Chapter 6. This is just a small selection of the enormous range of hides available in their retail shop in Wimbledon.*

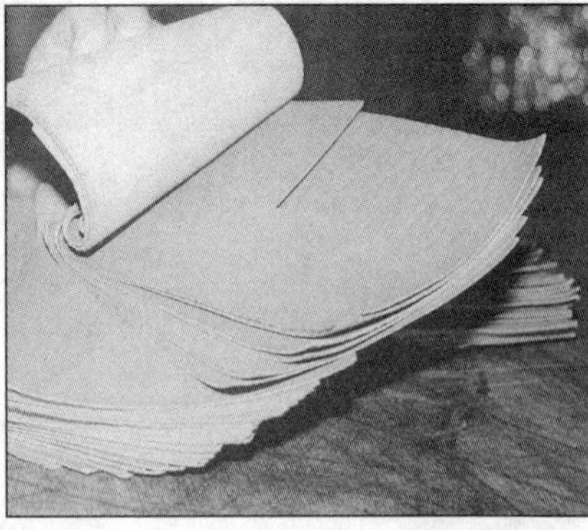

▲4.9. *Even if your car's Connolly leather upholstery is many years old and features an unusual grain, the firm will be able to match it from their huge range of samples.*

▲4.10. *This huge press squeezes the leather against a mould embossed with the appropriate grain pattern, thereby recreating a finished product looking identical to the original, which may have been produced 60 or more years ago!*

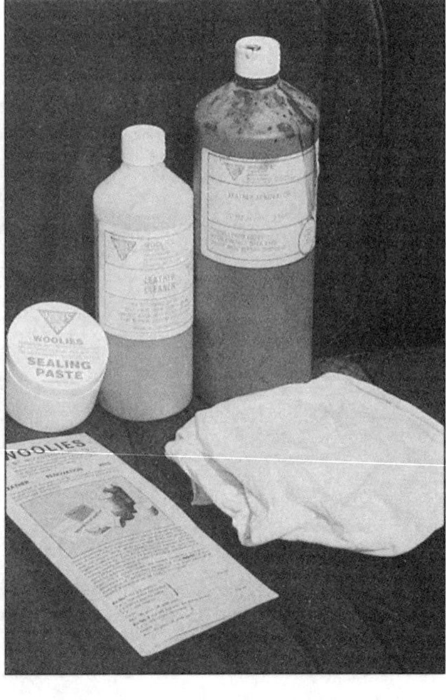

WOOLIES' DIY LEATHER RENOVATION KIT

There are several leather renovation kits made specially for the DIY market, and the following step-by-step picture sequence shows how, by using one or other of these, you can tackle the renovation of typically 'tired' (but basically sound) leather upholstery.

The kit used was supplied by the well-known firm of Woolies (I. & C. Woolstenholmes Ltd), of Market Deeping, near Peterborough. As Woolies say: 'The purpose of this well-tried kit is to restore leather to its original colour, with uniform finish and without giving the just-been-painted appearance.'

Four sizes of Woolies Leather Renovation Kit are available (No. 1, for two/three seaters, No. 2, for four/five seaters, 'Jensen' for four seats plus trim panels, and 'Limousine' for a complete interior). All are available by mail order. They are reasonably priced and all come with generous amounts of the product and materials needed to carry out the job.

Each kit contains cleaning solution, colour-matched renovator, sealing paste and the cloth required for application, plus instructions. Woolies require a sample of *cleaned* original leather for colour-matching purposes, and the mixing takes around ten days. They stress that, although they endeavour to accurately match the samples supplied, some 'artistic tolerance' (i.e. slight variation in shade) must be accepted by the customer.

The following sequence shows the use of a kit on some sad but sound seats from a Mark II Jaguar:

◀4.11. *The kit contains cleaning solution, colouring agent and sealing paste, plus the necessary soft all-cotton cloth for applying the products. Full instructions are also included. Woolies will colour-match a sample of your original leather, and specially mix the colouring agent to achieve the correct shade.*

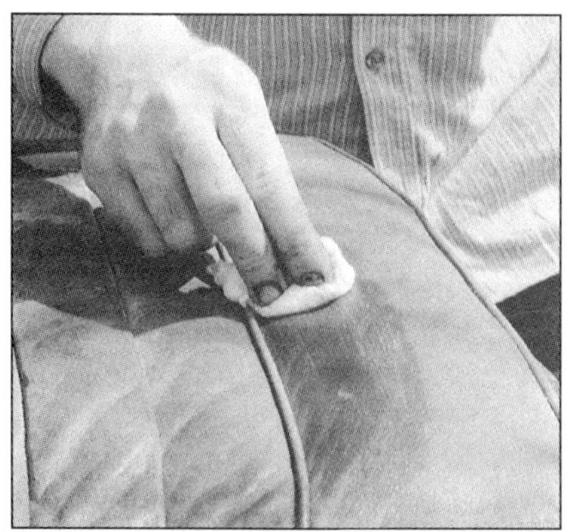

▲ 4.12. *Thorough cleaning of the leather is necessary to enable the renovating dye to penetrate the hide. Using the cloth provided, apply the leather cleaner, rubbing lightly. Where necessary use a small brush to lift ingrained dirt. Try to avoid 'flooding' the leather. Next, wipe all surfaces clean, using a fresh piece of cloth. After this first clean, and if the leather has been neglected, apply hide food, then allow 48 hours for this to soak in, and remove surplus with the leather cleaner solution.*

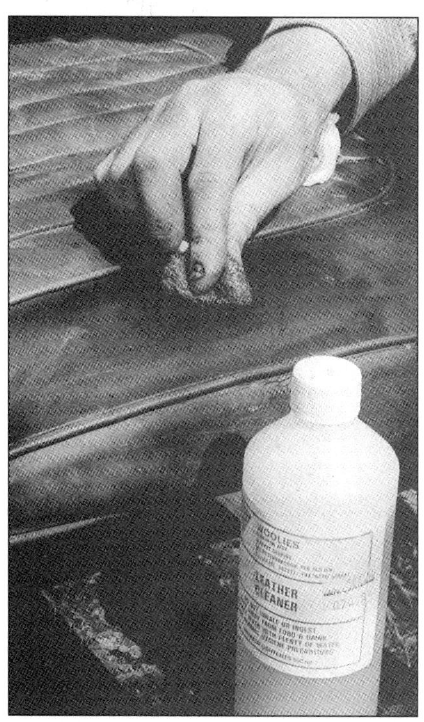

▲ 4.13. *It can be useful (especially when the surface is very smooth) to use fine grade steel wool, in conjunction with the cleaner, to provide a 'key' for the colouring agent.*

▲ 4.14. *It is surprising how much better the cleaned leather looks, even before application of the dye. This seat hadn't been cleaned for many years, but after a few minutes it looked altogether better.*

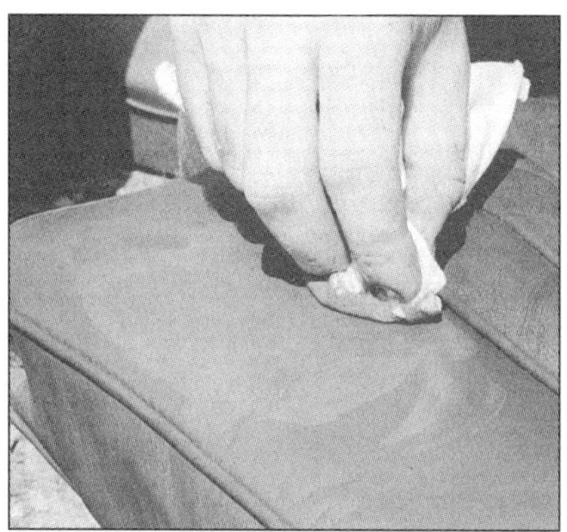

▲ 4.15. *Using a soft pad of cloth (rather than a brush), apply the colour renovator dye, having first thoroughly stirred this. Make sure that the solution reaches the depths of all the nooks and crannies, and that it adequately covers the whole of the surface of the leather, but don't worry if the coat looks a little thin. Tackle small areas at a time.*

▲ 4.16. *After leaving the first coat to dry for at least 30 minutes at normal room temperature, apply a second coat. This can be applied by cloth or, without further thinning, by spray gun (as shown). Apply several very light coats to avoid excessive build-up of the liquid. Ensure that the spraying pressure is not too low, or the renovator tends to dribble out of the gun. Conversely, if the pressure is set too high, excessive build-up will result.*

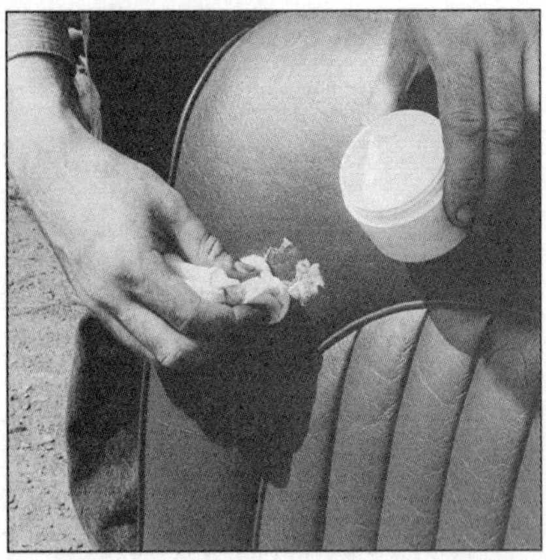

▲ *4.17. The next, and crucial, stage is to apply the sealing/polishing paste, but only after the renovator dye has fully hardened. This aspect of the job requires very great care, or the renovator dye will be removed. Apply the paste very sparingly, and use only extremely light pressure. An alternative – and successful – approach is to apply a tiny amount of paste to a cloth, allowing it to dry almost completely before very gently buffing the leather. The finished surface will have a water-resistant sheen.*

▲ *4.18. Before long the Jaguar seat looked like this – smart, comfortable and colourful, and ready for years more service.*

▲ *4.19. The treated seat compared with its untreated partner (left). The revived seat has an altogether brighter appearance and feel.*

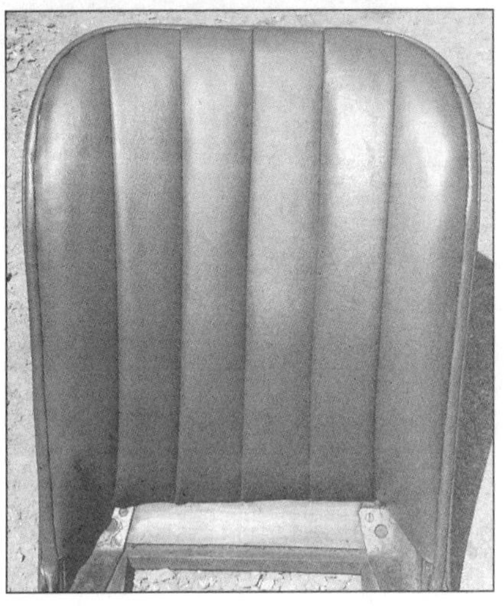

▲ *4.20. This seat from an Austin Ten had been made in sections of leather showing slight colour variations. Using Woolies' colour renovator dye and polishing paste, the seat was given a uniform hue. Woolies say that although their kits are not intended for completely changing the colour of trim, they can be used for this purpose. Try a test piece first.*

It is worth noting that, after renovation with the Woolies kit, the surface of the leather will not be completely sealed. Therefore hide food can still be applied on a regular basis to keep the hide supple.

Although not designed for use on vinyl, the renovator dye seems to work well on very old, porous rexine and leathercloth, which soaks it up. Try a sample section before getting too ambitious!

LEATHER REPAIR?

Even if the leather on your car has suffered to the extent that it has become holed, all may not be lost. It may still be possible to carry out localized repairs, rather than scrap an original seat covering because of, perhaps, one or two small areas of damage.

Patch repairs for small areas of damage can be effected by cutting a replacement piece of leather from spare material, usually found underneath a seat or behind a panel, and gluing it in place to bridge the damaged section. The techniques are similar to those outlined in the 'Patch repair' section in Chapter 6.

However, such repairs are seldom unobtrusive. For maximum chances of an 'invisible' repair which blends with the surrounding leather, first smooth any rough edges of leather surrounding the damaged area, either using fine wet-or-dry (silicon carbide) paper (used dry) or wire wool.

It is also possible to 'feather' the edges of both the patch and the original leather (immediately around the damaged section) by tapering the thickness of each piece of hide, using a sharp trimmer's knife. **Take very great care during this operation, and always cut away from your fingers, and always work on a clean, solid workbench.** When tapering the leather around the hole, always cut towards the centre of it.

Where possible, apply the repair patch underneath the original hide, and glue firmly in place using contact adhesive.

The Eastwood Company can supply a repair kit for leather which is designed to deal with small imperfections. It contains 1-oz bottles of cleaner, liquid rubber and various leather colouring agents, plus all the tools and full instructions necessary to tackle such repairs.

The following photographs show the kit being tried on an old leather seat from a Jaguar. It is advisable to practice on a small area before tackling a full repair.

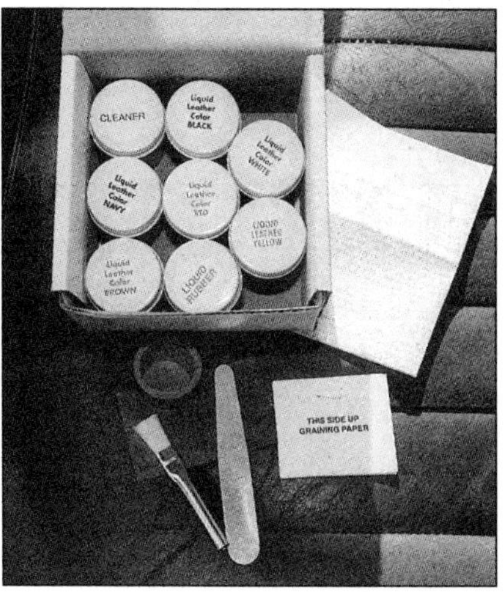

▲ *4.21. The Eastwood kit contains everything necessary to tackle small repairs on leather seats (and trim panels). Comprehensive instructions are included.*

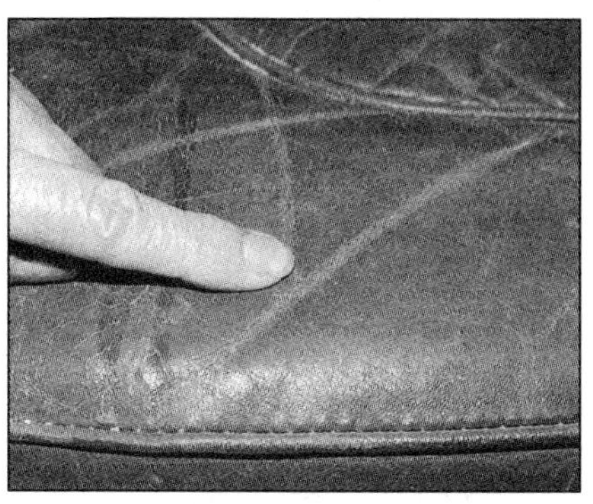

▲ *4.22. As leather ages, cracks form in the surface, and eventually the material will split. Taking early action can avoid such damage.*

▲ *4.23. The first step is to clean the surface of the leather, applying the cleaner provided in the kit (or any proprietary leather cleaning fluid) using a soft cloth.*

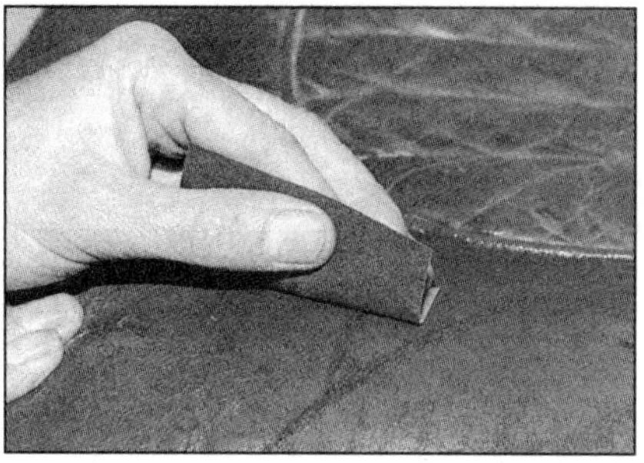

▲ *4.24. Using the abrasive paper from the kit, carefully smooth the rough edges of the cracked leather. In some cases it may be necessary to use an abrasive paper with a coarser grit.*

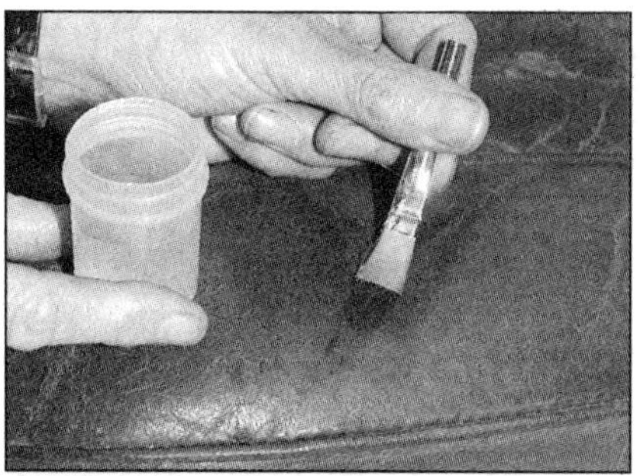

▲ *4.25. Now apply the 'liquid rubber' leather mending solution, brushing it into the valleys forming the cracks (a brush is provided in the kit). Several applications may be needed. Allow to dry fully between each application. Ensure that the solution is spread so that it blends fully with the surrounding leather. Clean the brush after use. If you require a grained finish, then before the last coat of liquid rubber is dry ...*

▲ *4.26. ... choose a graining paper with a pattern as close as possible to that of the original leather, and apply to the liquid rubber, if necessary taping it firmly in place until the rubber has fully dried (normally after two or three hours).*

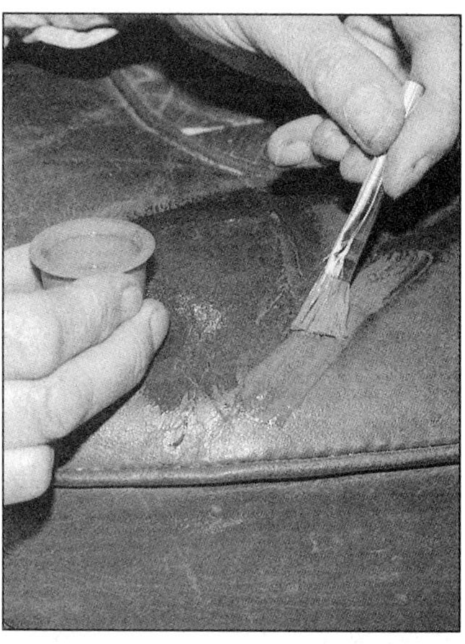

▲ *4.27. Leave the repair(s) for several hours (preferably overnight), then mix the colouring agents in the mixing bowl to match the correct shade of your original leather – this can take some time! On this repair we deliberately mixed a contrasting colour to make it more visible in the photograph. Next, paint the colour on to the repaired sections, and on to the adjacent material. Only apply to cleaned surfaces. Apply in several coats, allowing each to dry fully before applying the next.*

On completion, the seat will look and feel better, and should survive for far longer than an untreated example.

EMBOSSED LEATHER

It is especially important to take care of older leather bearing embossed features, such as those found in many pre-war cars, and also some post-war Vauxhalls, etc. The traditional, harder types of leather were more easily embossed than the softer varieties of today, and it can be impossible to duplicate an emblem built into the original upholstery.

Providing the leather from which any embossed panels are made is in sound structural condition, it can be recoloured to match surrounding panels made from new materials. Recolouring is the subject of the next chapter.

Chapter 5

Recolouring trim

It is quite often useful (or even necessary) to be able to recolour the trim components in your vehicle. Just one such occasion could be when second-hand trim panels have been acquired – they may be in good condition but completely the wrong colour for your car.

PAINTS

There are several options available when it comes to recolouring. One is to buy one of the special paints intended for use on PVC, etc., and to paint it on to the panels by brush. This will colour the surface of the panels (provided that they have been fully cleaned beforehand), and can look good and last for years.

Such paints are usually available in fairly small tins from motor accessory shops. However, a little of this paint can go a long way. I once successfully recoloured a second-hand trim panel for the rear door of an estate car by brush-painting with two coats of PVC paint from a seemingly tiny tin. Although I sold the car seven years ago, I still see it now and again, and I'm pleased to say that the trim panel still looks good!

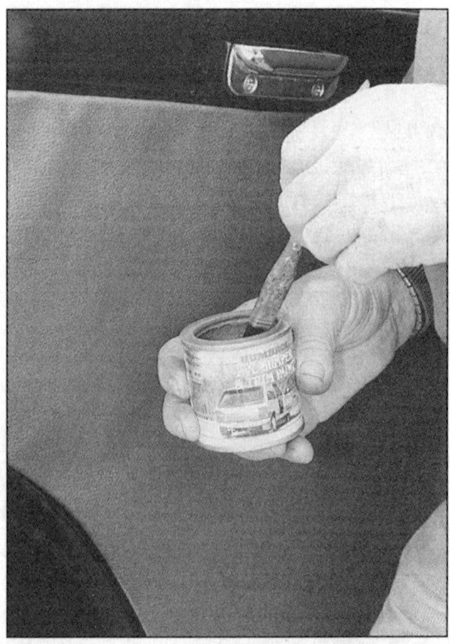

▲ *5.1. For recolouring small areas, or touching-in black trim panels, etc., PVC paint can give very good results. If the paint is applied carefully, the brush marks will disappear to leave a smooth, glossy and tough surface.*

For dealing more easily with larger areas, or where it is required to colour match the paint with existing trim, Woolies of Market Deeping supply a cellulose-based PVC/leathercloth renovating paint, which can be applied either by brush or (preferably) using a small spray gun, such as a modelling air brush, to give a quick-drying, tough, flexible and durable surface.

Woolies will colour-match sample material supplied (subject to the acceptance of a possible slight variation in shade). They say that thorough cleaning of the surface to be painted is necessary, especially to get rid of silicone-based surface treatments, etc. For this they advise using their special 'Leather Cleaner' liquid, rather than proprietary cleaners or white spirit, the latter of which can leave a film on the surface.

Woolies also supply Leather Renovation Kits which, while not primarily intended for recolouring leather, *can* be used for this purpose, depending on the colours concerned. Full details of application methods are given in Chapter 4.

PENETRATING COLOUR

A relatively new system of colouring vehicle trim is that offered by Bradleys Plastic Finishers under the Vinylkote name.

Unlike traditional paint products, Vinylkote is said to penetrate the surface of the trim being coloured, leaving the surface pattern 'as original'. The coating forms a chemical bond with the molecules of the material being coloured, thereby changing the pigmentation of it and eliminating the chances of flaking, peeling, cracking, and wearing off. It can be used on trim panels, seats (vinyl or leather), and on the soft plastics used in modern vehicles.

Available in any colour (Bradleys can match to your sample), and in gloss, satin, matt and textured finishes, Vinylkote can be used for revitalizing existing trim by bringing its appearance back to original condition, or by completely changing its colour.

The colouring agent is a pre-thinned, single-pack product which comes ready-to-spray. It is said to contain no CFCs, cadmium, zinc, formaldehyde or isocyanates, and that it gives a non-toxic finish. However, rubber gloves and goggles are required when handling Vinylkote, as it contains petroleum distillates. It should also only be applied in a well-ventilated area. Detailed health and safety information is given in Bradley's 'Mixing Scheme' leaflet, and the advice contained therein should be followed.

CLEAN IT!

It is essential to clean any trim panels being re-coloured. Dirt, grease and silicones can first be removed by using Vinylkleen. In cases where the surface may previously have been painted or lacquered, a product called Vinylprep should be used as well. This should only be used sparingly on ABS or PVC type plastics.

If dirt is really ingrained in the trim, and conventional cleaning has had little or no effect, it may be worth trying a very little cellulose thinners, applied with a clean rag. Take great care, however, and try a small unobtrusive area first – thinners can melt some plastics very quickly!

After the surface of the trim panel/seat has been cleaned, the Vinylkote is sprayed on – it is best to try a small area first. After 15 minutes or so, a length of sticky tape should be stuck on to the newly recoloured section, and then lifted off. There should be no Vinylkote on the tape, and in virtually every case, there won't be! However, if there *is*, the product has not penetrated the surface, and reference will then need to be made to Bradleys or their 'Mixing Scheme' leaflet for what action to take.

The Vinylkote should be applied in 'mist' coats (between two and five in number, waiting from 10 to 15 minutes between coats) using a fairly low air pressure setting. It dries quickly, and can usually be handled within half-an-hour of spraying. Full curing time is usually between 16 and 20 hours. Higher temperatures will reduce drying times. Damp/humid conditions can cause poor adhesion and/or 'blooming' of the product.

Vinylkote is particularly useful for reviving items of trim vital to the car's character but which cannot be reproduced by DIY methods. Bear in mind, though, that although the product gives excellent results on good condition leather and vinyl, etc., it will not hide deep cracks on old coverings.

The following photograph sequence depicts how a special panel from a 1959 Cadillac (which had for many years been standing in the Arizona desert) was recoloured to match the rest of the interior, which had been retrimmed. Since the panel could not be replaced with a new item, the only option was recolouring. In this case the panel was removed from the vehicle. This is always the best option, although a delicate item *could* be left in the vehicle, provided that masking is fastidious!

▲ *5.2. Neglected and dirty, this panel from a 1959 Cadillac was looking very sorry for itself. To revive it, Vinylkote of the appropriate colour was mixed by Bradleys, using a sample of the new leather in which the rest of the vehicle had been retrimmed.*

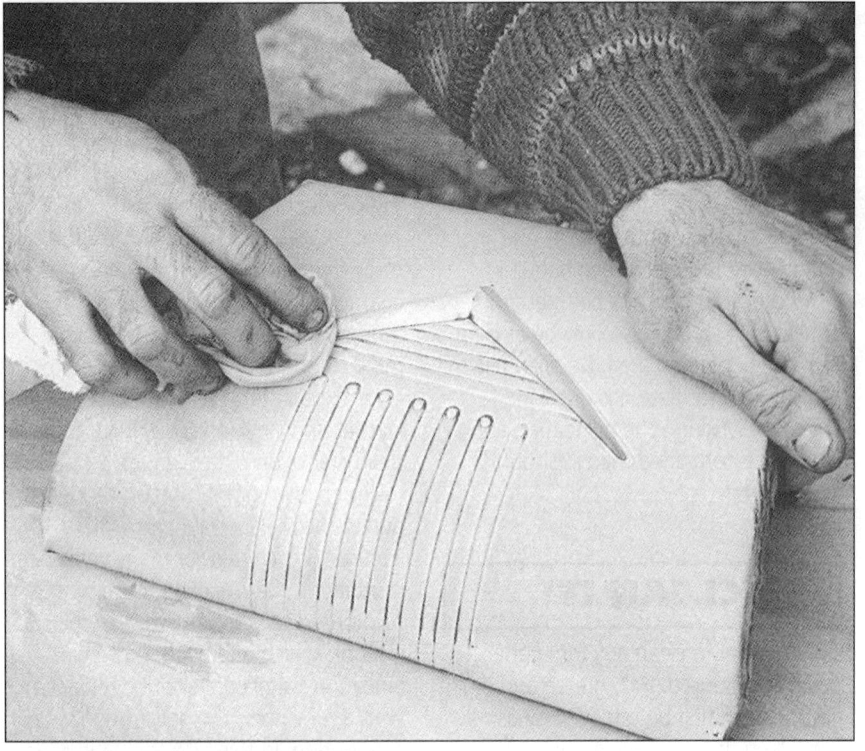

▲ *5.6. This recoloured Cadillac panel not only now precisely matched the shade of the rest of the trim, but was completely transformed – a shining example of what can be achieved for comparatively little effort.*

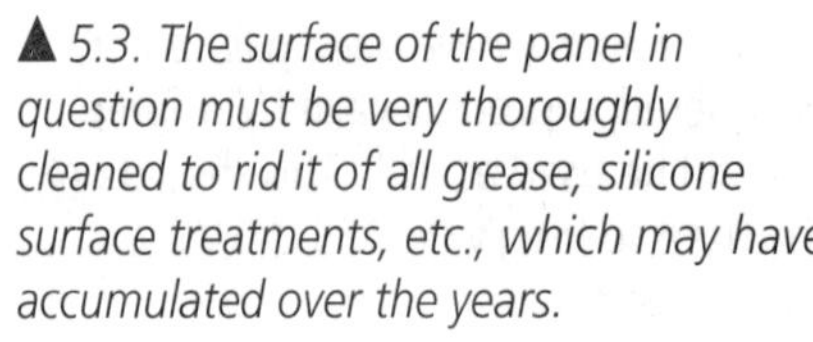

▲ *5.3. The surface of the panel in question must be very thoroughly cleaned to rid it of all grease, silicone surface treatments, etc., which may have accumulated over the years.*

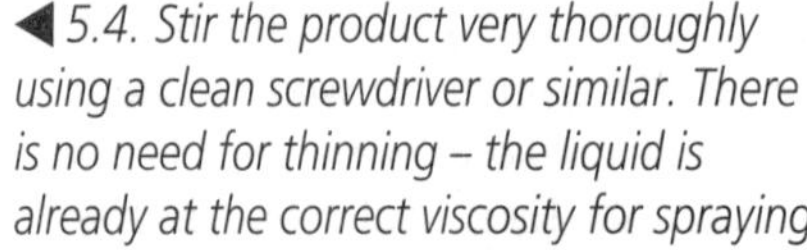

◀ *5.4. Stir the product very thoroughly using a clean screwdriver or similar. There is no need for thinning – the liquid is already at the correct viscosity for spraying.*

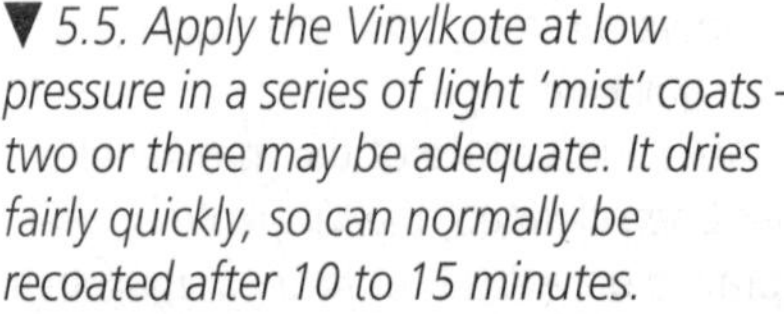

▼ *5.5. Apply the Vinylkote at low pressure in a series of light 'mist' coats – two or three may be adequate. It dries fairly quickly, so can normally be recoated after 10 to 15 minutes.*

CHANGING COLOURS

The section above showed how to use Vinylkote to re-apply 'as original' colour to a trim panel. In the following sequence a colour change is dealt with. Should you have to use a trim panel from another car, the chances are it will be of the wrong colour. By using Vinylkote you can very easily and permanently recolour it to match your existing trim.

The experimental piece this time is a scrap door trim panel from an old Triumph, to which was added a dramatic 'arrow' shape – just to show what can be achieved.

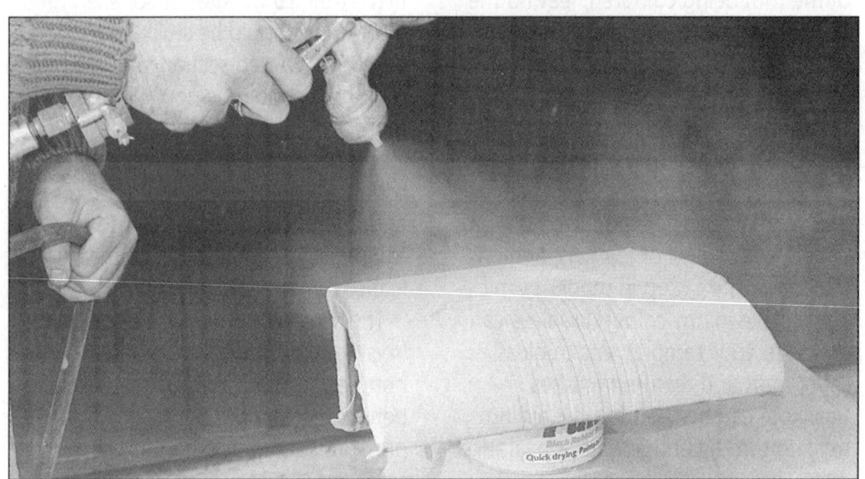

▲ 5.7. *Before the experiment the panel was just plain black vinyl.*

▲ 5.8. *To brighten it up it was decided to form an 'arrow' shape in the centre of the panel, and to spray it in a contrasting colour. Having first thoroughly cleaned the panel (as described in the previous section), the required shape was formed by using masking paper and masking tape.*

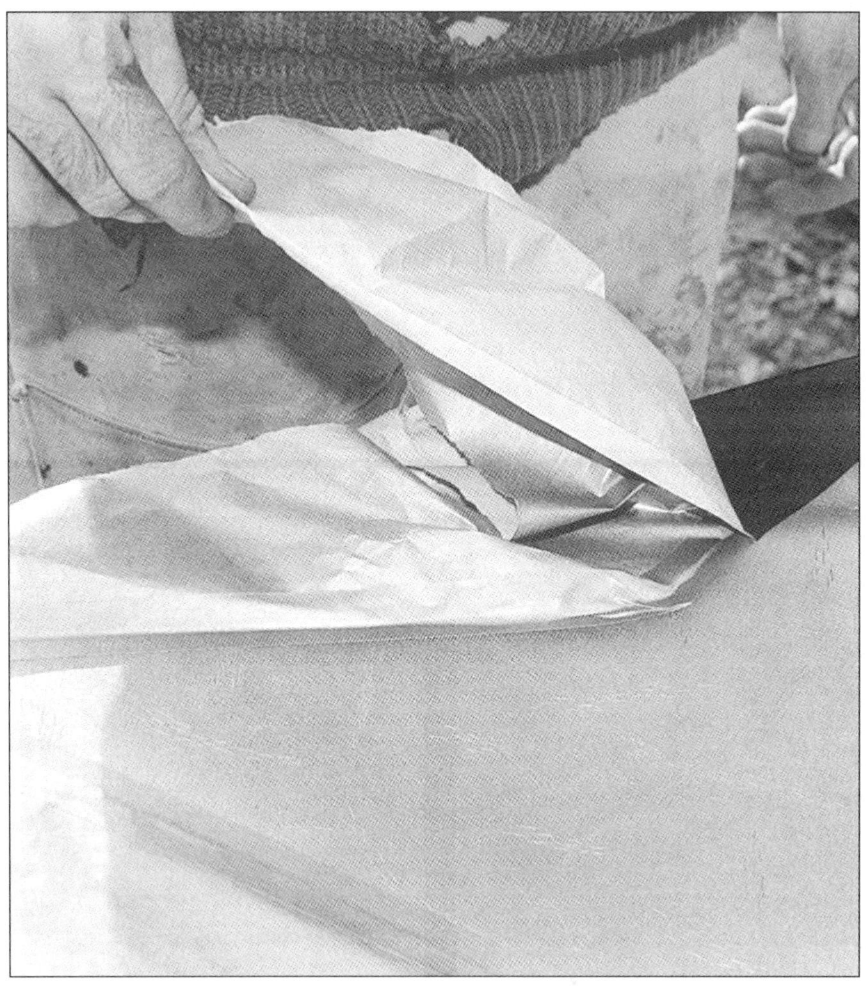

▼ 5.9. *The Vinylkote of contrasting colour was now applied in several 'mist' coats, each being allowed to dry before application of the next.*

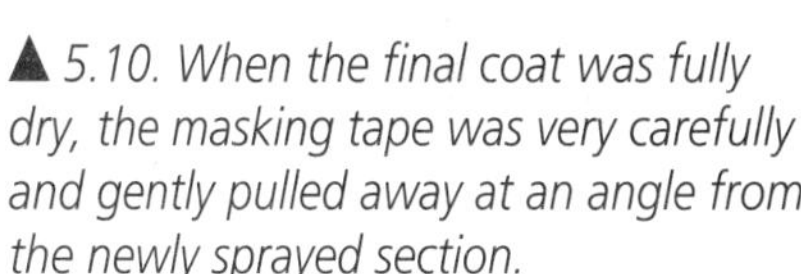

▲ 5.10. *When the final coat was fully dry, the masking tape was very carefully and gently pulled away at an angle from the newly sprayed section.*

▼ 5.11. *The finished result. The coverage was remarkably good, showing what can be achieved when completely changing colours.*

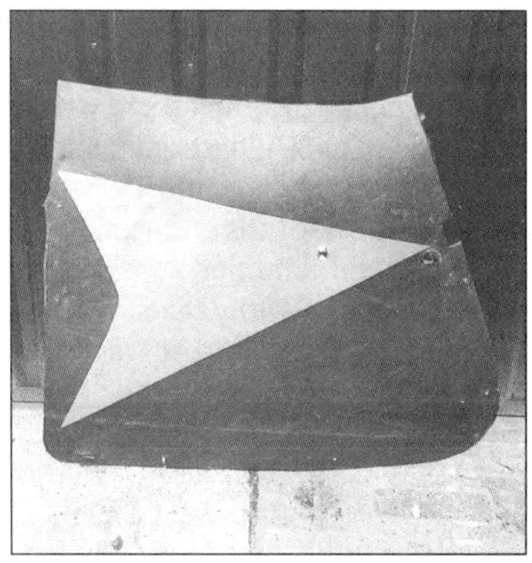

Chapter 6
Seats

The importance of the condition of the seats in your car should not be underestimated. Naturally, you want them to look good – particularly in a classic car – but your comfort when in the vehicle depends on them being in sound condition and properly padded. Filthy seats, with sagging springs and broken frames, make for very unpleasant, and potentially unsafe, travelling.

So, for all reasons it is wise to ensure that the seats in your car are restored with great care and attention to detail. That way they will look right, feel comfortable on the longest of trips, and last a long time.

There are several basic rules to observe in the dismantling and restoration of car seats. For a start, when working on pairs of seats (usually front ones), leave one seat intact while working on its opposite number so that you have a pattern to work to should problems arise – they usually do!

Also, make a detailed study of the methods of construction of the seats you are dealing with. Unless you have a very good idea of how the seat was put together originally, there is little hope of your being able to properly rebuild it. To this end it is a good idea to take photographs and/or video film – or at least make easy-to-understand sketches – of the seat in its original form, and during the various stages of dismantling.

When taking a seat apart, do the job carefully and try not to destroy the original materials, retaining clips, and so on. Items such as the retainers are often unique to the seats and it is therefore very difficult (if not impossible) to obtain new replacements, so the originals will need to be kept for reassembly.

When removing securing clips beware of sharp edges, as they could cause damage to you and the seat material if carelessly and hurriedly levered off.

Keep your workbench clean. Inevitably, as an old seat is dismantled, dust and rust will fall out of it. Clean this up as you go (a vacuum cleaner is usually the best tool for the job). Not only will it make for a more pleasant working environment, but it will prevent any damage from grit, etc., to new materials.

In every case, remember that patience is a virtue. Dismantling, repairing and reassembling seats is not a job which can be rushed, especially when you are new to such work. Take your time, concentrate on what you are doing and this job – which after all is not easy – will be enjoyable, and the reward will be seats you can be proud of.

VARIATIONS IN SEAT MANUFACTURE

Over the years the construction of car seats has changed dramatically. Early cars – typically those made up to the late 1930s – had wood-framed seats (ash usually being the wood). To the framework was attached the sprung/padded cushioning – often suspended within a wooden case or stitched to a webbed chassis. This in turn was covered by layers of calico, horsehair, more calico, cotton stuffing and, finally, the outer cover – usually of leather, although cloth seats were used on cheaper cars.

Before the Second World War, manufacturers turned to steel framing for their seats. Variations included tubular and pressed steel frames and, in place of inter-linked coil springs, foam padding in the form of shaped Dunlopillo assemblies gained in popularity. Some car manufacturers, including Austin, used pneumatic cushioning – rubber air bags being incorporated into the seat base.

After the war, foam bases were used, supported either by rubber webbing strips or rubber diaphragms, in each case stretched across the seat frame to provide the requisite tension.

During the 1950s, leather upholstery gradually gave way to vinyl, except in luxurious/sporting models, and stitched panels were discarded in favour of heat-welded units. In the 1960s and 70s, flat Z-profile springs were used, joined together across the seat base.

Different methods of construction led to a wide number of variations on the main themes, and one has to be realistic and accept that it will be very difficult – impossible, even – to obtain the original materials to rebuild a seat exactly the way it was first constructed. Improvization may be necessary to get as close as possible to the original design. For example, rubber foam padding may have to be used in place of badly damaged and irreplaceable pneumatic cushions.

Usually, seats show signs of wear by obvious damage to the covering (fraying, stretching and abrasion damage, etc.), lack of support within the base (due to broken springs, etc.), and by broken framework – the backrest frame often parts company with that of the base unit. In almost every case, the problem can only really be solved by stripping the seat to its bare components, so that the trouble can be fully assessed and the appropriate action taken.

SEAT DISMANTLING

The sequence of pictures which follows shows the dismantling, renovation and reassembly of a seat from a Jaguar Mark II. Although slightly more complicated than average, the basic construction of this particular seat is typical of a wide cross-section of car seats, and at the same time it incorporates many features likely to be found on classic luxury cars.

▲ *6.1. This sad seat from a Mark II Jaguar had seen many years of use, followed by a long period of neglect. The leather covering had disintegrated, the stuffing was in a bad way, and the steel frame within had broken.*

▼ *6.2. Carefully lift out the seat base, ensuring that all the relevant bits are kept together – both now and during any prolonged storage.*

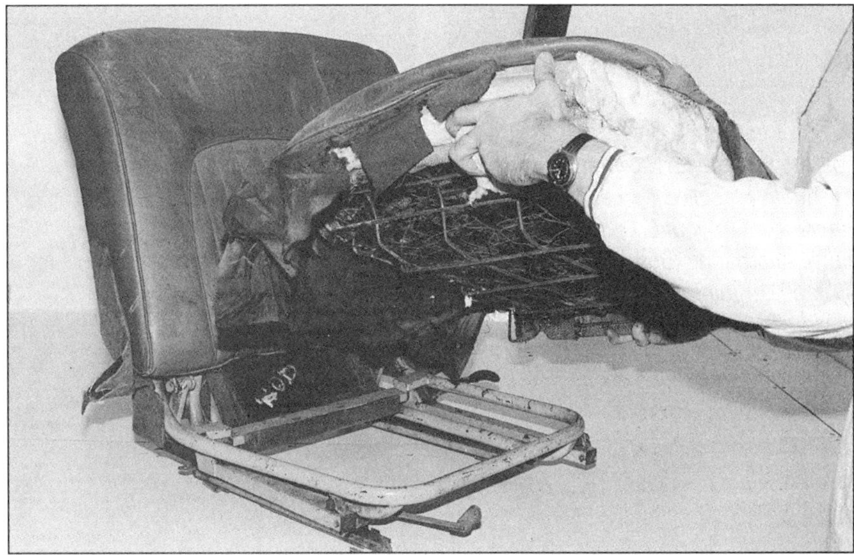

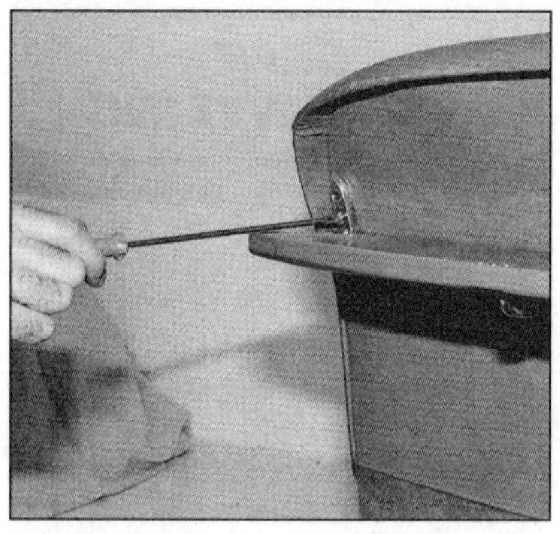
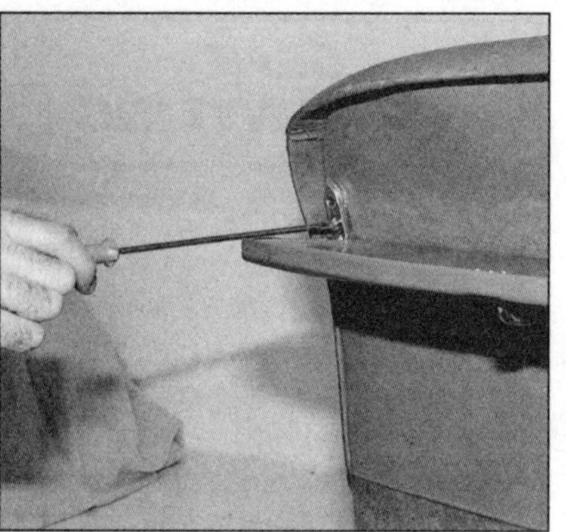

▲ *6.3. Tackle the backrest first, removing any extra accessories, such as this picnic table. Ensure that items like this – on which the wood finish was in excellent condition – are stored very carefully to avoid damage. Make detailed notes of the positions and numbers of any spacers found beneath brackets, etc.*

▲ *6.4. Keep all brackets, screws and spacers together in receptacles which are adequately labelled for easy future reference. Old yoghurt pots, jam jars and butter/margarine tubs make ideal storage containers.*

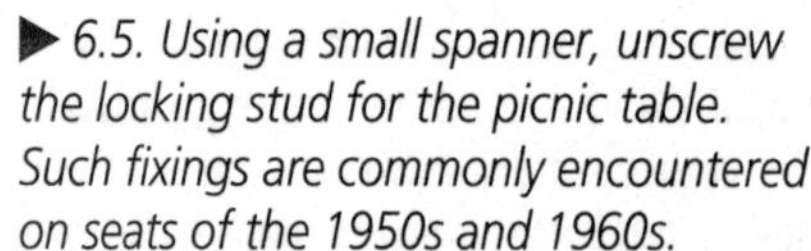

▶ *6.5. Using a small spanner, unscrew the locking stud for the picnic table. Such fixings are commonly encountered on seats of the 1950s and 1960s.*

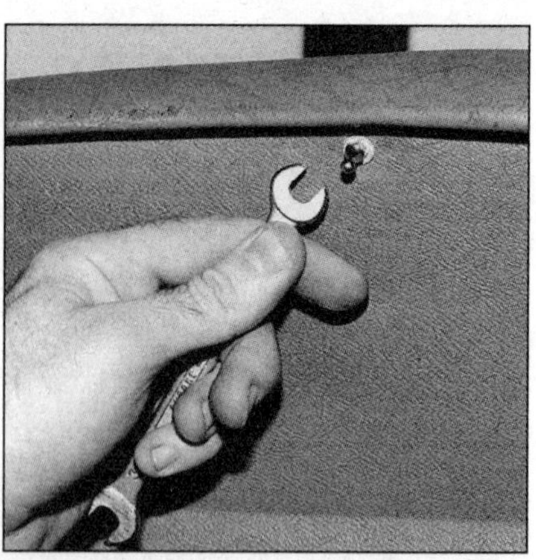

▼ *6.6. Taking very great care to avoid damage, remove the rear panel from the seat frame. Usually the clips will be in serviceable condition and can be used again – unless of course they are 'graunched' off during dismantling.*

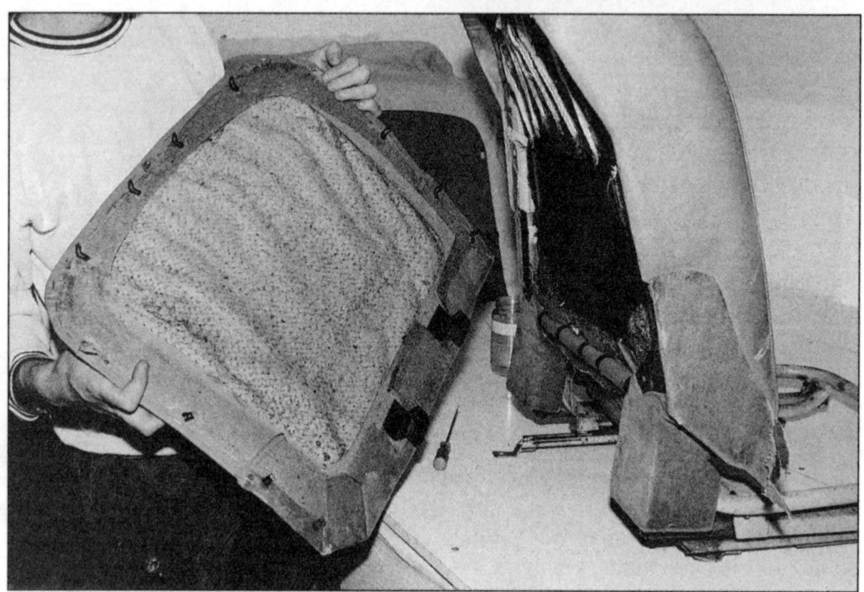

▼ *6.7. Some seats incorporate trim panels around the base, and these have to be released. They are often screwed on. Again, carefully retain all fasteners.*

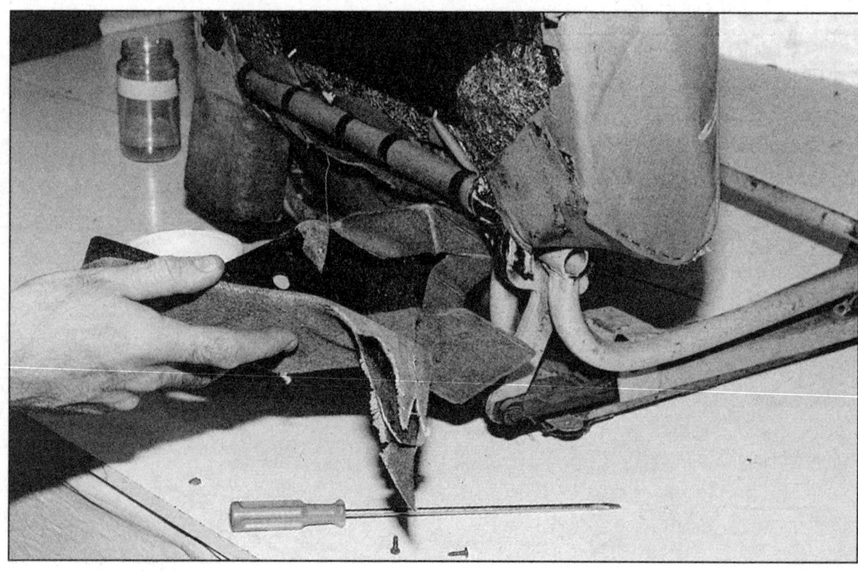

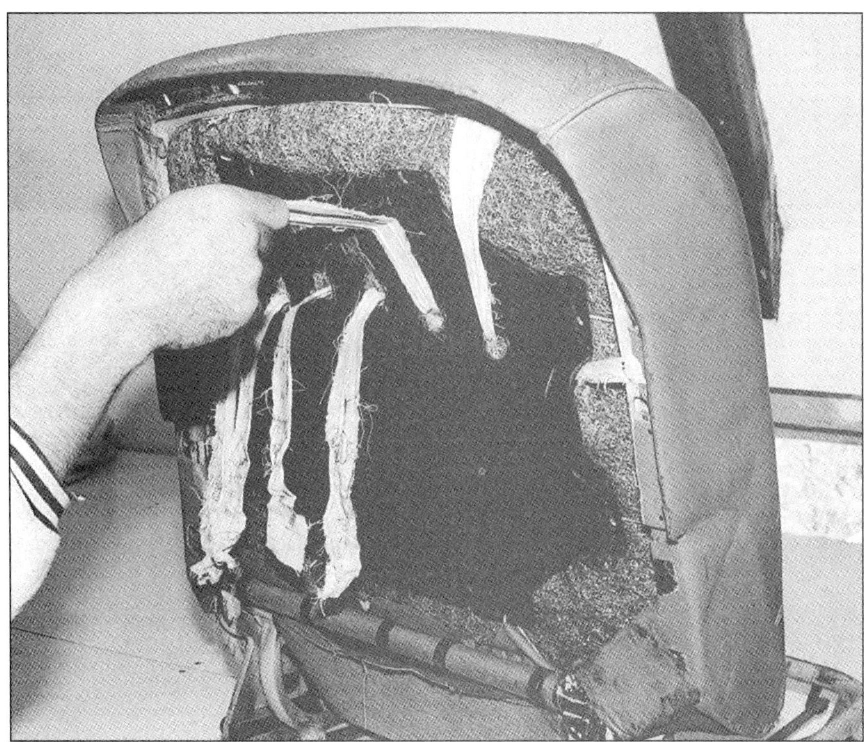

▲ *6.8. This Jaguar seat incorporates calico strips which effectively tension the centre section of the seat back. These are extensions of the backing material for the fluted section of the seat at the front face of the backrest. The calico strips may be nailed or – as in this case – glued in place. Carefully release them at the back of the seat.*

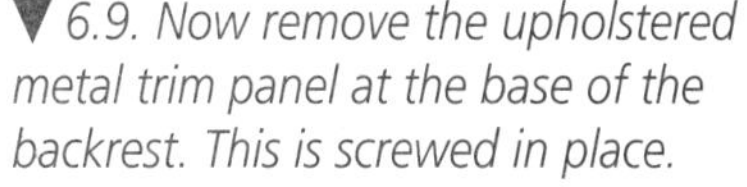

▼ *6.9. Now remove the upholstered metal trim panel at the base of the backrest. This is screwed in place.*

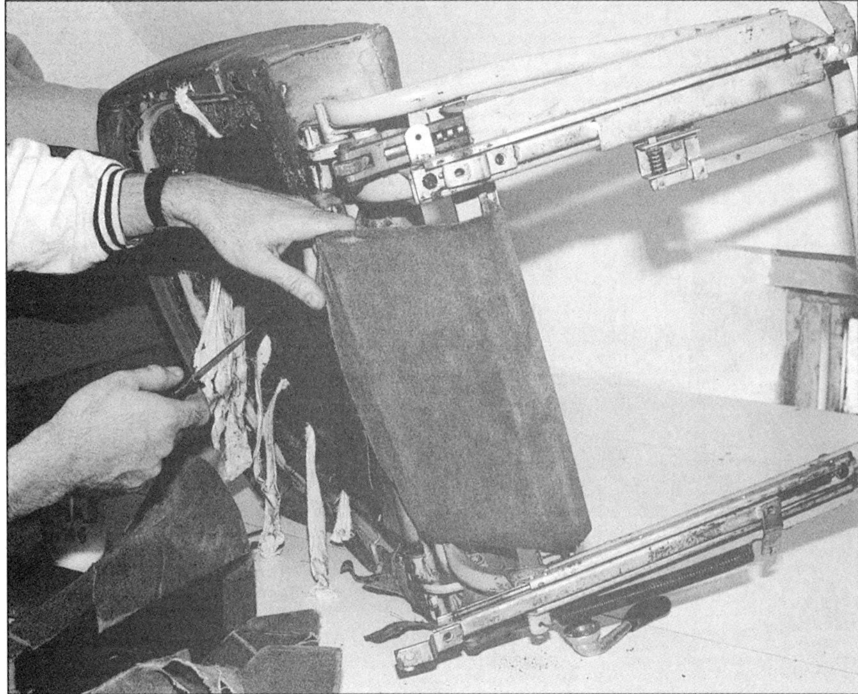

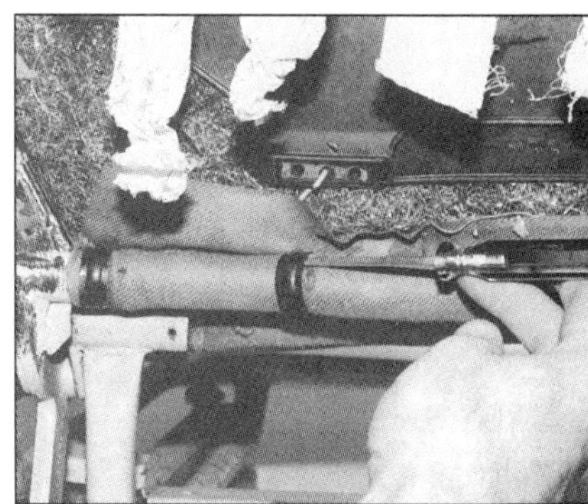

▲ *6.10. The way is now clear to release the C-shaped clips securing the cloth/vinyl (forming the lower section of the rear of the backrest assembly) to the lower rear cross-member of the frame. Take great care when releasing the clips, which can be gently levered off with an old screwdriver. Save them all in a suitable, marked container.*

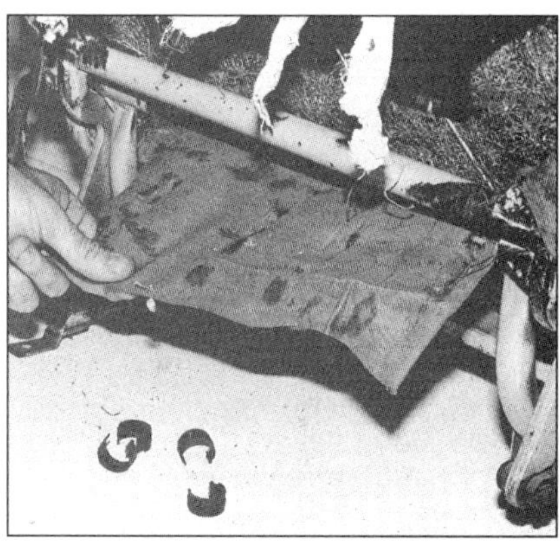

▲ *6.11. The cloth/vinyl can now be unwrapped from the cross-member.*

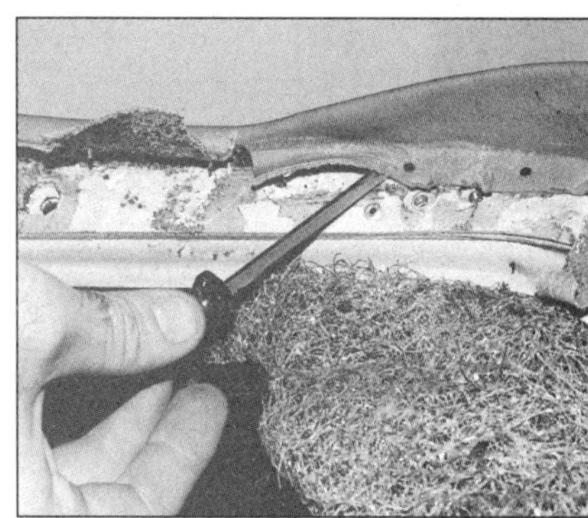

▲ *6.12. The leather side-panels are glued and nailed in position along the sides of the frame. Gently release them. Once more, an old screwdriver is a valuable implement.*

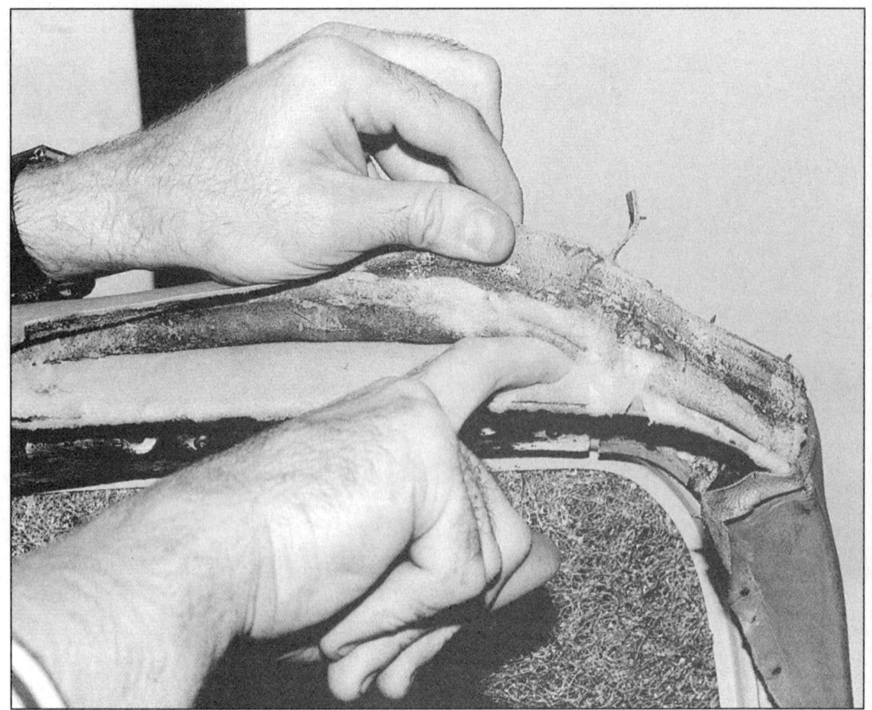

▲ *6.13. The next task is to separate – using your fingers – the foam rubber padding from the inside of its leather cover around the top of the seat. The foam at the sides forms part of the cover, and therefore it doesn't matter if at this stage the foam comes away with the leather.*

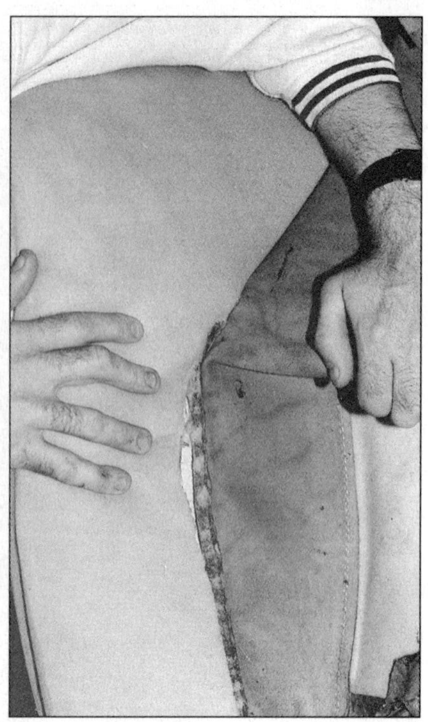

▲ *6.15. Separate the foam from the leather covering, taking very great care to save the foam, as it is specially shaped to give the seat its form, and can usually be re-used. On this Jaguar seat the foam within the back rest was shaped like an inverted U.*

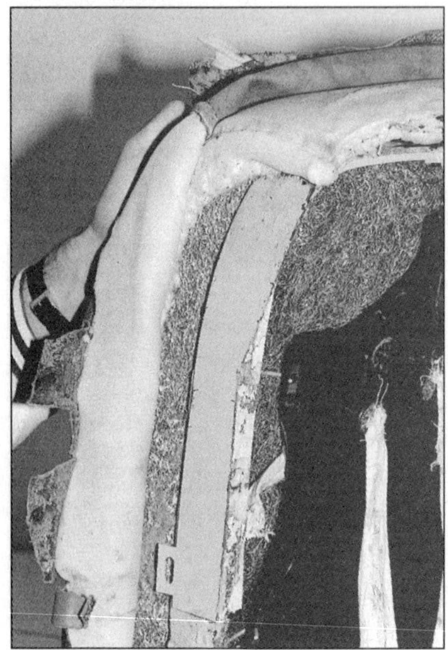

▲ *6.14. Now peel away the leather. Start in one corner and roll it off the frame.*

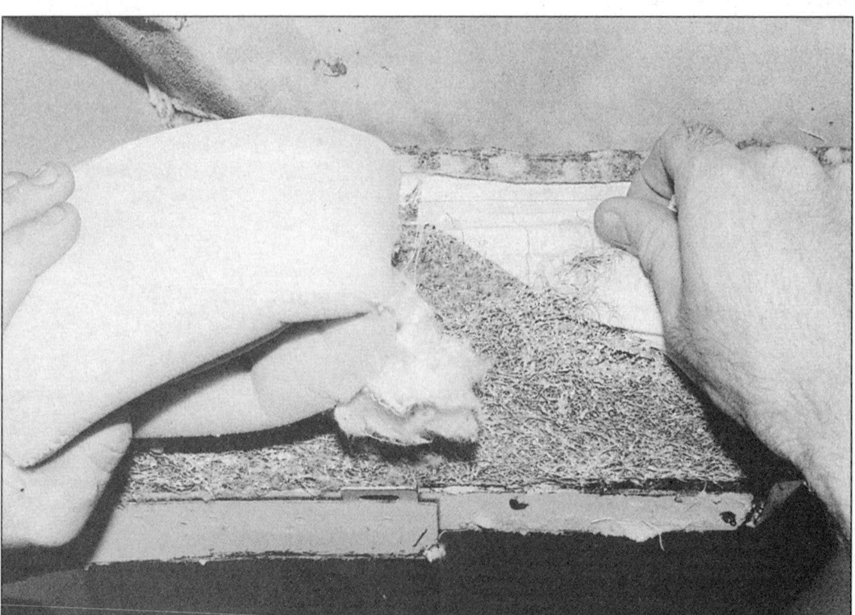

▲ *6.16. Next, gently release the calico side-flaps which secure the centre section of the seat covering to the rubberized horsehair backing.*

▲ *6.17. Now, carefully pull out the calico strips (shown in picture 8) forwards and through the foam.*

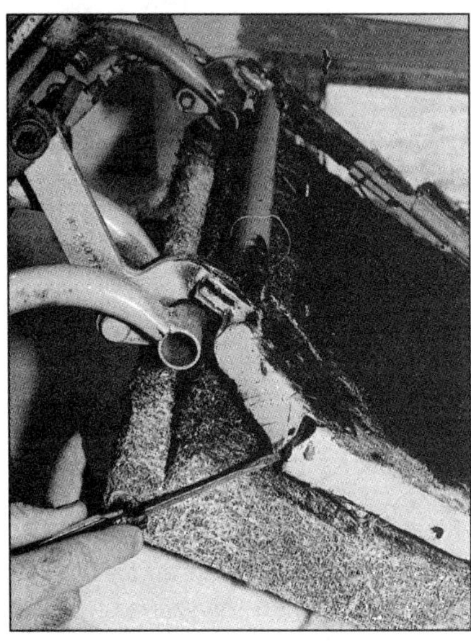

▲ *6.18. At this point, carefully inspect the seat frame for damage. This corner on our frame was not joined – and it should have been – resulting in diagonal distortion/twisting of the frame.*

Normally, there is no need for further dismantling, but if, as in our case, the frame needs to be repaired by welding, all coverings obviously must be removed first.

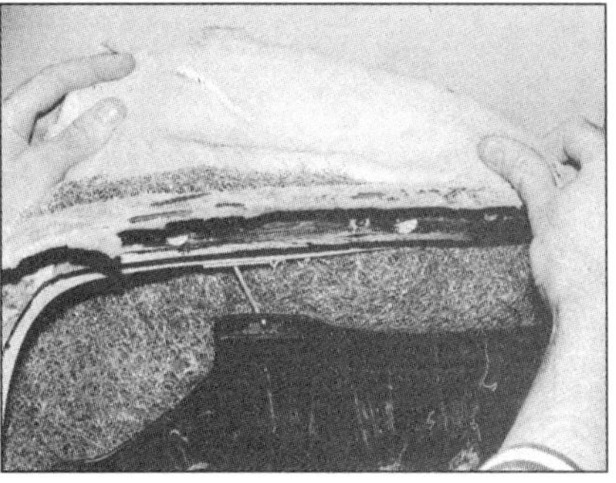

▲ *6.19. Carefully separate the padding from the outer edge of the seat frame.*

▲ *6.20. Unhook the rubber support pad from the perimeter of the frame, and gently pull the pad clear, with the rubberized horsehair still attached. Incidentally, not all seats incorporate rubber pads.*

▲ *6.21. Welding (MIG or oxy-acetylene are suitable) can now be carried out to repair the frame. Ensure that the frame assumes its correct profile before welding takes place, and make sure that the joint is strongly made.* ***Always wear protective gloves and goggles when welding.*** *Treat the weld and surrounding metal with protective paint after welding, and allow the paint to dry fully before proceeding.*

▲ *6.22. Now that the backrest assembly has been stripped to its basic components, work can start on the base of the seat. First, remove the retaining hog rings securing the cloth to the base of the seat at the rear. A pair of pliers or side cutters is useful for this operation.*

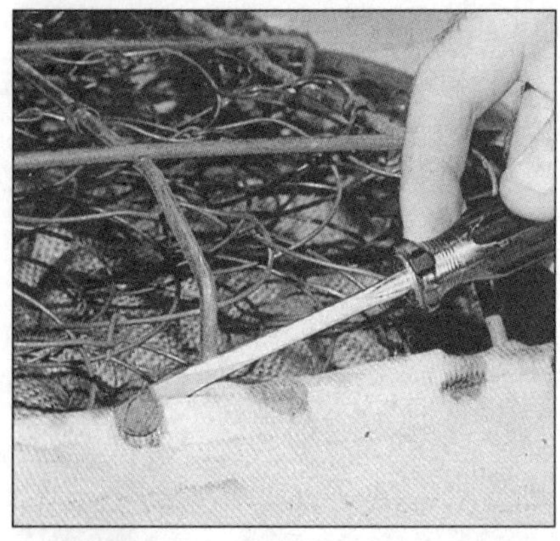

▲ *6.23. Next, ease out the clips securing the material to the sides of the steel frame. As always, retain the clips in a safe place.*

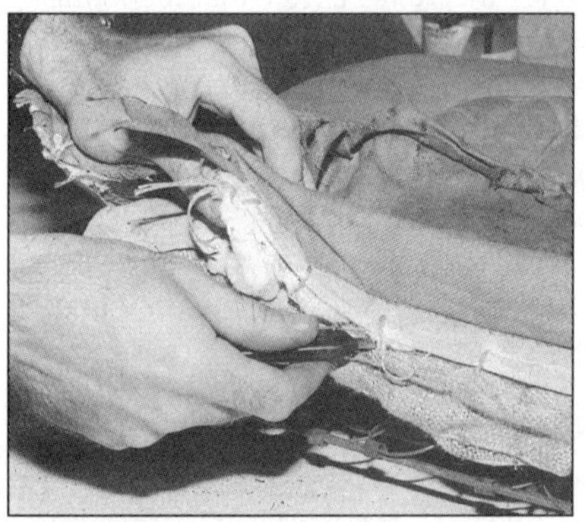

▲ *6.24. Using a sharp knife, cut the stitching at the rear of the seat base.*

▼ *6.25. Carefully peel back the cover, ensuring that this and the foam within are not damaged in the process.*

SEAT REBUILDING

Once a seat has been dismantled, a replacement cover can be made by using the original sections as patterns. It is vitally important that the material you use is as close as possible in texture and strength to the original.

Modern stretch vinyls can be easier to work with than traditional materials with less inherent 'give', and they certainly cost less (which is attractive if you are working to a tight budget). However, since a decision to use vinyl will almost always be regretted in the future, it is far better to do the job properly at the outset.

Of course, there is nothing wrong with vinyl for a car in which it was used originally, but a car trimmed in leather when new will never look, feel or smell the same if its seats are replaced with vinyl covers.

The extra outlay on leather will be compensated for by the fact that the job should only need to be done once and, if the work is diligently carried out, should look good indefinitely. This will be appreciated every time you – or anyone else – takes a look at the interior of your car. The voice of experience speaks here – I once had a car reupholstered in a plastic leather substitute material, and have regretted it ever since. The only way round the problem now, of course, is to start all over again!

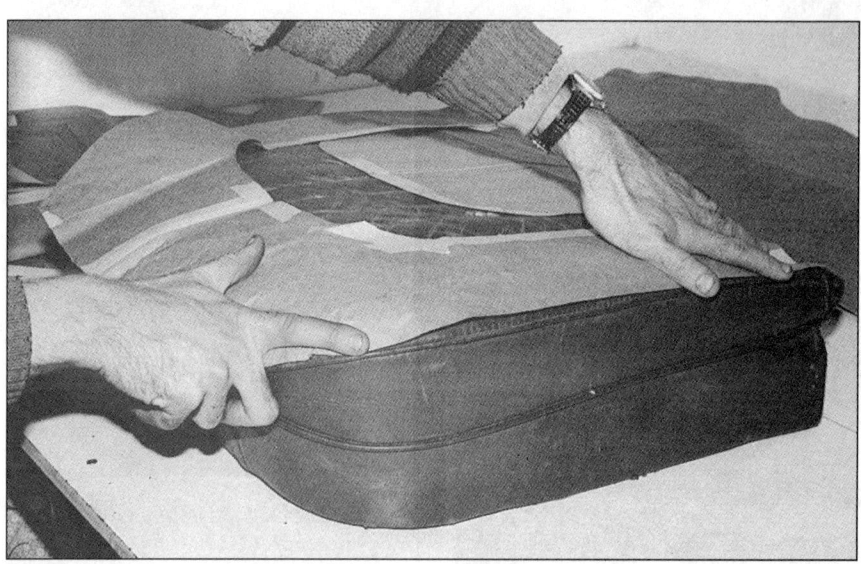

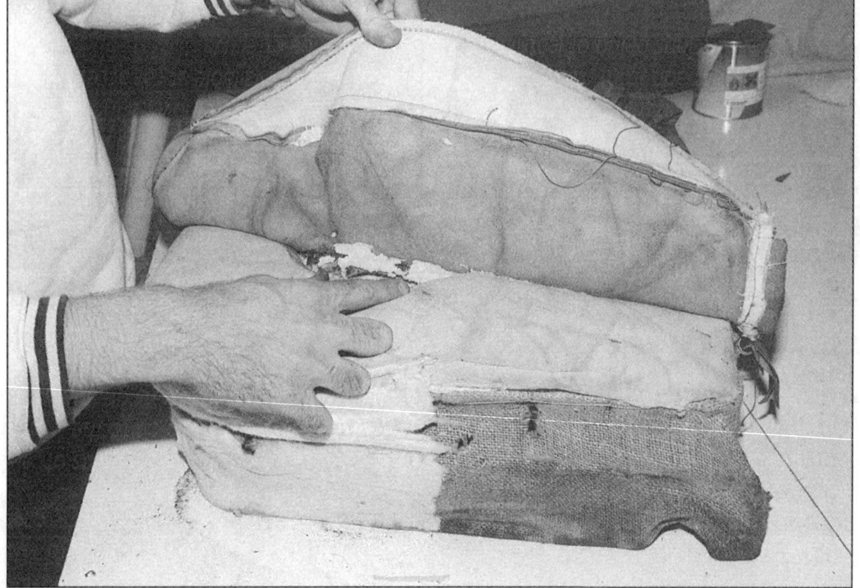

▲ *6.26. It is vital that an accurate template is made for each large, unpleated section of the seat coverings – brown paper is a flexible, practical and inexpensive material for this. If necessary, mark and cut the template for the section a little larger than the original, to allow for final trimming to the correct shape. In this case, the pattern has been made for the horseshoe-shaped outer section of the base of the Mark II Jaguar seat.*

FLUTING

There are no two ways about it – the measuring and making of fluted sections for seat coverings is an involved procedure, and the potential problems are many. Frankly, if you are not a patient person, it may be better to seek professional help for such work.

Success in this field requires great accuracy, application and attention to detail, and the ability to be able to calmly count to ten and start again if things go wrong, as they may well do, at least to start with.

Always allow plenty of time for this work – rushing will get you nowhere. Also, especially if you are working with leather, bear in mind that miscalculations and mistakes will be costly; so take care, and double-check at each stage of the operation. Having said all that, persistence pays off, and practice really does make perfect. The experience of producing quality, good-looking fluted upholstery yourself is a rewarding one, and worth all the effort.

There are several ways of achieving a pleated, or fluted look on seats (and sometimes also on door trim panels, etc.). The traditional method is to sew the seat covering material to a backing cloth, with a series of parallel stitching lines, such that a series of long, narrow pockets is created between the two. These pockets are subsequently stuffed with a soft, cotton-wool like substance, to give the seats a unique, supple feel.

Each pleat in the covering material overlaps the next one, in such a way that the stitching is hidden from view by the folds in the material. Obviously, these folds mean that each flute requires a greater width of covering material than the finished product would suggest, and gauging the amount of extra material required is a matter for practice as well as accurate calculation – more of this later.

A less complicated method of creating flutes is to lay a sheet of cotton stuffing on top of the backing cloth, and in turn cover the stuffing with the covering material, folding and stitching these three elements together along the edge of each pleat.

Easier still is using a backing cloth which can be bought with a covering of stuffing already bonded to it. In this case the covering material is simply sewn to the combined backing assembly. However, it has to be said that neither of these two alternatives really quite live up to the original method in looks and feel. What follows, therefore, deliberately concentrates on the traditional, more complicated sequence of operations, so that best results are achieved.

MATERIALS AND MEASUREMENTS

It cannot be emphasized too strongly that only top quality materials should be used when re-creating pleated or fluted upholstery. This applies to covering materials, backing cloths and to substances used for stuffing.

Inferior quality materials are almost always a poor long-term investment, and could mean that the job may have to be tackled again rather sooner than you would wish. Fluted sections of seats are almost always in the areas which have to withstand the highest stresses, and poor quality materials may not be able to stand the strain for long.

As already explained, it is vital for a good finished result that measurements are taken most carefully from the original upholstery and applied to the new materials. In particular, it is necessary to establish the precise width of each individual flute, and for this purpose it is best to take measurements at the front and back of each flute, rather than in the centre. This is because the weight of a seat's occupant is usually concentrated in the centre of it, leading – eventually – to stretching of the material and therefore providing an inaccurate width dimension.

Always measure all flutes – not just one or two – just in case they are not all the same. Interestingly, the numbers and widths of flutes can vary between seats taken from similar models of vehicle, and it is not unusual to find variations between different flutes on the same seat!

To double check the average width of each finished flute required, measure the overall width of the fluted section of the original seat, and divide the figure obtained by the number of flutes it comprises. It is also, of course, vital that the length of the fluted section is correctly established, i.e. taking into account the sag of the original seat. A flexible tape measure is the best implement for this job.

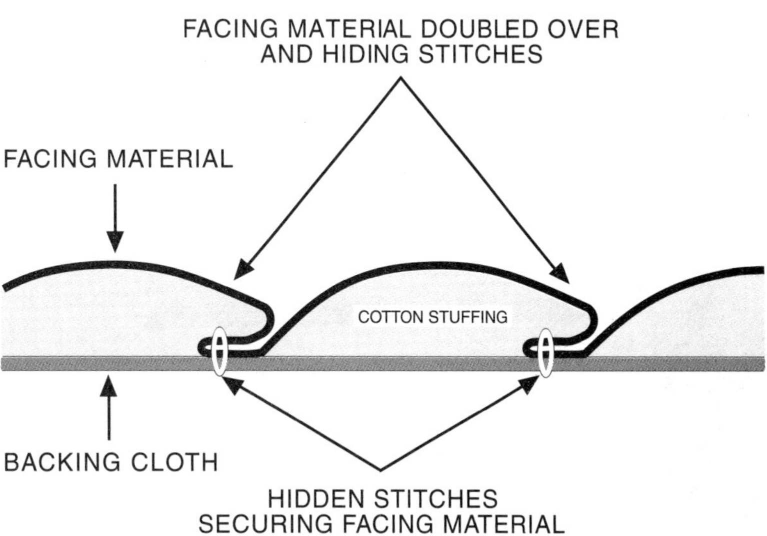

▶ *6.27. The traditional method of creating fluted upholstery is to form a series of 'waves' across the material. In each case the covering material is stitched to a backing cloth (e.g. calico), but the doubled-over folds in the covering material ensure that the stitching is not visible from the face side – clever but complex.*

▶ *6.28. It is necessary to take measurements of the overall width of fluted sections, such as these, as a vital reference when rebuilding. The dimensions of such sections should be transferred to the backing cloth, as described in the text. Measuring and marking out the flutes onto the seat covering material is much more complicated, since each flute has to be marked out wider than the finished items to allow sufficient material to create 'stuffing' pockets and folds within each flute. This measuring and forming is a complicated operation which requires time and patience, but it has to be right. Making a paper pattern for the whole of such a section can be a useful guide to the size and shape of the finished fluted section.*

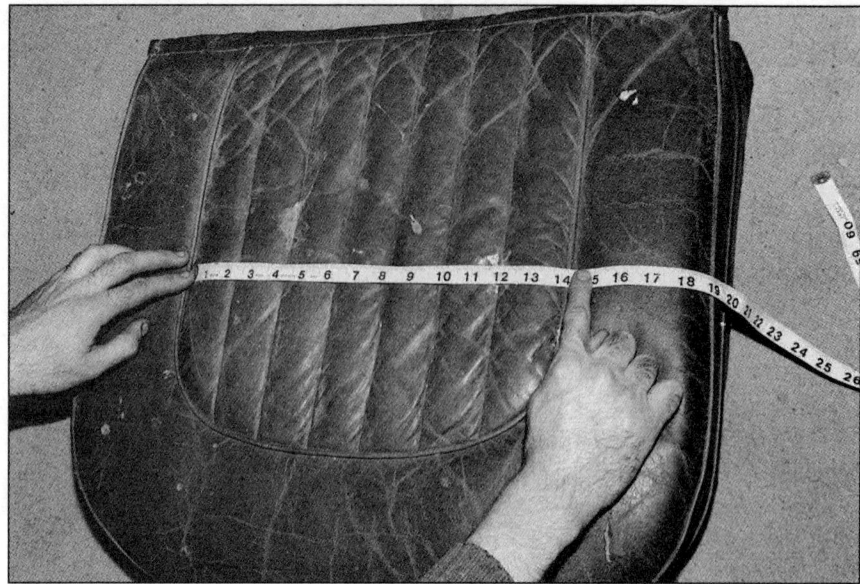

Once the overall measurements of the fluted section have been established, the perimeter of the replacement section, and the individual flute lines, can be marked out onto the backing material (usually calico), using chalk, a fairly fine point ball pen, or a fine nib felt tip marker.

This operation is fairly straightforward since, of course, even when the fluted assembly is completed, the backing cloth will sit relatively flat. Therefore, the width and length dimensions of each flute can exactly match those taken from the original seat.

Ensure that the backing cloth is free from folds before you start, and mark the positions of the flute lines so that they run parallel with the 'weave' of the material, so that it doesn't stretch in service.

Always mark out on a piece of backing cloth a little larger (normally, by about two inches/five centimetres) all round than the original section, making it easier to work with. However, don't just guess how much to allow. In all cases, refer to the original for guidance on how much extra material is required at each side, and at the top and bottom of the fluted section.

These 'extension' pieces are often fairly substantial, since they have to be glued to the body of the seat and help hold the assembly together. For example, on some backrest assemblies – like those of the Mark II Jaguar – in which extensions of the calico are fed through the horsehair backing and rubber diaphragm for securing at the back, make sufficient allowance for these strips in your calculations, also for the 'wings' of the backing cloth at each side of the main fluted section.

▼ *6.29. Take great care when marking out the position of each flute onto the backing cloth – in this case top quality calico. Inevitably, creases will try to form as you mark out the material, and it is important to eliminate these as you go.*

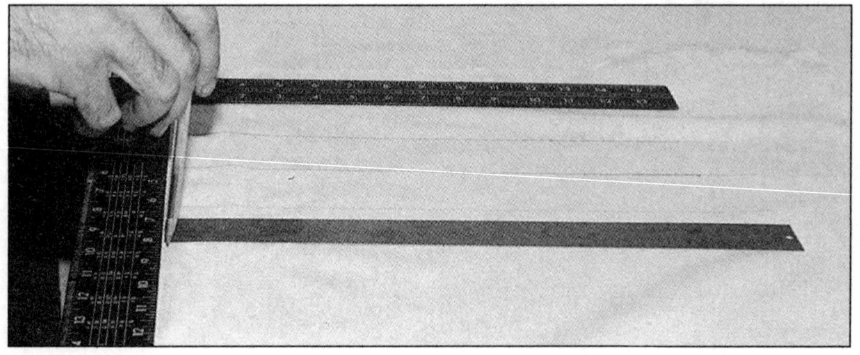

So far, so good, but producing the fluted section in the covering material is rather more complex. Having said that, if the job is taken step-by-step it is not so daunting.

Having established the precise width required for each finished flute, to this dimension must be added an allowance to provide sufficient extra covering material for the 'stuffing pocket' forming the outer wall of each flute, and to provide the seams/'doubled back' overlap at the edge of each one.

This is where calculations must be precise for a good-looking finished job to be achieved. The problem is that it is difficult to give exact instructions on how much to allow, in total, since there are several variables, including the thickness of the padding required in each flute. Obviously, the thicker the padding, the more covering material will be needed to form each flute, since the material has to wrap around the padding.

Other factors which affect the calculations include the width of the flutes themselves (on wide flutes, a little more overlap may be appropriate than with narrow ones), and the positioning of the stitches within the doubled-over edges of the flutes.

In any event, I would strongly recommend that before attempting to create a fluted section for real (and using materials costing real money!), you should create a few practice workpieces, using inexpensive vinyl as the covering material. The practice will help you judge how much allowance is needed in the measurements, to suit your individual application. It will also enable you to feel more at home with creating neat stitching in precisely the right place.

Only move on to the proper materials for practice pieces when you have gained confidence; and postpone attempts at actually making fluted sections of seats until you are really happy with what you are creating.

It is worth re-emphasizing that because the overall width of the covering material has to be slightly wider than that of the backing cloth (in order to allow for the thickness of the padding within each flute), an extra width allowance *per flute* has to be made when measuring.

In addition, a further amount must be allowed for the seams (and overlap) between each flute. As a general rule, this might be ⅛ in extra for the stuffing (although this will of course vary, depending on the required thickness of flute required), plus ¼ in for the seams/overlap, making a total of ⅜ in *per flute*.

If, for example, the fluted section comprises seven flutes, and has a total measured width of 14 in, with each finished flute therefore needing to be 2 in wide, the nominal width of the flute, to incorporate the allowance for the stuffing material, needs to be ⅛ in greater.

As already explained, an allowance also needs to be made for the seams/doubling-over of the edge – an additional ¼ in. This means that the extremity of each flute will need to be marked out on the covering material at intervals of 2⅜ in. (2⅛ in plus ¼ in).

In addition to the allowances already mentioned, for marking out purposes on the covering material, you should add an extra half an inch or so to the overall width, to provide a border to which adjacent panels can be joined.

This does sound complicated but, as already mentioned, experimentation and practice will help you gain confidence, and make easier the job of judging the correct width to mark out for the particular job you have to tackle.

With any seat covering material – and in particular in the case of leather – carefully inspect the material for flaws and ensure, if there are any, that they are kept well outside the area you will be working from. Leather hides can, for example, suffer from holes and marks which would spoil the appearance of a seat. Obviously it helps if you buy your hides from a reputable supplier, and if you carefully inspect them prior to purchase.

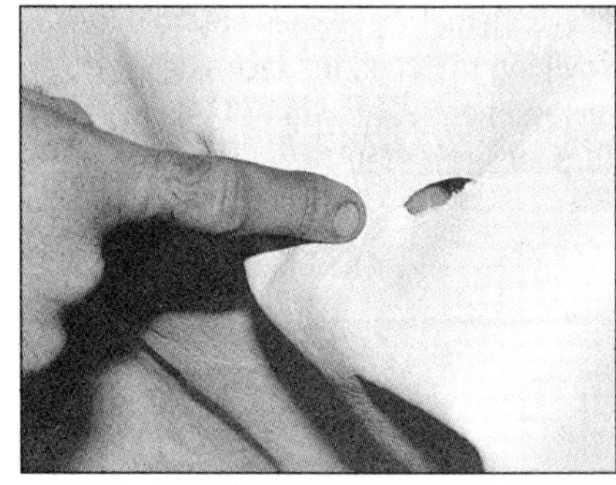

▲ *6.30. Holes like this are not uncommon in hides. Obviously such defects should be avoided when marking out the leather.*

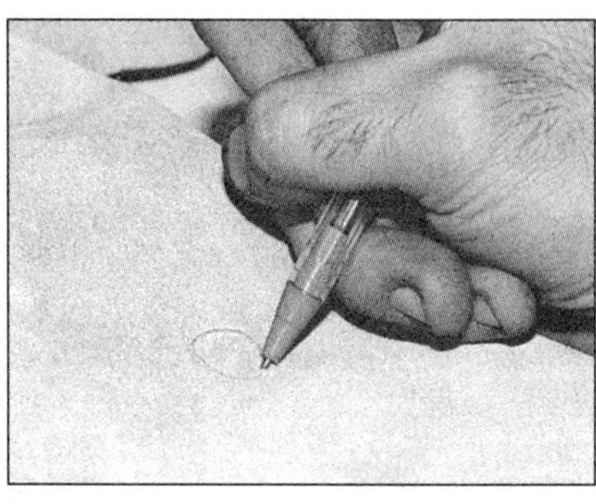

▲ *6.31. Less noticeable marks are best highlighted by circling with a pen. It is then less easy to overlook them when measuring and marking the hide.*

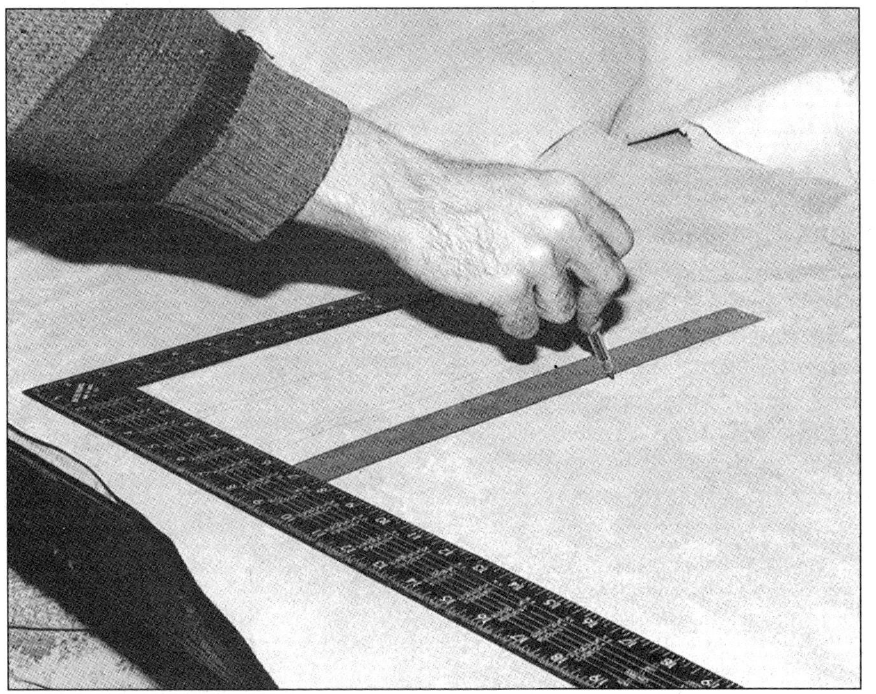

◀ *6.32. The next stage is to precisely mark out the reverse side of the hide, so that the flutes can be formed and stitched correctly. There are several approaches. Applying the measurements already quoted, and starting from the straight left-hand side line, representing the outside edge of the first flute, draw a line (B) at a distance of 2⅛ in from the left-hand side line (A) – 2 in being the width of flute and the remaining ⅛ in being the extra allowance for the padding. Draw another line (C) ¼ in further to the right, as shown. The two lines B and C, thus made, represent the stitching lines. The material is folded along the unmarked line (D) so that B and C are now adjacent (it may help when folding if you also mark line D on the material – midway between B and C). The covering material is then stitched through lines B and C, to the backing cloth (see photograph 6.34 on next page).*

NOTE: Remember, when you fold the covering material, the face side of it always meets, and you will sew from the 'unseen' side of it.

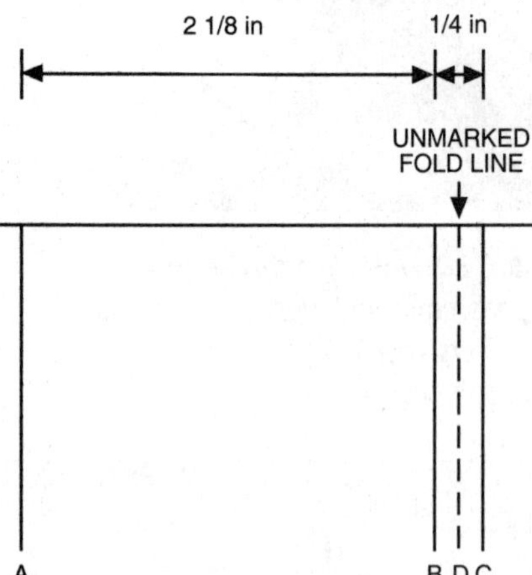

▲ *6.33 Having selected an appropriate, blemish-free area of the hide, mark out the positions of the flutes onto the back of it with tailor's chalk or a ball point pen. If using a ball point, take care not to press too hard or the leather may be marked on the other side, and avoid using inks which may soak through the leather.*

When the leather and backing cloth have been marked out, recheck your dimensions to make sure they are correct, and cut out the sections using a pair of shears designed for upholstery work. Take your time and be sure that you don't cut inside the lines marking the outer perimeter of the fluted section.

SEWING

Having marked and cut out the backing cloth and covering materials (not forgetting the extra half an inch or so around the covering material, to join it to adjacent panels), the two need to be joined together to form the basis of the fluted section.

Before starting, ensure that the sewing machine is correctly set up for the material being used, in terms of being loaded with thread of the correct type and colour for the material being sewn, thread lubrication, tension and length of stitch.

For leather, larger stitches are required than when working with vinyl. So, when working with leather, remember that any more than between eight and ten stitches per inch will lead to the material being cut as the stitching proceeds. In this case, fewer stitches will give a stronger result.

Lay the backing cloth (calico) with the marked lines uppermost, and on top of this sit the covering material (in our case leather), with the marked face downwards – i.e. towards the calico.

Now precisely align the marked lines at one end of both the backing cloth and the covering material. To achieve this, the covering material can be folded/doubled back on itself so that the first flute's perimeter line can be easily mated with that on the backing cloth. You may find it easier to hold the covering material in this position by using large paper clamps.

stitched line remains perfectly straight.

Stop every few inches and double check. At the other end of the flute, double stitch/over sew the last half-inch of stitching, to secure it. With the needle and clamp foot lifted, the materials can be withdrawn from the back of the machine (to avoid the thread catching) and the thread cut off.

▼ *6.34. Sewing the backing cloth and covering material together is obviously a critical part of the operation. Care, patience and time are needed to obtain good results. The two marked lines represent the outer edges of the two adjacent flutes (see also photos 6.32 and 6.33 above). In the picture you can see that these two lines are being sewn together and to the calico backing cloth.*

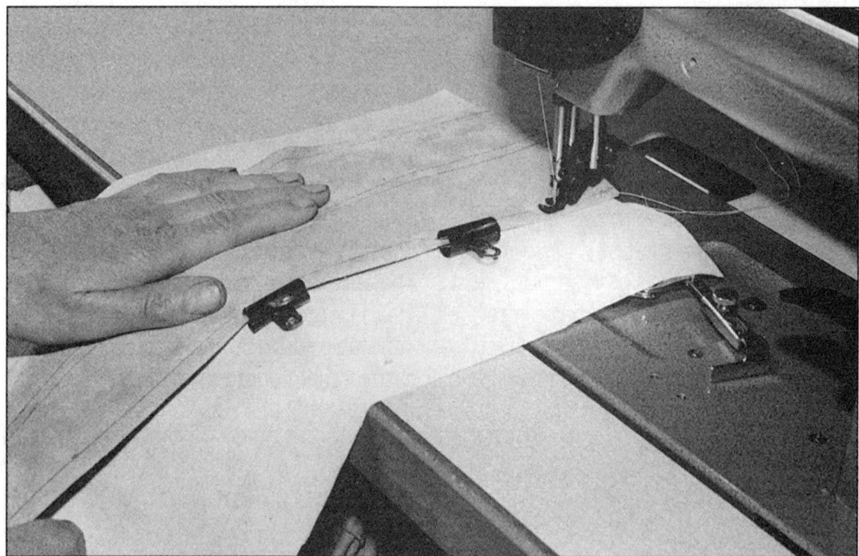

In fact, the first row of stitches needs to be made a fraction 'outboard' of the marked lines, so that at a later stage the adjacent border material and piping can be sewn precisely along the lines.

To create the first row of stitches, carefully feed the two thicknesses of material into position on the sewing machine (with the needle raised), and double stitch/over sew the end of the flute (for the first half-inch or so) to prevent the stitching from pulling undone.

Proceed carefully along the chosen line, gently feeding in the materials as you go, making sure that any creases are dealt with as they arise, and that the

▼ *6.35. Now clip together the material along the next flute line, and fold this line forward (to the right, as shown here) onto the next line marked on the backing cloth, then repeat the sequence as shown in 6.34. Repeat until all the flute lines are sewn up.*

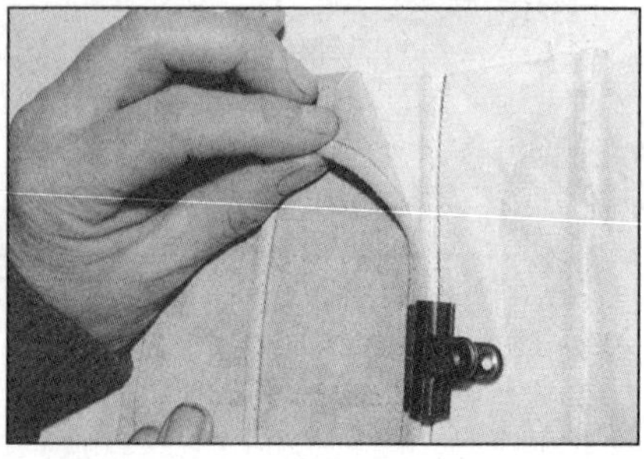

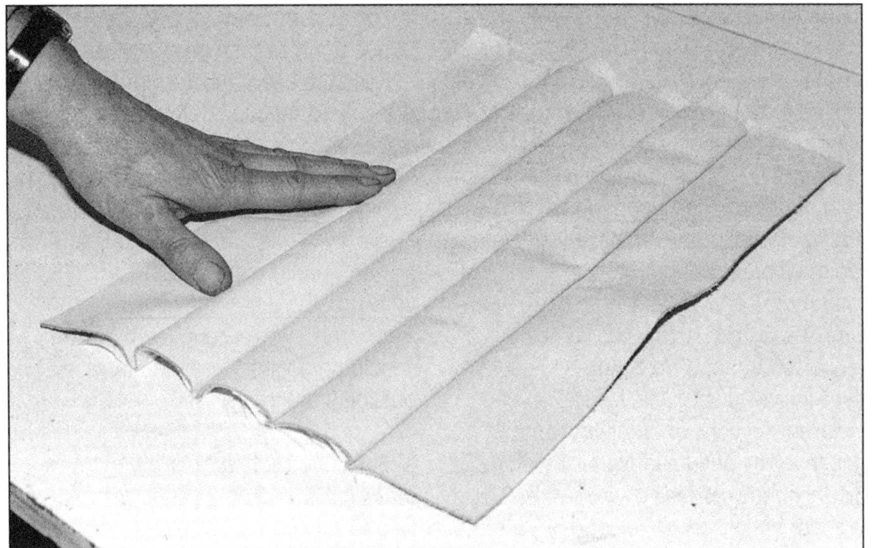

▲ *6.36. When the sewing is completed, the practice fluted section should look like this. Note that for this demonstration piece, we omitted the rows of stitches at the edges – these would obviously need to be included on a fluted section forming part of a seat.*

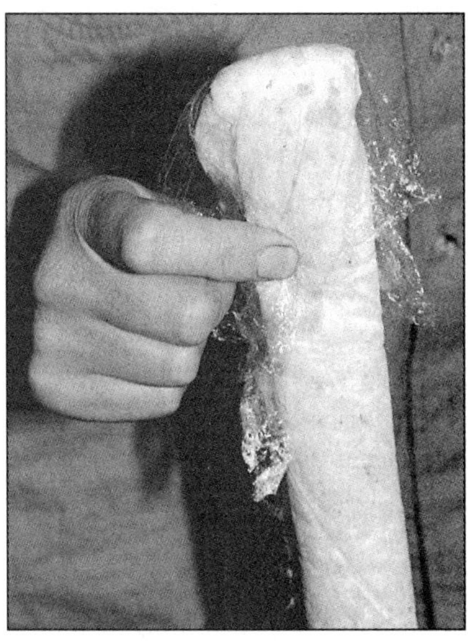

▲ *6.38. Lay the roll of padding material along the stuffing stick, and wrap a short length over the end, then cover this with a piece of cling-film.*

Nearly there – although at this stage the pockets formed by the fluting are still empty.

PADDING

Having joined the backing cloth and covering material, the pockets formed between them need to be filled with suitable stuffing material. Normally this is cotton-based wadding, although foam is sometimes used.

To create the appropriate thickness of stuffing within each flute, the material is rolled – typically two or three times, but more for thicker padding. Obviously, for a uniform effect, each flute requires the same amount of padding! Wherever possible, tear the stuffing to size, rather than cutting it, the random pattern at the torn edge helps to avoid hard lines which may be visible when the fluting is completed.

The wadding then needs to be fed into each flute. A specially designed stuffing stick can be used. This has a leather strap which doubles back along the length of the stick, and holds the padding in place against it as the stick is fed through the flute.

Once the padding is in position, the strap can be unwound from the stick, which is then very carefully pulled out of the flute (while holding on to the stuffing to prevent it from 'walking').

An alternative, if you don't have a stuffing stick, is to use a wooden rule or similar length of wood. The wadding is placed on top of the rule, the end wrapped over the wood and held in place by means of cling-film, as the stuffing is inserted into the flute. The plastic film helps the stick to slide easily through the flute, and keeps the padding in position as it does so. Simple but highly effective.

Eventually, a row of stitches needs to be applied across the open ends of the fluting to keep the wadding in position.

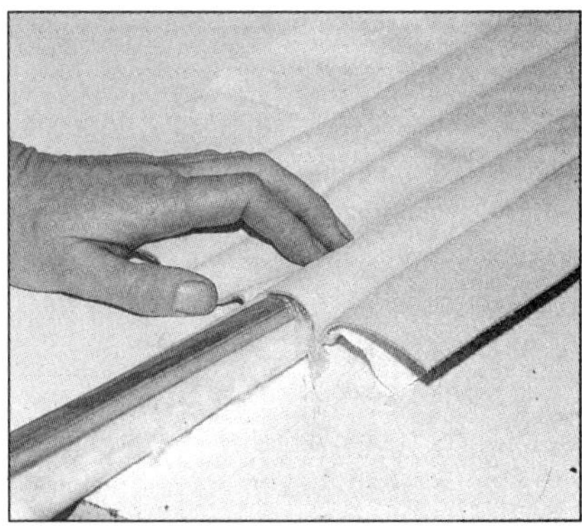

▲ *6.39. Now feed the stick, together with the padding, fully into the flute.*

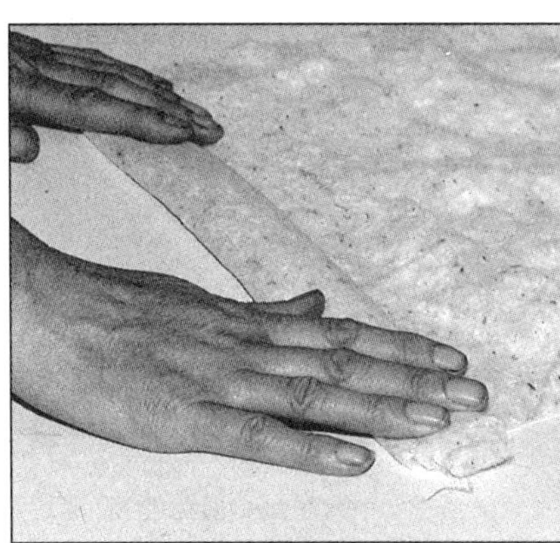

▲ *6.37. Carefully roll the padding material to create an appropriate thickness for the flutes you are filling. Flatten the rolls as you proceed.*

▲ *6.40. When the stick protrudes from the flute, simply remove the film and slide the stick out, while holding the padding in place.*

PIPING

To finish the fluted section and to add strength and provide a defining boundary between this and adjacent sections of the seat, a length of piping is employed. On older cars this is effectively a length of tightly packed, twisted paper (piping cord) or cotton, enclosed within a tube of covering material which matches or contrasts with the colour of the adjacent sections of the seat.

From the 1950s onward the piping in most cars consisted of wrapped 'plastic string', although some models – including Rovers – had piping with a steel base.

For cars of the 1970s and later models, ready-made plastic piping can be acquired, but for the larger diameter piping of earlier models, it will usually be necessary to fabricate your own. This involves wrapping a strip of covering material, approximately 1 3/16 to 1¼ in wide, over the piping cord so that the cord is fully enclosed.

The covering material is sewn together (and sometimes first glued as well) immediately adjacent to the cord. The extra flanges of the covering material are used to stitch the finished piping to the adjacent seat panels.

To form a length of piping, first mark out on the covering material a strip a little longer than the length you require, and carefully cut this out. This can then be wrapped over a similar length of piping cord of the appropriate diameter, and glued/sewn in place. You may find it beneficial to use a little glue to hold the materials together prior to sewing. In any case, the glue provides extra security.

Sewing together lengths of piping is not difficult, but does require the use of a special 'piping foot' on your sewing machine. This enables the strip of covering material to be stitched very close to the cord, pulling the cord and the material together to make a neat job.

There are a number of other factors to consider when creating piped edges. For example, when working on particularly long edges (perhaps on very wide rear seats) there is the possibility that you may have to join together two (or more) lengths of piping. However, this can generally be avoided if you always mark the lengths of piping required on your chosen covering material, before you cut out seat bases, etc. – so that a greater length of material is available.

If you do have to join two pieces of material, it is wise to position the joint where it is relatively unobtrusive, and at a point where it will not have to withstand maximum abrasion and stretching stresses. In fact, such joints can be disguised by applying a plug-and-socket type joint – at least ⅜ in long – between adjacent sections of outer covering. By tapering the outer surface of the plug and the inner surface of the socket (using a sharp upholstery knife), and by carefully gluing/sewing them together, the resulting joint will be barely visible.

When negotiating corners with piping, the material will tend not to want to go round smoothly. Therefore, for dealing with external (convex) radii, a series of V-cuts can be made along the flange of the covering material, while on internal (concave) turns the width of excess flange material is simply reduced as far as possible by trimming away.

A simpler alternative is to cut nicks in the flange of the covering material – but ensure that these don't reach the main part of the piping!

Once the piping has been formed, it has to be sewn into position. Often it will form the boundary between, for example, fluted and unpleated sections of a seat. Start by sewing the piping flange to the unpleated section, keeping the stitching close to the piping.

The next step is to attach the fluted panel, during which process it is again essential to keep the stitching as close as possible to the piping. It is vitally important that the fluted panel is stretched to its correct length before sewing on the piping – the natural tendency of the fluting is to shrink, and if it isn't pre-stretched as described, it won't properly fit the piping.

When this job is completed, there should be no stitches visible from the outside (you hope!)

▼ *6.41. To create border piping for seats, cut a strip of covering material (leather or vinyl, in a colour to match or contrast with adjacent panels) and wrap around the piping cord (in this case, having a diameter of 3mm), with the cord at the mid-point of the fold.*

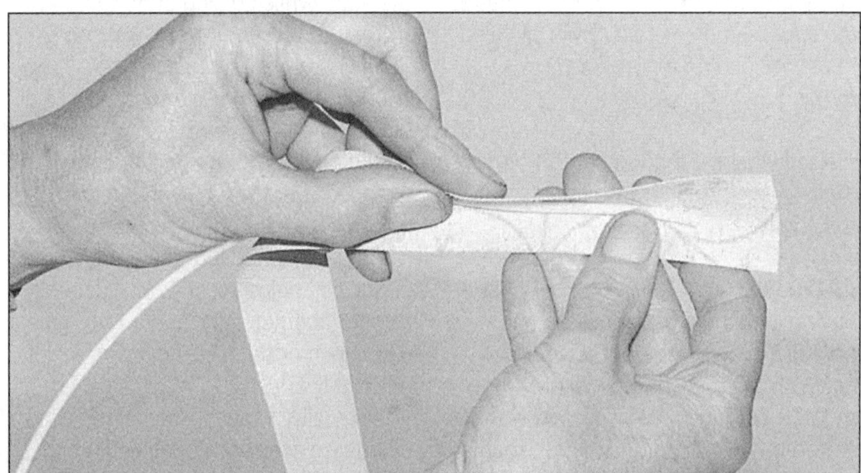

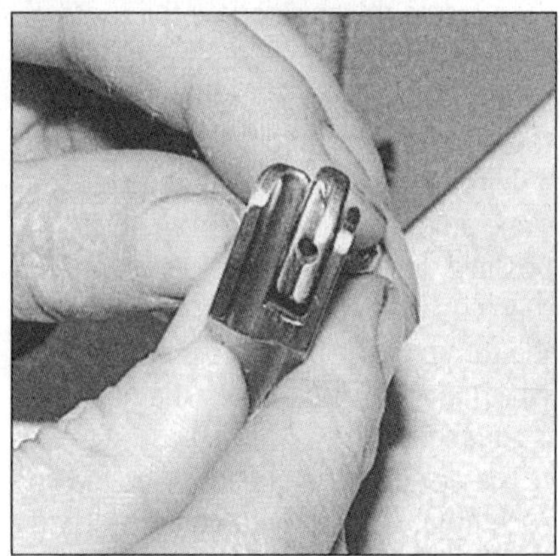

▲ *6.42. This special 'piping foot' is designed to pull the piping cord and the cover material close together while stitching, to give a taut, even appearance.*

▶ *6.43. Holding the covering material strip and the cord together, and gently feeding them towards the needle, sew the two together. The stitching is intended to run very close to the cord, leaving a fairly wide flange to aid attachment to adjacent seat panels. The two halves of the flange can be glued together to avoid an extra run of stitches along the inner edge.*

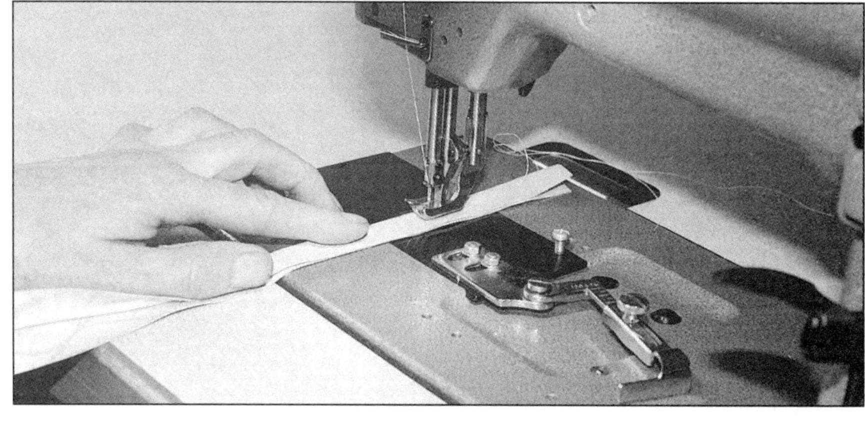

▲ *6.44. Lay the assembled length of piping along the edge of the unpleated section to which it is being joined, with the flanged side towards the machine.*

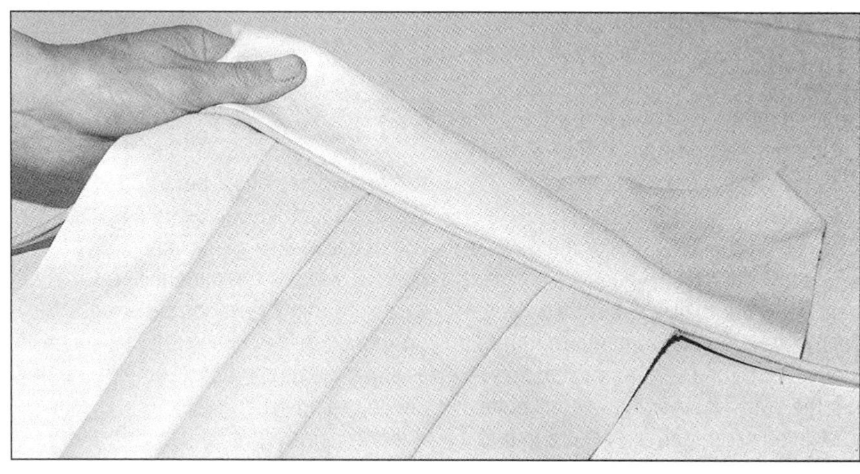

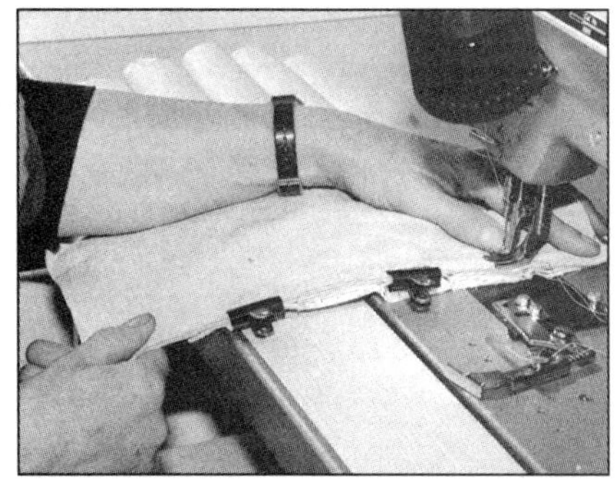

▲ *6.45. The next step is to join the unpleated section (now with piping attached) to the fluted section. Lay the fluted section, face upwards, on the machine base, with the pleated section, face downwards, on top of it, with the edges to be joined in line. When the stitching is completed, it should only be visible from this (the reverse) side. Effectively, now, the piping is sandwiched between the unpleated and fluted sections. It is helpful to use 'bulldog' clips to hold the sections together while they are sewn. It is also wise to stretch the materials in order to keep them taut during sewing.*

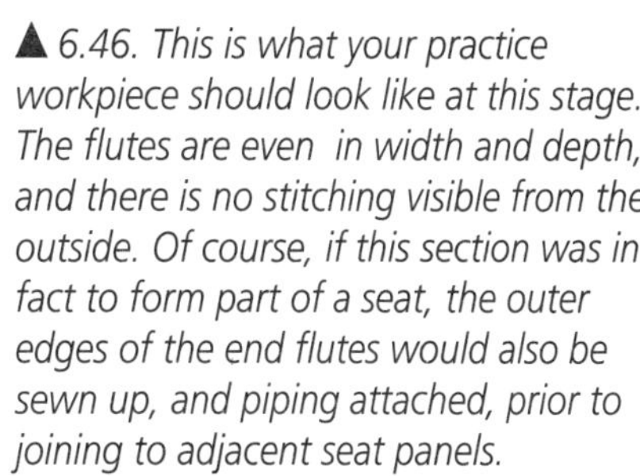

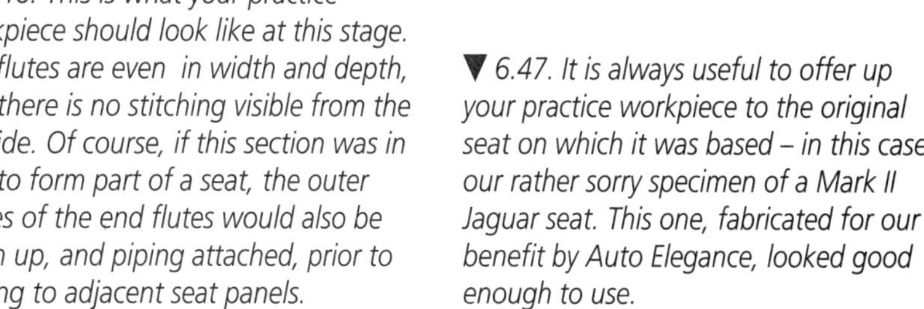

▲ *6.46. This is what your practice workpiece should look like at this stage. The flutes are even in width and depth, and there is no stitching visible from the outside. Of course, if this section was in fact to form part of a seat, the outer edges of the end flutes would also be sewn up, and piping attached, prior to joining to adjacent seat panels.*

▼ *6.47. It is always useful to offer up your practice workpiece to the original seat on which it was based – in this case our rather sorry specimen of a Mark II Jaguar seat. This one, fabricated for our benefit by Auto Elegance, looked good enough to use.*

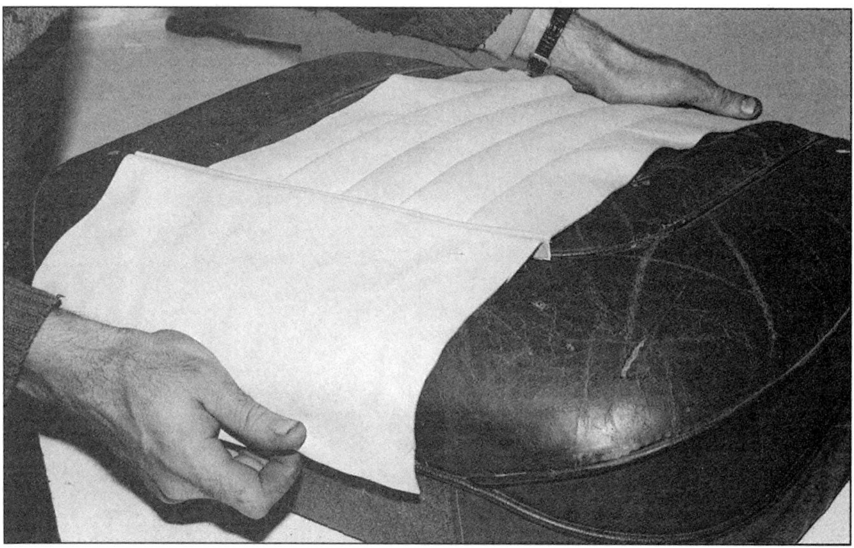

FITTING NEW SEAT COVERS AND REASSEMBLY

Having made replacement sections for all those forming the seat, it is almost time to assemble them. However, depending on the state of your original seats, you may wish to clean and repaint the seat frames, and wash the rubberized horsehair.

If you do decide to wash the horsehair, it is a good idea to place the various components into a pillowcase or similar before loading them into the washing machine. This way, none of the bits can make a bid for freedom!

If the foam base of your seat is almost complete but has, for example, odd chunks missing, it is possible to cut a replacement section from a block of foam, and glue it in place. The main problem here is matching the shape and compression characteristics of the original.

For some cars, ready-made replacement foam bases are available, but take care when buying, for not all conform to the original shape and texture, with the result that the seat will never look or feel quite right. In any event, always ensure that any foam you employ is fire-resistant – much old stock is not.

In the following sequence, mention is made of gluing at each stage, as appropriate. However, I feel that – especially on your first job – you may find it beneficial to first carry out a dry trial-fit (i.e. without using glue) to ensure that everything fits as it should.

If any adjustments are necessary, it is easier to make them before the components are glued together! Similarly, if using clips and tacks, only push/drive them halfway home, until you are sure that all components are correctly positioned. Otherwise, if the clips/tacks are fully fitted, it can be very difficult to remove them again without causing damage to surrounding materials.

When using upholstery grade contact adhesive, ensure that there is adequate ventilation in the working area, and take a break as often as you can. Implicitly follow the product's safety and application instructions.

Normally, a coating is applied to both surfaces to be joined. These are then left for ten minutes or so, before being brought together. Remember that such contact adhesives give a very strong bond as soon as the materials touch – so ensure that everything is correctly positioned before final contact is made, as adjustments can be extremely difficult to make.

It is imperative, of course, that the flute lines align between the seat base and backrest sections, when the two are brought together. You may find it easier to assemble the base first, then deal with the backrest cover, and adjust its position, as necessary. Normally, only very minor readjustment is required.

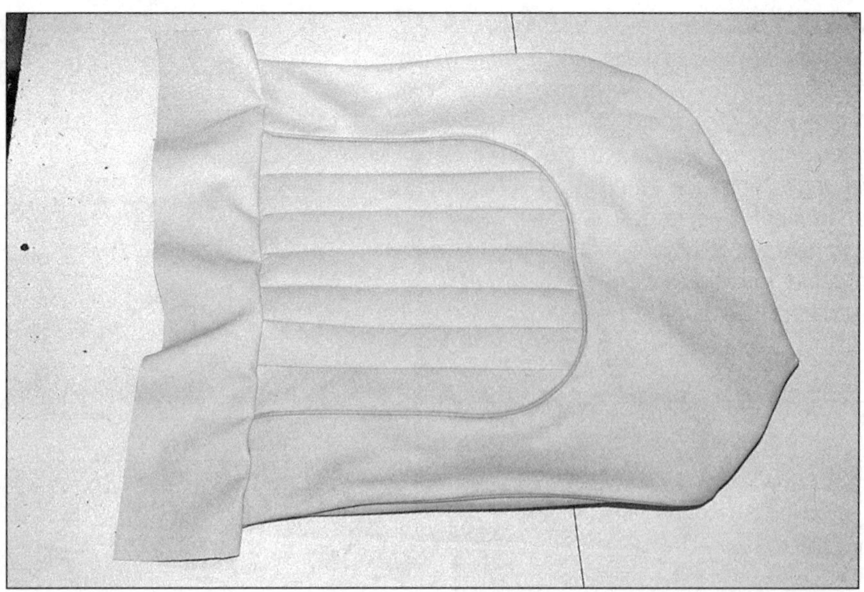

▲ *6.48. The replacement cover for the seat base – in this instance in a very light coloured leather – should look similar to this, prior to reassembly.*

▼ *6.49. Although in the majority of cases it is possible and sensible to re-use the original, pre-shaped rubberized horsehair and foam padding (since making new padding of the correct profile is extremely difficult!), sometimes it is necessary to add a little extra wadding, to compensate for wear/compression of the original items. Lay the wadding onto the original materials in a uniform layer, and ensure that it is wrapped neatly around all curved sections. Pictured here is a back rest, but the comments apply equally to the seat base.*

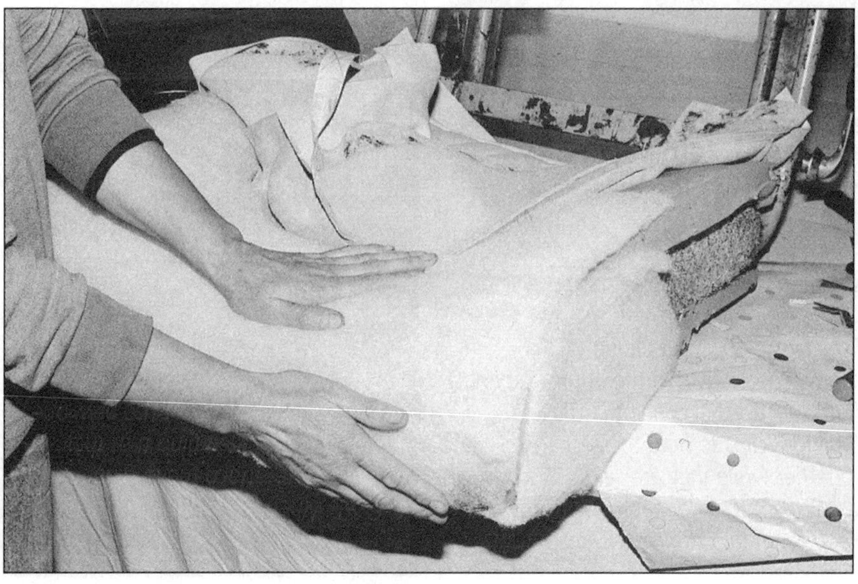

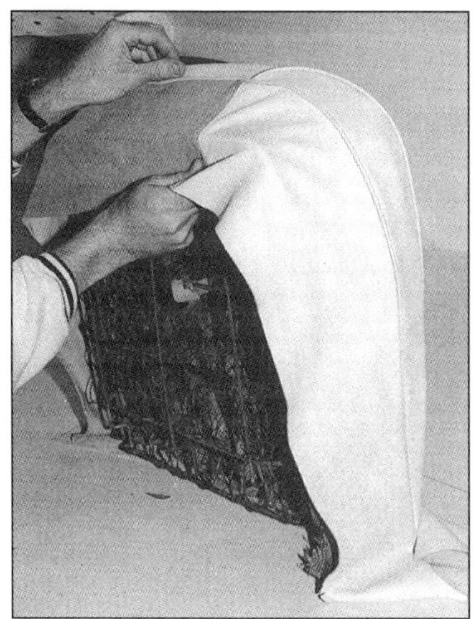

▲ *6.50. Fitting the replacement cover is, in effect, the reverse of the dismantling procedure. The cover should be trial-fitted to the base, ensuring that it fits snugly up to all perimeter boundaries, and that wrinkles in the covering material are eliminated as you proceed. If the cover is reluctant to slide over the foam base, apply a little soap to the recalcitrant section of foam – things should start to move then.*

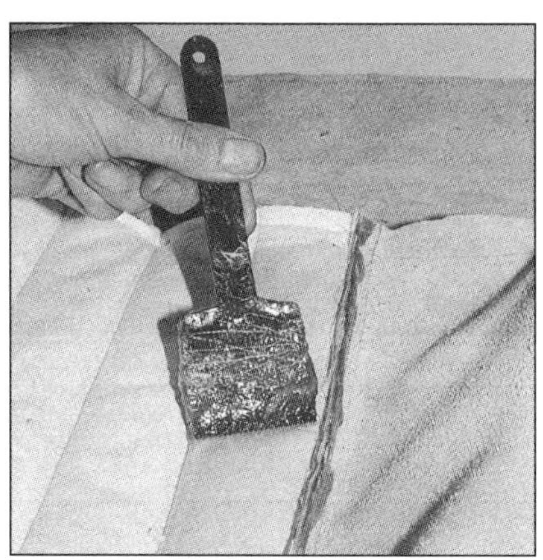

▲ *6.51. If all is well with the trial fit operation, remove the cover from the base, and apply glue to the underside of the perimeter of the fluted section of the cover, and to the corresponding section of the padded base. After a few minutes, bring the two together again, ensuring that they are in the correct position as they make contact! Fit one corner of the front (i.e. most visible) section of the cover first, and work your way across and backwards, rolling the cover into place as you go. Don't apply glue across the whole of the central (in this case, fluted) section, since some flexibility is required in this area, to allow some 'give' as an occupant sits on, and gets up from, the seat.*

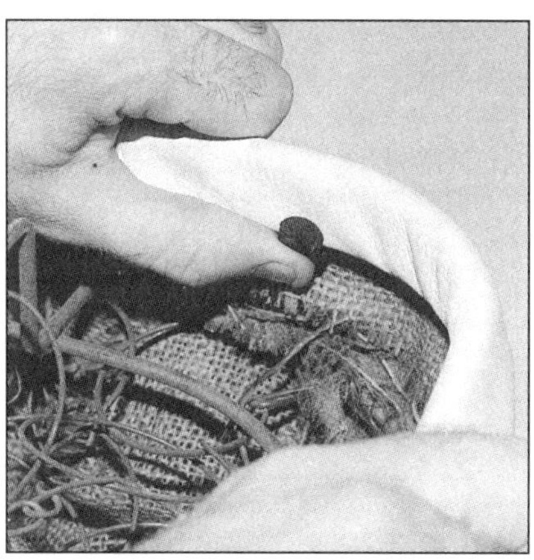

▲ *6.52. When the cover is correctly positioned, re-attach the original retaining clips – assuming that they are fit for further service – or use new ones if you can obtain them. Ensure that the cover is perfectly positioned before the clips are pressed fully home.*

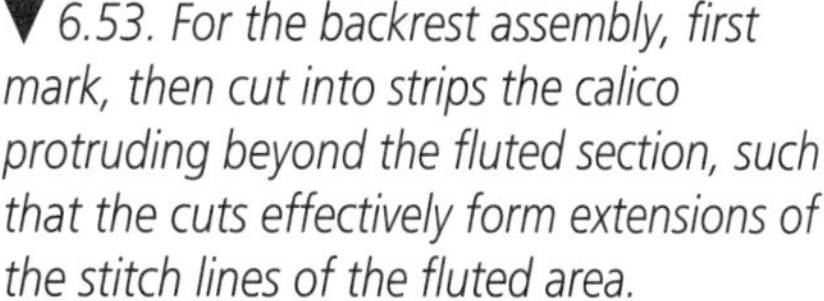

▼ *6.53. For the backrest assembly, first mark, then cut into strips the calico protruding beyond the fluted section, such that the cuts effectively form extensions of the stitch lines of the fluted area.*

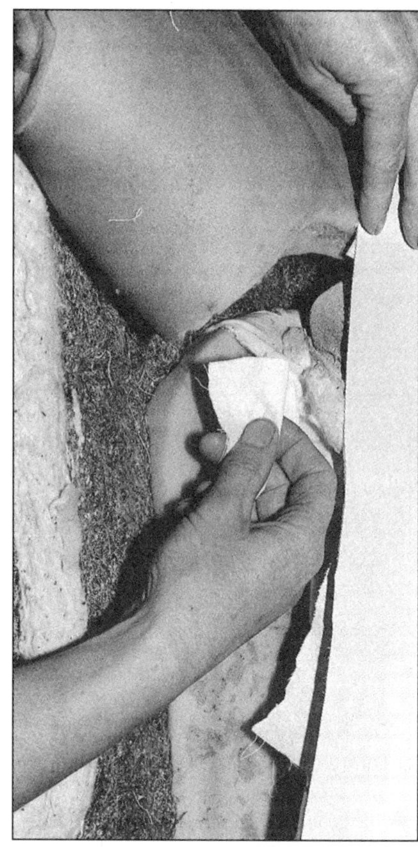

▲ *6.54. With the new backrest cover assembly offered up to the seat frame (with the foam rubber and rubberized horsehair padding still/already attached to the frame), carefully feed the calico strips through the back of the seat, to protrude from the rear. This is a fiddly operation, but not difficult.*

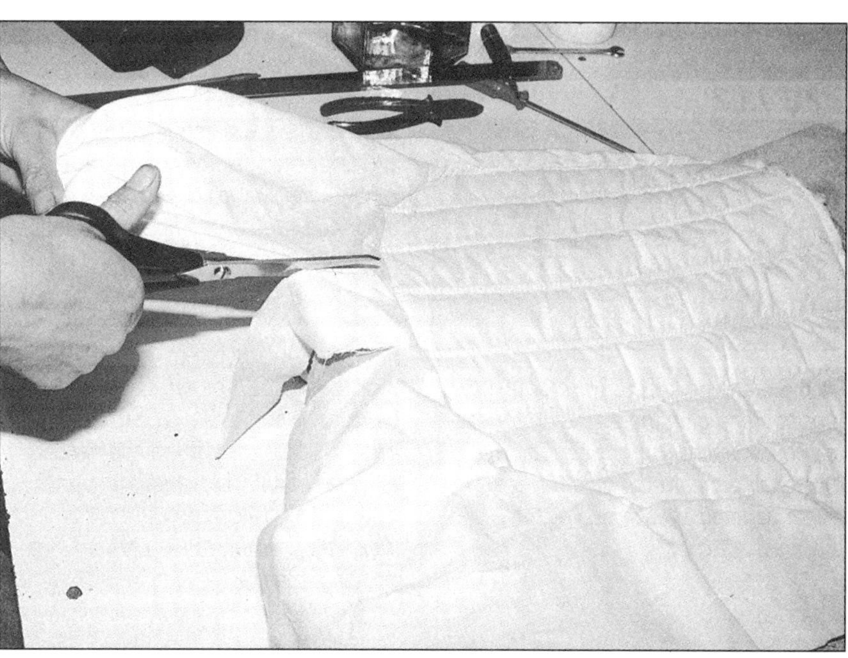

▶ 6.55. *This is the same operation as shown in 6.54, viewed from the back of the seat.*

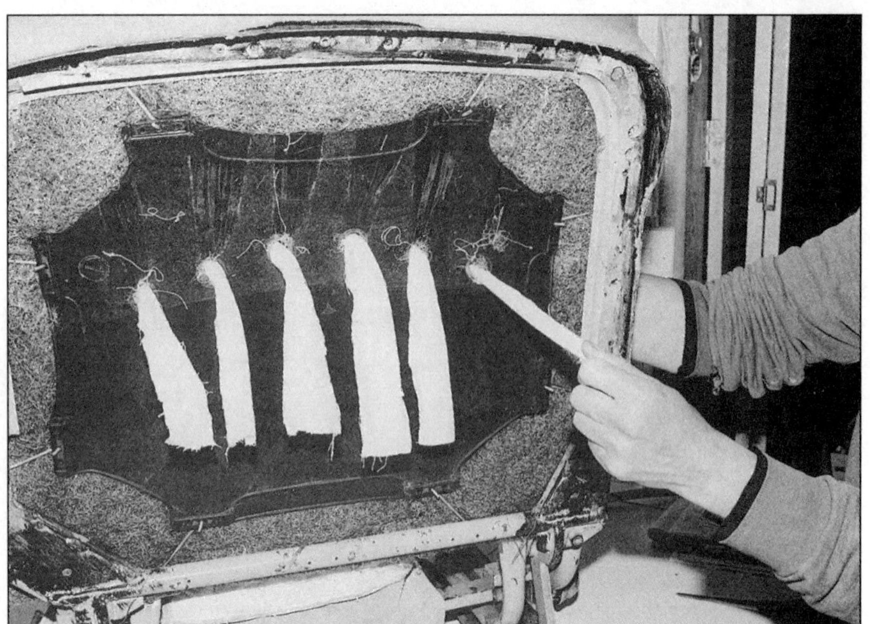

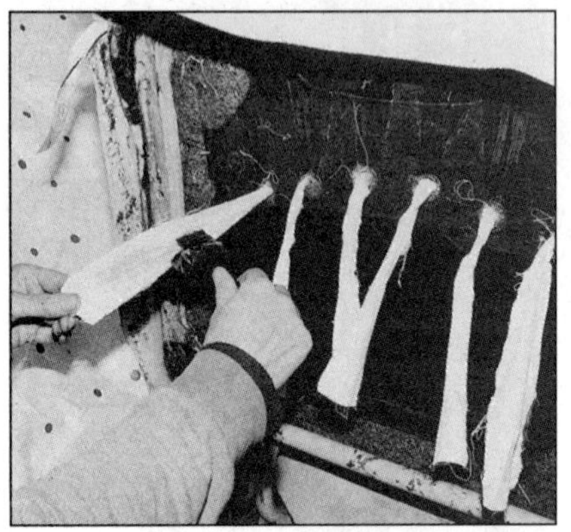

▲ 6.56. *The strips are then glued firmly to the upper section of the rubber seat diaphragm to assume the position shown in photograph 6.8.*

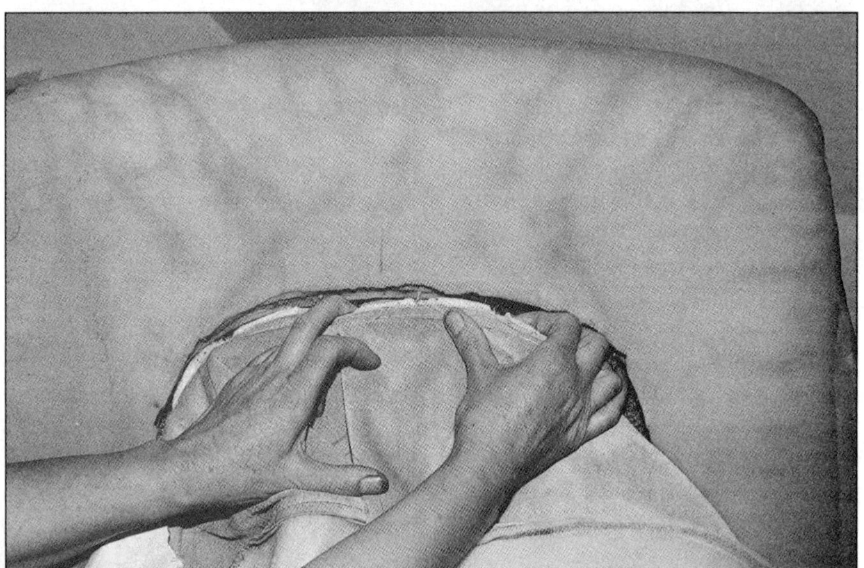

▲ 6.58. *The seam between the fluted and unpleated sections of the outer cover is now carefully positioned, then glued to the inside edge of the horseshoe shaped foam pad forming the outer section of the body of the backrest.*

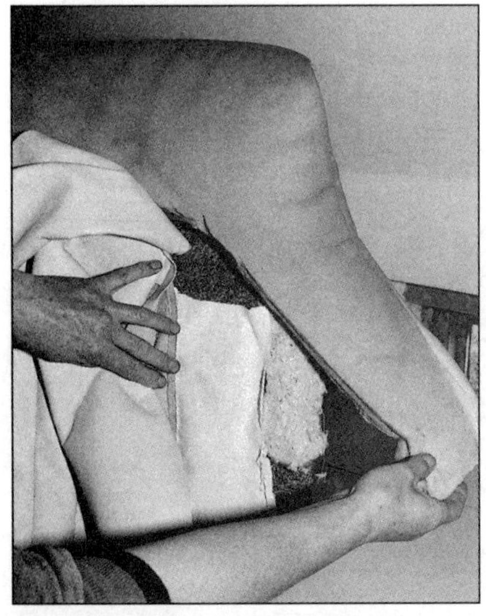

▲ 6.57. *The next job is to smooth into position and glue the extensions of the calico backing cloth to the rubberized horsehair beneath the outer layer of foam padding at each side of the backrest assembly.*

▶ 6.59. *Now roll the cover assembly over the top of the seat, flattening out wrinkles as they arise. As with the seat base, in some cases it may be necessary to install additional wadding/foam as you fit the cover, to compensate for wear/compression of the original seat padding material.*

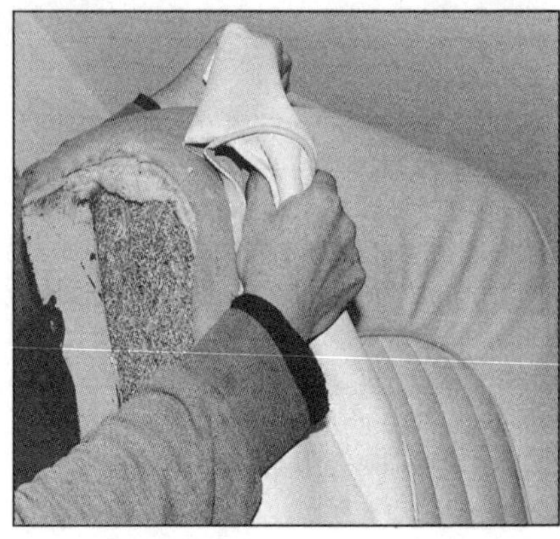

▶ *6.60. Glue is now applied to the underside of the covering material, along the top edge of the backrest …*

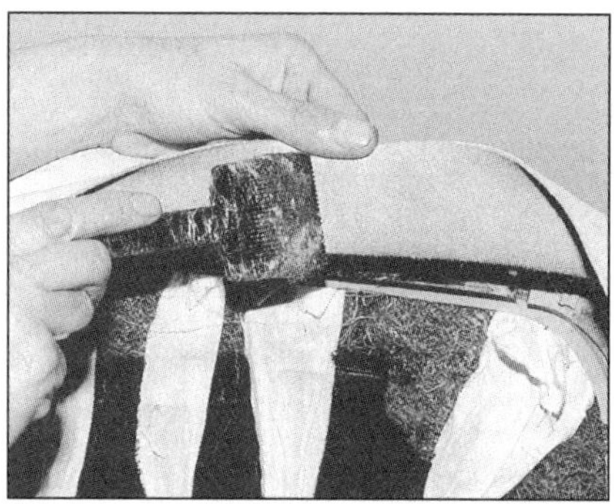

▶ *6.61.… and along the corresponding section of the seat frame. After allowing the glue to dry for a few minutes, bring the two together, ensuring that the cover is stretched reasonably tightly (to eliminate wrinkles) as you do so.*

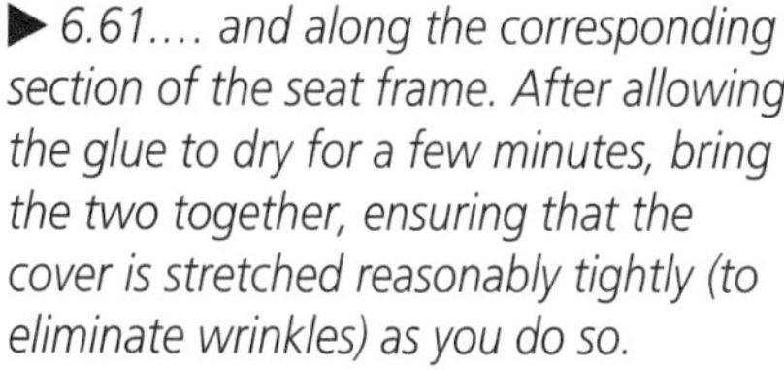

▼ *6.62. In addition to gluing, tack the cover in position on the frame, where the original was secured in this manner.*

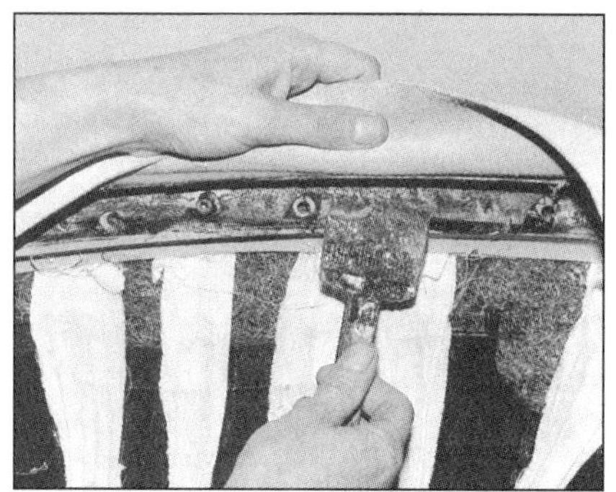

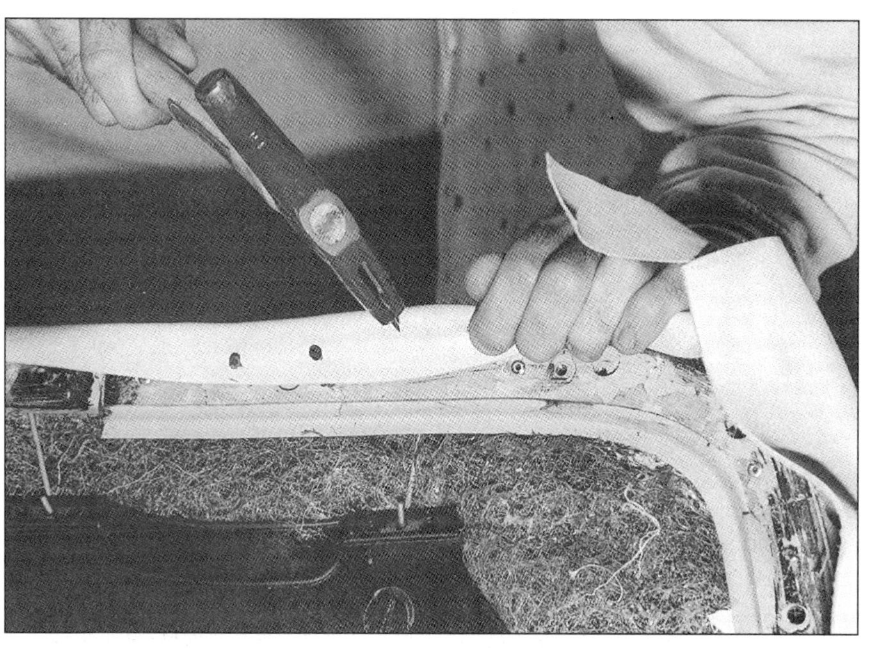

PICNIC TABLES

Many sports/luxury cars, like the Mark II Jaguar, featured picnic tables built into the backs of the front seats. These are relatively straightforward to deal with, provided you allow plenty of time for the job.

▼ *6.63. First, unscrew all fittings (including the hinges) and store in a receptacle containing only fittings from that table. Label accordingly and – especially if re-assembly is going to be some time in the future – put somewhere safe.*

▼ *6.64. Release the screws retaining the wooden base of the table to the frame. Retain the fixing screws.*

▼ *6.65. Carefully separate the wood from the frame, and then take out the screws securing the handle. These are only accessible with the wood removed, so on reassembly, make sure that the handle is screwed on before the wood base is refitted.*

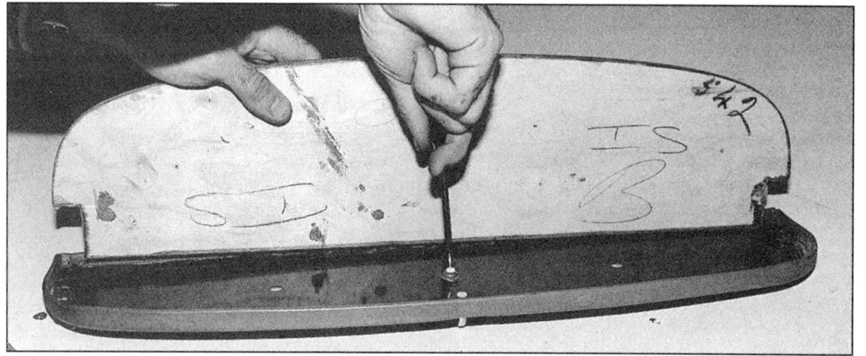

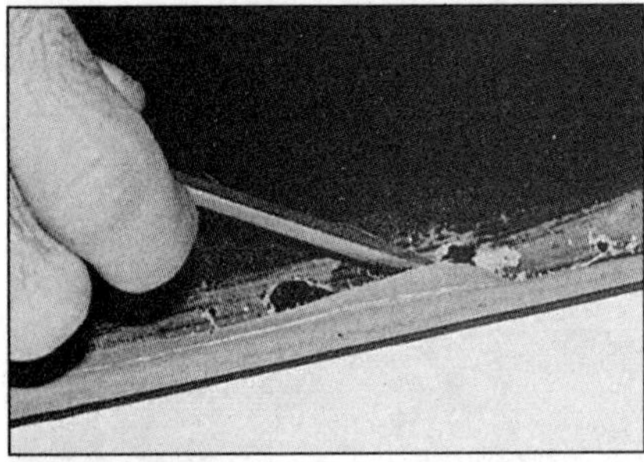

▲ 6.66. *Using an old, blunt screwdriver or similar tool, carefully release the leather covering from around the perimeter of the table; the leather was originally glued in place here.*

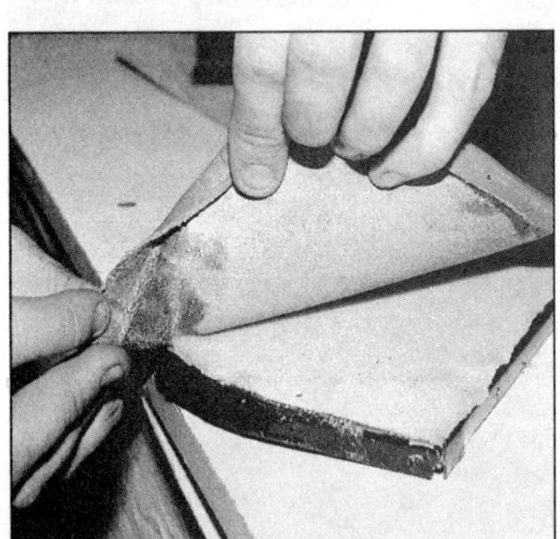

▲ 6.67. *Now very gently peel back the leather covering, if possible leaving the foam padding in place on the table.*

▼ 6.68. *Now use the table (placed on the back of a suitable area of hide to match the leather used on the rest of the seats) as a template for marking out the shape of the replacement covering. Use tailor's chalk, a crayon or a ball point pen – don't press too hard, or the face side of the leather could be marked.*

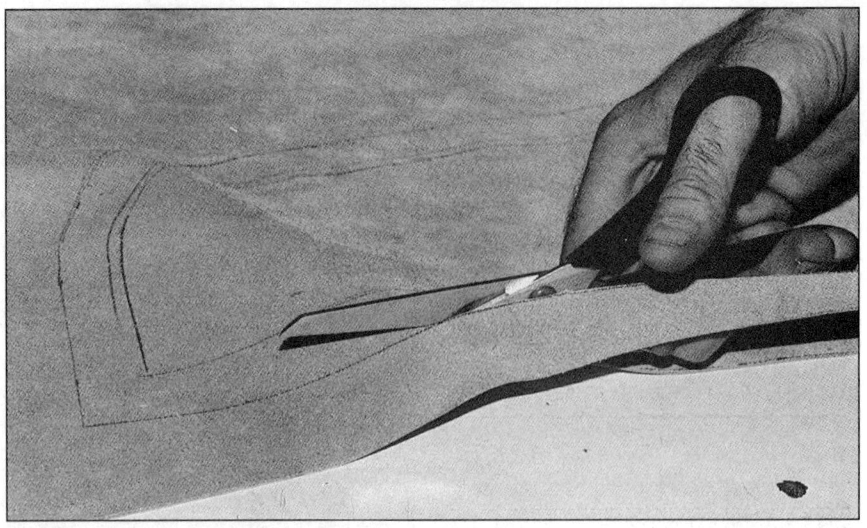

▲ 6.69. *Mark an additional line, approximately one inch larger than the exact dimensions of the table, all round. This extra flange will be wrapped over the edge of the table and glued to it. Use sharp scissors/shears to cut the new covering from the hide.*

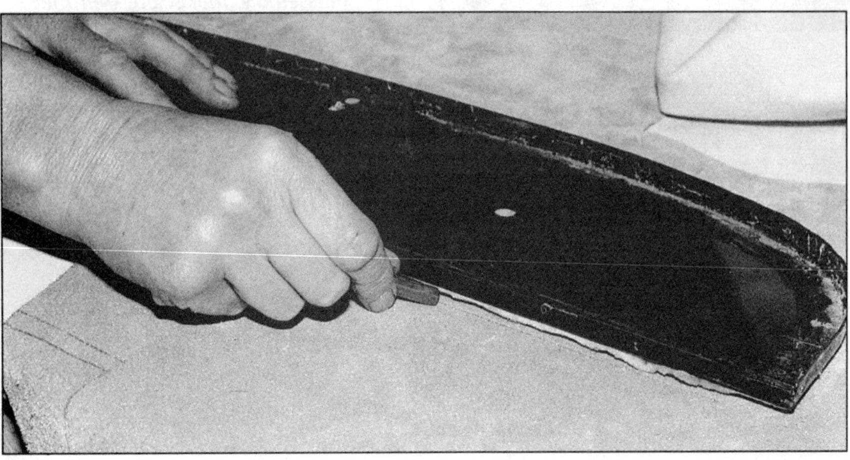

▲ 6.70. *Cover the workbench with a large sheet of masking paper, place the leather covering face down on top of it, followed by the picnic table frame, in the correct position. Spray both the edge of the picnic table and the corresponding flange on the new leather covering with a light coating of glue from an aerosol – for relatively small areas this can be quicker and easier to use than the traditional 'brush-on' type of contact adhesive, although that is less expensive.*

▶ *6.71. Using your fingers (make sure they are clean and free from glue), tension the leather covering from side to side, then along the flat edge at the bottom of the table, and along the top of the table, starting in the centre and working outwards. Aim to get a nice, even tension across the entire outer surface of the leather. At the edges, start to roll the leather over the flange.*

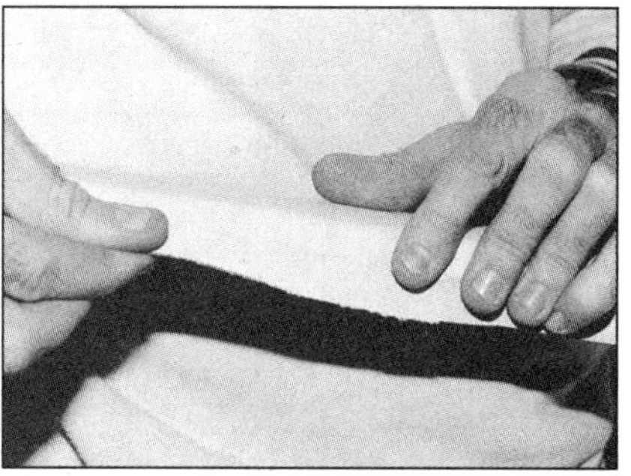

▼ *6.74. Fabricate separate, short sections of leather to fit around the hinges. Double these over, then tack in position. Reference to the original material used here will give the precise size and shape required.*

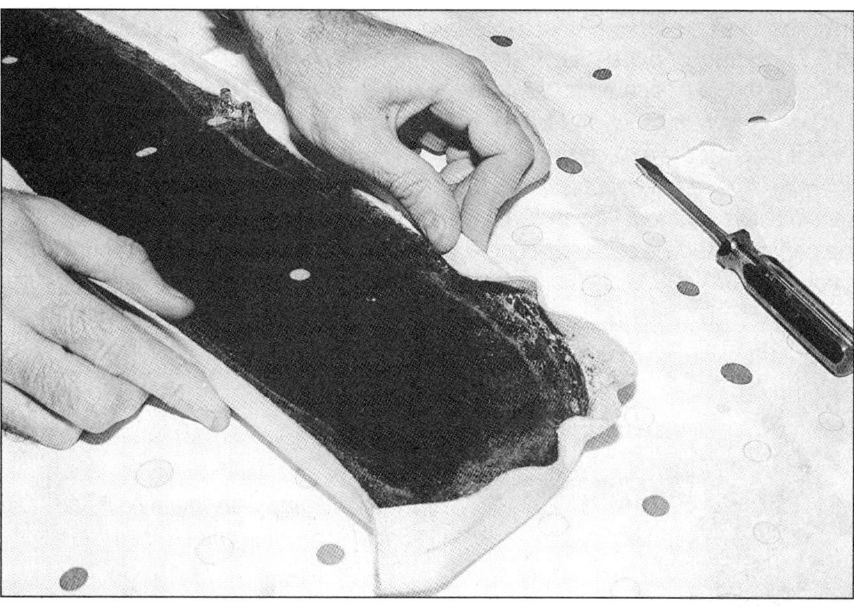

▲ *6.72. Turn the table over, and continue to roll the leather onto the glued flange. Press down all around the flange as you proceed, ensuring that the leather is properly tucked in, and that all the outer corners of the table are adequately covered by it.*

▼ *6.73. Trim off the excess leather on the inside, using a sharp knife.*

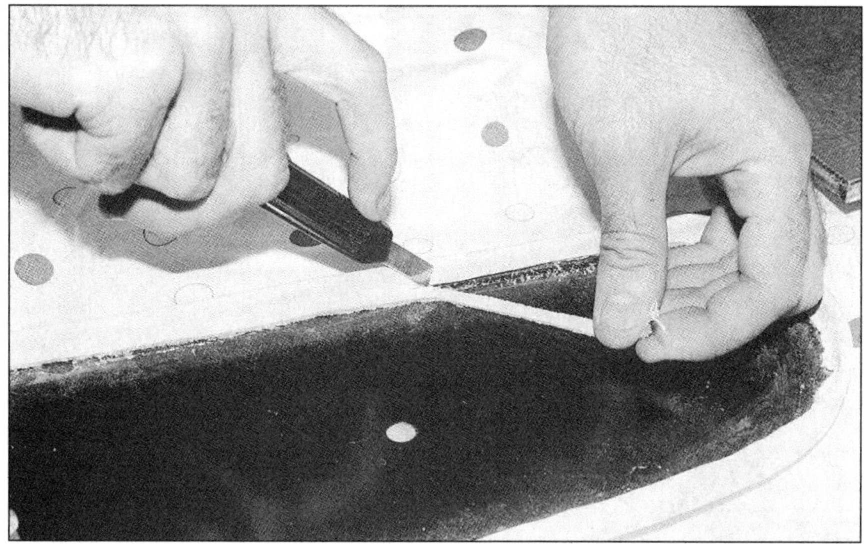

▼ *6.75. Refit the handle, the wood base and then the hinges. This can be a difficult operation, so first line up the existing screw holes in the wood, and make small holes in the leather in corresponding positions, at the bottom of the table. The hinges are often a tight fit within a newly renovated table, so take care when refitting them.*

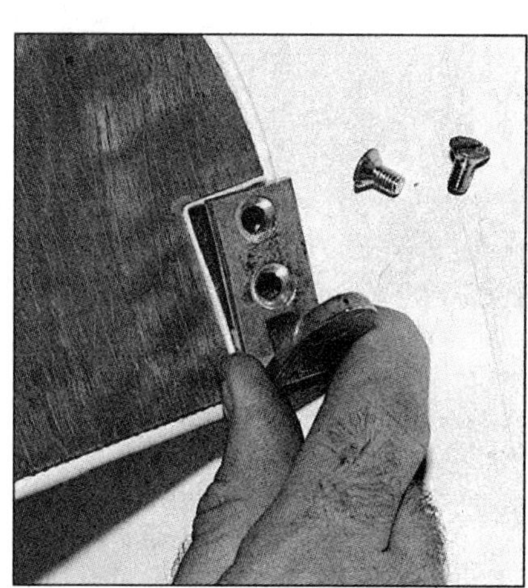

TRIM PANELS

Many seats incorporate additional trim panels, and these should be covered to match/contrast with the rest of the seat. In most cases the panel itself can be used as a template for marking out the new covering material, and the original covering material, once removed, can also provide invaluable clues to the methods of construction used.

▼ *6.76. Lay the metal trim panel on top of the covering material – in this case moquette – reverse side uppermost, and mark out the profile. Allow an extra inch or so around the edge and mark a second, outer line. The material between this line and the inner one forms the flange which will be glued to the trim panel.*

▲ *6.78. Aerosol or brush-on contact adhesive should be applied to the outer surface of the trim panel, and to the inner surface of the replacement covering. After a few minutes the two should be brought together and any creases in the surface of the covering smoothed out.*

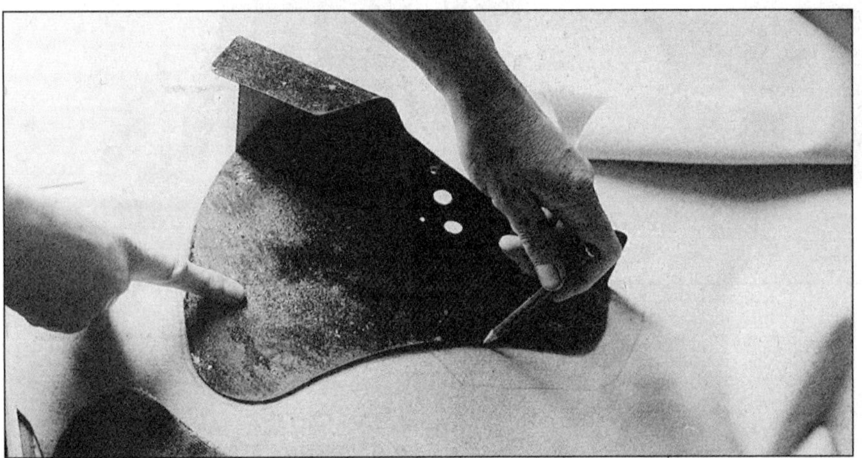

▲ *6.77. Sometimes the panel is sandwiched in a pocket of covering material. In this case the two halves of the pocket need to be sewn together – inside out – along their outer edges. The pocket can then be turned right-side out and trial-fitted over the trim panel.*

AMERICAN CAR SEATS

To cope with the high volumes required, the mass-production techniques employed in making seats installed in older American cars were generally more advanced than those of the European car makers.

To illustrate some of the differences in a typical unit, here we show the salient points of a rebuild of the bench type seat base from a 1959 Cadillac. Many of the general points relating to the stripdown are as covered in the previous section on Jaguar seats.

To avoid unnecessary duplication, I have concentrated here on the differences in construction between the two types of seat, and corresponding variations in the methods employed during restoration.

▼ *6.79. Many years in the heat and bright sunlight of the southern states of the USA had taken their toll of the upholstery of this 1959 Cadillac. The bench type seats were first removed from the car, then dismantled; all components – including the various electric motors built into the seat – being carefully stored for future use/reference.*

▶ 6.80. By contrast with the Mark II Jaguar seat, the base section from the Cadillac is built around a metal base with zig zag profile steel springs. To ensure that this seat lasts indefinitely, this base section was sent for sand-blasting and powder coating prior to reassembly. Shown here is the rear seat base.

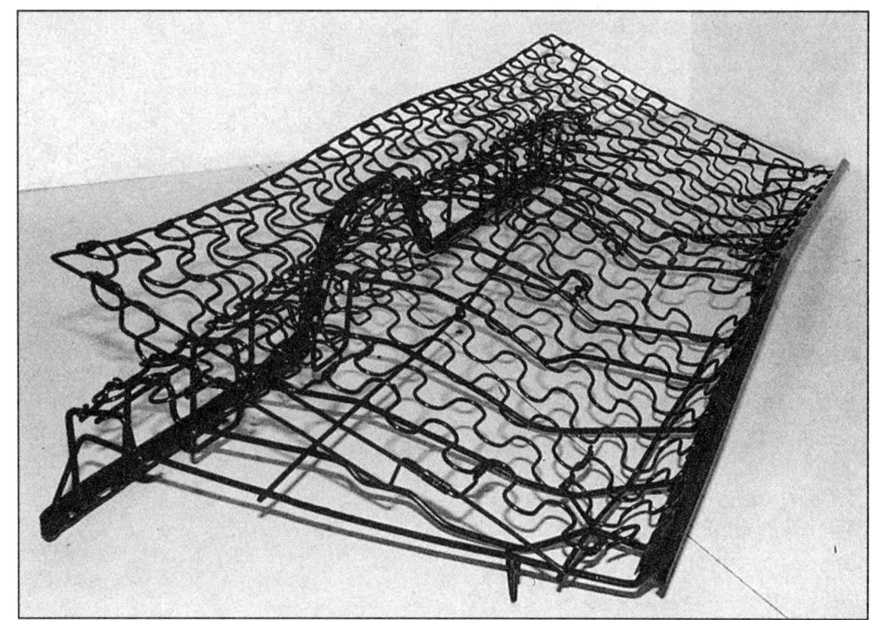

▶ 6.81. The hessian covering of the seat base (front shown here) incorporates reinforcement by cross-wires. The construction of the new hessian covering has been made by reference to the original, shown on the left. Before the hessian is sewn onto the outer edge of the frame, the edges of the frame should first be padded with strips of felt.

▶ 6.82. As with many cars, the sprung base on this seat was originally covered with shaped rubber foam. The foam often completely disintegrates with age, so new sections need to be fabricated from blocks of new foam having similar structure and feel to the original. Building the shape and depth of the seat takes time, and in some cases it is necessary to form replacement padding using different varieties of foam, having varying densities.

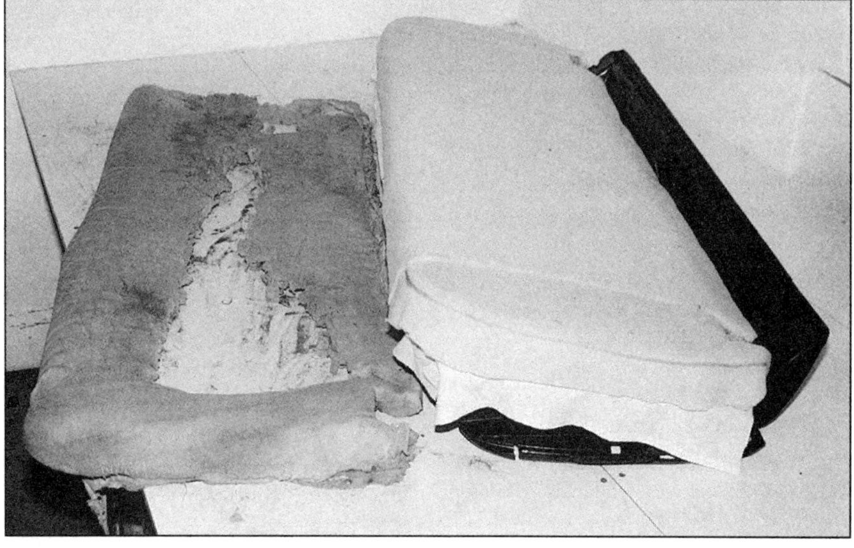

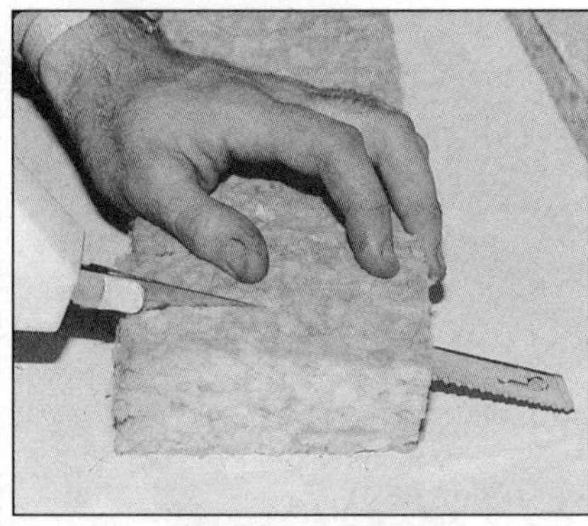

▲ 6.83. *In most cases the foam forming the main body of the seat needs to be quite dense. This is then covered with a softer foam to give the final profile and feel. Initial cutting to size of the denser chipped foam can successfully be carried out using an electric carving knife (**take care during cutting operations**).*

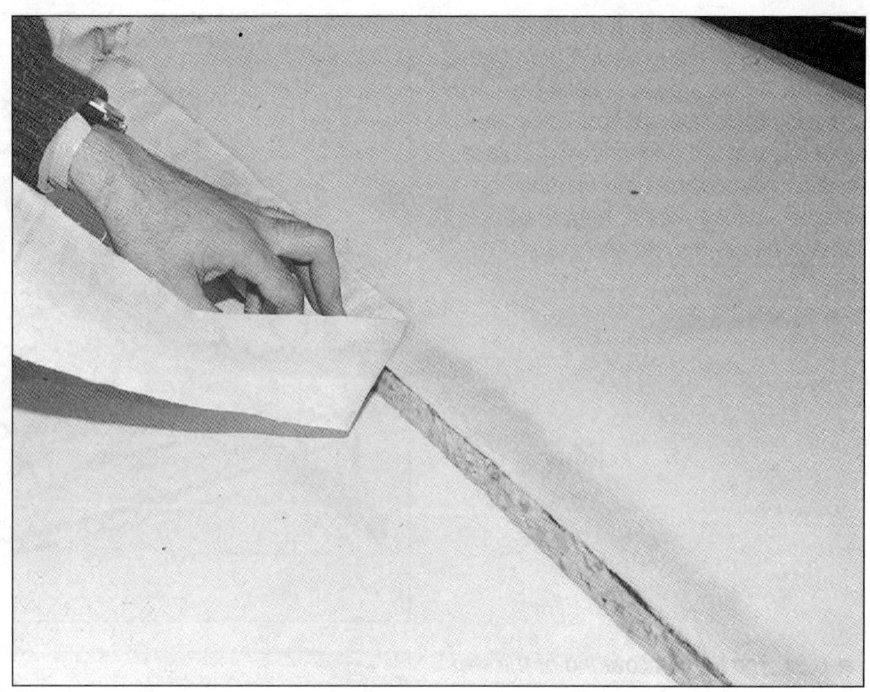

▲ 6.85. *The softer foam is easier to trim to shape (scissors can be used). This foam can be wrapped over the denser material to give the required rounded contours along the seat edges.*

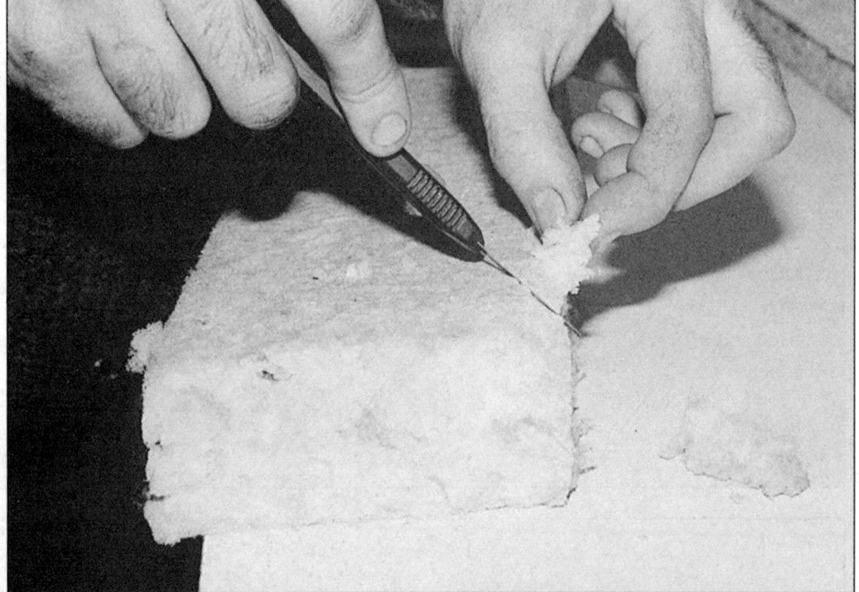

▲ 6.84. *Cutting a bevelled edge on the denser foam is relatively straightforward, if a very sharp, long-bladed craft knife is used (**take care**).*

▼ 6.86. *On the Cadillac a strip of calico had originally been glued to the back of the seat base. This strip was then secured by hog rings to the back of the seat frame. Therefore, during reconstruction, a new strip of calico should be cut and glued in position on top of the foam.*

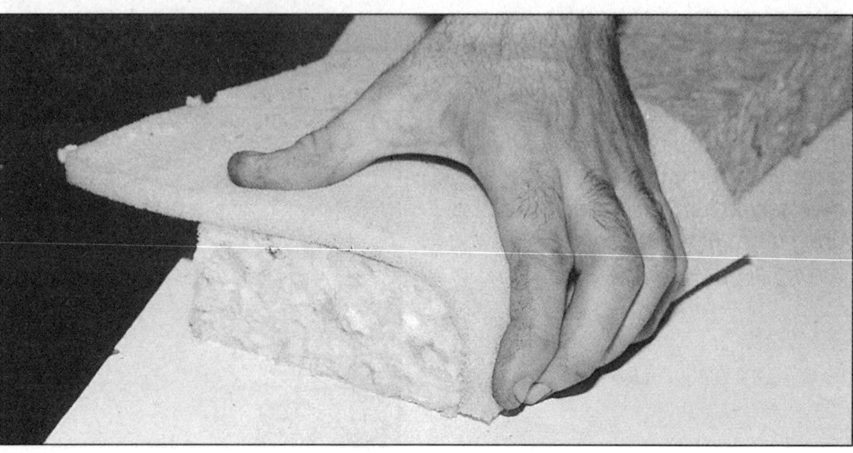

It is worth noting that British and European hog rings can be much smaller than early American ones. Therefore, if restoring an old car made in the USA, it is best to buy American-type hog rings.

▲ *6.87. Hog rings are often supplied in strips, and are C-shaped. The individual rings are broken away from the strip as required. To fasten hog rings, they are first fitted into the jaws of the special pliers made for the purpose, as shown.*

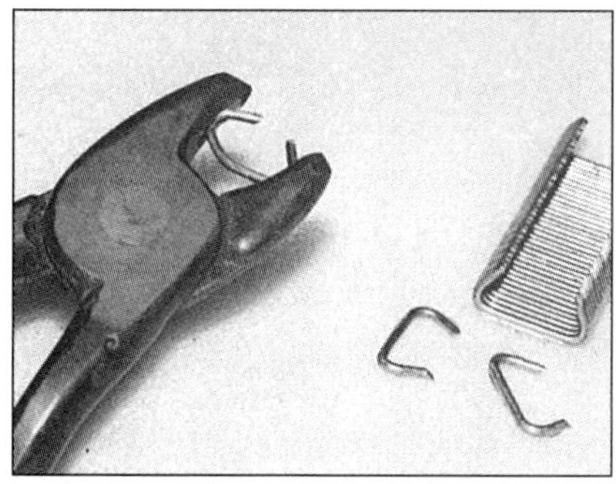

▲ *6.88. The rings are compressed in the jaws of the pliers – in practice, of course, the rings would first be passed through the material to be fastened, and around the seat frame. As the rings compress, they gradually ...*

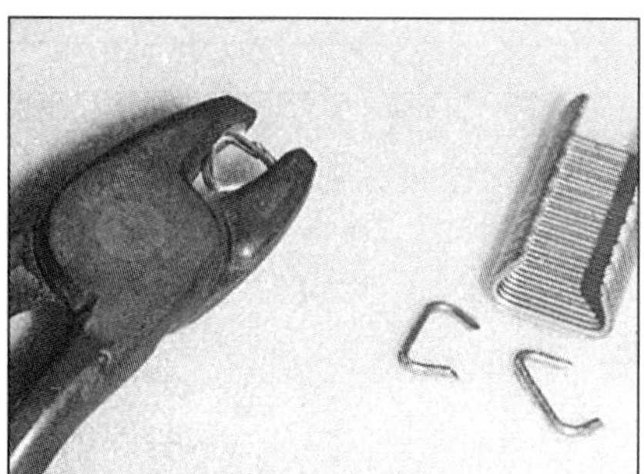

▲ *6.89. ... assume a triangular profile, effectively locking the material to the seat frame.*

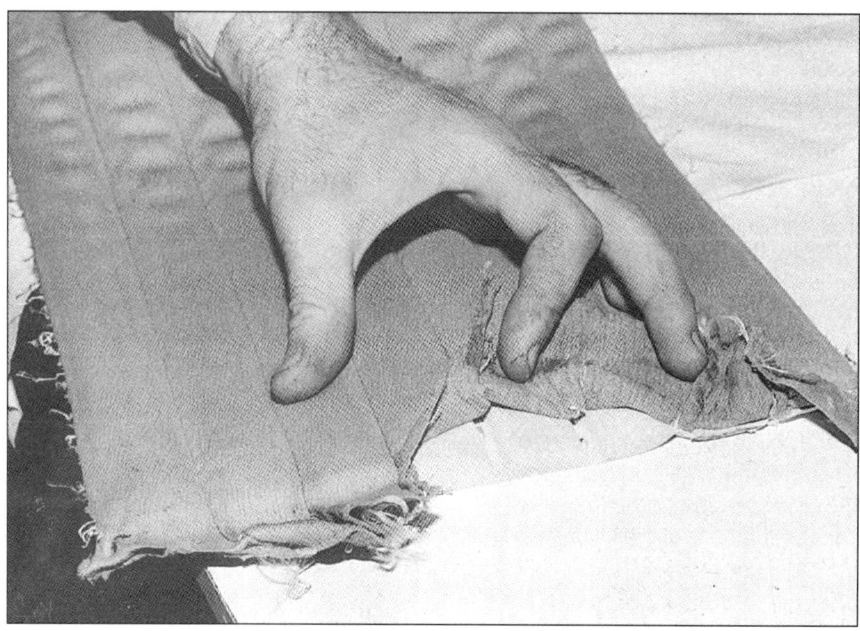

▲ *6.90. It can be quite a tedious job installing hog rings, since often the seat frame is rather inaccessible beneath the foam padding.*

The flutes employed on many American car seats – like those of our 1959 Cadillac – are much narrower than those of the Jaguar seats, and were formed at the factory in a very different manner. It would be very difficult to form and stuff narrow flutes like these in the same way as those in the Jaguar seats, and a different technique is needed to reproduce them.

▼ *6.91. In the case of the Cadillac the flutes are very narrow. Originally, these were made from pre-channelled foam, which was machine-grooved after being stuck onto a calico backing sheet. Alas it is not possible to buy pre-channelled foam like this, so an alternative method of construction has to be adopted.*

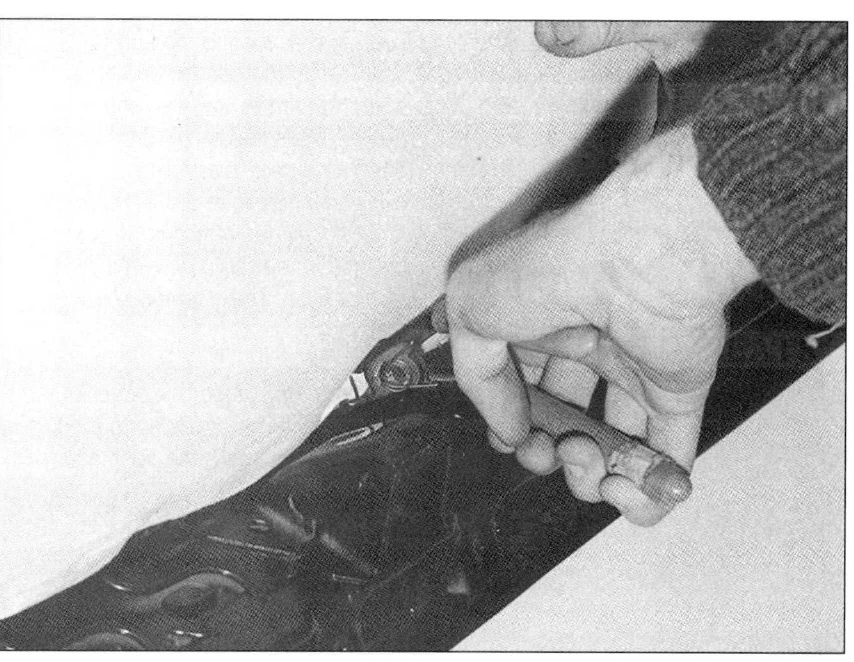

▶ *6.92. First, cut out a sheet of calico, large enough to form the covering for the seat base. Now, using measurements taken from the original seat as a guide, mark off very carefully the required width of each flute. In this instance, it was necessary to mark flutes at one-inch intervals, with 0.25 in between each flute, to provide the tucked effect required. It can be helpful to highlight the appropriate divisions on a steel rule, to assist in the marking out process.*

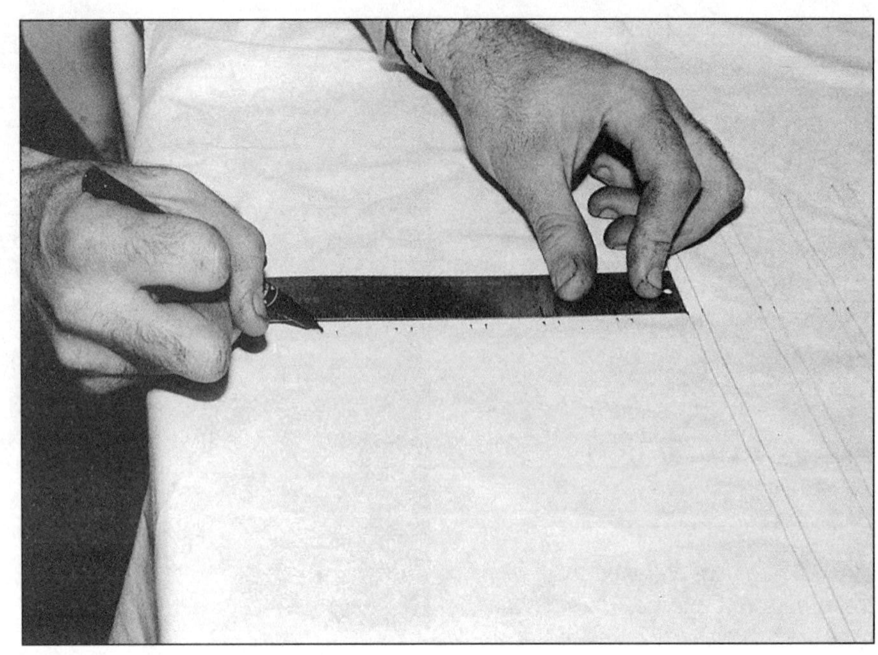

▼ *6.93. Next, count the number of flutes required (from the markings on the calico backing cloth), then mark and cut sufficient numbers of strips (in this case, one-inch wide) from foam rubber of similar density and thickness to the original.*

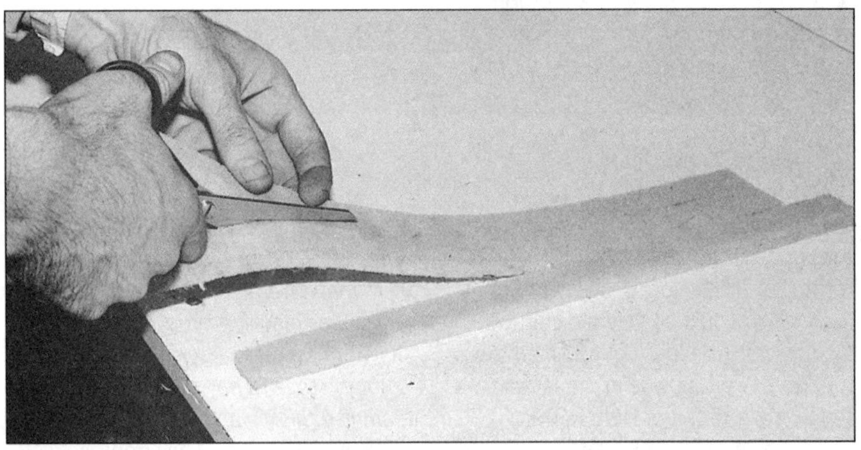

▼ *6.94. Now – very carefully – glue the foam strips to the calico, ensuring (by reference to the marked lines) that the strips are all parallel and in their correct places!*

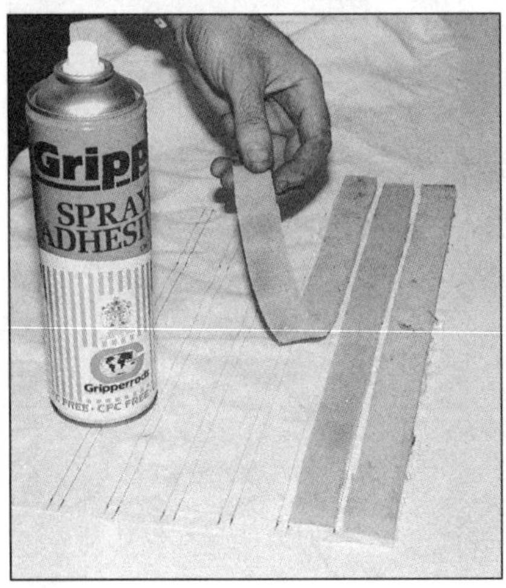

▶ *6.95. Initially, form and sew up the flutes in the covering material (as described in the section on Jaguar seats), but at this stage leaving off the backing material (calico). When the flutes have been thus formed in the covering material, re-sew along the same stitch lines, attaching the covering material to the calico between each strip of foam. The assembly should then look like this.*

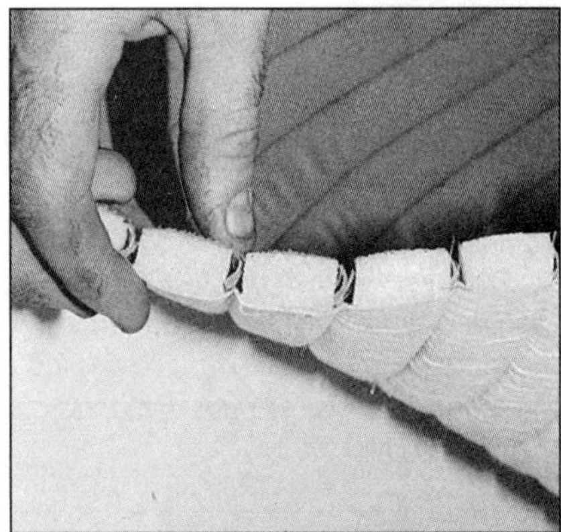

▶ *6.96. At this stage, the edges of the seat covering can be added to the fluted panel, sewing across the open ends of the flutes.*

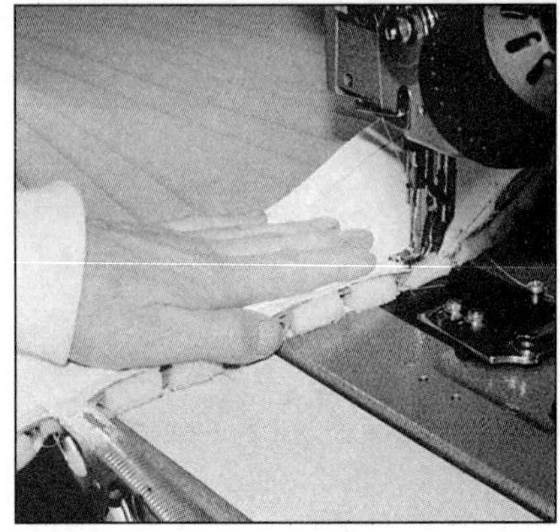

▶ *6.97. The completed seat covering (into the edges of which wire strips have been sewn, to add strength) can now be gently stretched into position. When all is well (and not before!), the covering is secured to the edge of the seat frame, using hog rings.*

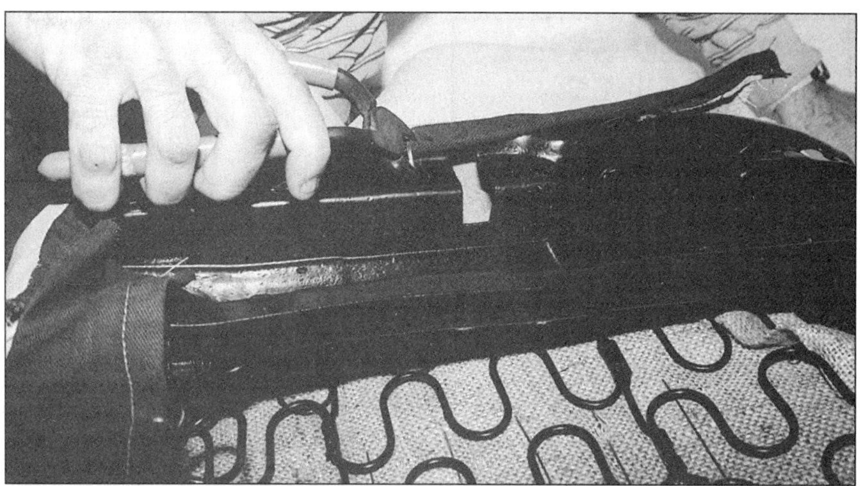

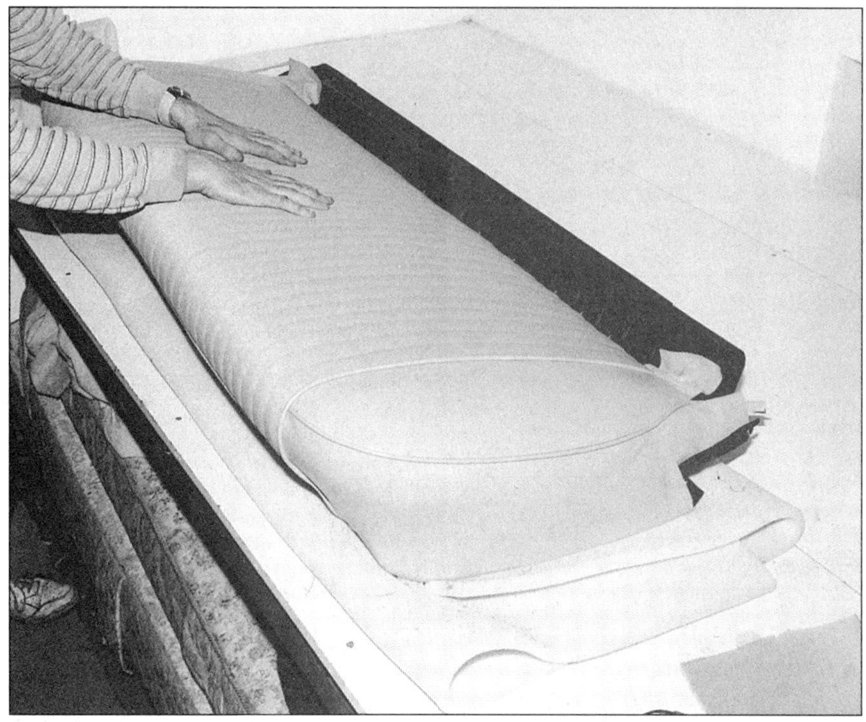

▲ *6.98. In due course the finished seat base should look like this. The rebuilt unit will now give many years and miles of comfortable motoring once again.*

▶ *6.99. Old and new. Just a reminder of the rotten state of the original covering, which could now be consigned to the waste bin!*

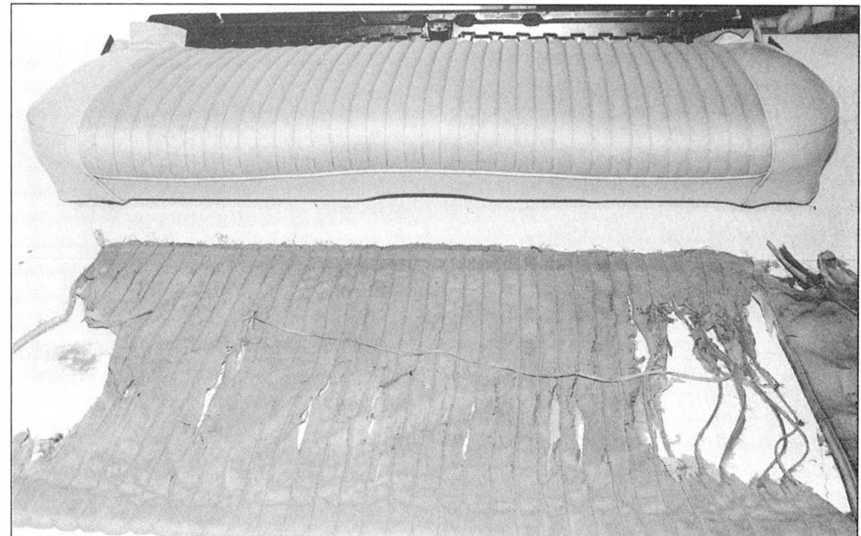

PRESSED STEEL FRAMES

Many cars, including some pre-war models and sports cars of the 1960s/70s, had their seats (especially the back rests) constructed around a pressed steel frame, covered with moulded foam padding, and – usually – a fluted outer covering in leather or vinyl (sometimes cloth).

In some cases the pressed steel frame forming the back rest is covered with millboard tacked onto wooden runners (often of plywood, and usually rotten!) which may be attached to the frame with bifurcated rivets.

Each bifurcated rivet has two legs which are opened out to secure the wood to the steel, once the rivet has been passed through a hole drilled in both materials. When dismantling, these are easily released to allow the steel frame to be cleaned, de-rusted and painted, and for the wood to be replaced, if necessary.

The back rests are often sharply curved, and the replacement plywood sections have to be very carefully shaped to follow the profile of the back rest. To achieve this, start at one end, securing the wood with the first new rivet, then gently bend the wood to shape, installing rivets as you proceed. It can help if the wood is allowed to soak in hot water, or is bathed in the steam from a boiling kettle (**take care**) before you attempt the job – otherwise it may split.

When fitting the new securing rivets, carefully prise apart the legs with an old screwdriver, then knock them flat using a hammer, with a wood or steel block to react against on the opposite side of the back rest.

TECHNIQUES

The techniques involved in dismantling the seats and in making replacement coverings are generally similar to those already described. However, the method of construction means that some areas require a slightly different approach. To show this, the seat from a 1964 MG Midget (a typical sports car seat) is used, but to avoid duplication, techniques already covered above are not repeated here.

▲ *6.100. This battered example was once a smart seat in a 1964 MG Midget. The car had not been used for several years, and the seat covering was breaking up.*

▶ *6.101. The first step is to separate the two halves of the seat. A close examination of the backrest revealed that it was in a sorry state, and the only answer was to make and fit a new covering. Ready-made coverings are available, but take care when buying as some fit better than others. The alternative is to make your own, using the fluting and other construction techniques already described.*

▶ *6.102. With the covering material removed the seat looks like this. Often the foam is found to be in good condition, and can be re-used. Check its condition very carefully.*

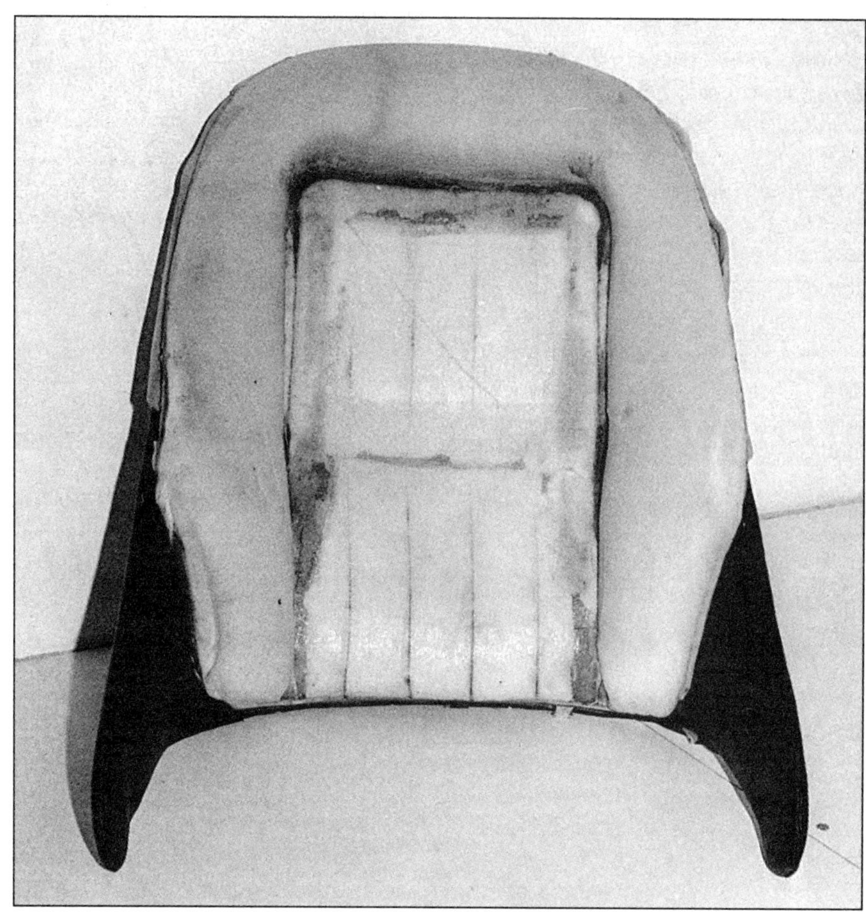

▼ *6.103. If it is necessary to replace the thin layer of foam stuck to the back of the steel pan, the next step is to carefully peel back the original foam to use as a template for the replacement section.*

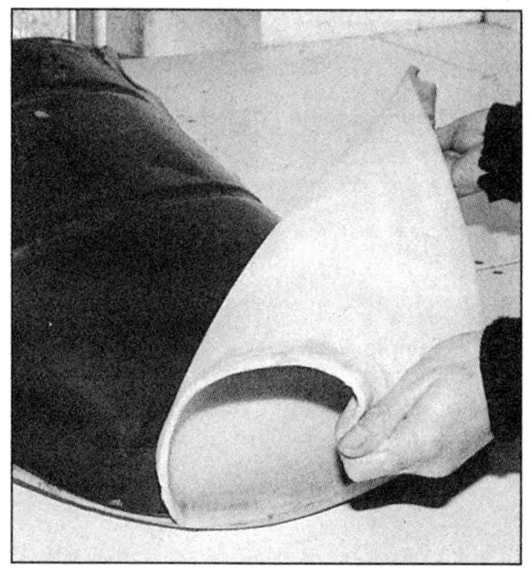

▼ *6.104. When reassembling, ensure that the foam padding is securely glued to the steel frame, then apply glue to the inside edges of the horseshoe-shaped foam forming the centre of the backrest. Note the addition of a thin layer of wadding around the outer edge of the backrest foam. This can give extra body to the seat where the original foam is found to have compressed slightly over the years.*

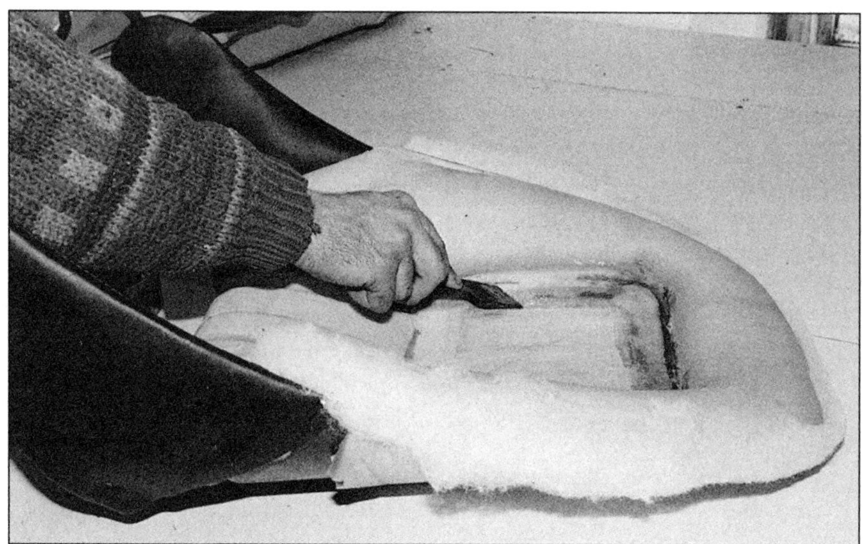

▶ *6.105. Apply glue also to the inside of the new cover assembly (in this case, made from scratch), in places corresponding to the adhesive applied to the backrest foam.*

▶ *6.106. The cover assembly can then be very carefully slid onto the backrest and, once correctly positioned with all wrinkles smoothed out, the securing clips can be refitted along the lower edge. It can be helpful to wrap cling-film over the foam as the cover is fitted – the leather/vinyl will slide more easily over the plastic film.*

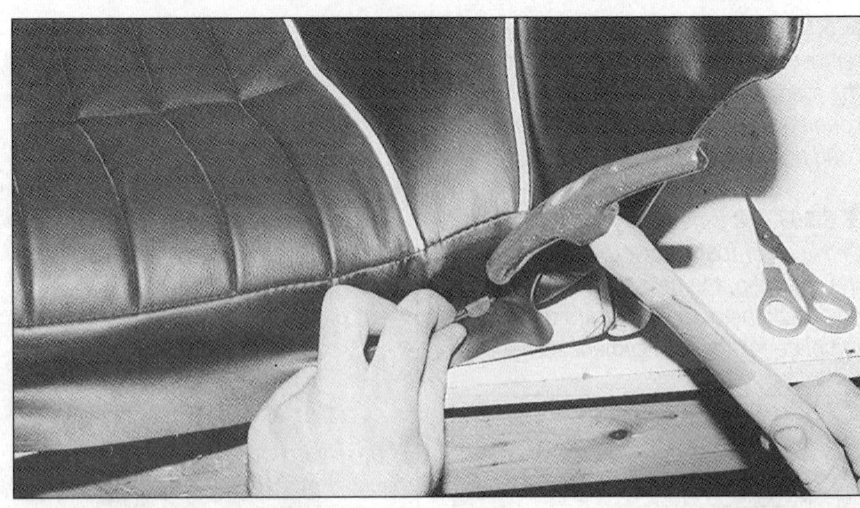

▼ *6.107. This seat base was in an even worse state than the backrest. Again, there was no alternative but to strip the assembly and re-cover it.*

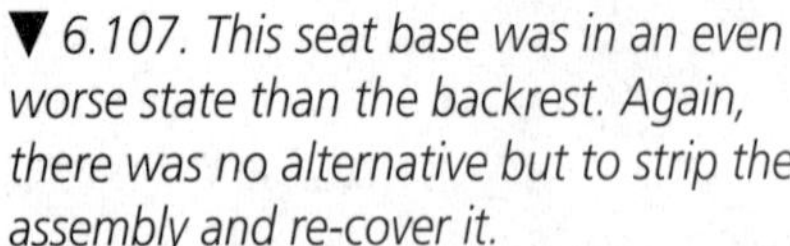

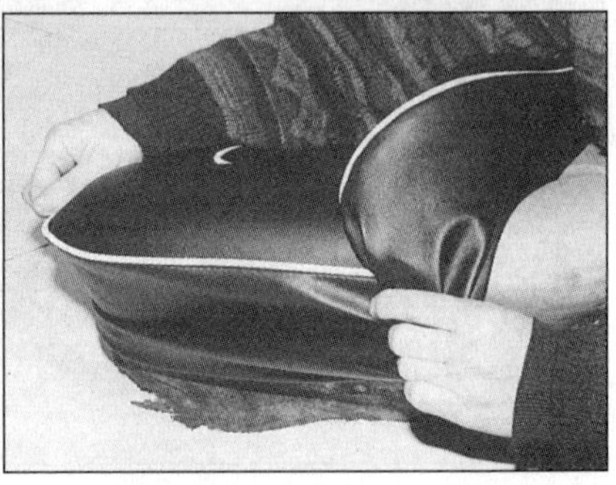

▲ *6.109. Trial-fit the replacement cover (made from scratch), ensuring that it fits snugly and without wrinkles. If all is well, remove the cover, renew the material covering the lower section of the foam base (if necessary), then reassemble using adhesive on the foam and the inside of the cover to hold everything together.*

▼ *6.108. The foam beneath the covering is often found to be in good condition, which is just as well as replacements can be hard or impossible to find, and very difficult to duplicate. The material covering the lower section of the foam base is easily replaced.*

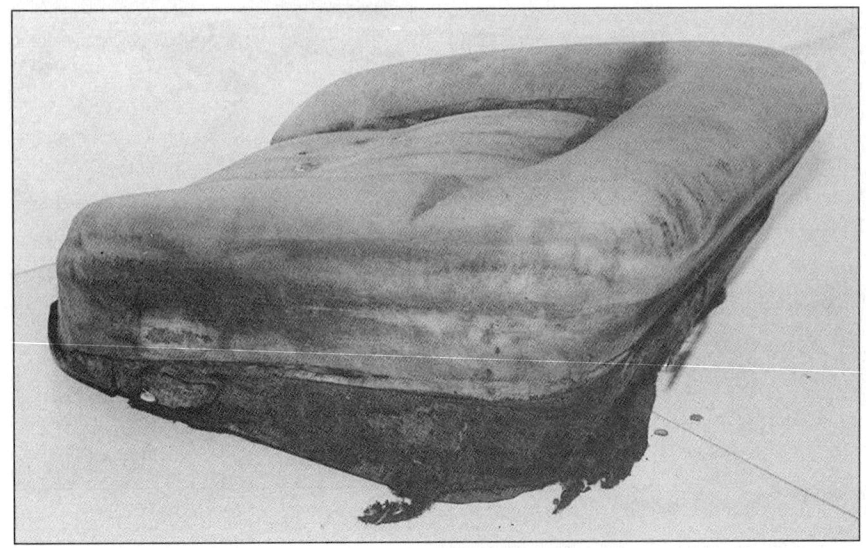

PRE-WAR MODELS

Seats from pre-war cars (and some immediate post-war models, which were essentially similar) can usually be dismantled using the techniques already outlined. However, there are some differences in construction. Notably, many early cars had seat frames made from ash.

Where the framework has deteriorated it will be necessary to have new sections made, cut to size and inserted. For the supply of the new wood, and cutting to size (but not necessarily final shaping), contact a hardwood specialist and ask for advice and help. If carpentry isn't your strong point, engage a professional to remake the frame for you, ensuring that the wood is treated against woodworm, etc.

Other differences in pre-war seats can include the methods of trimming the edges of back rests, etc. In particular, beading made of lead-filled brass or soft aluminium alloy may have been used for finishing strips.

▶ *6.110. If the wooden framework on your pre-war seats (or indeed the main wood frame of the vehicle's body) is in poor condition, replacement sections can be obtained from hardwood specialists who can offer advice and also cut the wood to size. This is just a small section of the vast stocks held by Oakwood of Sherborne, Dorset.*

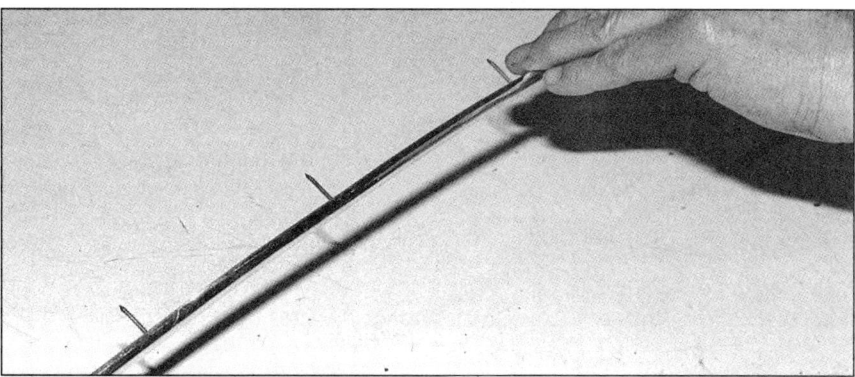

▲ *6.111. On many pre-war cars the joint between the material covering the rear face of the pressed steel back rest and the fluted front-facing covering is concealed by means of half round profile, lead-filled brass beading. This can be covered with leathercloth or hide, or can be plated or polished. Soft alloy pin beading does a similar job. Both types are flexible, allowing them to be bent to follow the contours of the seat, and both have built-in nails positioned every few inches. Finishing strips like this can be obtained from trim suppliers such as Woolies.*

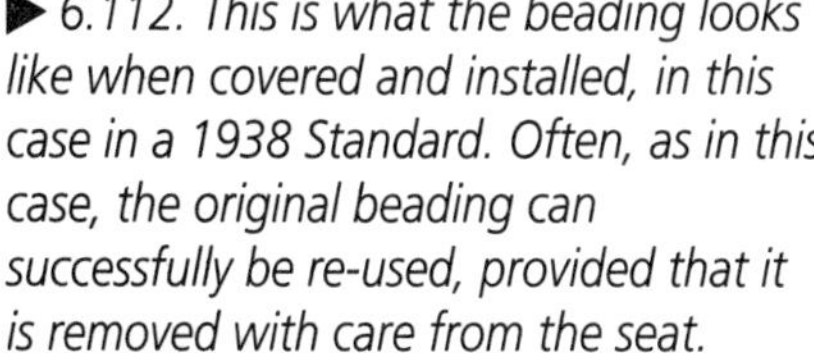

▶ *6.112. This is what the beading looks like when covered and installed, in this case in a 1938 Standard. Often, as in this case, the original beading can successfully be re-used, provided that it is removed with care from the seat.*

PATCH REPAIRS

It is very difficult to make invisible patch repairs to car seats. In general, if a panel is damaged, the only real answer is to remove and dismantle the seat, as described in earlier sections, and to make a new panel or complete seat covering.

Having said that, provided that you are prepared to accept that a repair may be visible, to a certain extent, it is quite possible to improve a seat by patching where a small area of damage exists. This may be preferable where it is difficult to match the seat covering material, or where the rest of the seat is in perfect condition and replacement of a panel or complete covering is not justified.

If the covering material is split rather than holed, a reinforcing piece of calico, cut to overlap the split on all sides by an inch (25mm) or so, can be very carefully slipped inside the split. Smooth the calico into position and firmly glue in place, using contact adhesive on both the calico and the underside of the seat covering material.

For repairing plastic covered seats and panels, it is worth noting that Loctite produce a special adhesive (Vinyl Bond) designed to bond vinyl and PVC. Said to be suitable for both small and large repairs, the adhesive dries clear, giving a permanently flexible and waterproof bond.

The following sequence shows a typical patch repair on the cloth-covered seat of a Ford Escort Mexico.

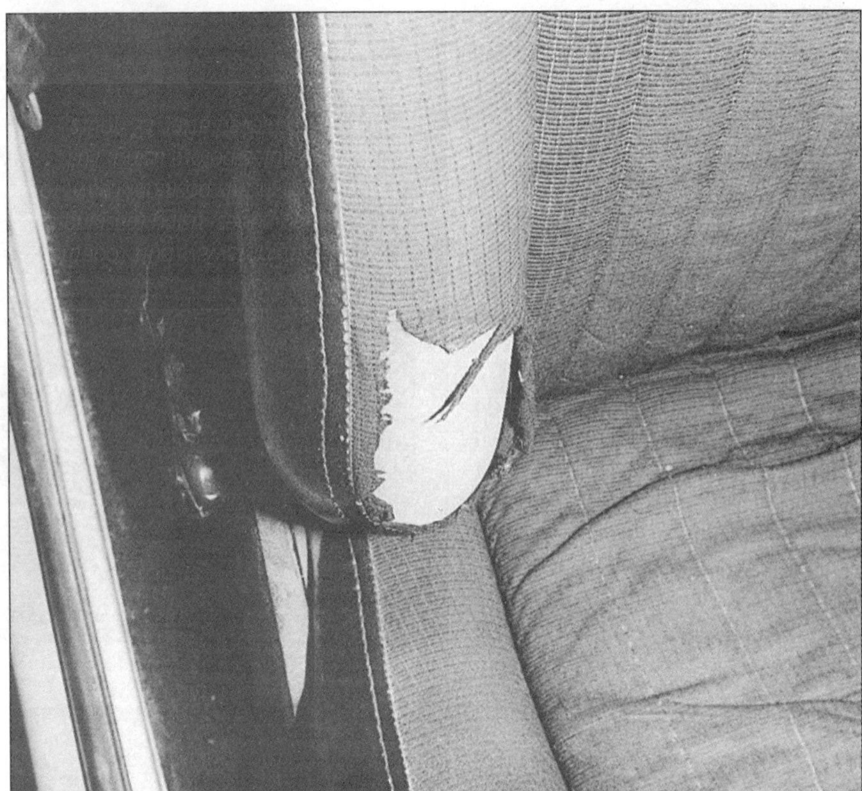

▶ *6.113. This driver's seat in a 1970s Ford Escort Mexico was badly worn on the outside edge of the wrap-around side-panel. However, the rest of the seat was in good condition and the owner didn't want to dismantle the seat. In any case, it was not possible to obtain seat covering material to match the original, so replacement of a complete panel, or the covering of just one front seat, would have made the interior look odd. The decision was therefore taken to patch repair the damaged panel as unobtrusively as possible.*

▼ *6.114. A small piece of material, in the same colour and as close as possible in texture to the original seat covering, was cut out so that it was larger than the hole in the covering by approximately one inch all round. This was then carefully fed into the aperture, so that there was an equal amount of overlap all around the edge.*

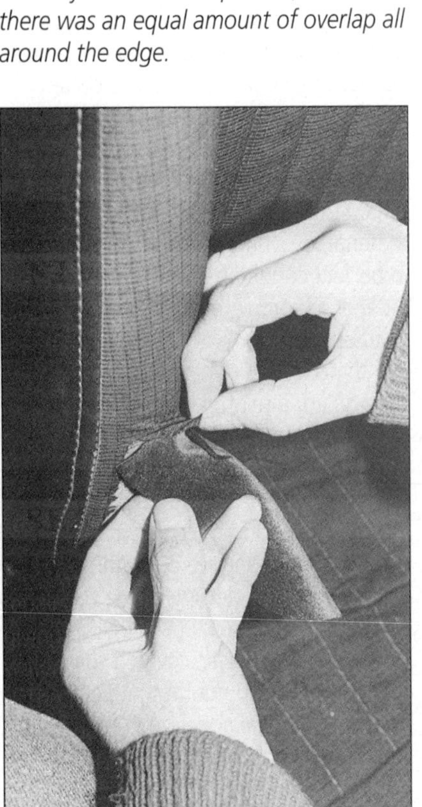

▼ *6.115. The uneven edges of the hole in the original covering material were carefully trimmed, then the excess material around the aperture was doubled back and tucked out of sight.*

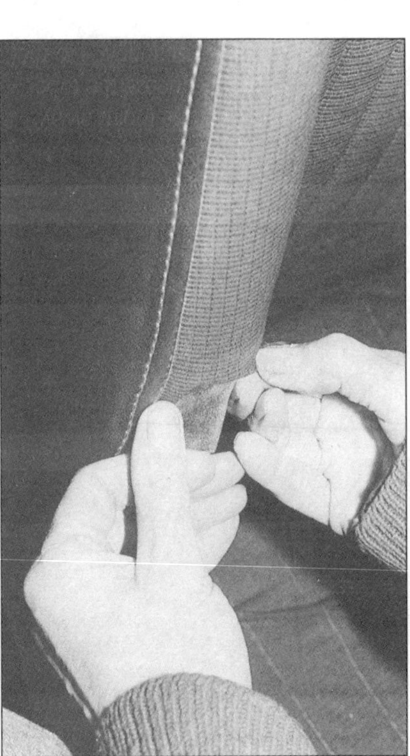

▼ *6.116. It was a simple matter to hand-stitch the repair patch in place. While the patch is not invisible, it is certainly preferable to a gaping hole in the seat, and a repair like this will stop the damaged area from spreading.*

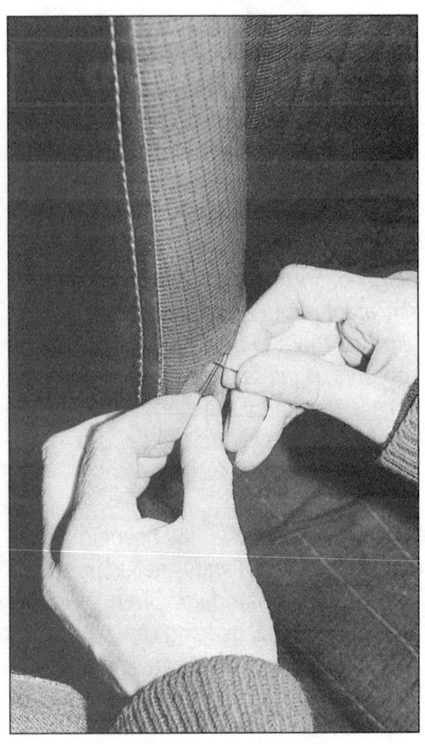

VINYL BOND

Loctite's Vinyl Bond adhesive has been developed specifically for the bonding of vinyl and PVC, and is ideal for small, permanent and flexible repairs to seats and trim panels with coverings made of these materials.

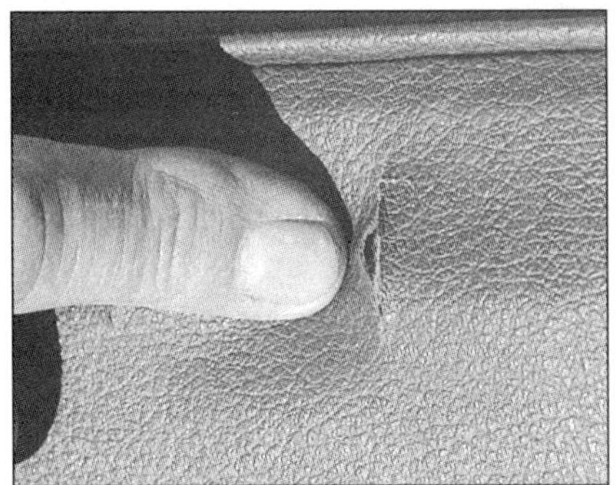

▲ *6.117. Tears and cracks like this often appear in plastic-covered seats. Ensure first that the adjacent edges are clean, dry and free of grease.*

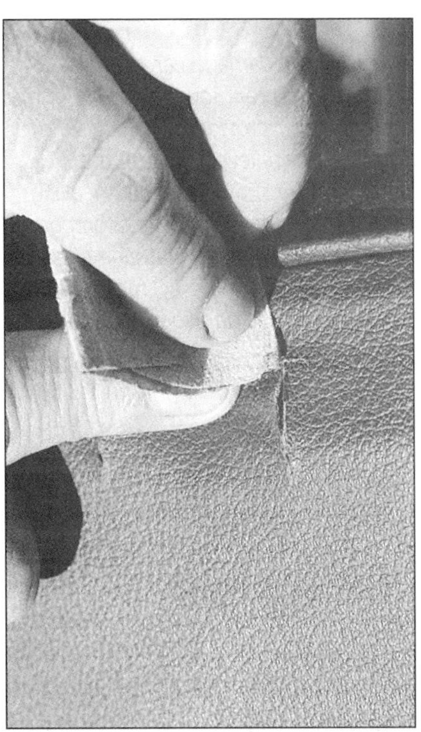

▲ *6.118. Use fine sandpaper to prepare the broken edges of the material, to provide a key for the adhesive.*

▼ *6.119. Open the tube (point away from you and don't squeeze the tube), then apply the glue – sparingly – to the edges of the damaged area.*

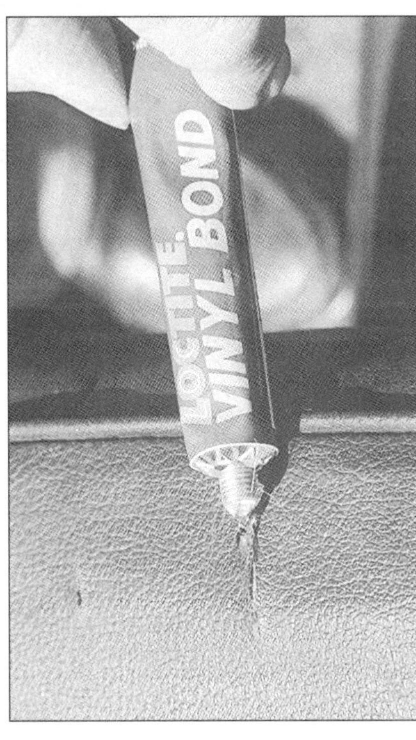

▼ *6.120. Straightaway, butt together the damaged edges, using masking tape to hold them in this position. Leave for up to 45 minutes before using. Full strength is achieved after 12 hours.*

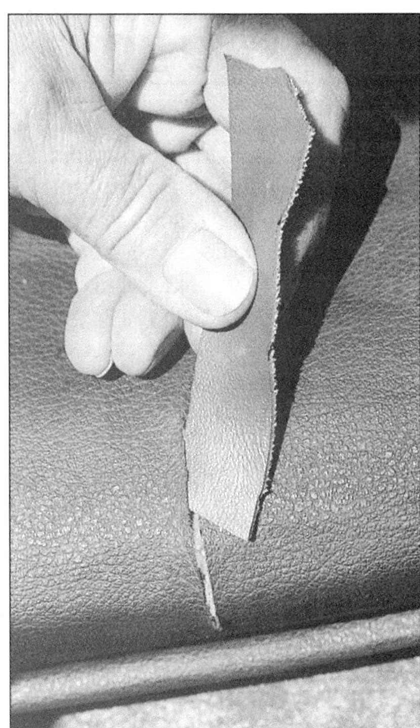

▲ *6.121. If the damaged area is larger, Vinyl Bond can be used to attach a backing patch to the back of the material, to add support.*

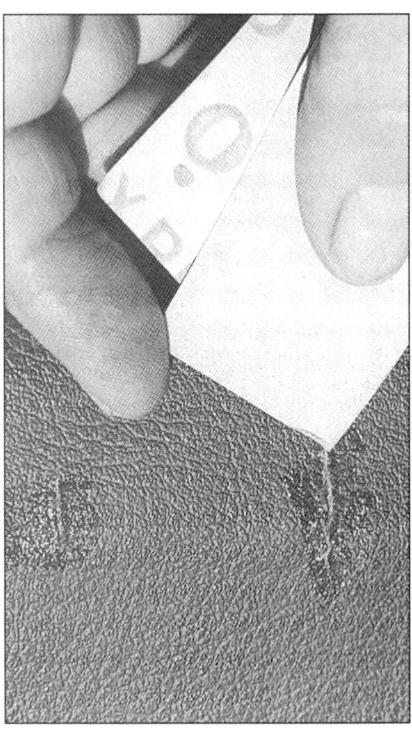

▲ *6.122. Use fine sandpaper to remove excess adhesive and to smooth the joint.*

REPAIR KIT

There are several kits on the market to enable small repairs to be carried out on vinyl and leather trim. The following photograph sequence shows the Vinyl and Leather Plastic Repair Kit, from Frost Auto Restoration Techniques Ltd, in action on the rear seat from a Ford Cortina Mark I.

For best results it is wise to follow implicitly the instructions provided with the kit.

▶ *6.123. The Frost kit contains urethane filler, colouring agents, graining papers and full instructions. It can be used on leather or vinyl seats or trim panels, and can also be used on facias. Unlike some kits, it does not require heat to cure the compounds used.*

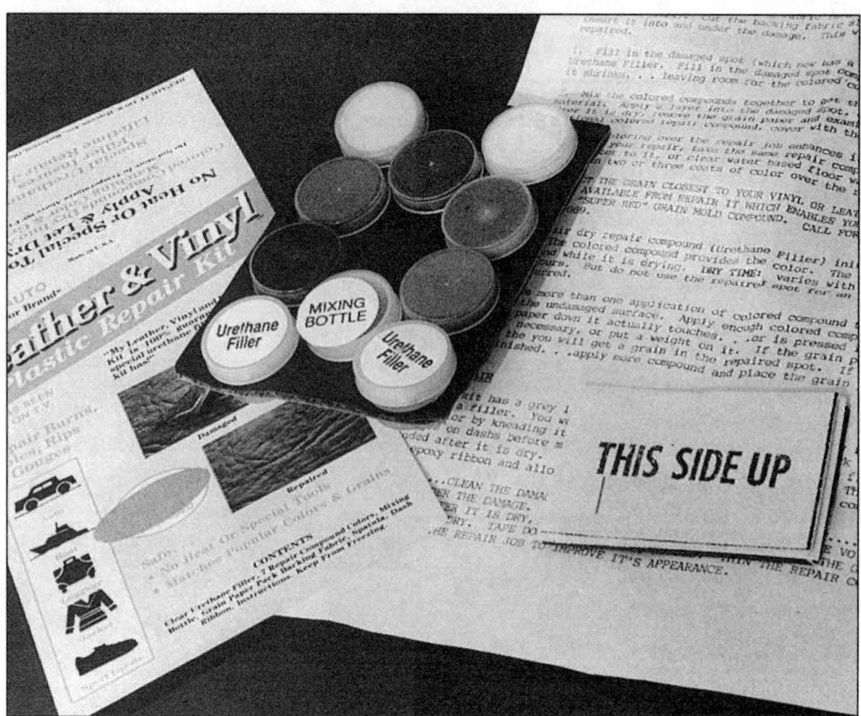

▼ *6.124. The Cortina's rear seat base was suffering from two minor imperfections, in the form of tiny holes with sharp edges.*

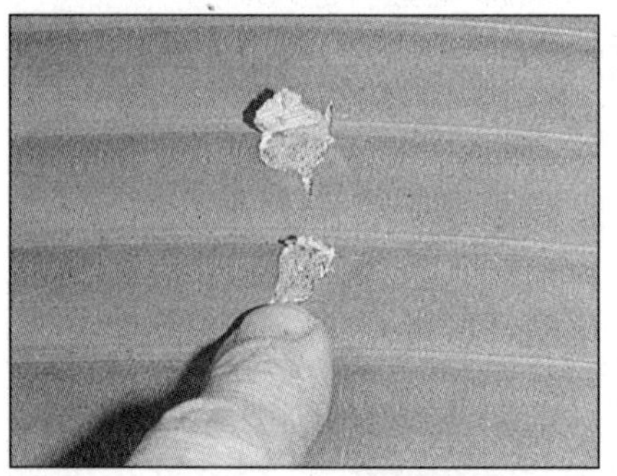

▼ *6.125. The first step is to cut two circles of backing fabric (any thin cloth can be used) slightly larger than the areas of damage.*

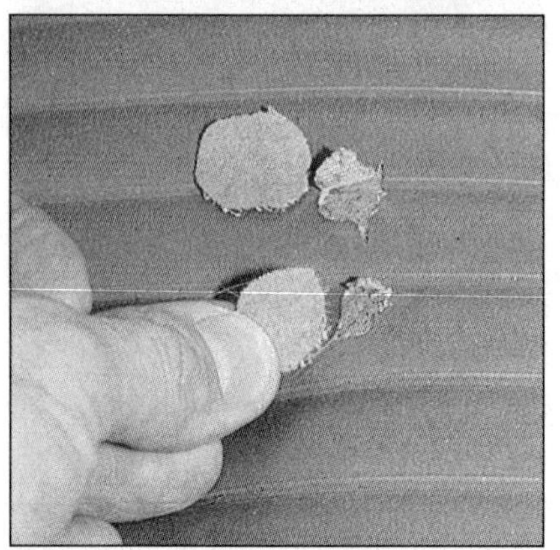

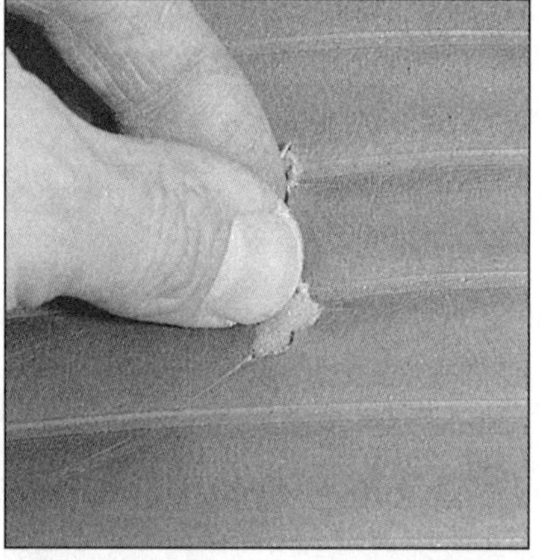

▲ *6.126. Fill any voids beneath the damaged area with foam, then very carefully slide the backing fabric beneath the edges of the surrounding seat covering material so that the edges of the fabric overlap the perimeter of the hole by an approximately equal amount all round. Ensure that the fabric lies flat before proceeding. This is a tedious operation when dealing with small areas.*

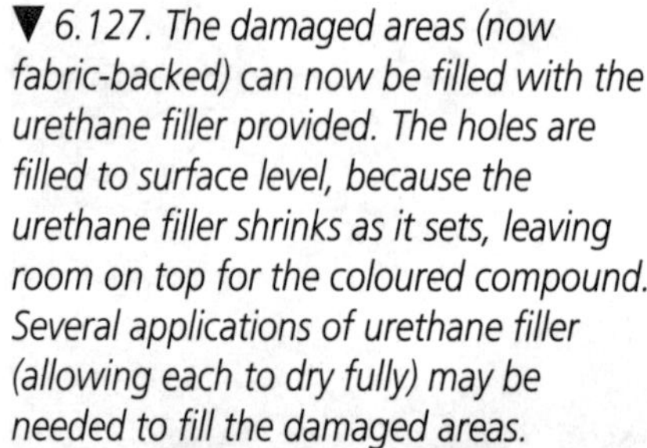

▼ *6.127. The damaged areas (now fabric-backed) can now be filled with the urethane filler provided. The holes are filled to surface level, because the urethane filler shrinks as it sets, leaving room on top for the coloured compound. Several applications of urethane filler (allowing each to dry fully) may be needed to fill the damaged areas.*

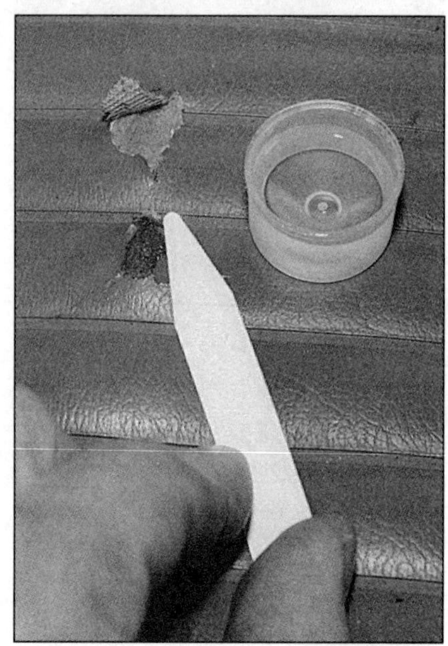

▶ *6.128. The colouring agents provided now need to be mixed to produce a compound of the same colour shade as the seat covering being repaired. Only a few drops of each colour are normally required, mixed together in the pot which comes with the kit. Take great care to keep the coloured pots apart (so that no accidental mixing can take place) and clean – always replace the lid immediately after use. Arriving at precisely the right colour can take a long time!*

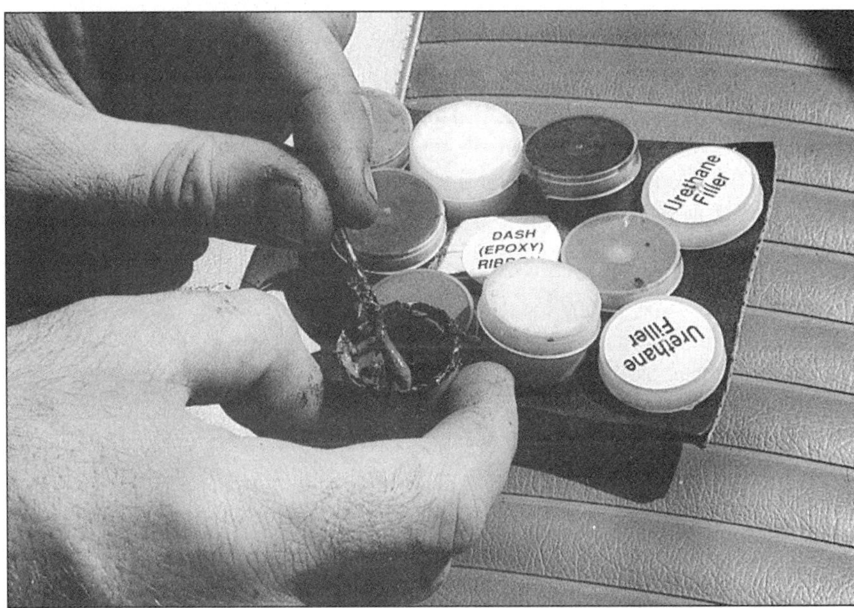

▶ *6.129. The coloured compound should be spread into the repairs as soon as possible after mixing. Ensure that the edges of the repaired sections are adequately blended with the original seat covering.*

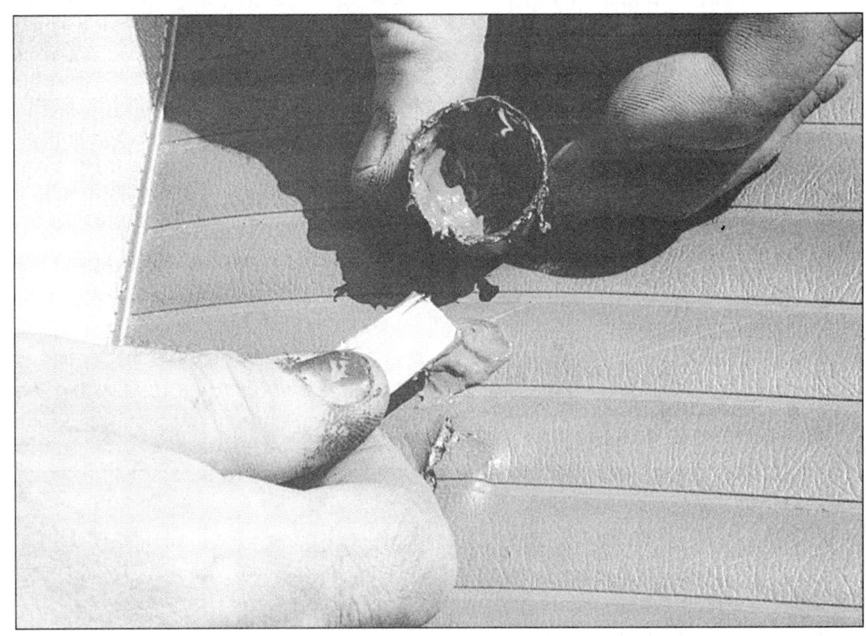

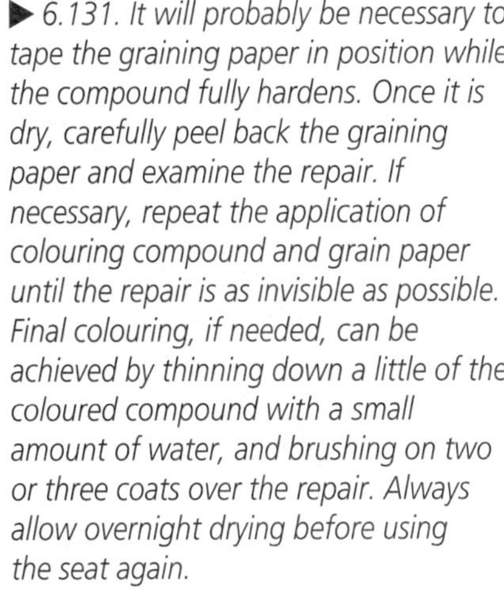

▲ *6.130. Select the graining paper having the pattern closest to the grain on your seat, place it face down on top of the repaired area(s), and allow the compound to dry.*

▶ *6.131. It will probably be necessary to tape the graining paper in position while the compound fully hardens. Once it is dry, carefully peel back the graining paper and examine the repair. If necessary, repeat the application of colouring compound and grain paper until the repair is as invisible as possible. Final colouring, if needed, can be achieved by thinning down a little of the coloured compound with a small amount of water, and brushing on two or three coats over the repair. Always allow overnight drying before using the seat again.*

REPLACING COIL SPRINGS

A problem often encountered when renovating the interior on an older car is breakage or disappearance of one or more of the coil springs forming the sprung base of a seat.

It is often impossible to buy suitable new replacements, in which case the only option is to employ a similar spring from a second-hand seat. In each case, try to ensure that, as far as possible, the replacement spring is of the same type, size and wire diameter as the original.

The following photographs show the sprung base of a seat from a car scrapped long ago, being used as a donor for springs to rebuild the seat base from a Triumph Roadster. Often such donor bases are available very cheaply – especially when the covering material is damaged or missing – simply because nobody else wants them! However, they can be invaluable for restoration work.

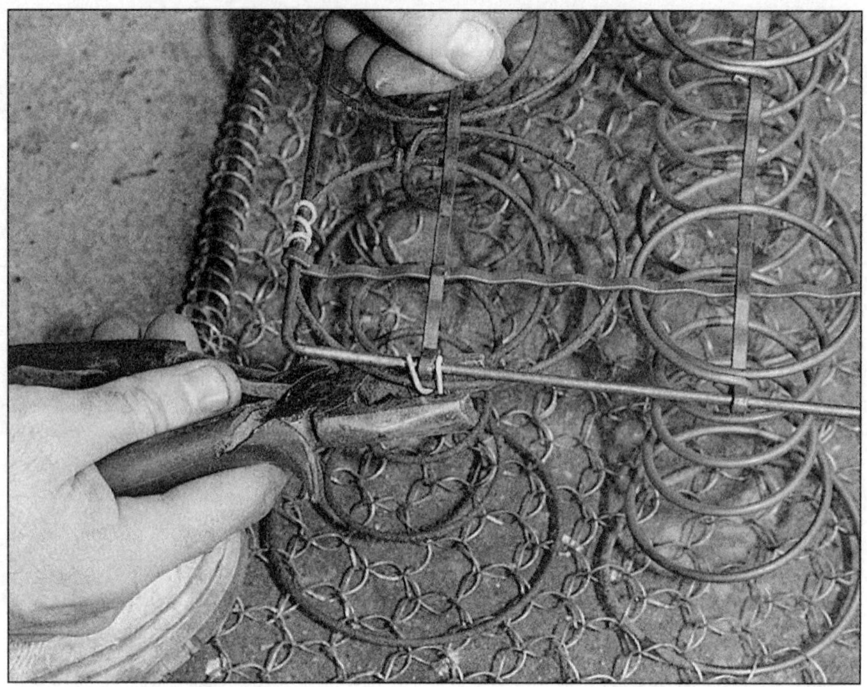

▲ *6.132. Having ensured that the 'new' spring is of the required type, shape and size, the first step is to release it from its old home. Methods of attachment vary. However, in most cases a screwdriver and a pair of tin snips and/or wire cutters will do the trick.*

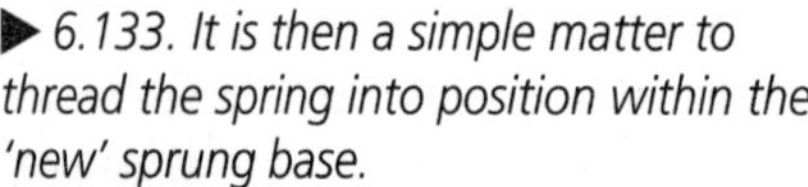

▶ *6.133. It is then a simple matter to thread the spring into position within the 'new' sprung base.*

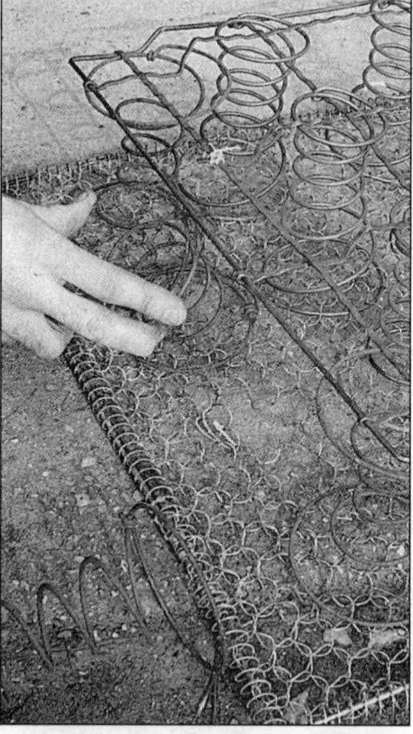

◀ *6.134. The spring can be attached to the perimeter of the frame and, where necessary, to adjacent springs, by the use of home-made clips. These can be fashioned from ordinary single wire (using the original clips as patterns), and installed using a pair of pliers. The springs fitted into this Triumph seat were almost identical to the originals.*

CHANGING THE CHARACTER OF A SEAT

Owners often wish to change the character of the seats in their car, while retaining similar overall profiles and sizes. One obvious example is to upgrade from vinyl to leather coverings, or from cloth to leather. One step further is to introduce fluted panels where none were originally used.

Obviously, this approach is not appropriate where complete originality is desired (as with concours old cars), but it can certainly help to improve the interior on more recent vehicles.

To illustrate what can be achieved, the following photographs show the transformation of a seat from a Fiat X1/9. This was originally cloth-covered and without fluted panels. The owner specifically wanted leather seats, and flutes!

Here's how the job progressed. Again, to avoid repetition of stages covered earlier in this chapter, only the salient points are described. Incidentally, this seat shows further variations on the themes already covered in terms of construction. In particular, tensioning straps are employed to give the seat its dished shape.

▼ *6.135. Before and after! On the left is the original cloth-covered seat from the X1/9. On the right is its partner, after having been re-engineered with a new leather covering incorporating fluted panels.*

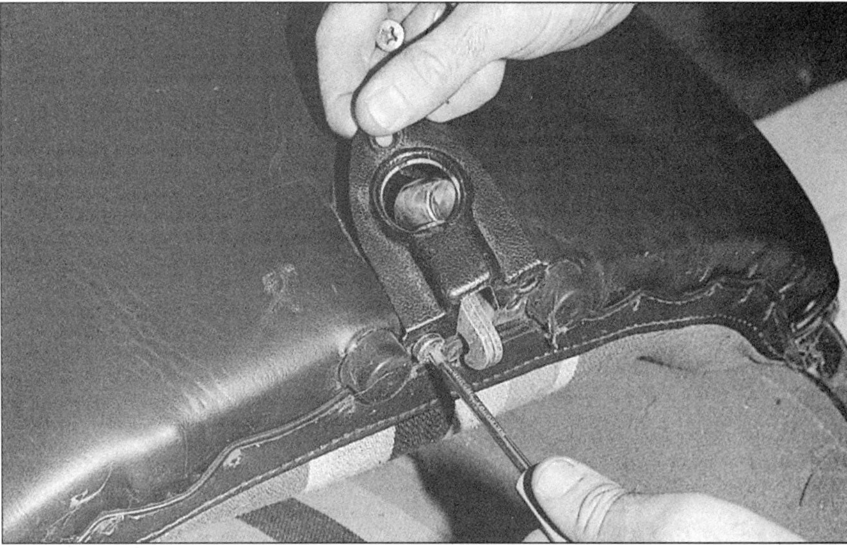

▲ *6.136. Start dismantling by taking out the screws securing the handle on the back rest.*

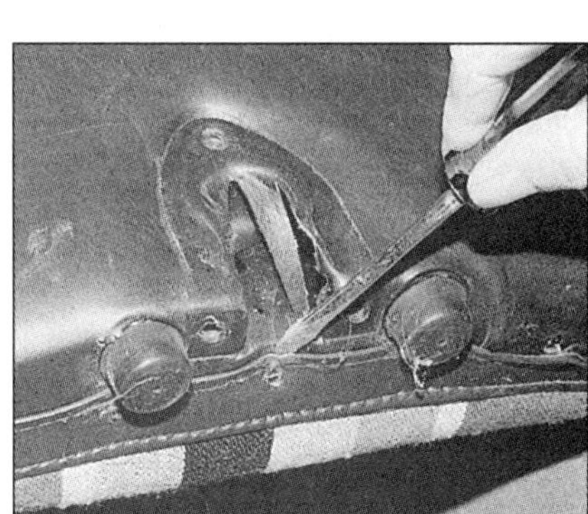

▲ *6.137. Release the steel tabs securing the material at the base of the back rest – an old screwdriver is useful for this.*

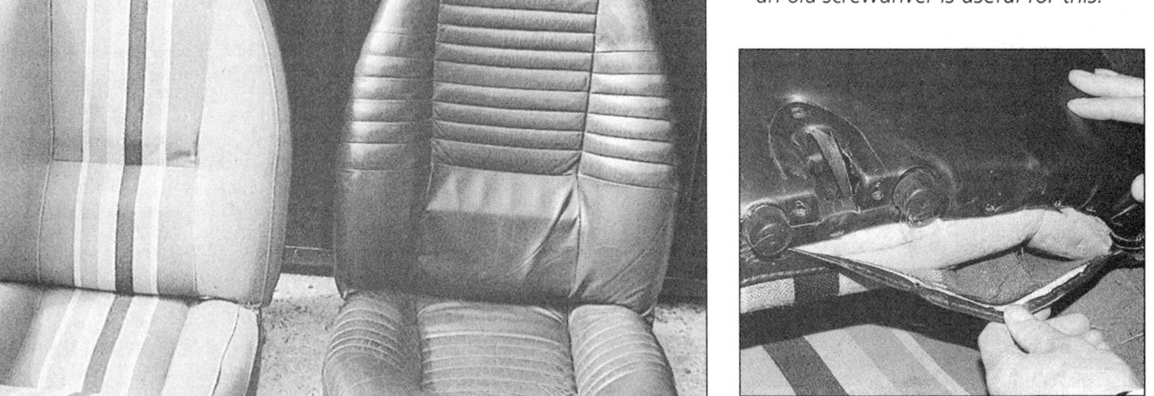

▲ *6.138. Detach and pull down the edge of the material, which effectively forms a bag over the back rest, the open end of the bag being joined at the bottom.*

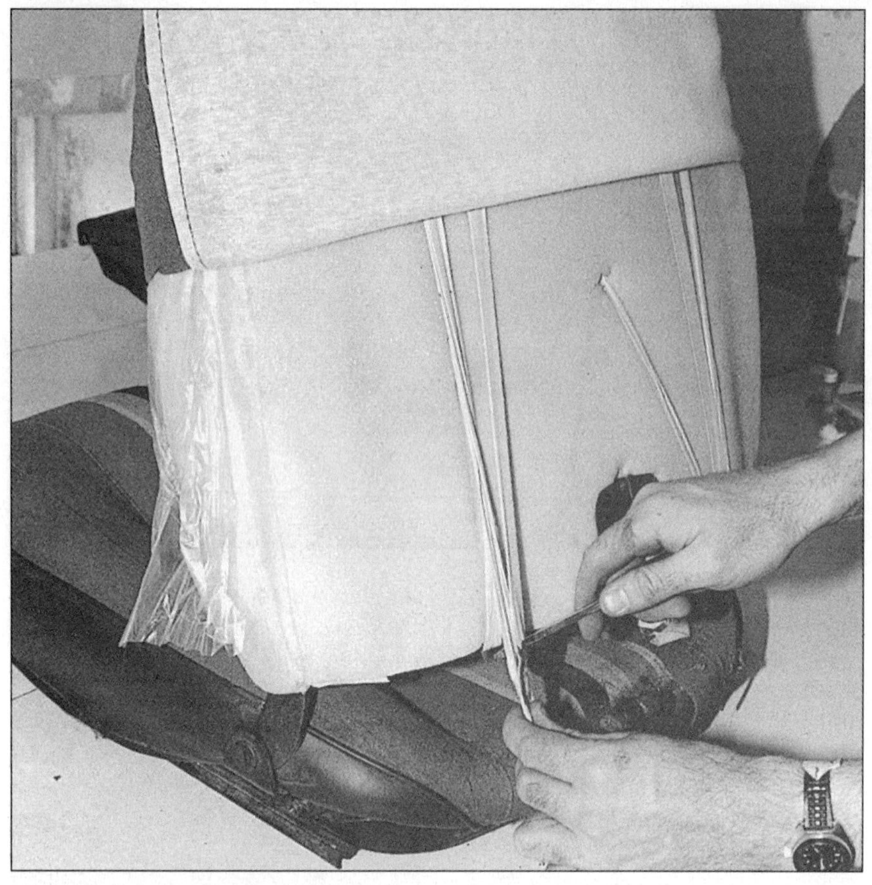

▲ *6.139. Now carefully unroll the back rest cover, and unclip the tensioning straps that are revealed.*

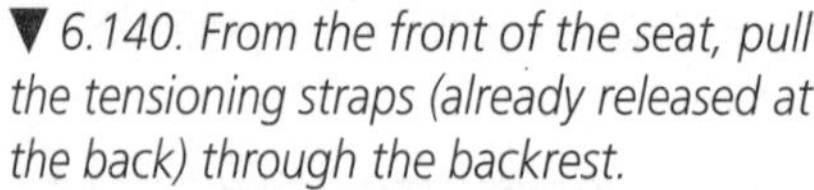

▼ *6.140. From the front of the seat, pull the tensioning straps (already released at the back) through the backrest.*

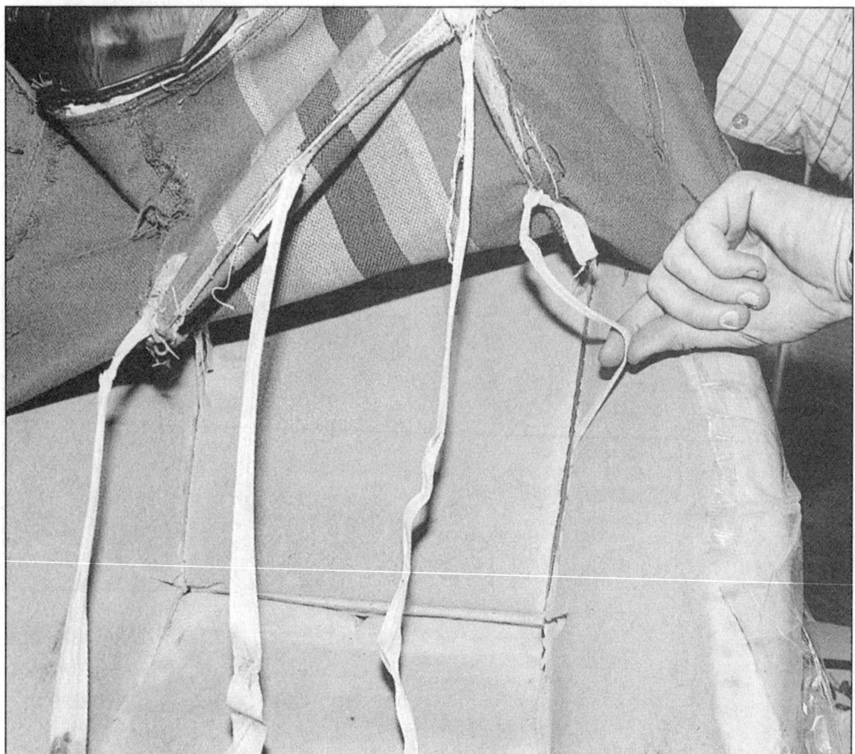

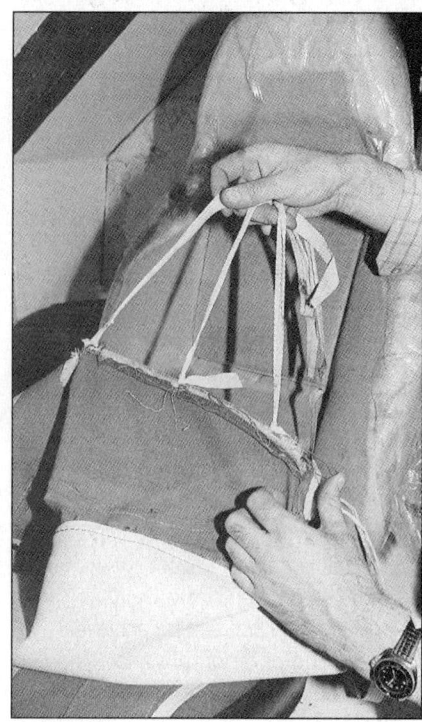

▲ *6.141. The tensioning straps are secured to steel bars – as the straps are pulled taut and secured, within the foam forming the main part of the backrest, they pull the seat into shape, giving the dished appearance.*

▲ *6.142. The seat base is of different construction, with hog rings securing Z-springs to steel bars within the base. Release the hog rings to separate the components.*

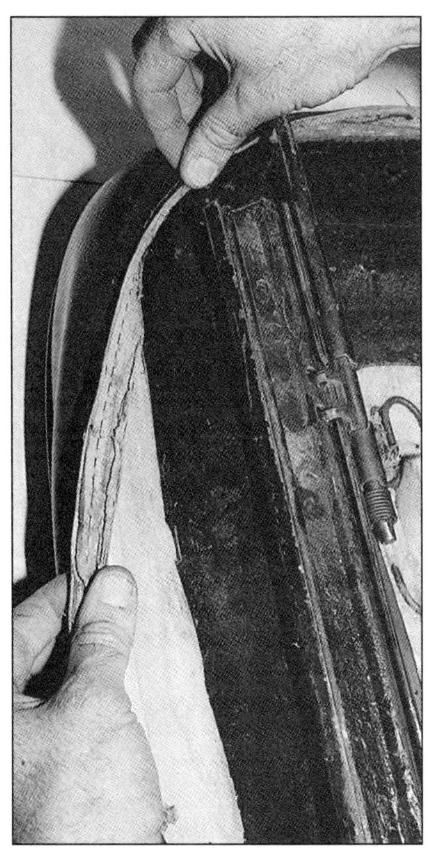

Patterns need to be made for each of the new sections required. These are best made from vinyl, because it stretches, thereby more easily allowing for the curvature of the foam forming the seat base. Experimentation can be carried out at this stage to achieve the desired look and structure of the new sections. Next, the vinyl patterns can be laid flat onto the new covering material, and the required shapes marked out, then cut to shape.

▶ *6.145. Patterns can be made for the new sections, and marked on the foam of the seat structure, using a felt-tip pen. Proposed fluted sections, etc., can also be marked on the foam as references.*

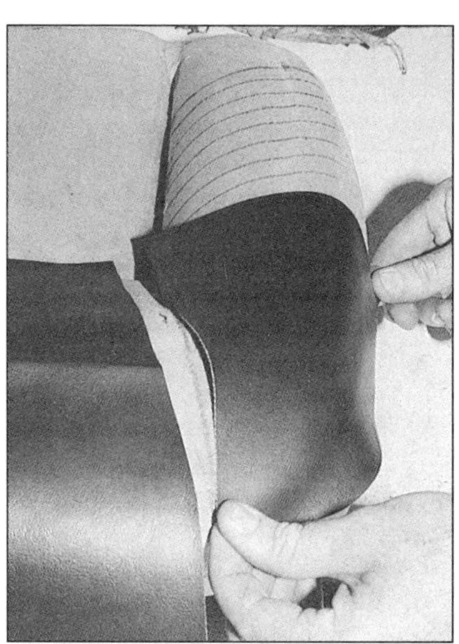

▲ *6.143. Cardboard edging is sewn into the seat base cover, and this locates within clips in the metal backing of the seat. The cover is secured by hooks at the rear. Carefully detach all the way round.*

▼ *6.144. Withdraw the steel bars (and the cover) from the apertures in the foam base.*

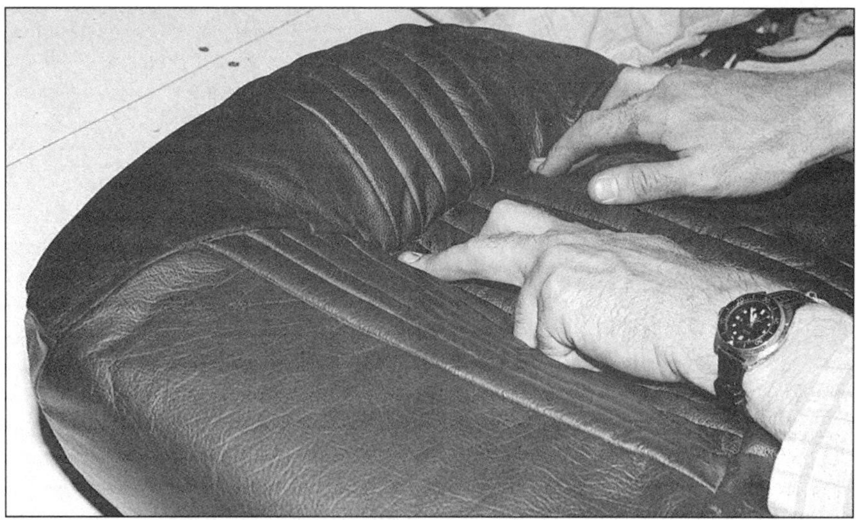

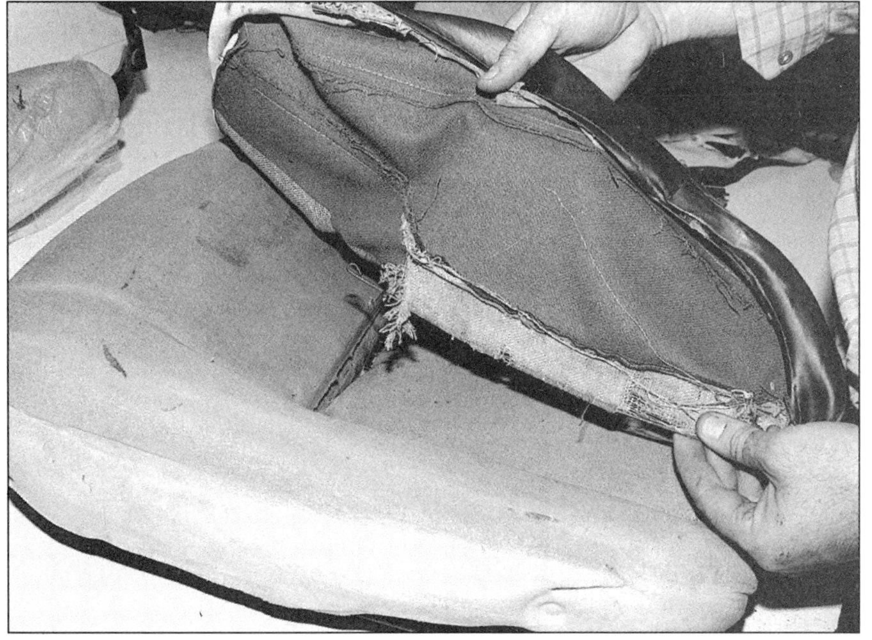

▲ *6.146. Construct the replacement seat covering (using the techniques shown earlier in this chapter) and trial-fit it, pressing in at the points where the tensioning straps will act, to see how well the covering will fit. Note that before attempting to fit the back rest cover, cling-film or thin plastic sheeting should be wrapped over the top of the foam, enabling the covering to slide more easily into position. The film can remain in the seat.*

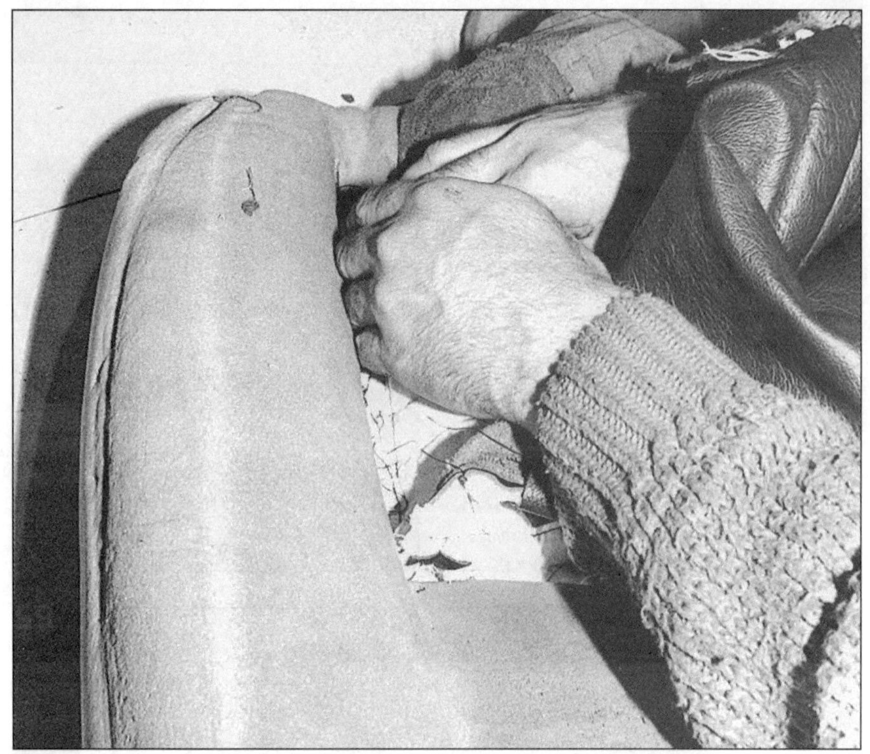

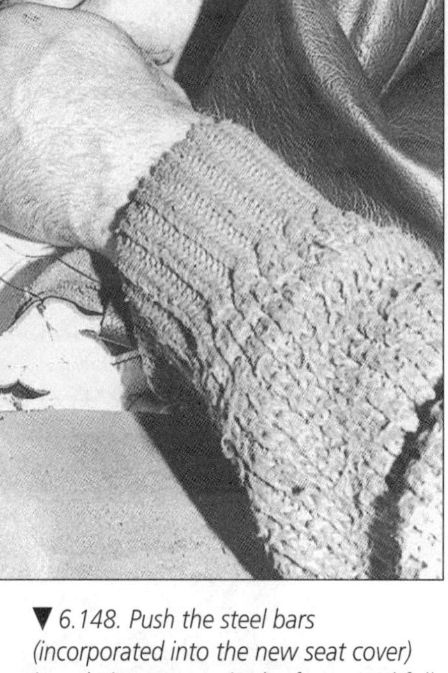

▲ *6.147. If all is well, push/pull the tensioning straps through the assembly in the reverse direction to that which applied when dismantling.*

▼ *6.148. Push the steel bars (incorporated into the new seat cover) into their apertures in the foam, and fully into position.*

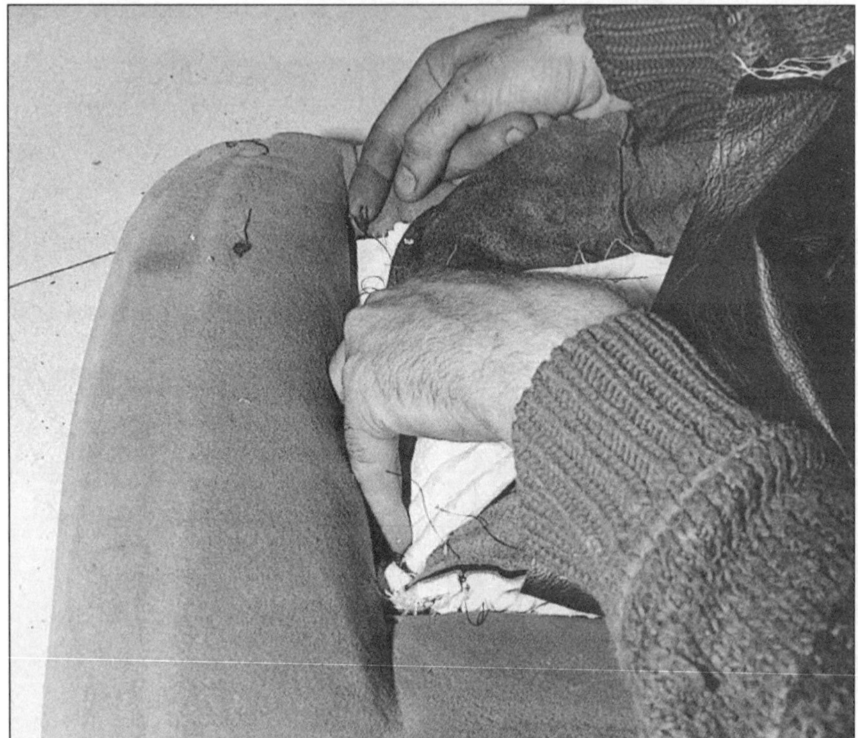

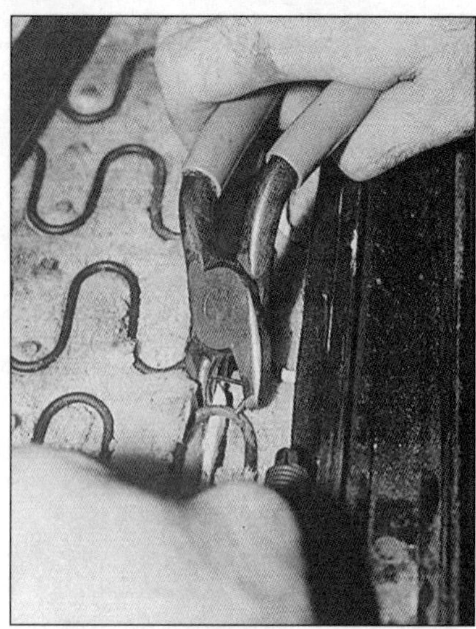

▲ *6.149. Using hog ring pliers (these were from Frost Auto Restoration Techniques Ltd), fit new hog rings to hold together the Z-springs and steel bars.*

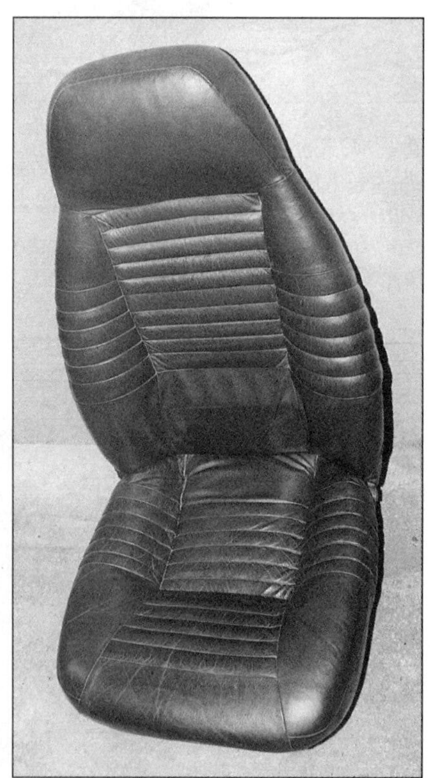

▲ *6.150. The completed seat looks and feels far better than the original. With its new leather covering it should wear well, too.*

GENERAL NOTES AND HINTS

In this chapter I have endeavoured to include most of the areas you are likely to encounter when tackling seat restoration. However, the following general notes may also be of assistance.

Seats originally fitted with rubber (Pirelli) webbing (a series of straps running under and across the seat) as the means of suspension for the seat base can be rebuilt either as original, by cutting to length and installing new lengths of webbing, or they can be modified.

One alternative to the original set-up is to attach a solid steel base pan (with a few small holes drilled in it for ventilation) to the original frame (by riveting or welding in place). A block of foam, cut to shape and about 4 in (100mm.) thick, mounted on top of the pan, is then used as the means of suspension for the seat. This method of construction tends to give a firmer seat which can also be less prone to sagging if the occupant is fairly heavy!

If the original foam in a seat is past redemption, and replacements in good condition cannot be located, new items can often be made using chipped foam as the main ingredient.

With this cut to the shape of the back rest rear panel (which is often of steel), and the forward face cut as close as possible to the original profile (an electric carving knife is useful for this), the final contours can be achieved by applying a thin layer of ordinary foam to the front face of the chipped foam. Don't rush this job – care is needed to get it right!

The seats on some cars, including some BMWs, incorporate plastic tapes which originally were heat bonded to the foam padding. However, such tapes can be sewn in place during restoration of such seats.

The following tools (referred to in Chapter 1) will also be of assistance:

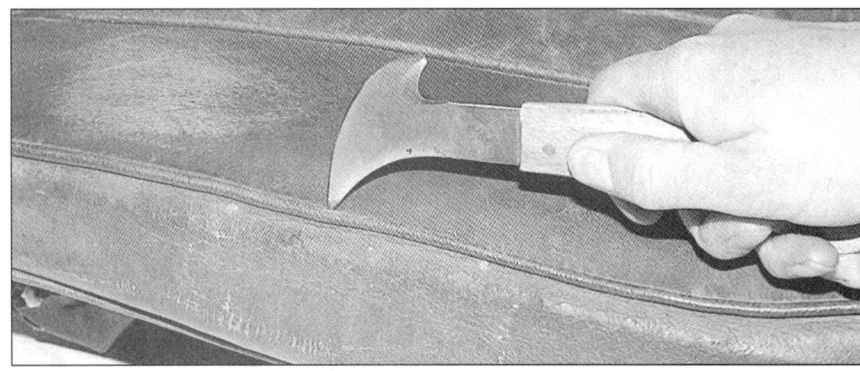

▲ *6.151. When dismantling seat coverings, or other sections of trim which are sewn together, the use of a trimmer's knife, like this one from Eastwood allows precise cutting of the stitching, without damaging the adjacent panels, which can then be used as patterns, or possibly can be kept for re-use. Keep sharpened for maximum effect.*

▼ *6.152. For gripping material and pulling it tight around seat frames, a pair of upholsterer's pliers, like these from Frost Auto Restoration Techniques Ltd, are a great help. Their jaws exert a strong grip yet are designed not to mark the material.*

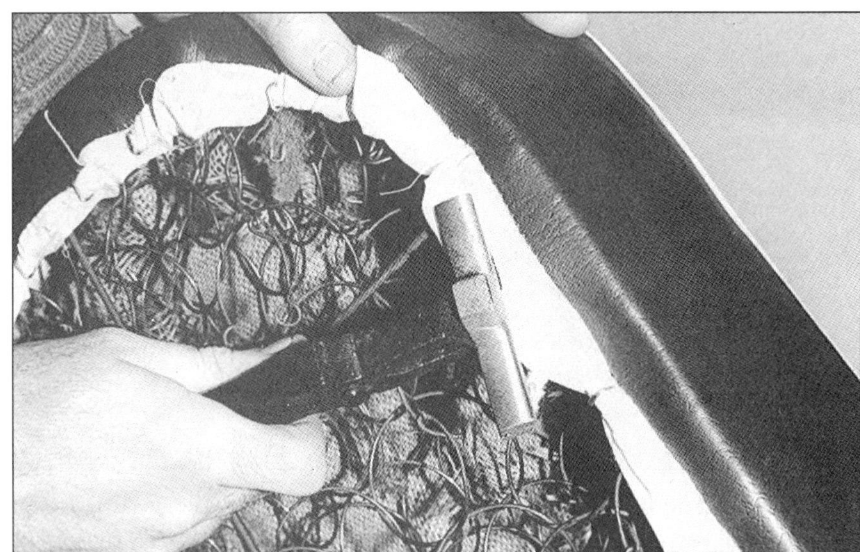

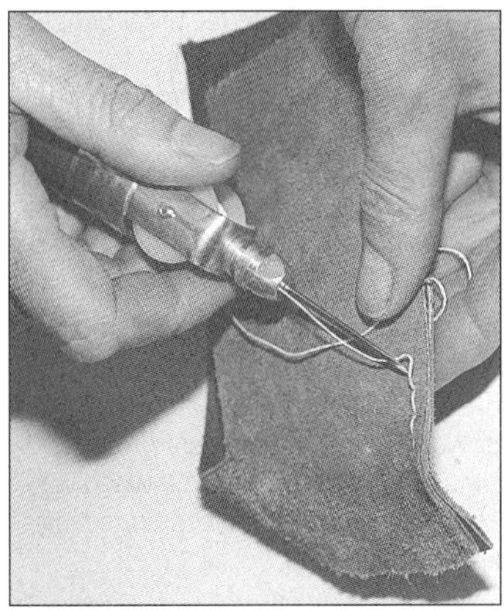

◀ *6.153. This versatile little automatic awl, from Eastwood, is useful for a number of jobs where access is available from both sides of the material being tackled, including attaching hessian to seat bases, etc. The technique for sewing with the awl is soon mastered. It requires waxed thread for optimum ease of use.*

Chapter 7

Facias and cappings

The finish used on the facia and door cappings will vary according to the age, type and quality of the vehicle. Most cars built during the last 20 years or so incorporate large, moulded plastic finisher panels in these areas. Earlier family cars featured painted metal interior panels, and many cars of the 1930s/40s had metal facias and door cappings/window frames, finished with an imitation wood grain effect.

Upmarket cars – in the old days and now – incorporate wood veneer finishes. Wood veneer is a very thin slice of grained wood (often walnut) attached to a backing board, and varnished to give a shiny and pleasing appearance.

In good condition, wood veneer interior fittings can look really superb. Conversely, deteriorating old veneer can make an otherwise perfect interior appear shabby. Age, exposure to moisture and sheer neglect on the part of successive owners can lead to discoloured, lacklustre veneer which looks awful.

Some older vehicles incorporated solid wood facias and door cappings, etc. In fact, it is more common to find door cappings made of solid wood, with dashboards often constructed from plywood to which a veneered top surface has been added. The wood was usually varnished to provide protection and a gloss finish.

Each type of finish has its own advantages and drawbacks, in terms of looks, everyday use, and approach when restoration work is required. In all cases, however, prevention is better than cure, and regular attention using polish/preservative appropriate to the material will help it to last intact for many years.

MAINTENANCE AND RESTORATION

Plain, painted metalwork can be treated in the same way as exterior bodywork, with an occasional cleaning, 'cutting back' and wax polish usually being all that is required to keep it looking smart. This is covered in Chapter 2.

When the paintwork has been allowed to become chipped or badly faded, a rub-down and respray – again, as for exterior bodywork – will restore the appearance relatively easily. However, it is usually best to remove the panels from the vehicle for the work to be carried out, and in the case of a facia panel, this often involves releasing wiring, instruments and so on.

If you take this approach, always disconnect the vehicle's battery, before starting work, and be very careful to label all wiring which is disconnected, to aid reassembly.

The alternative to removing the facia from the car is to very carefully mask all instruments, switchgear and surrounding interior fittings prior to respraying. However, this can be so fiddly that the time taken is likely to exceed that required to remove the dash and do the job properly.

Panels and window surrounds, etc., bearing imitation wood grain effects can usually be maintained in good condition by the occasional application of wax polish. However, they can be virtually impossible to restore precisely as original, since in many cases the factory finish was achieved by means of printing/transfers which have long since ceased to be available.

In such cases, the use of a wood graining kit can impart a suitable finish which will look smart and will be in keeping with the style of the original design, even if it does not precisely match what was created at the factory. Reapplying this type of finish is shown later in this chapter. Once again, it is best if the dash and other affected panels are removed from the vehicle where possible.

Where a vehicle has a plastic facia, an occasional cleaning and coating with an anti-ultraviolet solution will help to preserve its looks and slow down the adverse effects of sunlight (including a tendency to become brittle, with cracks opening up, etc.)

When the damage has already been done, remedial work can be carried out using one of the dashboard repair kits which are available nowadays. Details of the technique are included in this chapter.

Varnished, solid wood panels can suffer from a number of maladies, including cracking and peeling of the varnish, and the appearance of white areas caused by the wood grain filler (originally used to fill small surface imperfections in the wood) being bleached.

If the wood (including veneered finishes) is basically sound, recolouring to the original hue (where necessary) using a wood stain, and revarnishing, will effect a complete cure. In the case of a dashboard, the most difficult part of the job (as already mentioned) is removing the instruments, switches, wiring, etc., to enable the panel to be removed from the vehicle. The alternative is to release these items as far as possible, and to carefully mask them while restoration work is in progress.

The full restoration of facias and door cappings with wood veneer finishes can be rather complex, and the job is often thought to be too difficult to tackle by many DIY restorers. However, I hope that I can show that it is fully within the realms of DIY restoration, without the need to spend a fortune.

It should be noted that the method of veneer replacement shown later in this chapter is only one approach. It is included because it is relatively straightforward – and it has been proved to work.

WOODWORK RENOVATION

If the woodwork in your vehicle is structurally sound, but lacking in finish, it is usually not difficult to regain the good looks which may have disappeared years ago. However, as with most aspects of interior renovation, it is a job which requires patience, and it takes time to achieve good results.

The first step is to remove all traces of the original varnish. This can be done using paint stripper, but be very careful not to get the stuff on your skin or in your eyes (wear rubber gloves and protective goggles), and don't use the sort of stripper which turns some woods (including walnut and mahogany) a dark colour. Test on a small, unobtrusive area first.

Wire wool can be used to agitate the paint stripper, to speed up the removal of the old varnish. On completion, be sure to thoroughly neutralize any stripping agent remaining on the wood, following the instructions on the container. It is often difficult to completely purge the wood of all the chemical.

An alternative to the use of paint stripper is to employ a wood chisel, or a suitable scraper, to physically remove the original varnish. This can be very effective and, if the varnish is old and brittle, it often flakes off very easily. However, extreme care is needed to avoid making nicks in the surface with the chisel/scraper.

When all the old varnish has been removed, smooth the surface of the wood with very fine sandpaper to give a keyed surface ready to accept the new varnish. Follow up with very fine wire wool, working with/along the grain.

REPAIRS?

At this stage you will quite likely discover imperfections in the surface, such as scratches, dents, burn marks and sections which require repair by gluing the wood back together.

On veneered finishes, if the damage has breached the surface, unobtrusive repair can be very difficult, although it is sometimes possible to let in a small piece of veneer to match as closely as possible the original finish. Failing this, you will either have to live with the damaged section, or replace the veneer, as described later in this chapter.

Small scratches in solid wood panels are best abraded out, using progressively finer grades of sandpaper. Sometimes the whole panel will have to be resanded to obtain a uniform appearance.

Dents can be more difficult to eradicate. Sometimes, the application of steam from a boiling kettle or steam iron (take great care) can help to bring slight depressions out of the wood. Otherwise, attempts can be made to fill the dent, using a wood substitute filler. Furniture restoration firms may be able to assist with the supply of suitable materials for this. However, bear in mind that it can be extremely difficult to get filled areas to match the appearance of the original wood (even when revarnished) because of the different properties of the filler material. Experiment first.

Very minor burn marks can sometimes be scraped from the surface of the wood, alternatively it may be possible to bleach out the darkened sections, using domestic bleach. This can also be used, where necessary, to lighten otherwise darkened areas of the wood. However, it is often more effective to simply sand down the wood until a uniform surface colour appears.

If you are very careful, machine sanding of a solid wood surface (using a random orbital sander) will often eradicate minor surface discoloration. If, however, such discoloration is because of the presence of oil, grease, etc., within the wood, try first to neutralize it – taking great care – by applying methylated spirits, white spirit or thinners to the surface. Use only the minimum amount necessary.

If repairs by gluing are required, be sure to use a waterproof, exterior quality adhesive – especially on convertibles!

WOODWORK REVARNISHING

With the surface prepared, revarnishing can take place, preceded where necessary by recolouring the wood using wood stains. These are easily applied by brush, but be sure to follow the instructions supplied with the product.

Ideally, choose an exterior grade, water-repellent varnish containing an ultraviolet (UV) protector. Using white spirit (or other agent, as specified by the product's instructions), thin the first coat approximately 50/50, mixing thoroughly.

Before applying the varnish, wipe the surface of the wood with a tacky cloth, of the type used when spraying exterior paintwork, to rid the surface of all dust. Brush or spray the varnish onto the wood. If brushing, be sure to smooth out the brush strokes as you go.

Allow the first coat to thoroughly dry (for at least 24 hours), then, using very fine sandpaper (preferably well-used, to avoid making deep scratches in the surface of the varnish), or special fine abrasive paper used by furniture makers/restorers, gently rub down the surface. Wipe with a clean tacky cloth before applying a second coat.

Repeat the process, using a smaller amount of white spirit with each successive coat, until the final coat can be applied neat. Usually it will be necessary to apply several coats – the first few soak into the wood, while later coats build up a deep gloss (you hope!).

Allow the final coat of varnish to dry for several days – preferably a week or so – then again gently rub down the surface with ultra-fine abrasive paper, followed by the application of fine grade paintwork cutting compound paste, then liquid paintwork colour restorer and finally wax polish. Always try a small section before attacking the whole of the panel – just to be sure that your efforts will have the desired effect.

▲ *7.1. At first glance this ancient wood door capping looked very sad, yet it was basically sound – an ideal candidate for revarnishing.*

▼ *7.2. The old varnish was easily removed from the surface of the wood by scraping. Be very careful not to damage the surface of the wood if you use this method.*

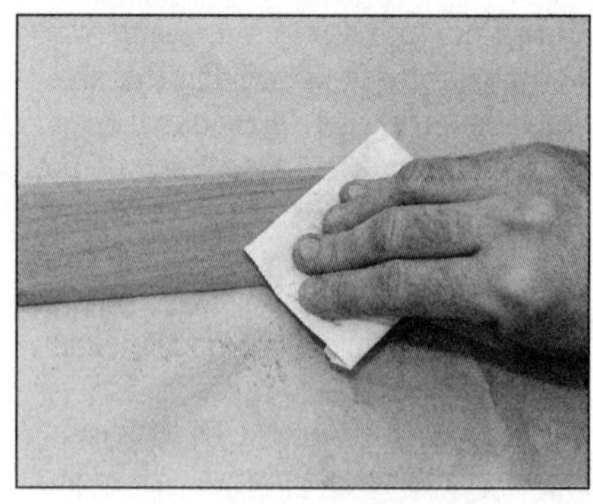

▲ *7.3. Rub down the surface of the wood, using medium grit sandpaper or 'production' paper of approximately 320 grade (to eradicate any minor surface irregularities). Then use progressively finer grades to achieve a smooth surface.*

▼ *7.4. Use very fine grade wire wool as a final preparation, rubbing along/with the grain.*

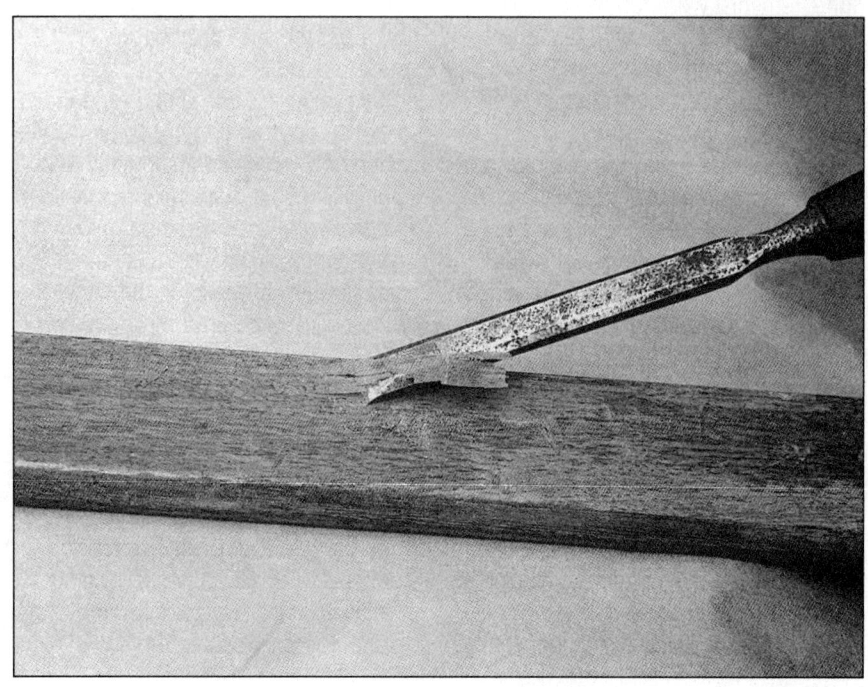

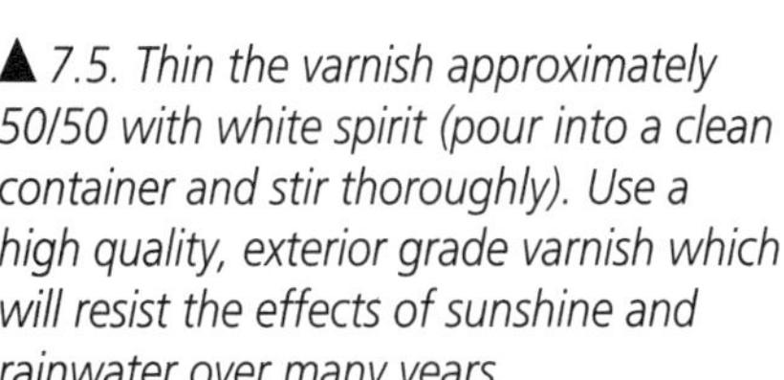

▲ *7.5. Thin the varnish approximately 50/50 with white spirit (pour into a clean container and stir thoroughly). Use a high quality, exterior grade varnish which will resist the effects of sunshine and rainwater over many years.*

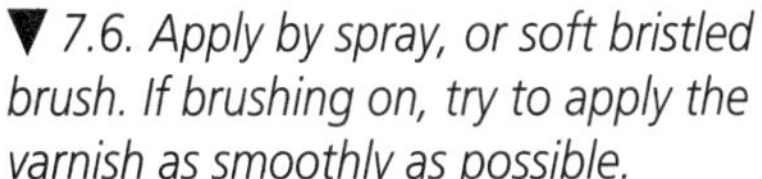

▼ *7.6. Apply by spray, or soft bristled brush. If brushing on, try to apply the varnish as smoothly as possible.*

▲ *7.7. Even with only two coats applied, the varnish brought out a surprisingly rich, natural colour in the wood, and highlighted its grain, thereby transforming its appearance. The section of the capping on the left-hand side of this photograph was deliberately left untouched to show the difference. Further coats should be applied until a deep gloss is obtained.*

STAIN IT?

Sometimes it is necessary to recolour the wood prior to revarnishing, to achieve a uniform finish. This is easily done, using readily available wood dyes/stains.

If recolouring is required, carry out all the preparation stages as already described, but instead of the varnish, first apply wood dye/stain of the required colour. Use a soft brush, and as far as possible keep the stuff clear of clothes, hands and other items you don't want coloured!

▼ *7.8. This capping was sound, but showed varying shades of brown. Recolouring, then revarnishing, would restore it.*

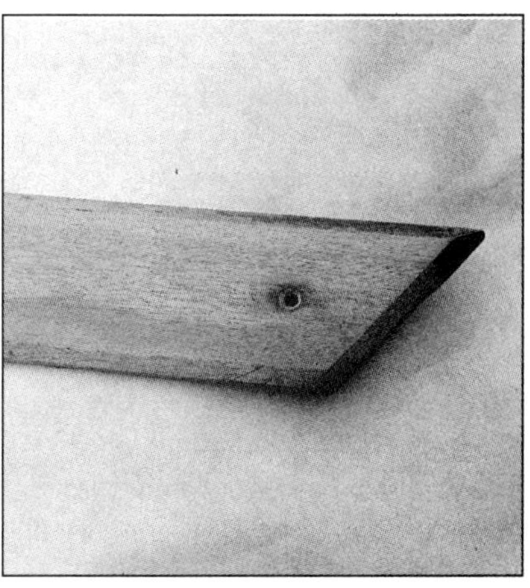

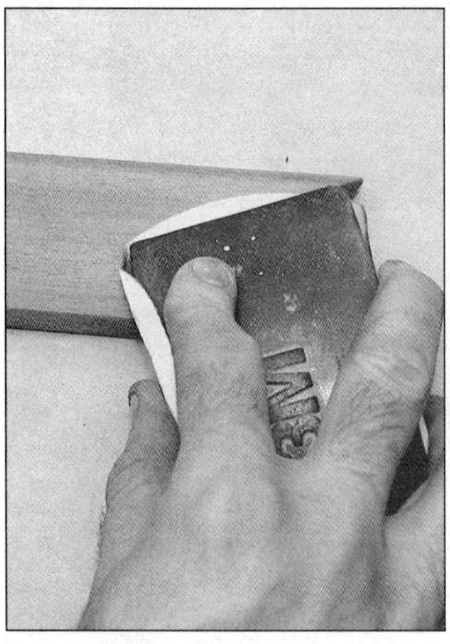

▲ *7.9. Using 360 grit, then progressively finer grades of 'production paper' or sandpaper, smooth the surface of the wood. This process often removes minor surface discoloration.*

▲ *7.10. The wood dye/stain can be applied using a soft cloth, and working the colour evenly into the grain. Wipe off excess stain, and allow to fully dry (according to the instructions with the product).*

▲ *7.11. The stained wood can then be varnished as shown earlier, to give a rich, beautiful finish.*

VENEER REPLACEMENT

There comes a time when just polishing, or even revarnishing a veneered panel is simply not enough to restore its good looks. Where the thin covering of veneer is badly scratched, peeling or severely cracked, the only real solution is to reveneer the panel.

Because of the time-consuming nature of the job, applying veneer to, say a dashboard, is an expensive operation if you go to a professional. This is understandable, for it is a job which normally takes many hours. Of course, time – in terms of professional man-hours – costs money!

However, with a little dedication, patience and attention to detail, superb results can be achieved at home, with the total outlay amounting only to the cost of the materials. Although this area of operations is one which you may not have thought about tackling, the work is, in fact, straightforward – it just takes time!

The following sequence of photographs shows the application of new veneer to the facia of a 1940s Triumph Roadster. This particular car had been sadly neglected for many years. The veneer finish was missing in many places and badly damaged in others. In fact, it was an ideal candidate for reveneering.

Often, the woodwork forming the main facia panel is sound, with just the veneer having suffered. However, in this case, it was also apparent that the wooden facia itself was crumbling (this is more likely on open-topped cars like the Triumph Roadster), and therefore, before the application of veneer could begin, a new facia panel had to be made, using standard woodwork techniques. In fact, a new facia assembly was constructed quite easily, using the original as a pattern.

If the plywood forming the main facia panel has only suffered in a few localized places (usually ply separation is the problem), but is generally sound, it is possible to restore the panel by squeezing strong wood glue between the laminations of the ply, then clamping the wood and allowing to set for 24 hours.

New veneer can then be attached to the facia panel, which on this Triumph was made from plywood. In fact, facia panels are frequently made from plywood (often birch-faced ply) since this provides a sound base on which to mount the veneer, and in most cases the wood used is not seen. Birch-faced plywood is obtainable from builders' merchants.

The photograph sequence begins by showing – as an example – how a glove box lid was tackled. Since the the edges are to view, either closed or open, the lid was originally made from a solid wood base rather than plywood.

▲ *7.12. This facia panel from a 1946 Triumph Roadster was in a very poor state, and the woodwork forming the main panel had to be replaced. However, the glove box lid was sound, and this was tackled as a separate item.*

▲ *7.14. A chisel with a bevelled edge can be used to very gently lever off the remains of the original veneer. The flat face of the chisel should be held against the wood as the veneer is carefully prised away. As you do this, take care not to damage the wood around the perimeter, or beneath the veneer.*

▼ *7.15. A chisel/scraper can also be used to scrape off old varnish from the wood. Sometimes this comes off very easily, sometimes it can take hours! Again, great care is needed to ensure that the wood is not scored or otherwise damaged.*

▲ *7.13. With the glove box lid removed from the main facia panel, the hinges and other fittings, screws, etc., should be carefully removed and stored in clearly labelled containers.*

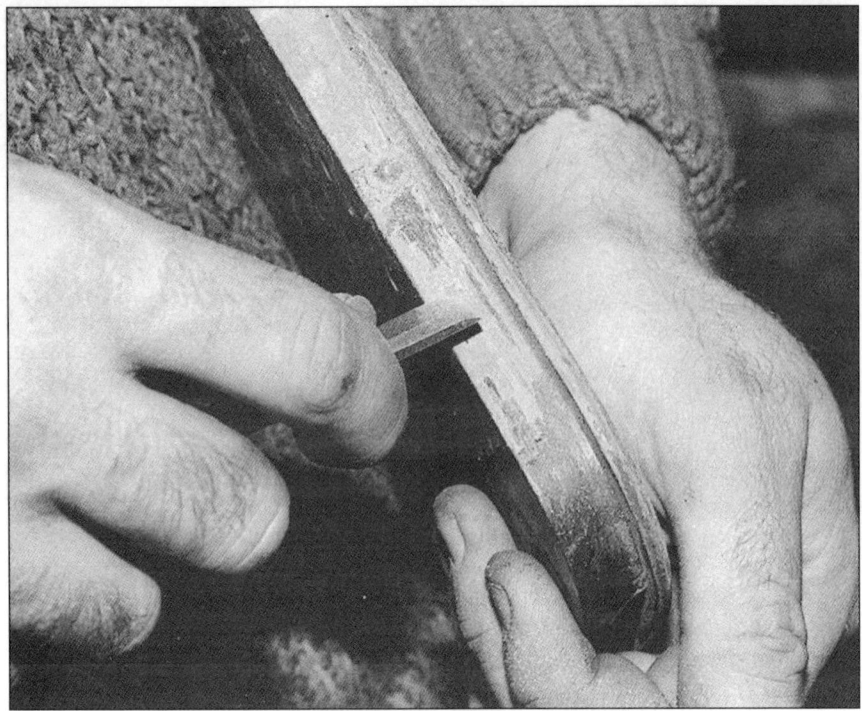

▲ *7.16. Use the side of the scraper/chisel to remove varnish from the edge of the panel. Take great care to keep your fingers well clear of the blade, and, again, take care not to damage the wood.*

▲ *7.17. Eventually, the wood will come completely clean, as shown here. It is quite in order to use an orbital sander on the flat surfaces. This will also considerably speed up the process of removing old varnish, etc. Damaged areas, such as depressions or holes, should be made good by gluing in new sections of wood. Circular holes can be filled using a short length of dowel of appropriate diameter. Glue in place, allow to set and then level the surface.*

▼ *7.18. The next stage is to create grooves in the surface of the wood for the glue (which will retain the new veneer) to sit in. An old, fine-toothed hacksaw blade is an effective tool for this job, and experience suggests that best results may be obtained by making grooves across the grain, rather than running with it. In any event, take the very greatest care not to damage the adjacent (and visible when complete) edges of the wood.*

WHICH VENEER?

The next aspect of the job is critical – choosing and marking out the veneer to be used. There are literally hundreds of different types of veneer, so choose carefully to match the original, and specify exactly what you require when ordering from specialist suppliers – veneers aren't cheap, and mistakes tend to be expensive!

It is perhaps obvious, but it can be very difficult to precisely match the grain of an original veneer, so for a perfect job it is usually easier and more effective to reveneer a complete dashboard (for example) than to attempt to replace just a section of it. However, if you are not concerned about the grain, you may more easily be able to match the colour of the original veneer, so that at least any replacement sections made will be less noticeably different.

For this Triumph, a European straight cut walnut type was required, as opposed to a burr walnut (i.e. with a multitude of wriggly bits visible). Normally, veneers are available in sections either six or seven inches wide, but in this case a 10-in width was required. Such widths can prove difficult to locate. However, persistence in the search pays off.

In all cases veneer is very delicate and it should be treated with the utmost respect, or it can easily become damaged prior to fitting.

Where the need is to create a similar-looking pattern on either side of, say, a centre line in the middle of a dashboard or door capping, adjacent layers of veneer from the same tree can provide the answer, in the form of book matched veneer. If two layers are peeled apart, it will be seen that the patterns on the adjacent faces of the veneer are virtually identical.

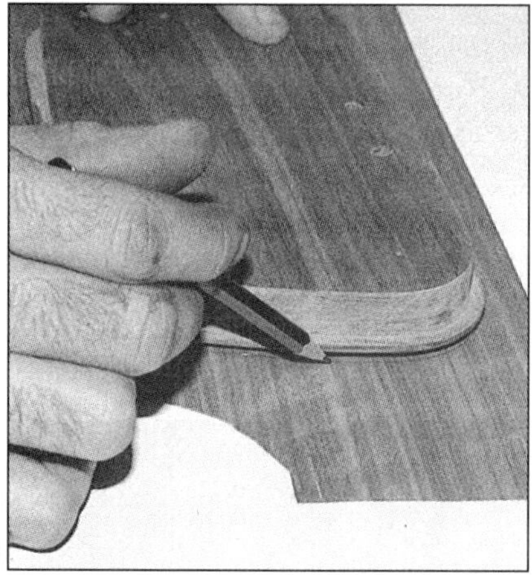

▲ *7.19. There are various ways of marking up the veneer. One way is to make cardboard templates and mark around these. Another is to mark the veneer on the reverse side, using the original panel as a template.*

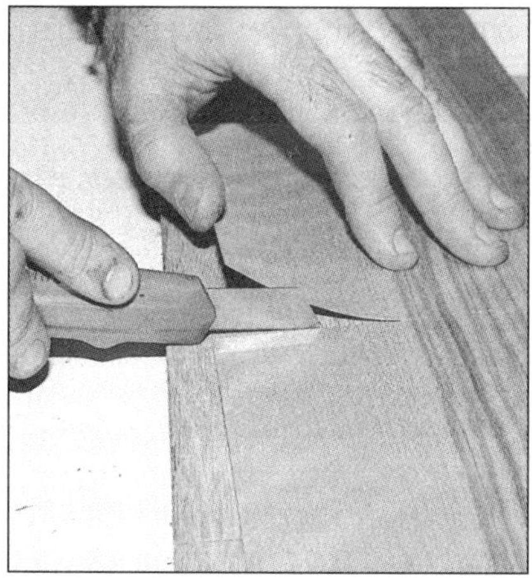

▲ *7.20. The veneer can be cut to the required shape using a very sharp knife (scissors can be used, if you are extremely careful). The veneer is less brittle, and therefore easier to cut, if wet.*

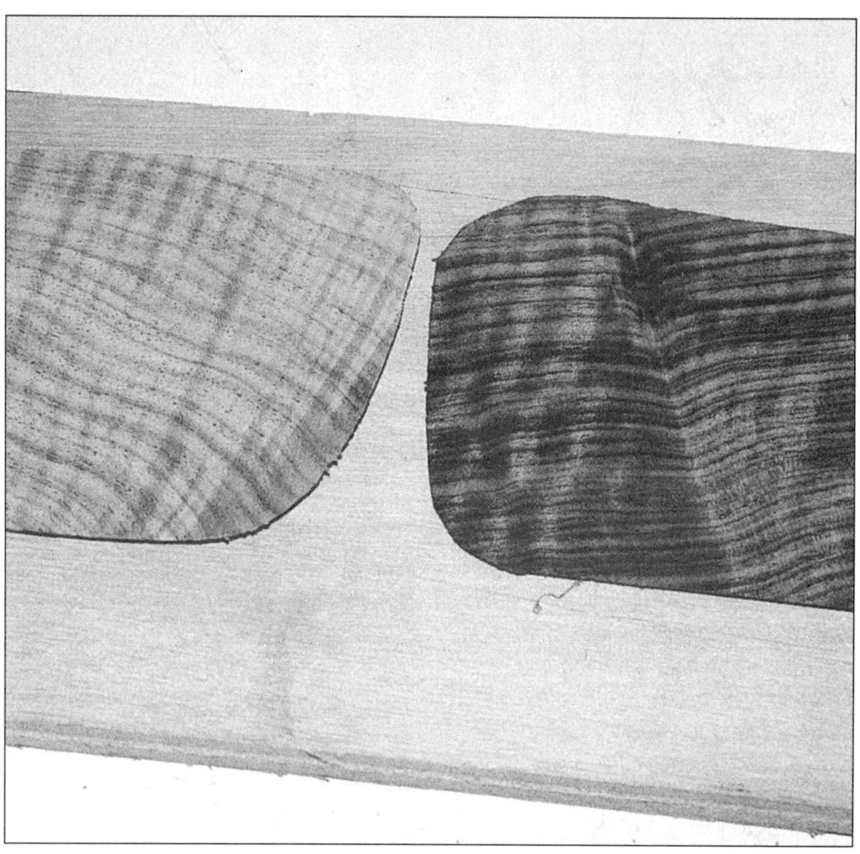

▲ *7.21. Another advantage of cutting the veneer when wet is that the grain shows up much more strongly.*

To attach the veneer to the panel, a strong adhesive is required and, for a long-lasting job, it is necessary to clamp the two components together until the glue has fully set. If the facia is flat, a flat piece of plywood can be used as a pressure pad to hold the components together. But if the facia is curved it will be necessary to make special moulds (three were used on the Triumph Roadster) to make the clamping more effective in its action.

▶ *7.22. It is vital that the new veneer is clamped firmly in place against the facia panel until the glue has fully set. On a curved dashboard, like this Triumph item, the job needs to be done in three separate stages. Here, the third and final centre section of veneer – in this instance, flat in profile – is being applied. The more clamps – and hence the more even the pressure – the better. This is a vitally important part of the operation.*

In order to accommodate the tight curves of this facia panel, curved moulds were made in addition to the flat central one. The curved sections were formed using glass-fibre paste, bonded to the flat plywood sheet forming the main part of each mould, and with plywood strengtheners built in around the corner sections. To prevent the glass-fibre bonding to the facia panel itself, sticky-backed plastic or similar material can first be stuck to the facia – the glass-fibre paste is therefore spread onto the plastic, rather than the wood of the dash panel. On completion of the mould-making, the mould and the plastic can be 'peeled' away from the dash together.

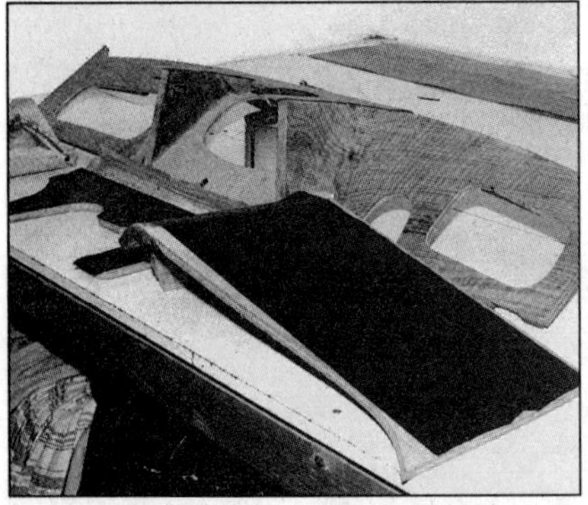

▲ 7.23. Each mould was built up gradually, and the glass-fibre was allowed to harden while the mould was clamped to the dash panel, thereby bonding the mould into an immensely strong unit of the correct profile. When the glass-fibre had fully set, the mould was unclamped and peeled off as an assembly. Only final trimming and finishing was then required to remove minor ridges and imperfections in the mould. Next, in each case, a layer of wide, sticky-backed plastic was stuck onto the back of the mould, to provide a barrier between the mould and the veneer, and to prevent seepage through the veneer of the adhesive. Otherwise the veneer could very easily have become permanently bonded to the mould!

▲ 7.24. Cascamite resin wood glue is ideal for sticking the veneer to the various panels. Available in powder form, it is mixed with water in a separate container to form a paste. Once it hardens (and it's best to leave it overnight in a relatively warm room), it forms an extremely strong bond. Always implicitly follow the instructions supplied with the adhesive.

▲ 7.25 The adhesive is spread evenly onto the wood of the panel being tackled, then ...

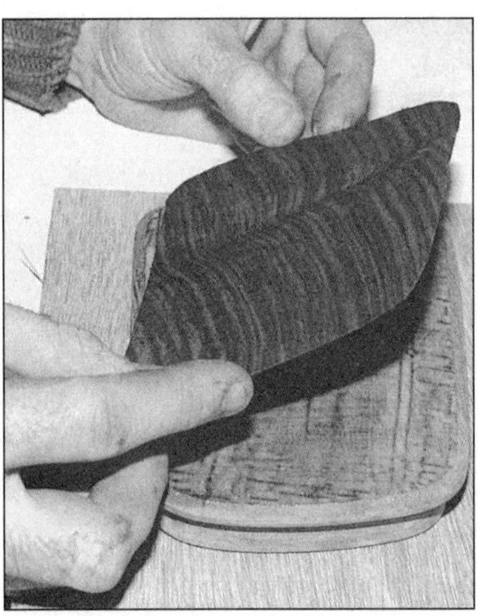

▲ 7.26. ... the pre-cut veneer is applied. For reasons explained in caption 7.27, the veneer is normally cut slightly over-size for later trimming back to precise dimensions. Since the Cascamite adhesive is water-based, it doesn't matter if the veneer is damp when applied. Also the glue is very forgiving until it hardens, allowing the veneer to be slid easily into precisely the correct position.

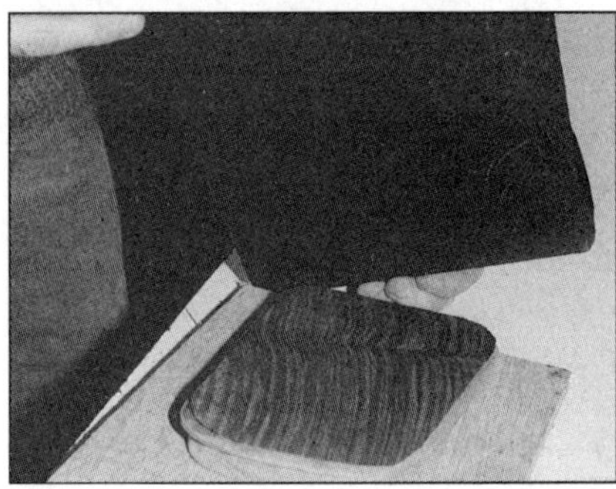

▲ 7.27. Next, the mould is very carefully applied. Effectively, in this instance, the glove box lid is made the filling in a plywood sandwich! It is absolutely essential that the veneer doesn't move from its correct position as the mould is fitted. If the veneer has been pre-cut to precise dimensions, you have no leeway at all in this. On the other hand, if the veneer is slightly over-size, the position of the edge of the veneer can be observed while the mould is being fitted, and it is not quite such a disaster if the veneer moves a fraction during this operation. Although not essential, proper veneer tape can be used to hold the veneer in position – this can easily be removed afterwards without damaging the grain. Other adhesive tapes can be more vicious in their grip, and may be reluctant to let go!

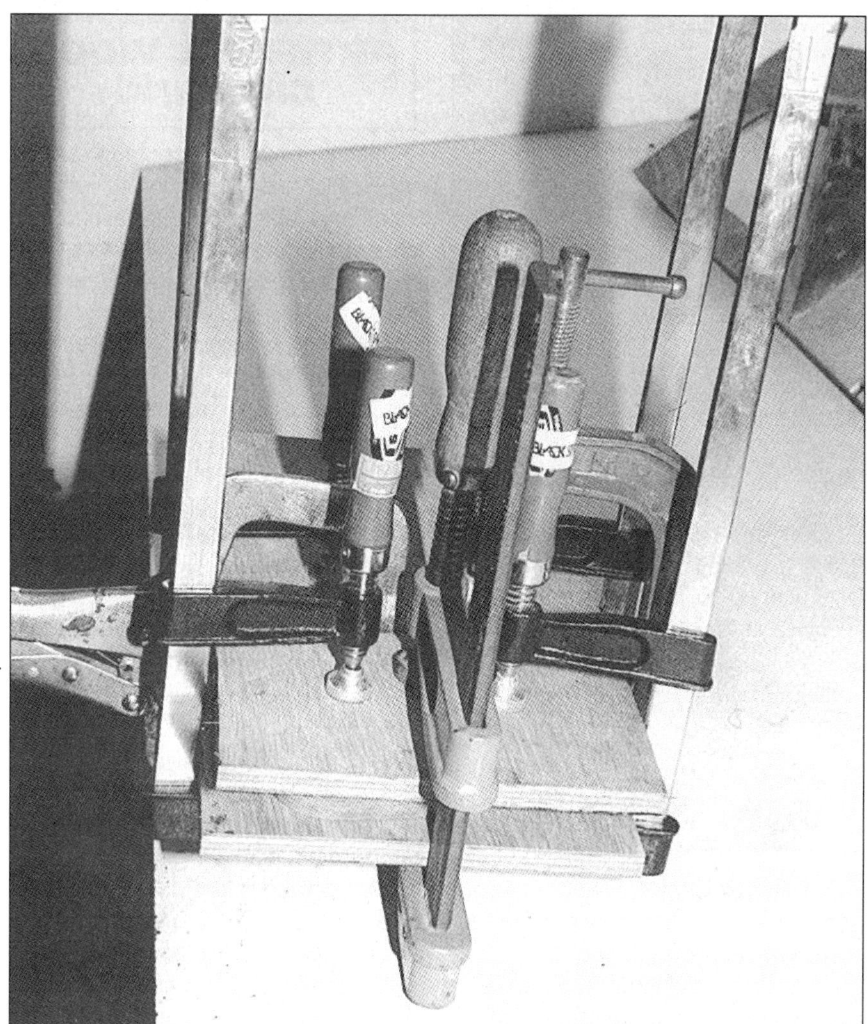

▲ *7.30. Extreme patience is required when tackling curved sections. Always try to ensure that there is support for the section of veneer being trimmed to size. Sometimes the curved part of the panel has to be rolled as work proceeds, to keep the veneer in contact with the shield board.*

▲ *7.28. The sandwich is now very carefully clamped together, once again ensuring that the veneer doesn't move from its correct position as the clamps are applied. A set of inexpensive clamps were used for this application – the more there are, the more even will be the pressure. Tighten them a little at a time in diagonal sequence.*

▶ *7.29. Where possible, leave the glue to harden for 24 hours before attempting to trim back the edges of the veneer. Put a discarded piece of plywood on the bench as a shield, and use a very sharp knife to score and then cut off the excess veneer. A sharp chisel could also be used for this job. If you do make a mistake, it is sometimes possible to glue unobtrusively in place small pieces which have accidentally been cut off, or to file smooth rough edges, etc.*

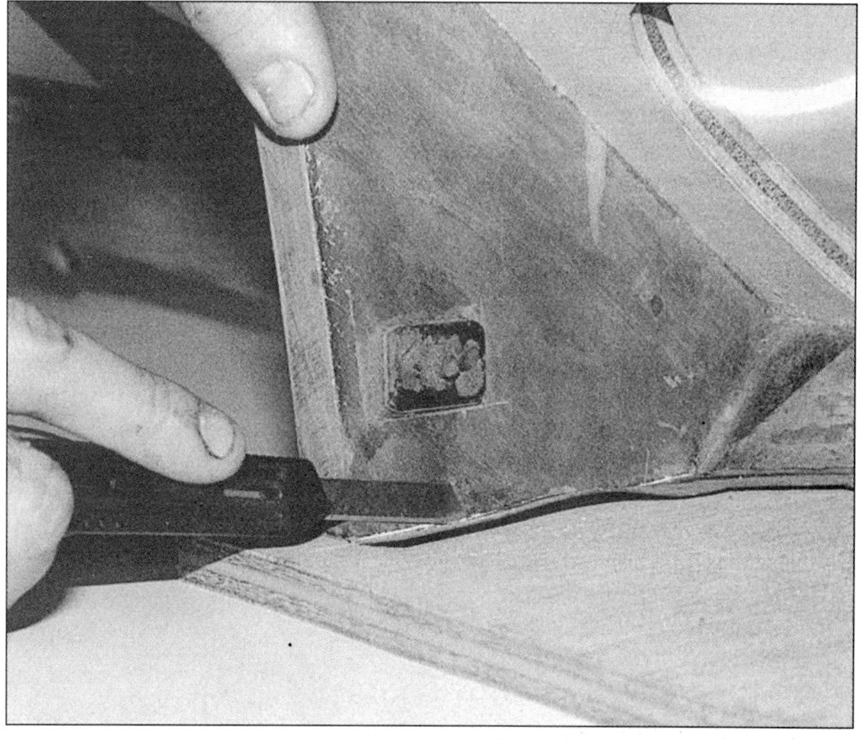

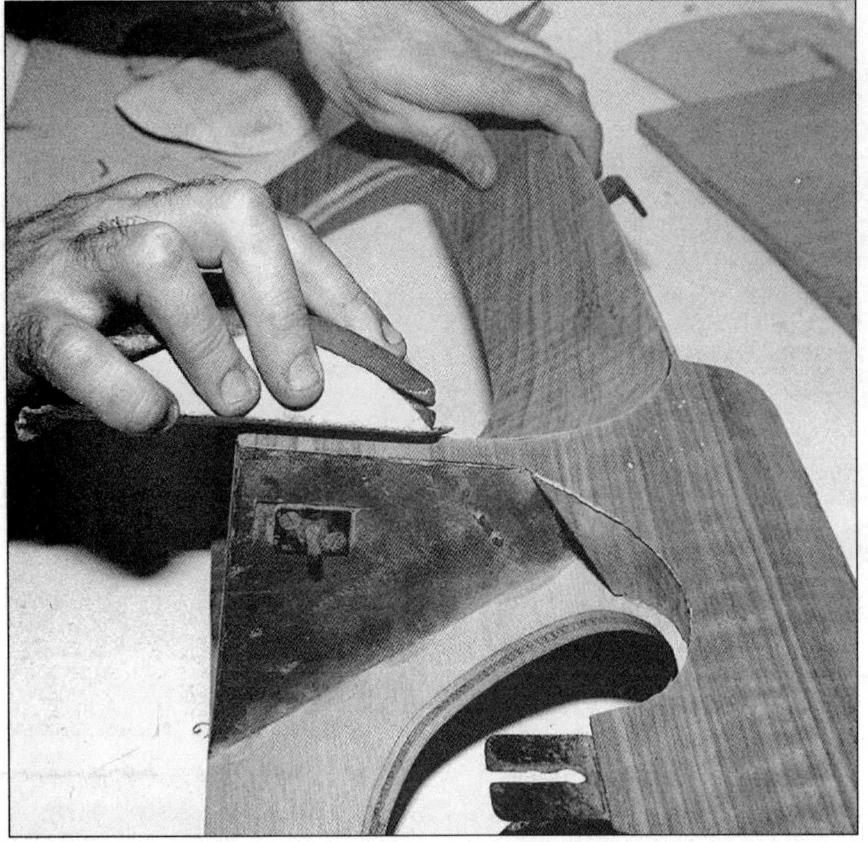

▲ *7.31. The edges of the veneer can be blended against the surrounding woodwork by the careful use of abrasive paper and a proper sanding block. Always use a block! Normally, fine grade sandpaper will be all you need. However, for the rectification of mistakes, and for smoothing very sharp edges, medium grit paper may have to be used first. In any event, take your time and don't rush this job.*

▶ *7.32. On completion, the finished dash requires coating with varnish to impart a beautiful shine. This Triumph Roadster panel was finished using several sprayed on coats of two-pack varnish (**an air-fed mask is essential when working with such materials**). A variety of less toxic varnishes are available – the choice being governed by personal preference. Suitable products can be purchased in DIY stores, and can be applied by brush, allowing each coat to dry fully before applying the next. Care is required to eliminate all brush marks, but excellent results can be achieved, and at low cost.*

As stated earlier, there are several approaches to applying veneer, of which that shown above is just one. For example, successful results can also be obtained using iron-on veneer, which can be purchased at DIY and hardware shops.

ARTIFICIAL WOOD GRAINING

As mentioned at the start of this chapter, many older cars were endowed with wood grain effects on their steel facias, door cappings and window frames. The graining was originally imparted by means of transfers, or by screen printing processes. Such finishes eventually deteriorate, and can be very difficult, if not impossible, to reproduce precisely as original.

Until a few years ago, a plastic grain pattern film called Di-Noc was available, but alas this is no longer the case. Restorers these days are faced with forgetting the wood finish, and simply painting the dash and window frames an appropriate plain brown, or attempting to create their own wood grain effect, or using a wood graining kit.

To do it yourself you need first to clean and respray the affected panels, normally in brown to match the original shade. Before removing the original finish forever, photograph or video it to provide a record of the grain you are aiming for.

If the graining effect on your car has all but disappeared, try to find another example of your vehicle in good, original condition, and use this as a guide to the type of graining you need.

The grain effect can then be added, perhaps using an acrylic or enamel paint, applied by means of various special tools. Some favour firm bristle paint brushes, with the bristles trimmed to form sharp spikes, while others prefer sponges (especially useful for creating knots), combs and so on.

When the paint forming the grain pattern has fully dried, it can be preserved by coating with clear varnish. It is possible to create some extremely realistic (if not entirely original) graining at home, providing you have the necessary patience. In all cases, practice on scrap metal panels before trying your efforts on the real thing.

TRY A KIT

Appreciating the problems of obtaining a true-to-life wood grain effect, Jay Products of Cleveland, Ohio, USA, have developed a kit specifically to help others having such difficulties.

In developing the kit, the firm experimented with many different types of paints and tools to arrive at what they feel is an effective and easy to use system.

Available in walnut (brown tint) or mahogany (red tint), the kit contains all the tools necessary for the job – a graining tool plus two brushes, and sufficient paint (base and finish coats) to cover, on average, the dashboard and window frames on two cars.

STUDY AND EXPERIMENT

Included with the kit is the useful booklet *Wood Graining Made Easy*. I would advise reading this fully, as well as the detailed instructions on the tins of special paint supplied, before you start.

In fact, there are minor variations between the advice given in the booklet and that on the tins. However, with wood graining, there is no definitive right or wrong way. Practice, experimentation and gaining experience to perfect your own technique is the way to achieve the results you will be happy with.

It is also worth noting that in addition to the brushes and graining tool supplied with the kit, other items can be used to impart different grain effects. These include paper towels, combs, rag, cheese cloth, different varieties and sizes of paint brush – and so on.

Jay Products recommend that the dashboard and window frames are all treated, since it is virtually impossible to precisely match the original finish and colour. They also say that a top coat is not necessary, but that a varnish (not lacquer) may be added, once the graining has been applied.

Jay have endeavoured to make their kit user friendly, and say that 'you cannot make a mistake, as any part of the operation can easily be re-done.' However, they also wisely advise experimenting first on a spare panel or sheet of steel, before doing the job for real.

It is always best if the panels to be tackled are removed from the vehicle and placed on a horizontal surface in good light. A portable work bench, covered with masking paper, is an ideal base on which to work. You can then get at the workpiece from all angles, and see into all the corners.

The kit was put to the test using the facia panel from an early 1950s Austin taxi, which had long since lost its original grain pattern. Three of us eagerly unpacked the Jay Products kit and studied the instructions, and were keen to see what could be done with the Austin's panel. However, to be honest, at the outset, none of us was convinced that we had the necessary skill to make the kit work effectively. Anyway, this is how we got on.

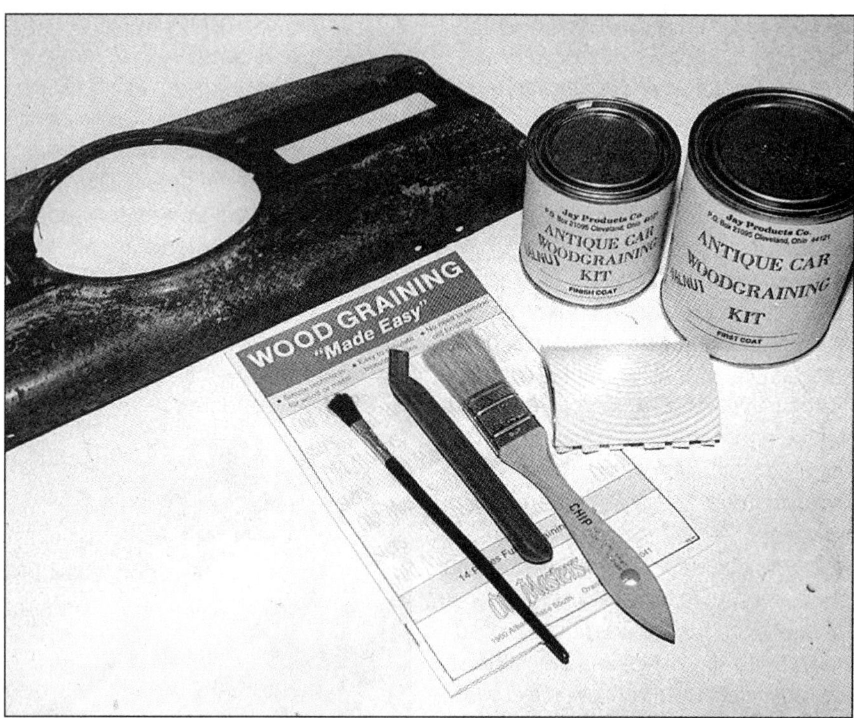

▲ *7.33. The Antique Car Woodgraining Kit from Jay Products contains all the necessary tools and paint, in addition to the fascinating booklet Wood Graining Made Easy. Pictured next to it is the dash panel from a pre-war Packard, which still bore traces of its original grain. In the absence of any visible original Austin grain, the taxi's owner decided to use the wood effect on the Packard dash as a model for the Austin panel.*

Unless the original coatings are particularly thick, in most cases it is not necessary to remove the original finish (where sound). However, the surface should be sanded smooth, with any chipped sections of paintwork feather-edged using fine grade silicon carbide (wet-or-dry) paper, used dry. All dust must be removed from the surface before painting it.

▲ 7.37. *To achieve the desired finish, we used the small round brush in a swirling action to recreate a similar effect to that on our model Packard panel. After some experimentation we discovered how to create several natural looking patterns. We found the best effect was created by applying plenty of paint to the panel, then using a near dry brush to form the swirls, interspersing these with some longer line patterns.*

▲ 7.34. *This is how the Austin dash panel looked at the start. Devoid of its original finish, it could only be improved! Using a little thinners on a clean rag, we carefully cleaned the panel to remove all traces of grease and dirt. Next, we wiped the surface all over, using a 'tacky cloth'.*

▼ 7.35. *Using the soft brush provided, we applied the first self-smoothing base coat, spreading the paint evenly onto the surface. One coat may be sufficient, but if a second is required, this can be applied approximately two hours after the first. Be sure to cover all surfaces, including the edges of the panels; and on window frames, include all the lips which may be visible. On completion, the brush can be cleaned in thinners. After 24 hours, the surface was lightly rubbed down using steel wool, and then all dust was again removed from the panel with a tacky cloth.*

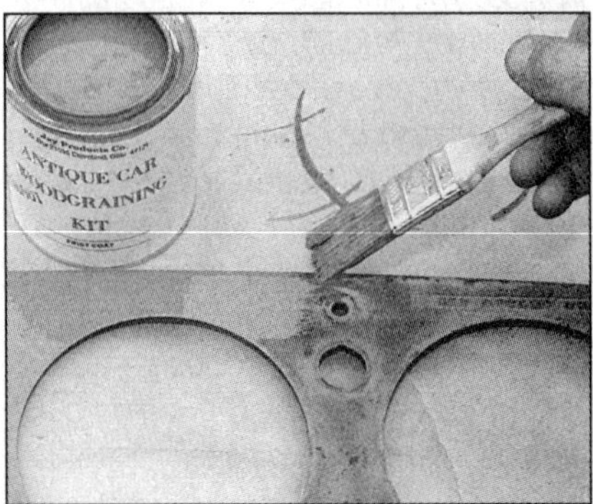

▼ 7.36. *The stain paint was applied using the small round brush from the kit. The instructions on the tin advise dipping just the edge of the bristles in the paint – a little of it goes a long way. Make sure that the whole of the surface area is adequately covered. Don't worry too much what the panel looks like at this stage!*

This was becoming more like fun and the three of us were starting to believe we could achieve good results! Jay Products' instructions advise using the brush in light strokes in V-shapes, curves, or straight lines, applying the brush lengthways across the surface. They also mention that on dash panels, the design can be created from the centre, working outwards, although this isn't essential.

They further advise against creating sharp lines, but rather to use a 'soft inter-mixing of curls and uneven lines'. If the finish appears to be too dark, the end of the brush can be wiped to create a lighter effect.

Fortunately – and deliberately – the paint used to create the grain effect is slow-drying, so that it remains workable for a long time, and any mistakes can be rectified (by smoothing out and starting again) without difficulty. Even if you are unhappy with the result when the paint has dried, it is a relatively simple matter to re-apply the base coat and start from scratch once more.

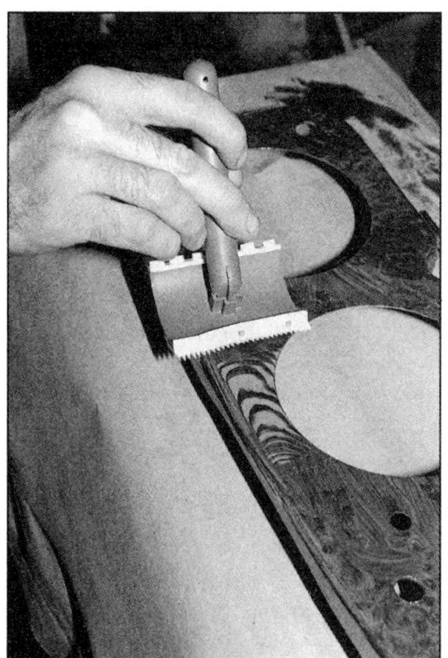

▲ *7.38. For dealing with larger areas, and for creating wider patterns, the ingenious graining tool supplied in the kit can be employed. This one tool can be used to form an amazing variety of types of grain, and is fun to experiment with. The booklet in the kit gives full details on creating different effects.*

▲ *7.39. This was how the Austin panel looked just an hour after starting. We now had a realistic looking wood grain effect which had truly transformed the dash panel. In addition, the kit had enabled us to easily recreate an effect very similar to that used on our model Packard dash. We were most impressed, and the three of us were anxious to continue experimentation with other panels!*

▼ *7.40. Ensure that your pattern is continued around all the edges of the panels you are graining. Don't worry if the swirls look a little odd when first applied. The paint settles down on the surface after a few minutes.*

When you are satisfied with the results of your efforts, clean the brushes (with care – our small brush disintegrated when rinsed in thinners!), then allow the workpiece to rest undisturbed for 24 hours or so. The surface can then be sealed with exterior grade varnish (containing UV protectors) – polyurethane types are suitable, sprayed or brushed on. As an alternative to varnishing, the panel could be wax polished.

DASH REPAIR KIT

Plastic-covered facias are prone to cracking as they age, and this can obviously spoil the appearance of an otherwise tidy interior. Options include re-covering the existing facia (but it can be difficult to achieve original looking results), obtaining a replacement facia top in better condition, or attempting to repair the crack(s).

The Eastwood Company sell a dashboard repair kit, and other kits are available for dealing with repairs to vinyl – these can also be applied to dash tops, etc. In this section we show the Eastwood kit as applied to the dashboard on a Ford Cortina of the early 1960s. A tidy car, it was suffering from a cracked dash just above the instrument panel.

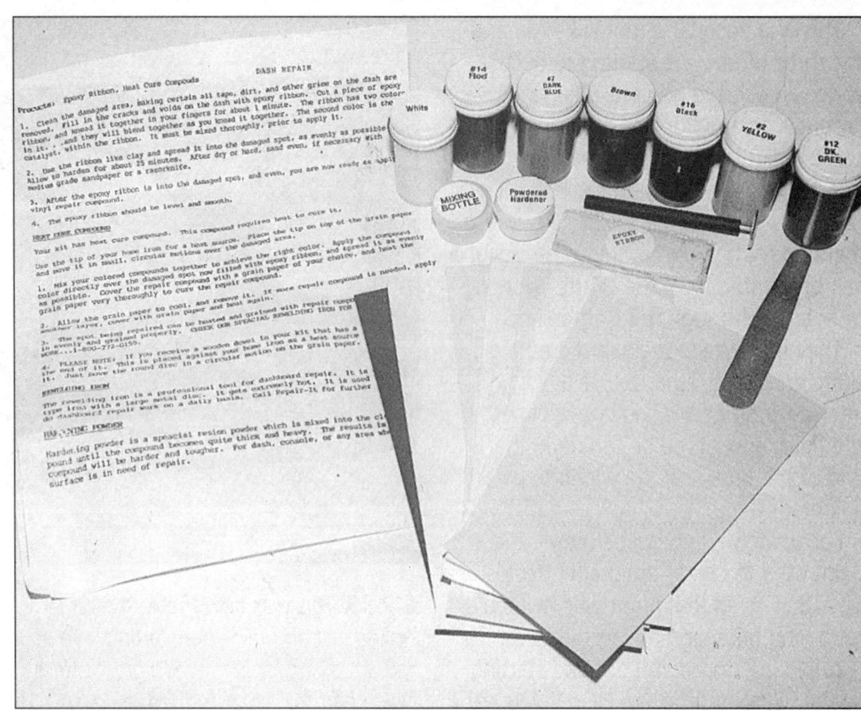

▲ *7.42. The Eastwood kit comes complete with instructions, epoxy ribbon, powdered hardener, a heat curing tool, various graining papers and a range of coloured vinyl repair compounds.*

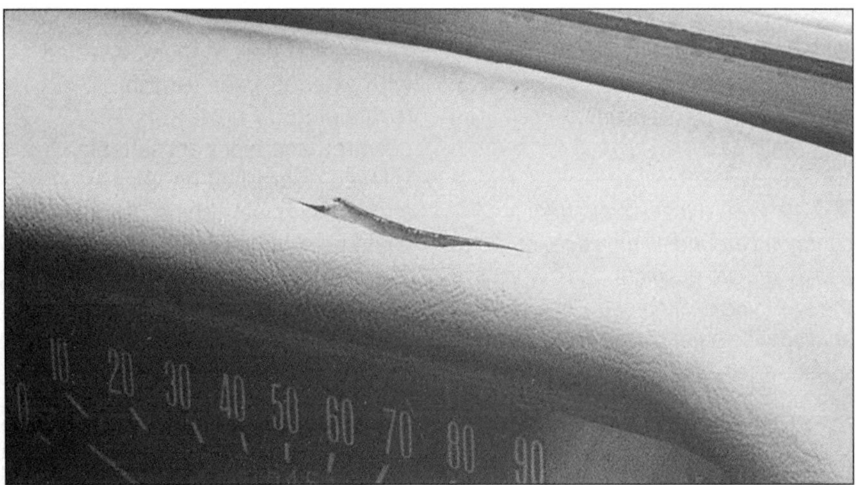

▲ *7.41. This is the unsightly crack afflicting the Cortina. The rest of the dash top was in perfect condition, so a repair, rather than replacement, seemed appropriate.*

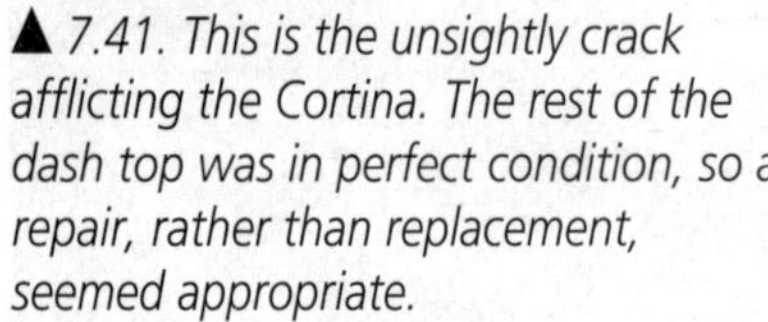

▼ *7.43. The first step is to thoroughly clean the area surrounding the damage. A little washing-up liquid solution, applied with a soft cloth, and then wiped off with a clean, damp cloth, is very effective.*

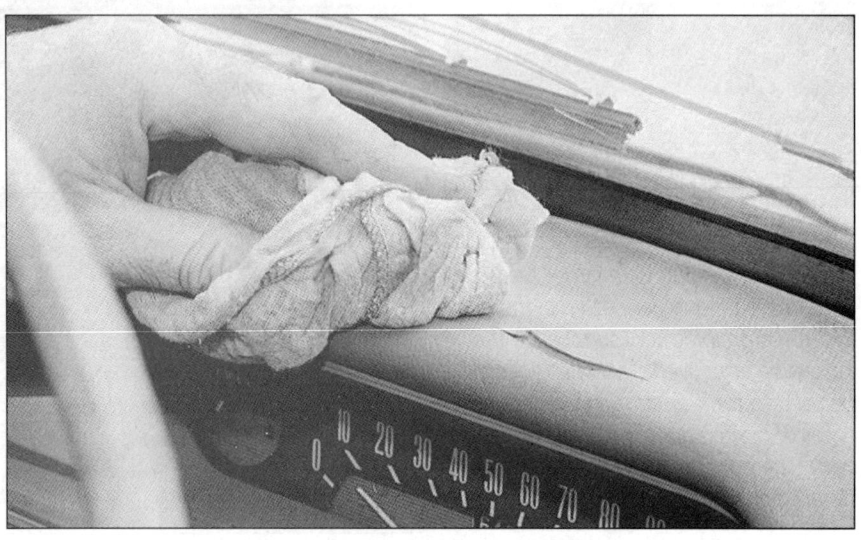

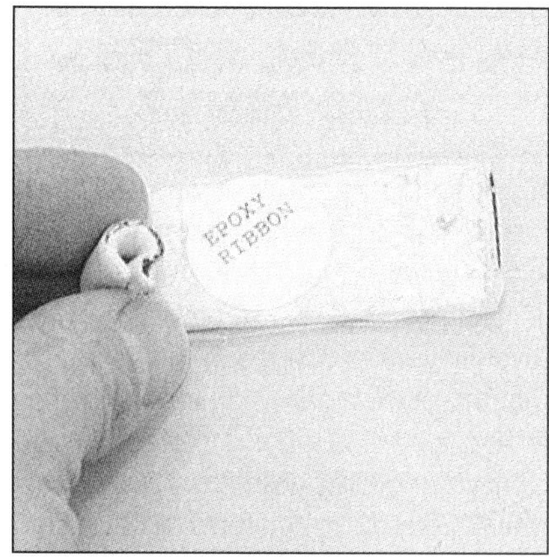

▲ 7.44. A short length of the twin-coloured epoxy ribbon is then cut from the strip provided, and moulded together until the colour turns a uniform grey, indicating that the two components in the ribbon are fully mixed.

▼ 7.45. The epoxy mixture is now spread firmly into the aperture(s) in the facia, until the surface is just proud of the surrounding material. If there are any protruding flaps of broken plastic, it is best to break them off before applying the compound. Leave the mixture top harden for approximately 25 minutes.

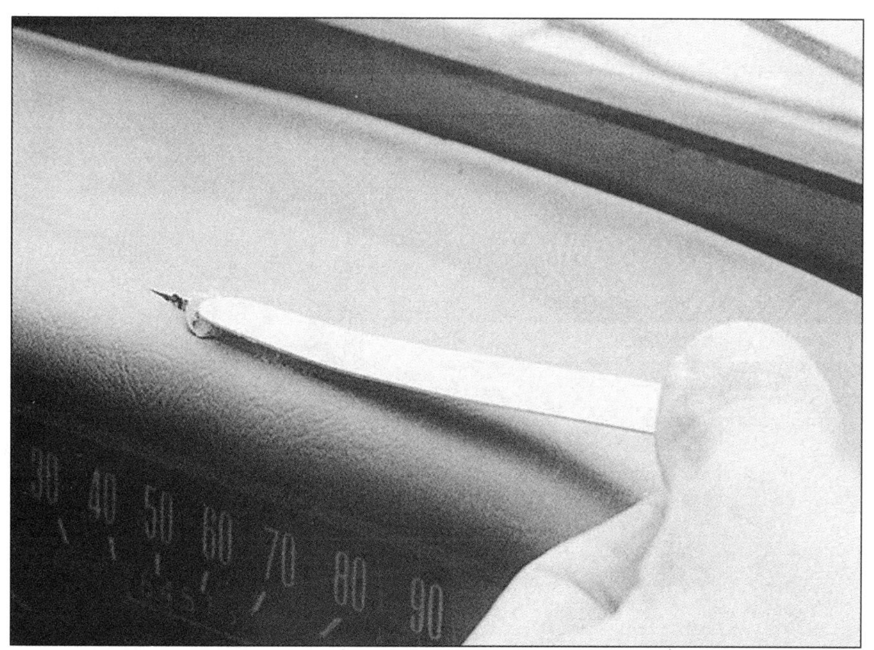

▲ 7.46. While the mixture is hardening, select and mix together (in the mixing bowl provided) the appropriate coloured repair compounds, to obtain a solution which precisely matches the shade of the original dash. An old screwdriver can be used as a mixing implement. Take care not to mix the colours in their own tubs – use an old, clean teaspoon, or similar, for extracting the necessary few drops of coloured agent, and immediately replace the lid. The colour mixing is very much a trial and error business, and can take some time. Persevere to obtain the correct colour. A little hardening powder should also be added, to make the finished repair tougher.

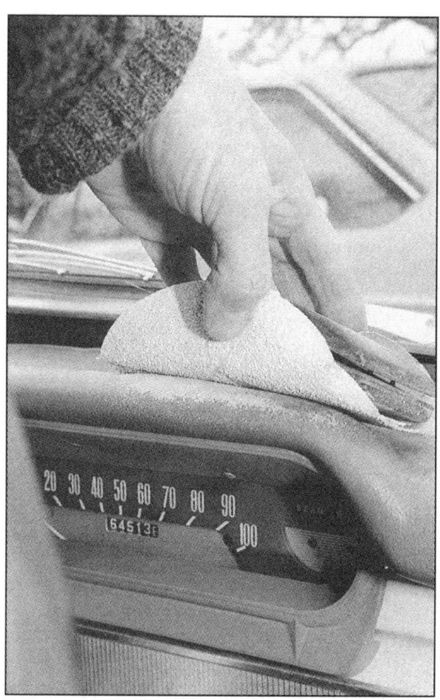

▲ 7.47. Using medium grit abrasive paper, wrapped around a rubbing block, level the surface of the epoxy filler previously applied to the dash – it should have hardened by now. Wipe off surplus dust with a tacky cloth (as used in vehicle refinishing).

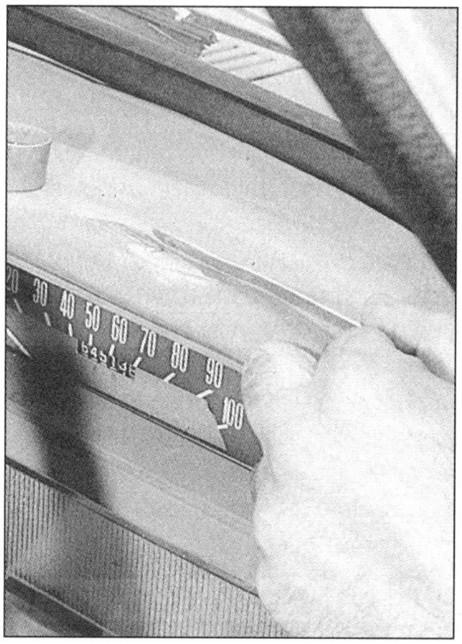

▲ 7.48. The coloured repair compound, mixed earlier, is now very carefully spread on top of the epoxy filler material, overlapping the repair by half-an-inch (13mm.) or so, all round, to enable the repair to blend easily with the surrounding dash.

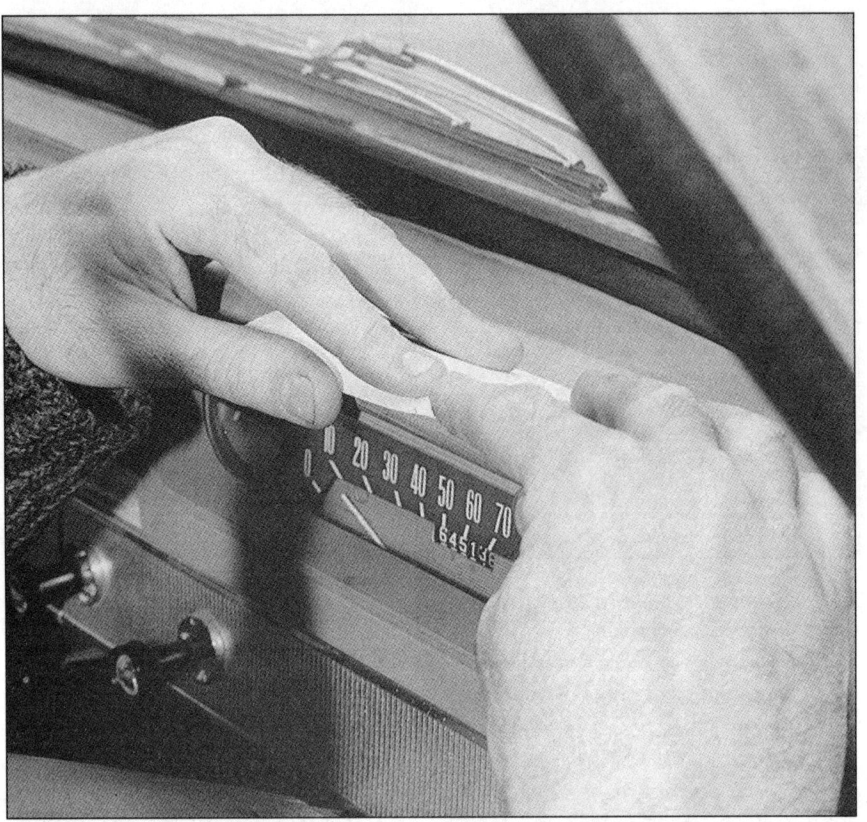

GENERAL NOTES AND HINTS

In addition to the types shown, some cars have vinyl or even leather-covered dash tops and centre consoles. The general procedures for renewing the coverings are as covered in the next chapter, on trim panels. In each case the original panel is used as a pattern for fabricating the replacement. Take care when choosing the material to be used, especially where the panels have surfaces curved in several directions; in which case stretch types are preferable.

Many sports cars have wrinkle finish dashboards. These can sometimes be rejuvenated simply by respraying with normal paint, although wrinkle finishes can now be recreated with special paints which reproduce the original surface texture. They are available in a range of colours, too.

▲ *7.49. Select a graining paper from those supplied, to match as closely as possible the original grain, then firmly but carefully place this face down on top of the coloured repair compound already applied.*

▶ *7.50. It is usually necessary to tape the graining paper in place, using masking tape. The graining paper must be heated very thoroughly to cure the repair compound beneath it. In theory this can be achieved by warming the end of the heat curing tool supplied with the kit by placing it against a domestic iron, or similar, but take care – it get's very hot. Rub the heat curing tool over the graining paper in a circular movement, so that the heat percolates through to the compound below. In practice this is a difficult operation and the repair compound can be very reluctant to solidify. Leave the graining paper in place until things have cooled down, then carefully release the masking tape and graining paper. Repeat the operation, as necessary, until a perfectly grained repair results.*

Chapter 8
Trim panels

The overall effect of a vehicle's interior can be made or marred by the appearance of items which, on their own, are relatively insignificant. Trim panels – such as those fitted to the doors and rear quarters of virtually all cars – are a case in point.

Often the seats and carpets are restored to a high standard, only to be let down by panels which are ill-fitting, poorly made or both! This is strange, since in many cases these panels are far easier to reproduce than other parts of a car's upholstery.

As with most aspects of vehicle interior renovation, to achieve good, original-looking results, it is wise to look closely at the panels as fitted to the car at the factory. These may be in poor shape, but will yield useful clues about their construction, and the materials used. Wherever possible, it is best to follow the makers' methods of manufacture, to produce a similar looking panel.

Materials used vary according to the age and quality of the vehicle concerned. Backing boards for trim panels can be made of millboard, hardboard or plywood. Millboard and standard quality hardboard warp badly when wet, so for long-term survival of your new panels, it may be worth investing in water-resistant oil tempered hardboard. Similarly, if your budget will allow, and your original trim panels were backed by plywood, it is preferable to use the highest quality wood when making replacements.

Water-resistant marine ply, which will also be able to cope better with temperature variations, is the best you can get, but typically will cost more than twice as much as standard grade material. If you cannot run to marine ply, at least aim for quality, multi-layer ply with some water resistance.

When cutting backing boards to shape, a jig-saw with a fine blade can be used, alternatively a hand saw. Again, a fine blade is preferable. In every case, ensure that the panel being cut is well supported, and ensure that basic safety precautions are observed – including keeping electrical cables, fingers and clothing out of the path of the saw blade.

Many quality cars had trim panels covered in leather. In such cases, nothing less than leather will ever really look right, although, of course, this is more expensive than vinyl.

Where vinyl-covered panels were fitted originally, replacements should be made using similar looking materials. However, in addition to the original non-stretch types of material used on many cars of the 1950s and 60s, modern stretchable vinyls are available. These can be easier to work with, and put less strain on stitched joints, etc., since they possess an inherent ability to flex.

Occasionally it may be possible to re-use the original covering materials – for example, in cases where the backing board has become distorted or has disintegrated, yet the covering material is still in good condition. In such cases the material may shrink when removed from its original backing panel, and gentle stretching, aided by heat from a hair dryer or fan heater, may be needed when fitting the material to the new board.

It may sometimes be necessary to dismantle a panel to see how its components are fitted together. This is especially true of items which incorporate complex features such as map pockets, and so on. If you do this, be sure to leave at least one panel intact for reference.

STRAIGHTFORWARD PANELS

Many cars have straightforward, uncomplicated trim panels which are comparatively easy to reproduce. The first step in each case is, of course, to release the panel from the car, then to remove all the staples from around the perimeter of the panel, and all the original trim clips. Save the clips for future use, if you cannot obtain new replacements.

Now gently peel the covering material away from the wadding/foam padding material, and the backing board. The covering materials and the padding may come away together. Retain all the materials at this stage, for possible use as templates.

Often, the original backing board can be used as a pattern. However, before using this as a template, ensure that it actually fits the vehicle! Differences can arise through shrinkage and warping, partial disintegration, and sometimes by the attempts of previous owners at making new panels! If in any doubt, make a paper or cardboard template, using the vehicle, rather than the panel removed from it, as a guide.

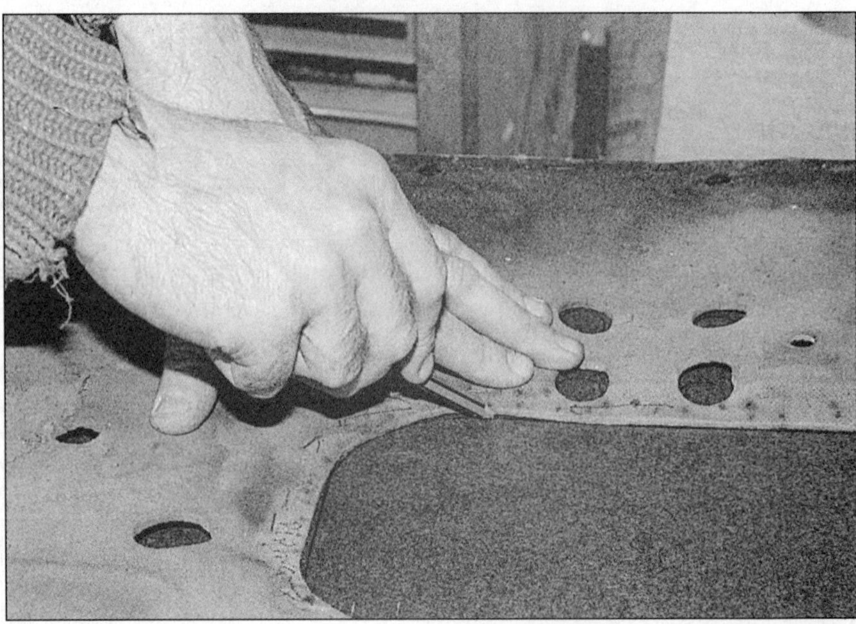

▲ *8.1. Having established that the original backing board is of the correct dimensions, or otherwise having made a paper/cardboard template, lay your pattern onto a sheet of new board, and carefully mark out the shape required, and the positions of all apertures, including those for door handles, window winders, trim retaining clips, and so on. Always use new material of the same thickness as the original, to avoid problems with attaching panel retaining clips, etc. If unsure of the precise dimensions, make the new panel slightly larger than the original – it is fairly easy to trim off material at a later stage, but impossible to add it on!*

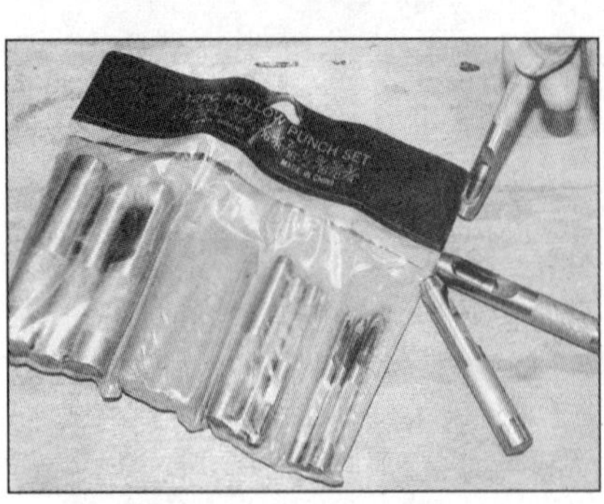

▲ *8.2. For cutting out small diameter, circular apertures, a set of hollow punches of varying diameters (with a block of lead placed underneath the panel as each hole is cut out) is invaluable for this work. Alternatively …*

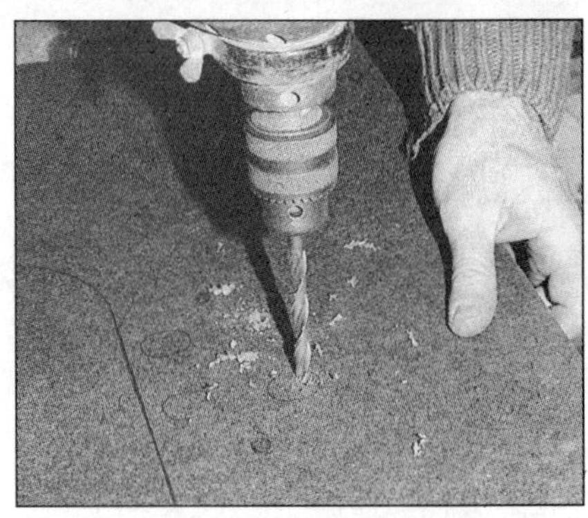

▲ *8.3. … drill bits of appropriate diameters can be used.*

▲ *8.4. For the larger and irregular shaped apertures, in each case start by drilling a hole, about ¼ in (6/7mm) in diameter, just inboard of the edge. Then,* ***wearing a dust mask and goggles****, use a jig-saw or hand saw (in each case choosing a fine-toothed blade) to cut out the aperture. Trim off excess material from around the perimeter of the new panel, too.*

▲ *8.5. The panel should now look something like this. In this case the holes around the perimeter of the panel (to accommodate the retaining clips) had not yet been made in the hardboard.*

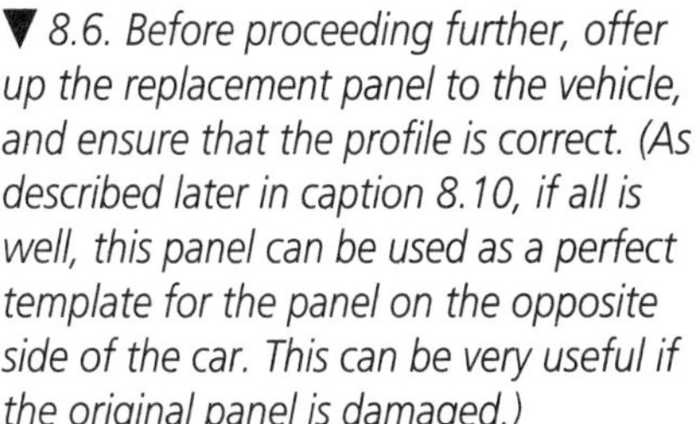

▼ *8.6. Before proceeding further, offer up the replacement panel to the vehicle, and ensure that the profile is correct. (As described later in caption 8.10, if all is well, this panel can be used as a perfect template for the panel on the opposite side of the car. This can be very useful if the original panel is damaged.)*

▲ *8.7. The holes for the retaining clips can now be made, by the use of a hollow punch, or with a drill.*

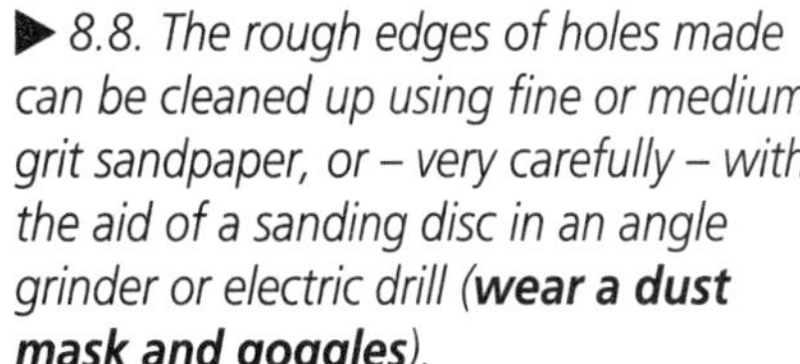

▶ *8.8. The rough edges of holes made can be cleaned up using fine or medium grit sandpaper, or – very carefully – with the aid of a sanding disc in an angle grinder or electric drill (**wear a dust mask and goggles**).*

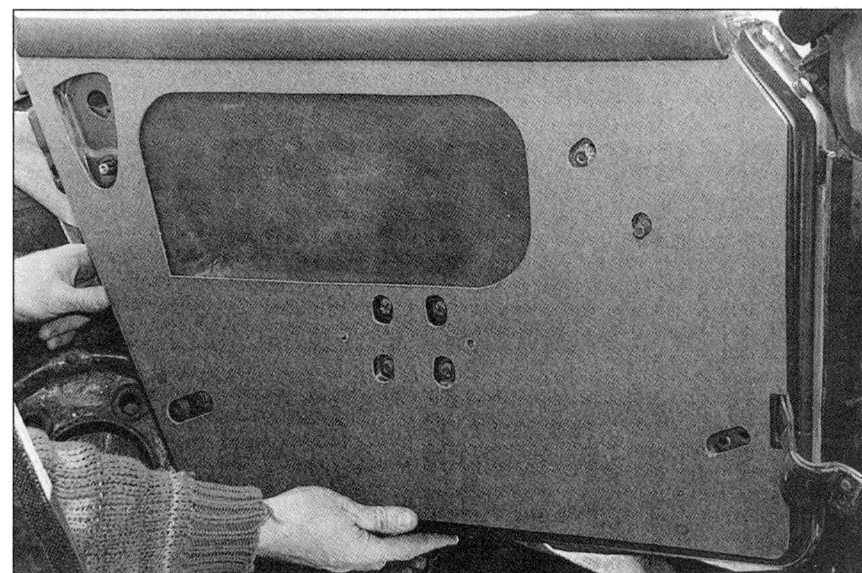

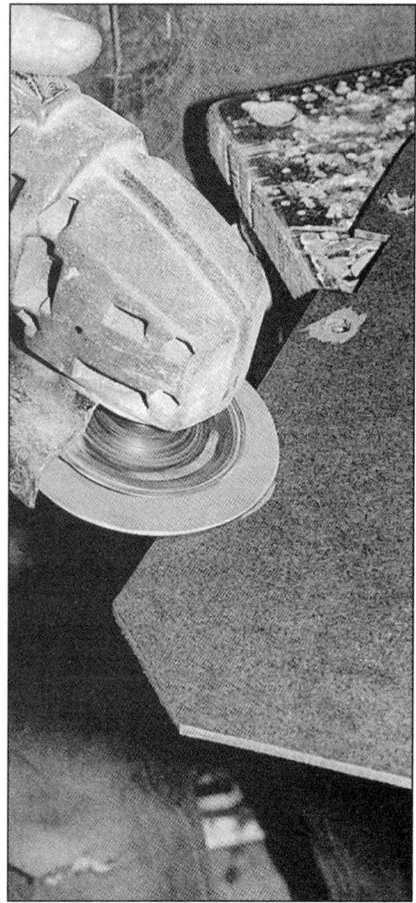

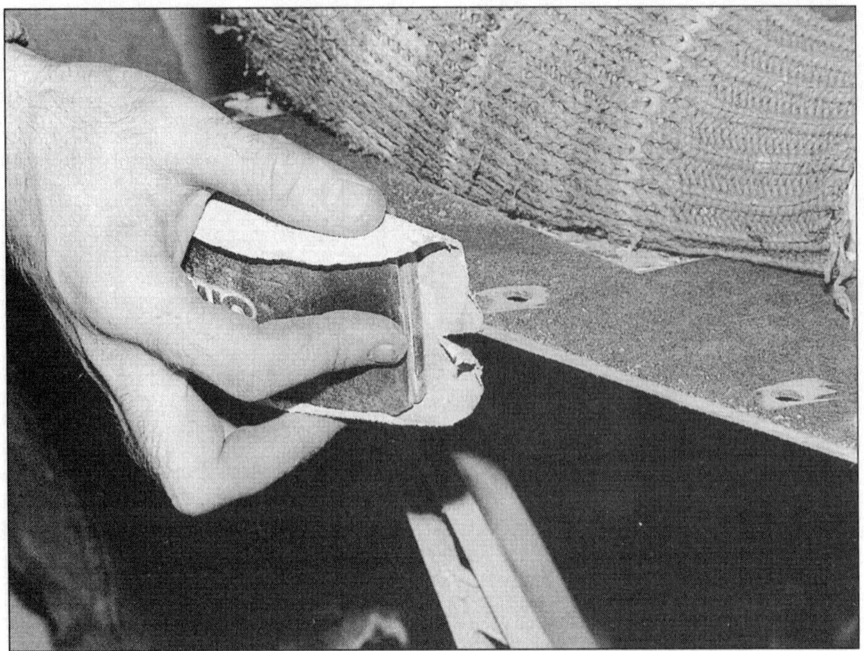

▲ *8.9. The rough edges of the new panel can be tidied up using a sanding block and fine or medium grit sandpaper.*

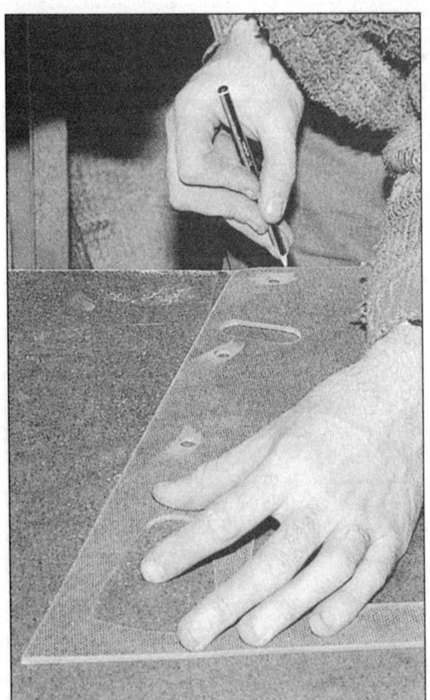

▲ *8.10. In this case the newly made backing board was used as a template (complete with all apertures, etc.) for marking out the replacement board for the opposite side of the car. Note that the board for the other side needs to be placed the opposite way up to the board just made.*

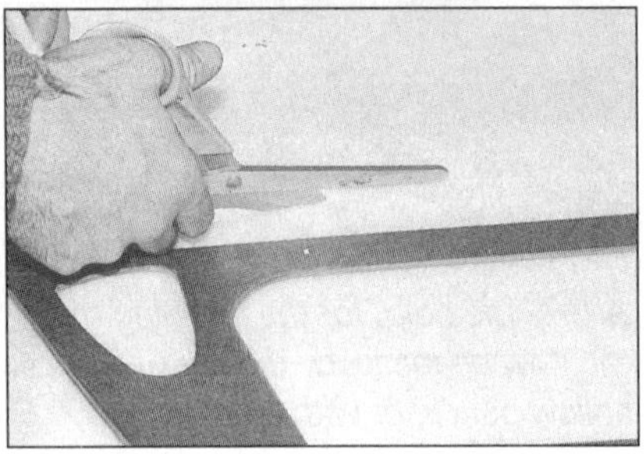

▲ *8.11. The backing board can now be laid onto a sheet of foam or skin wadding, and its profile marked on the padding material, which can then be cut slightly larger than the board.*

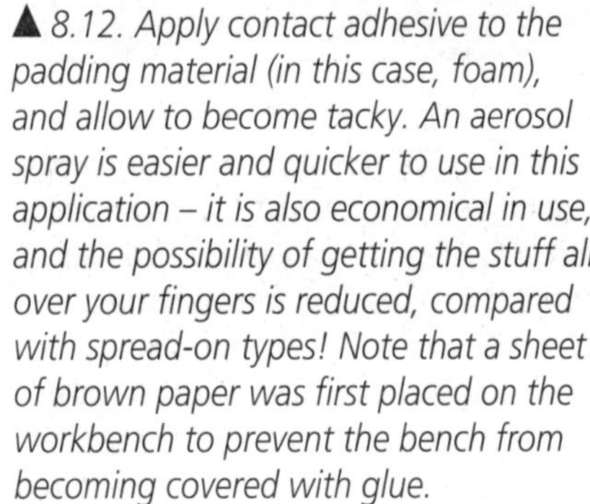

▲ *8.12. Apply contact adhesive to the padding material (in this case, foam), and allow to become tacky. An aerosol spray is easier and quicker to use in this application – it is also economical in use, and the possibility of getting the stuff all over your fingers is reduced, compared with spread-on types! Note that a sheet of brown paper was first placed on the workbench to prevent the bench from becoming covered with glue.*

▼ *8.13. Similarly, adhesive is applied to the backing board, and allowed to become tacky.*

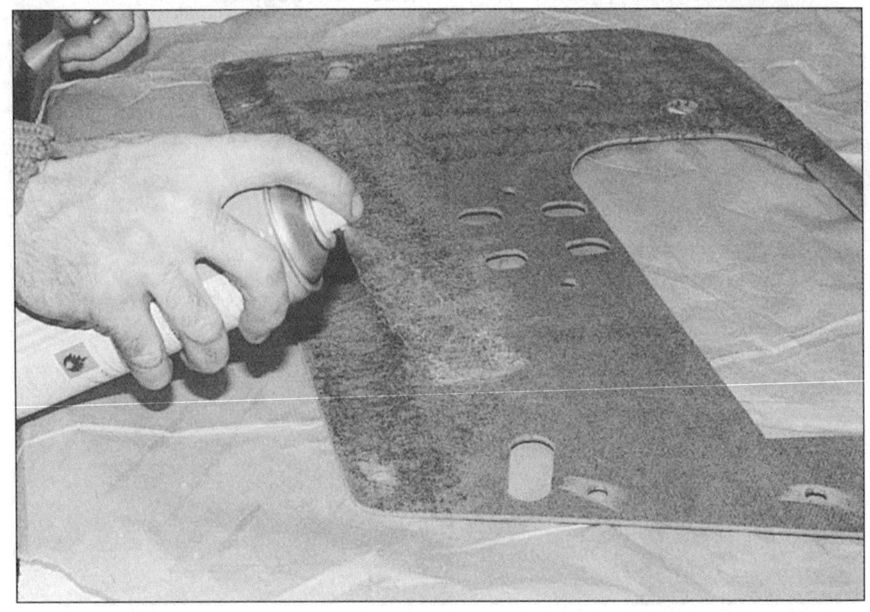

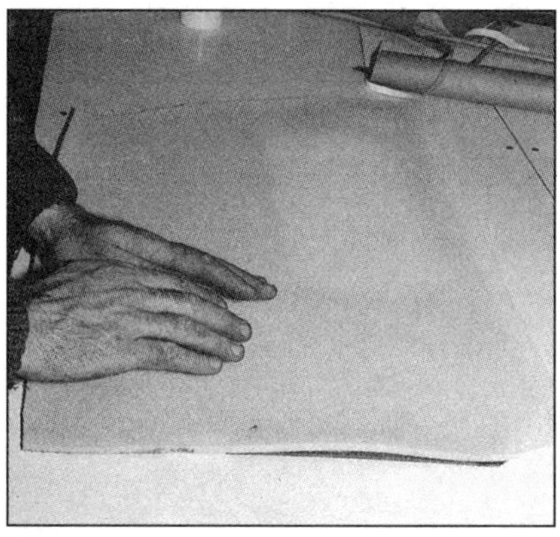

▲ *8.14. The foam can then be fixed in place. Take care to ensure that alignment is correct at the first attempt, for once the adhesive bites it is difficult to release for a second go!*

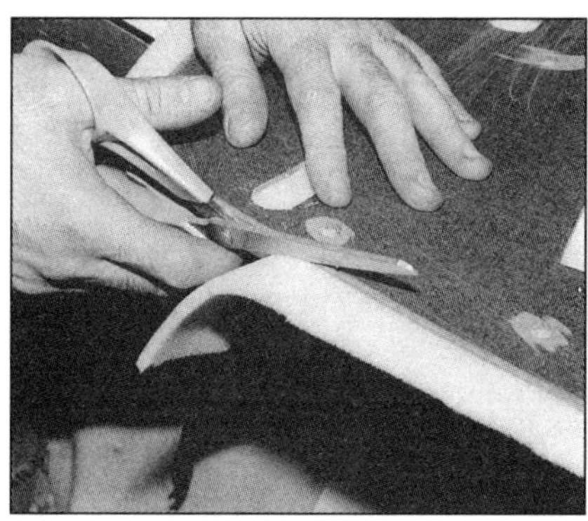

▲ *8.15. The foam can now be trimmed precisely to the shape of the panel, using scissors, or a trimming or craft knife.*

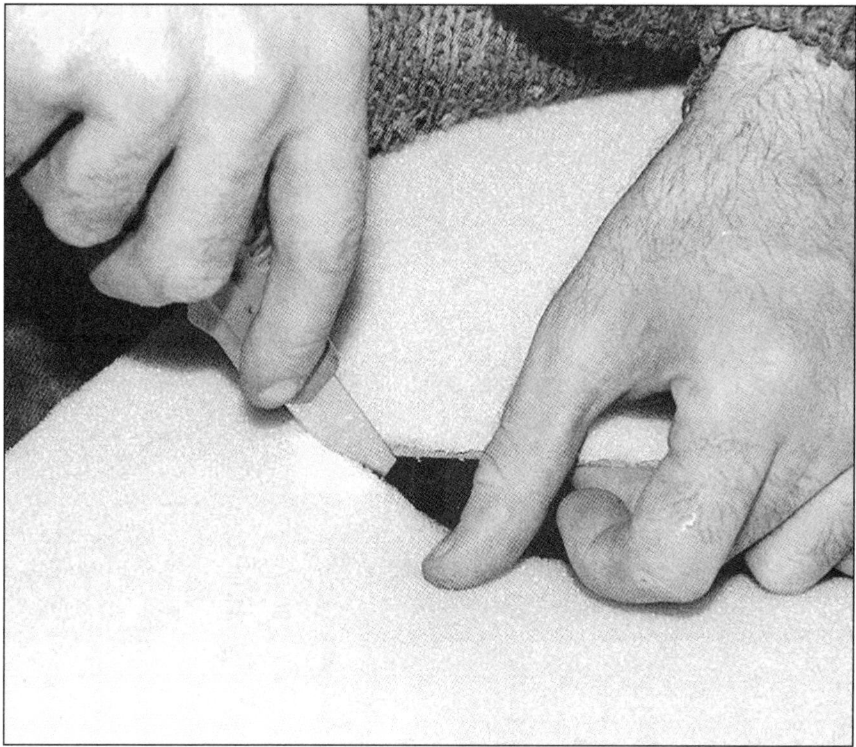

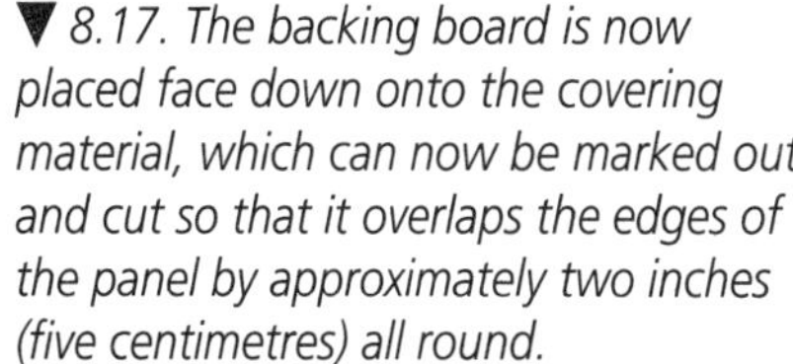

▲ *8.16. Carefully cut out any apertures within the panel, from the foam, using a sharp knife.*

▼ *8.17. The backing board is now placed face down onto the covering material, which can now be marked out and cut so that it overlaps the edges of the panel by approximately two inches (five centimetres) all round.*

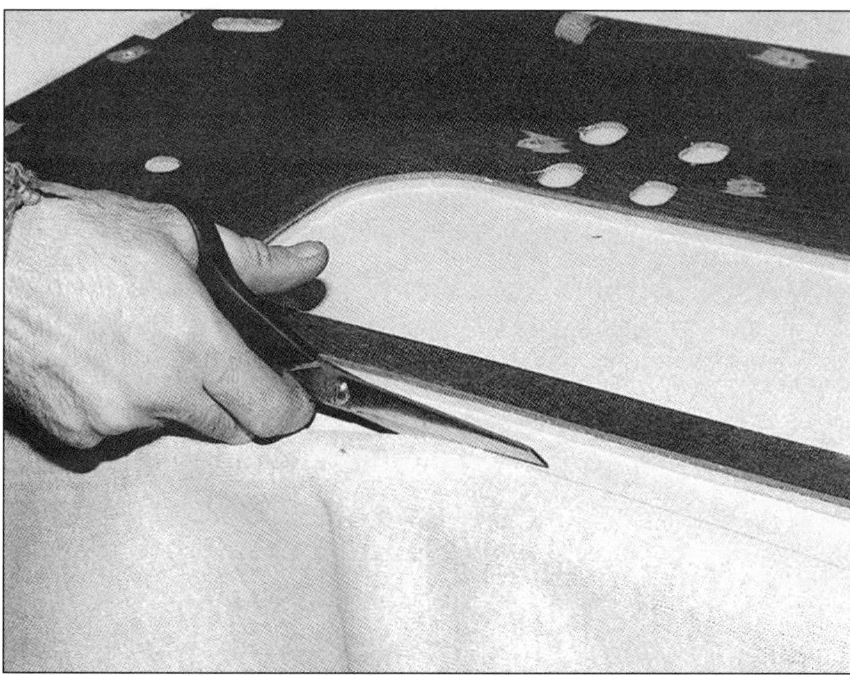

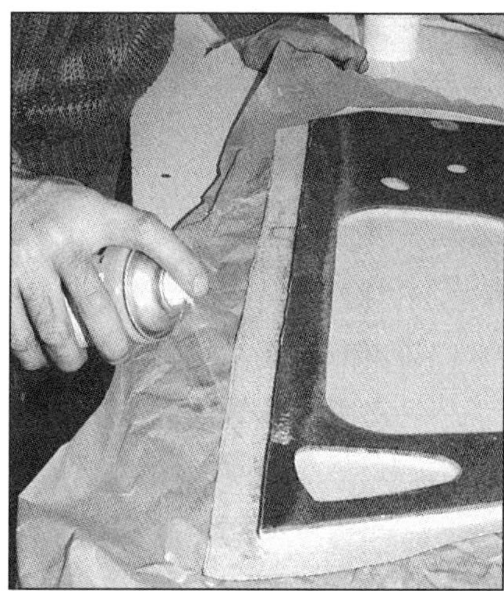

▲ *8.18. Next, adhesive – either spray-on or brush-on – is applied to both the overlapping flange of the covering materials, and to the perimeter of the backing board, and allowed to go tacky. The edges of the covering material can now be wrapped over the perimeter of the board. (Note that if re-using the original covering material, and this has shrunk – as is often the case – it can usually be encouraged back into position by stretching with the aid of heat applied by a hair dryer or fan heater.) In every case, the straight edges of panels are easy enough, but …*

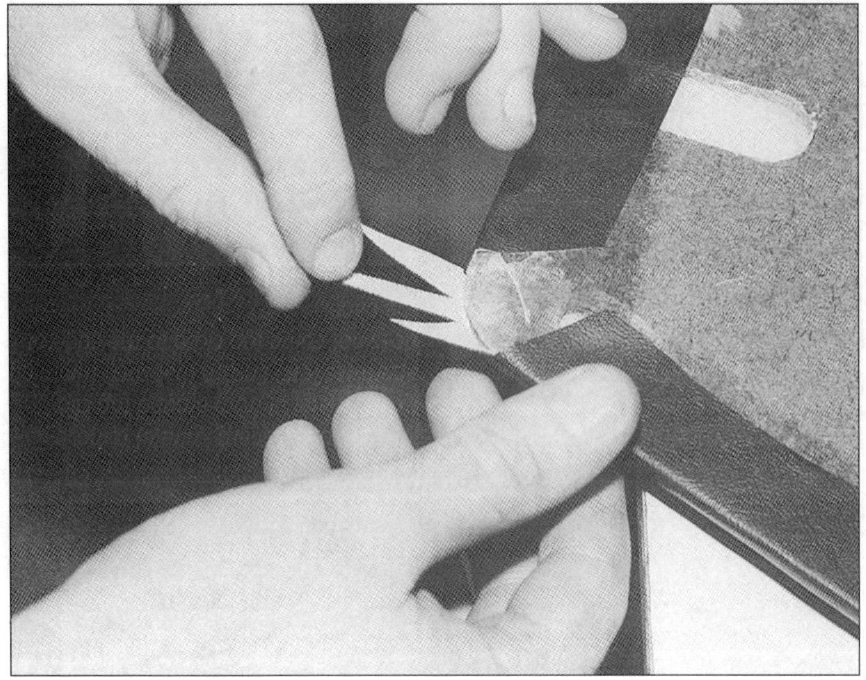

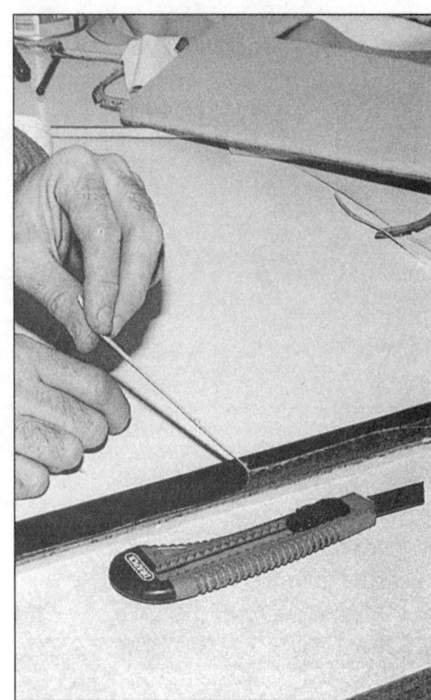

▲ 8.19. ... the corners need special care. To enable the covering material to easily run round the corner without wrinkling, etc., make a series of short V-cuts around each corner. This effectively removes excess material, and enables the covering to sit flat. Take very great care to ensure that the narrow end of each V-cut finishes on the reverse side of the panel, or else each will be visible from the face side.

▼8.20. Similar techniques are applied when negotiating apertures for window winders and door handles, etc., and flaps also need to be cut when working around cut-outs for door retaining straps, and so on. In each case, work slowly and methodically, and a first class finished result will be obtained.

▼ 8.21. In each case, try to start smoothing and folding the flaps into position from the face side of the material, then turning the board over so that they may be pressed firmly in place from the reverse side.

▲ 8.22. Where apertures come close to the edges of the panels, carefully trim back excess material from the wrap-over edge of the covering material, using a sharp knife, before finally sticking the material in place to the reverse side of the backing board.

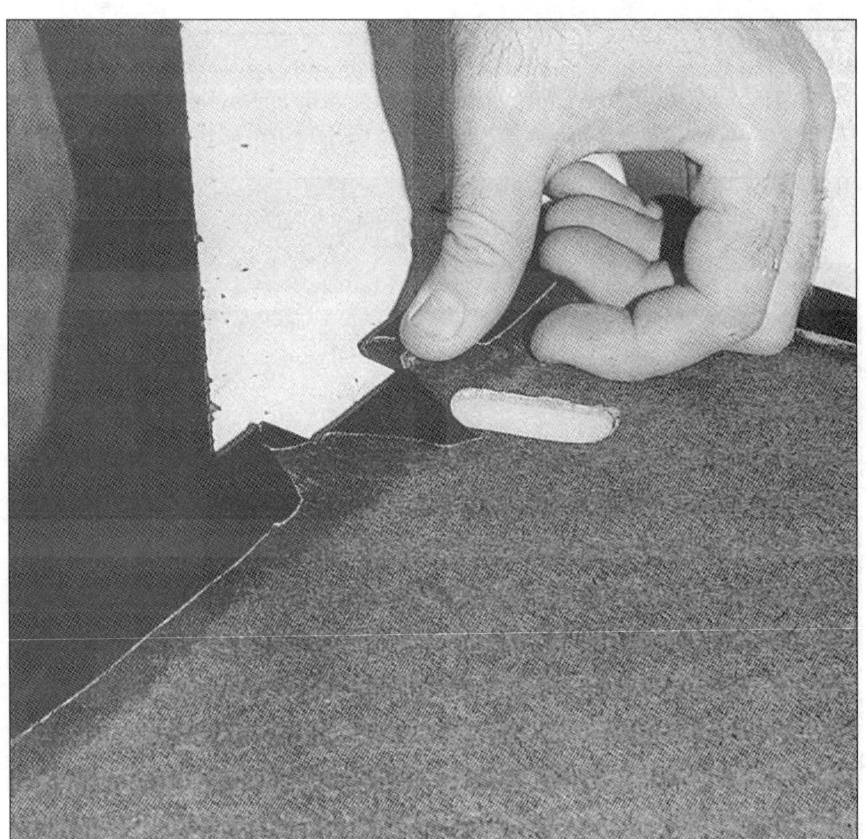

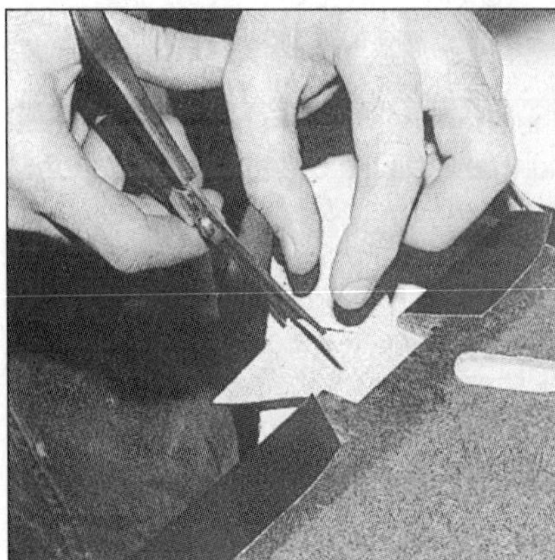

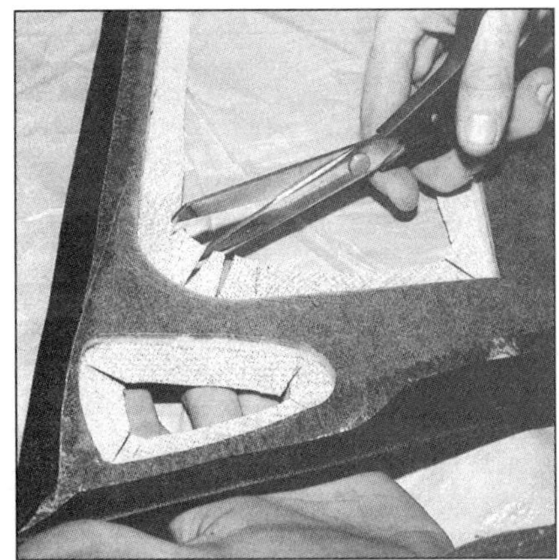

▲ 8.23. *Cut material from within each aperture in the panel, again leaving an overlap to wrap around the edges. Carefully relieve each corner by cutting V-shaped slots in the covering material. Take care to ensure that the base of each V does not come too close to the backing board, or this will show when the flange of the material is wrapped over.*

▼ 8.24. *Once more, apply adhesive to the backing board and the flanges of the material, and allow to go tacky.*

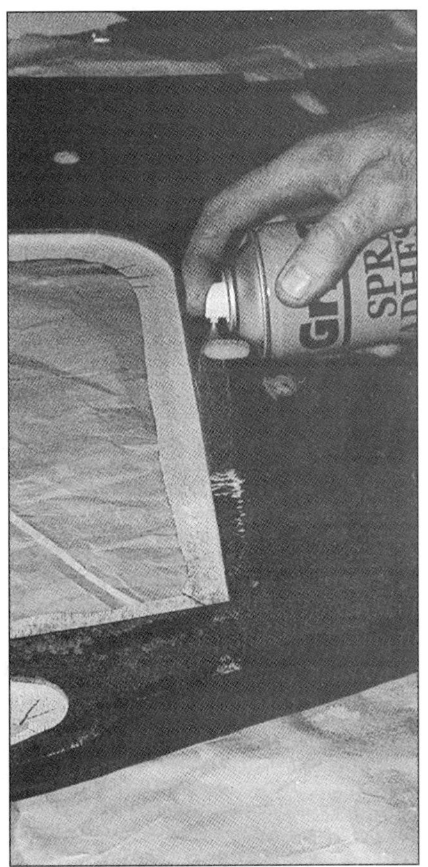

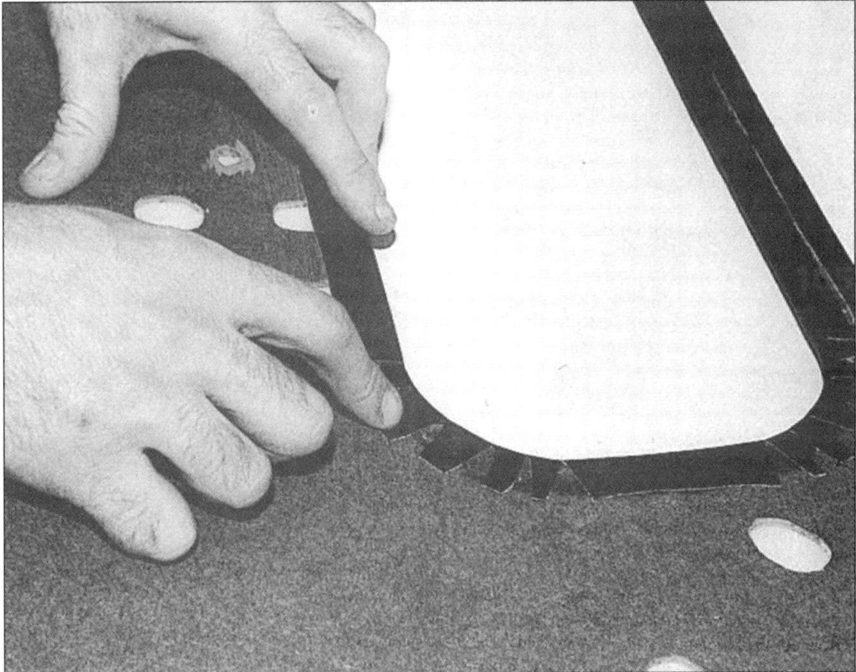

▲ 8.25. *Now carefully fold over the edges of the material around each aperture, eliminating wrinkles and air bubbles beneath the material as you do so. Push each flap of material fully home against the backing board. Check the appearance from each side of the panel.*

▼ 8.26. *For additional security, staple each flange in place. If working with standard thickness hardboard, ensure that the legs of the staples are no deeper than* $\frac{1}{8}$ *in, or they may penetrate the covering material. Always opt for galvanized staples, available from builders' suppliers or timber yards.*

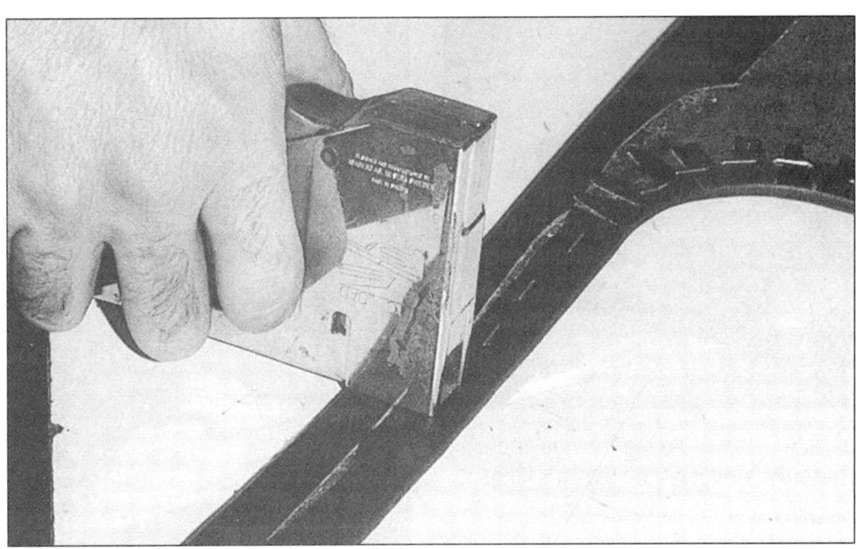

▼ 8.27. *Use a sharp knife to remove excess material from around trip clip apertures, etc. Ensure that such trimming does not come too close to the edge of the panel.*

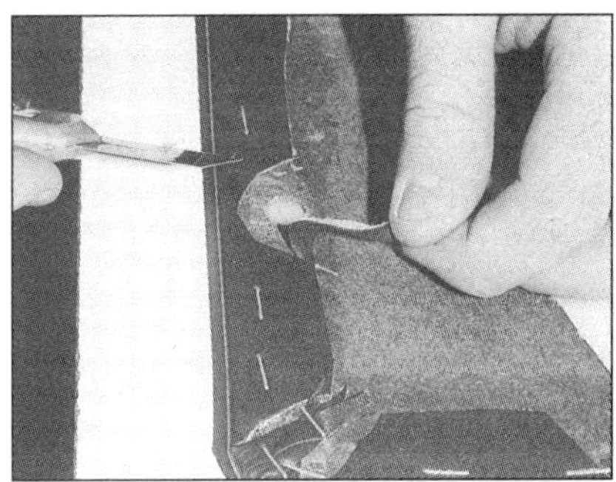

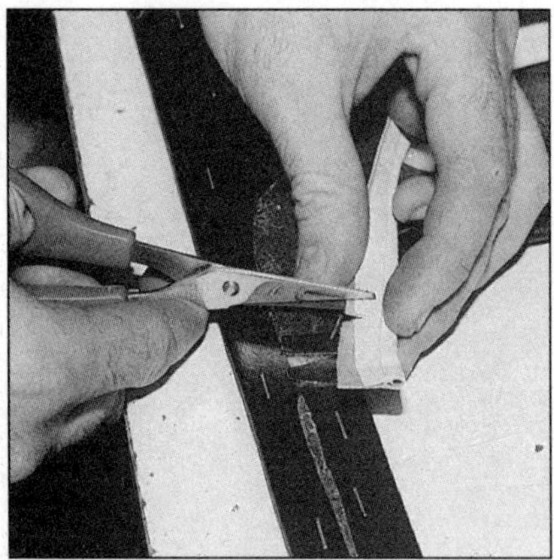

▲ 8.28. Some panels, such as these MG items, incorporate piping around the edges of the larger apertures. Having made the piping (as described in Chapter 6), cut slots in the flange to enable it to negotiate the corners of the aperture.

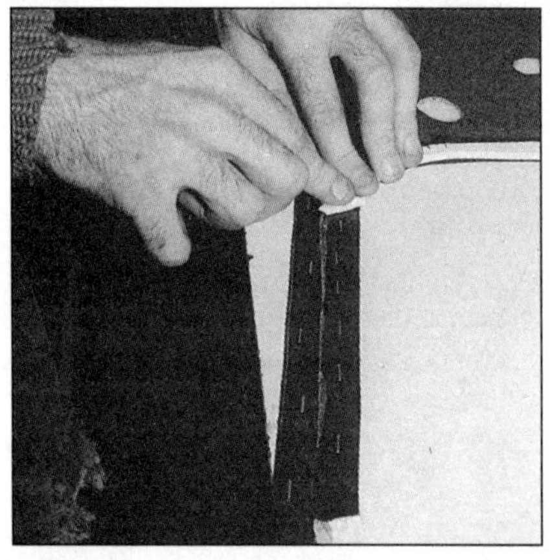

▲ 8.29. The piping can then be glued in place.

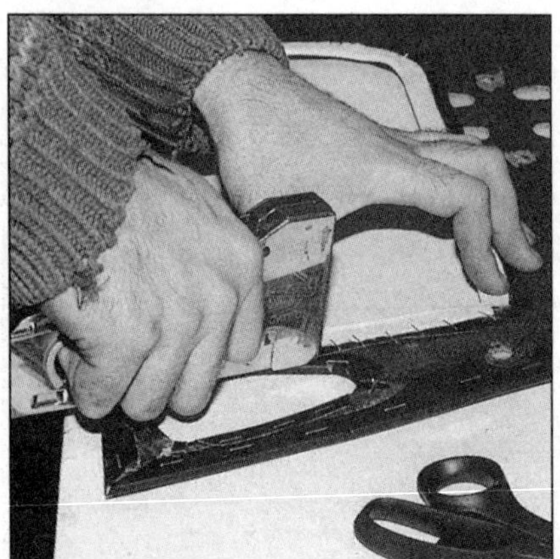

▲ 8.30. Staples should then be applied, between the piping's flange and the backing board, as extra security.

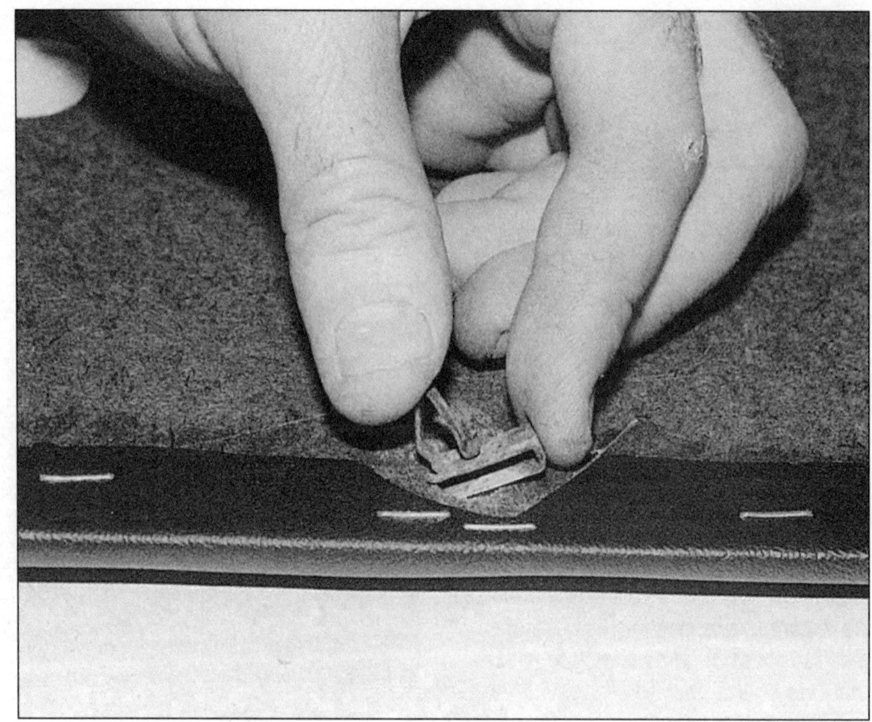

▲ 8.31. When the panel is complete, new trim clips can be fitted. If difficulty is experienced in obtaining new, the old ones can be re-used, or alternative types may have to be adapted. Sometimes, a screwdriver may be needed to push the clip fully home. Final readjustment of position is usually necessary when fitting the panel to the car.

▼ 8.32. If the original clips are to be re-used, they usually benefit from de-rusting (with medium grit wet-or-dry silicon carbide paper, used dry), followed by applications of anti-rust primer and then top coats. These are usually most easily applied by aerosol spray.

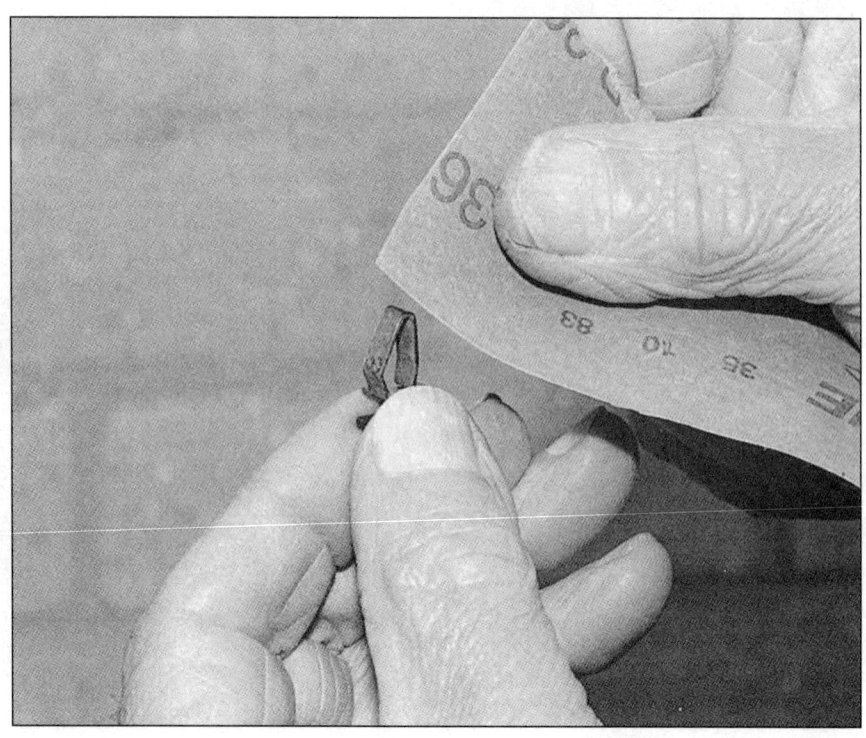

▲ *8.33. On some cars, like this MG, a small section of covering material is glued directly to the door frame, to act as a backing for the large aperture in the main door panel. Ensure that you cut the material sufficiently large that the edges of it are not visible when the trim panel is fitted.*

▼ *8.34. The completed panel can now be finally offered up to the vehicle, then X-apertures can be cut in the appropriate positions (established by gently pressing the panel assembly against the door) to accommodate the operating shafts for door handles, window winders, etc. Where possible, cut inwards, towards the centre of the X.*

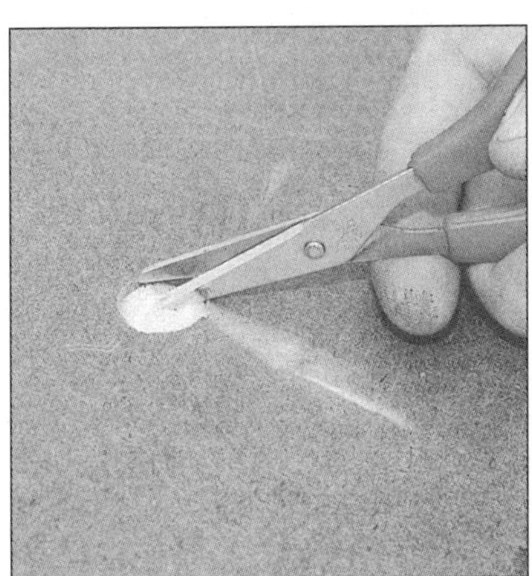

▲ *8.35. On completion, the new panel can be refitted to the car, and door handles, etc., re-installed. As already indicated, slight adjustment of the positions of the panel clips within their apertures is often required as the panel is fitted.*

▼ *8.36. New and old! Just a reminder of how bad the original panels usually are – a strong, good-looking replacement can be made with comparatively little outlay, plus a few hours of effort.*

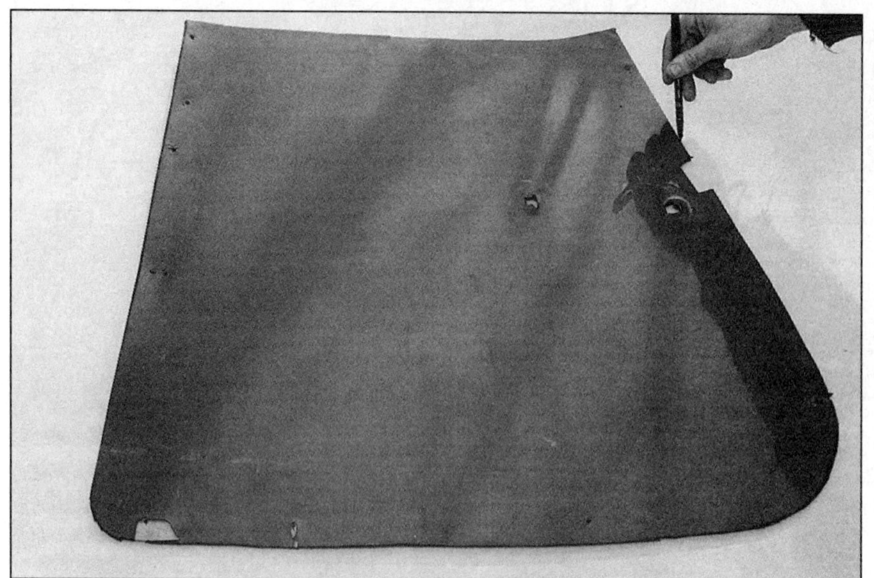

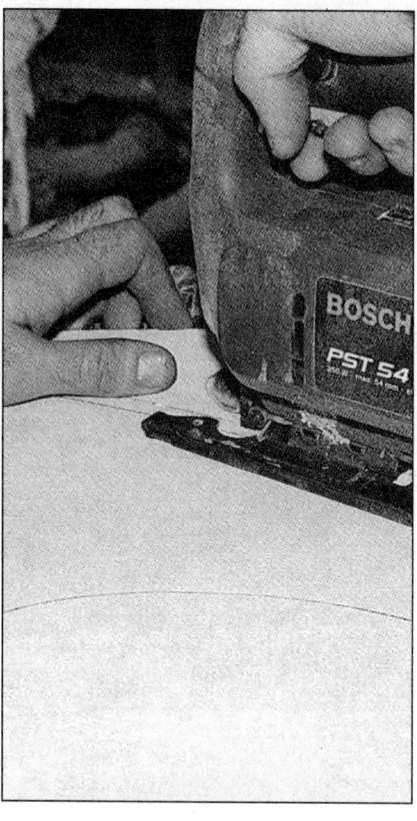

MORE COMPLEX PANELS

Many trim panels, especially on older, quality cars, incorporate additional adornment and practical features, like map pockets. In such cases the originals should always be your guide.

While it may not be possible to match exactly the materials used many years ago, you will at least be able to reproduce the methods used in construction, to achieve a finished product which looks and feels right.

The following sequence shows tackling the door trim panels from a 1940s Triumph Roadster. In the past the original panels had been lost and replaced with totally incorrect hardboard items, covered with similarly inappropriate cheap vinyl. However, at least the panels were of the correct overall size, and were therefore useful as templates.

To get the rest of the detail construction correct, details and measurements were taken from another Roadster with original type panels still fitted, and paper templates made as guides. Looking at other examples of your car – preferably unrestored ones – will often give valuable information on how the panels should be. This is especially important if your own vehicle has been altered over the years.

▲ *8.37. Although this trim panel is wrong in terms of construction, it is of the correct profile, and can therefore be used as a template for marking out the shape of the new panels onto a sheet of marine or weatherproof thin plywood the same thickness as the original factory-fitted panel.*

▼ *8.38. Using paper templates made by reference to an original car, apply details of cut-outs (in this case for a map pocket), etc., to the panel. Photographs and sketches of an original vehicle are also invaluable aids to detail.*

▲ *8.39. An electric jig-saw is the ideal implement for cutting round the lines marked on the plywood, indicating the outer perimeter of the panel.* ***Always wear a dust mask and protective glasses during this operation, and keep fingers and clothes well clear of the blade.***

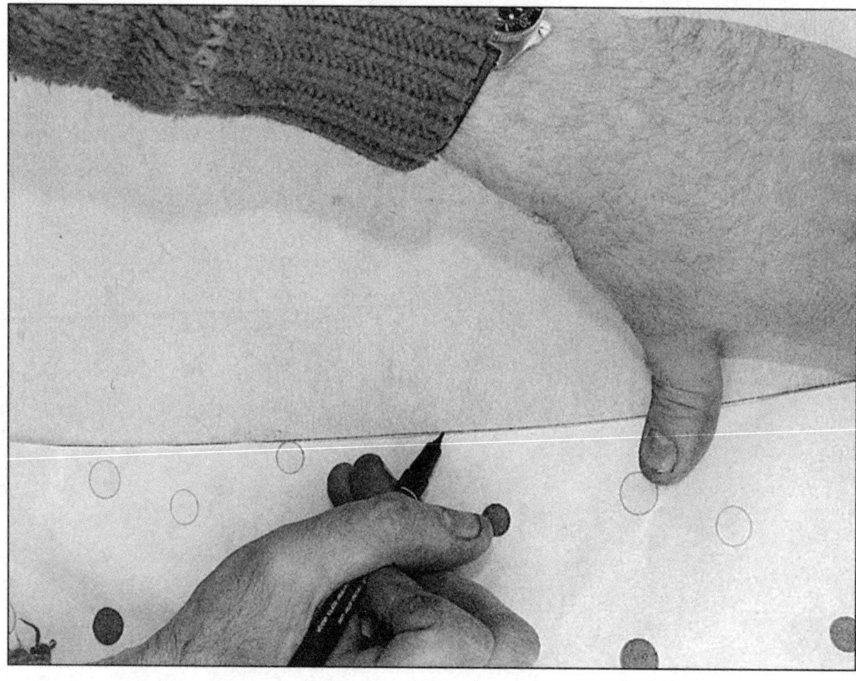

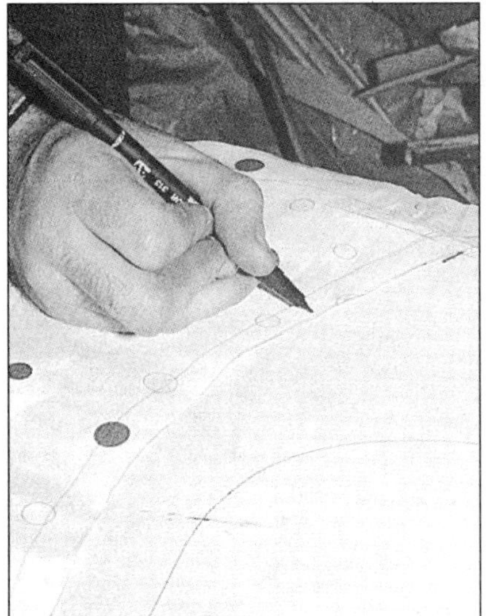

▲ *8.40. More detailed information can now be marked onto the panel, including, for example, the precise positioning of carpet sections to be added at the bottom, also such features as keyhole-shaped apertures used to fasten the panel to the door frame – and so on.*

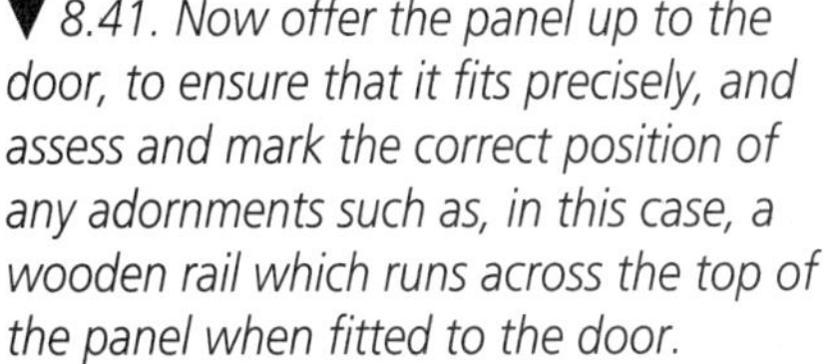

▼ *8.41. Now offer the panel up to the door, to ensure that it fits precisely, and assess and mark the correct position of any adornments such as, in this case, a wooden rail which runs across the top of the panel when fitted to the door.*

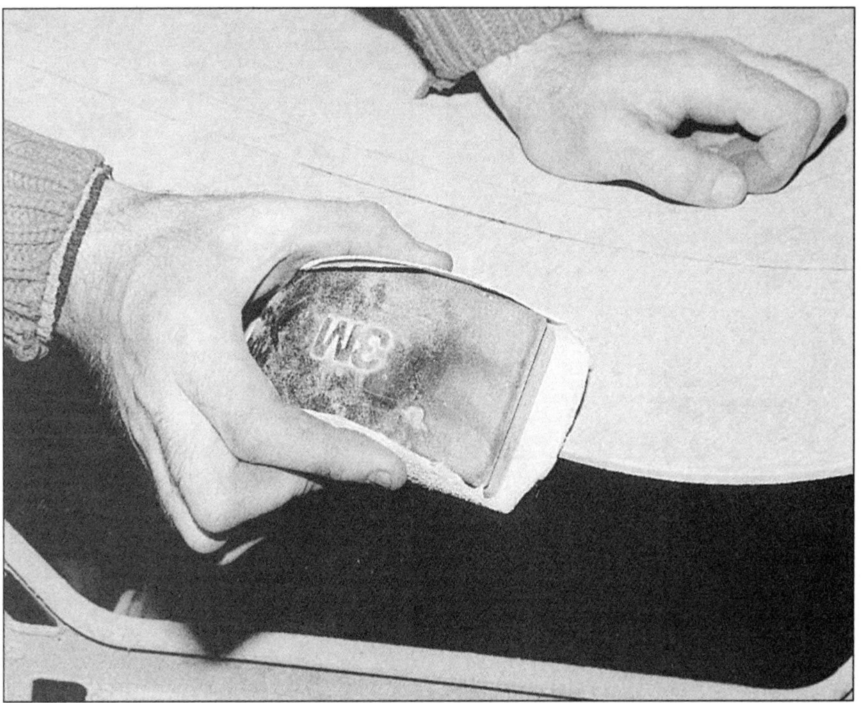

▲ *8.42. Carefully sand smooth the edges of the panel, creating a very slight bevel in the process.*

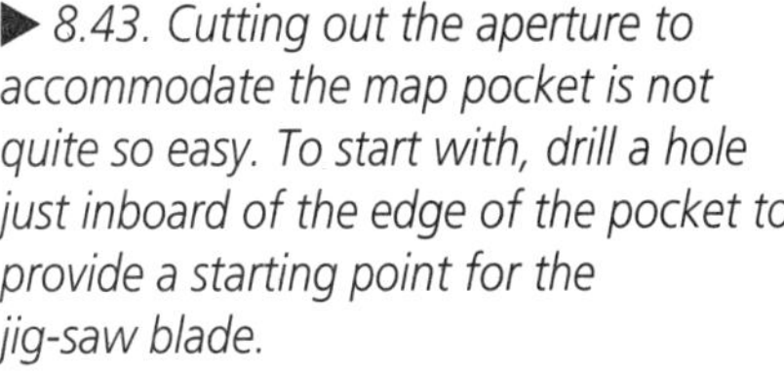

▶ *8.43. Cutting out the aperture to accommodate the map pocket is not quite so easy. To start with, drill a hole just inboard of the edge of the pocket to provide a starting point for the jig-saw blade.*

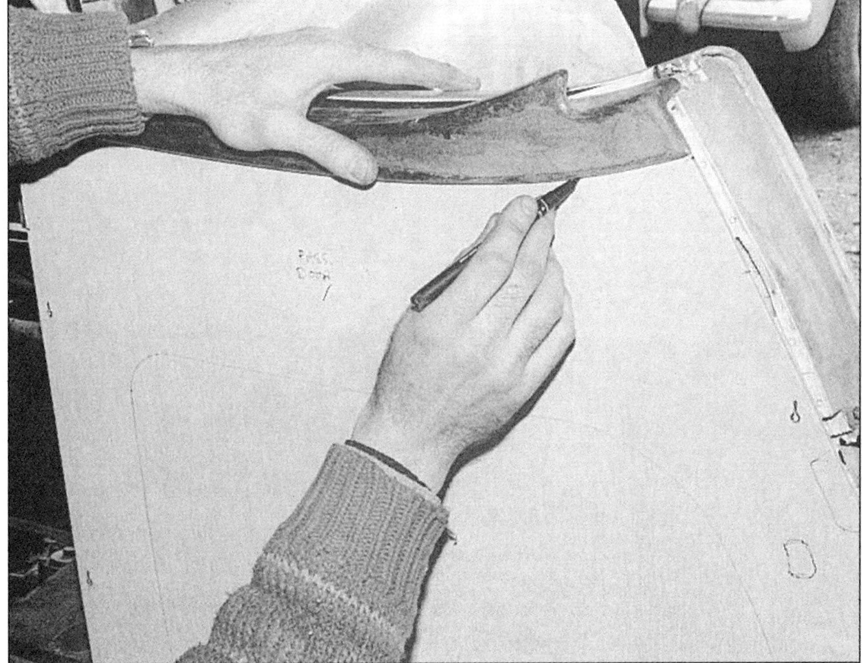

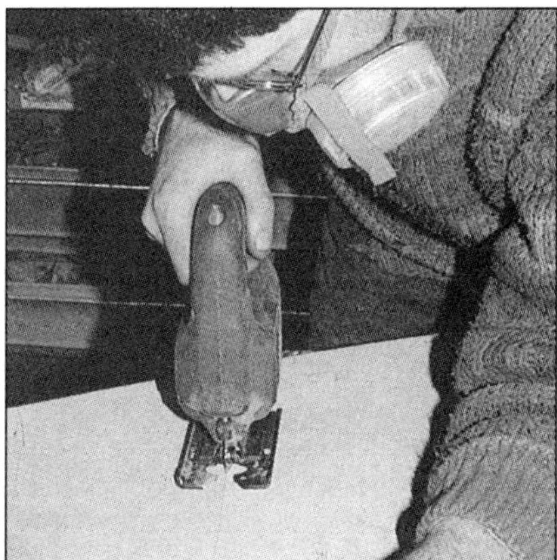

▲ *8.44. Once the cut has been started, carefully guide the jig-saw around the perimeter of the map pocket aperture.* ***Always wear a dust mask and protective glasses during this operation, and keep fingers and clothes well clear of the blade.***

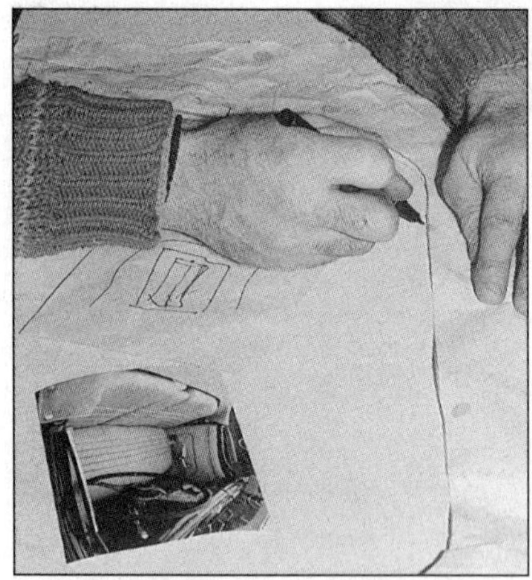

▲ *8.45. To form the map pocket in the Triumph door, a second ply panel has to be made up as a backing board. This is attached to the back of the main trim panel. Photographs and sketches of, and measurements taken from, original cars can help a great deal in ensuring that the new panel is precisely the right shape and size.*

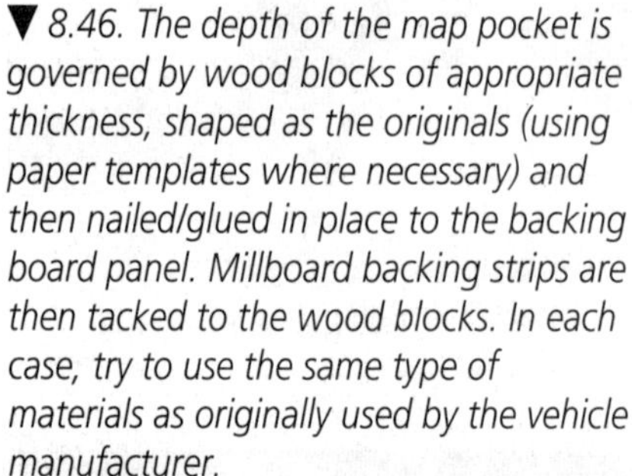

▼ *8.46. The depth of the map pocket is governed by wood blocks of appropriate thickness, shaped as the originals (using paper templates where necessary) and then nailed/glued in place to the backing board panel. Millboard backing strips are then tacked to the wood blocks. In each case, try to use the same type of materials as originally used by the vehicle manufacturer.*

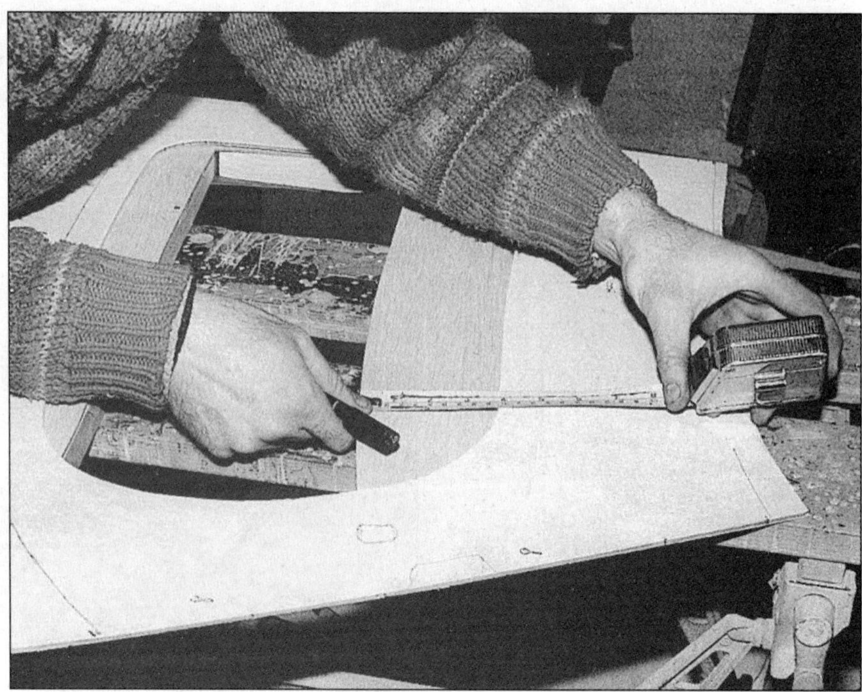

▲ *8.47. It is essential that measurements are double-checked at each stage. Here, the precise position of the backing board of the map pocket in relation to the main trim panel is being assessed.*

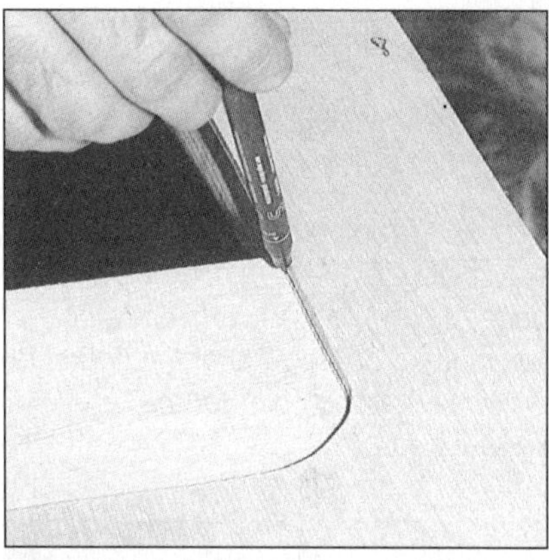

◀ *8.48. Once the correct position has been established, mark the front of the backing board so that in subsequent operations it is straightforward to align the two panels. Next ...*

▲ *8.49. ... turn the two panels over – together – and again mark their relative positions on the reverse side to aid assembly.*

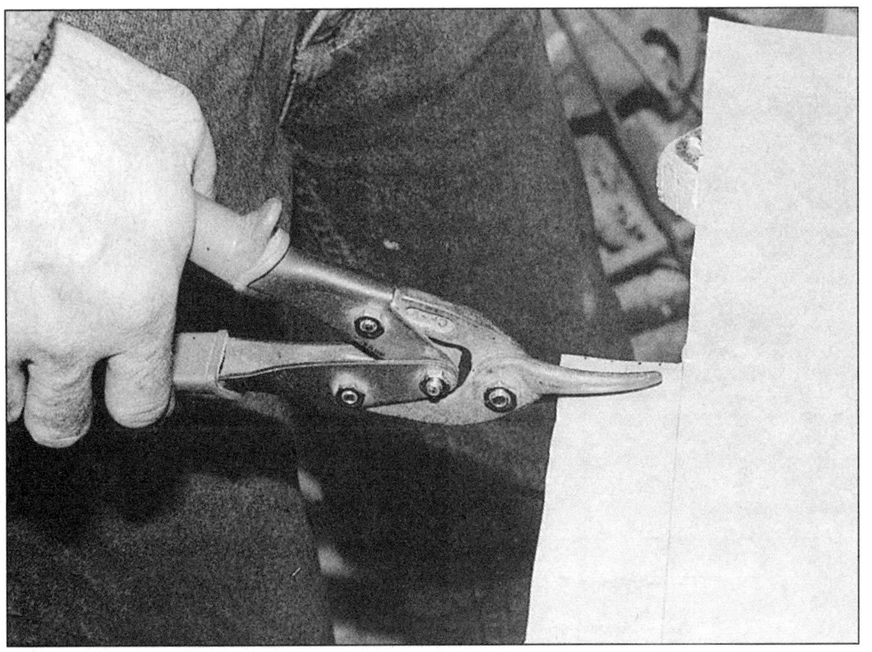

▲ *8.50. Where intricately shaped trim clips are required, these may have to be made up to suit the application. In this case, all the correct panel holder clips (used to secure the map pocket's backing board to the back of the main trim panel) were missing, so new ones had to be fabricated, using those on an original car as a guide. The first step was to cut rectangular strips of steel (in this case galvanized, to help prevent rusting) from a large sheet. The dimensions were obtained from the clips used on an as-original car.*

▼ *8.51. Now the position of any holes can be marked precisely on the clips, and then the metal can be centre-punched and held steady in a vice while the holes are drilled. Always start by drilling a smaller hole than required, and build up to the correct size in small steps. This will help to give a clean edge to each hole, and prevent undue distortion of the metal.*

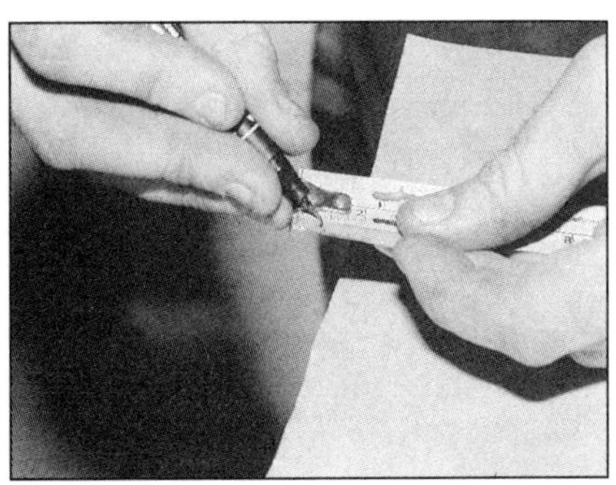

▼ *8.52. In this case, the clip, when finished, had to assume an S-profile. This was achieved by cutting two blocks of solid metal, the same width as each leg of the S, and placing them on opposite sides of the rectangular clip (so far, flat in profile). This assembly was then carefully positioned in the vice, and …*

▲ *8.53. … then the vice was fully tightened. The squeezing action of the jaws formed the clip around the metal blocks, giving the correct profile.*

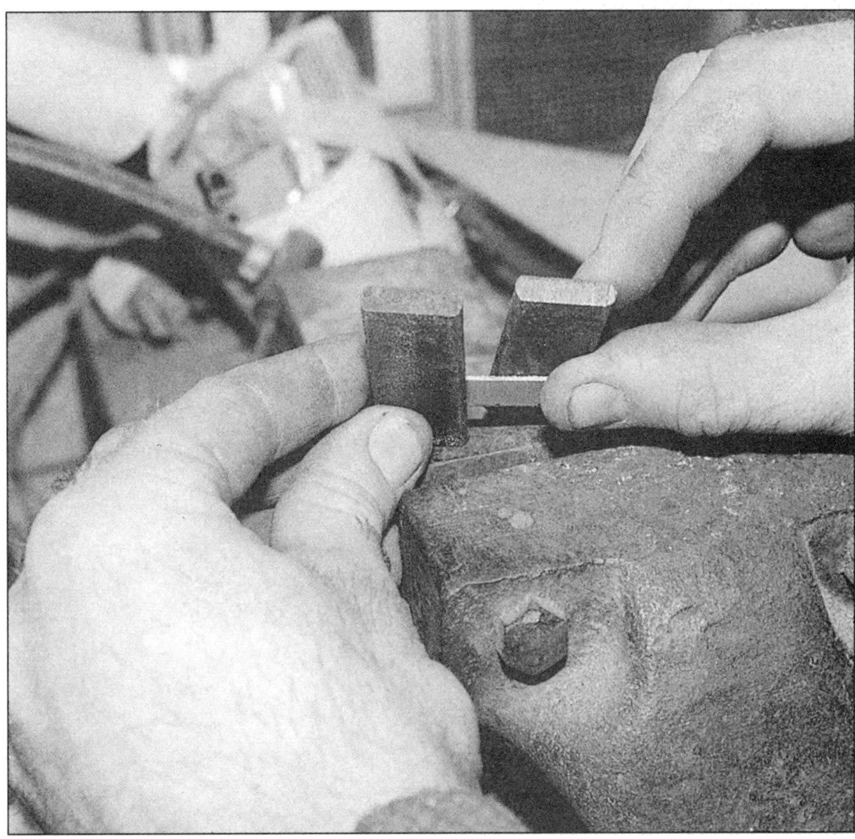

▶ 8.54. *Here are some we made earlier! Some of the clips needed to be wider than the rest. These were formed in the same way as their narrow companions.*

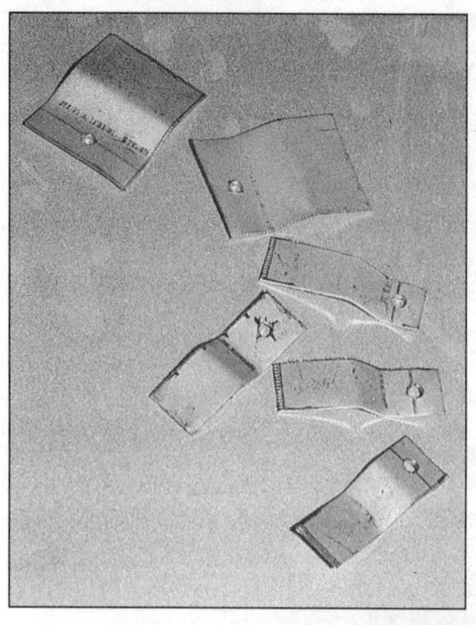

▼ 8.55. *The clips could now be offered up to the trim panels in their correct positions, and holes drilled in the main panel, through the hole already made in each clip. In this case the holes were ⅛ in diameter, and made right through the panel, to accept blind rivets.*

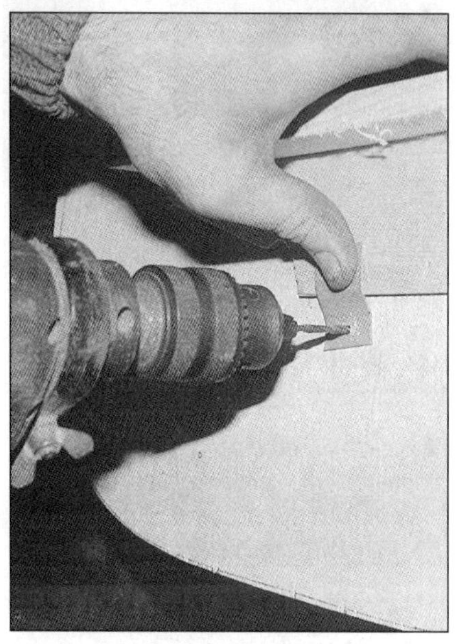

▼ 8.56. *The clips could then be riveted in place, onto the main trim panel. Always ensure …*

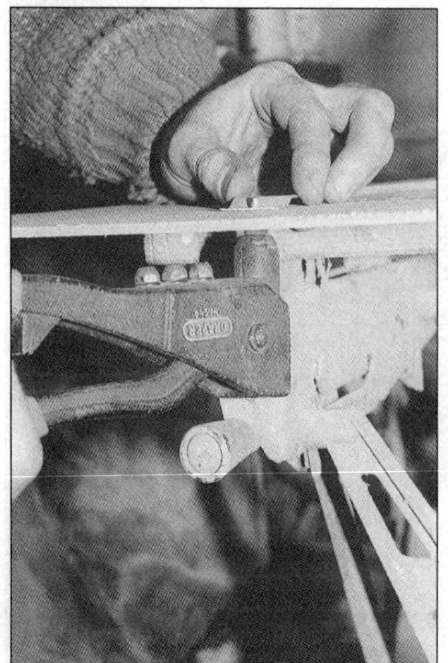

▼ 8.57. *… that the flush end of the rivet is on the outer (or face) side of the trim panel.*

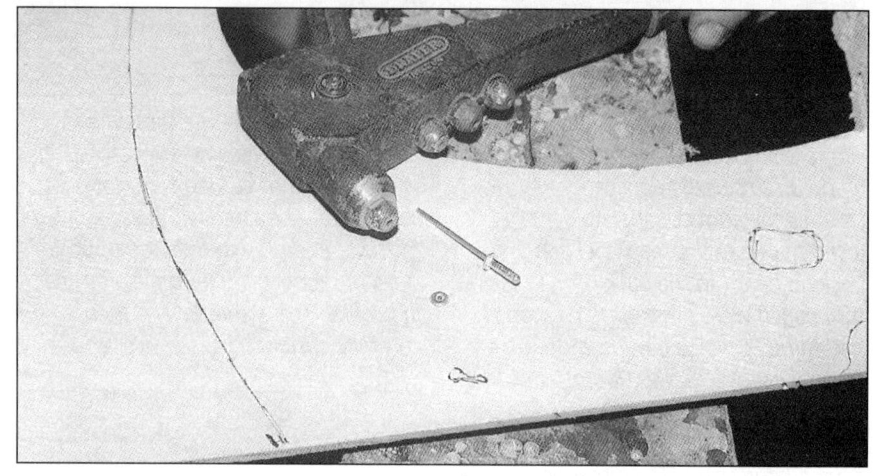

▼ 8.58. *The new clips can be twisted through 90 degrees, using a pair of pliers, to allow the backing board of the map pocket to be slid into position on the back of the main trim panel. The freshly riveted clips will be quite stiff to swivel.*

▲ 8.59. A series of keyhole clips had to be made for the Triumph's door trim panels. These have keyhole-shaped apertures which allow the panel to be hooked into place over the heads of screws in the door frame. It is probably easier to visualize what is meant, by looking at some clips. So here are two different varieties, both of which have been hand-made.

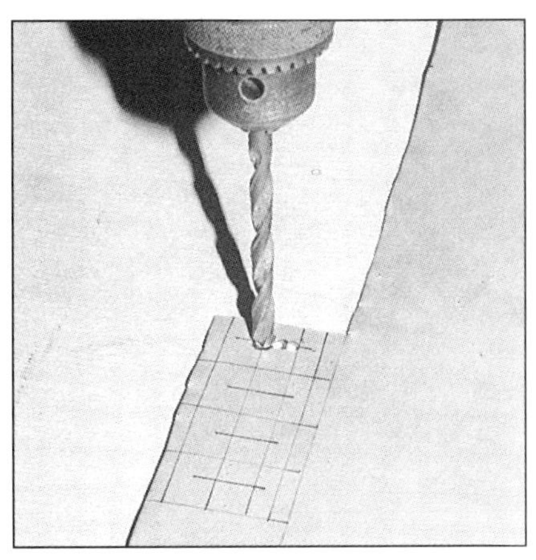

▲ 8.60. Once again, a series of rectangular steel strips are required. Each is marked with a vertical line indicating the centre of the strip, and four horizontal lines. The points at which the inner two of these lines cross the vertical line represent the positions of the centres of the two holes forming the basis of the keyhole shape – this must be central in the clip. The two outer lines are references for drilling the holes for the securing rivets. The holes are then drilled in the sheet – the sizes needed can be gauged by reference to an original panel, or the diameters of the heads and shafts of the screws in the door frame (where fitted).

▼ 8.61. It is always easier to drill the holes before separating the clips from each other. This is a row of completed clips, ready for separation with a hacksaw (or a pair of tin snips can be used), and showing the two drill bits used to create the upper and lower diameters of the keyhole aperture. The short section between the two circles can be removed by initially using the small diameter drill bit, then a tiny file, to create the parallel sides of the aperture.

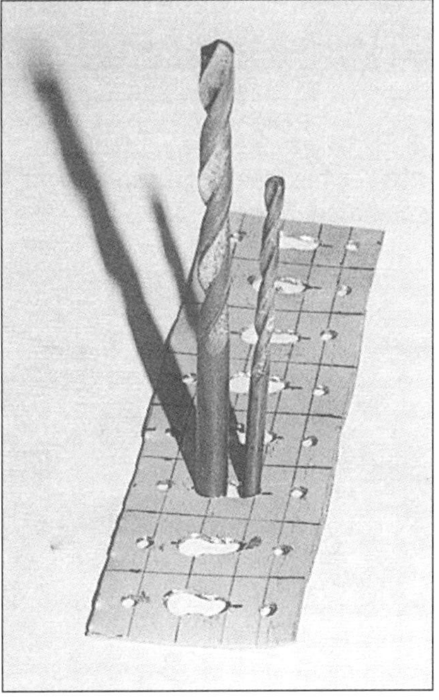

▼ 8.62. Each clip should be offered up into position on the trim panel. All must fit vertically on the panel in order to operate together as the assembly is fitted to the car. This inevitably means that some parts of some of the clips will overhang the edge of the trim panel, and will have to be trimmed to shape.

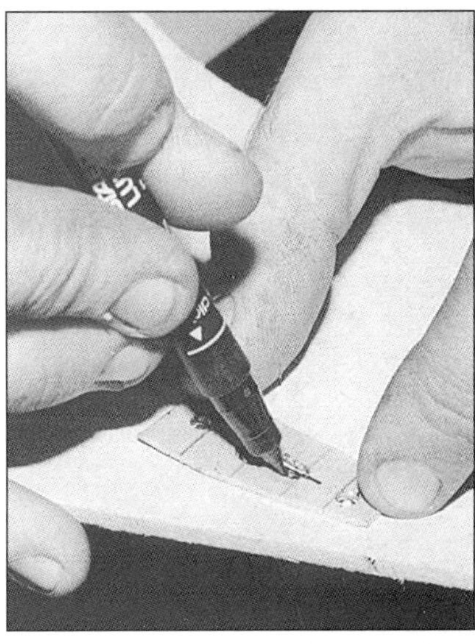

▲ 8.63. When all trimming has been carried out, offer up the clips again, mark their positions on the panel and …

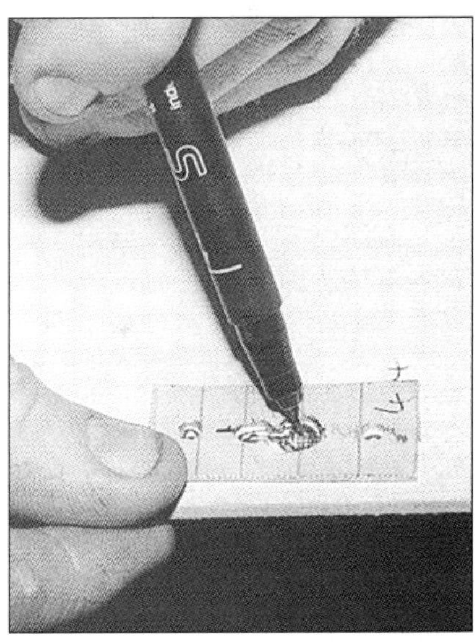

▲ 8.64. … number both them and their marked locations, so that they can be fitted in the right places.

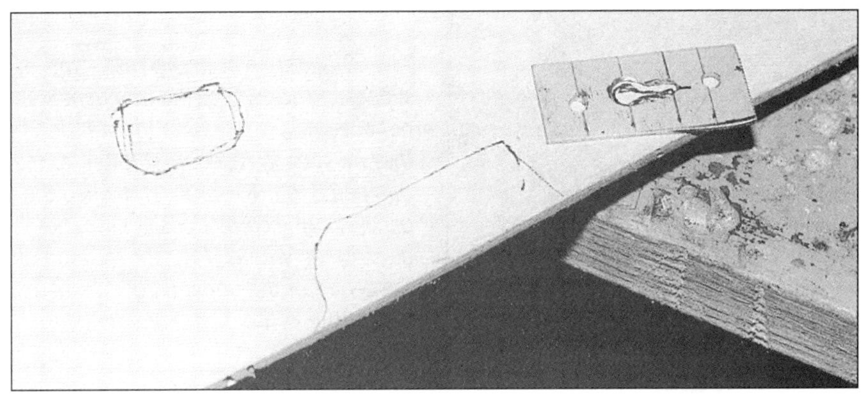

▲ *8.65. The holes in the trim panel can now be drilled in their marked positions, to accommodate each of the screw heads around the door frame when the panel is fitted to the car. The holes must be the same width as the diameter of the larger drill bit used when making the keyhole clips, but must be elongated (using the drill bit) so that they are the same width throughout the depth of the keyhole aperture. This is much easier than it sounds! Two ⅛ in diameter holes must also be drilled in the marked positions to take the securing rivets.*

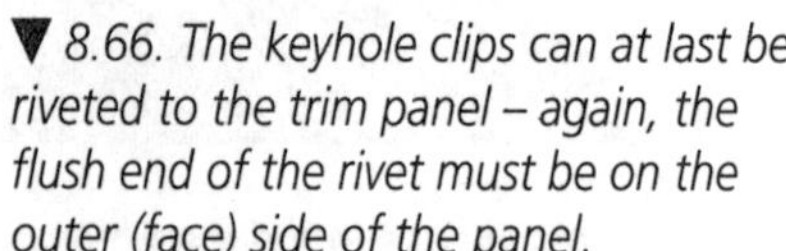

▼ *8.66. The keyhole clips can at last be riveted to the trim panel – again, the flush end of the rivet must be on the outer (face) side of the panel.*

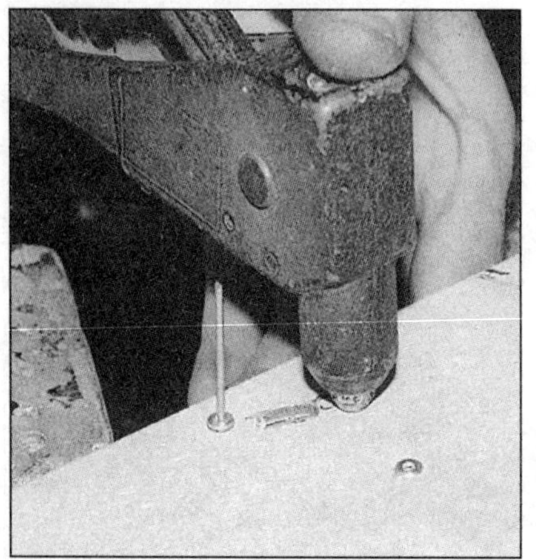

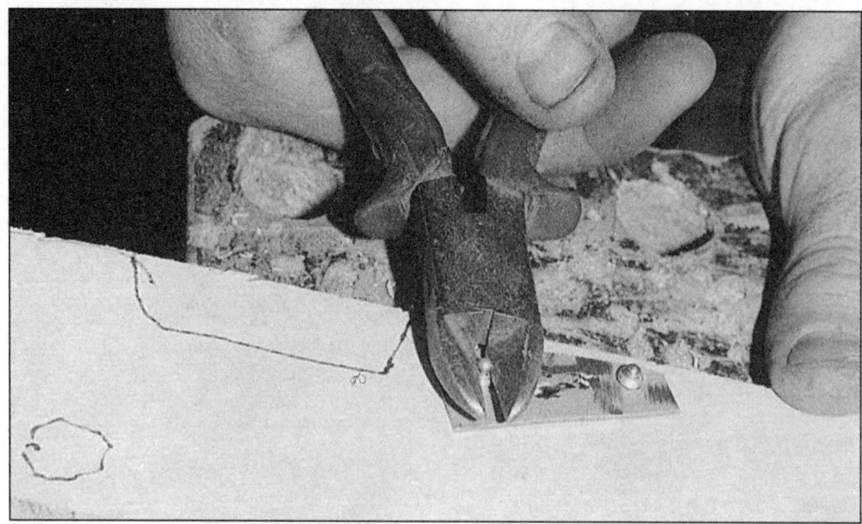

▲ *8.67. Where necessary, roll out the steel centre of the rivet, using a pair of side cutters, then …*

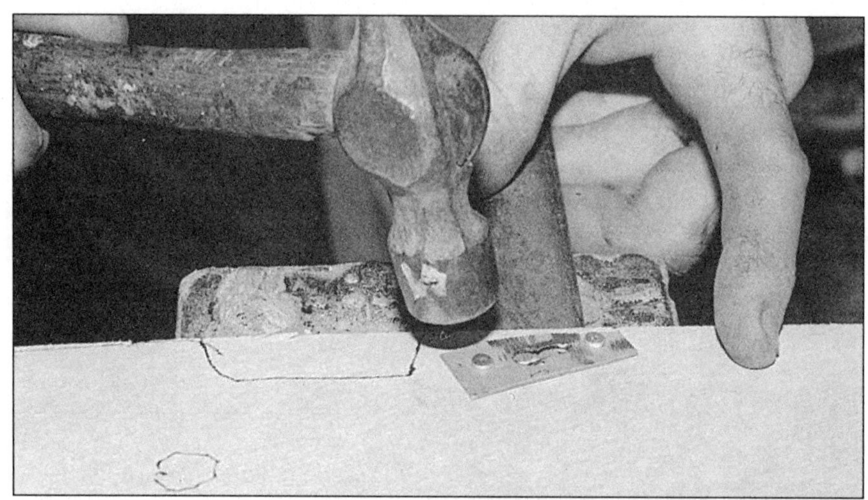

▲ *8.68. … with a stout steel bar placed beneath the panel, squarely tap the end of the rivet with a hammer, to flatten the aluminium casing of the rivet, leaving a smooth profile.*

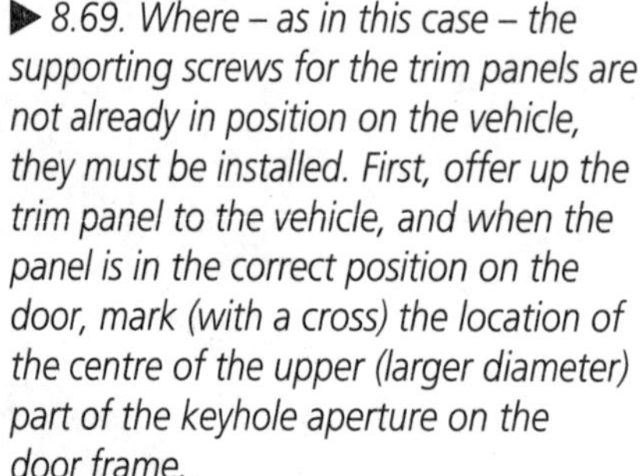

▶ *8.69. Where – as in this case – the supporting screws for the trim panels are not already in position on the vehicle, they must be installed. First, offer up the trim panel to the vehicle, and when the panel is in the correct position on the door, mark (with a cross) the location of the centre of the upper (larger diameter) part of the keyhole aperture on the door frame.*

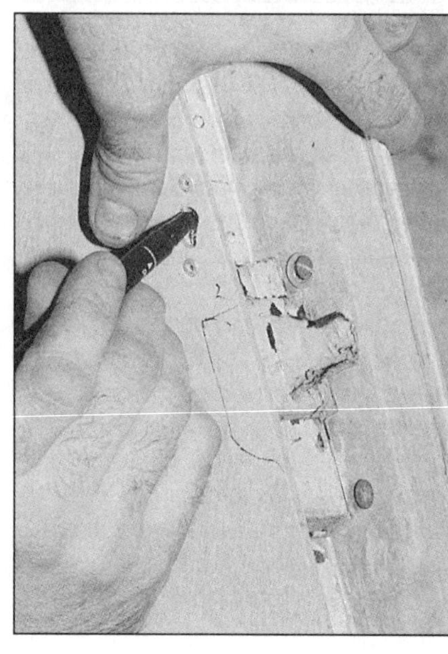

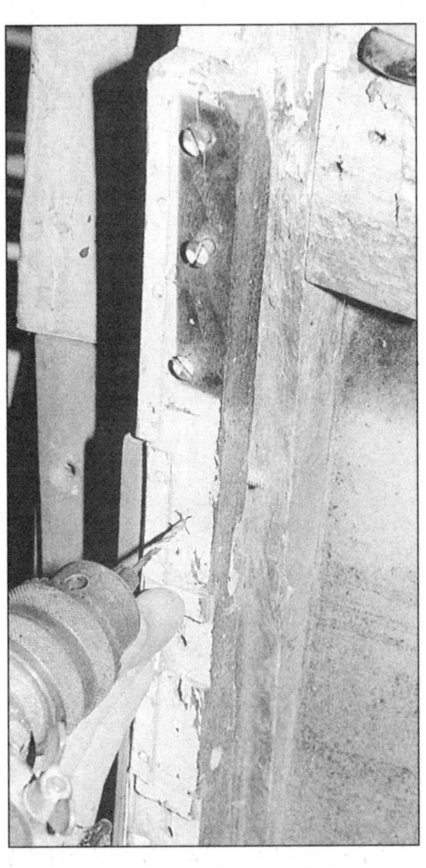

◀ 8.70. The door frame can now be drilled to accept the panel retaining screws, in the positions already marked. Use as small a diameter of drill bit as reasonably possible, to ensure that the screw grips firmly in the wood.

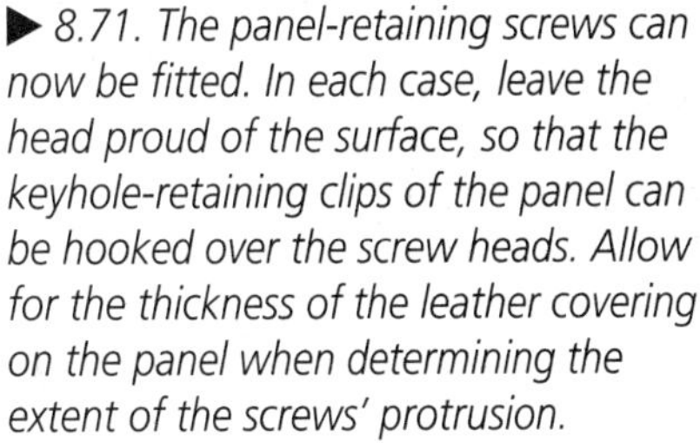

▶ 8.71. The panel-retaining screws can now be fitted. In each case, leave the head proud of the surface, so that the keyhole-retaining clips of the panel can be hooked over the screw heads. Allow for the thickness of the leather covering on the panel when determining the extent of the screws' protrusion.

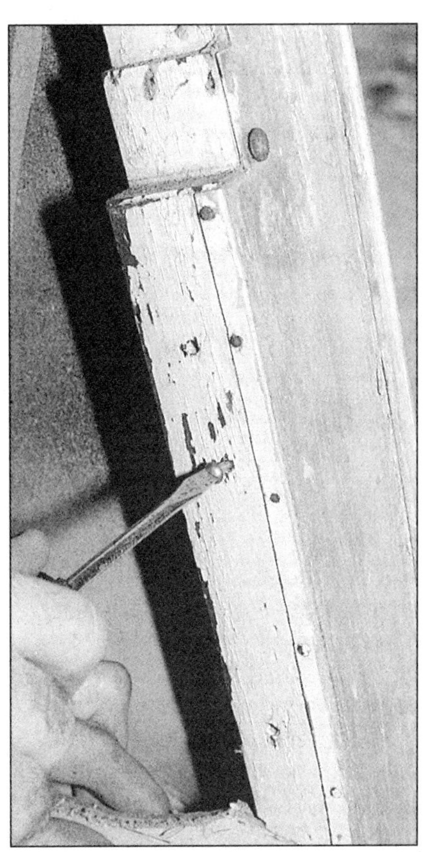

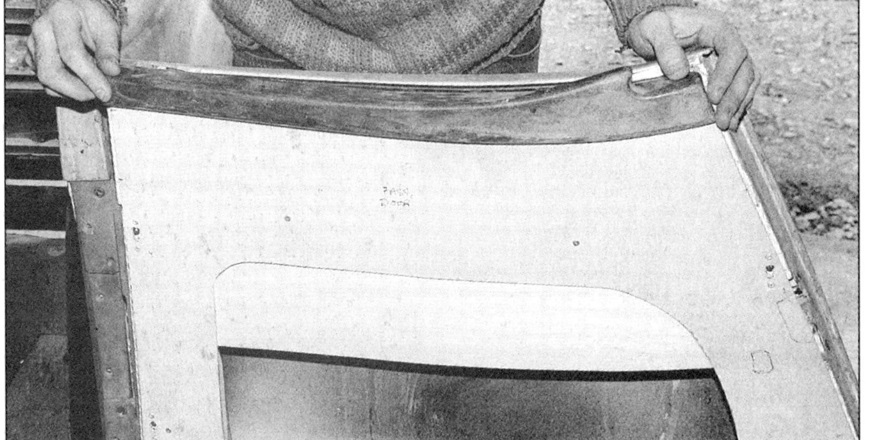

◀ 8.72. With the panel fitted to the door, accessories such as the wood cappings, can be trial-fitted. It is very rewarding when everything fits as it should!

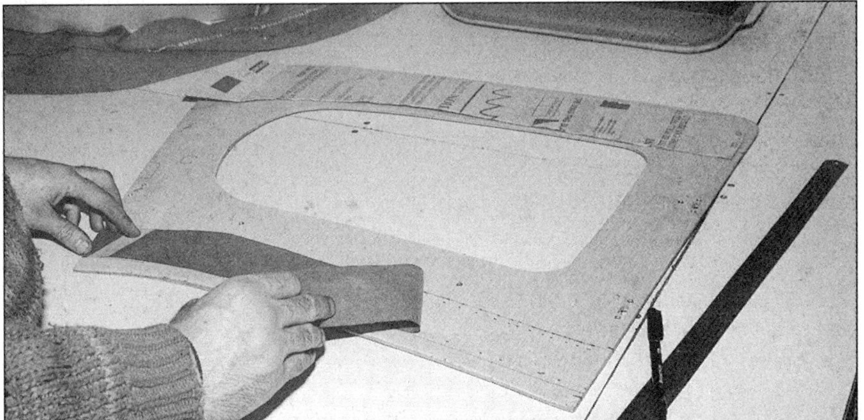

◀ 8.73. Having ensured that all is well in terms of fit, remove the assembly from the vehicle and separate the main panel from the map pocket backing board. Using paper or cardboard templates made by reference to an original panel, mark the positions of – in this case – the section of carpet at the bottom of the main panel, and fluted leather at the top.

▶ *8.74. Contact adhesive should now be applied to the panel – aerosol types are quicker and easier to use in this application.*

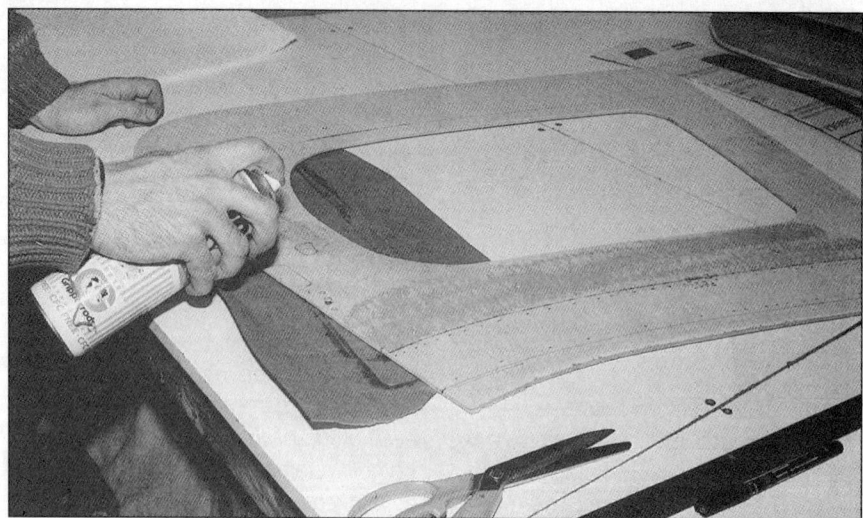

▶ *8.75. When the glue is nearly dry, attach a layer of padding to the panel (leaving gaps for any carpeted sections, etc., to be applied later). Originally, cotton wadding was used, and this can still be obtained if you prefer total originality. However, you may prefer to use ¼ in thick foam sheet, which is easier to handle. Make the foam sheet a little larger than the area to be covered; it is more easily trimmed precisely to shape when in position.*

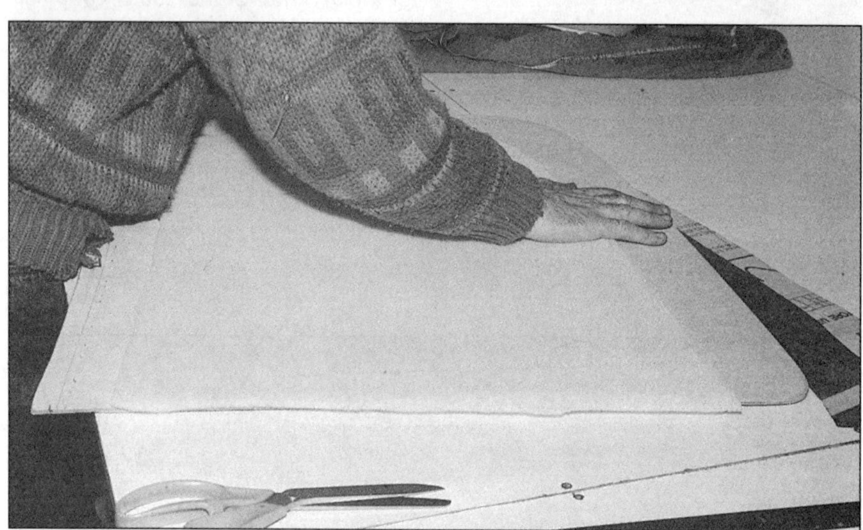

▼ *8.76. In order to gauge exactly where to cut the foam along the bottom of the door, re-apply the template of the carpet section, and mark its upper edge on the foam.*

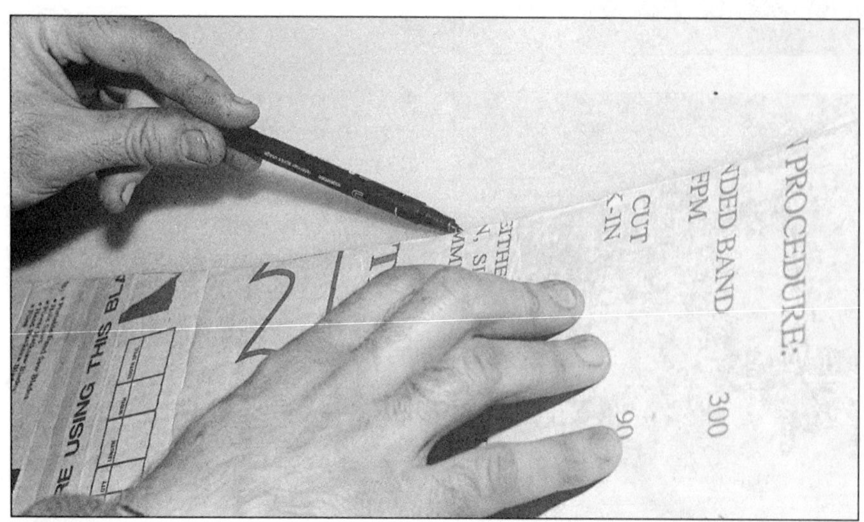

▶ *8.77. Now use a sharp trimming or hobby knife to trim off excess foam along the perimeter lines already marked.*

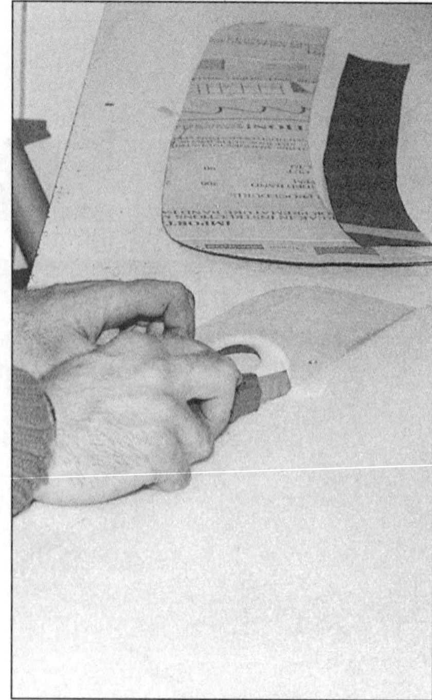

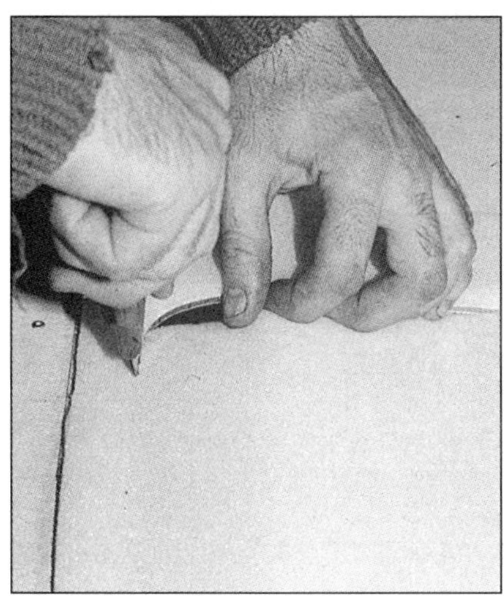

▲ *8.78. Similarly, cut out the aperture for the map pocket.*

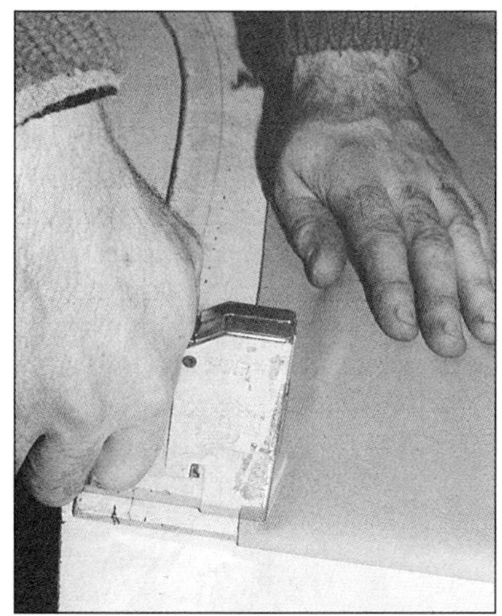

▲ *8.79. The leather covering for the main (central) area of the panel can now be cut to shape – including allowance for the main aperture, in the centre of the panel. Here – as around the outer perimeter of the panel – a flange about 2 in (5cm) wide should be left for wrapping over onto the back of the panel. The leather is stapled to the front of the plywood along its upper and lower edges. Ensure the material is kept free of creases as you work your way along. The flanges of the leather can be wrapped around the perimeter of the main aperture in the panel, and can be secured on the back of the panel as described earlier in the section of this chapter covering straightforward panels.*

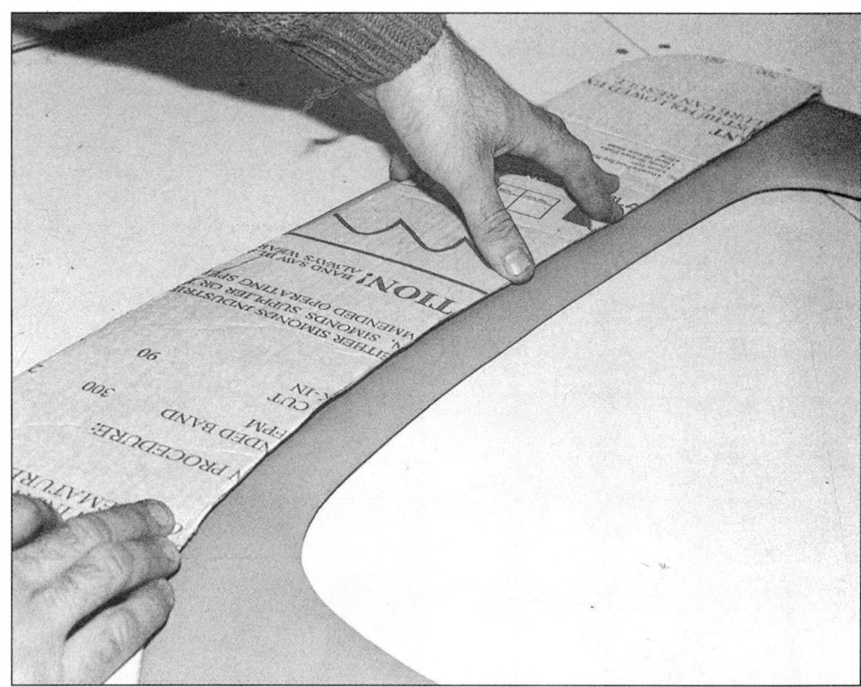

▲ *8.80. Once again, the template for the carpet section can be offered up to the panel, to ensure that all is well.*

▼ *8.81. The lower section of carpet can now be cut to shape and bound around its edges, as described in Chapter 10. The carpet can then be secured to the panel, and piping added around the perimeter of the panel, as described in Chapter 6.*

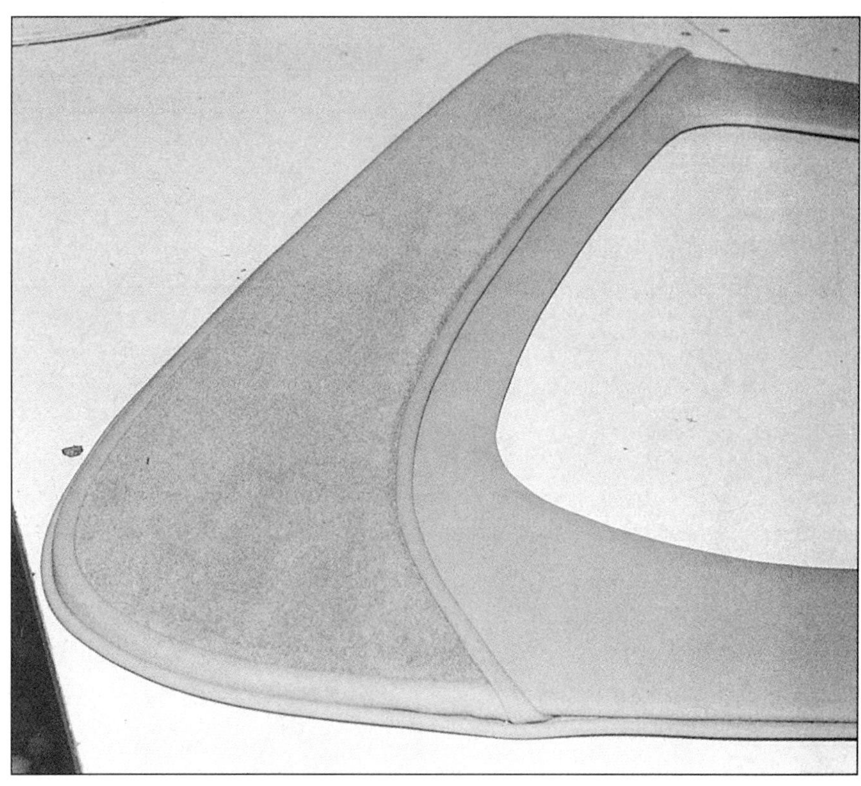

▼ *8.82. Similarly, the fluted section at the top of the panel is fabricated and secured to the panel. Note that staples are used along the upper edge.*

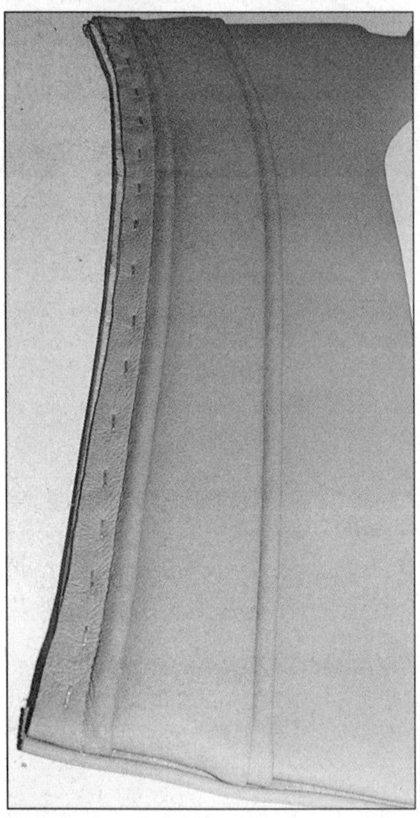

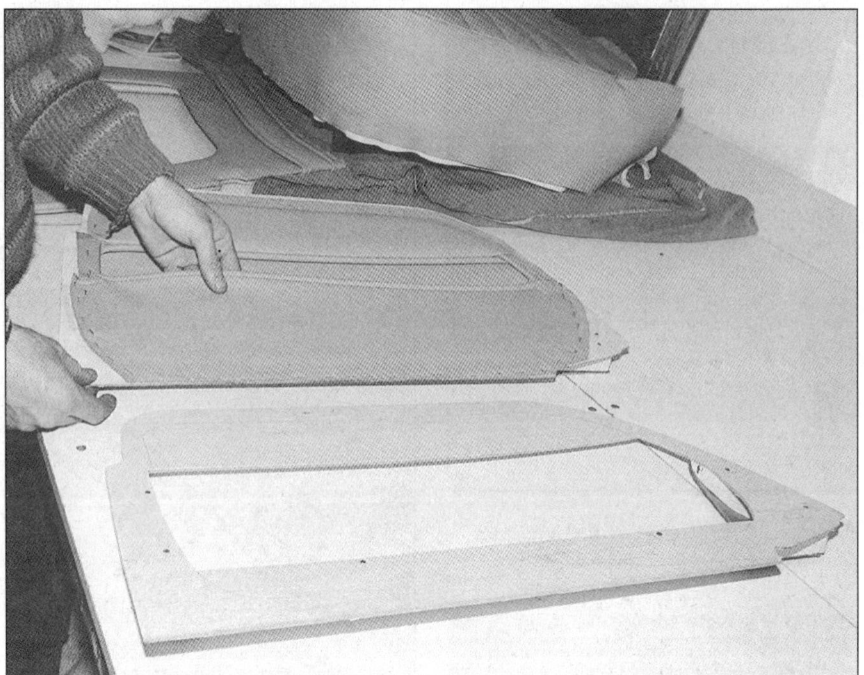

▲ *8.84. Using similar techniques to those already described, the leather coverings and their piping are built up as assemblies, and attached to the backing boards for the map pockets. The board in the foreground is in its raw state, that in the background has had the leather covering attached.*

▼ *8.83. Note that in addition to being glued in place, the piping is also stapled to the back of the panel to form a strong and secure edge.*

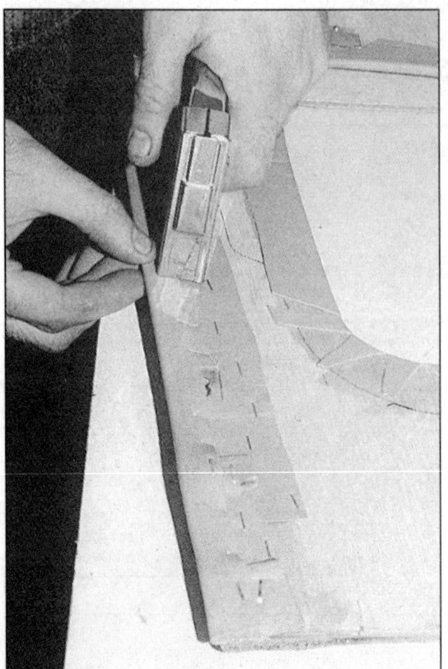

▼ *8.85. This is what the map pocket backing board looks like from the rear, with the leather covering stapled to it. Use plenty of staples for a secure job. Once complete, the assembly is simply clipped to the main door trim panel, using the clips made earlier.*

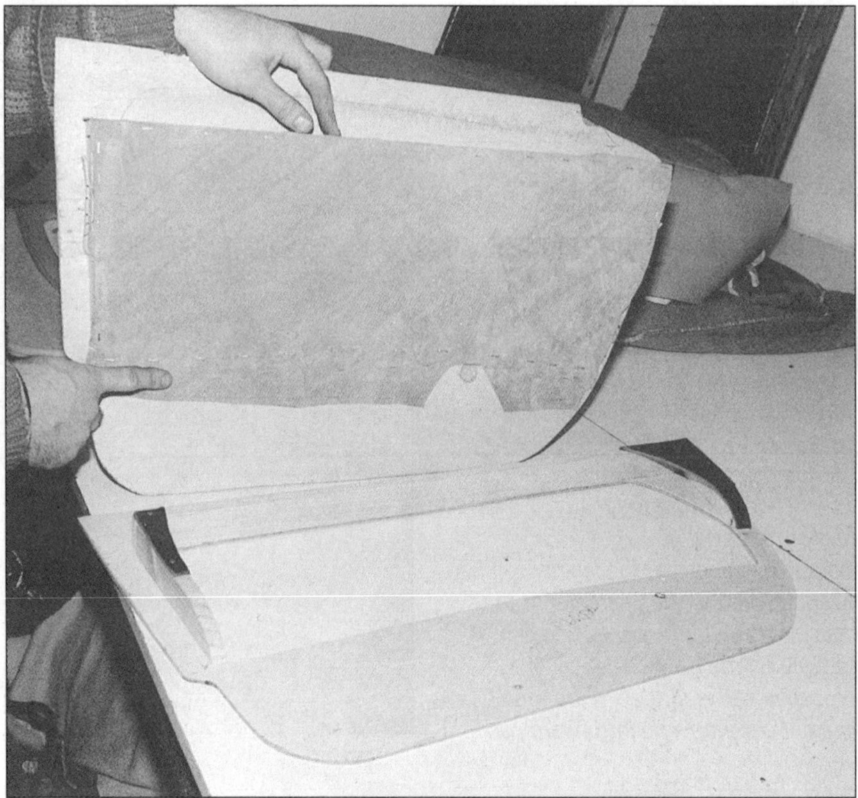

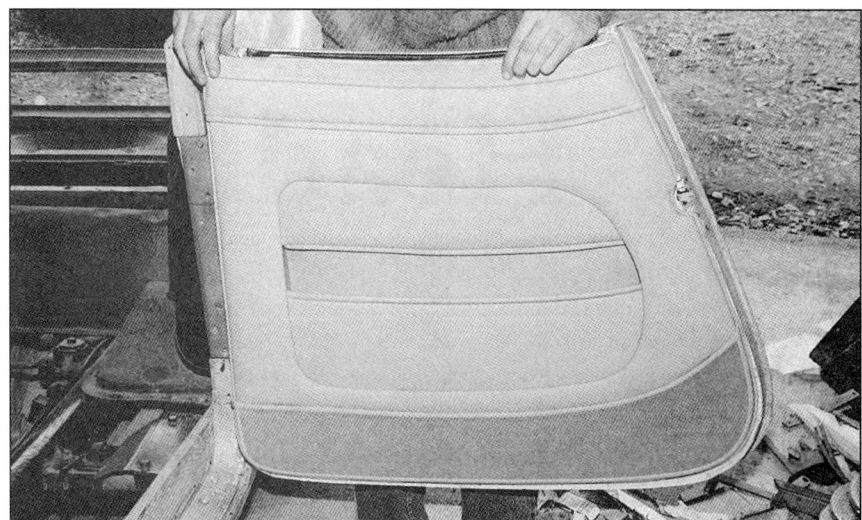

▶ *8.86. The finished panel. Results like this really do justify the time and effort put in. Assembled with care, your trim panels should be on show for many years to come, and it is very rewarding to know that they are all your own work!*

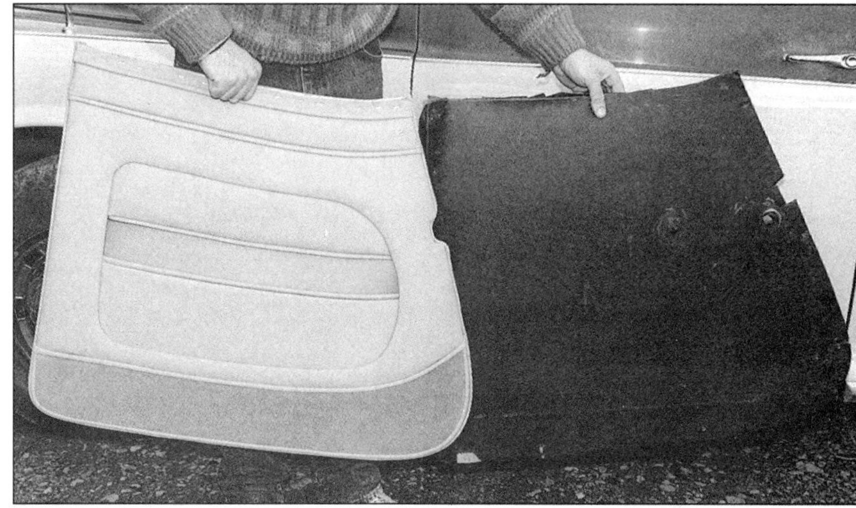

▶ *8.87. Just a reminder of the panel (plain, covered in vinyl and totally incorrect) as fitted to the car when acquired (on the right), and the new as-original, leather-covered panel, complete with map pocket, carpet trim and fluting (on the left). Well worth all the effort.*

▼ *8.88. Similar techniques can be applied to producing any trim panels for the vehicle, including those in the boot. Cardboard templates, made from old packing cases, etc., can be invaluable. Their inherent flexibility makes them easy to work with.*

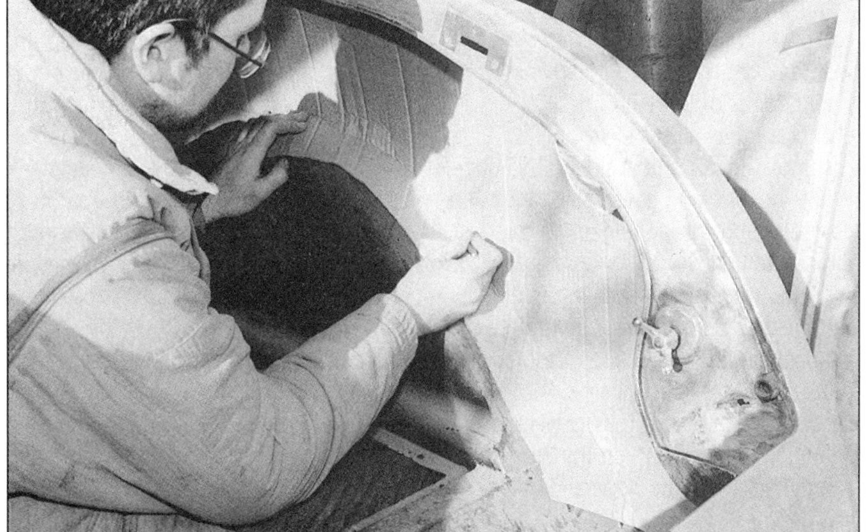

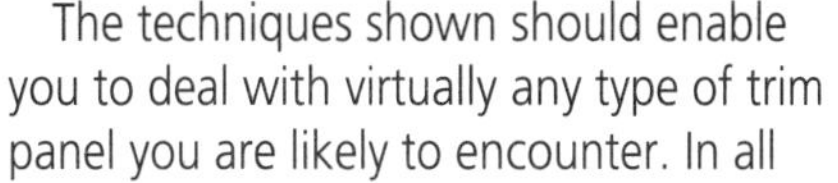

The techniques shown should enable you to deal with virtually any type of trim panel you are likely to encounter. In all

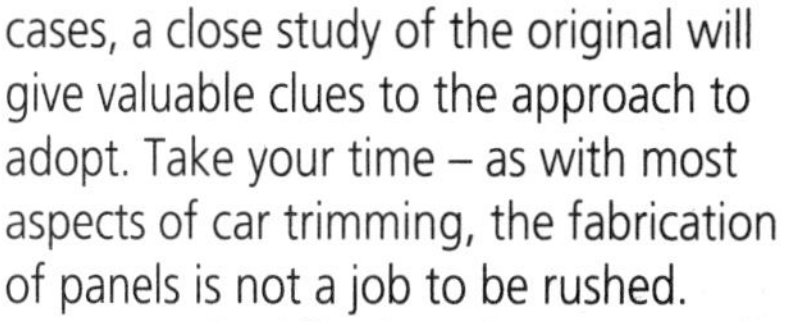

cases, a close study of the original will give valuable clues to the approach to adopt. Take your time – as with most aspects of car trimming, the fabrication of panels is not a job to be rushed.

It is usually difficult to disguise a badly damaged trim panel by patching. Normally re-covering or replacement will be required if the affected area is extensive. However, small areas of damage can be made to look less conspicuous by careful patching, using similar techniques to those shown in Chapter 6 under the sections entitled 'Patch repairs' and 'Repair kit'.

One final tip – sometimes it is difficult to insert items such as ash trays, bright finishers, grilles and so on into newly made trim panels. In such cases, the application of a little thread lubricant will often aid fitting.

Chapter 9
Headlinings

All cars have some form of headlining (headliner) which serves to insulate the roof panel of the vehicle, and to give a warm, comfortable feel to the interior. Perhaps surprisingly, headlinings likely to be encountered are all variations on a remarkably small number of main themes.

In many older (especially pre-war) vehicles, specially made folds in the headlining material were simply nailed to the wooden cross-members within the car's roof. More recent alternatives include the fixing of the headlining material to a sprung steel frame, or looped onto cross-bars (lists) which hold the material taut across the roof.

Modern cars (and some older models – like Jaguars from the late 1960s on) almost invariably have one-piece headlinings, often comprising compressed fibreboard covered by a foam-backed nylon (or similar) lining.

Regardless of the type fitted, eventually they all suffer from accumulated dirt and accidental damage. While the dirt can be removed, tears and disintegration through ageing are difficult to conceal.

There comes a point when the only sensible course of action is to replace the headlining with a new one. Although this is usually seen as a very difficult job, it can prove far easier than generally imagined – depending on the type of headlining fitted and how careful/lucky you are!

GENERAL TIPS

In all cases, reference to the original headlining should be made when planning to fabricate a replacement. Before you take out the old unit, make notes – especially with regard to unusual items – of the positioning of accessories (such as interior lamps, sun blinds and their clips, vanity mirrors, and so on). It is also a good idea to take a number of photographs, and/or some video footage, of the interior before you start work.

Try to remove the old headlining unit as a whole, and carefully label and store all related items. Keep them all in one place so that they can easily be traced when the time comes for reassembly.

It is perhaps obvious, but it is best to remove all the seats from the car before attempting to remove the headlining. Not only will this give you more room in which to work, but in some cars (especially small ones, and those with the linings mounted on frames) it is just not possible to remove the headlining with the seats in position.

If the original headlining material has been completely destroyed, or even if just a single section is missing, be sure to measure (or take a pattern from) the original frame/bars while still in place in the vehicle.

In all cases, it is essential to keep the new headlining material as clean as possible during fabrication and fitting operations. In particular, avoid touching the material with greasy hands – wash them frequently.

If you do mark the material, the chances of rectification will depend on the type of material you are using. However, in most cases, gentle use of the appropriate proprietary cleaning agents will do the trick.

For stubborn grease marks on cloth linings, a *little* spirit wipe solution (as intended for removing grease, dust, etc., from car bodywork prior to respraying), applied sympathetically with a soft cloth, can work where other methods fail.

PRE-WAR HEADLININGS

To illustrate the techniques applying to many pre-war cars, the following sequence shows removal and refitting of a headlining on a Rolls-Royce 20-25HP model. Although this beautiful old coachbuilt car incorporates some fixtures not found on all cars, its headlining is typical in terms of construction and fitting.

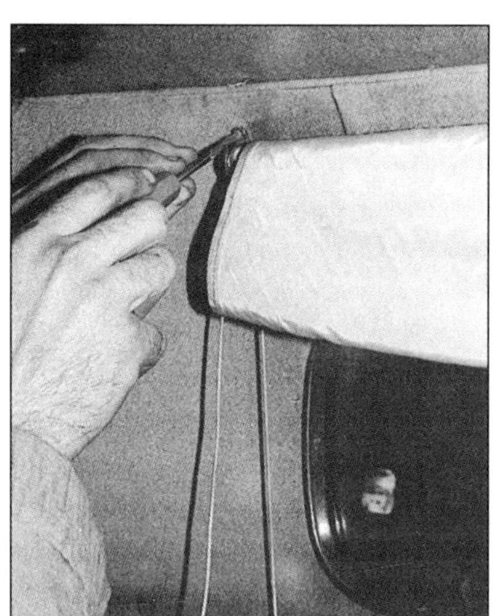

▲ *9.1. Start by removing the rear window blind, where fitted. Take out the screws securing the blind to the wood framing within the roof, and also the operating cord and supporting clips for this, where used. In some cars, like this Rolls-Royce, the operating cord passes through an aperture in the headlining, and into a hidden tube (visible in picture 9.25). The tube runs behind the headlining to the front of the car, where the cord emerges.*

▶ *9.2. On many older cars the rear window frame is secured around its perimeter by screws (although sometimes tack-on braid is used as an alternative). Remove the screws ...*

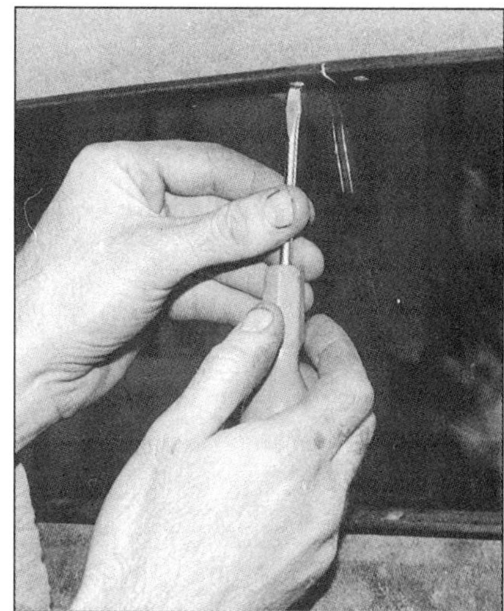

▼ *9.3. ... and then carefully extract the frame. It may need to be gently prised out of its aperture.*

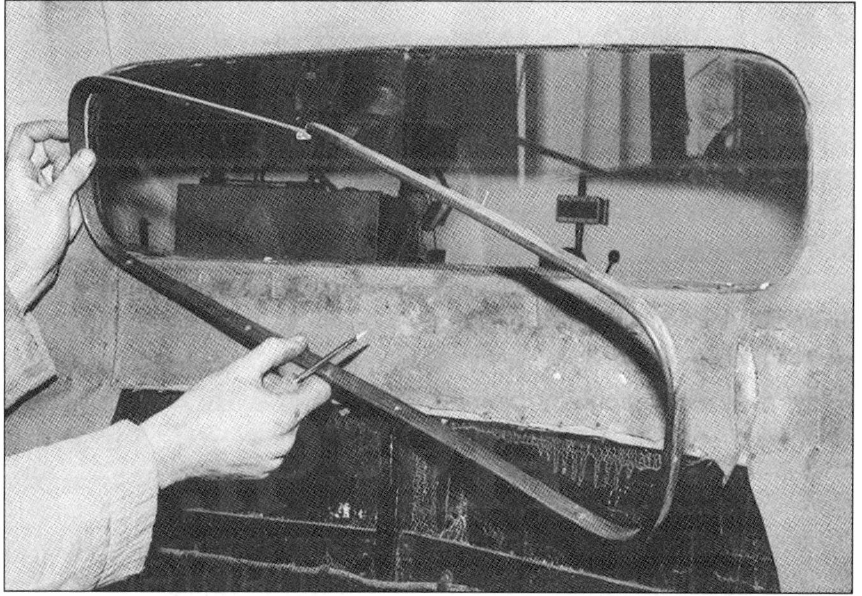

▲ *9.4. The ashtrays, where fitted, must also come out. Lift out the tray, unscrew the backing and lift these parts away.*

▲ *9.5. The wooden frames surrounding the ashtrays must also be gently encouraged from their surroundings.*

▲ *9.6. The rope pull handles are released by removing their securing screws.*

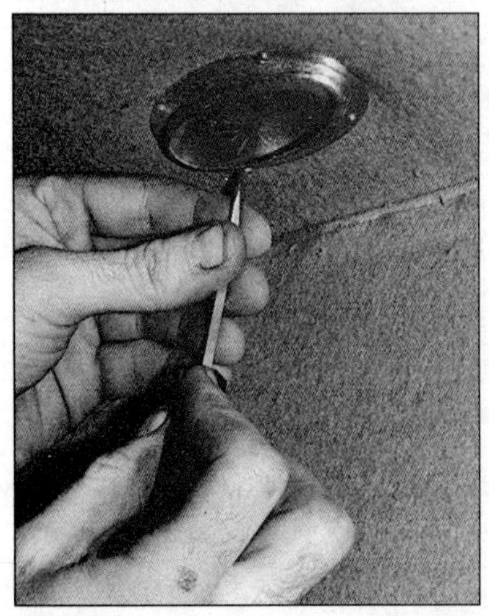

▲ *9.7. Take care when removing the interior lamp(s) that the glass does not fall and break. The bezel is usually secured by screws around its perimeter which, once slackened, release the lens into the hands of gravity!*

▲ *9.8. Gently ease the lower sections of the rear part of the headlining away from the edges of the roof. It is essential that the lining material is salvaged in one piece (for use as a template for the replacement headlining) so take great care, especially if it feels very brittle.*

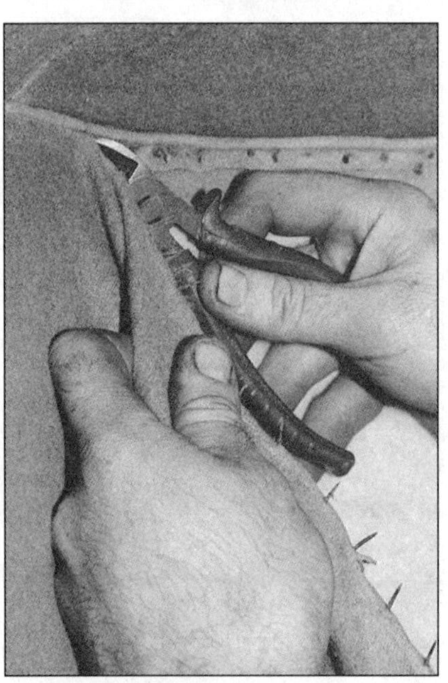

▲ *9.9. Reluctant tacks can be encouraged from the wood by careful levering with a pair of side cutters, or similar implements. Again, avoid damaging the headlining material.*

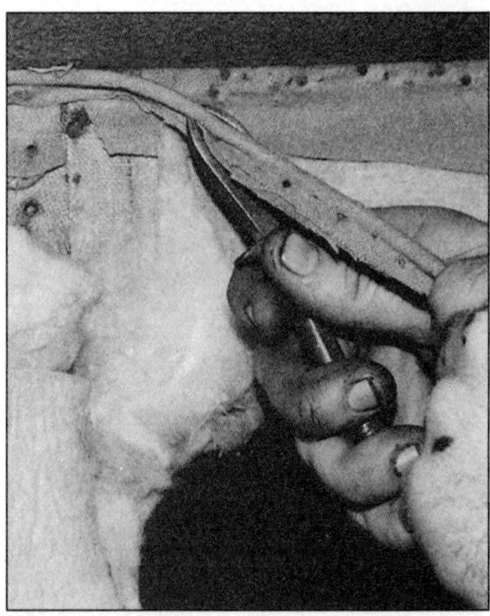

▲ *9.10. The piping between the vertical and horizontal sections of the lining can now be gently pulled away. Again, a pair of side cutters can be a great help during this operation. Try to remove as many tacks as possible as you go. Inevitably, though, some will remain behind and will have to be withdrawn later. This car had been reupholstered previously, and the original set of tacks had been left in place at that time!*

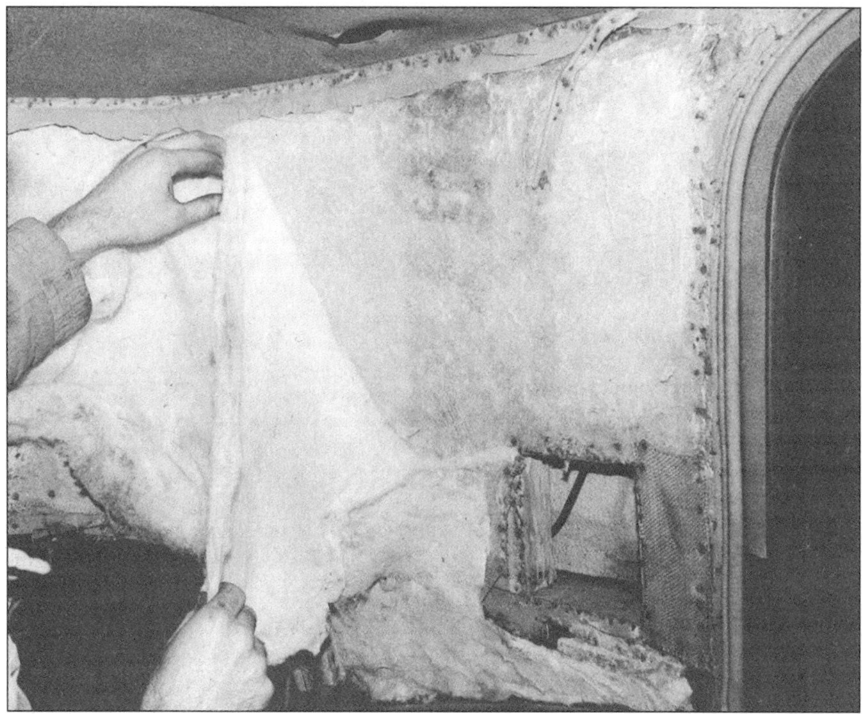

▲ *9.11. The padding can now be pulled away from the wood framework to which it is tacked. For now, the topmost section of the rear headlining can remain in place, while attention is focused on the front end.*

▲ *9.13. The door pillar trims are next to go. In most cases these are simply screwed in place.*

▼ *9.14. The closing latch for the sun roof, along with the locking catches and rails, must be unscrewed and safely stowed away.*

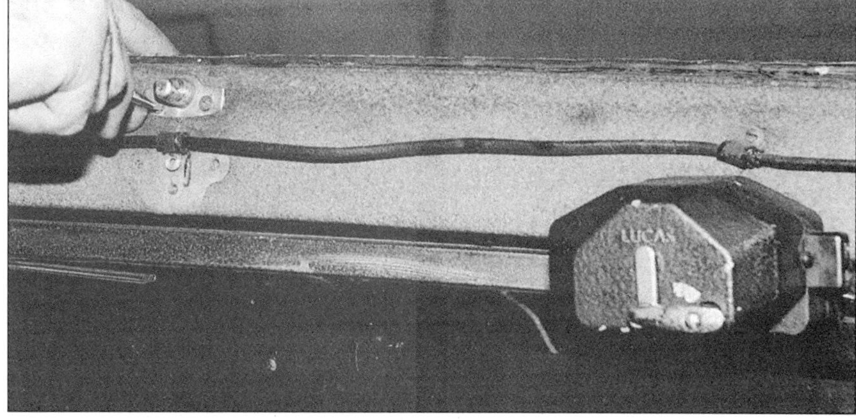

▼ *9.12. The cover strips along the sides of the sun roof (where fitted) must be removed to free the headlining, which is also secured here.*

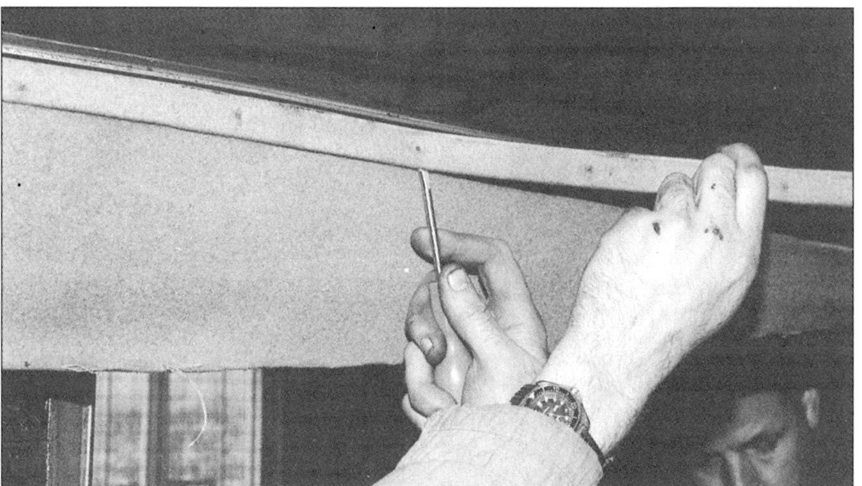

▼ *9.15. Off, too, must come the wiper motors and wiring, where mounted on top of the headlining as in this Rolls-Royce.*

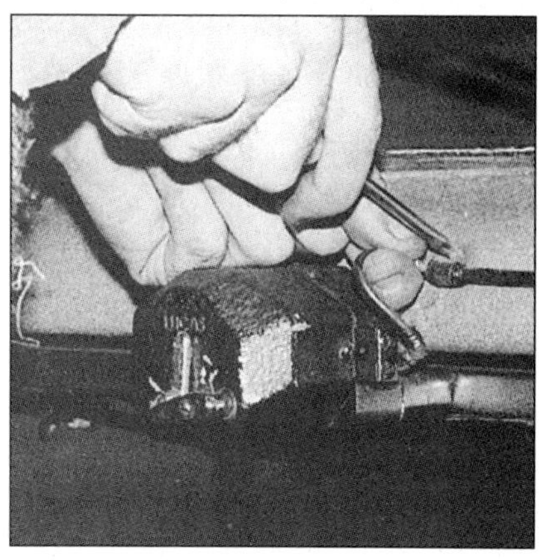

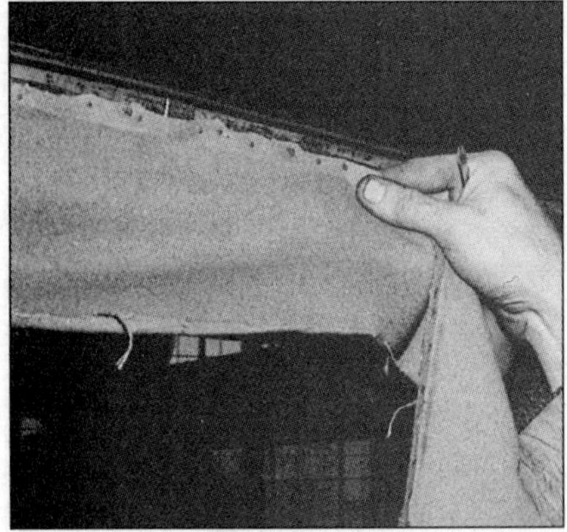

▲ *9.16. The cloth-covered board above the windscreen header rail, and the two wings of the headlining on either side of the sun roof, can be detached next. Try to keep the material intact.*

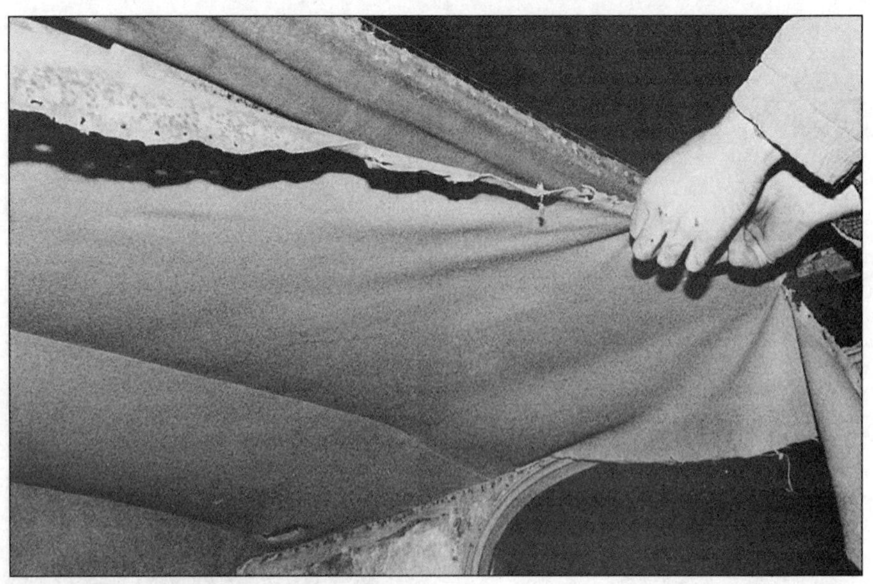

▲ *9.19. … while the material is freed from the rear edge of the sun roof aperture.*

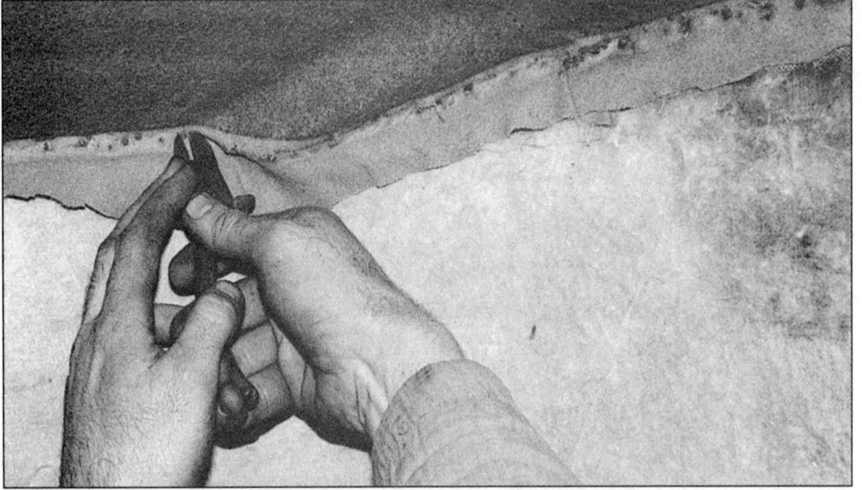

▲ *9.17. The tacks securing the extreme rear section of the headlining can now be eased out.*

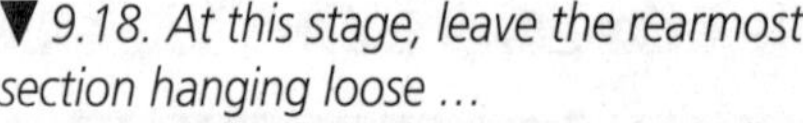

▼ *9.18. At this stage, leave the rearmost section hanging loose …*

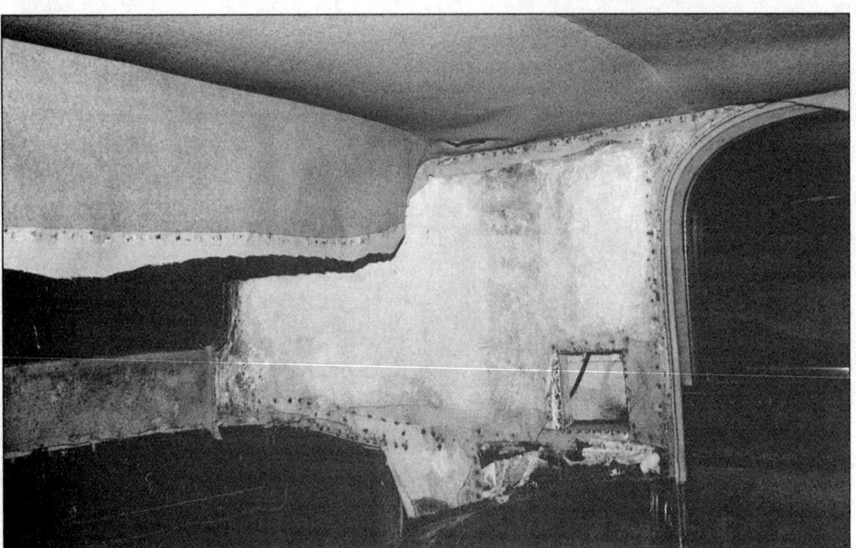

▲ *9.20. With the forward and rear ends of the main section of the headlining now freed, it is a relatively straightforward job to detach the folds in the material and their securing tacks from the wooden cross-members in the roof.*

▶ 9.21. *The piping above and around the door apertures now needs to be removed. Once again, side cutters are useful for this job.*

▼ 9.22. *Now the laborious task of taking out all redundant tacks can begin in earnest. This staple and tack removal tool from Frost Auto Restoration Techniques Ltd can help in this job.*

▼ 9.23. *Using the removed headlining sections as patterns, mark out the new material in the same way as described in the previous chapter so that replacements can be fabricated. Always aim to use materials with texture and quality as close as possible to original.*

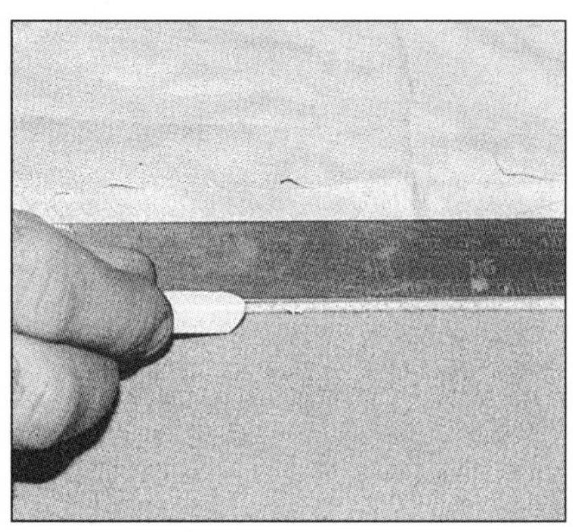

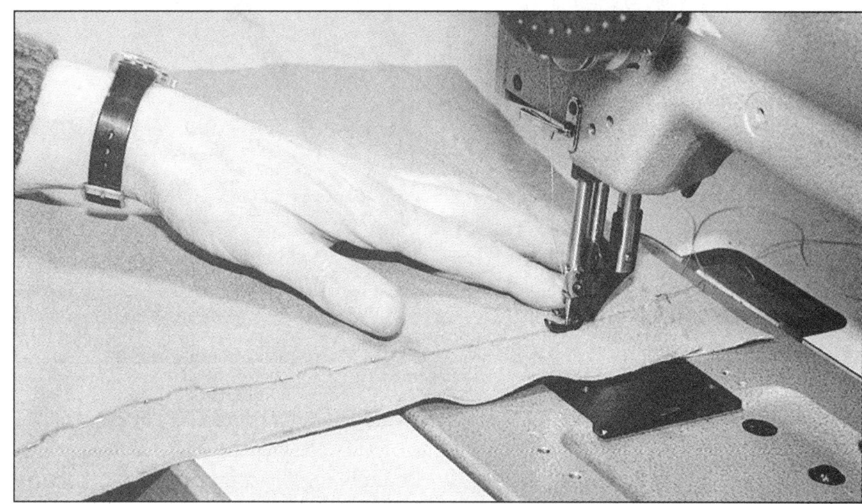

▲ 9.24. *Using the original headlining as a guide, again, folds must be sewn into the new assembly at the appropriate points, to provide the means for fastening to the roof of the car.*

Always make a thorough check on the condition of the woodwork forming the framework within the roof, also the inside of the roof panel itself, and items such as sun roof drain tubes, etc. Remedial work to these items – and to accessories – should obviously be carried out while the headlining is out!

Installing the replacement headlining assembly must be carried out in the reverse order to dismantling. Ensure that you have available a proper, magnetic hammer and an adequate supply of tacks. A staple gun can be an invaluable aid in this work, too. It is particularly useful if you are working on your own, for holding material in the correct position until a series of tacks can be applied.

To avoid duplication of all the stages shown under the dismantling procedures, in the following sequence I have concentrated on the techniques required for reassembly, and have deliberately not included shots of *every* operation.

▶ 9.25. On the Rolls-Royce the first section to be installed was the vertical panel at the rear, having first cut to shape and tacked in place cotton padding material and hessian to match the originals. This was initially stapled, then tacked in position to the wooden rails across the top of the window and around the back of the seat. Where there are to be several layers of material tacked in place along the same rail, leave sufficiently large gaps between the tacks in the first row, since each layer of material adds further tacks, and available space for them is soon used up! Ensure that, initially, the aperture cut for the rear window is rather smaller than the actual dimensions of the window – final trimming can take place later. Just visible at the top left of the picture is the tube which accommodates the roller blind operating cord, as described in caption 9.1.

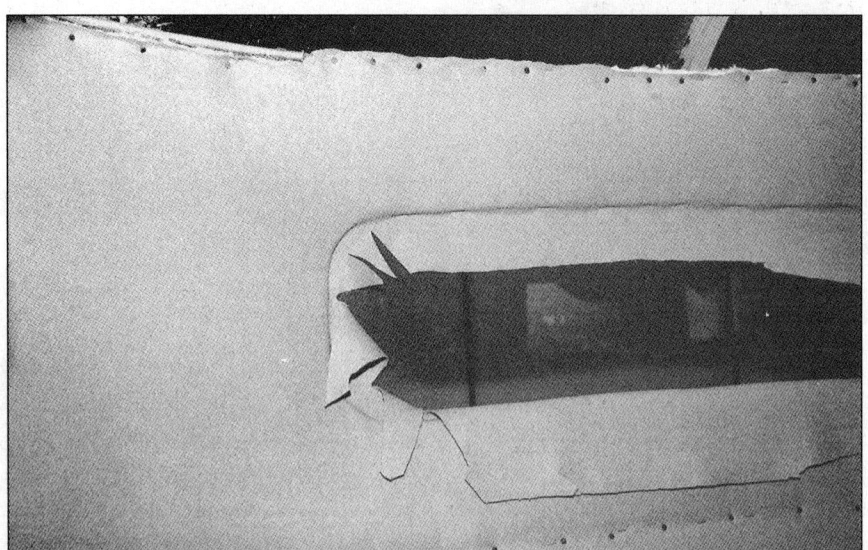

▶ 9.26. When installing the main, uppermost section of the new lining, start at the rearmost wooden cross-rail, tacking the headlining to the frame using a magnetic hammer designed for the job. Always start in the centre of the rail, and work outwards towards each side of the car, ensuring that all creases are eliminated as you do so. Stretch the material gently and evenly towards the front of the car, and repeat the process on the next rail.

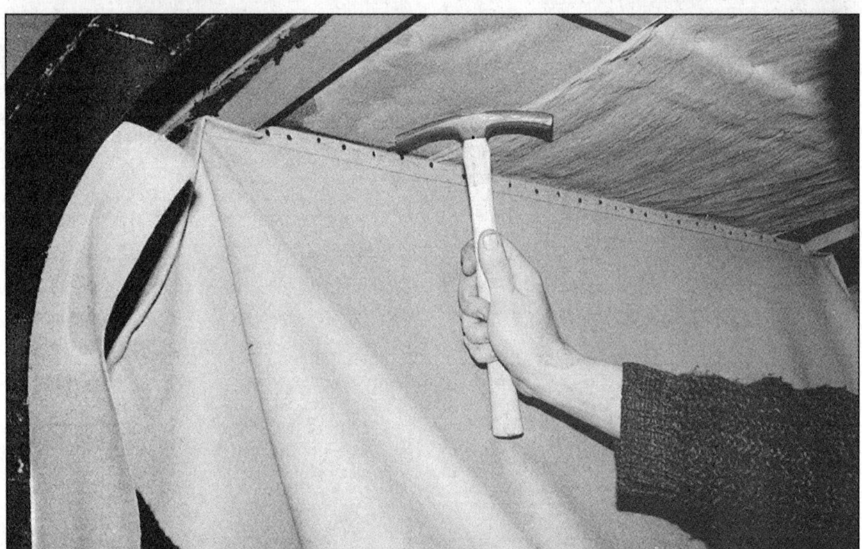

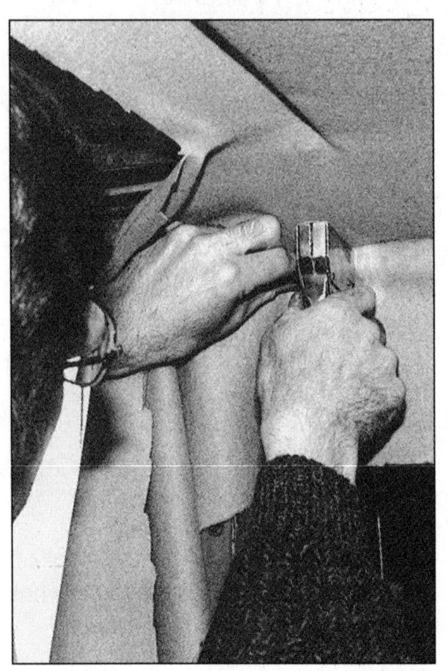

◀ 9.27. Taking great care, again pull the material towards the front of the car, and temporarily staple in place along the rail at the rear of the sun roof aperture (fine adjustments can then be made to the positioning of the cloth, if required). The material can now be secured along the sides of the roof. Again, the staple gun can be used, initially. Don't use too many staples in these early stages – just in case they have to come out again!

▶ 9.28. The wings of the headlining running forwards on either side of the sun roof aperture can now be secured, too.

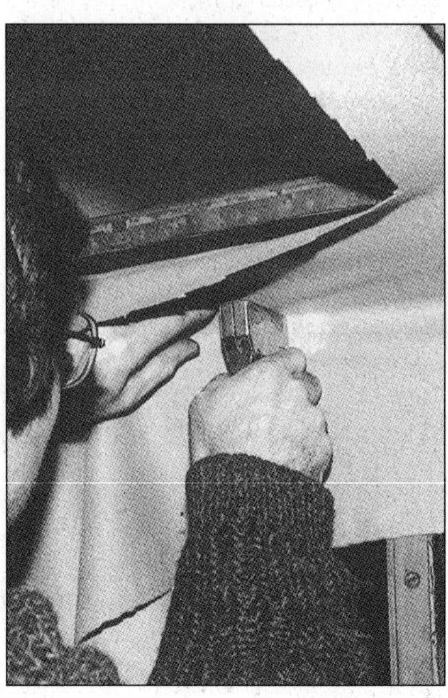

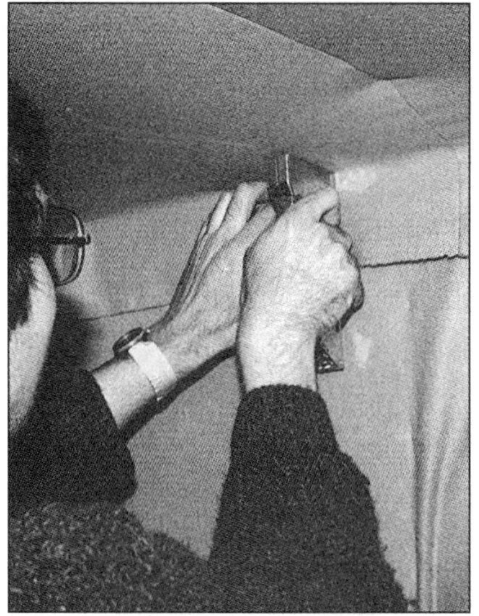

▲ *9.29. Similarly, work backwards along the edges of the main section of the roof lining which, as can be seen, is positioned here on top of the rear, vertical section of the lining. Note that, depending on the construction of the headlining, often the rear section of the lining can be positioned on top of the main section of the roof lining. In every case, close study of the original will give clues to the best approach.*

▼ *9.30. Check on the fit of the material, in particular looking for creases and undue stretching. If necessary, carefully remove the staples and re-position the cloth. When all is well – and not before – secure the lining in the correct position by means of tacks. Here the lining is being secured to the rear edge of the sun roof aperture.*

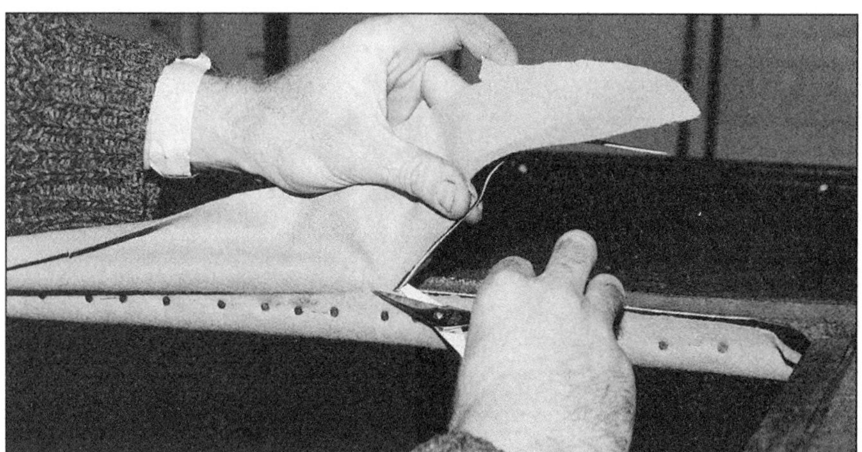

▲ *9.31. Using a sharp craft/upholstery knife and/or a pair of scissors, carefully trim the excess material from around the sun roof aperture.*

▼ *9.32. The rear of the interior will now look like this, and further trimming is required …*

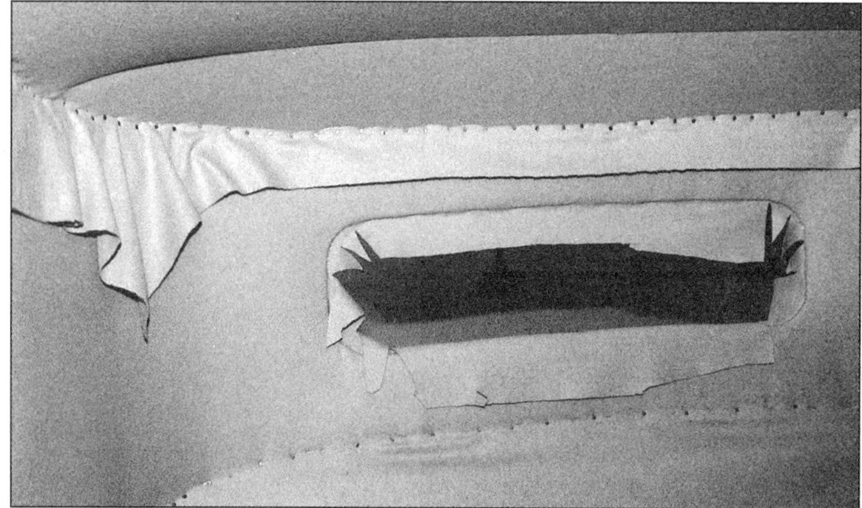

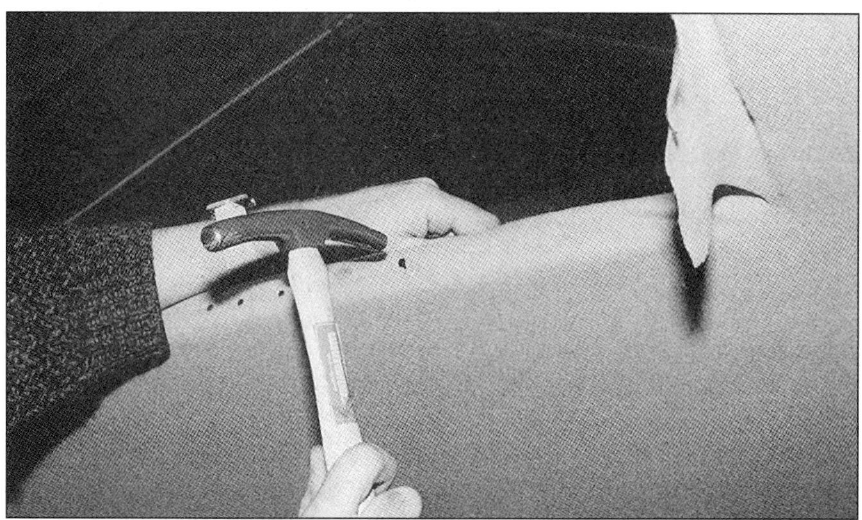

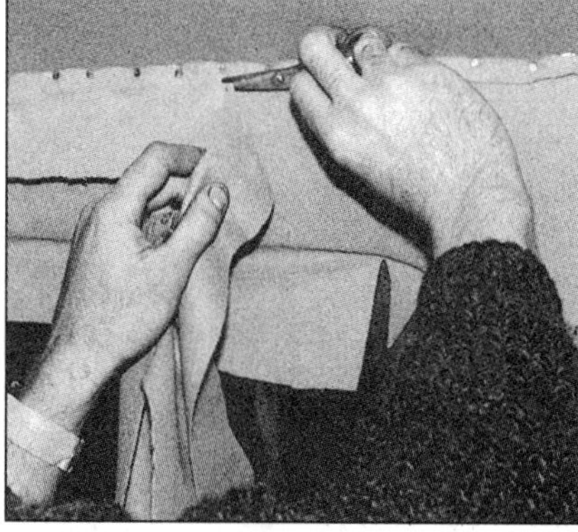

▲ *9.33. … around the perimeter of the main section of roof lining. Take extreme care not to damage the adjacent material during this operation. At this stage, leave in place the excess material around the window aperture.*

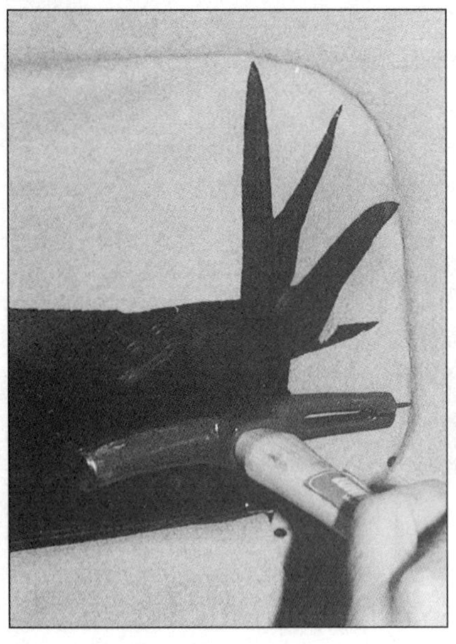

▲ *9.34. Now install a series of tacks to secure the headlining material around the rear window aperture, having first trial-fitted the window frame and marked on the cloth the positions of the fixing screws, using a sharp pencil applied through the holes in the frame. This will show where not to put the tacks, and will avoid the awkward situation in which a retaining screw cannot be fitted because a tack has been installed in its way! Use the magnetic hammer to apply the tacks. Go very carefully here, to avoid breaking the window!*

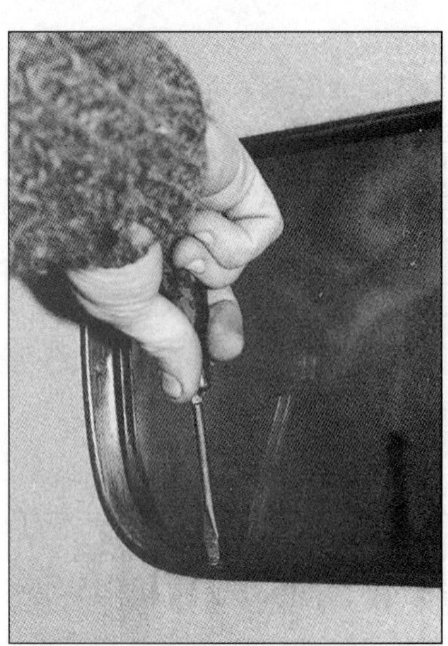

▶ *9.36. When the frame is correctly positioned, its retaining screws can be fitted and fully tightened.*

Note that there are many ways of fixing the edges of the headlining in place, including, on some cars, the use of cellulose strips wrapped into the perimeter of the headlining material and tacked in position, or by the application of 'hidem' banding.

In every case, a close study of the original components is worthwhile, and will determine the method used at the factory (or by the last restorer!). The owner of this Rolls-Royce specifically wanted to use 'hidem' banding.

▼ *9.35. The excess material around the window can now be trimmed off, and the window frame re-installed. This may require a little gentle 'push and shove' to make it fit properly!*

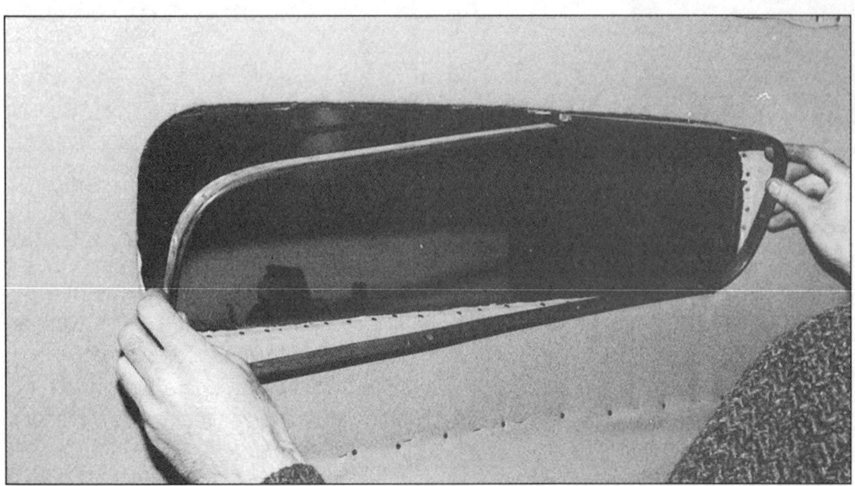

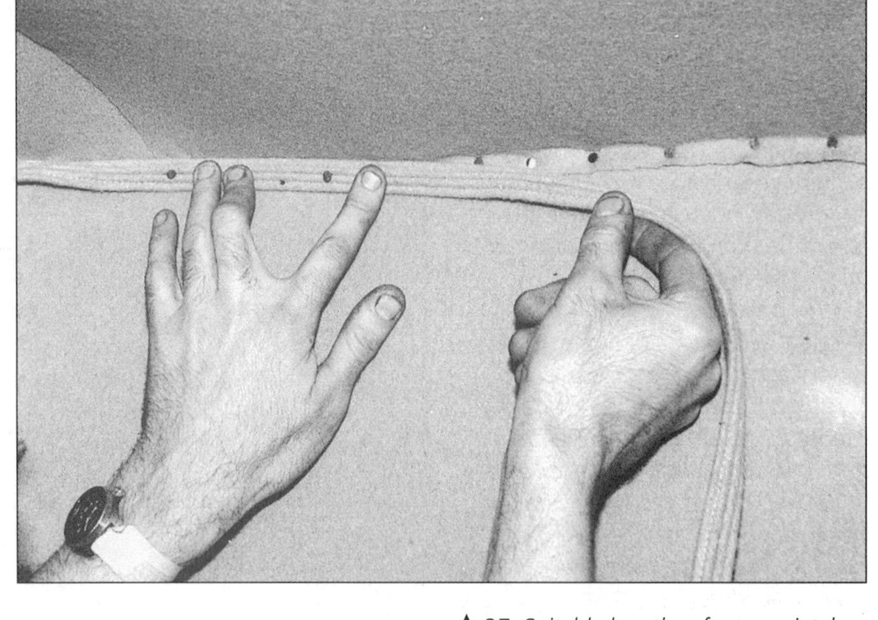

▲ *37. Suitable lengths of appropriately named 'hidem' banding can then be fitted to cover the row of tacks around the upper section of the headlining. When the banding is correctly positioned, a small parallel punch can be used to drive the securing tacks fully home between the two flexible rails of the banding, which then conveniently close together over the heads of the tacks. Try to apply the 'hidem' banding as neatly as possible, and in a straight line, as errors in fitting will show! Note that where 'hidem' banding is to be used around the door apertures, the draught excluder must be tacked in place first.*

FRAMED HEADLININGS

Some cars – including a number of British models of the 1950s – were fitted with steel frames upon which the headlining material was mounted. The lining material was usually fitted to two, separate frames (front and rear), and each was installed as a complete unit once the headlining material was attached to it.

In theory, it should be relatively easy to remove the frames (which are sprung/screwed into place), and to refit them once the replacement lining has been made. However, when reinstalling, special care is needed so that the frames are not bent out of shape, and the new cloth lining is not damaged. Refitting can take time, too.

As previously stated, it is preferable – and in many cases imperative – to remove the seats from the vehicle, to allow more room in which to work, and to enable the large steel frames to be extricated from the bodywork without damage to either the frames or the seats.

Where separate front and rear frames are employed, the front unit is normally clipped to the rear frame. The clips can either face to the front or the rear, and it may not be apparent from a visual examination which applies. Always consult the workshop manual or, where available, the parts list for your vehicle. Often these give invaluable information, diagrams and so on, relevant to the construction and fitting of the headlining frames.

Another important aspect which should be borne in mind is that usually, where framed headlinings were fitted during manufacture of the vehicle, the material was glued to the body shell around the rear window aperture. This means that the rear window will have to be removed before the headlining is taken out, and can only be refitted after the new headlining has been installed. Conversely, it is in some cases a definite advantage to refit a front windscreen, if removed (for example during a major restoration) *before* refitting the headlining. However, it is impossible to generalize, and in each case a study of the vehicle and the relevant technical data (workshop manual, etc.) will give an indication of the best way to approach the job.

Removal and refitting of front and rear screens is usually not difficult, but again it depends on the type of rubber seal employed. In most cases, once the bright trim strips (where fitted) have been released, and the original bond between the body and the rubber seal has been broken (this can be achieved by running an old, blunt screwdriver around the perimeter of the window between the seal and the body), the glass can be encouraged from the vehicle by the application of firm but gentle pressure.

It is wise to have at least one assistant on hand on the opposite side of the glass to which pressure is being applied, as sometimes the glass is released suddenly, and needs to be caught before it breaks! Study the workshop manual before you start work – sometimes the glass is released into the vehicle from outside, although in most cases the glass was originally fitted from the outside.

When refitting screens, a length of nylon cord, a foot or two longer than the length of the perimeter of the rubber seal, can be used. Start by fitting the screen seal to the glass, gluing the cut ends of the seal together where the seal is not supplied as a one-piece unit. Now, by threading the cord into the groove in the seal which accommodates the steel lip around the window aperture (with, initially, the two ends of the cord emerging at the same point), the glass and its seal can be encouraged into position.

With the window positioned centrally within its aperture, and with an assistant applying firm pressure to hold the screen and rubber seal in the correct position, on the opposite side of the glass the two ends of the cord are gradually pulled outwards from their groove, in opposite directions. In so doing, the external lip of the rubber seal is also pulled out and over the bodywork flange, thereby holding the screen in place (this is shown in photograph 9.76).

This can be a time-consuming, nerve-racking job. If you are at all doubtful about tackling it, it would be best to leave it to the professionals – get them to remove the glass before you start work on the roof lining and, once the lining has been refitted, engage them again to refit the screen and its seal. More expensive, it's true, but probably cheaper than replacing a broken window glass.

Finally, on refitting the screen, sealing compound should be re-applied between the glass and the rubber seal, and between the rubber seal and the car bodywork, to keep out moisture.

To illustrate a typical headlining renovation on a car with a framed lining, the following sequence depicts the relevant stages on a 1955 Austin Cambridge. It should be noted that, to make it easier for photography, we removed the doors on this vehicle. In practice, this is not strictly necessary, although it does give easier access to the interior.

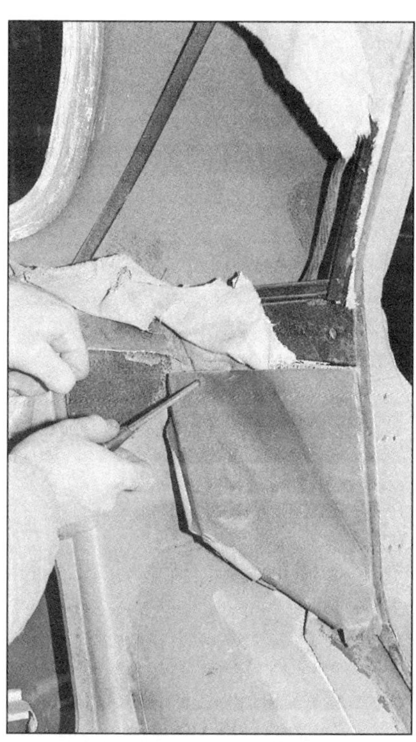

9.38. Unscrew/unclip any trim panels, etc., near to the headlining frame(s), to give more room in which to work. Items such as sun visors, interior mirrors and so on also need to be removed at this stage. This panel was obscuring the lower section of the rear headlining frame, and its retaining screw.

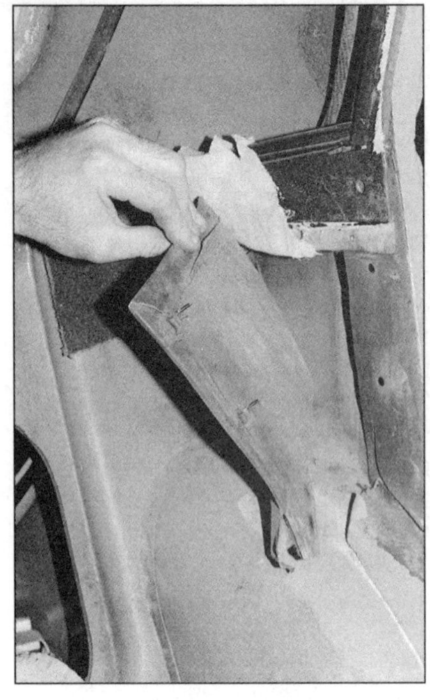

▲ 9.39. *This panel was screwed in at the rear, and clipped in at the front. Carefully pull away, preserving the panel so that it can be refitted later, or at least used as a pattern.*

▼ 9.40. *Now take out the retaining screws securing the headlining frame to the vehicle. Store the screws in a suitable receptacle, clearly labelled.*

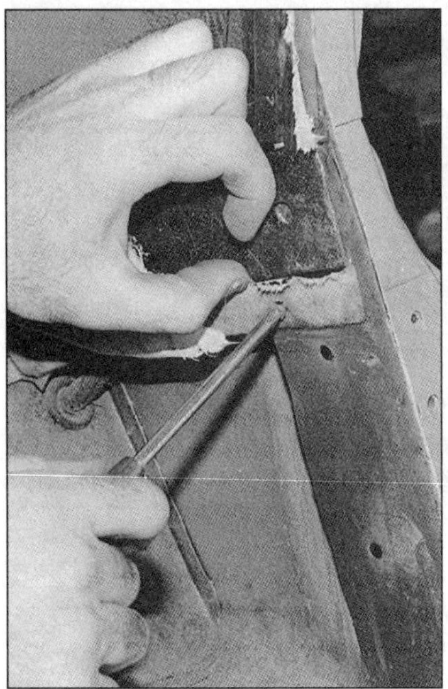

▲ 9.41. *On this Austin, the front frame, which has clips at its rear edge to engage with the rear frame, has to be removed first. Gently ease downwards the forward corners of the front frame, then ease the lining forwards to disengage the clips at the rear.*

▼ 9.42. *Use a long screwdriver or similar implement to encourage the side runners of the frame away from the roof of the vehicle. Take very great care not to bend the frame or damage the vehicle's roof.*

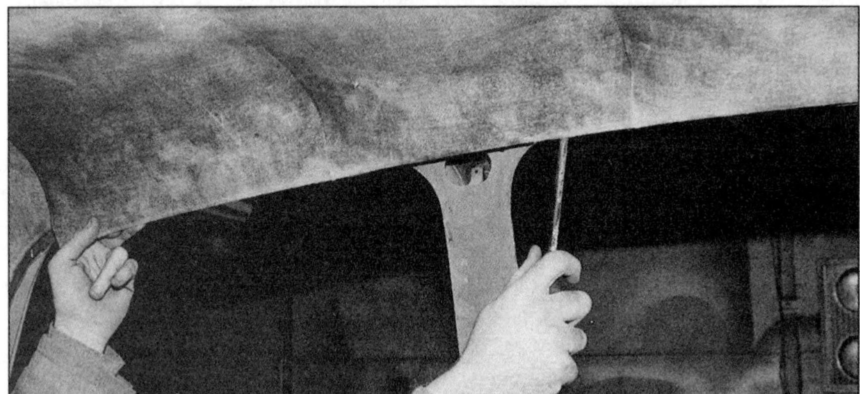

▲ 9.43. *Once the frame is relieved of tension around its perimeter, it can be gently lifted down from the roof of the vehicle, carefully disengaging any interior light wiring, etc., from the frame as it is lowered. The headlining unit can then be removed from the car.*

▶ 9.44. *The rear frame can now be disengaged from the side rails of the roof, and from the clips, where present, securing the rear edge of the frame to the rear parcel shelf. You may find screws in this area, too. Take care not to damage the frame or the rails in the removal process.*

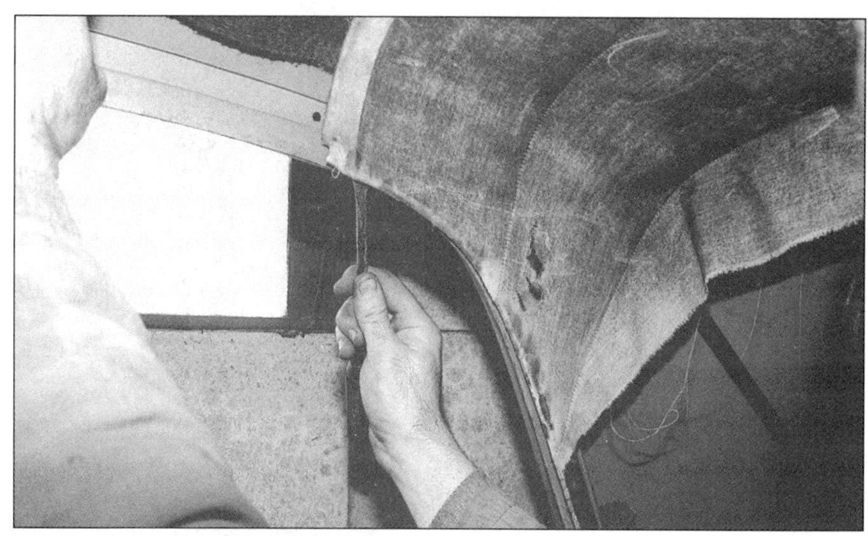

▼ 9.45. *The rear frame can now be removed. It is also wise to take out any sound deadening felt to assess the condition of the inside of the steel roof panel. In this car, the sound deadening fell out as the headlining frame was removed!*

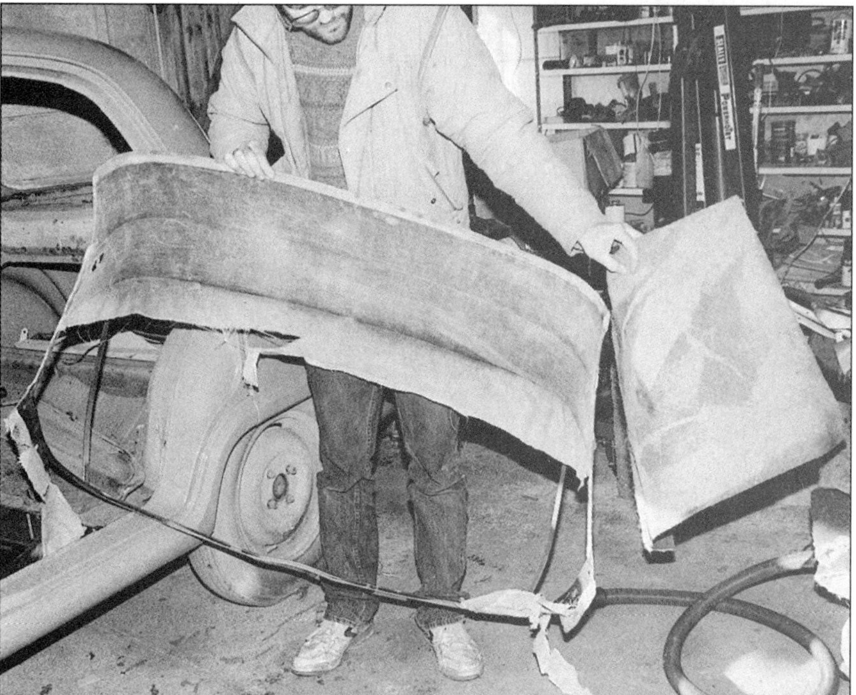

▼ 9.47. *Inspect the state of the steel panelwork forming the roof of the vehicle. If rust is found, this should be abraded away, using fairly coarse grit abrasive paper (wear goggles – gravity dictates that the debris will fall downwards, towards you!). The affected areas should then be treated to several coats of anti-rust paint, and be allowed to dry. In this case the roof was generally in excellent condition, with only a few patches of very minor surface rust, which were dealt with.*

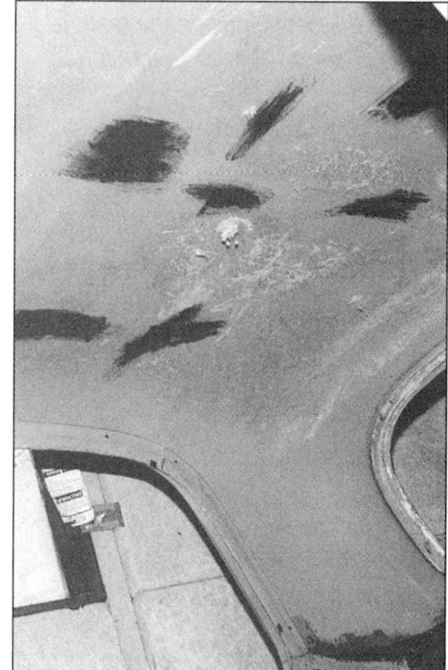

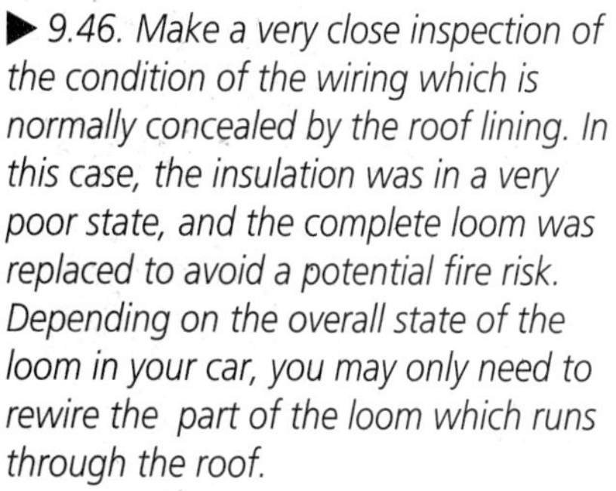

▶ 9.46. *Make a very close inspection of the condition of the wiring which is normally concealed by the roof lining. In this case, the insulation was in a very poor state, and the complete loom was replaced to avoid a potential fire risk. Depending on the overall state of the loom in your car, you may only need to rewire the part of the loom which runs through the roof.*

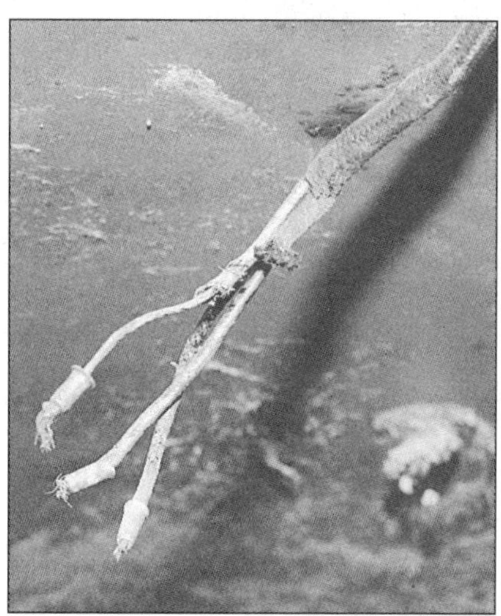

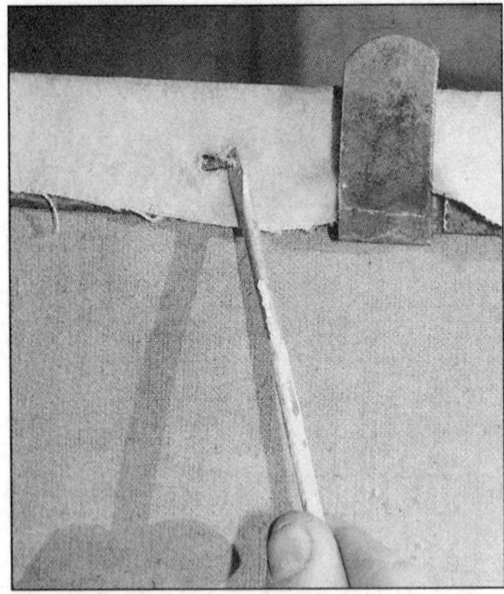

▲ 9.48. *Attention can now be turned to the headlining frames. Start by disengaging the retaining clips/spikes from the material, using a screwdriver, and taking care not to catch your hands on the sharp points of the clips. Go gently – these clips don't like being bent around too much, and can snap off.*

▼ 9.49. *The headlining material was originally stapled together around each of the cross bars in the frame. Carefully remove each staple, taking care to preserve the precise shape of the original lining. In this case the staples were so rusty that a gentle pull on the material was all that was needed to free it from the frame.*

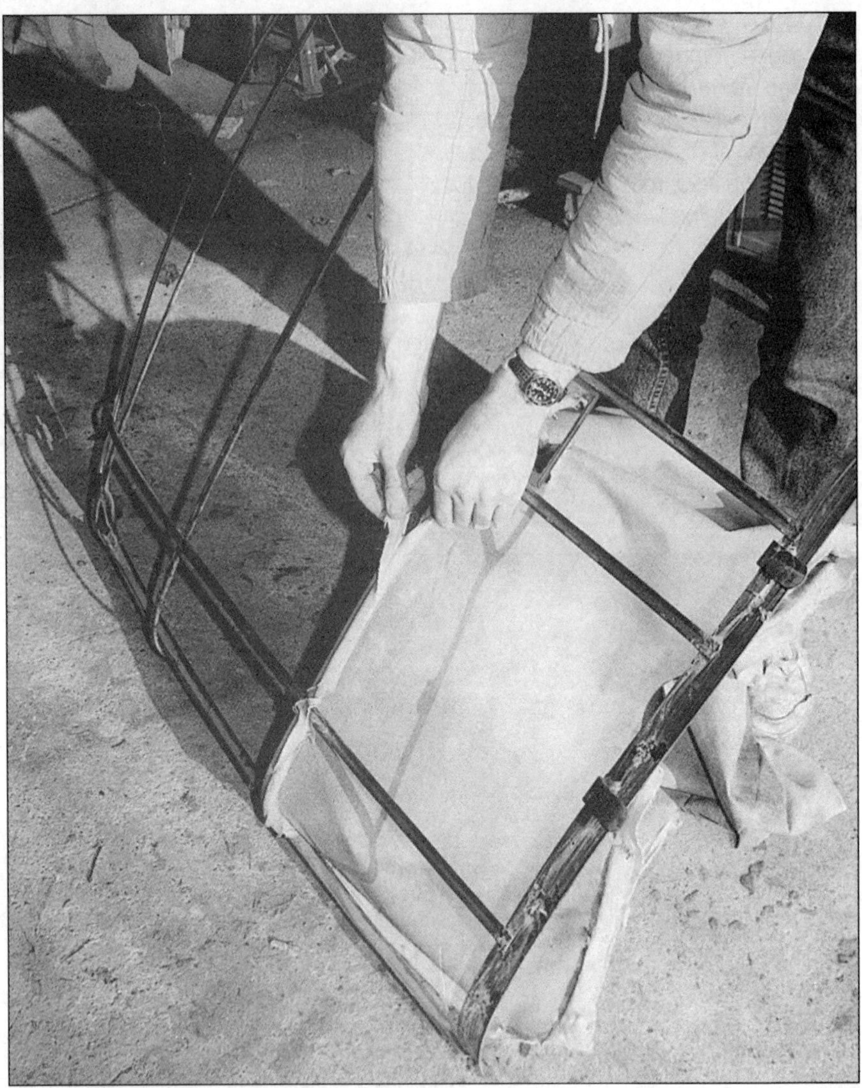

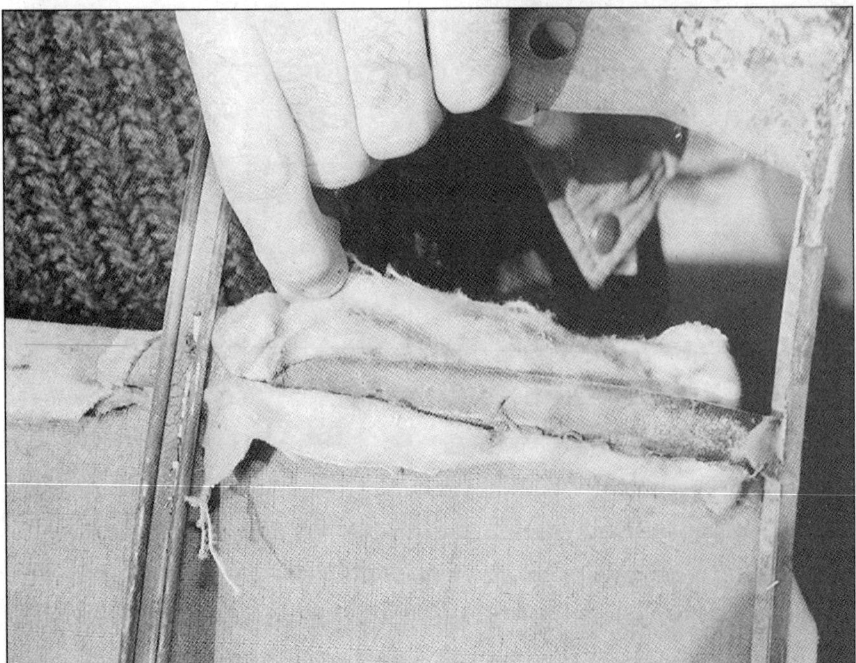

▲ 9.50. *Systematically work your way along the frame until all the lining material is free to be removed.*

▼ 9.51. *The next job is to examine the structure of the headlining frames, and to rid them of any rust which may be evident. Clean off all surface rust using a fairly coarse grit abrasive paper.*

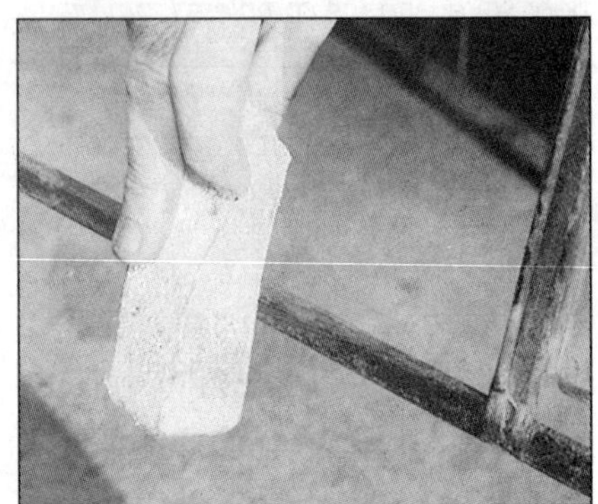

▶ *9.52. When all rust has been removed, brush on a rust-inhibiting paint, or apply primer and top coats, using an aerosol. Beware – some anti-rust paints react violently with some adhesives! If in doubt, form a test piece, applying the paint, allowing to dry, then coating the paint with adhesive.*

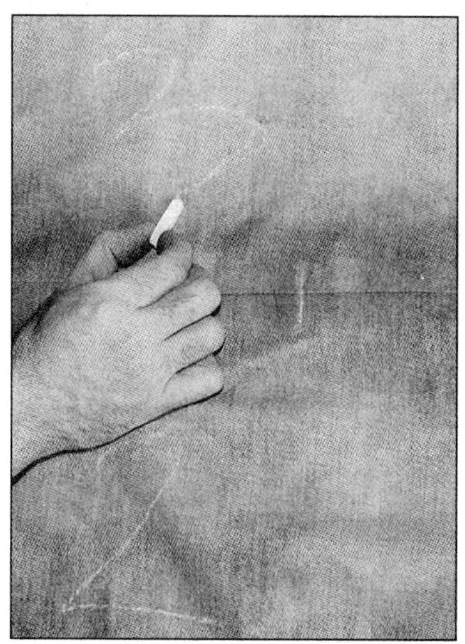

▲ *9.53. While the paint on the frames is drying, carefully mark adjacent sections of the original headlining with tailor's chalk, or a crayon. Along the border of each section, mark short lines between adjoining sections (as a guide to alignment), and number each section from the front to the rear of the car. This will help identify which piece goes where when constructing the new lining.*

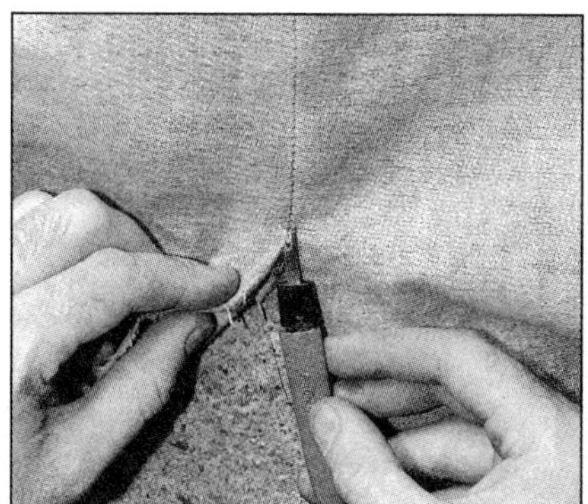

▲ *9.54. Now cut through the stitching joining together the original sections of lining, so that the lining is now split up into its constituent components.*

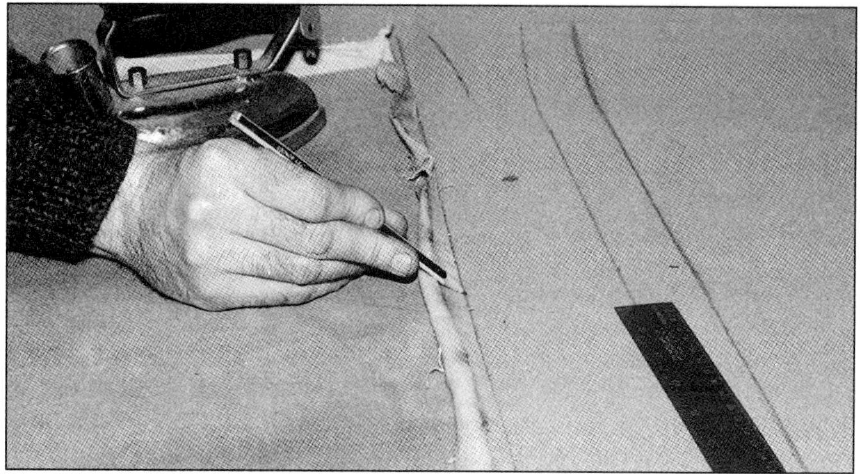

▲ *9.55. Use each section of the original lining as a template for the new material, which should, as far as possible, match the original in texture and colour. Using tailor's chalk or a pencil mark the position of the boundary of each section on the reverse of the new material. An old iron is useful to flatten and hold in place the original material, while you are marking out the perimeter of the section. As you proceed, mark each section of new material with the corresponding section number marked on the original lining. This should help to prevent mistakes.*

▼ *9.56. Make allowance for the width of the seam flange at the edge of each section, using the original as a guide, and mark on the material in the form of a line of dots. In this case the flange is very wide. When the various sections of the headlining have been sewn together, these flanges will be wrapped over the cross-bars of the headlining frames, and stapled/stitched in place to hold the material in the correct position on the frames.*

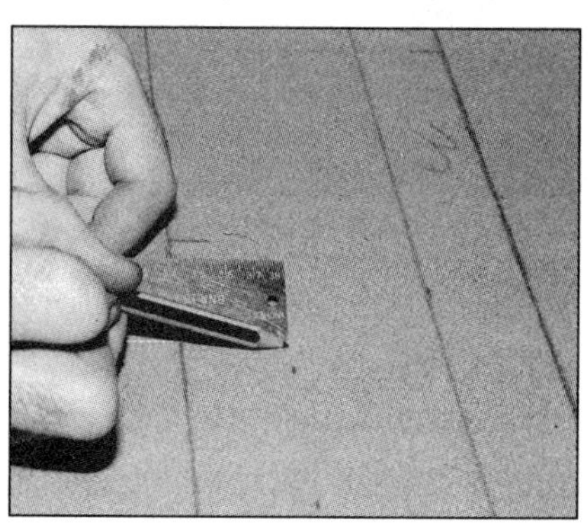

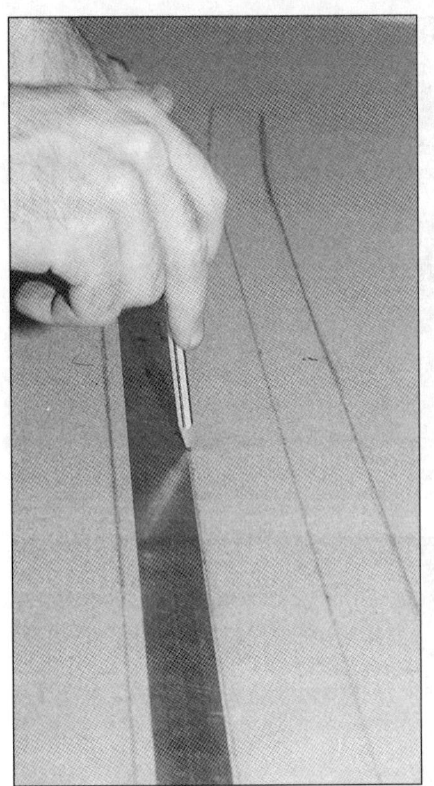

▲ *9.57. Now join up the dots to form a continuous line on the material.*

In some cases the material sections may be damaged or may even be missing. If so, use the frame to make paper patterns, which in turn can be applied to the new material.

▼ *9.58. When you are satisfied that you have marked out all the sections to the correct profile, they can be very carefully cut out using a sharp pair of shears or scissors.*

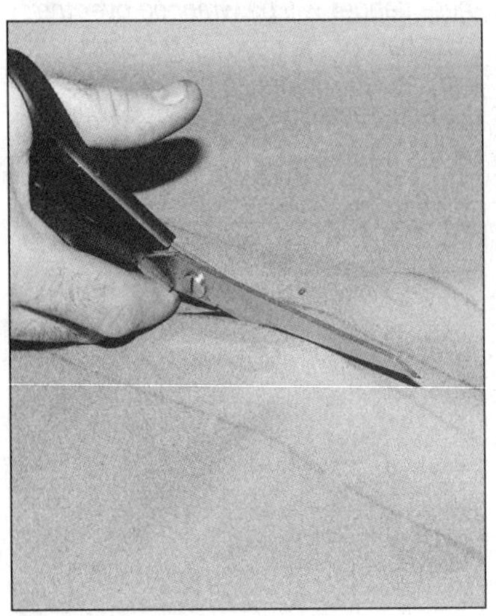

▶ *9.59. The next stage is to pin together the adjacent sections (as identified by their numbers) along the seam lines marked along their perimeters.*

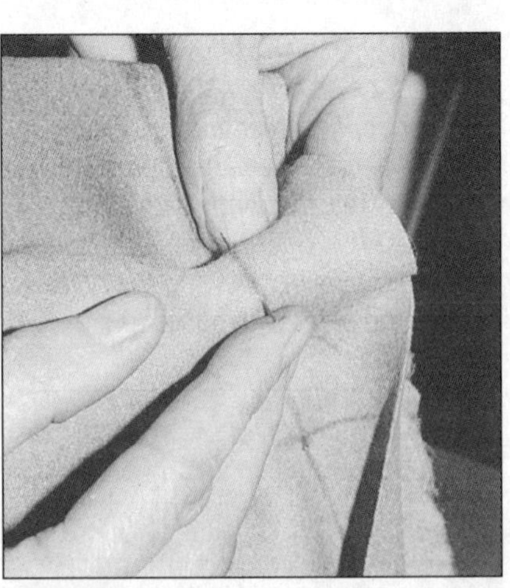

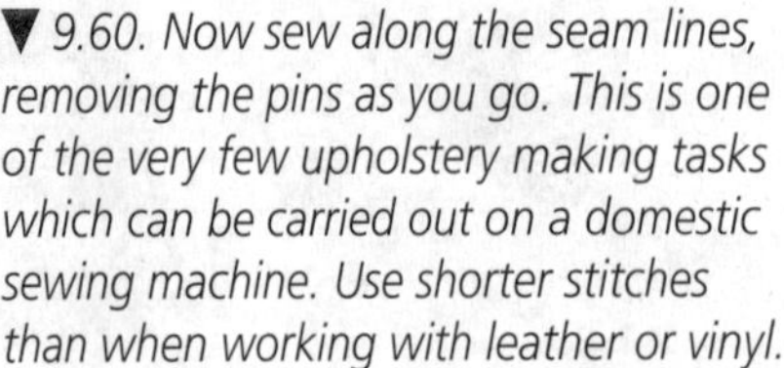

▼ *9.60. Now sew along the seam lines, removing the pins as you go. This is one of the very few upholstery making tasks which can be carried out on a domestic sewing machine. Use shorter stitches than when working with leather or vinyl.*

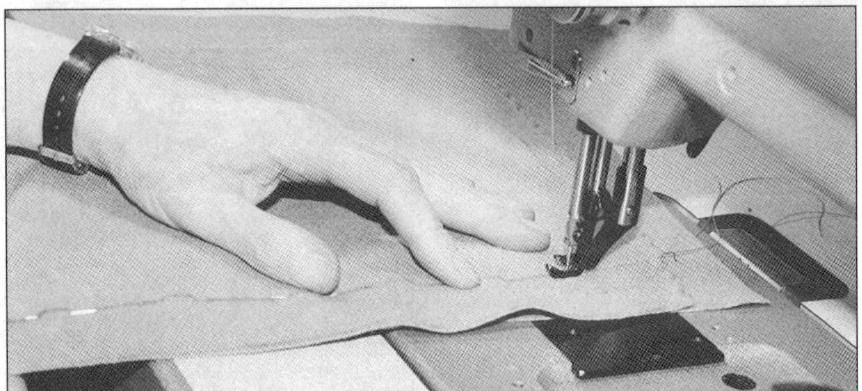

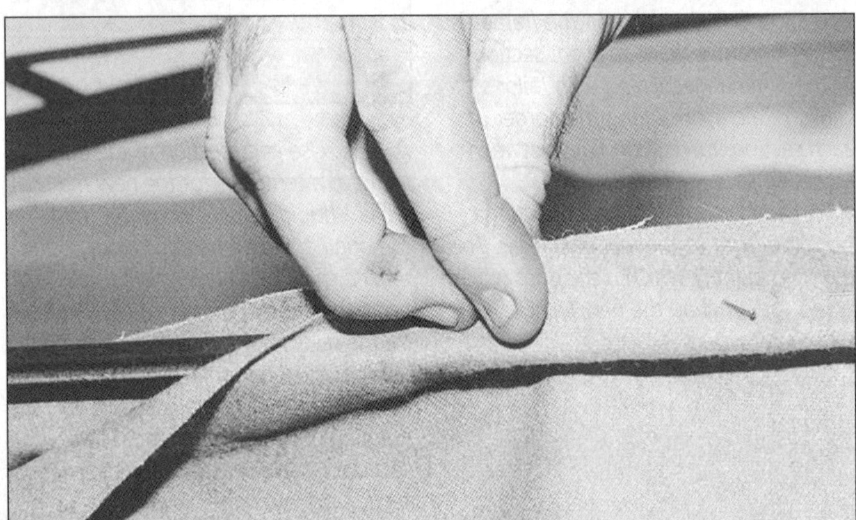

▲ *9.61. When all the sections of the lining have been sewn together, the lining can be fitted to the frame. The loose flanges at the edges of each section are wrapped around the frame's cross-bars and pinned. Then, when you are confident that each section is sitting squarely on the frame, and looks right, they can be hand-sewn in this position. The sections were originally joined together by staples on this car, but standard staples eventually rust, so sewing is a better long-term alternative. Avoid using glue to join adjacent flanges – by doing so you will lose the flexibility to rotate the material around the cross-bars, and it will prove to be more difficult to correctly tension the material on the frame.*

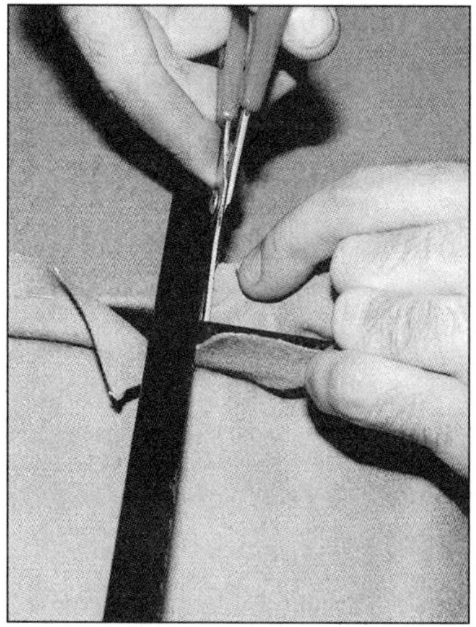

▲ 9.62. The flanges of the material have to be trimmed in the vicinity of the fore and aft runners. Simply cut small slits in the flange at the appropriate points.

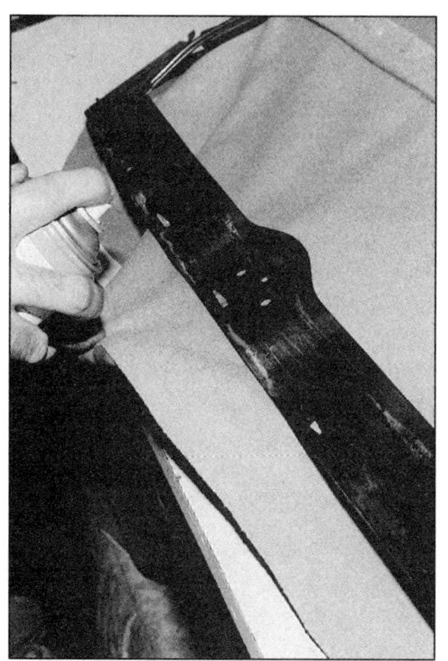

▲ 9.63. Pull the lining material from the front and rear of each frame unit, to tension the material, glueing this in place on the front and rear cross-bars, and/or using the original retaining clips/spikes. An aerosol adhesive is easy to use, and is less likely to soak through the material than some traditional types.

▶ 9.64. Similarly, wrap the material over the side runners of the frame, and glue/clip in place.

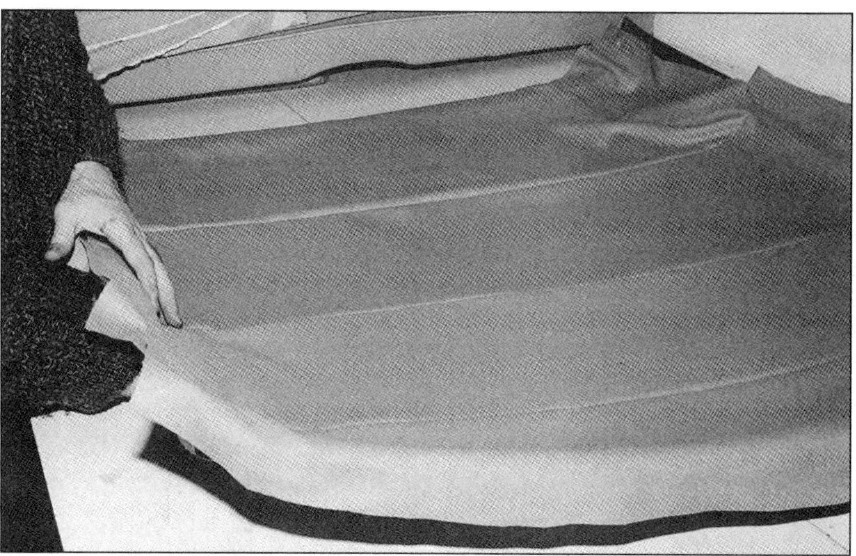

▲ 9.65. Be sure to pull out all creases as you work your way along the frame, re-securing if necessary, to re-tension the material. If care is taken at this stage the headlining should look good for many years. A creased lining always looks awful!

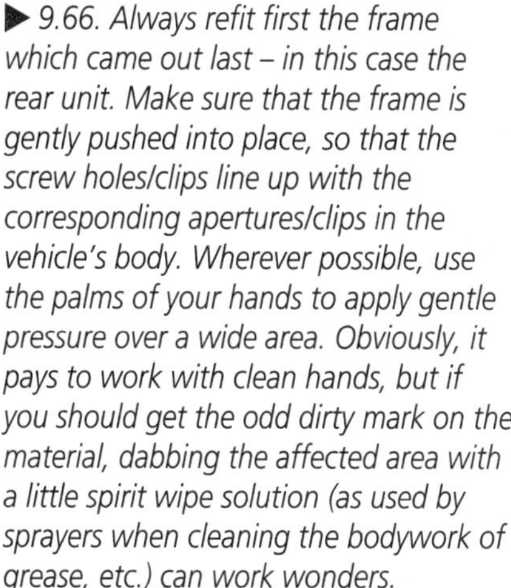

▶ 9.66. Always refit first the frame which came out last – in this case the rear unit. Make sure that the frame is gently pushed into place, so that the screw holes/clips line up with the corresponding apertures/clips in the vehicle's body. Wherever possible, use the palms of your hands to apply gentle pressure over a wide area. Obviously, it pays to work with clean hands, but if you should get the odd dirty mark on the material, dabbing the affected area with a little spirit wipe solution (as used by sprayers when cleaning the bodywork of grease, etc.) can work wonders.

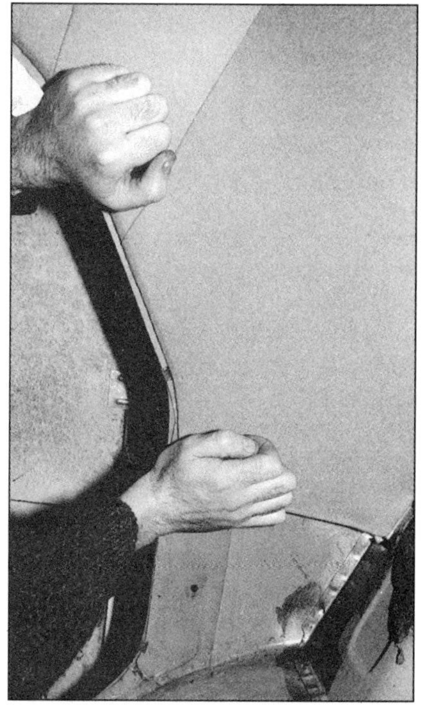

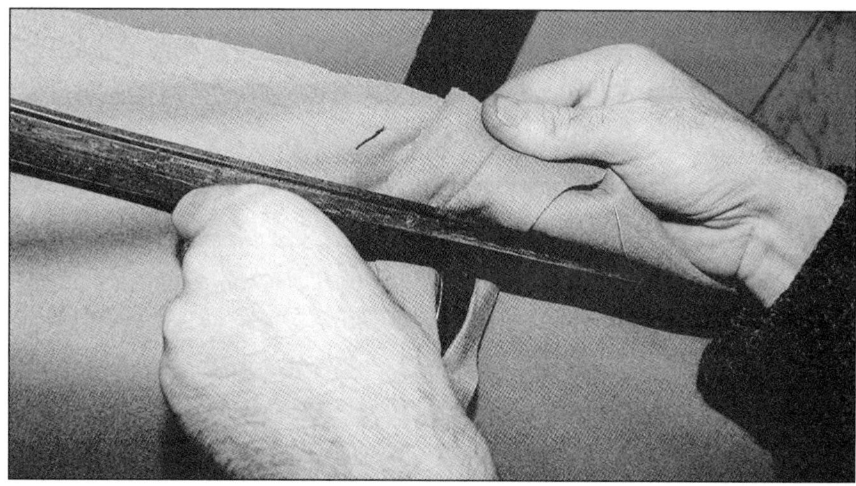

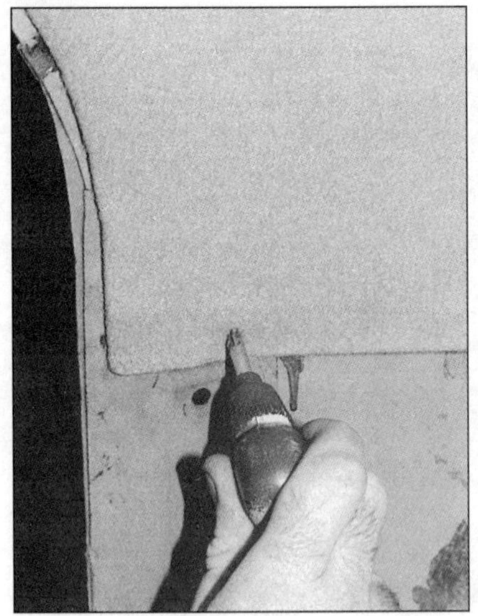

▲ *9.67. Use a pointed implement to make the necessary tiny hole in the material, and to precisely align the screw holes in both the frame and the vehicle. Now reattach the fixing screws securing the rear lining frame. Before proceeding further, ensure that all locating clips are fully home, and check that the lining has not acquired new creases – if it has, find out why and re-position as appropriate until the material is once again reasonably taut (but not over-tight) on the frame.*

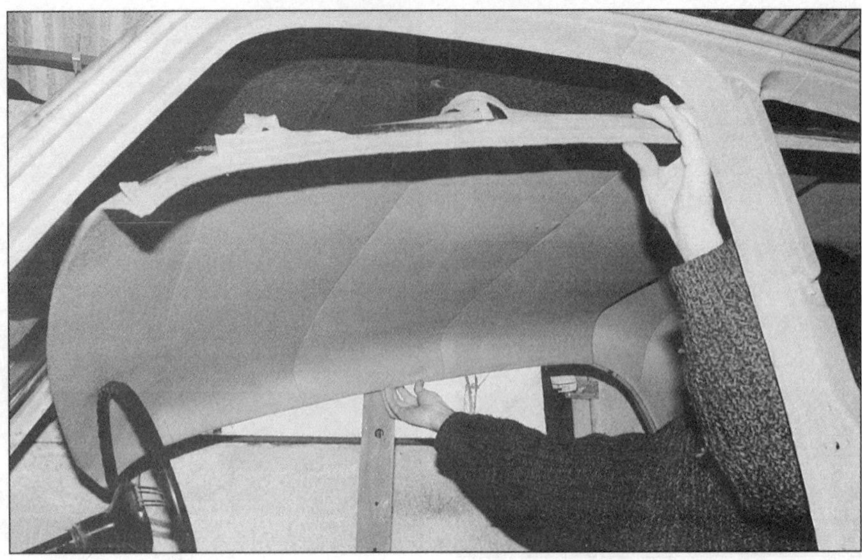

▲ *9.68. Carefully lift the front headlining assembly into position, taking very great care not to catch the material on any sharp projections.*

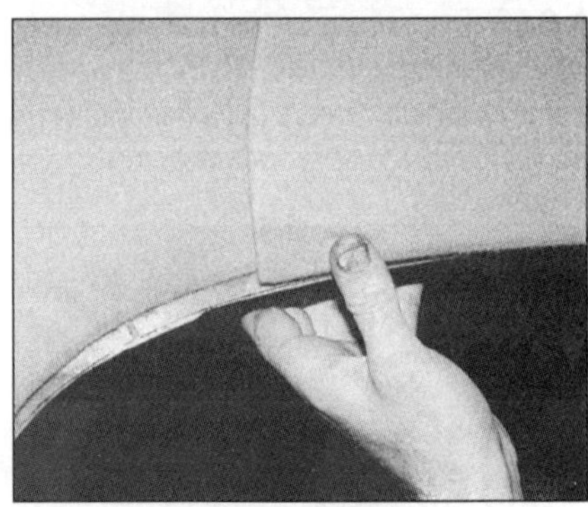

▲ *9.70. Once the rear end of the frame is fully home, guide the sides of the forward lining into their correct positions (working towards the front of the car) along each side.*

It is possible to re-install the rear window at this stage (i.e. *before* fitting the front headlining frame), but experience has shown that the act of installing the forward frame can disturb the rear unit, thereby creating unsightly wrinkles, notably above the rear window.

In fact, what often happens is that when pushing the front frame towards the rear, to fully engage with the retaining clips, the rear frame is effectively compressed, so that the material covering this frame loses its tension, and sags. If the rear window is already fitted, these wrinkles can be impossible to lose.

It is therefore far better first to install the front headlining frame assembly – then, if necessary, re-tension the material on the rear frame, by adjusting its fit around the rear window aperture. My advice is that only then should the rear screen be refitted.

▲ *9.69. As the forward lining is raised and moved backwards into position, ensure that the clips engage fully with the front rail of the rear headlining assembly. It is helpful to have an assistant on hand during this operation!*

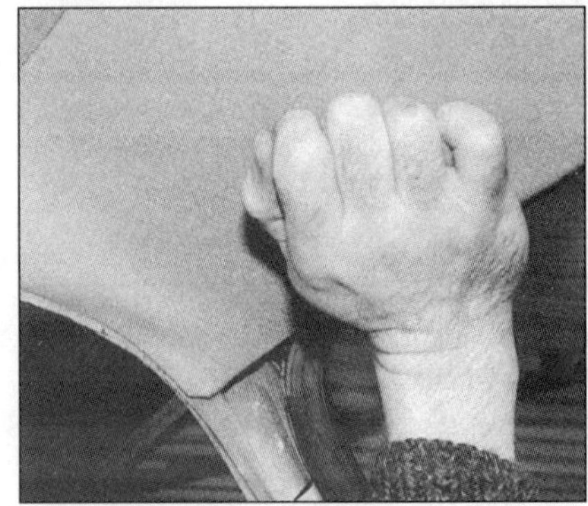

▲ *9.71. Push the front of the forward lining upwards until it is sitting in the correct position, then check very carefully for signs of either over-tight material or sagging. Such problems can often be corrected by slight re-positioning of the headlining frames.*

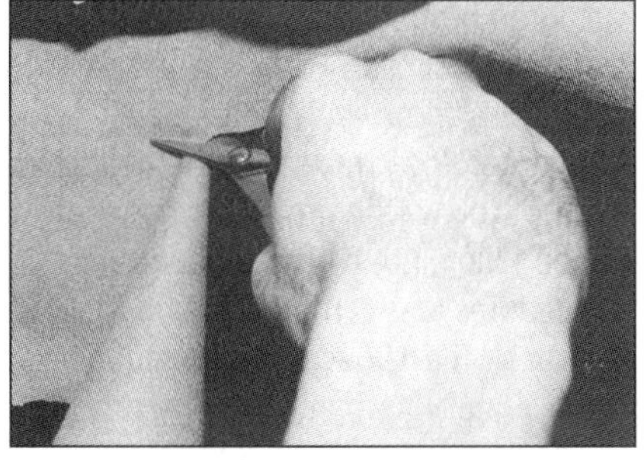

▲ *9.72. An aperture needs to be cut in the material for the rear window. Start by cutting slots, well inboard from the perimeter of the window's aperture in the bodywork, then gradually work outwards, a little at a time, towards the edges of the aperture. Always ensure that there is more than sufficient material to wrap over the window aperture's bodywork lip, to be glued in place on both the inside and the outside of the flange. Go easy – mistakes at this stage are expensive!*

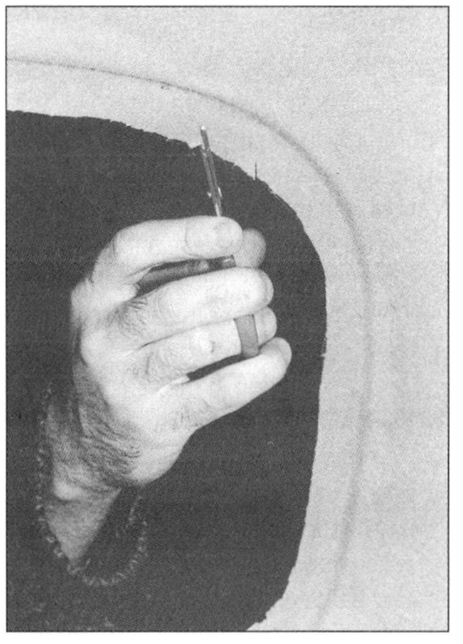

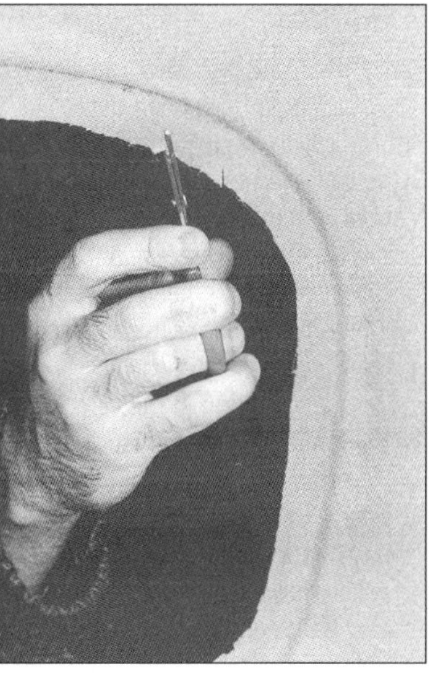

▲ *9.74. Cut short slits in the material around sharp corners to relieve stress at these points when the material is folded over the window's aperture flange.*

▼ *9.75. Now apply contact adhesive to the external side of the window aperture lip, and to the corresponding area of material around the aperture. After a few minutes, when the glue has become tacky, the headlining material can be folded over the lip to be firmly stuck on the outside. This will help to hold the lining in place (not least when the rear window and its seal are fitted!), and will be hidden by the rear screen seal, when this is installed.*

▲ *9.73. Apply contact adhesive to both the inside of the lip in the bodywork, and the corresponding area of headlining material. Allow the glue to become tacky, then, while pulling the material gently towards the rear of the car (to eliminate wrinkles) stick it to the inside of the steel lip. Avoid stretching the material too much during this operation. Excess material can now be trimmed off, but leave half-an-inch or so (sometimes more, depending on the depth of the lip, and of the rubber screen seal's outer flange) to be wrapped over the lip towards the outside of the car.*

▼ *9.76. Using a length of nylon cord, as described in the introduction to this section, the rear window can be installed and its rubber seal encouraged into its correct position. The nylon cord is used to pull the outer flange of the screen seal over the bodywork lip and into place. Take great care not to split the rubber seal during this operation. (Note – in this car the window was fitted from inside the vehicle. In most cases the screens are fitted from the outside.)*

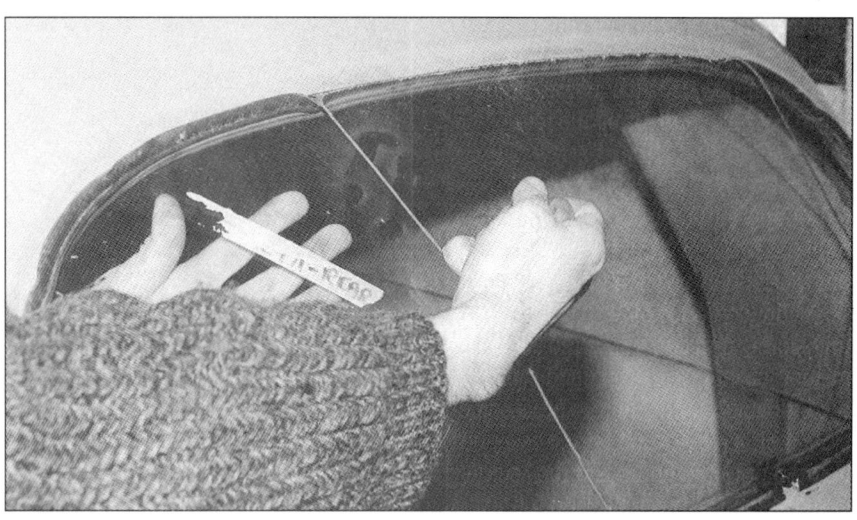

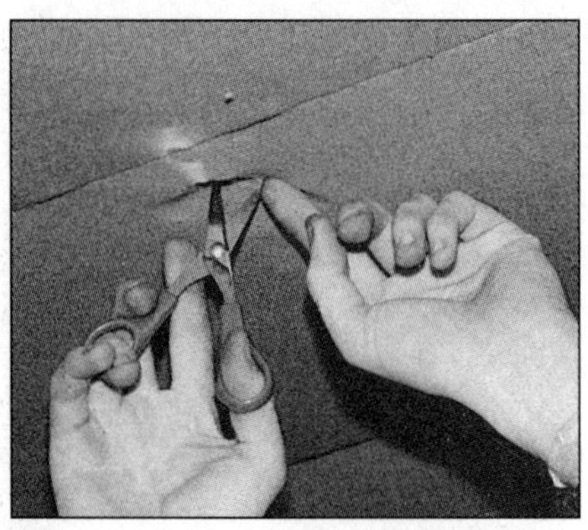

▲ *9.77. Finally, a small X-shaped aperture can be cut to gain access to the interior lamp wiring/mounting, and items such as the sun visors and rear view mirror can be refitted.*

LIST RAIL HEADLININGS

The most commonly encountered type of headlining fitted to classic cars is that in which the material is supported on cross-rails (list bars or wires) which run across the vehicle through pockets formed in the headlining material, where adjacent sections of it join.

Each list rail is supported at each end (at the sides of the vehicle at roof level) by means of clips, sockets or screws. Methods of attaching the headlining to the vehicle at front and rear, and along each side, vary.

Often, the headlining material is supported at the front and rear of the vehicle by being glued to the tops of the screen apertures, in which case the glass will have to come out. An examination of the vehicle will confirm whether or not this is necessary. If it is, the notes above on framed headlinings will be of assistance.

Methods of attaching the lining material along each side of the car also vary. Sometimes the material is attached by glue to the upper edges of each door aperture (and covered/held in place there by the door aperture trims). Alternatively, the material can be crimped in position, stapled or tacked in place. Some manufacturers employed tacking strips made of relatively soft material – such as wood, rubber, or compressed fibre board – for this purpose.

REMOVAL

Once the front, rear and side edges of the headlining have been detached, the list rails, with the lining still attached, need to be removed from the car. Take care during this operation to maintain the rails in their correct relative positions, and try to keep the headlining intact – it will then be far easier to use it for pattern-making.

When in position in the vehicle, the list rails – almost always curved to assume an inverted U profile within the roof of the car – follow the profile of the roof. They are normally held in tension against it, with felt or similar material acting as a barrier between the rails and the roof panel. To detach the rails, therefore, they must be rotated through 180°, then detached from their brackets/clips/ retaining screws, to enable them to be removed from the car.

The precise set-up varies from vehicle to vehicle, but in a typical example, one would start at the back of the car, and work towards the front. In each case, roll each list rail forwards through 180° to free it from the roof.

As each rail is extracted from its pocket in the lining material, it should be identified (numbered) so that it can be returned to precisely the same position in the car, and the same way round! This is vitally important, for in some cars there are large numbers of list rails, all of which look similar. However, they all vary slightly in length and degree of curvature, and if mixed up the headlining will not follow the profile of the roof!

The following, typical sequence of procedures was carried out on a Mark II Jaguar of the 1960s. The techniques apply equally to many other models.

The marking out and cutting out procedures for the lining material are similar to those covered in earlier sections. As always, reference to the original lining will yield invaluable clues as to the method of construction, and the sequence of assembly of the lining.

In the case of the Jaguar the main headlining is made from a single piece of material, with pinch folds sewn into it at intervals corresponding with the spacing of the list rails. At each of these points, a calico pocket, attached to the upper side of the material, is incorporated (being sewn to the pinch folds) to accommodate the list rails.

In all cases, take care to be precise, and to make the most economical use of the lining material.

▼ *9.78. The first step is to remove all ancillary fittings (including, in this case, the front and rear screens, door aperture trims, sun visors and so on). The lining is then ready to be detached from the upper edges of the screen and door apertures.*

▲ *9.79. If any sections of the lining are missing, make paper templates at this stage, before the list rails are removed. This will help to ensure that the replacement lining is made to the precise size and shape as the original.*

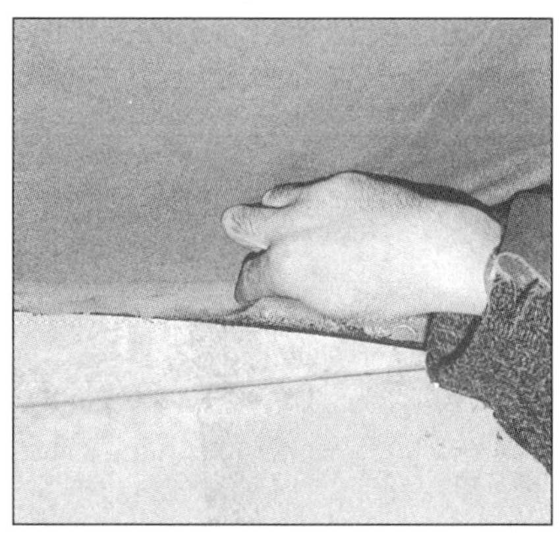

▲ *9.80. Now carefully detach the lining at the front and rear, and along each side. The lining in this Jaguar was stapled to the tacking strip. Take great care not to damage the material, which can be used as a pattern for the replacement lining.*

▶ *9.81. With the Jaguar it is appropriate to start at the rear of the car when removing the list rails. Roll each rail through 180° towards the front of the car. The rails may at first be reluctant to move, as they …*

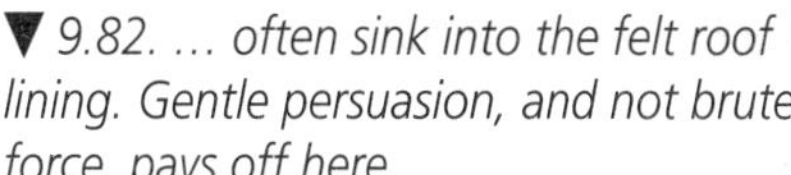

▼ *9.82. … often sink into the felt roof lining. Gentle persuasion, and not brute force, pays off here.*

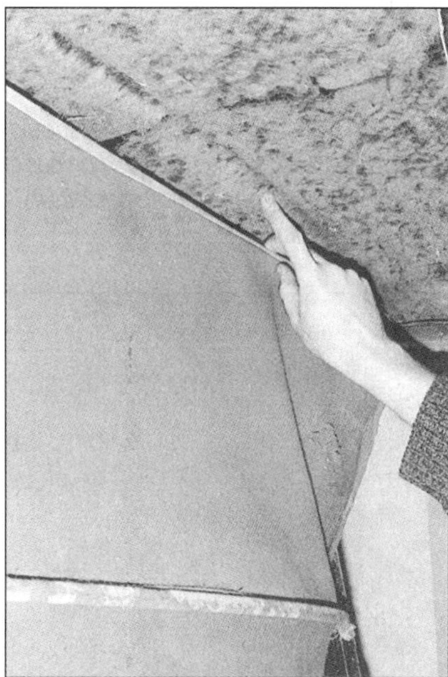

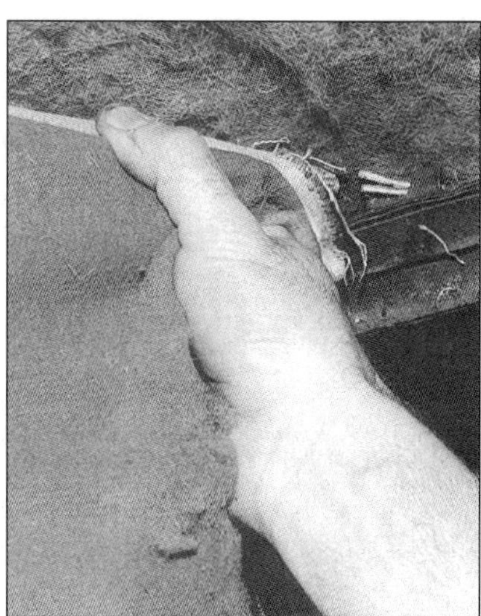

▲ *9.83. Now detach one end of the list rail from its socket (or other attachment), taking care not to damage the rail, the socket or the headlining assembly in the process.*

▼ *9.84. The end of the list rail just released can now be lowered, making it easier to detach the opposite end.*

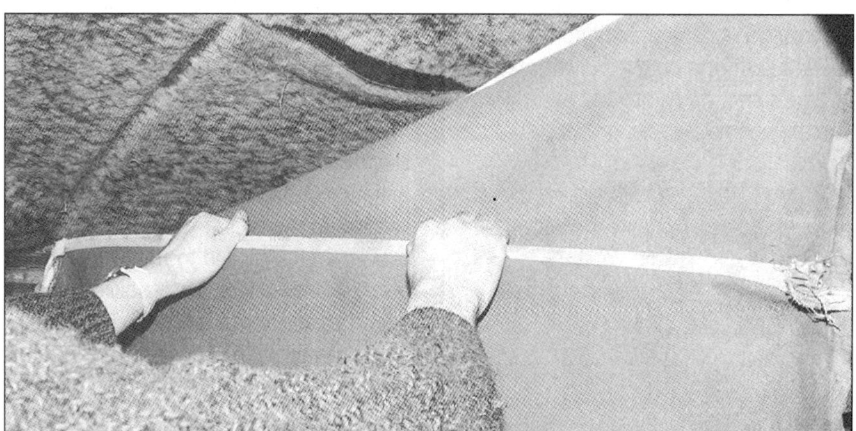

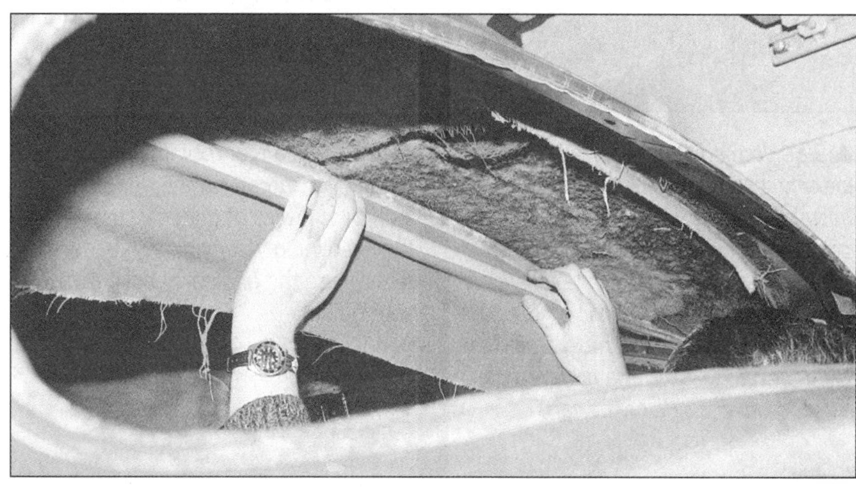

▲ *9.85. With the lining assembly freed from the car, the list rails can now be withdrawn from their individual pockets in the lining. Often the rails have become very rusty over the years, and the rust takes a firm grip on the pocket material. All the same, try not to use excessive force when releasing.*

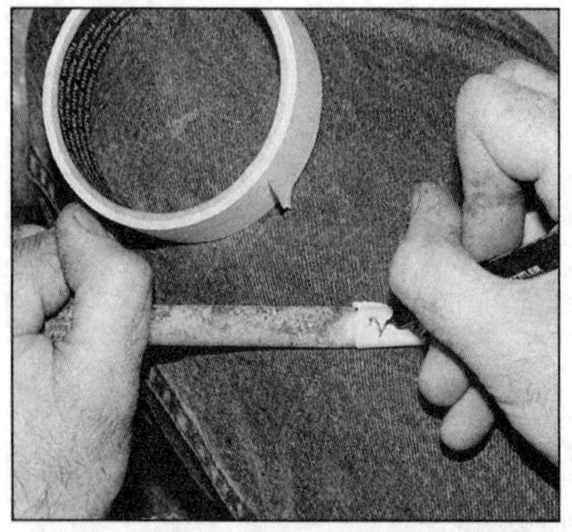

▲ *9.86. Immediately each rail is freed, identify it so that there can be no mistake later regarding its correct position in the vehicle. One way is to wrap the rail with masking tape, and write the number of the rail on the tape (it's perhaps safest to number from the front, and to keep all the numbers on, say, the driver's side of the car).*

▶ *9.87. Using medium grit abrasive paper remove all traces of rust from each list rail. Follow this with a chemical rust killer, then paint with primer and top coat. These are easier to apply by aerosol spray. (Wear goggles and appropriate masks when rubbing down/spraying.) Allow to dry fully! The rails, thus protected, should last for a very long time, and will be easier to slide into their appropriate pockets in the new headlining.*

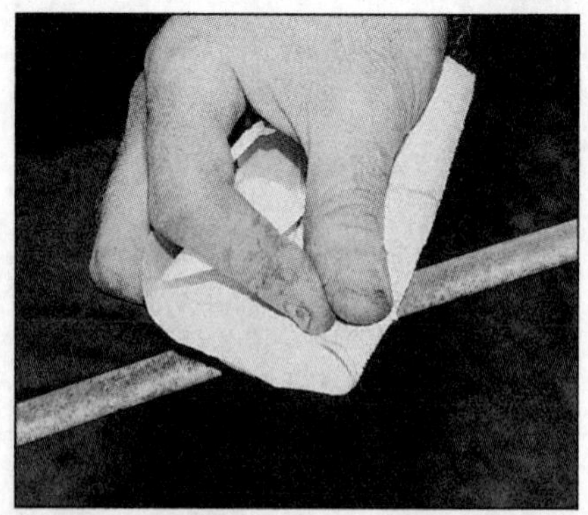

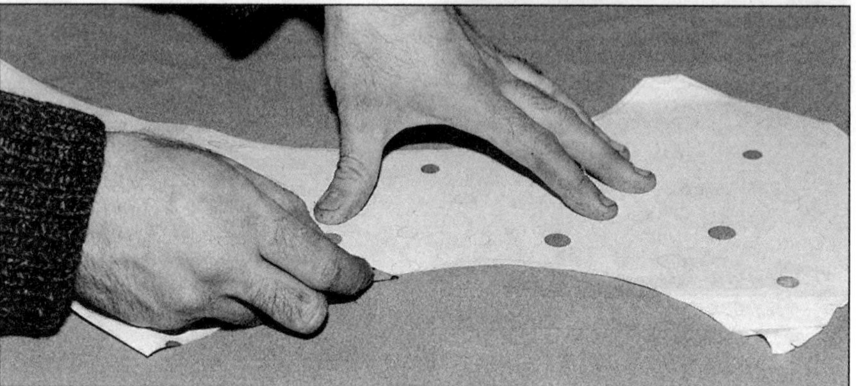

Using the original headlining as a pattern (and including any paper templates necessitated by the original panels having long since disappeared!) mark out the exact shape of each section of the lining onto the new material. However, allow and mark an additional half inch (13mm) or so at the end of each section. In the case of the Jaguar, this extra material is used to form pinch folds at the points where calico pockets will be added to accommodate each list rail.

It is always helpful to mark a centre line on the material, in addition to the perimeter boundary.

On this Jaguar the headlining comprises one main, large piece of material (sub-divided by the pinch folds, as described) sewn to an additional smaller piece (accommodating the sharply curved rear roof line). Individual models vary greatly in the numbers of individual pieces of material from which the headlining was originally made. Always use the original headlining as your guide.

▲ *9.88. Mark out the profile of the new headlining with care and precision. This paper template had been made up by reference to the vehicle itself, since the rearmost panel of the original headlining on this Jaguar was missing.*

▲ *9.89. At the end of each section of the headlining (each section corresponding to the spaces between the list rails) form a pinch in the material, and attach with a series of Bulldog clips a strip of calico, folded to form a U profile, as shown. In all cases use the original lining as your guide to dimensions and the precise positioning of the material. Sew each calico pocket in place before proceeding to the next one.*

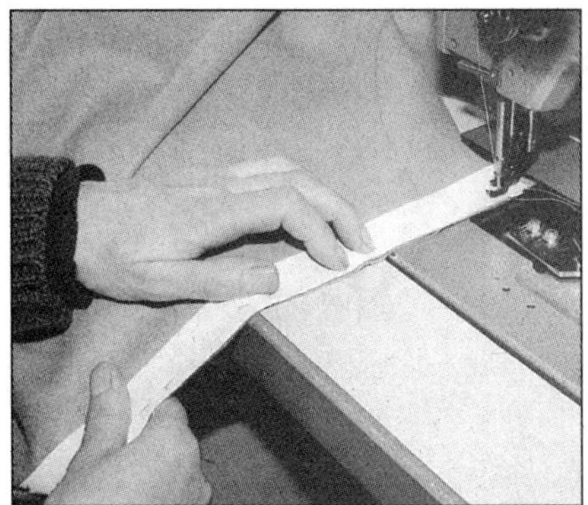

▲ *9.90. For ease of sewing, pins can replace the Bulldog clips when the time comes to join the calico pocket to the main headlining material. This is one of the few occasions in vehicle trimming when a domestic sewing machine may be used.*

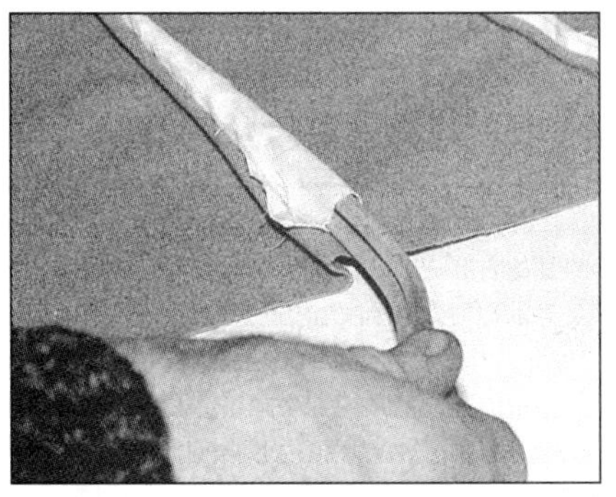

▲ *9.91. The smart reconditioned list rails can now be fed into their appropriate pockets in the new headlining. It is essential that they are correctly centralized within the material.*

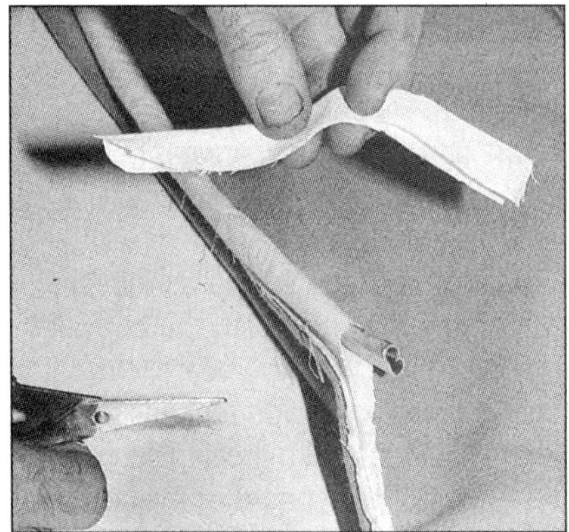

▲ *9.92. Trim back the open ends of the pockets so that the list rails just protrude at each end. Further trimming may be necessary when the headlining is offered up to the vehicle.*

▲ *9.93. When fitting the new lining assembly, start at the opposite end of the car to the one you started removing the original unit from. In the case of this Jaguar, reassembly was started from the front. With the first list rail effectively upside down, insert the ends of it into its sockets/pegs, then rotate the rail towards the rear of the car and into its correct, inverted U position, so that the material is tensioned as you work rearwards. Repeat the procedure for each rail.*

Note: As each rail is fitted, the position of it within its calico pocket must be checked, and adjusted if necessary to ensure that it is central.

As you work backwards through the vehicle, ensure that the material is kept evenly tensioned from front to back (at this stage, with the sides of the material unattached to the vehicle, there is nothing to provide tension from side to side of the material). It can be useful to use a series of Bulldog clips (with rounded, rather than sharp-edged jaws, to avoid damaging the headlining) to maintain tension in the lining material as you work.

Ensure, too, that the stitch line marking the boundary of each section of the lining hangs immediately below each list rail, and that it takes the form of a straight line across the car. Rectify any twisting at this stage.

As the lining assembly is installed, it may be necessary to further trim back the ends of the calico pockets to allow more flexibility in positioning the headlining on the list rails.

▼ *9.94. After a few minutes your headlining should look something like this – nearly there! Obviously the material will only be fully tensioned when the front and rear sections, and those at the sides, are attached to the vehicle.*

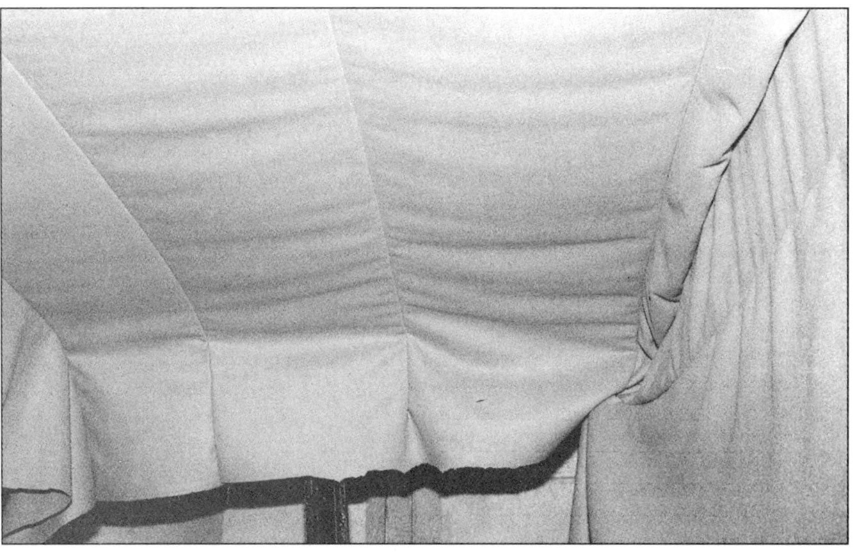

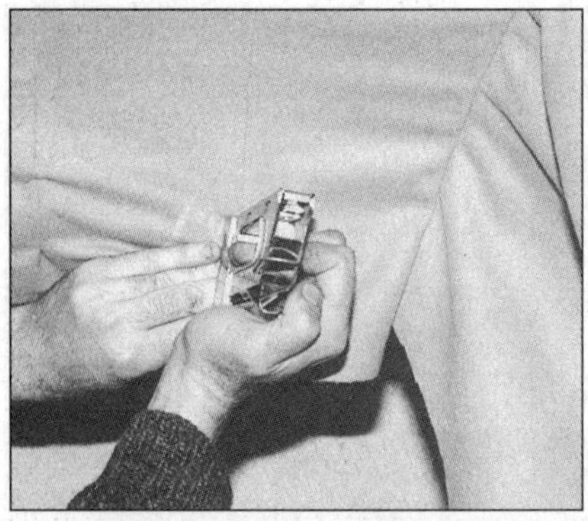

▲ *9.95. When even tension has been achieved, the lining can be stapled or tacked in place along the sides of the roof.*

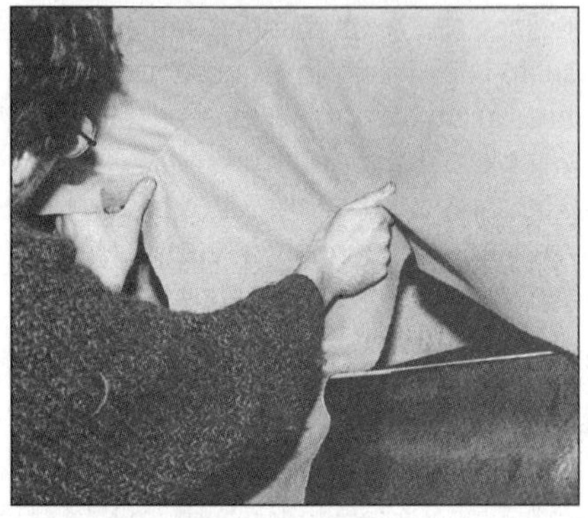

▲ *9.96. Stretch the material into position around the front and rear screen apertures, and glue in place using contact adhesive.*

▼ *9.97. The excess material at the front, rear and sides of the headlining is then carefully trimmed away (as shown for framed headlinings) and the exposed boundaries then concealed under window rubbers or Furflex piping, etc., glued in position using contact adhesive.*

▲ *9.98. When finished, the lining should look like this – the results of your efforts will be admired for many years to come.*

Almost inevitably you may be left with a few slight creases in the lining material, but, provided these are not simply the result of poor tensioning of the material on your part, they can often be steamed out. Simply boil a kettle within the vehicle, and allow the steam to play on the headlining for a few minutes (**Take great care not to scald yourself or others with the steam or hot water**). You should find that the creases simply drop out. As an alternative, a steam iron, of the type which 'puffs out' steam, could be held near to the offending creases. Again, they should fall out of the material.

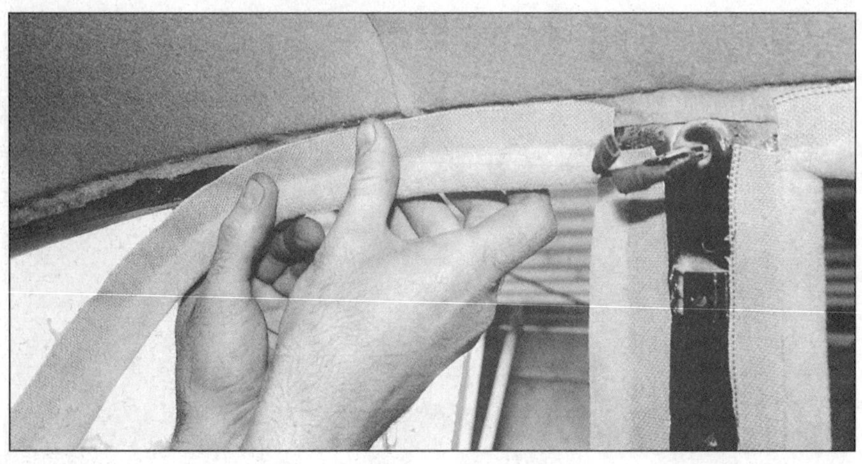

ONE-PIECE HEADLININGS

On many modern vehicles – and a number of older ones (for example, Jaguars and Daimlers from the mid-1960s on) – the headlining is made from a simple one-piece board covered with the lining material – often foam-backed nylon.

The compressed fibre backing boards usually used have the manufacturing advantage that they are light in weight and simple to install.

From a restoration point of view, they do have some disadvantages. One is that, being one-piece items, they are large (especially on bigger vehicles) and relatively cumbersome. Also, since they are usually made from relatively thin, brittle fibreboard, they are easily damaged. The corners and edges are especially vulnerable.

As if this weren't enough, problems can occur when removing the original lining material from the board. No matter how careful you are, it is almost impossible to avoid removing some of the fibre from the board as the covering material is peeled away from it. Extreme care is needed during this operation.

If you do end up with a series of shallow depressions across the surface of your backing board, you can attempt localized filling of the affected areas (using a carefully applied flexible filler, for example), although this is a difficult operation and success isn't guaranteed. Alternatively you could stick a comparatively thick section of foam over the whole of the surface of the backing board, to disguise the depressions, prior to applying the covering material. Another option is to try to purchase a new replacement backing board (in many cases impossible), or try to find a second-hand one in better condition than your own (unlikely).

Another interesting aspect of working with this type of one-piece lining is that it can be impossible to remove the board from the vehicle through the door apertures, even with all the seats removed from the car. The alternatives are – if you are really keen – to take out the front or rear screen, or to fix replacement lining material to the backing board while it is still in the vehicle.

Having said all that, the one-piece headlinings do have the overriding advantage of simplicity in re-covering, since it is fairly straightforward to mark out, cut and fit the material required. Normally a foam-backed material is used, and this is quite easy to work with.

The following photograph sequence shows the fitting of a replacement headlining in a Daimler Sovereign (XJ6 type). The principles can be applied to most cars with one-piece linings.

In this case the car's owner did not want the windscreen(s) removed from the vehicle, so the lining was fitted with the backing board still in the car. In view of the possibility of breaking the windscreen during removal/refitting, also the chance of destroying screen seals which are in good condition and doing their job effectively, this is in any case probably the best route to take for DIY replacement of the lining.

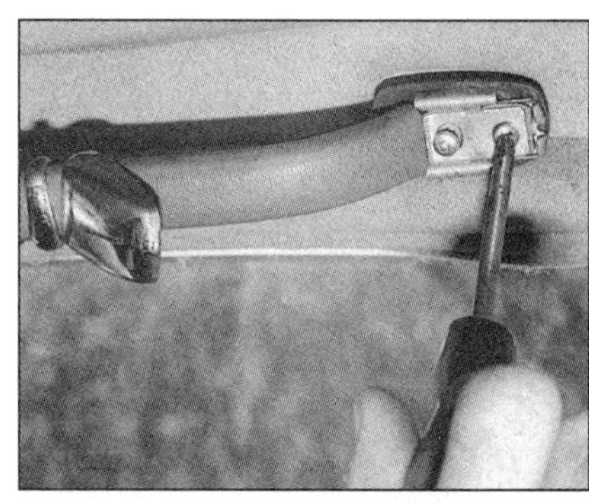

▶ *9.99. The first step is to remove the grab handles from the trim panels immediately beneath the headlining, on each side of the car. On the Daimler these were held in place by screws hidden beneath a chromed capping. As the handles are removed, make a note of the relative positions of the plastic spacers beneath them – these are tapered. Keep all components together in a safe place.*

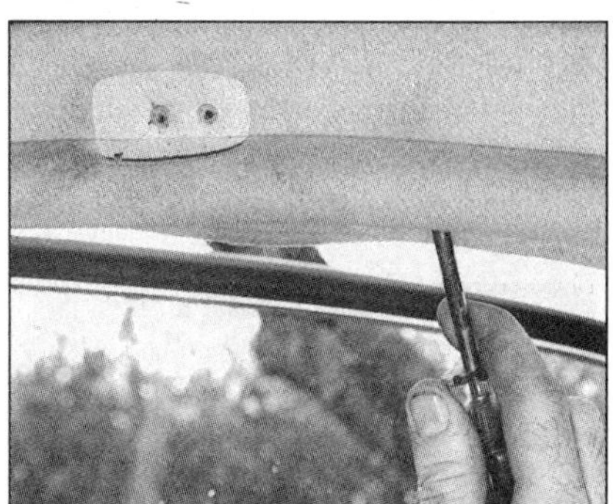

▶ *9.100. With extreme care, prise the trim strips on each side of the car away from the bodywork. The securing clips are easily broken, and the trim strips can be damaged unless care is taken.*

▲ *9.101. The rear seats need to come out to provide access to the rear parcel shelf area. In any case their removal gives more room for working within the vehicle. The retaining screws are released and the seat base lifts out. The back rest is also held in place by screws, and fits onto clips built into the rear panel.*

▶ *9.102. The rear seat belt mounting bolts (where fitted) also need to be removed – on the Daimler they pass through the rear parcel shelf.*

▲ *9.103. Next to go is the rear parcel shelf itself. Take care to support all its length as it is removed. The trim panel beneath the rear window can also come out now.*

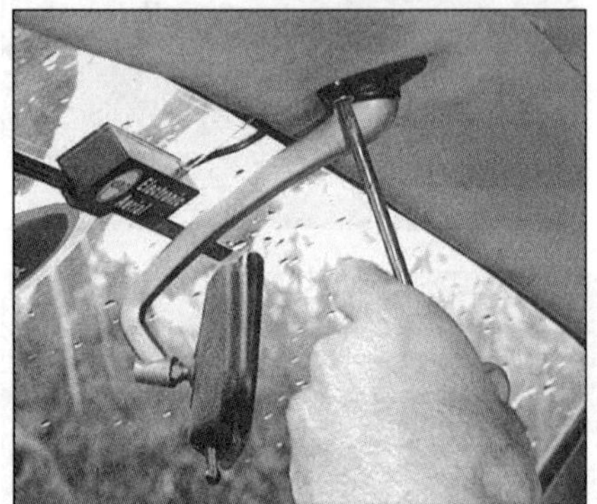

▲ *9.104. At the front of the car, unscrew and take out the rear view mirror, also the sun visors. Don't lose the screws!*

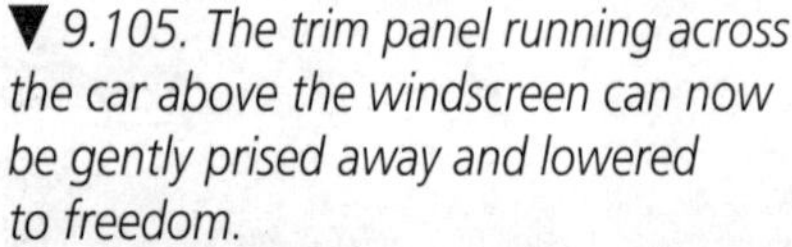

▼ *9.105. The trim panel running across the car above the windscreen can now be gently prised away and lowered to freedom.*

▲ *9.106. Similarly, the trim panel across the top of the rear window can be removed.*

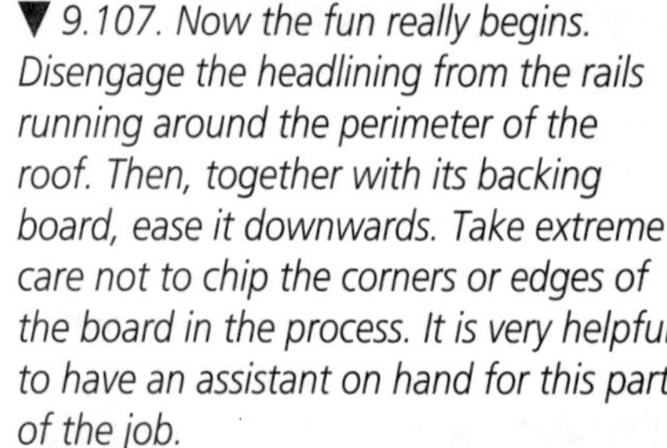

▼ *9.107. Now the fun really begins. Disengage the headlining from the rails running around the perimeter of the roof. Then, together with its backing board, ease it downwards. Take extreme care not to chip the corners or edges of the board in the process. It is very helpful to have an assistant on hand for this part of the job.*

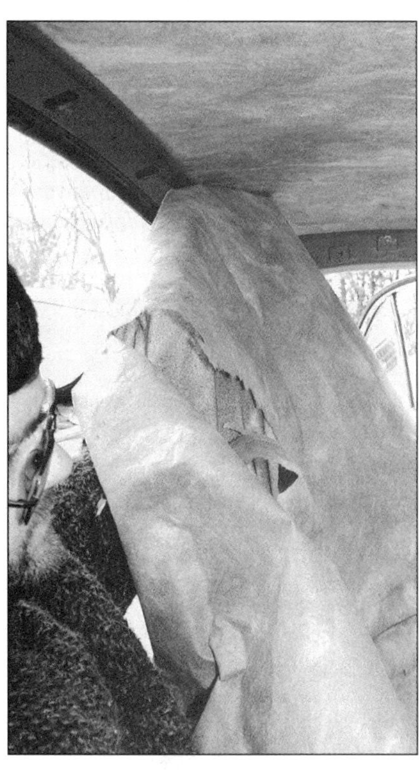

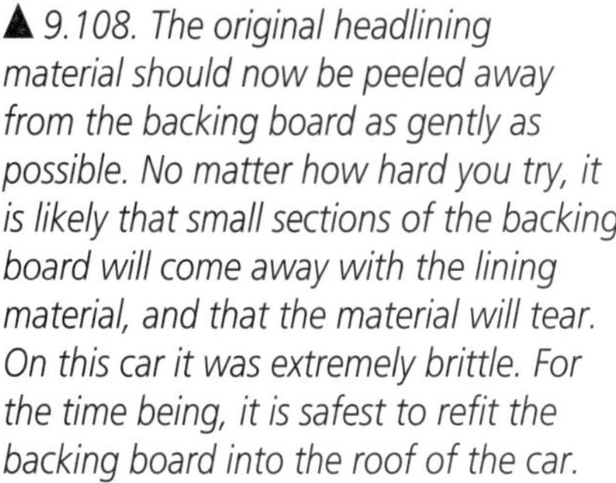

▲ *9.108. The original headlining material should now be peeled away from the backing board as gently as possible. No matter how hard you try, it is likely that small sections of the backing board will come away with the lining material, and that the material will tear. On this car it was extremely brittle. For the time being, it is safest to refit the backing board into the roof of the car.*

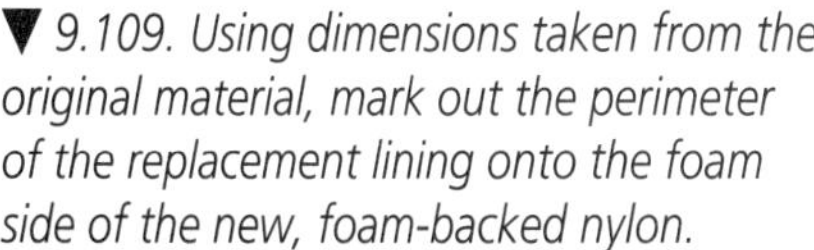

▼ *9.109. Using dimensions taken from the original material, mark out the perimeter of the replacement lining onto the foam side of the new, foam-backed nylon.*

▼ *9.110. Cut out the new lining slightly oversize – by perhaps three inches (75mm) all round.*

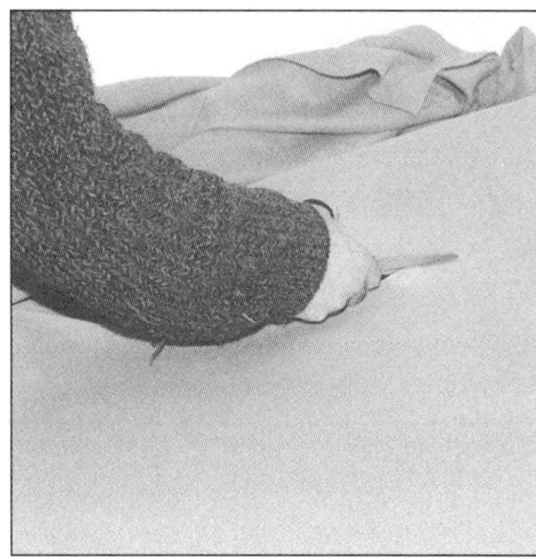

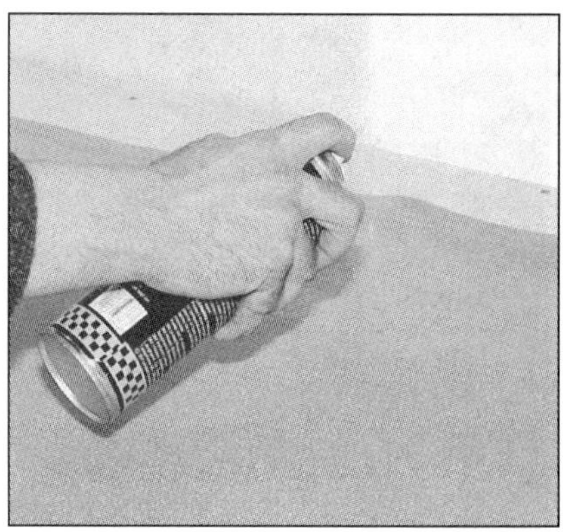

▲ *9.111. Apply contact adhesive both to the back of the new lining material and to the lower side of the backing board.* **Wear a mask and ensure adequate ventilation while doing this.** *Aerosol glue is easier to apply on this job. Make sure that the seats and carpets within the vehicle are covered with sheets, etc., to prevent them being covered with glue.*

▲ *9.112. When the adhesive has turned tacky, bring the lining material to the vehicle (very carefully) and position it precisely against the backing board. It is best if the board is left in place in the roof of the car while the covering material is pressed home. Work from the centre of the panel outwards, smoothing the material and ensuring that all wrinkles and bubbles are removed.*

▲ 9.113. Now trim the edges of the material a little closer to the actual size required. A minimum of an additional half inch (13mm) or so should be left all round.

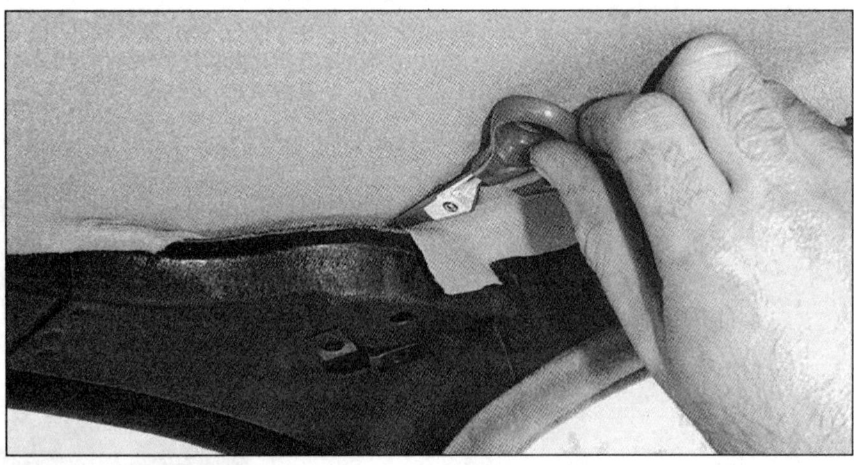

▲ 9.114. Starting in the corners, tuck the extra material out of sight and against the backing board, ensuring that no creases are created in the process. A pair of scissors, preferably with rounded blades, is useful for this job.

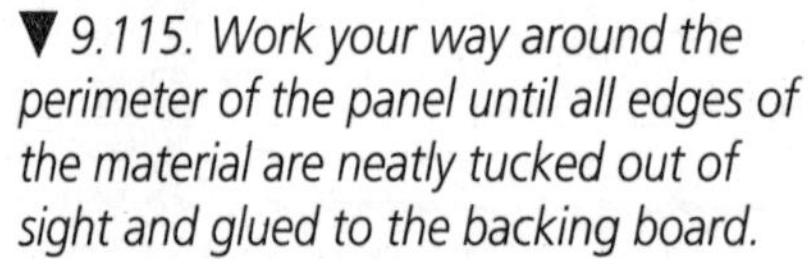

▼ 9.115. Work your way around the perimeter of the panel until all edges of the material are neatly tucked out of sight and glued to the backing board.

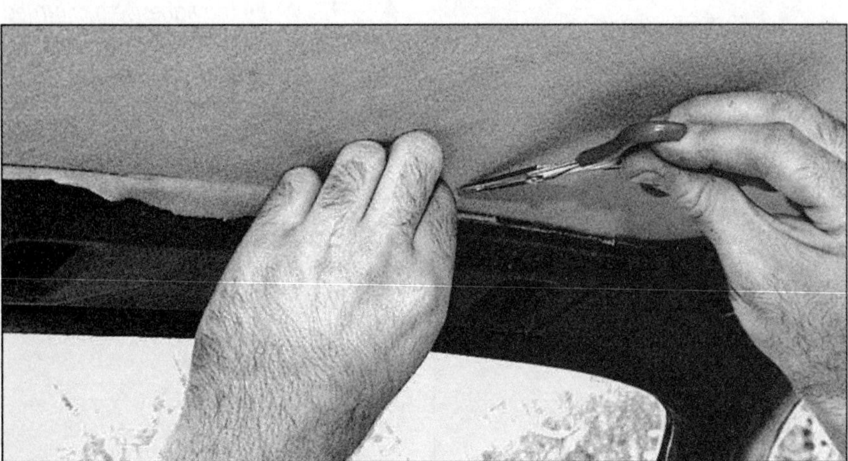

▼ 9.116. The trim panels which fit at the front and rear, and on each side of the roof panel now have to be re-covered. Lay each item in turn onto the new material, and mark out the shapes onto the foam side, ensuring that you allow sufficient material to fully cover the panels.

▼ 9.117. Once again, carefully cut around the lines marked, then stick the covering material sections to each panel in turn, using contact adhesive. Finally, trim off excess material.

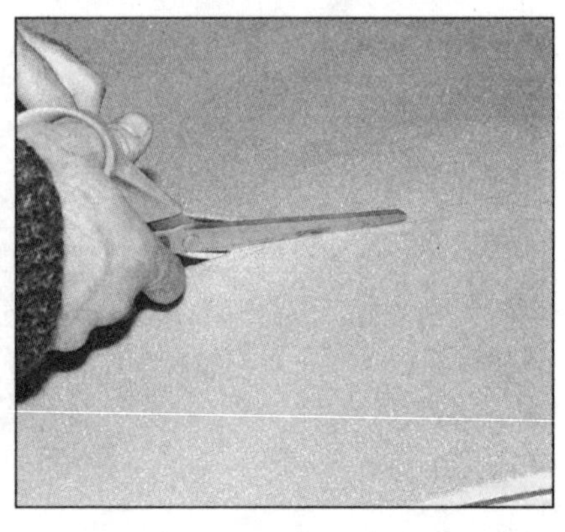

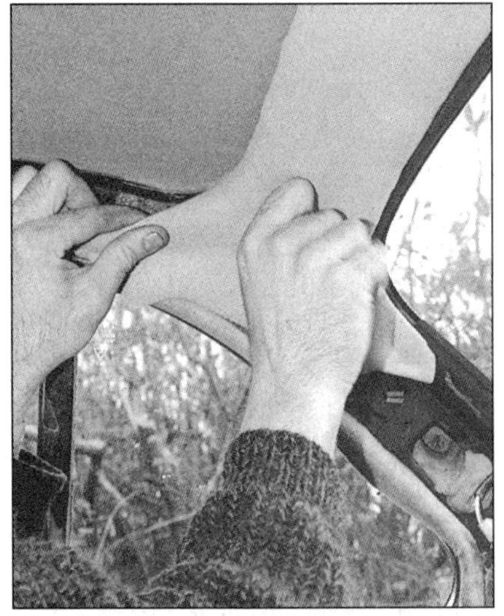

▲ *9.118. The front and rear trims are refitted first, making sure that the retaining clips are properly located and pressed fully home.*

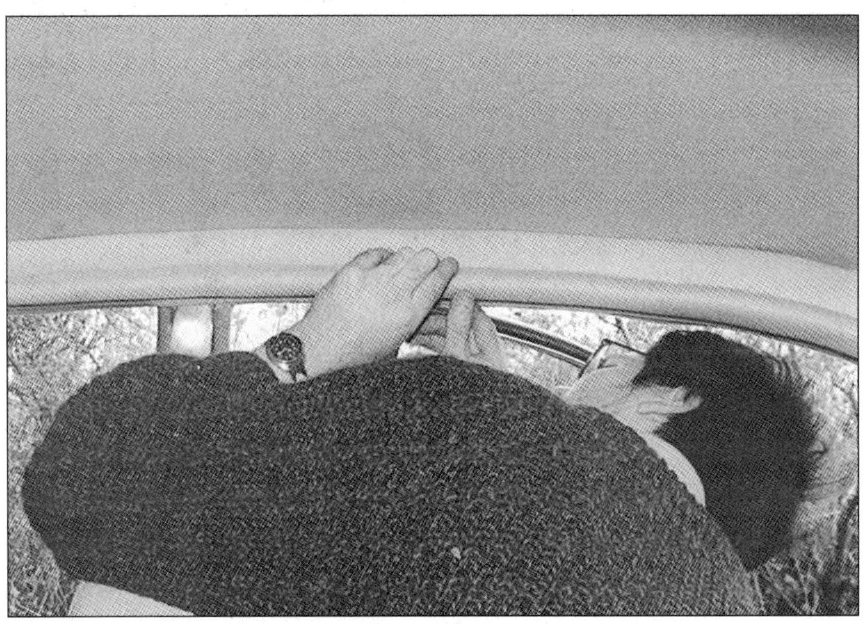

▲ *9.120. The side trims are next to be refitted. Properly locating the retaining clips in their holes can be a time-consuming task.*

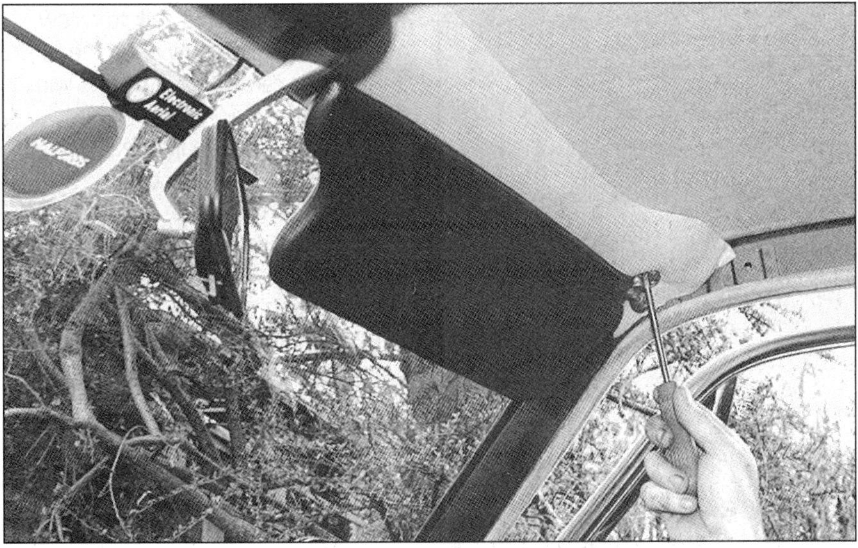

▲ *9.119. The rear view mirror and sun visors can now be added. If necessary, use a needle or trim regulator tool (such as that available from Frost Auto Restoration Techniques Ltd) to help relocate the screw holes.*

▼ *9.121. The final job is to refit the grab handles. The whole operation, from start to finish, took under six hours.*

Chapter 10

Carpets

The floor coverings are a vital part of the interior trim in any car, and when dirty and worn they can seriously detract from the pleasure of travelling in the vehicle.

Many older cars – especially the more basic models in a range – were originally fitted with rubber mats, and these eventually broke up as they aged. In such cases, obtaining an original pattern replacement, either new or in good condition, can be difficult.

One alternative is to make replacements from sheets of fluted rubber matting, and another is to fit carpeting. Neither will be as original, but will certainly be preferable to unsightly mats with great chunks of rubber missing!

For cars originally fitted with carpets there may be more options available to you, depending on the make of vehicle. The more popular classic sports cars, including MGs, Jaguars, Triumphs and so on, are well catered for in terms of ready-to-fit trim (including carpet sets) available from specialist spares suppliers for the individual marques.

There are also ready-to-fit sets on offer for many other popular vehicles, but *don't buy without seeing a sample* of the carpets and, if possible, talk to fellow owners to establish how good the fit and finish of the carpets is, compared with the originals.

I know from personal experience that some of the so-called ready-to-install carpet sets can be of the incorrect texture, ill-fitting and of poor overall quality. Indeed, it sometimes takes almost as long to rectify a poor set of carpets as it does to make a proper set from scratch.

MAKING YOUR OWN

If you do decide to make your own carpets, don't discard the remains of the originals as these will be an invaluable guide to how the new ones should be made.

The first step is to find new carpet with the appropriate weave, the correct texture, pile type (e.g. loop or close-knit pile) and material, and in the same colour as the originals – unless, of course, you are changing the colour of your car's trim. Sometimes you may have to compromise, such as when the original weave or colour is no longer available.

By asking the various suppliers for samples of the carpets they sell (they are usually only too pleased to oblige), you should be able to obtain a near-match of the original. It is worth bearing in mind that rubber-backed carpets are often used today. The one big advantage of these is that they don't fray.

Before ordering the carpet, you must work out exactly how much you are going to need. Don't forget to take into account the width of the carpet as supplied. Some carpets are supplied in rolls wider than others (often 57 in, compared to the standard 40-in width).

Where there is a choice (as with some types of black carpet), it can be easier to cut the replacement sections from the wider roll. Having established this, one way of working out the length required is to carefully place all the sections of the original carpets on the floor, within the width of the carpet to be purchased, and to measure the overall length of the pieces when so laid out.

When doing this, arrange the pieces of original carpet so that the weave runs in the same direction for corresponding pieces on opposite sides of the car (e.g. left-hand and right-hand side floor carpets), and for adjacent sections.

The original carpets can be used as templates for cutting out the shapes required from the new carpet. Where the shape of the carpet is complex – over a transmission tunnel hump and similar obstacles, or where the original carpets are very badly damaged, or missing – paper templates can be made, using the shape of the vehicle floor itself as a guide. Use large sheets of brown paper, or a roll of the masking paper (obtainable from vehicle paint factors) normally used when spraying a vehicle.

Where necessary, complex template shapes can be made up in a number of small sections subsequently stuck together with masking tape. Heavy weights are useful to hold the paper flat when making patterns. It is imperative to be precise when marking and cutting out, and to use sharp blades when cutting the paper, to ensure clean edges.

For cutting the new carpet to shape, use a sharp hobby knife or a pair of scissors or shears. Whichever you use, make sure that the carpet is cut cleanly, and not torn apart. A clean edge is better looking and less likely to fray if unbound. Take your time when cutting templates and the new carpet, and double-check at each stage. The future appearance of the carpets depends on getting it right now.

Bear in mind that carpets often shrink during years of use, so before using them as templates always check that the original carpets still fit the floor of the vehicle. If in doubt, make new patterns – using the vehicle body as a precise guide to the measurements required.

Another aspect to consider is that of soundproofing. If you intend to use underlay/soundproofing felt thicker than that of the original, it is important to allow for this when making your new carpets. The profile of the carpet may need to be modified as, in effect, it will be sitting higher up in the vehicle, where the dimensions may be a little different from those nearer the floor level! In such cases, first cut out the underlay/soundproofing, lay this in position in the car, and make templates of the shape of the raised floor.

When matching colours, always use a piece of the original carpet which has been taken from a part of the car not subject to excessive sunlight – under a seat, for instance.

There can be complications where control pedals, handbrake lever, and so on, emerge from the floor; and around seat belt mountings and where the original carpet featured a sewn-in heel pad.

The original carpets will quite likely have been bound with suitable reinforcing material around apertures and along their edges. Also several sections of carpet were often joined together – for example, where front floorpan carpets join those covering the transmission tunnel.

In each case, a heavy duty sewing machine will be required. A domestic machine is useless for such work. If you don't possess an industrial machine, you can still create the shapes required and ask a professional upholsterer to join them together, or apply edge binding, heel mats, etc., as required.

Carpet sections which are vertically applied to inner sill panels, kickboards, and so on, are usually glued in place – make sure that the sections will all fit together perfectly *before* you apply the adhesive.

Make sure, too, that where carpet is fitted to inner sills (for example) that it is cut sufficiently low along its top edge to allow the refitting of aluminium trim panels, etc. These are often fitted to the upper flanges between the inner and outer sills, and their presence can be forgotten when trimming a car with a stripped out interior (guess how I know?)

When making and fitting replacement carpets – and especially when there are no original patterns to work to – think carefully about how each section will fit in the vehicle. Just one example of where complications can arise is in the relationship between carpet covering the transmission tunnel and that on the floor of the vehicle. In this case, for a neat appearance the edges of the carpet on the tunnel should sit on the floor on either side of the tunnel, and the flat sections of floor carpet should sit *on top of* the edges of the transmission tunnel sections.

FIXINGS

For floor-mounted carpets, many were originally fastened to the vehicle with three-pronged, circular fasteners. These are made in three sections. A metal ring, from which the prongs (locking tabs) extend, is passed through the carpet (with the ring sitting on top of it) and locks on to a lower, securing socket ring, which sits below the carpet.

To lock the two rings together, the prongs from the upper ring pass through slots in the lower one, and are then bent over to secure it in place. To prevent the carpet from moving within the car, the lower socket rings are clipped on to floor-mounted buttons, which are screwed to the car.

The positioning of existing buttons on the floor will give a guide to where the fasteners will need to be installed in the new carpet – normally at all corners.

Where no existing buttons are present, one way of ensuring alignment is first to attach the socket assembly to the carpet, then apply chalk to the lower (socket) ring. With the carpet placed in the correct position in the car, a chalk impression will be made on the floor. The centre of this shows the correct position for drilling the hole for the button's retaining screw.

Alternatively, fix the button to the vehicle floor, chalk the head of the button, and then lay the carpet in the correct position on top of it. The button will leave a chalk mark on the underside of the carpet, indicating the correct position for locating the socket assembly.

Always ensure that there are no brake pipes, fuel lines or electrical wiring anywhere near the part of the floor you need to drill for the button's screw. If there are, mount the carpet retainer in another part of the floor.

Where underfelt is used, cut holes in it in appropriate positions to allow the fixing button/screw to pass through so that the carpet can be securely clipped to the button without placing excessive strain on the carpet, and without unsightly changes of gradient around the button.

Where the underfelt is very thick, the retaining buttons may have to be raised a little from the floor by means of spacers, or, if you do not intend to remove the underfelt very often, by mounting the buttons on top of large washers, in turn placed on top of the underfelt. Effectively, in this case, the underfelt is screwed to the floor.

A modern alternative to using button-type fasteners is the adoption of hook-and-loop material (Velcro). This is easily attached and released, and is effective if maybe not original.

Once the carpets have been fitted, and the car is back in use, you will find that they shed pile in quantity for the first month or two. Gently vacuum-clean them at frequent intervals, and thereafter clean the carpets in this way at least once a month to prevent abrasive grit from causing damage to the structure of the weave.

The following photograph sequence illustrates the stages involved in recarpeting a typical mid-1950s Austin saloon. These techniques can be applied to any vehicle.

MAKING CARPETS

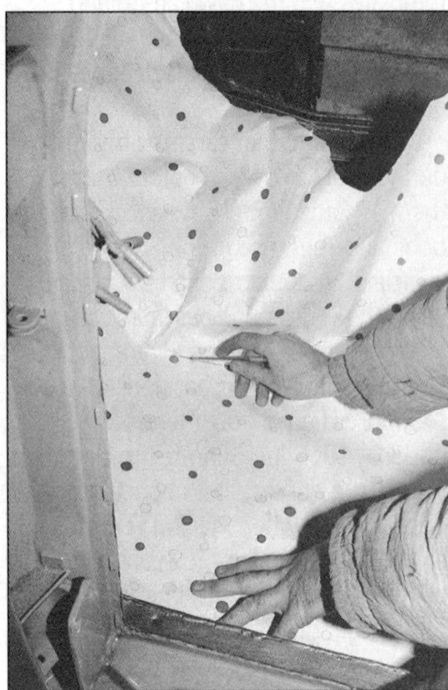

▲ *10.1. If you have no original patterns to work from, make your own using sheets of masking or brown paper. Press the paper firmly against the bodywork so that impressions are made on the paper around the perimeter of each section. Mark these lines clearly on the paper.*

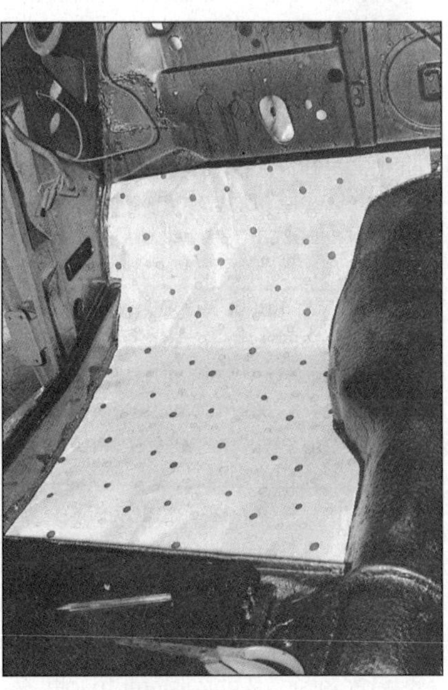

▲ *10.2. Cut around the lines so drawn, then double check that the template thus formed fits the floor of the car as it should.*

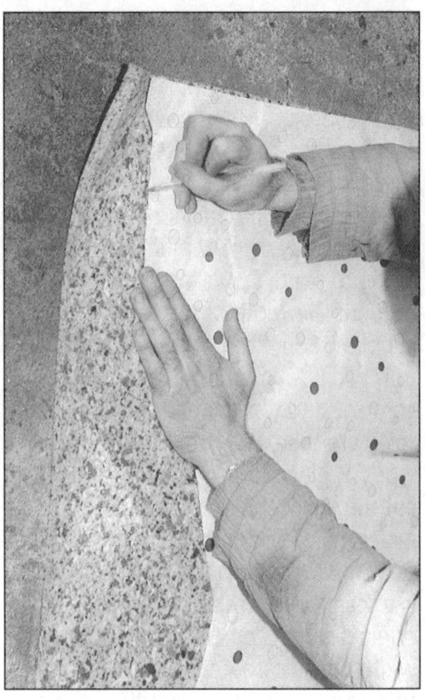

▲ *10.3. Transfer the shape thus formed to the soundproofing/underlay, keeping the pattern and the soundproofing material as flat as possible in the process.*

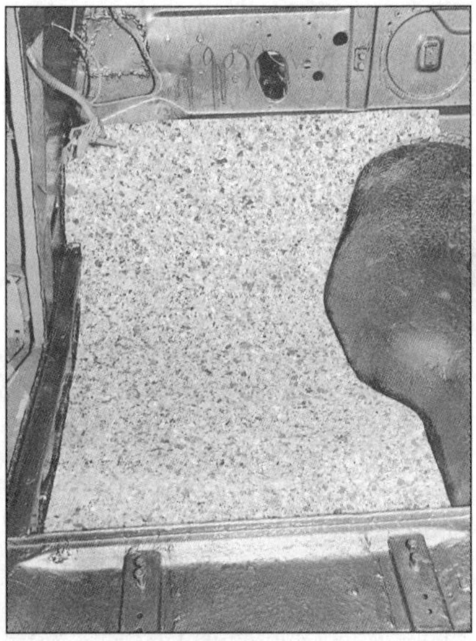

▲ *10.4. Very carefully cut out the required shape, then offer up the soundproofing material to the vehicle, ensuring that it fits properly. It is obviously better to cut the material a little too large, rather than too small – it can then be trimmed precisely to shape.*

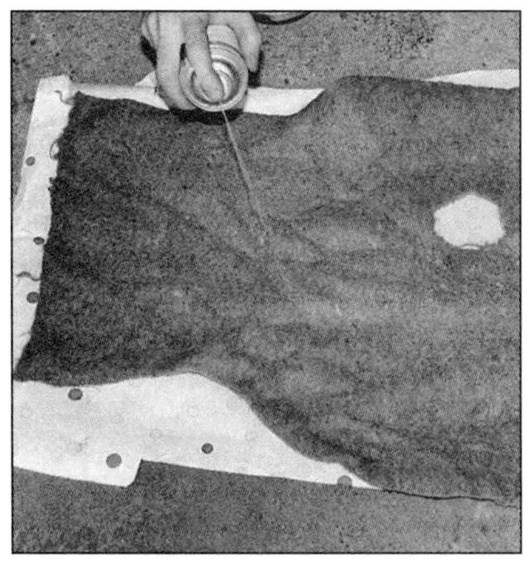

▲ *10.5. It is difficult to correctly shape thick soundproofing material over multi-curved surfaces, like transmission tunnels. Here it may be preferable to re-use the original manufacturer's felt, if in good condition, or to cut to shape a new section of suitable thin felt. This can be glued in place on the tunnel – apply contact adhesive by spray to both the felt and the tunnel.*

▼ *10.6. Offer up all the pieces to ensure that they fit together as they should. Any adjustments can be made at this stage. (Note: In this case original underfelt has been re-used on the transmission tunnel, but a modern, cellular foam soundproofing material has been employed for the main sections of the floor. The application of such soundproofing materials is one area in which modern technology can benefit the owners of older cars!)*

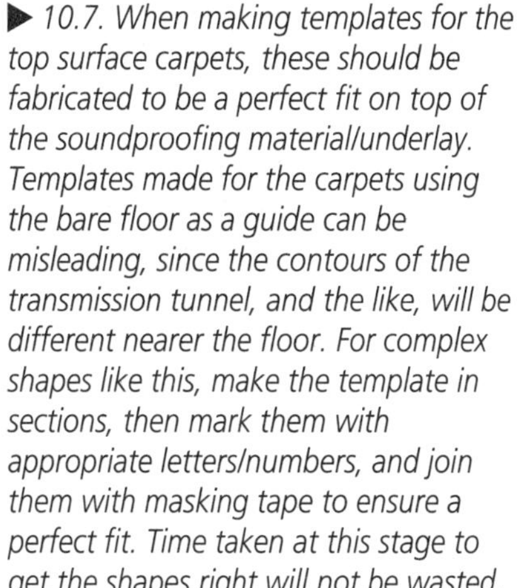

▶ *10.7. When making templates for the top surface carpets, these should be fabricated to be a perfect fit on top of the soundproofing material/underlay. Templates made for the carpets using the bare floor as a guide can be misleading, since the contours of the transmission tunnel, and the like, will be different nearer the floor. For complex shapes like this, make the template in sections, then mark them with appropriate letters/numbers, and join them with masking tape to ensure a perfect fit. Time taken at this stage to get the shapes right will not be wasted.*

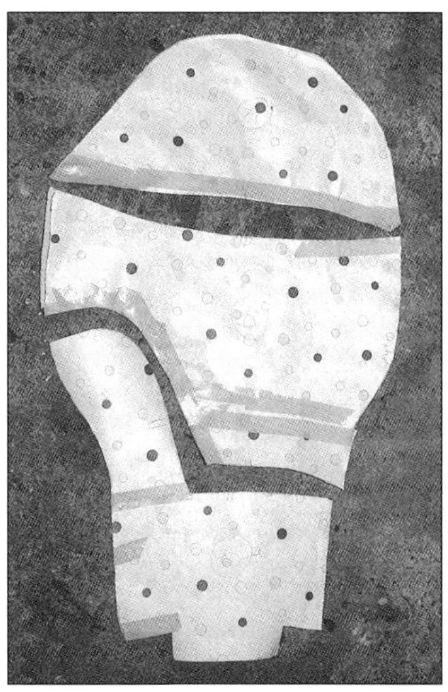

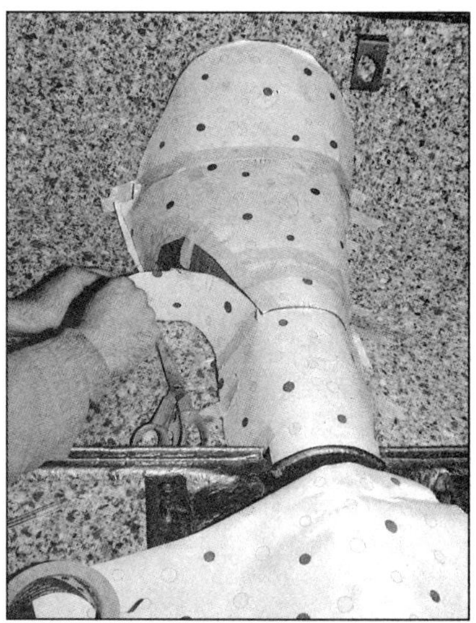

◀ *10.8. When you are satisfied that the profile is correct, separate the three components once again. It is vitally important to get the shapes precisely correct. As can be seen, when laid flat, the various sections take on an entirely different shape from their profiles when wrapped over the curved surface of the transmission tunnel.*

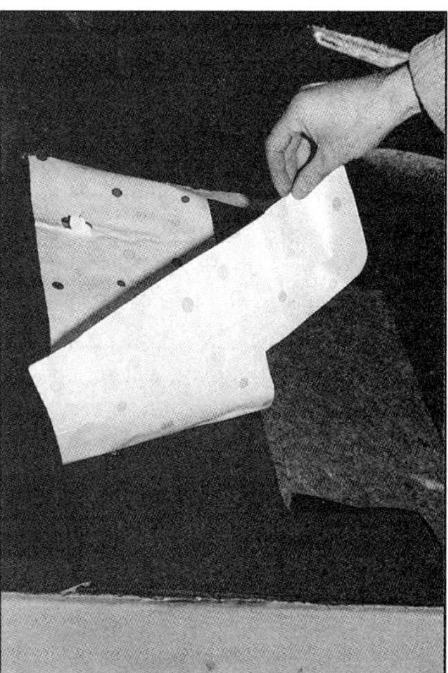

▲ *10.9. Make similar paper patterns for all the sections of carpet required, and ensure that each fits perfectly into its allotted space in the vehicle. Often – but not always – the profiles of the left-hand side floor sections are mirror images of those on the right-hand side.*

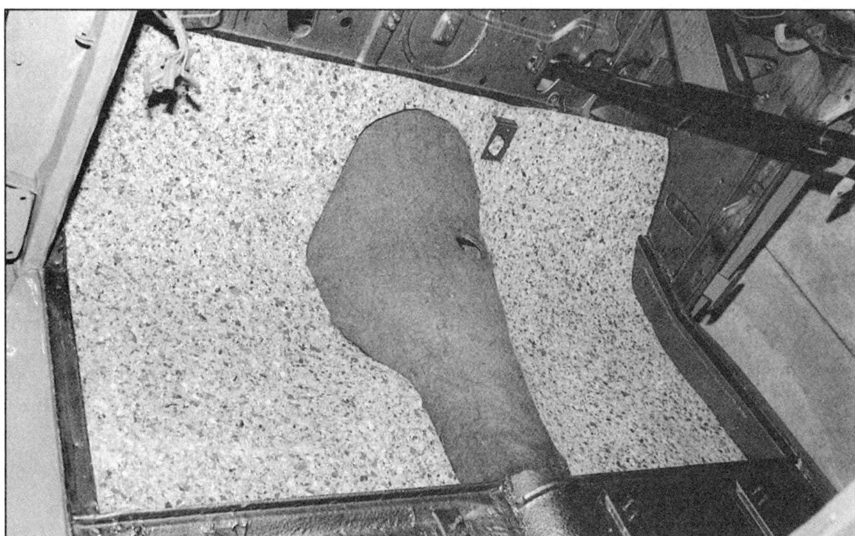

▲ *10.10. Believe it or not, the two adjacent sections of carpet shown above are from the same roll, but one section is placed at 90° to the other. The difference in the reflected light and therefore the appearance/colour is because of the different directions in which the weave/pile runs. Therefore, when transferring the shapes from your paper templates to the actual carpet to be used, ensure that the pile runs in the same direction for all sections, or the finished carpet set will look very odd!*

▼ *10.11. Before actually marking out on the carpet, ensure that the template is the correct way up, or the carpet section will effectively be upside down! When marking the profile of each section, lay the carpet face down on a clean surface, securely hold the template against the carpet, and – preferably using tailor's chalk – carefully mark around the edge of the template so that the correct shape appears on the carpet.*

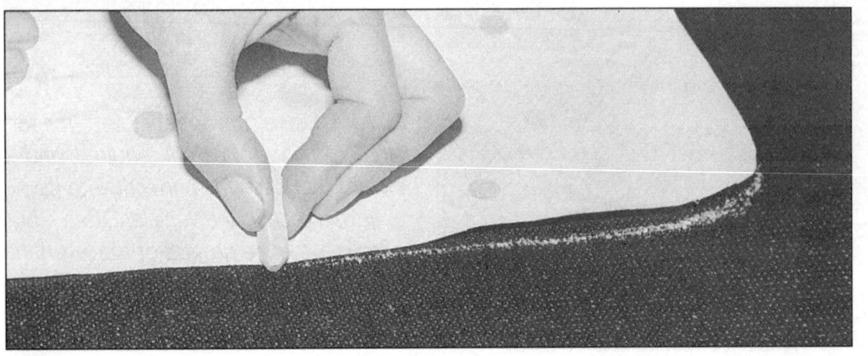

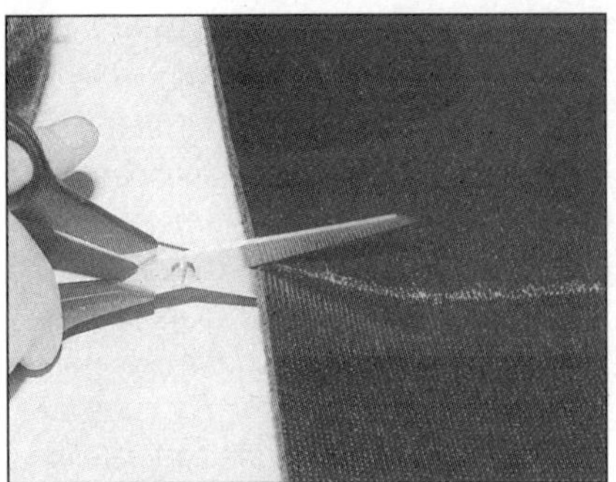

▲ *10.12. Now comes the critical task of cutting out. Take great care to ensure that the carpet is cut to exactly the same shape and size as the template, by cutting on the inside of the chalk line (in effect, this represents the outside edge of the template).*

BINDING

Carpet edges look far better when bound, and are less prone to fraying. Whichever method of binding you choose, the two ends of the binding material used will have to be joined. The easiest method is to simply overlap the ends of the material. However, this can leave an obvious high spot, best positioned in an unobtrusive section of the carpet.

An alternative, especially useful when all of the carpet is highly visible or vulnerable to heavy use, is to feather the adjacent, overlapping ends of binding material by reducing their thickness towards their ends. Use a craft knife *(taking great care, and always cutting away from you)* to form mating tapers on each end, then glue/sew in place.

There are several methods which can be adopted when binding carpets – in each case, ensure that the stitching which secures the binding is not too close to the edge of it, or it may not hold fast for long.

READY-MADE BINDING

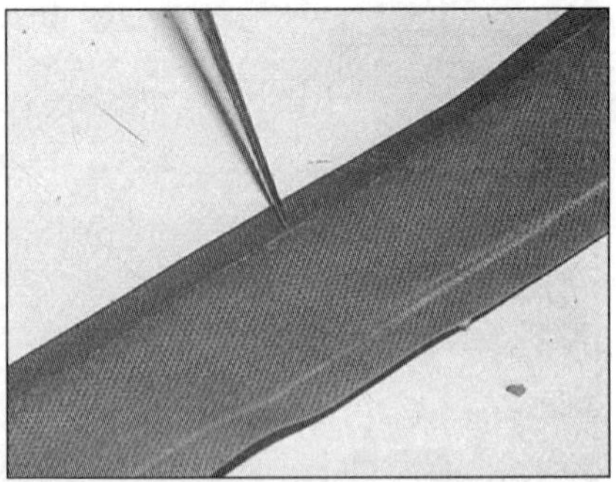

▲ *10.13. Firms such as Woolies can provide ready-made binding. This takes the form of a strip of binding material with one edge turned over and pre-glued in place.*

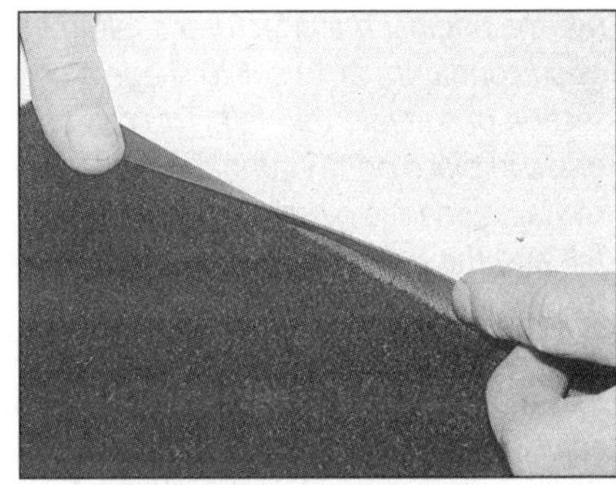

▲ *10.14. Wrap the binding over the edge of the carpet, ensuring that the width of the binding is uniform all the way along. If necessary, the binding can be glued on the reverse side, to hold it in place.*

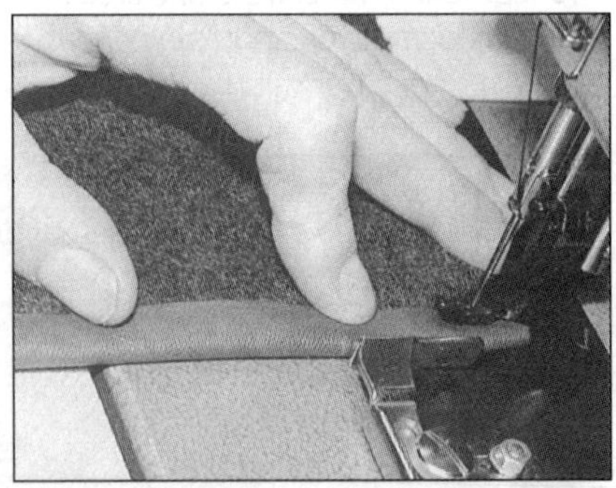

▲ *10.15. With the binding now carefully folded over onto the top of the carpet's pile, sew in position through both sides of the binding, just inboard from the edge. Note the metal guide in place on the sewing machine deck – the carpet and binding material are held against this as they are fed through the machine.*

MAKING YOUR OWN BINDING

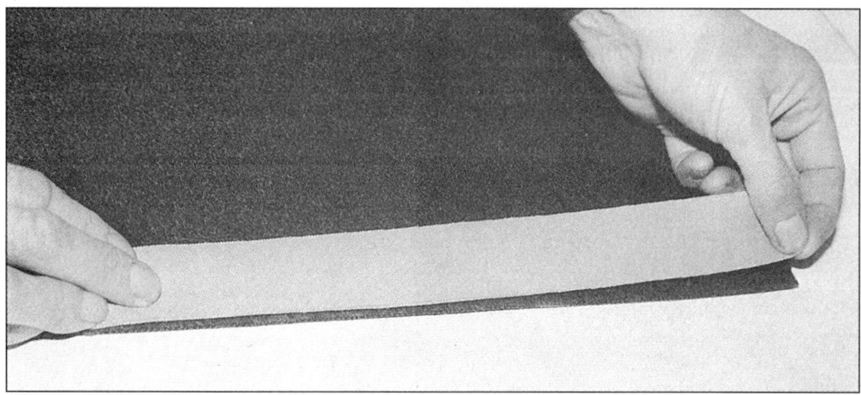

▲ *10.16. Cut a strip of leather or stretch-vinyl of sufficient length for the perimeter of the carpet you are binding, and approximately 1.5 in (4cm) wide. Place this face down onto the pile of the carpet, along the edge.*

▲ *10.17. Sew the binding strip to the carpet, making the seam approximately 0.3 in (0.75cm) from the outer edge.*

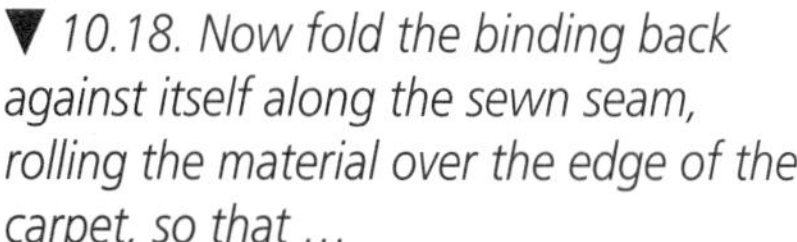

▼ *10.18. Now fold the binding back against itself along the sewn seam, rolling the material over the edge of the carpet, so that …*

▼ *10.19. … from the back of the carpet it appears like this.*

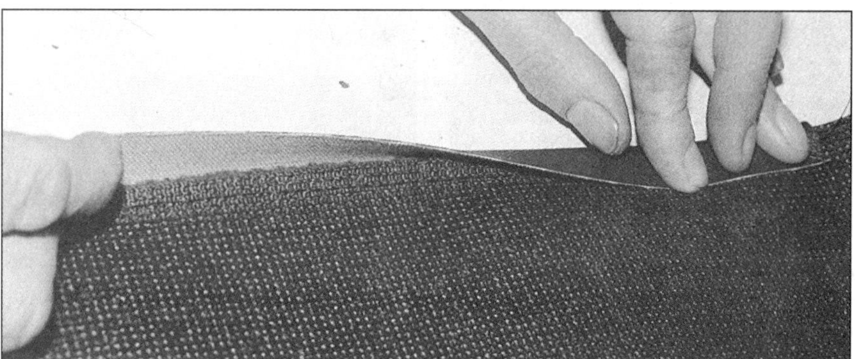

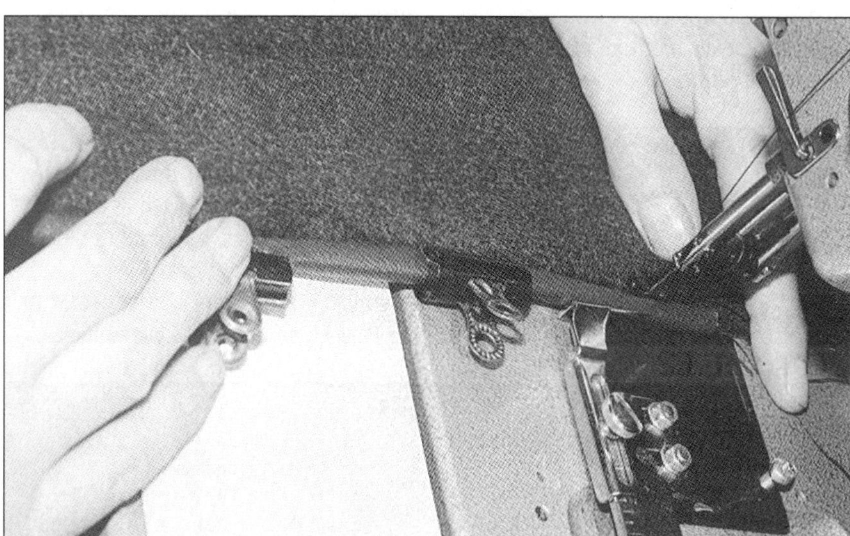

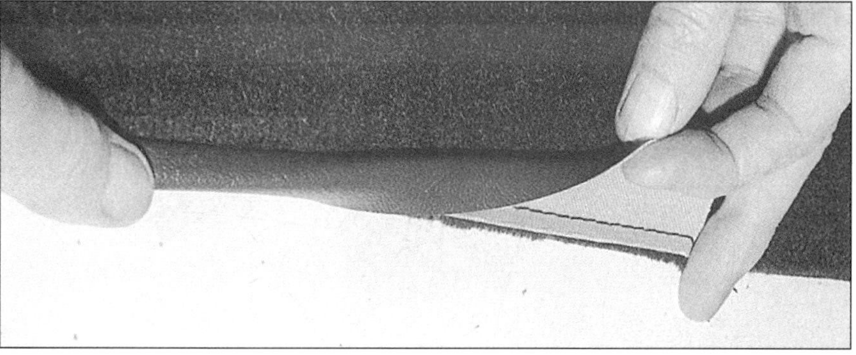

▲ *10.20. Firmly hold or clamp the newly-formed binding in place, and sew through the pile of the carpet to stitch the binding in position. Run the seam just inboard of the binding material so that the stitches pass through the folded over edge of the binding beneath the carpet, yet are not visible from the pile side.*

▶ *10.21. The finished binding should then look like this from the pile side. It is wise to do a trial run on a test piece, like this, before committing yourself to the actual carpets to be used.*

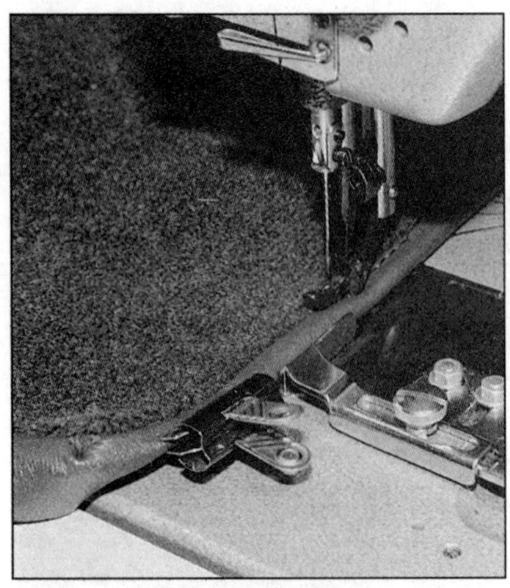

▲ *10.22. An alternative is to stitch the final seam so that the stitches pass through the outer side of the binding material, and are therefore visible from the pile side of the carpet. Many feel this is a less attractive method, in terms of the finished result.*

▲ *10.23. A useful attachment is this automatic binding machine, which feeds the binding material onto the edge of the carpet, enabling it to be positioned and sewn in place in one straightforward operation. The binding material slides through the machine far more easily if lubricated on both sides with talcum powder. The machine works best with thin materials.*

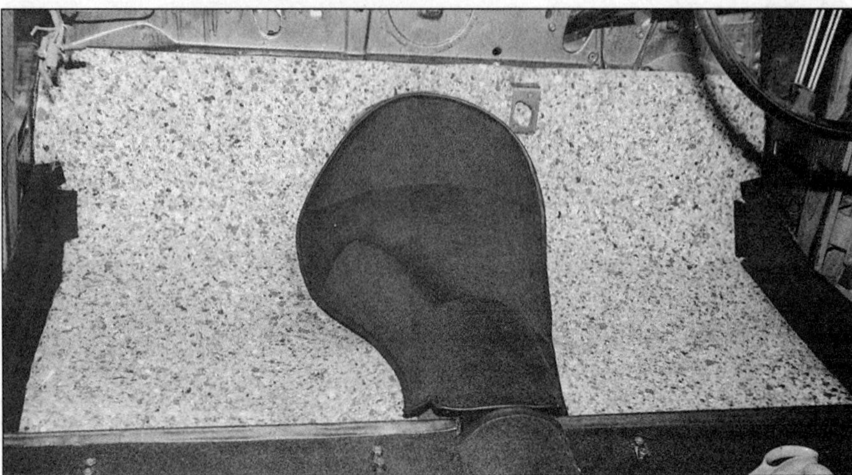

▲ *10.24. The forward section of the transmission tunnel is a complex shape in many cars. For this Austin A50 Cambridge, the carpet for this area was made in three separate sections, then sewn together, before finally being bound neatly around the edge.*

DEALING WITH OBSTRUCTIONS

Unfortunately, most car floors present unhelpful obstructions, such as control pedals, dip switches, handbrakes, steering columns and gear levers. It is essential that these are skirted neatly, or the finished carpets will look awful.

▼ *10.25. Use large sheets of paper to make the necessary patterns. Slots can be cut from the edges of the paper to the positions of the various obstructions, and circular holes/slots can be cut to accommodate the steering column and other large items. Ensure that the pattern fits perfectly, and trim as required in order to achieve this. Incidentally, the car shown here is a left-hand drive 1954 Ford Taunus.*

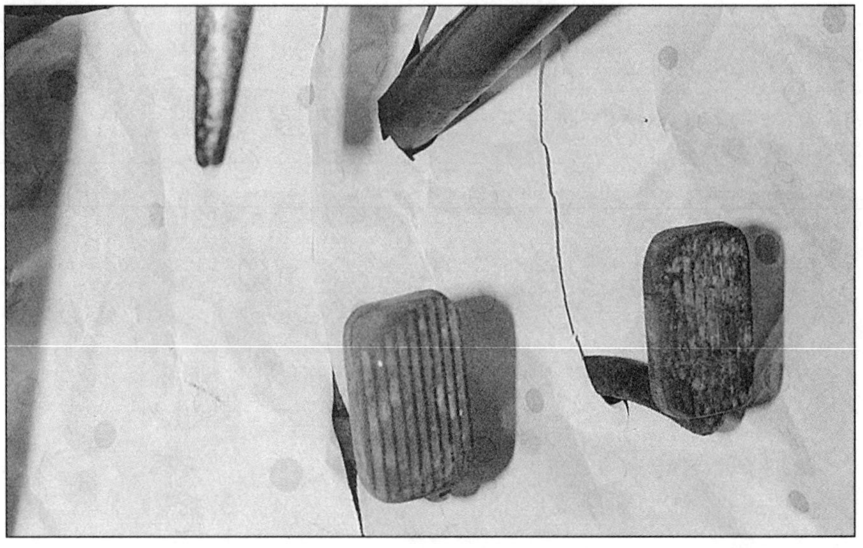

▶ *10.26. Floor-mounted dip switches are often found on older cars, like this 1954 Ford Taunus. Again, they can be negotiated by cutting circular apertures/slots in the paper.*

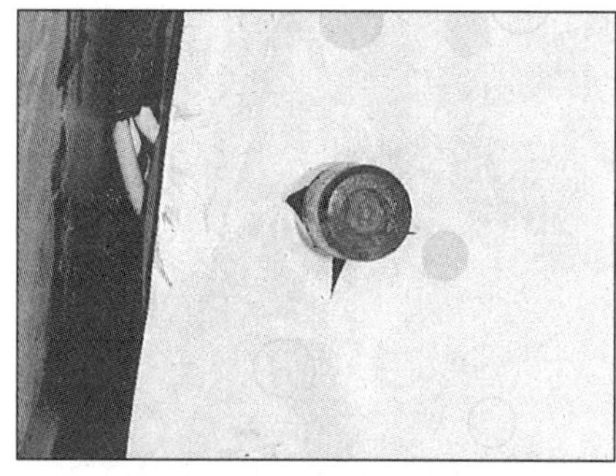

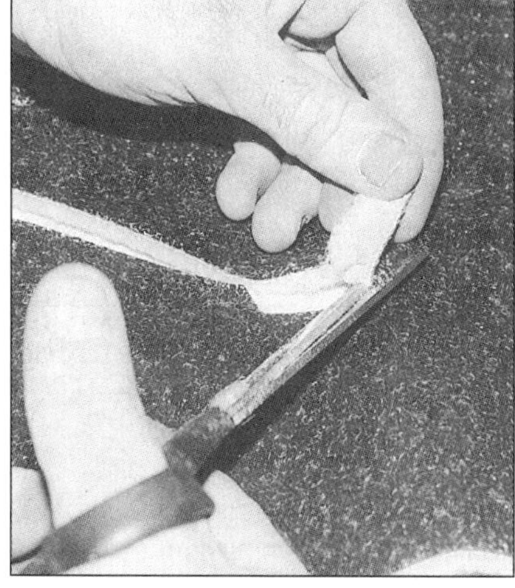

▲ *10.27. Transfer the shapes from the templates to the back of the carpets, as shown previously, then very carefully cut out the required slots and circles in the carpet.*

▼ *10.28. Now offer up the carpet to the car, once again ensuring that the holes are precisely in the correct positions (they must be!). Note that on this test piece an alternative method of accommodating the steering column and clutch/brake pedals has been employed, in which the slots from column to the pedals take the profile of an inverted V.*

▼ *10.29. The cut edges of the apertures made now have to be bound. This is carried out in the manner already described for normal binding. However, the binding in this case necessarily has to travel round very tight curves, and to allow this, slots need to be cut in the excess binding material on the outside of corner sections.*

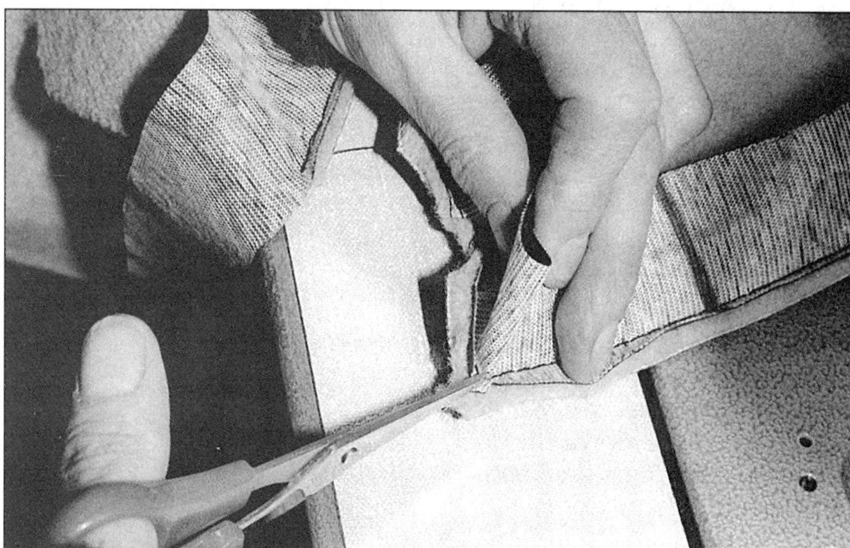

CIRCULAR APERTURES (AND OTHERS WITH TIGHT CORNERS)

Binding apertures which incorporate tight radii can be time-consuming, and care is needed to obtain a neat finished result.

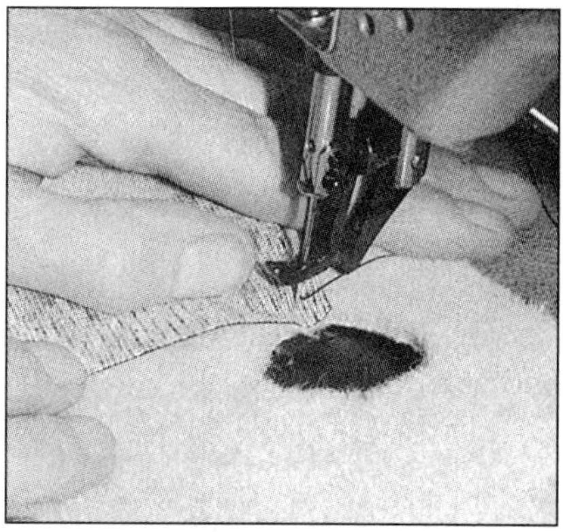

▲ *10.30. Start by sewing the binding material to the edge of the aperture. Place the material face down against the pile face of the carpet, close to the edge of the hole.*

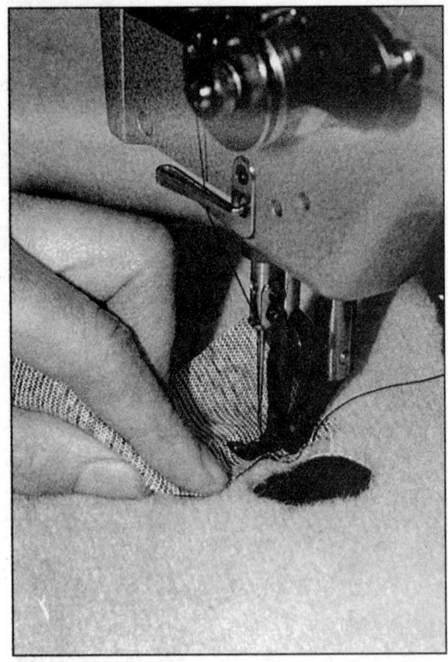

▲ 10.31. *Constantly turn in the seam around the edge of the carpet and binding material, so that the stitching follows the edge of the aperture as neatly as possible. It may be necessary to cut slots in the binding material to enable it to follow the profile of the circle.*

▼ 10.32. *Now feed the free edge of the binding material through the hole, and …*

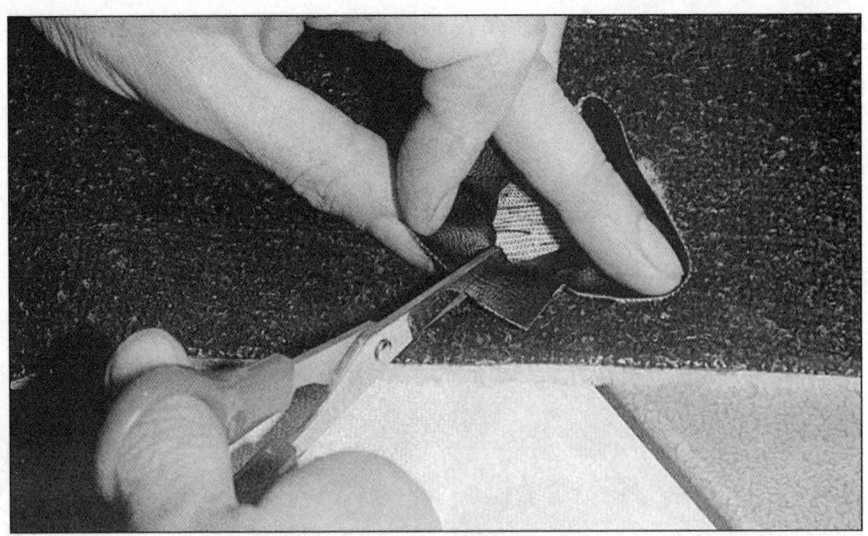

▲ 10.33. *… slot the edge of the binding as necessary to enable it to sit neatly around the edge of the hole. If necessary, glue the binding in place, then finally sew the edge to the carpet (from the back), trimming off excess material as required.*

▲ 10.34. *Here's one we made earlier! Once finished, the fully bound carpet looks smart and should last a long time. Once again, it is always wise to practice by making a test piece (or two!), before tackling a real carpet for your car.*

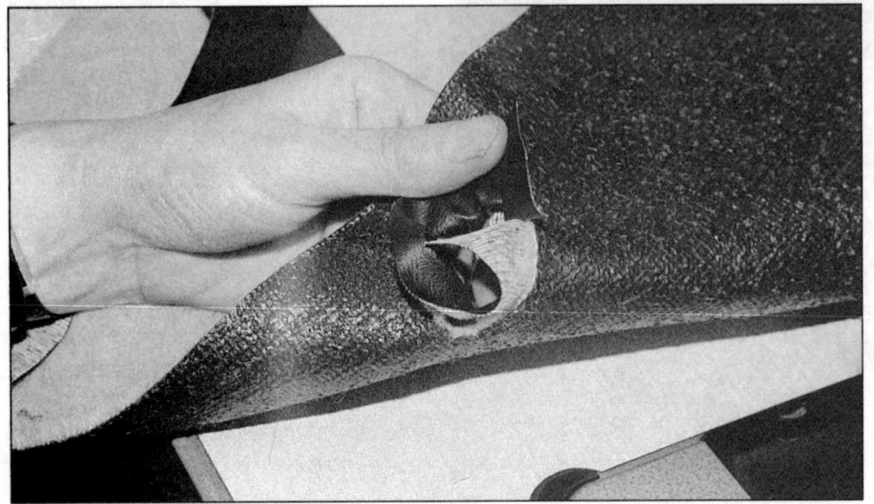

► 10.35. *An alternative method of binding awkwardly shaped apertures (or indeed carpet edges) – and easier to carry out, if less attractive in finished appearance – is to apply the binding material face up on top of the carpet pile, and to form the seam around the hole just inboard of the outer edge of the binding material. The snag with this is that the stitches are visible from the pile side of the carpet. The free edge of the binding material is then pushed through the hole and sewn in position from the reverse side of the carpet, again (as shown here) just inboard of the edge of the material. In this instance the binding has been formed by cutting two strips of vinyl to follow the awkward profile of the pedal aperture, with the join between them running around the inside of the hole where it is not easily seen.*

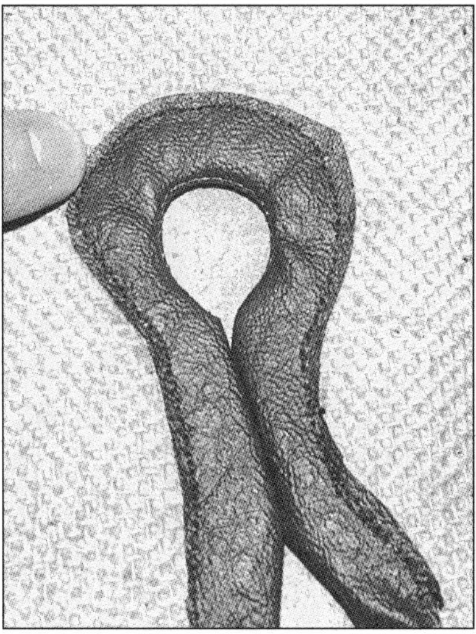

ATTACHING THE CARPETS

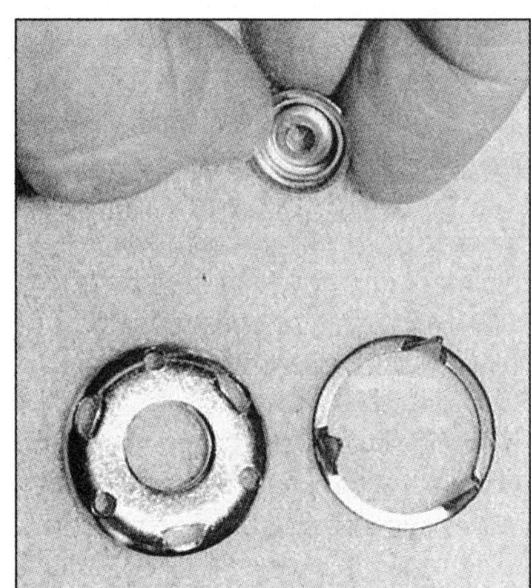

▲ 10.36. *Carpets are often secured to the vehicle by means of a floor-mounted button and carpet-mounted socket assembly, like these. Available from firms such as Woolies, they are easily installed (usually in corners) and prevent the carpet from walking. The button (top) is screwed to the floor, while the three prongs of the retaining ring (right) are passed downwards from the pile side, through the carpet, to mate with the lower section of the socket assembly (left). To secure the carpet, it, together with the socket assembly, is simply pushed downwards to lock onto the floor-mounted button.*

▼ 10.37. *In order to mount the button on the floor, a hole must be drilled to accommodate the retaining screw. Ensure that there are no brake pipes, fuel lines or electrical cables in the vicinity of the proposed hole, then carefully drill through the floor. In this Jaguar, the soundproofing felt installed was quite thick, so it was decided to drill the felt together with the floor, and to mount the button on top of the felt.*

▼ 10.38. *Use a large 'penny' washer under the head of the button, and screw the assembly to the floor. Apply a little copper-based anti-seize compound to the threads, to help combat corrosion and to make the screw easier to release next time.*

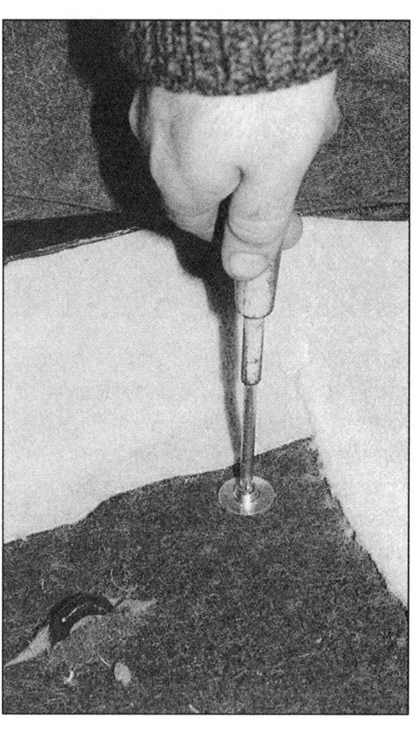

▼ 10.39. *Establish the correct position for mounting the socket assembly in the carpet. It can help to mark the head of the button with chalk, then to place the carpet on top of it, leaving a chalk impression in the correct position for mounting the socket assembly. Alternatively ...*

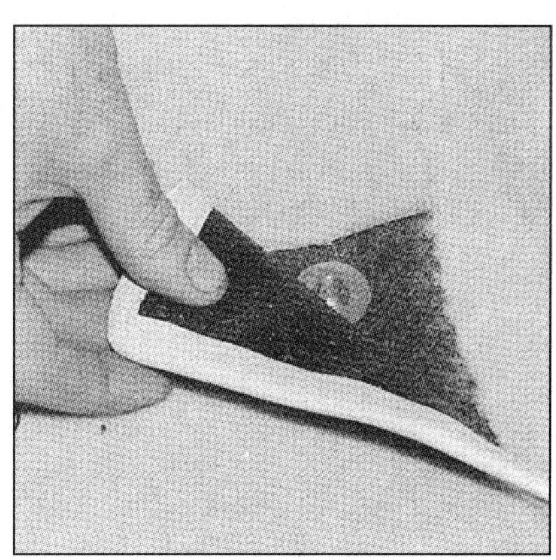

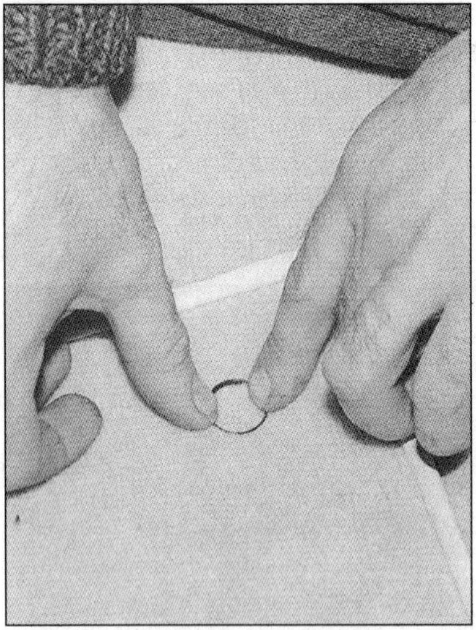

▲ *10.40. … push gently down on the carpet to establish where the hump formed by the button is. Now place the three pronged ring, forming the upper component of the socket assembly, around the button and push the prongs downwards and through the carpet.*

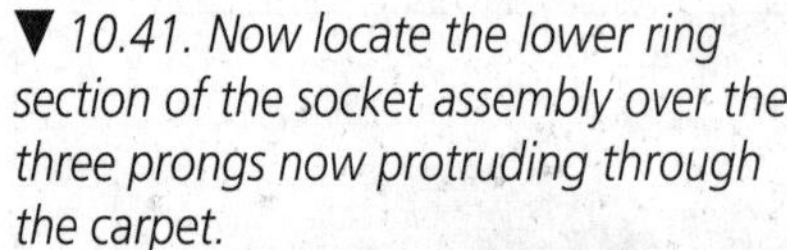

▼ *10.41. Now locate the lower ring section of the socket assembly over the three prongs now protruding through the carpet.*

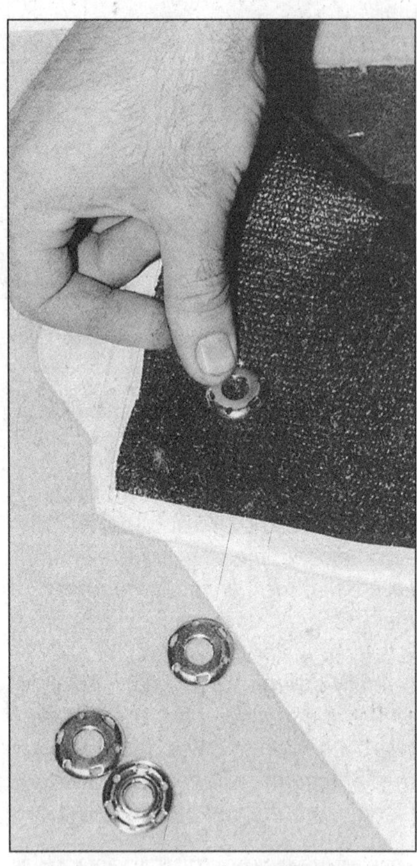

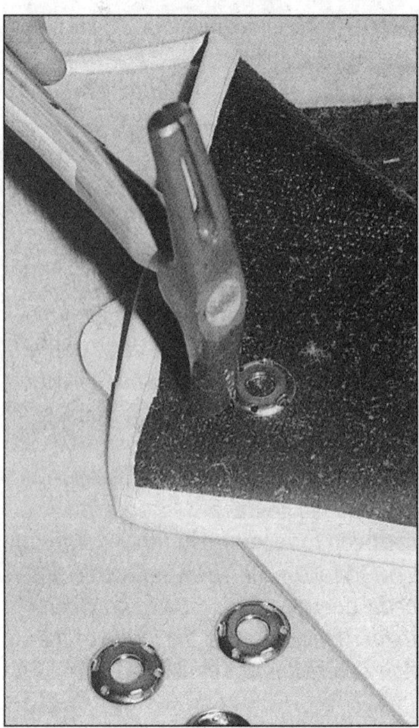

▲ *10.42. Once in position through the lower ring, use a hammer to bend the prongs from the upper ring to a horizontal position on the underside of the carpet, having first placed a wood block beneath the pile side of the carpet, to react against. This locks the rings together to form the carpet-mounted socket part of the assembly. The carpet can now be clipped to the floor.*

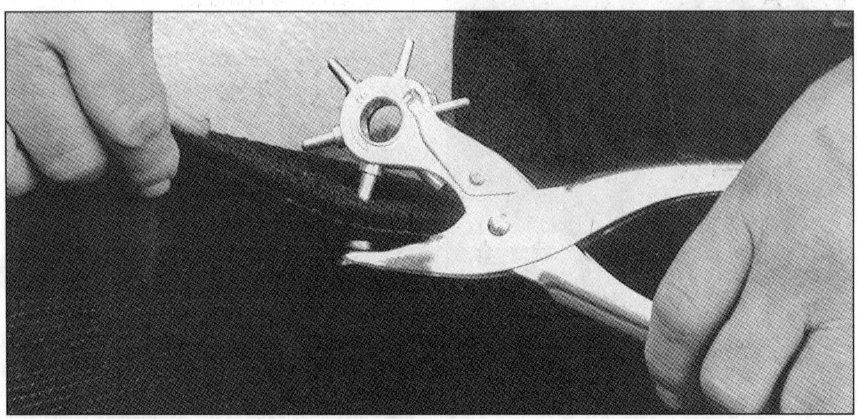

◀ *10.43. Some vehicles feature carpets which are screwed in place (for example, on the lower sections of the doors), and holes need to be made in the carpet to accommodate the screws. It is best to make such holes using a proper punch, like this one from Frost Auto Restoration Techniques. The use of a normal drill for making holes in carpets can result in the pile tearing away from the carpet and wrapping itself around the drill bit!*

Chapter 11

Soft tops and sun roofs

Perhaps for obvious reasons, convertible cars have an extra appeal, and in recent years their popularity has increased. The ability to be able to drop the roof and take full advantage of pleasant weather and fresh air (whenever it is available) has made most drophead models desirable vehicles.

However, such models can be very much less desirable if the hood (soft top) is badly fitting and/or leaks cold air and rainwater into the interior. I once drove a borrowed Austin Healey over 100 miles on a cold night, with icy air blasting around my neck from poor joints in the hood, and it's not an experience I would like to repeat!

For a convertible car to be really enjoyable to drive in all weathers, the hood must be of the correct type, properly put together, fitted with care and in perfect condition.

Many older convertibles have had their hoods replaced several times, and replacements are not always of the best quality, in terms of materials used or workmanship. It is far better, in a way, to have an original hood, albeit in poor condition, than a 'cheap and cheerful' replacement in better shape. At least with the original you have a chance of duplicating the manufacturer's design features.

REPAIR OR REPLACE?

It should be fairly obvious from a close examination whether the hood on your car is a candidate for replacement, or whether it will be possible to effect repairs to localized damage.

If the hood is sound (and perhaps original), but suffering from a few fairly small tears and holes, with perhaps an opaque rear window, it might be possible to repair it by replacing the window and carrying out patch repairs to the localized damage.

It has to be said that if damage is any more extensive than that described, it may be preferable to buy or make and fit a replacement hood assembly. Repairs are nearly always visible, especially those affecting larger areas of damage. Of course, a great deal will depend on your budget and how concerned you are with a perfect looking hood.

For many popular convertibles – especially sports models – replacement hoods are available off-the-shelf from a variety of suppliers. Prices vary from the expensive to the surprisingly cheap, and the quality of the products offered often varies directly in proportion to the cost! So, if you are considering buying a ready-made replacement hood, first take a look at exactly what you might be buying.

Consider – in relation to the original hood – the type and thickness of material used, the way in which the replacement has been made and whether vitally important areas, subject to stresses and strains in everyday use, are adequately reinforced. Look for the quality of binding along exposed edges. Ensure, too, that the fasteners employed on the replacement hood are compatible with, and of similar quality to, the originals on your car.

Take a close look at the rear window and the way it is fitted into the hood. If it is a very thin plastic screen, it may not last long. Similarly, if it is badly stitched in place, leaks won't be long in coming – and so on. In fact, most hoods today have the rear windows heat-sealed in place – look at the window and ensure that the sealing looks sound.

If you are a member of the one-make club(s) appropriate to your vehicle, talk to fellow owners and look at their cars. You should soon be able to arrive at a consensus of opinion regarding the best suppliers in terms of quality of product and fairness of price.

If there are no suitable suppliers of ready-to-fit hoods for your car, your options are either to have a hood made by a professional trimmer, or to make one yourself. The former is likely to be expensive, while the latter will take longer and may be more stressful!

Certainly, making and fitting a hood – and getting it right – can be a complex business, but patience will pay off and you should be able to achieve a result to be proud of. As in many cases when it comes to trim work, very often the original hood will be a useful source of information, so take measurements, notes and photos/video (inside and out) before dismantling. On the other hand, if your hood is a hopelessly bodged replacement by a previous owner, try to find a fellow owner with a correct original-style hood and take your measurements, etc., from this.

GO FOR GOLD

When considering the type of material to use on your replacement hood, my advice is to go for the best quality you can afford, consistent with the type of hood originally fitted. The vast differences in looks, feel, insulation qualities and longevity of good hooding material are out of all proportion to the relatively small additional cost, compared with a budget-quality item. The extra outlay at the start will be outweighed by the enjoyment of a product which is superior in every respect.

Good quality material is usually far stronger in every respect (being less prone to splits and other damage), and will therefore last longer, but it will also provide better heat and sound insulation, and in winter it will give a far more snug feel to the cockpit than inferior grade alternatives.

The type of hood material involved will depend on the age of the vehicle, and whether or not its hood is original. Early models used leather, waterproofed canvas or rubberized fabric, whereas many later cars have plastic-based hoods. If you are unsure of what was originally appropriate to your particular car, again, talk to fellow owners and/or join the relevant owners' club – another member may know the answer.

Beware of buying 'new old stock' hoods that are very old and may have been exposed to sunlight, etc., while in storage. Sometimes the material may *look* fine, only to show previously hidden weaknesses when it has been in service for a short time. Where possible, buy only products that appear to have been carefully wrapped, and even then, inspect all edges for damage and all folds for signs of weakness.

While on the subject of potential problems with folds in the material, it is always wise to store a convertible with the hood erected since this prevents severe creases from forming and helps to keep the hood in shape. A few years ago, while exploring a breaker's yard, I came across an old Austin drophead coupé which I estimated to have been in the yard for probably 20 years. The bodywork was all but rusted away, but there, proud and intact, stood the hood, which had been left in the raised position, and which had survived better than the rest of the car!

MATERIAL TYPES

The array of different materials on sale from which hoods can be made is bewildering, so it is worth taking a look at some of the types on offer, their construction and their cost.

Everflex hooding material is relatively inexpensive, and comprises a single coating plastic sheet with a cotton backing. It is available in a variety of colours. There are several cheaper materials on offer (for perhaps two thirds the cost of Everflex) but not all of them of good quality.

For about twice the price of the Everflex hooding, Cabriolet material is available. This is a double layer, PVC-coated fabric, with 100 per cent cotton backing, and the quality is naturally superior.

Those seeking more traditional materials can buy Duck. This comprises two sheets of vat-dyed cloth (with the weaves running in opposite directions), with a rubber sheet sandwiched between them. The price is on a par with Cabriolet hooding. Cheaper imitations are available. All varieties have a tendency to fade, and can also shrink when wet, making the hood difficult to attach to and detach from its fasteners.

At the higher end of the quality and price scale come the mohair ranges, and the modern mohair equivalents. Essentially these comprise 100 per cent polyester covering material, with a cotton lining. They are available in various grades, including a lightweight version (which is a little more expensive than Duck hooding) and heavier types. The advantages of these better quality materials are that they are less prone to shrinkage, have less tendency to fade and are not so likely to crease – in fact, they are better all round!

Note that although the mohair materials just described are essentially modern materials, they have in fact been around since World War Two. The heavier types are equivalent to the likes of Mercedes, Porsche and BMW original equipment grades, and can cost more than twice as much as lightweight versions or Duck.

There are other in-between types of hooding available, for example 100 per cent acrylic materials, costing a little more than Duck.

Colours available vary with the type of hooding. The Everflex range has 12 colours, compared with the two (black or fawn) of Duck, and the four of the cheaper mohair types – black, navy blue, blue or beige. Acrylics provide a choice of five (or so) colours.

It is worth noting that hooding suppliers often recommend making a two-per-cent shrinkage allowance for plastic-based materials, such as Everflex, etc. Shrinkage when wet is a feature of virtually all types of hooding.

CONSTRUCTION

Many older cars had their soft tops supported on a few hood sticks – originally wooden cross-members, later replaced by steel tubes. A number of models – including some British sports cars – have hoods and sticks which are completely removable. By contrast, other cars employ folding mechanisms – some of which are quite complex – to enable the hood to be raised and lowered more easily. A further complication, on some convertibles, including the Ford Zodiac and many American models, is power operation of the hood.

Where hood sticks are employed, the sticks are sometimes held in place by clip-on pockets on the inside of the hood, or just by the tension in the hood material itself.

With any hood the aim must be – consistent with the original design, of course – to minimize the number of seams (all of which are potential starting points for leaks), and to form any seams which *are* necessary in such a way that water is discouraged from entering the joint. Again, a close examination of the original will give invaluable clues to both aspects. Often a hood will be made in three distinct sections – a large central area, flanked by two, narrower side panels.

Early hoods were made in several sections (from front to back of the car), held in position on wooden cross-frames and with the adjacent, overlapping sections of hooding material joined together by being tacked to the frame. To hide the join, and to prevent the ingress of moisture, the seams thus formed were covered with trim strips – often of brass or bronze, with lead fillings from which built-in tacks protruded. These were simply tapped into place over the top of each join.

Appropriate replacement trim strips can be obtained from trim suppliers, and can be fitted at home, although great care is needed to avoid damaging the soft strip. A protective block of wood, or a soft-faced mallet, should be used when tapping such strips home.

On later convertibles, hoods were nearly always attached only at the header rail (across the top of the windscreen), at the rearmost frame hoop, and on the rear deck panel, behind and below the rear window.

Sometimes, where these attachments are achieved by nailing in place, and the nails are visible, 'hidem' banding is used to conceal the line of tacks. This is most obviously seen on the rear hoop, this being tacked onto the frame, often with millboard attached to the steel frame for use as a tacking strip. On pre-war types the rear hoop is often made completely of wood.

The 'hidem' banding can be attached by using small-headed, parallel-sided gimp pins, carefully inserted into the valley of the banding, every inch or so along its length. Where necessary, widen the valley by using a flat-bladed screwdriver, or similar implement, to allow the gimp pins in. Drive them home using a small punch (take care not to damage the surrounding hooding or 'hidem' banding material). Always start from the centre of the car and work outwards.

More recent cars have steel hood frames, to which the hood itself is attached by means of loops attached to the lower side of the hood.

In many cases the hood will be made from three, separate sections, joined together. These take the form of a large, central portion and two side pieces, all running from the front to the rear of the vehicle, and with the seams between them overlapped to prevent the ingress of moisture.

FASTENERS

A wide variety of fasteners has been used over the years to secure vehicle soft tops to the bodywork. It is, of course, essential that the fasteners are carefully fitted to both the hood and the bodywork, and that they align perfectly.

Fixings at the front and rear of the hood sometimes vary from those at the sides. For example, some hoods incorporate steel strips, sewn into the covering material, and which locate within channels above the windscreen and/or on the rear deck panel. Alternatively – and often on pre-war cars – the front edge of the hood frame sits neatly over the windscreen rail, to be secured by threaded wing bolts or similar fixings. There are many variations on these themes.

Around the sides and rear edges of the hood, various methods are used to secure the material, to make it weatherproof and to prevent flapping in the breeze! Your choice of fastener will largely be governed by what was originally used on the car – not necessarily what you find fitted when you acquire the vehicle! Again, if in doubt about this, talk to fellow owners.

Holes will have to be made in the hooding material to accept the fasteners, and these are best made by using hollow punches of the appropriate diameters. Use a lead block (covered with masking paper or a plastic sheet, to prevent the hooding material being marked) placed on the bench underneath the material, in order to achieve a clean cut. It is vitally important that the apertures made are only just big enough to accept the fasteners. Indeed it is usually advantageous to make the holes fractionally smaller, so that the fasteners are a nice, firm fit (without excessively straining the material).

It is useful to note that the push-button types of fastener require the correct special tools to fit them to the hooding; other varieties don't.

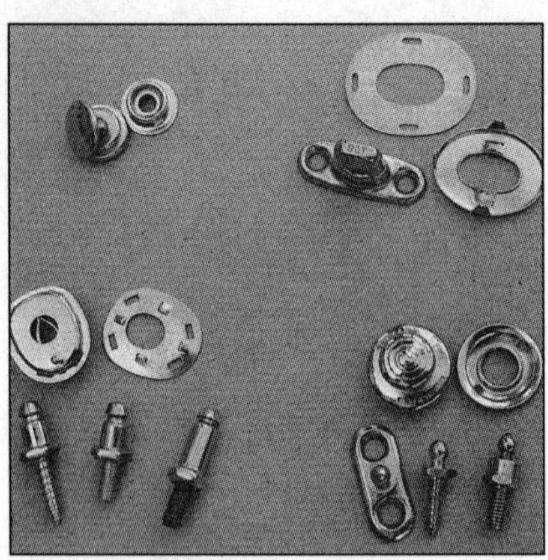

▲ *11.1. These hood fasteners – available from Woolies of Market Deeping, near Peterborough – are just four of the more commonly encountered varieties. They are, from top right and in a clockwise direction: Turnbuckle, Tenax, Lift the Dot and Durable Dot types. The way in which each type is installed and operates is described in this order in the text.*

Pre-war type cars often used Turnbuckle type fasteners. These comprise a spring-loaded turn section, mounted on the car's body, and a corresponding socket fixed within the hooding material. The socket is made from two interlocking components attached from either side of the material (the four prongs from the outer section locate into corresponding slots in the mating, inner component – the prongs are turned over to hold the socket assembly firmly in place). The hooding is retained in place by placing the socket assembly over the turnbuckle, and rotating this through 90°. Releasing the hood is a simple reversal of this process. These traditional types are effective at securing the hood but are not leak-proof!

More effective in keeping out water, and perhaps neater in appearance (yet, of course, not original on some early cars) are the Tenax fixings. With this type, a spring-loaded socket assembly, made in two, screw-together sections, is attached to the hooding by sandwiching the material between the two parts of the socket, which are screwed tightly together to hold them to the hooding.

With Tenax type fixings, the hood is attached to the bodywork by clipping the socket assembly to a corresponding metal spike screwed to the car's body. The spikes can be self-tapping varieties, or threaded to take a nut on the reverse side of the body panel (both these types incorporate spanner flats to enable them to be tightly fitted), or they can be attached to pre-drilled brackets, which in turn are screwed to the car.

Lift the Dot fasteners employ spikes attached to the bodywork, similar to the more recent Tenax types, and the socket section attached to the hooding comprises two components – as with the Turnbuckle types, four prongs from the upper section locate into corresponding slots in the lower half. The prongs are turned over to hold the socket assembly to the hooding. However, by contrast with the Turnbuckle variety, the Lift the Dot fasteners are snapped into position, and – as the name implies – are released by simply lifting one edge of the fastener, incorporating a raised dot. These are secure, easy to operate fasteners, but not rainproof.

Durable Dot (snap-on/off type) fasteners are extremely simple in concept and operation, with a socket attached to the hooding material, which is clipped firmly onto a corresponding stub, screwed or riveted to the bodywork. These are waterproof, but can be very difficult to release without hurting your hands, especially if the hooding is a very tight fit (when wet, for example).

Many variations on these main themes may be encountered. If those on your car are too far gone for re-use, the specialist suppliers listed in the Appendix at the end of this book should be able to supply the variety you need. In addition to the traditional, metal fasteners described, you may, on modern cars, encounter additional or alternative fixings, including the use of Velcro hook-and-loop type material. This is sometimes used to secure the hood frame members to the underside of the hooding.

Finally, it is perhaps obvious but, when installing new fasteners, make sure that the hood is properly installed on the vehicle before committing yourself to making holes for them. The positioning of the fasteners on the hooding and car body *must* align precisely, or the hood will never look right, nor will it be weatherproof!

MAKING AND FITTING A HOOD

There are many variations in the way car hoods are constructed; some are simple single-layer types – intended purely for occasional use in keeping showers at bay – others incorporate an inner lining (similar to the headlining on saloons) and the more sophisticated varieties have additional interlinings between the inner lining and outer covering. Obviously, the types with interlinings provide better insulation against noise and temperature variations than less elaborate hoods, and are also – naturally – more expensive and complicated to make.

Hoods also differ in the manner in which they are supported (for example, by removable hood sticks, or on a folding frame assembly) and attached to the vehicle. Because of these variable factors, it is impossible to generalize on methods required for making and fitting a new hood. In any case, there are usually several ways in which the job can be tackled. However, there follows a suggested sequence of working for the construction of a hood (whether or not an original pattern exists to base it on) and its fitting to the car.

The techniques shown are those applied to making and installing a typical multi-layer hood. They should be useful as a guide for most types, but bear in mind that variations on the main theme shown will need to be brought into play to cater for differences encountered on individual vehicles.

To recap: a close study of the old hood (where available) will be helpful in determining how the original was constructed, providing that the hood you remove is, in fact, the original. If you have any doubts, try to find another car of the same type of yours, in 'untouched' form, to use as a guide. Fellow members of the appropriate one make owners' club may be able to assist in this. Take detailed measurements, photographs and/or video film footage from an original hood/lining assembly, to help you later.

I stress again that the following method is only one approach. Later in this chapter there is an abbreviated section showing various hints, tips and alternatives, which can be used in addition to/instead of the methods outlined in the following paragraphs.

It is advisable to read right through the rest of this chapter before attempting any practical work!

STARTING POINT

Faced with constructing a complete hood assembly, it can be rather daunting trying to work out where to start. It is a good idea first to deal with the inner (head) lining, where fitted.

If you don't have an original lining to use as a pattern, paper templates can be made, using the shape of the inside of the old roof, or even the hood frame. It is quite possible to fit an inner lining to a car not originally so equipped, provided that there is sufficient room in the available compartment to stow the thicker hood when folded back.

One of the most difficult aspects of constructing a lining assembly – especially where none was fitted previously – is dealing with the vertical side sections above and behind the doors. One way round this is to incorporate lengths of stout cord into the headlining, at the top and bottom of each side section. They are often tacked in place, under tension.

The cord tensions the lining, and – at the bottom on each side – is required to provide a positive lower boundary to the lining. This is because, unlike the conventional lining in a saloon car, the hood, together with the inner lining, must fold, and there is nowhere fixed for attaching the lower edges of the side sections. In addition, the upper cord on each side marks a convenient dividing line between the horizontal roof panel and the vertical sections which join with it.

Typically, from the front of the car (on each side, at the outside edge of the windscreen header rail) the upper cord runs backwards, over the top of the door to a point above the rear corner of it, then in stages to the rear of the vehicle. The divisions between each stage correspond with one or more of the hood frame hoops, although it does not follow that *every* hoop marks a division.

The lower cord starts from the door shut pillar, at a point just behind the lower rear corner of the door window, and runs to the back of the vehicle, often attaching to the rear of the wheel arch panel, or rear deck/bulkhead (where possible, use an original lining as a guide). It can be helpful to attach (by sewing) a short length of elastic to the back of the lining material, approximately midway along the lower cord, the other end of the elastic being fastened to the lower part of the car bodywork. The elastic will then keep the cord taut, regardless of the position of the hood, and will allow the hood to fold.

The rest of the lining can be built on these foundations.

▲ *11.2. Lined hoods often incorporate padded bolster sections like these, fitted (usually) on top of the support rails (sometimes they are suspended on webbing straps running from the front to the rear of the vehicle). These interlinings – taking the form of calico bags, filled with horsehair or wadding material – tension the frame assembly, provide insulation and give a smoother line for the external hood material to follow. They are screwed, riveted or tacked in position. On some cars these interlinings cover the full width of the vehicle. On many later types they only cover the outer (side) sections of the frame. The centre section for this roof had yet to be made and fitted.*

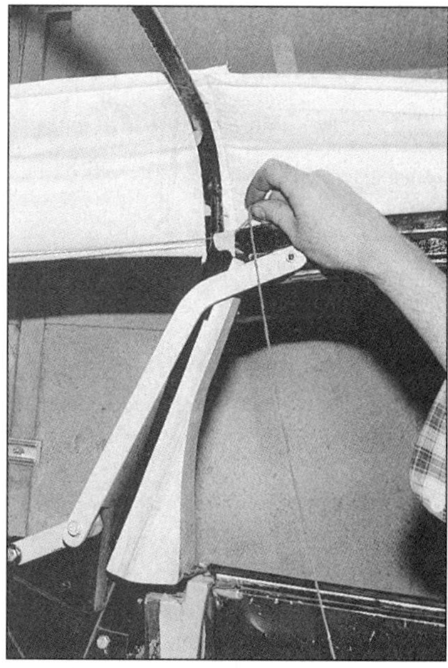

▲ *11.3. The first step in making the inner lining (headlining) is to run lengths of ordinary string along each side of the vehicle, in the positions where the tensioning cords forming part of the lining will sit. The string can be held in place with masking tape. Take your time to accurately position these lines.*

▼ *11.4. Now, using large sheets of brown paper (or similar), make up a pattern for the lining in sections, with already installed strings used as boundary markers. Carefully build up the precise shape of the lining, installing one section of the pattern at a time.*

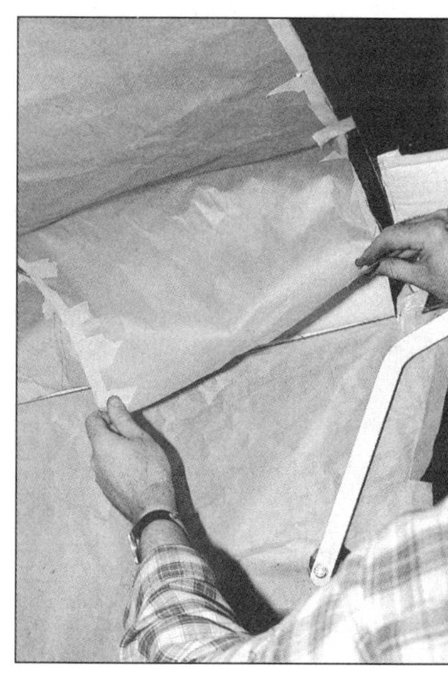

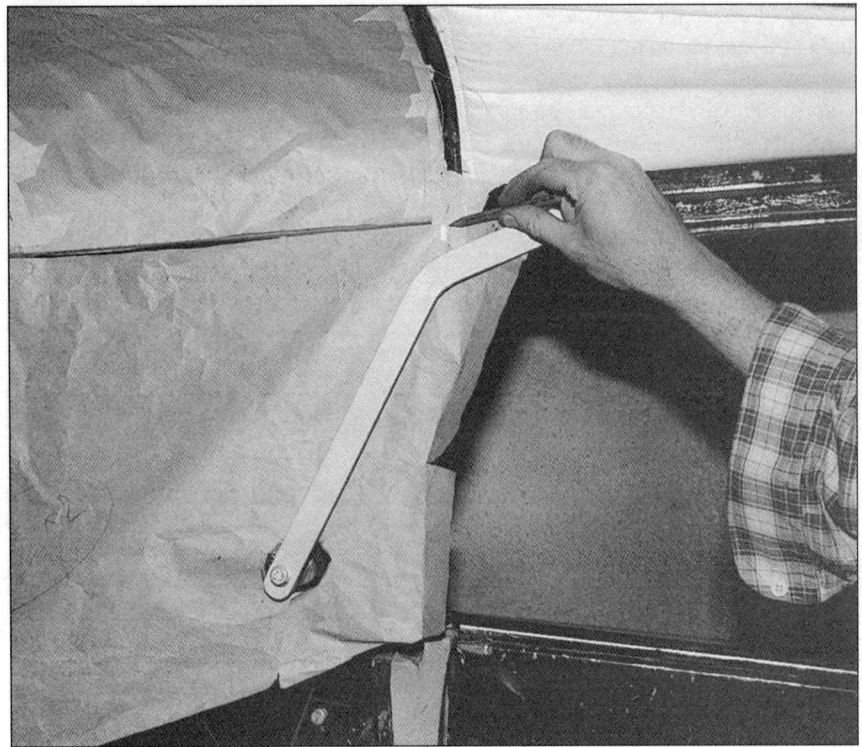

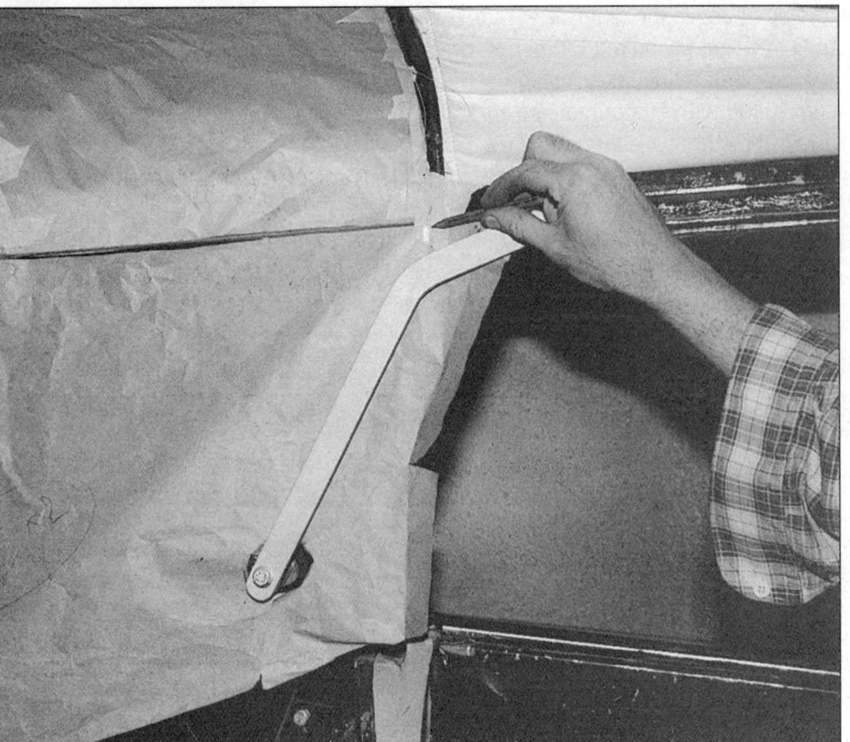

▲ *11.5. Use a pencil to mark adjacent sections of the pattern (make these alignment marks at each roof frame member), so that the sections can be accurately re-joined for reference later. Ensure that each section is marked so that its position can easily be identified.*

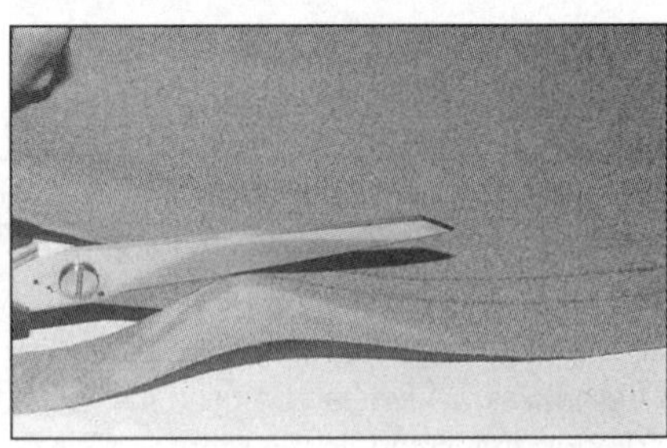

▲ *11.8. Next, very carefully cut out the material along the outer line. Be sure to mark the lining material sections so that they correspond with the markings on the templates, for easy identification.*

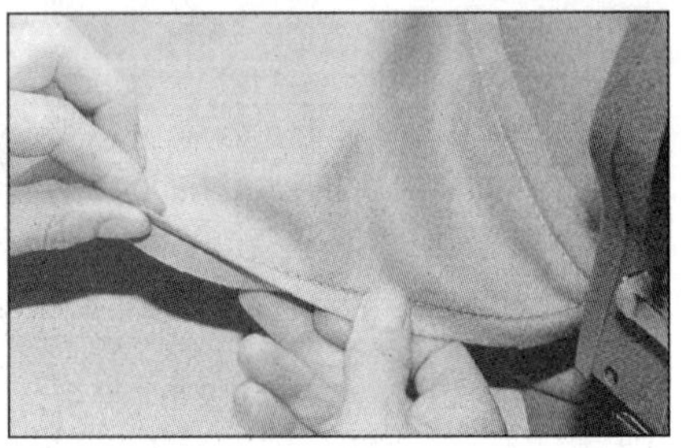

▲ *11.9. Adjacent sections of the lining can now be sewn together along the (inner) seam lines, marked previously.*

▼ *11.7. Now mark an additional line approximately $\frac{3}{8}$ in (1cm) outboard of the first, to form a seam allowance around the perimeter of each section.*

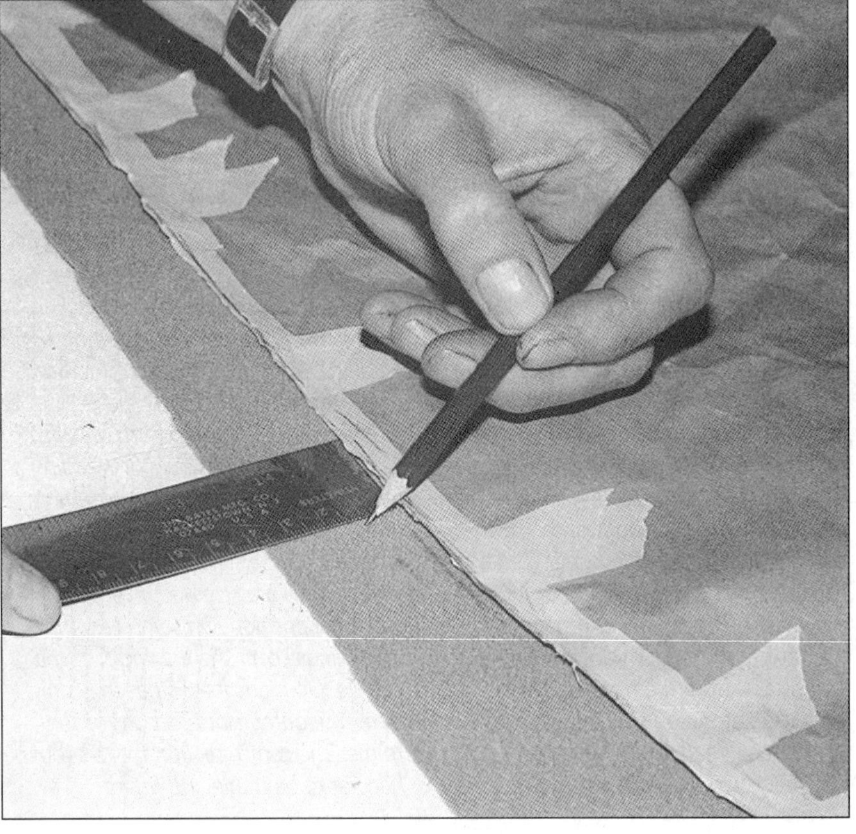

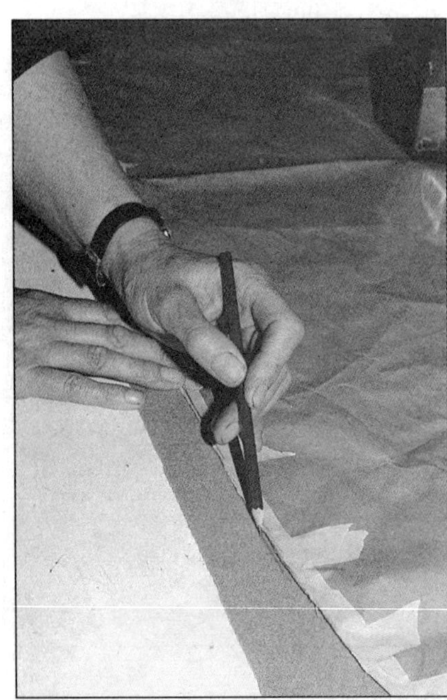

▲ *11.6. Mark the shape of each section onto the lining material.*

The next stage is to make up pockets to accommodate the tensioning cords. This is similar to forming piping for seats, as described in Chapter 6.

▼ *11.10. For each length of tensioning cord, cut a strip of the headlining material, greater than 1.25 in (3 cm) wide, and long enough to cover all the cord. Double over the material and sew the cord into the pocket so formed, using a piping foot on the sewing machine. Suitable nylon cord (very strong and virtually indestructible) can be purchased at DIY and hardware shops.*

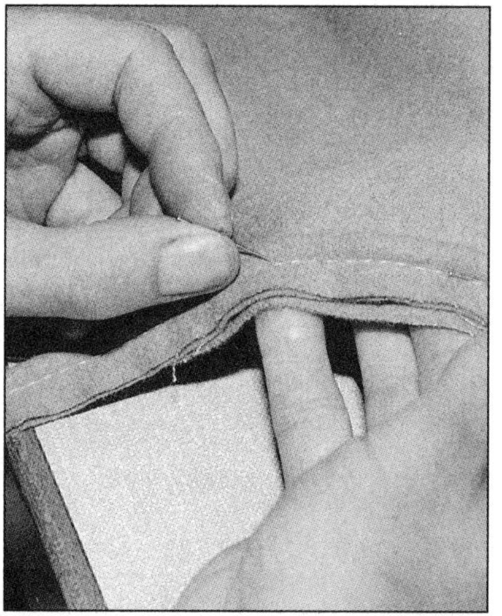

◀ *11.11. The cord piping can now be pinned in place along the appropriate edges of the headlining sections. Note that when the sewing is completed, the flange of the material will be tucked underneath the assembly, as viewed here, so that the piping will form a neat boundary to the lining.*

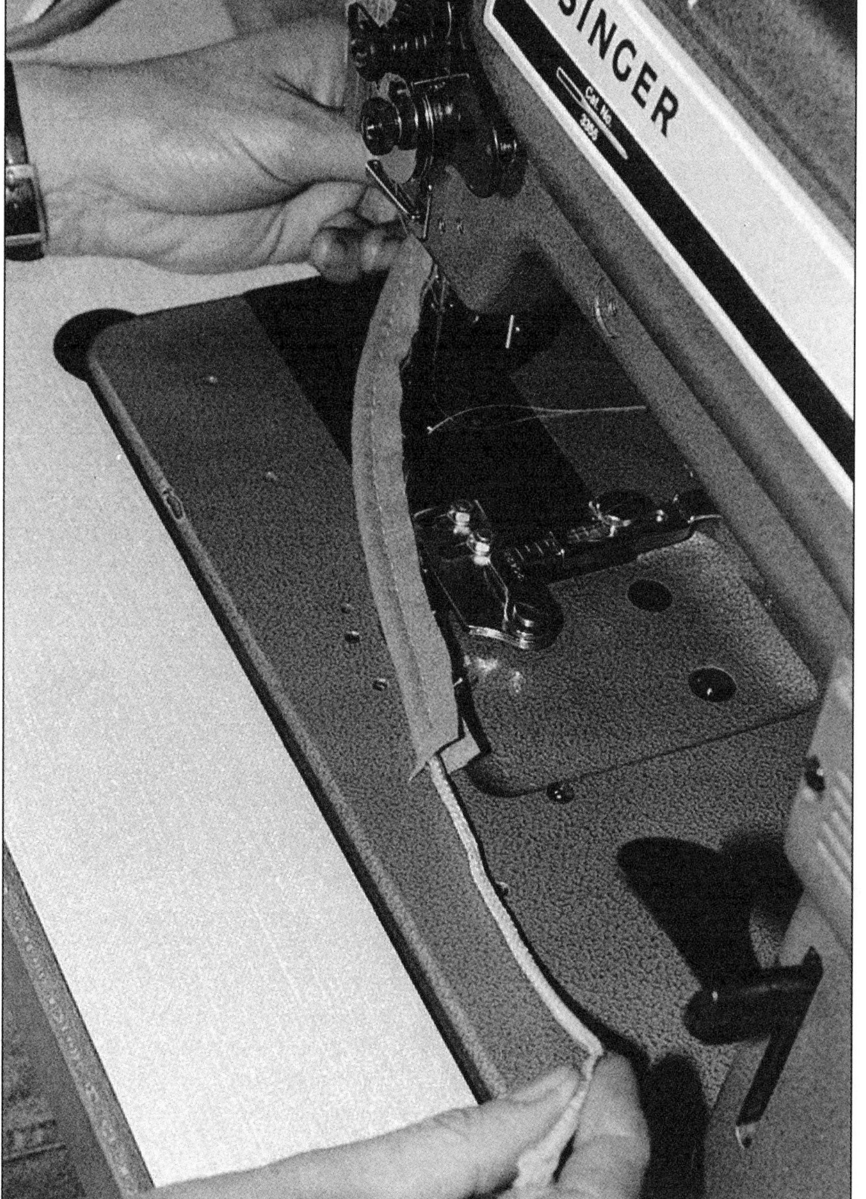

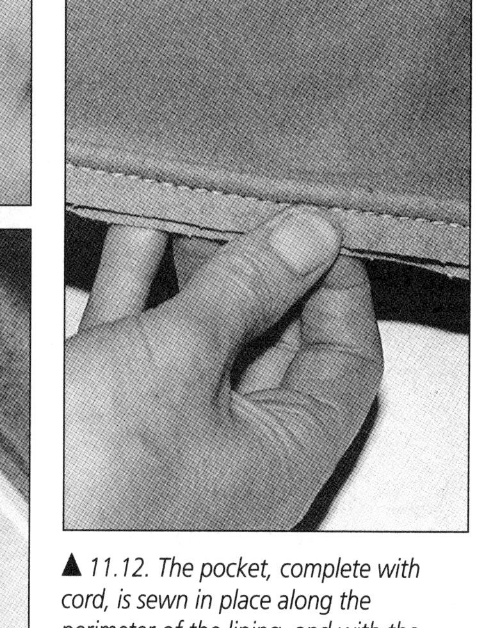

▲ *11.12. The pocket, complete with cord, is sewn in place along the perimeter of the lining, and with the hem of the material tucked underneath …*

▲ *11.13. … the finished edge looks like this.*

▼ *11.14. The rear quarter side sections, which fit behind the doors on each side, can now be sewn to the main (roof) assembly. In some cases, as here, apertures need to be made for the hood supporting irons to pass through. The precise positions of these will be evident from the paper patterns made at the outset. A circle of material, of appropriate diameter, can be sewn around the edge of the aperture (once cut out), then doubled back and secured on the reverse side of the main panel, by sewing in place, to form a neat edge.*

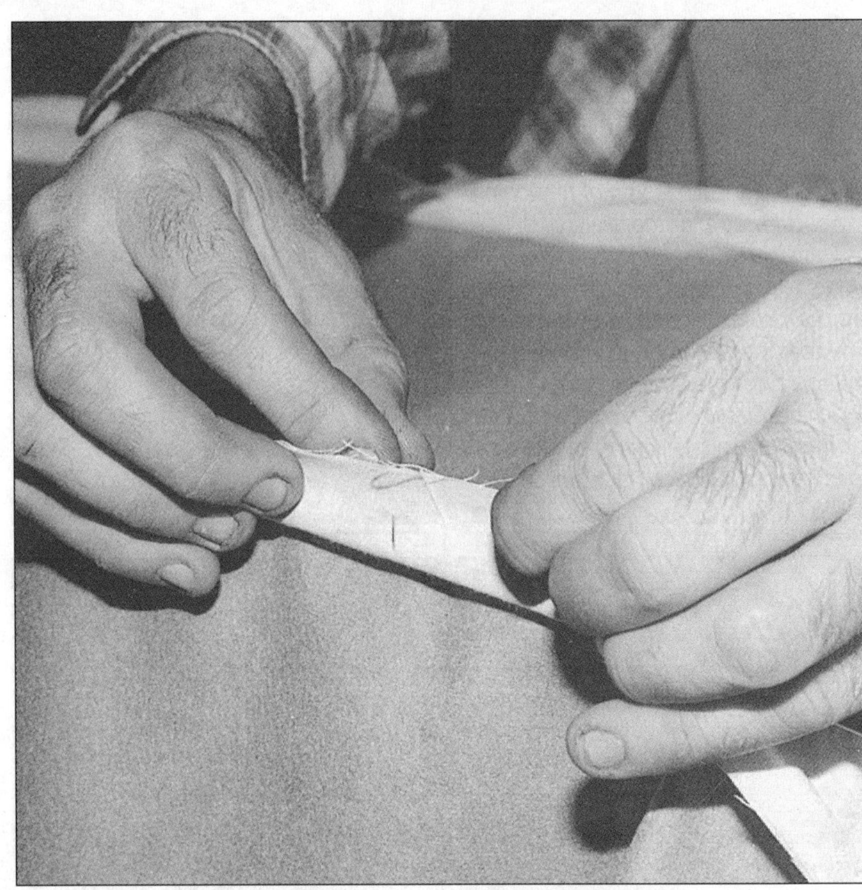

▼ *11.15. Once the lining is fully assembled it can be trial-fitted. It helps to have an assistant on hand during this operation. Ease it very carefully into position, taking particular care not to strain it when feeding the material into place over hood support bars, etc.*

▲ *11.16. If all is well, the lining can be pinned to the frame. If not, establish exactly where the problem is – sometimes minor adjustments need to be made to lose creases, etc. It is usually best to work from the centre, outwards.*

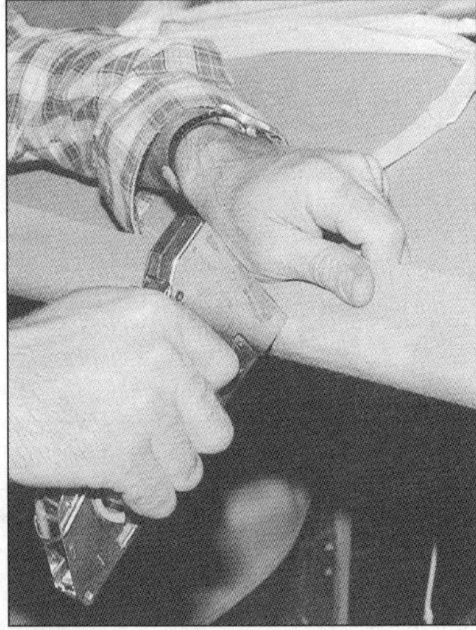

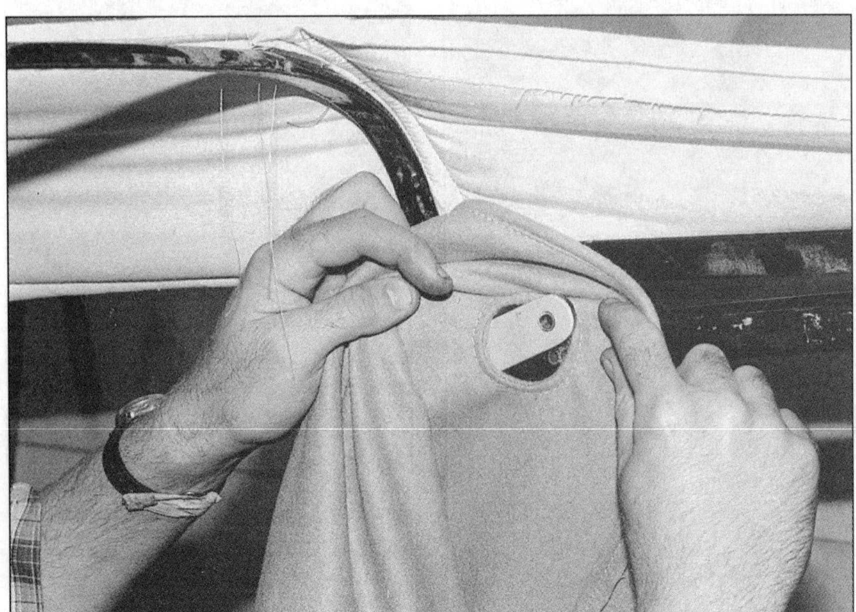

▲ *11.17. Where wood battens are a feature of the design, the lining material can be stapled or tacked to the frame. Staples are quickly installed, but many feel that tacks are in fact preferable, since, if only tapped halfway in initially, they are more easily removed and re-positioned than staples, which can also cut the material unless care is exercised.*

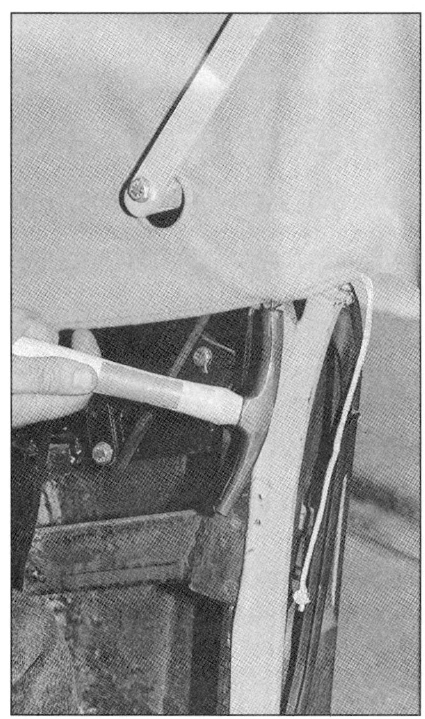

▲11.18. *Again, where wooden sections are incorporated, the forward part of the rear section of the lining can be tacked to the frame, giving a secure grip and tensioning the material.*

▼ 11.19. *The lining should now look something like this. Try the hood in the open and closed positions, to ensure that the headlining folds neatly in both directions, before final tensioning and tacking in place.*

With the inner lining fitted, attention can now be turned to the outer sections of the hood.

▼ 11.20. *If you haven't already done so, the centre section of the interlining can now be made and installed. As with the outer (side) sections depicted earlier, the lining takes the form of a wadding sandwich – i.e. a calico bag stuffed with wadding (horsehair was used on very early cars). It is stitched at the sides and in the centre to prevent migration of the wadding, and tacked in place to the front and rear rails of the hood frame.*

The outer covering of the hood can now be made. Once again, you can start by making paper patterns, either from the original hood, where available, or directly from the frame (covered, where appropriate, by the padded interlining already described). The shapes can then be transferred directly to the hooding material. Note that the paper used for pattern making will not be as forgiving in terms of stretch, as the hooding material.

As an alternative to using paper patterns, you could use inexpensive vinyl or cloth, which will stretch more

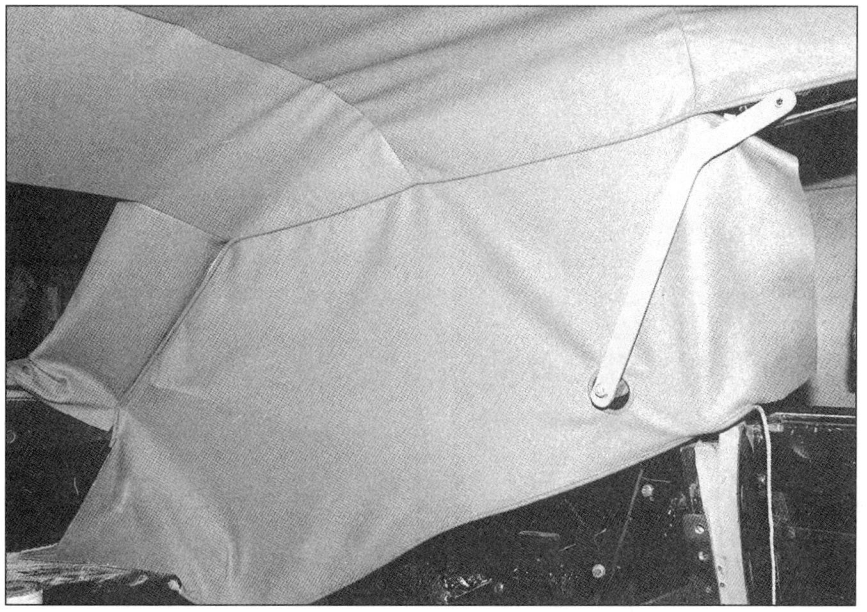

like the hooding. Another practical way of making the hood is to start with the material forming the actual outer covering, and to lay the centre section of it (the canopy) on the frame as the basis for the new hood. This method is expanded upon in the 'Hints, tips and alternatives' section later in this chapter.

One of the most critical factors in achieving good fit and finish is correctly establishing the width of the main (centre) section of the hood. Normally, this should be made as wide as possible, but should stop just short of the turn downwards at each side – the separate side sections will cover these areas.

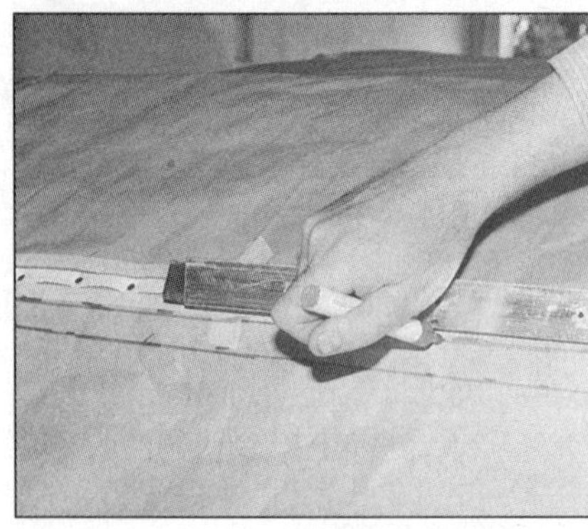

▲ *11.21. The shape of the rear window should be marked on the appropriate section of the pattern.*

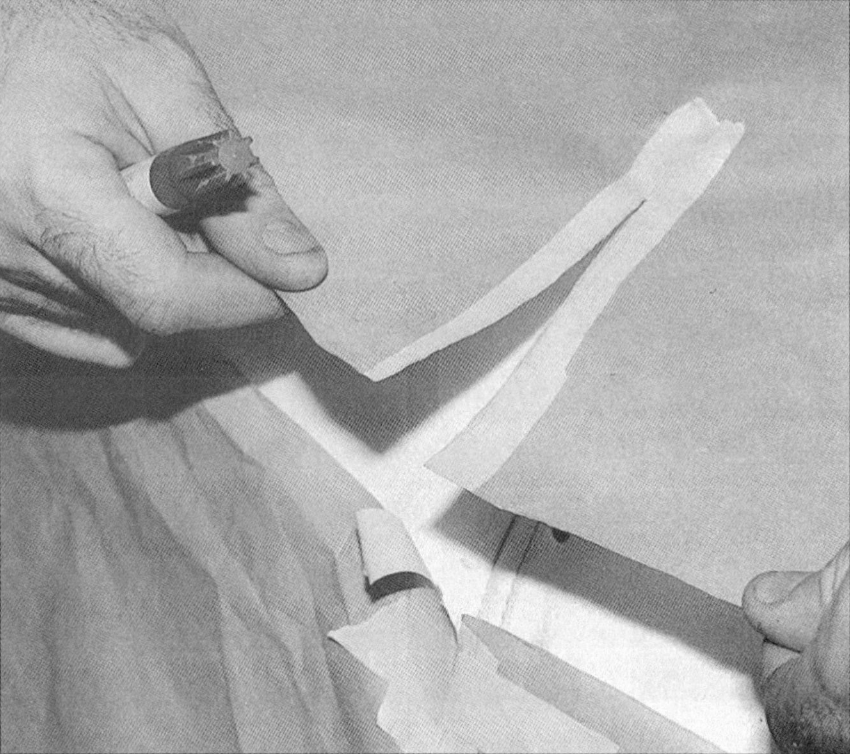

▶ *11.22. It is sometimes necessary to form darts (essentially, tapering folds, to take up excess material) in the hood, for example when negotiating sharp curves, or hood support bars. These allow the material to more easily change direction at such points. Mark and cut out the dart positions on the pattern.*

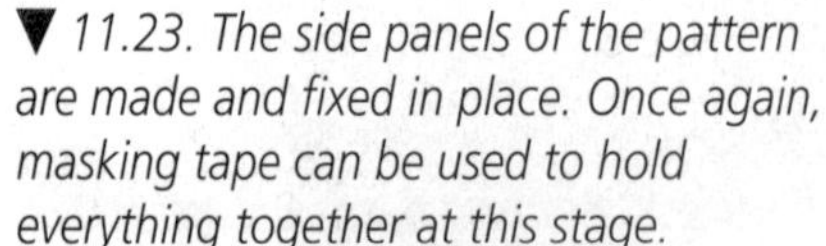

▼ *11.23. The side panels of the pattern are made and fixed in place. Once again, masking tape can be used to hold everything together at this stage.*

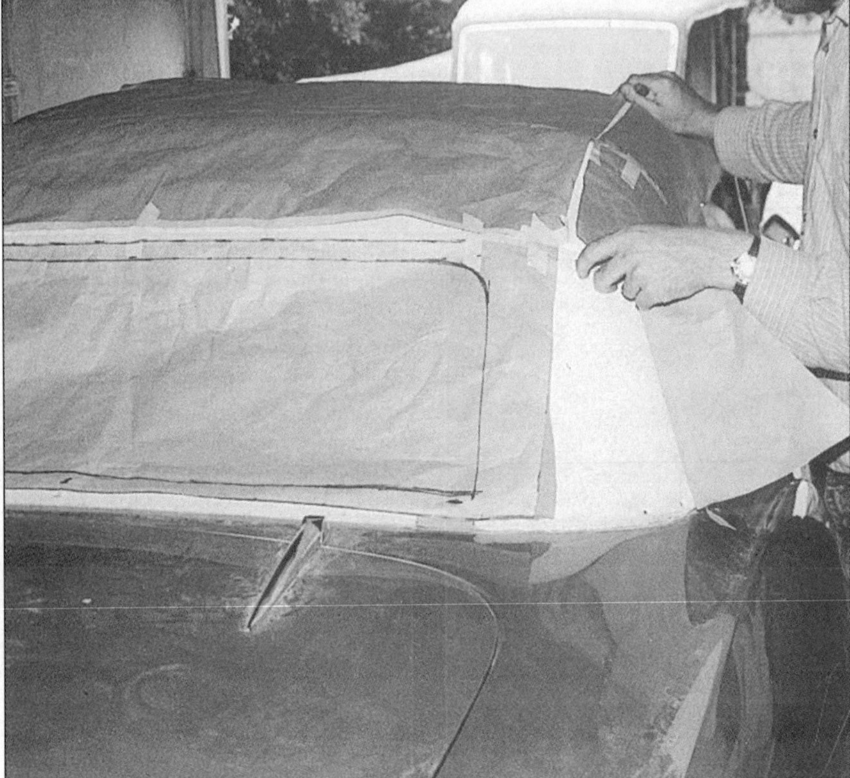

The profiles of the pattern sections can now be transferred to the hooding (in the same manner as described for the headlining material) and the hood itself can then be assembled.

Note that if you intend to finish the outer edges of the hood by folding over the perimeter of the material (as shown in the section on edging – specifically in photographs 11.33 to 11.35), sufficient extra material must be allowed for the hem when marking and cutting out, otherwise your hood could end up with insufficient depth at each side, and around the back!

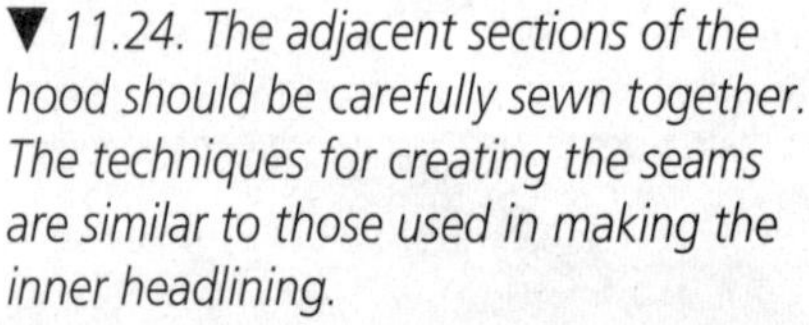

▼ *11.24. The adjacent sections of the hood should be carefully sewn together. The techniques for creating the seams are similar to those used in making the inner headlining.*

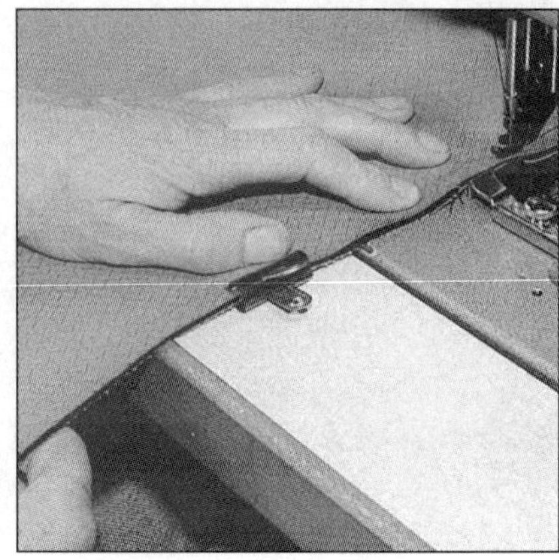

▼ *11.25. To create a dart, the hooding is first sewn so that a pocket is formed on the inside of the material at the appropriate point. In effect, this takes the form of a tapering fold, wider at the outside of the material and narrowing to a point. The pocket is sliced along the centre, using a sharp knife, so that two flaps are created. These can then be folded back onto the inner lining, and glued in place. Don't slice the material right into the narrow end of the fold or a small hole may appear, which can then grow larger. Note that, ideally, darts should only be made in the side sections of the hood, and not the main canopy.*

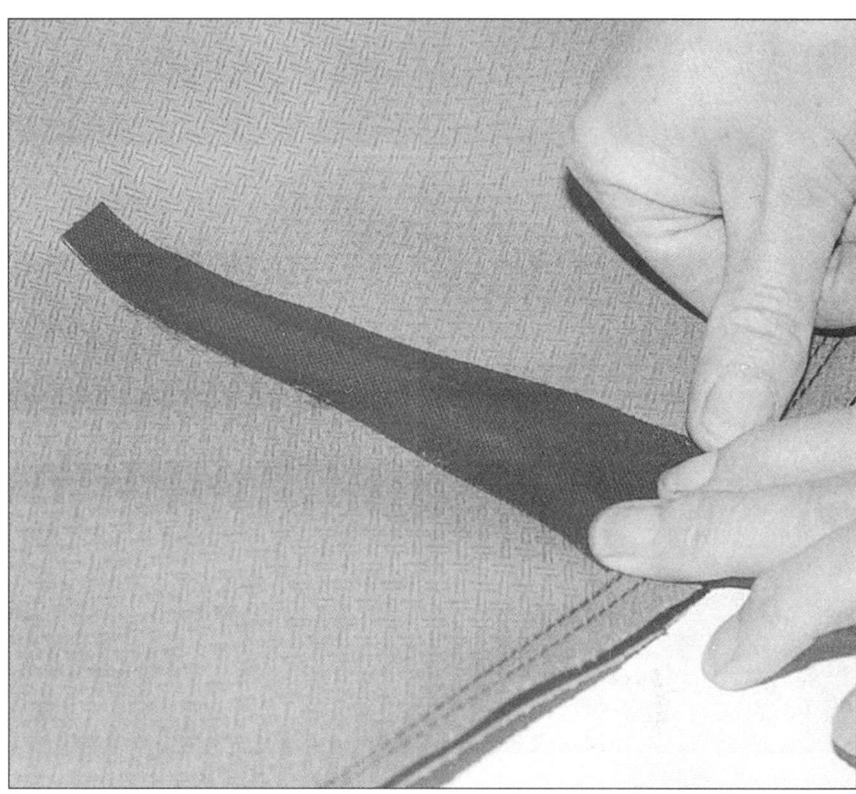

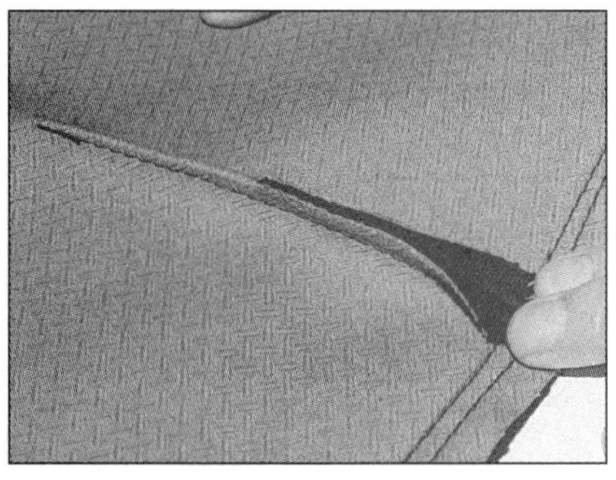

▼ *11.26. Contact adhesive is used to secure the flaps in the folded back position.*

▲ *11.27. A triangular piece of hooding – large enough to fully cover the dart, and to overlap its outer edges by ⅜ in (1 cm) or so all round – is then cut out and glued onto the dart. Finally, the assembly is sewn together.*

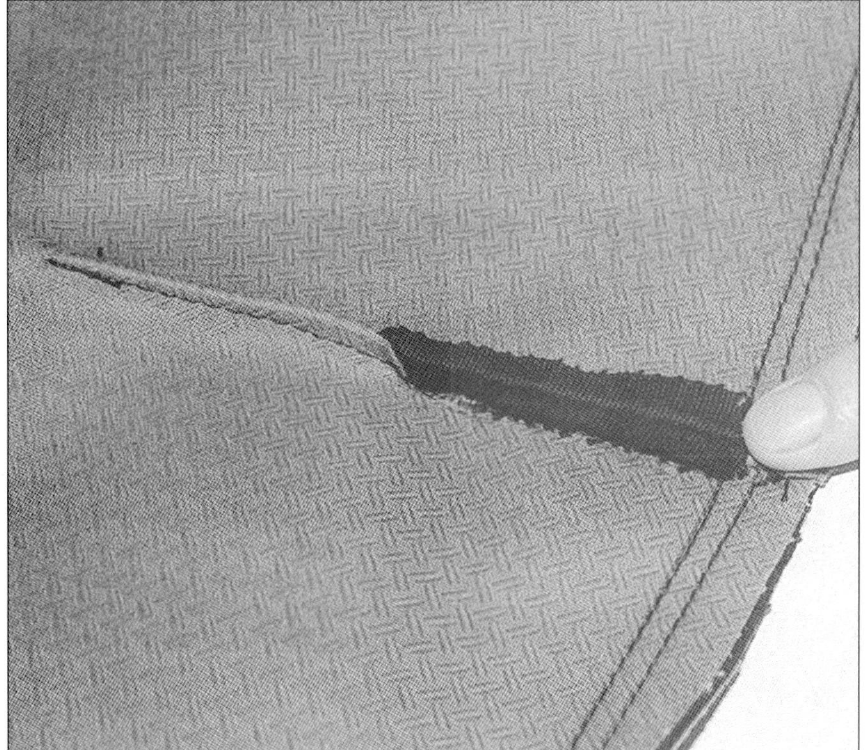

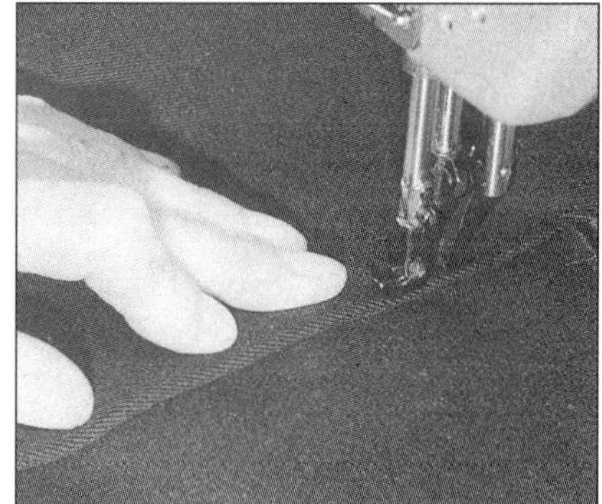

▲ *11.28. The seams around the hood are then top-stitched together – this is how a seam looks from the outside, and ...*

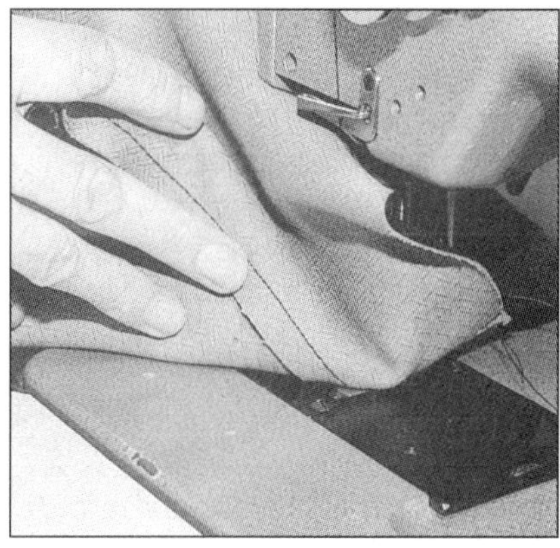

▲ *11.29. ... from the inside.*

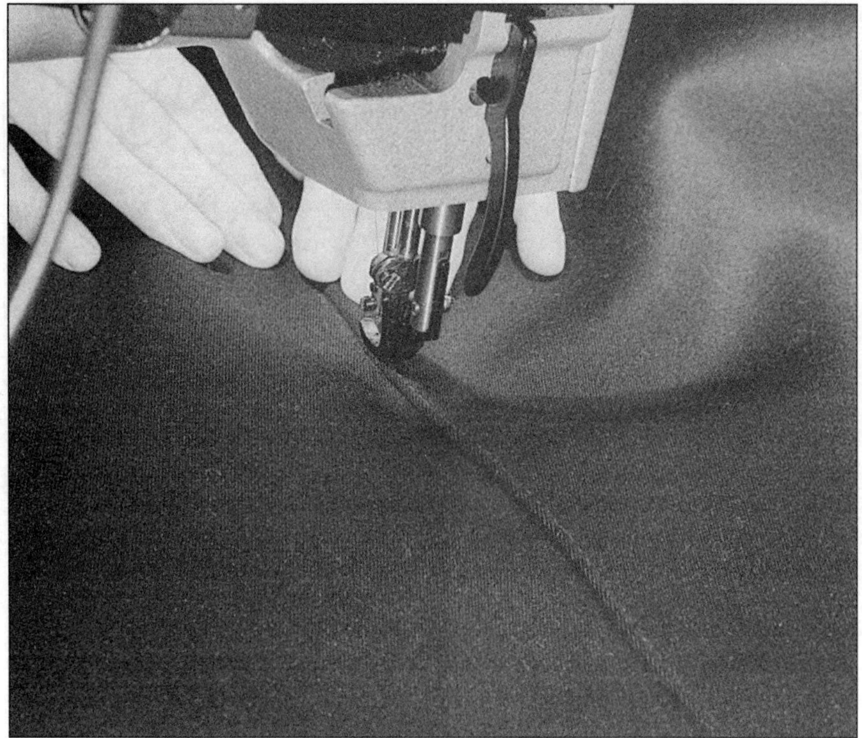

▲ *11.30. The seam should appear like this when partly completed.*

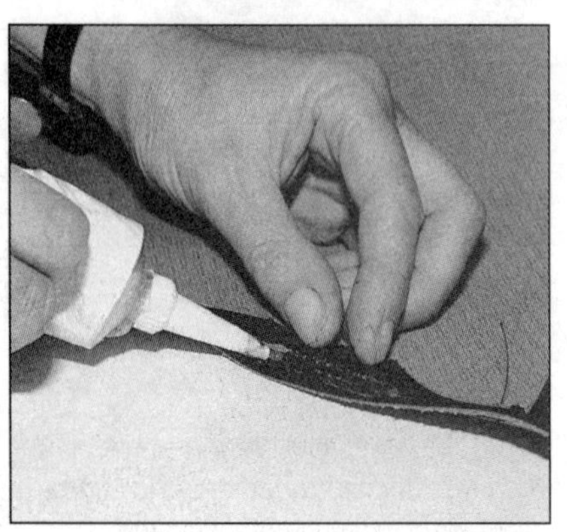

▲ *11.31. Waterproof seam sealer (in this case Dunlop S1718) is applied to all sewn seams on the hood, to prevent water from entering through the stitching holes. This is vital to ensure that the hood is weatherproof!*

▶ *11.32. It is wise to trial-fit the hood at this stage, and helpful to have an assistant on hand during this operation. Make sure that when the material is stretched evenly over the frame it assumes the correct profile and reaches the surrounding bodywork all the way around its perimeter.*

EDGING

There are several different approaches which may be followed when edging/binding the hood. One method is to bind the perimeter of the hood in the same way as a carpet is bound, as described in Chapter 10. A strip of hooding material – of the required length – is first cut out.

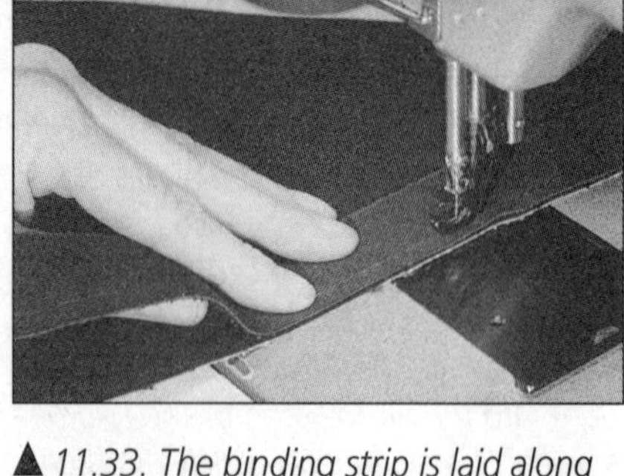

▲ *11.33. The binding strip is laid along the edge of the hooding material, (outer side to outer side) and sewn close to the edges of both.*

▼ *11.34. The strip of binding is then folded over the edge of the hood material, clamped in place and sewn in place on the inside of the hooding.*

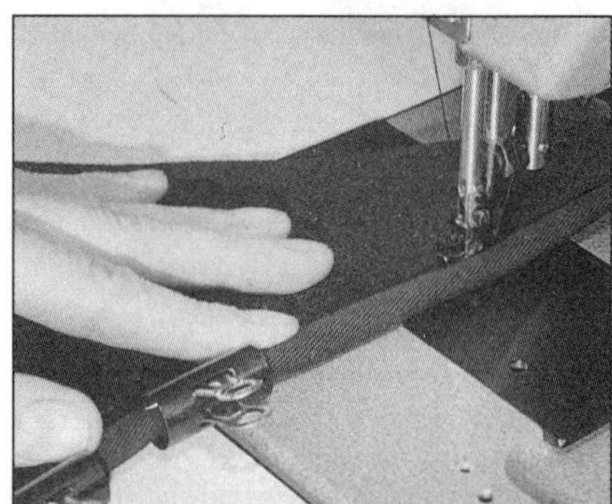

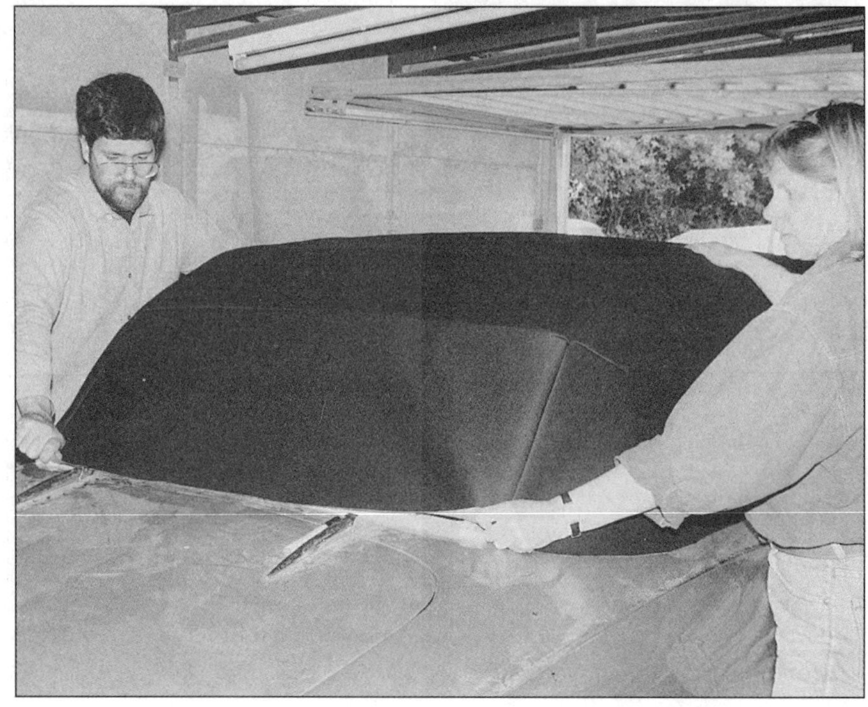

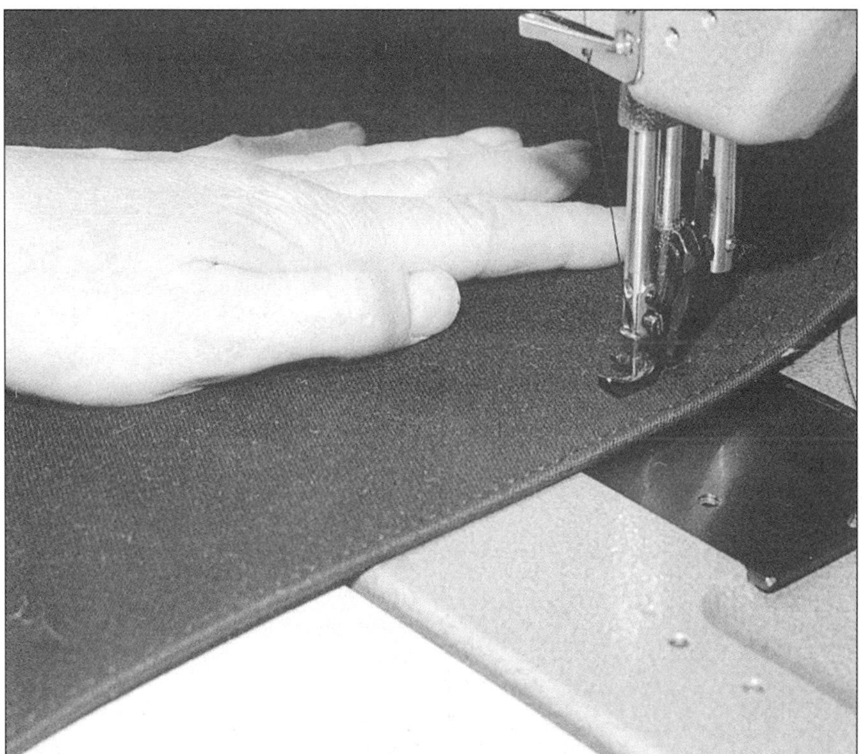

▼ *11.38. Weather pockets, where needed, are easily created by cutting two strips of hooding material and sewing the two strips together. They are then fitted in place around the upper edges of the door window aperture. Note that if the window aperture is curved, the inner strip of material forming the pocket will also need to be curved. The strips can be attached when the edge of the hood is bound. The diagram shows the layout.*

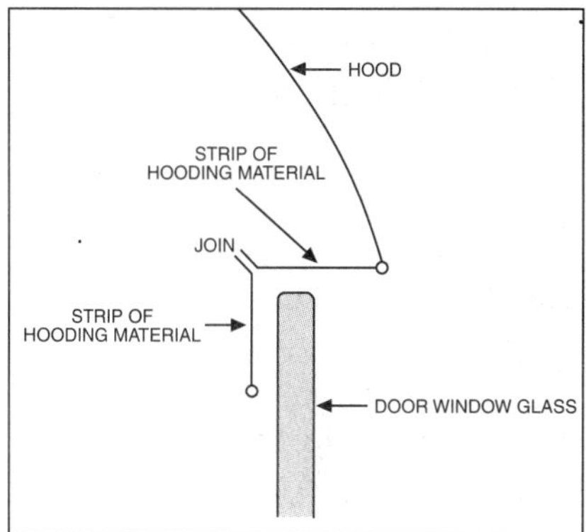

▲ *11.35. An alternative method is simply to create a sewn hem all around the perimeter of the hooding – this is folded over (towards the back of the material) and sewn in position close to the fold, also near to the outer edge of the turned over hem.*

▲ *11.36. This is a turned over edge, as viewed from the front, and …*

▶ *11.37. … as seen from the rear of the hooding.*

WEATHER POCKETS

On some hoods – including those of Morris Minor Tourers, for example – a pocket is created around the door windows, so that when the door is shut the window sits within a channel formed in the hooding, with a flange on the inside. This helps to keep the hood weatherproof.

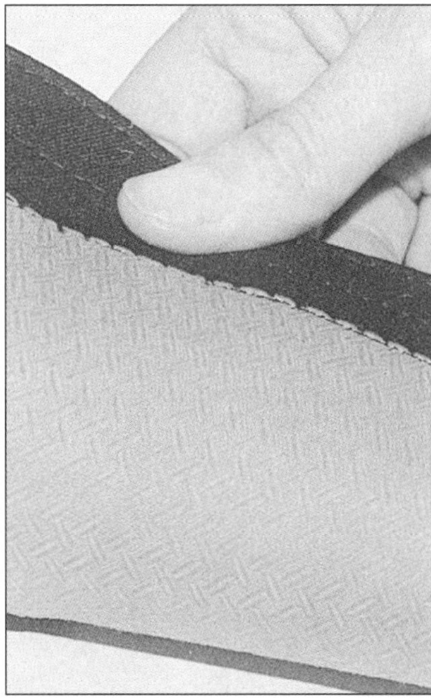

▼ *11.39. This is how a typical pocket appears from the front …*

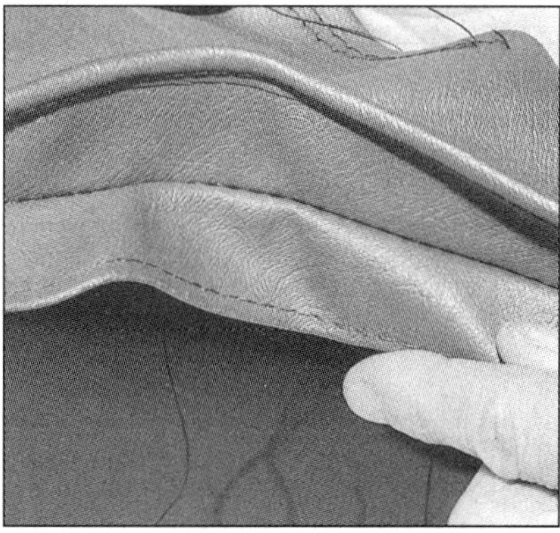

▼ *11.40. … and from the back.*

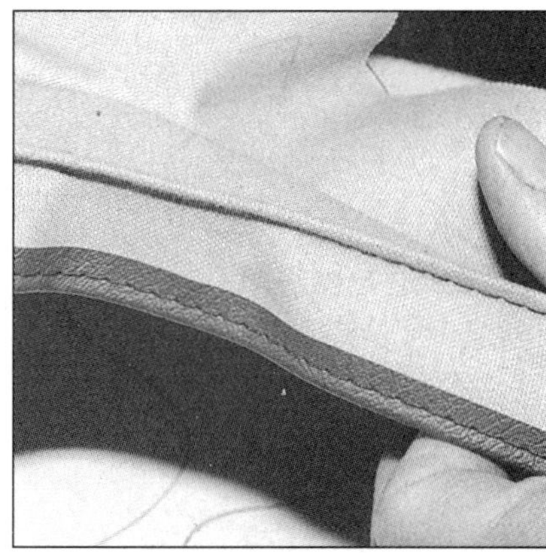

REAR WINDOW – MAKING AND INSTALLATION

With the exception of the very few hoods which incorporate real glass windows, within separate frame assemblies, the vast majority of soft tops have see-through plastic windows. When buying, aim for quality, and ensure that the window material is strong – thin plastic is more vulnerable to tearing. Vybak flexible window sheeting is available from upholstery suppliers, and is both durable and easy to work with.

Having first marked out the required shape, a new window can be constructed and installed in the hood. To illustrate the techniques, the following sequence shows how a test piece Austin Seven sized window was made. Throughout the manufacturing and assembly operations, try to avoid touching the surface of the window, as it can become covered in minute scratches if carelessly handled.

▼ *11.41. Start by marking the perimeter of the proposed window (if necessary, using the paper pattern marked earlier), and plot the exact centre of the window with a cross, as shown here, for alignment reference.*

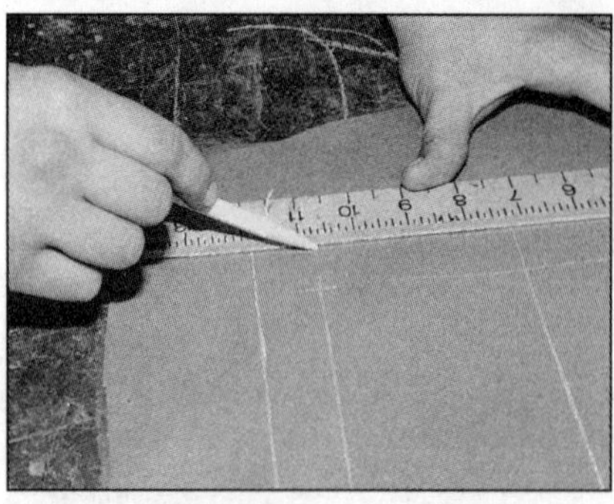

▲ *11.42. Next, mark a border 1 in (2.54cm) all the way around the outside of the marked window.*

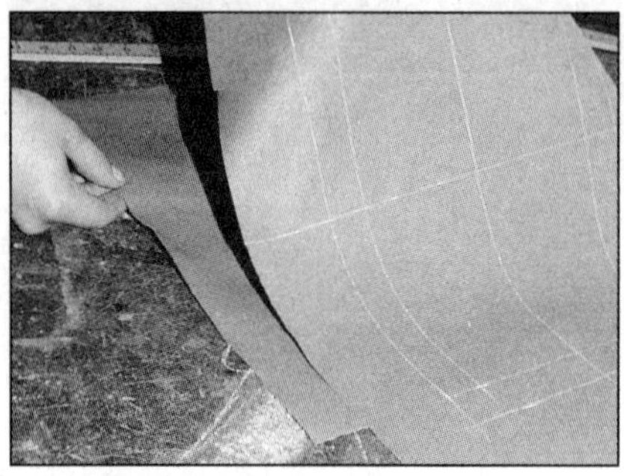

▲ *11.43. Cut a backing piece of the same material as the main part of the hood, a little larger than the marked perimeter of the window plus border, all round, and lay this, face up, on the workbench, with the marked section on top of it.*

▲ *11.44. Using just four tacks, tapped halfway in to the workbench or backing board, secure the two pieces of material together.*

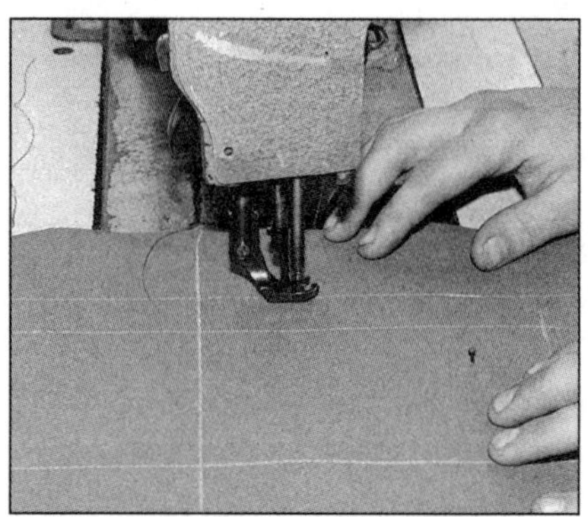

▲ *11.45. Carefully lift the assembly to the sewing machine table, and run a single line of stitches around the outer perimeter line.*

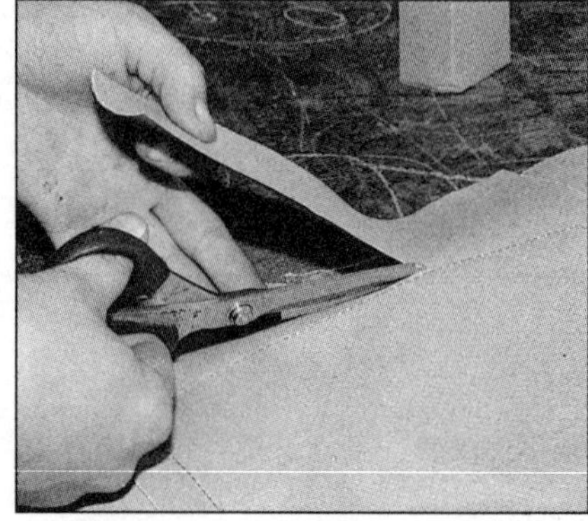

▲ *11.46. Turn the assembly over, then carefully and neatly trim off excess backing material quite close to the stitch line.*

▲ *11.47. Starting in the centre of the outer panel, cut diagonally towards each corner in turn, cutting right to the corner of the window opening (but not the outer border!) in each case. Leave a narrow flange – about ¼ in (6cm) wide – in place all along each side of the window aperture, as shown.*

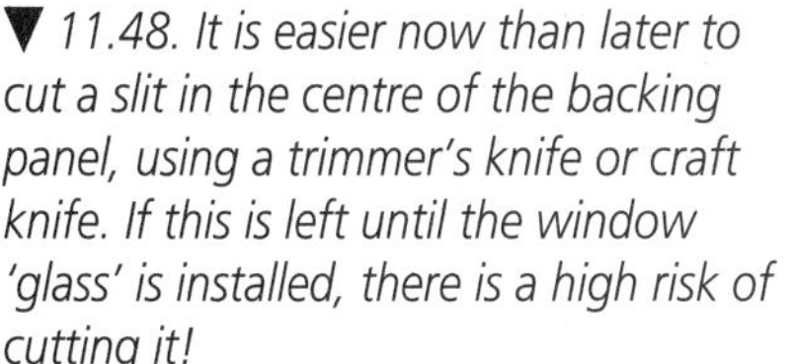

▼ *11.48. It is easier now than later to cut a slit in the centre of the backing panel, using a trimmer's knife or craft knife. If this is left until the window 'glass' is installed, there is a high risk of cutting it!*

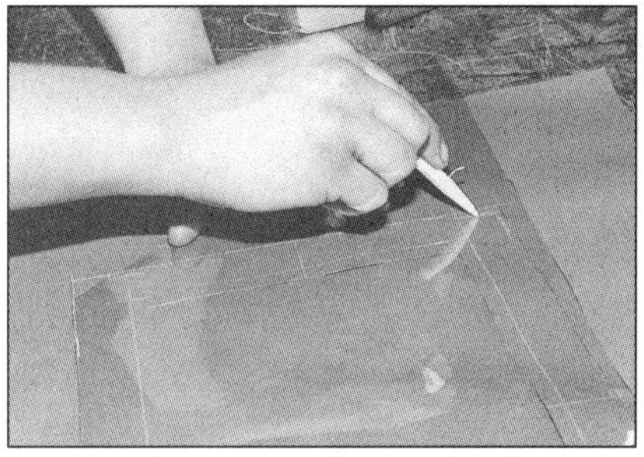

▲ *11.49. Mark and cut out the window 'glass' material just inboard of the outer perimeter (stitched) line, all the way round.*

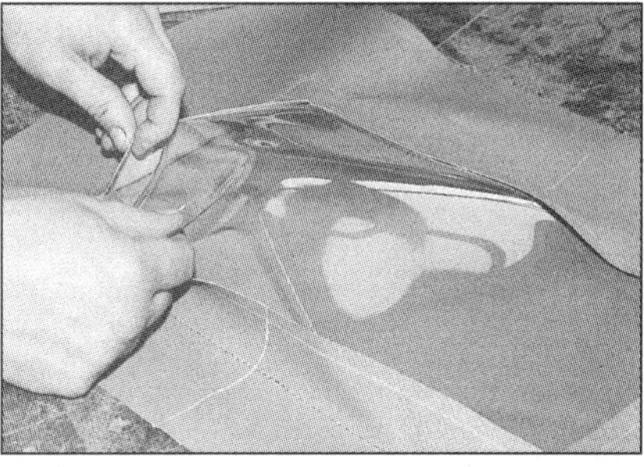

▲ *11.50. Now carefully feed the plastic glazing material into position within the pocket formed between the inner frame and the outer hooding. Try to avoid excessive hand contact with the glazing material.*

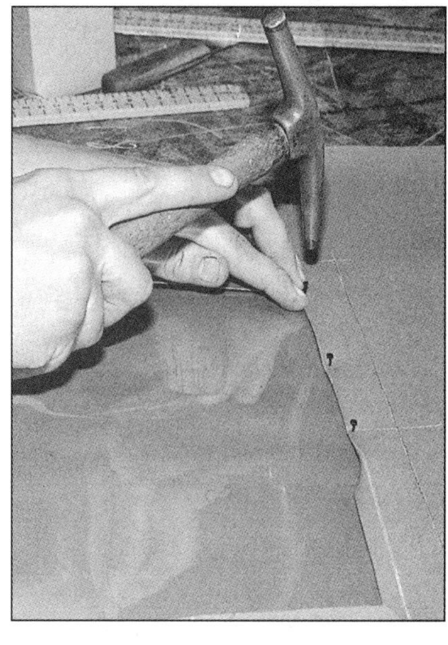

▲ *11.51. The next stage is to tuck the flange underneath the edge of the border, as shown, and secure using tacks tapped halfway in at intervals all the way round. (The holes made by the tacks will be covered by stitching.)*

▲ *11.52. Removing the tacks with side cutters (or similar) as you proceed, sew a single line of stitching all the way around the inner edge of the window's border. Try to keep the stitch line close to the edge of the border – approximately ⅛ in (3mm) or so inboard is ideal. Don't make the stitches too small or the plastic glazing material may tear.*

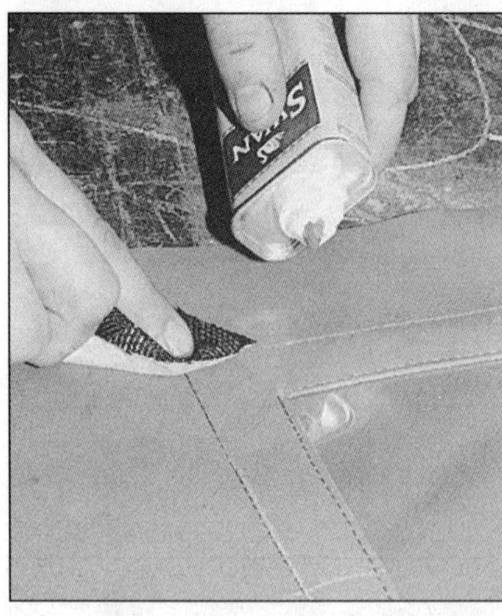

▲ *11.53. Use lighter fuel, applied with a soft cloth, to clean reference marks from plastic and leather hooding materials. In the case of mohair, marked with tailor's chalk, a little water and a stiff brush will remove the markings.*

▼ *11.54. Place a clean, soft cloth on the bench, and place the window assembly face down onto the bench. Using a sharp trimmer's knife or craft knife, very carefully slice out the remains of the centre of the backing panel, and lift this clear. It is best not to use scissors for this, as they may scratch the 'glass' panel.*

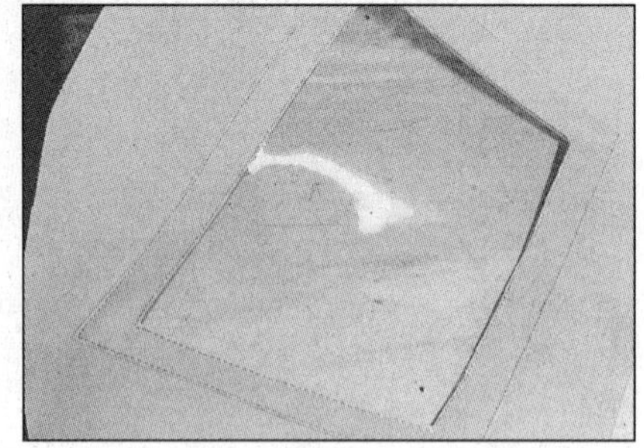

▲ *11.55. The finished window and inner frame is now a very strong unit. Making the window assembly in this way ensures that any pulling forces within the hood are taken by the frame assembly and outer hooding, rather than the glazing material itself. The assembly looks as neat from inside the hood …*

▲ *11.56. … as it does from outside.*

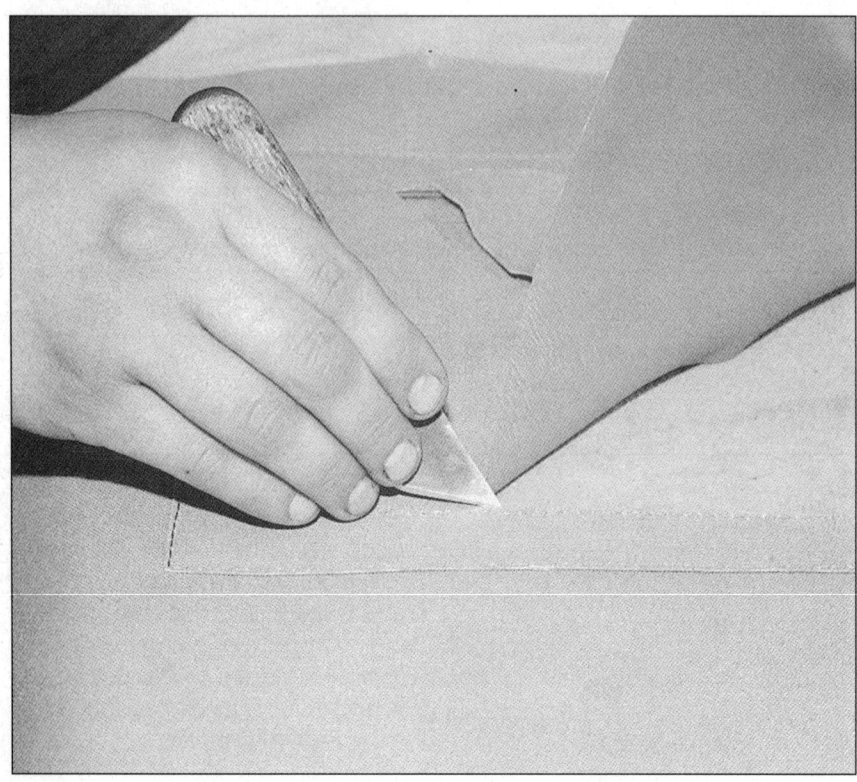

REAR WINDOW REPLACEMENT

It is reassuring to know that replacing a damaged rear window in an otherwise sound hood is quite possible, although the hood will have to be removed from the vehicle. The techniques are generally similar to those just described for installing a rear window within a hood. However, there are some additional points to note.

If your reason for wanting to replace the window is simply because it has become opaque, first try applying liquid cutting compound, as designed for 'cutting back' car paintwork – or alternatively chrome cleaner. These can improve matters dramatically. If a plastic window is badly creased, try gently warming it with a hair dryer. Again, this can work wonders. However, if the window is torn, you have little option but to replace it – or else the complete hood!

If the original window was heat sealed into the hooding material, you can still replace it with a sewn-in window. The heat-sealed original will have to be cut out, and your replacement will have to be slightly larger than the window removed (because of the heat sealed flange, around the original window's perimeter, which you have removed from the hood).

Before removing the old window from the hood, one approach is to stick masking tape across and up/down the window aperture (on the outside) so that the window shape and size won't alter as the glazing is removed. Alternatively, a possibly easier method is to sew the new window in place *before* removing the old one.

To remove the window, the stitching needs to be cut between the inner, strengthening panel and the original plastic window. Use a sharp trimmer's knife or craft knife, and take very great care not to damage the hooding during this operation. When the stitching has been released, the strengthening panel and then the window can be gently released, leaving the masking tape in position across the window aperture.

The new window (if not already installed) and the strengthening panel can now be fitted, temporarily taping the panel in place with masking tape, to hold it in position. Stitching (removing the masking tape as you proceed) will then secure the assembly.

HOOD FITTING

Once complete, the hood should again be trial-fitted to the vehicle, making sure that it is positioned centrally, and that it is gently stretched in all directions to assume its correct profile. The hope is that when you do this you will find that all creases are eliminated and that the hood sits snugly on its frame.

When fitting the new hood, always refer to the original bodywork fixings (where still fitted), and ensure that the fasteners on the hood itself are installed in precisely the correct, corresponding positions. Always start from the centre fixing and work outwards. Note that the fasteners are only installed at the final fitting stage, when everything else is correct!

If you have no original fixings to work to, ensure that the fasteners are evenly spaced and, in any event, make sure that the hooding material is not stretched too much between fasteners. Apart from the risk of tearing the material, creases may be formed. If in doubt, space the fasteners fairly closely, to spread the load evenly around the edge of the material.

Note that if you need to make marks on the exterior of the hood, these should be made on pieces of masking tape stuck to the hooding, rather than on the material itself. Such marks can be impossible to remove!

Try to avoid extremes of temperature when fitting the hood and, in particular, avoid working in very low temperatures when the hooding will be less flexible. If necessary, warm the hood material before you start work, and keep it warm by placing a fan heater in the vehicle while fitting the hood.

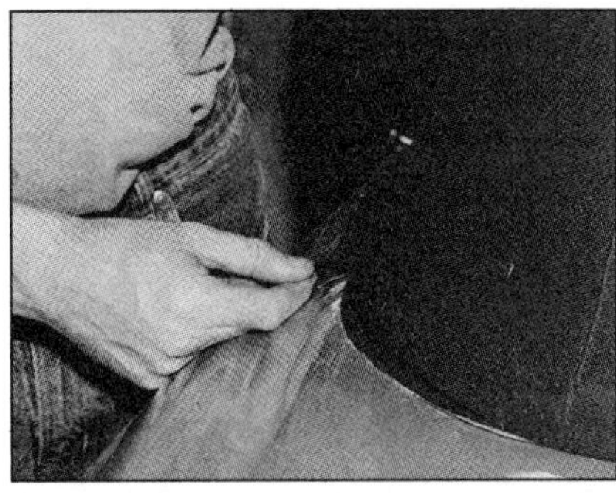

▲ *11.57. Carefully trial-fit the completed hood assembly. During the initial stages the hood can be pinned in place at the back, using four or five layers of masking tape to push the pins into to avoid scratching the bodywork. Working forwards from the back of the vehicle, check that the hood fits snugly all round on both sides, and especially that it sits neatly and closely above the doors/side windows.*

▼ *11.58. It is vital to ensure that the rear corners run in nice, smooth curves, with no creases, and that the hood is tensioned evenly across the rear of the vehicle, and from front to back, along the seams. The hood must stretch evenly when pulled at the front, with no creases being evident. When all is well, it can be secured at the rear edge by tacking the lower border in position. Don't be in too much of a hurry to start tacking. If in any doubt, drive the tacks only halfway in, so that they can be easily removed if they need to come out again.*

▼ *11.59. In this case (a 1940s-style assembly) the lower edge of the hood incorporates a separate inner strip of hooding material, through which the tacks are driven, and which is concealed by the outer covering of the hood. Once the rear of the hood is finally tacked in place, through the inner strip, the lower edge of the hooding can be rolled down into place, and secured by gluing. An alternative method (where a separate strip is not incorporated) is to tack through the main hood, afterwards covering the row of tacks with 'hidem' banding. On some cars, including MG Midgets and MGBs, the rear of the hood is held in place with a metal strip, built into the structure of the roof.*

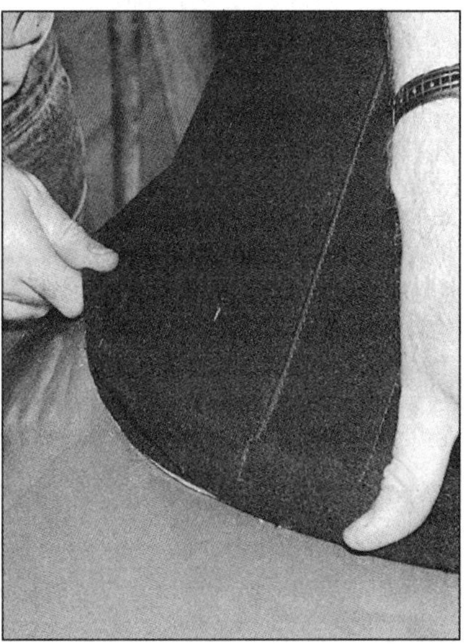

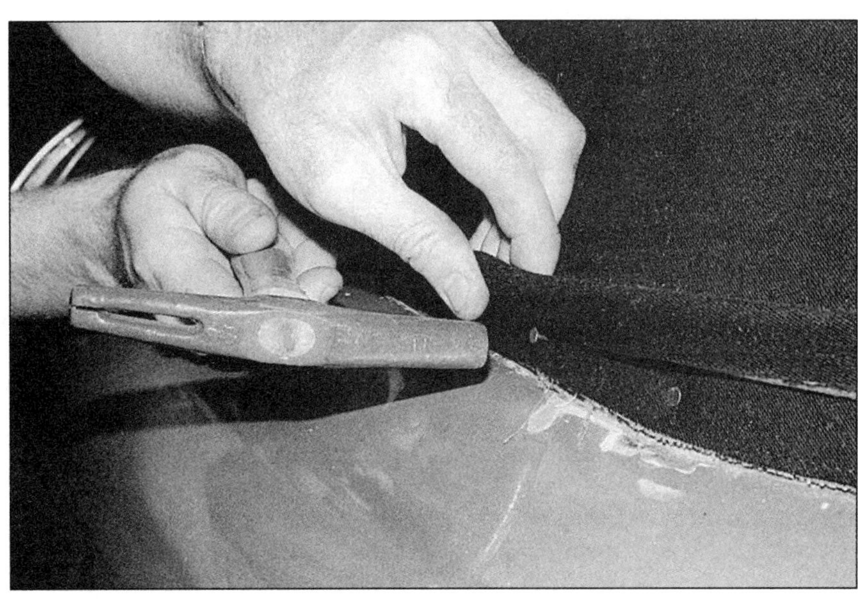

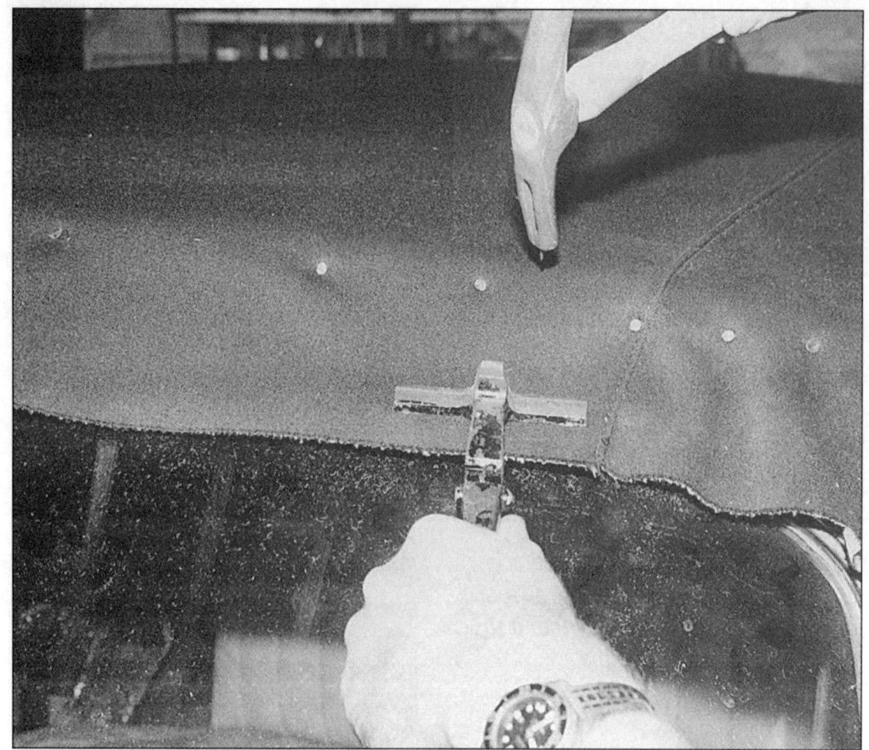

▲ *11.60. The forward edge must also be secured to the frame. Again, in this case, it is tacked in place, having employed a tensioning tool to pull the hooding material to the front. Tension tightly. Where possible, start in the centre of the frame and work outwards to the corners.*

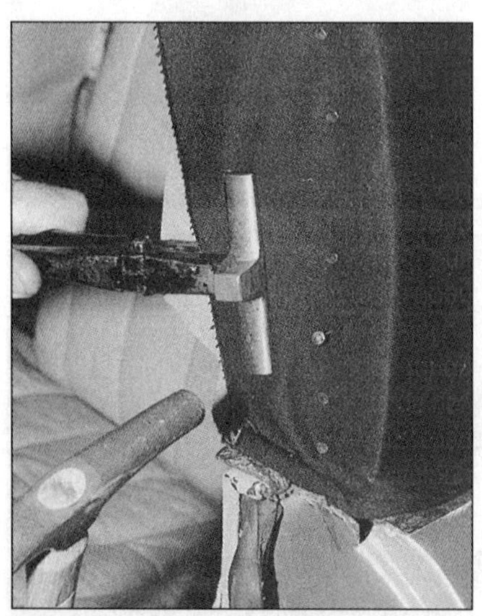

▲ *11.61. The forward sections of the rear side panels must be fastened to the front faces of the (rear) door pillars. Again, the hooding material needs to be tightly tensioned before being tacked in position.*

▼ *11.62. In this case the hood was now tacked to the wood bar across the top of the rear edge of the roof. Usually there is only one such bar per roof to tack into.*

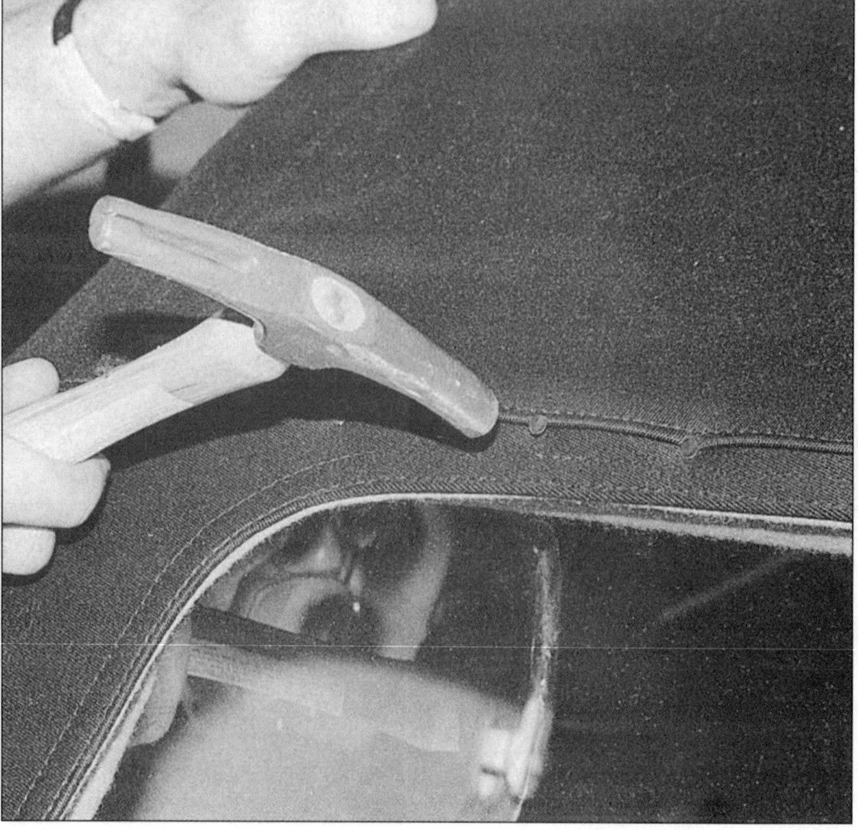

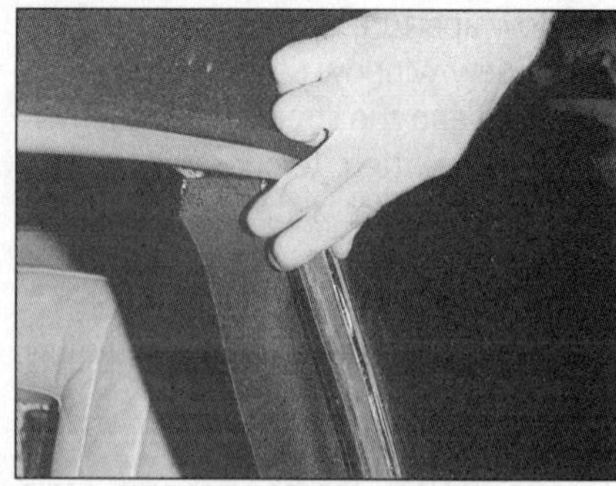

▲ *11.63. The trims covering the forward faces of the door shut pillars can now be fitted.*

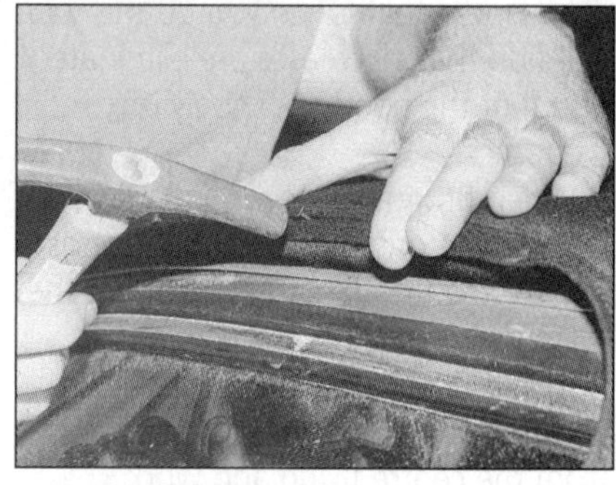

▲ *11.64. 'Hidem' banding is secured along the forward edge of the hood to cover the tacks.*

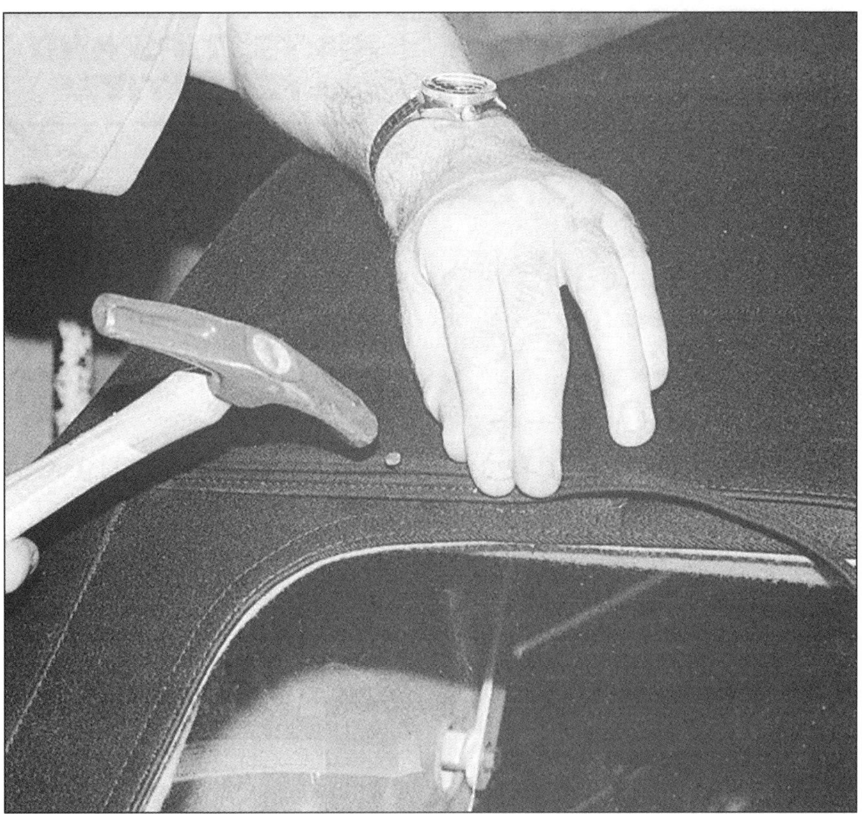

▲ *11.65. Similarly, 'hidem' banding is employed at the rear of the hood to conceal the tacks, and steel end caps then installed (at both front and rear). Any trim clips, etc., specific to the car can also be fitted/refitted now.*

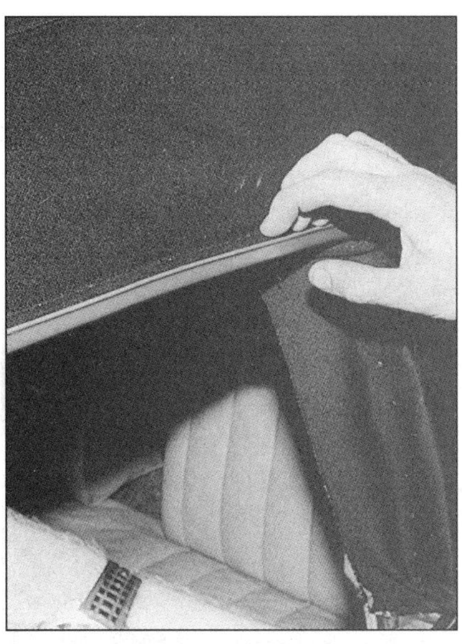

▲ *11.66. Double-check that the hood fits snugly all around its edges, and especially above the doors.*

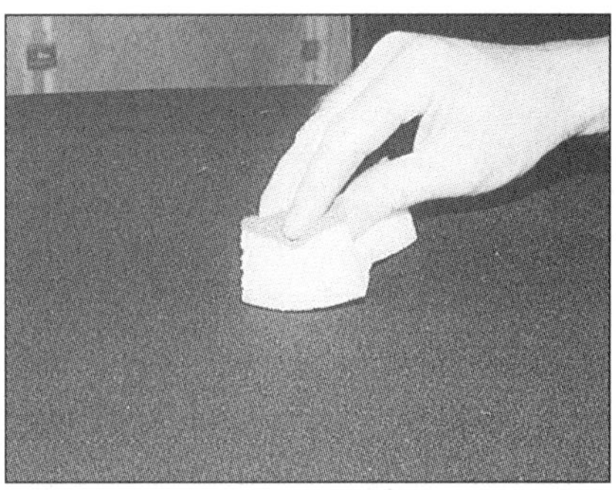

▲ *11.67. Carefully wipe off loose dust, etc., using a sponge which grips the dirt without damaging the hooding.*

▲ *11.68. Have a look inside to make sure that all is well here, then …*

▲ *11.69. … step back and admire the exterior. The finished hood should be a joy to behold!*

SINGLE LAYER AND EARLY HOODS

Many early hoods and those of less expensive sports cars were single layer items. These are easier to construct than the lined varieties (although – as a rule – smaller hoods are more difficult than larger ones) but there are some important points to note.

In many hoods, webbing straps, running from the windscreen header rail to the back of the car, are used to support the hooding and to maintain the correct spacing between the roof support rails. Cover the front hood support stick first, and keep the webbing on the horizontal, centre section of the frame.

On older models which employ side screens, these should be made and installed first, and the hood aligned with them, rather than the other way round. It is obviously essential that the joins between the two are as close a fit as possible, or wind and rain will find an easy way into the car!

Side screen windows are generally made from a much more rigid see-through material (for example, Cobex) than the flexible rear window. When installing windows made of this tougher material, ensure that the stitches are not made too small (or the glazing material may tear).

It is also wise to round off the corners of semi-rigid window material, or the sharp right-angled edges may pierce the stitching of the pockets in which they sit.

It is a good idea to make the glazing material sit *just* inboard of the stitching, to provide a nice, tight assembly. A special half-a-foot attachment used in the sewing machine will enable the stitch lines to be positioned close to the edge of the frame.

▼ *11.70. The side screens – where employed – should always be made first and the hood fitted to them. There should be no gaps between the screens and the main part of the hood, and the forward edges of the side screen frames should abut the windscreen pillars. The screens are glazed with a semi-rigid material. This is the assembly on an early Austin Seven.*

▲ *11.71. The forward edge of the hood should incorporate a flap to wrap over the top of the windscreen, as shown here. The hood on this Austin also has flaps along the sides as additional weatherproofing.*

▲ *11.72. Make sure that the side screens overlap the doors and rear section of the main part of the hood in such a manner that wind and rain stay on the outside of the car, as indicated here. Designs vary between individual vehicles. Note the use of contemporary type Lift the Dot fasteners to secure the rear hood sides.*

▼ *11.73. From inside the car the stitch lines along the fore/aft seams are hidden from view, since they are placed directly on top of the hood webbing straps referred to in the text.*

HINTS, TIPS AND ALTERNATIVES

As indicated at the outset of the section on making and fitting a hood, it is impossible in just one chapter to show every variation in hood construction and methods of working. However, the following, necessarily abbreviated, section may help in providing additional information to that already given, and/or alternative methods.

HOOD-MAKING AND FITTING

As an alternative to making paper patterns, templates can be made from more flexible, inexpensive vinyl, to more easily gauge how the hooding will sit on the frame.

Another, perhaps easier and quicker, method of starting to make a new hood covering is to lay on the frame a length of the actual hooding material to be used. This can be positioned longitudinally on the vehicle (to form the main, central canopy of the hood), and the centre line of both the vehicle and the hooding can be marked with tailor's chalk. (Such chalk can be used on mohair hooding material, and the marks can easily be removed after assembly using a little water and a stiff brush.)

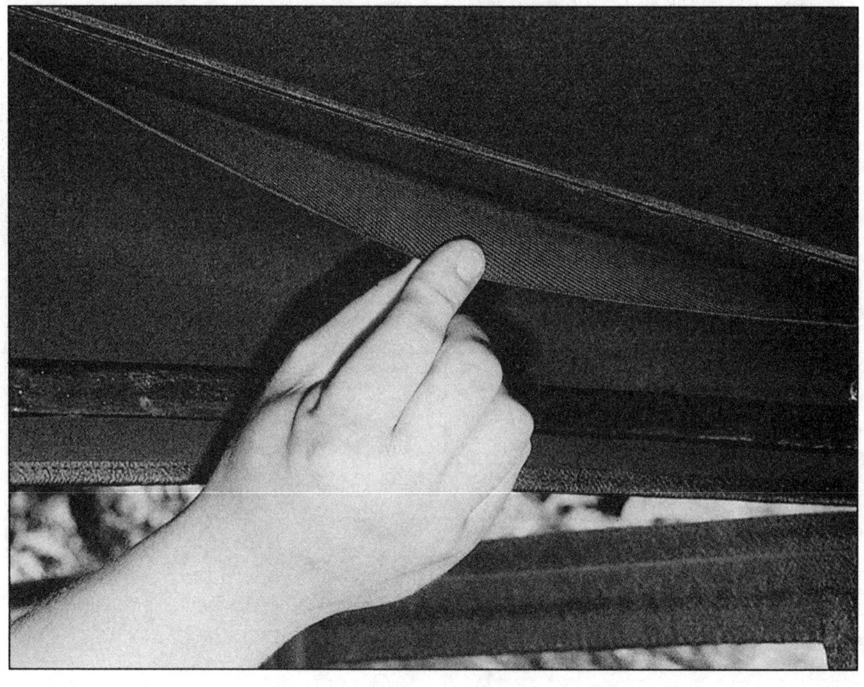

The material is pinned in place at the rear of the car (through four or five layers of masking tape, as described earlier, to avoid damaging the paintwork), then carefully pulled to the front of the car. The centre line marked will help ensure spot-on, square alignment during fitting operations.

The side sections of the hood can now be 'roughed out', using pieces of inexpensive vinyl, initially cut larger all round than the required sections. Using tailor's chalk, alignment marks can be made on both the main canopy and the side sections, every 3 to 4 in (7.5 to 10 cm), so that at any stage the correct relationship between all components can be confirmed.

Where necessary, any darts required can be made in the side sections *(not the main canopy)*, and at every stage the side pieces can be offered up to the main canopy and the vehicle, to check on progress.

It is essential to finish off the rear edge of the hood before tackling the sections around the doors. Once you have a good fit around the rear of the assembly, it is relatively straightforward to work towards the front of the car, pulling the sides taut as you do so. It is absolutely vital that the fit around the doors and side windows is perfect – take time to ensure that this is the case.

When assembling the main canopy and side sections of the hood, there are several ways in which the stitching may be arranged. In each case, it is essential that the 'grooves' between adjacent sections of hooding material are arranged so that rainwater cannot sit in them, looking for the easiest route into the car! Instead, angle the seams so that water runs harmlessly away from the joins.

INVISIBLE STITCHING

Where desired, it is possible to form seams in the hooding which are not visible from outside the car. This is, in fact, a very straightforward operation, as illustrated in the following sequence, which shows a test piece being made.

▲ *11.74. First lay the adjoining sections together, edge to edge, and make easily distinguishable alignment marks on both pieces, for instant recognition and realignment, if required. In this case, the mohair hooding was marked with tailor's chalk.*

▲ *11.75. Turn the adjoining sections face to face, and align the marks made previously. For easy lining-up, the marks can either be extended to the back of the material, or the hooding can be folded back, as shown, to establish where the next mark is. The sections can then be sewn together, with a line of stitches approximately ½ in (13mm) inboard of the adjacent edges. Recheck the alignment as you proceed.*

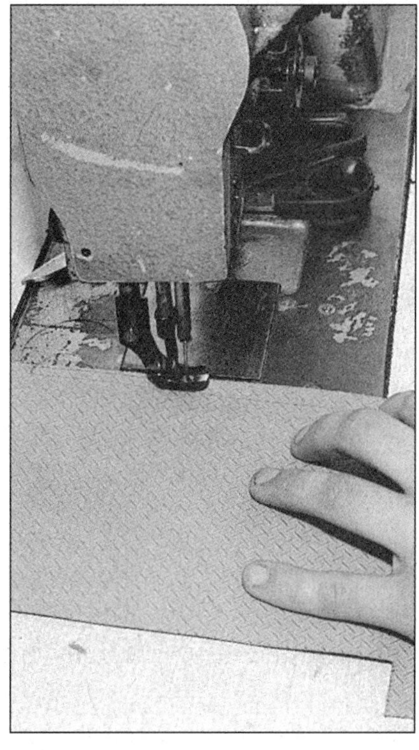

▲ *11.76. If you now run a second line of stitching close to the adjacent edges of material, the joint will be stronger and it will be easier to apply glue during a subsequent operation.*

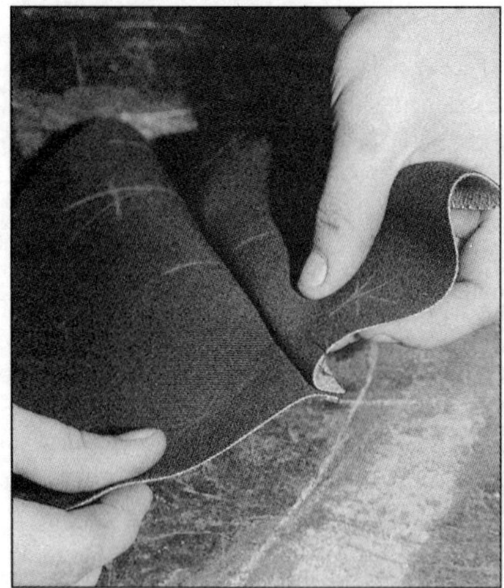

▲ *11.77. Always ensure that the outer side of the joint is angled so that rainwater will run away from the groove in the material. Imagine that, in the photograph, the lower part of the hooding is on the left-hand side. If the flange on the reverse side of the hooding (formed by the sewing operations shown in photographs 11.75 and 11.76) is bent towards the right (top), as shown – and then secured in this position by gluing – all will be well, since water will run away downhill to the left without becoming trapped in the groove.*

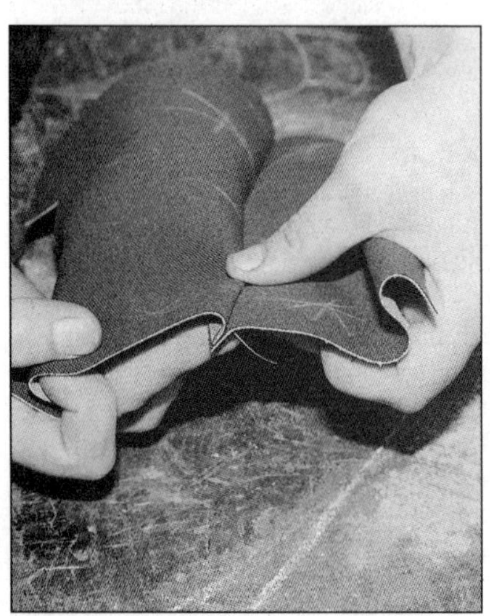

▲ *11.78. Still imagining that the lower section of the hooding is on the left-hand side, if the flange is bent to the left (downhill), the water will run down from the right-hand side and become trapped. This can be avoided by careful thought as you proceed.*

▲ *11.79. Having established which way the flange has to be bent, apply contact adhesive to the flange itself and to the corresponding section of the back of the material to which it is to be joined. Allow the adhesive to turn tacky, then ...*

▲ *11.80. ... carefully fold over the flange onto the pre-glued section of hooding, while at the same time gently pulling in opposite directions the adjoining sections of material, for a neat finish.*

▲ *11.81. Turn over the hooding and use a clean, rubber-faced mallet to tap down the seam. This will give a nice, crisp fold line.*

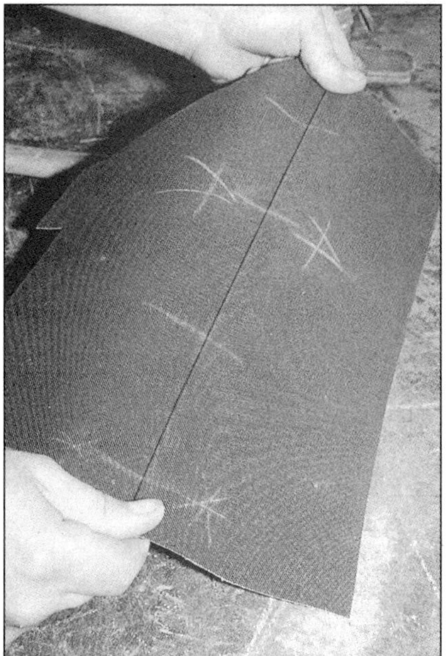

▲ *11.82. The result is a strong joint, with no stitches visible from the outside of the hood. If the hood is to be a single layer type, and it is desired that the stitching should also be invisible from the inside of the hood, webbing straps can be positioned on the hood frame directly beneath the seams, as shown in the section on single layer and early hoods.*

▲ *11.83. The chalk marks are easily removed from mohair by the application of a little water and a stiff brush.*

TONNEAU COVERS

As far as construction is concerned, tonneau covers are made in the same way as a single layer hood. To make a new one, first remove the original from the vehicle, and use it as a pattern to mark out the replacement on similar, new material. The techniques involved in sewing sections together, and in binding the edges, are the same as those already covered for the main hood. Sometimes, humps are incorporated for the steering wheel, also zip fasteners. Their methods of attachment to the tonneau cover will become obvious from a close examination of the original.

HOOD REPAIRS?

In most cases, once a hood is badly damaged – usually by splitting or tearing – a replacement is the best answer. It is sometimes possible to patch a hood which shows only minor damage, but there are potential problems. The first is that whatever you do, the stitching around the repair patch will be visible. Also, the hood will have to be removed from the vehicle for all but the smallest repairs, and if it is old (and therefore probably weak) it may be better to replace it at this stage.

If you do attempt a patch repair, an effective, if not invisible repair can be effected by attaching the patch to the inside of the hooding material. Make the patch – of the same material – around 1 in (2.5 cm). bigger than the damaged area, all round, and radius the corners of the patch. This will help make them less obtrusive, and less liable to lift.

Prior to gluing and then sewing the patch in position, tape together the damaged edges of the hood from the outside. This will help keep the edges in the correct relative positions while the contact adhesive is hardening, and will prevent any adhesive from reaching the outside of the hooding.

When the glue has fully hardened, sew around the edges of the patch, using thread to match the colour of the hood. Again, this will make the patch less obvious.

Finally, when the hood has been refitted to the car, and the hood is up, apply seam sealer to the repair seams to prevent the ingress of rainwater.

PROBLEM PREVENTION

Having made a hood to be proud of, it pays to look after it. As mentioned earlier, it is wise to store the car only with the hood raised, rather than folded back, or severe creases can form and the hood can become misshapen.

In addition, it is not a good idea to fold the hood down and leave it down when wet; wherever possible, allow it to fully dry after rain, before stowing it. Try to avoid storing the car in a garage with a wet hood, even overnight, and especially not for days on end.

SUN ROOFS

Sun roofs come in a variety of shapes and sizes, and it is impossible to generalize on construction and installation techniques. However, all have some similarities. In particular, most types are prone to leakage as they age, and in virtually all, problems can occur with water drain tubes (whether of rubber or steel) which are usually hidden and very often extremely difficult to get at unless large sections of the interior are removed!

Electrically operated varieties are usually fine when the car is relatively new, but problems can begin to occur as time passes, with clogging of the operating mechanism by dirt, and breakdown of electrical connections often being prime reasons for malfunctions.

Having cheered you up, it should be said that in most cases a detailed examination of the roof and the manner in which it was originally installed will provide valuable clues regarding the nature of the problems to be dealt with, and the required rectification work. Nearly always, this requires patience and attention to detail, rather than special skills.

STEEL, FABRIC OR GLASS?

In pre-war days, many sliding head models were equipped as standard with steel or fabric-covered panels. These sat on runners – sometimes external, sometimes concealed – on/within the main roof panel of the vehicle. Normally these can be removed by dismantling the runner assembly and removing the complete system from the car, or by unscrewing the locking handle and front rail of the sun roof, to enable it to be lifted out.

Many cars of the 1940s and 50s incorporated similar systems. In each case close study of the roof should provide clues, but it is always worth looking at the manufacturers' original manual for the car – sometimes 'factory fit' sun roofs are covered in great detail. It is also worth talking to other owners of cars similar to yours – they may have useful experience in this area to pass on.

Later models often have folding fabric roofs, or glass panelled tilt/slide roofs, either installed when the car was new, or retro-fitted later. The latter are often riveted in place within the vehicle, and extrication can take some time. In all cases, take very great care when the sun roof is removed – the raw edges of the steel roof panel of the car can have very sharp edges!

DRAIN TUBES

Rainwater drain tubes can take the form of steel or rubber tubes, designed to direct water away from the channel usually surrounding the sun roof, and typically down into the wheel arches to drain harmlessly onto the ground (in theory).

Troubles can include blockage of these tubes (normally small bore types which can become clogged with leaves, dirt, etc.) and physical deterioration of them, often accelerated by blockages! First signs of such problems include damp patches appearing in the corners of the headlining during heavy rain, eventually leading to the arrival in quantity of water in your lap or over your head during cornering.

Gentle probing of the drain tubes with a length of stiff wire can help to shift blockages, but if the tubes have become perished (rubber) or rusty (steel), the only cure is replacement or repair by welding in new metal, respectively. The problem here is that this almost always entails removal of the main headlining of the vehicle, to enable the affected areas to be reached.

COLD AND WET!

A few years ago I owned a 1950s Austin saloon with a standard-fit Pytchley steel sun roof. This was lovely in the summer, but one wet night during the first winter I had the car (when it was already 30 years old), the roof's steel drain tube, exiting from the driver's side front corner of the frame, succumbed to terminal corrosion, and what seemed like gallons of icy water cascaded all over me as I made a left turn!

The next day, out came the headlining (for there was no alternative) and the sun roof itself, and I made welded repairs to the steel section of the drain tube (and the others which were nearly as rusty), and replaced the original, rotting rubber sections of piping with reinforced nylon tube. It was expensive but should never rot again! Such tube can be obtained in various diameters from specialist suppliers of pipework and tubing.

If you do need to weld sections into rotten drain tubes, damage to nearby paintwork can be prevented by applying 'heat sink' compound to the outside of the roof. A similar, less expensive alternative can be to apply damp rags to the paintwork, redampening them when they start to steam. That's how I tackled the tubes on my newly resprayed Austin, and I was thankful that the paintwork didn't suffer.

In any event, if you have to tackle this sort of work, bargain also on replacing the main headlining of the vehicle (it will probably be water-stained anyway), also the miniature lining of the sun roof panel itself.

SUN ROOF RESTORATION

Usually, steel-panelled sun roofs are found to be in good condition. If not, rectification normally involves the eradication of rust, and repainting, as for any exterior bodywork panels. However, fabric-covered sun roofs can deteriorate, suffering in particular from tears and brittleness, as they age.

In such cases, good looks and weather-resistance qualities can be restored by removing the sun roof from the car (usually by unscrewing, or by drilling out the securing rivets), then replacing the inner and outer linings – using techniques similar to those already covered in Chapter 8 and Chapter 9.

The following photographic sequence shows dismantling an original Webasto folding type sun roof, taken from a 1970s Saab estate car. Many other types of roof are essentially similar in construction, but in all cases, a detailed preliminary examination is worthwhile, to establish how the roof was originally made and installed.

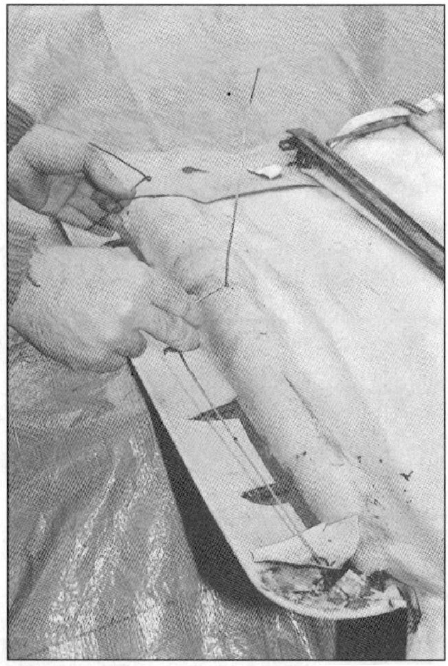

▲ *11.84. With the sun roof removed from the car, release the two sewn-in steel cables which tension the sides of the roof. On this roof, they are fastened at the rear of the assembly.*

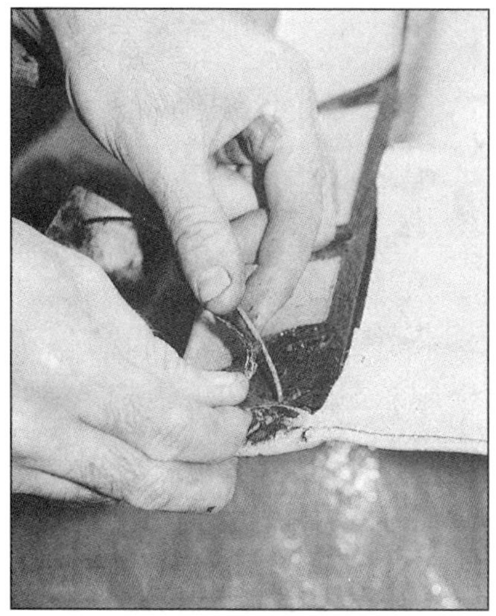

▲ *11.85. Carefully peel back each corner of the covering material (from around the cables), which is glued to steel cross-bars at the front and rear of the assembly.*

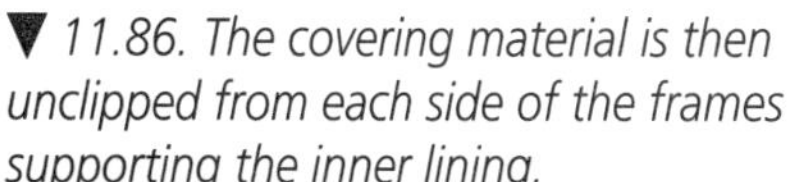

▼ *11.86. The covering material is then unclipped from each side of the frames supporting the inner lining.*

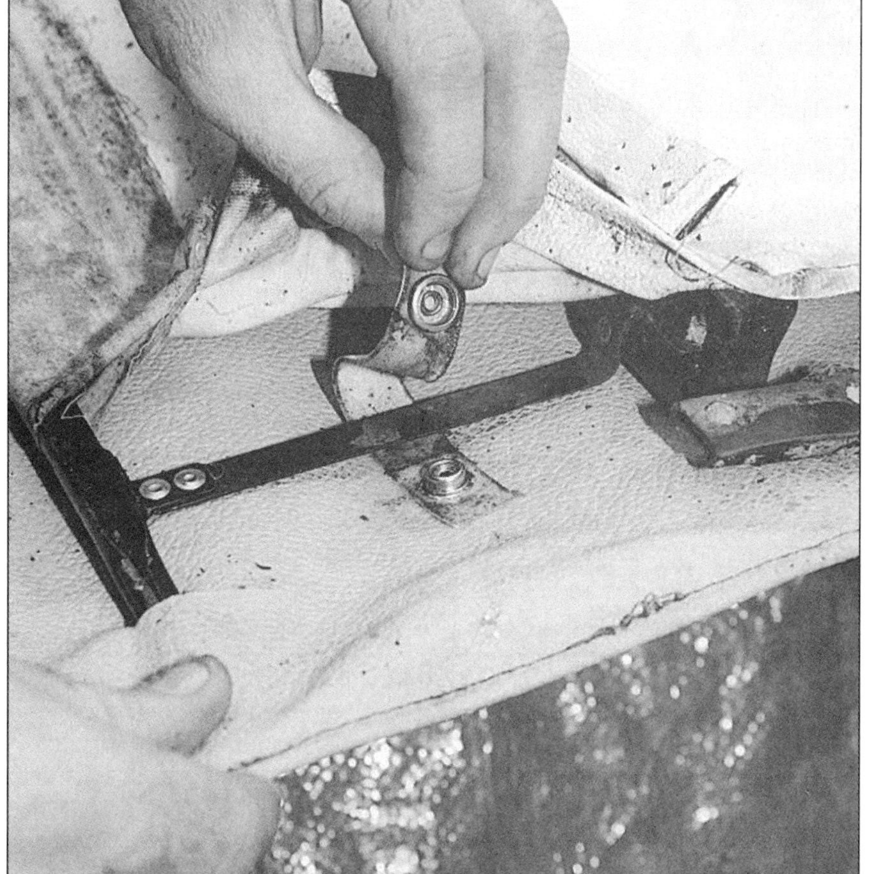

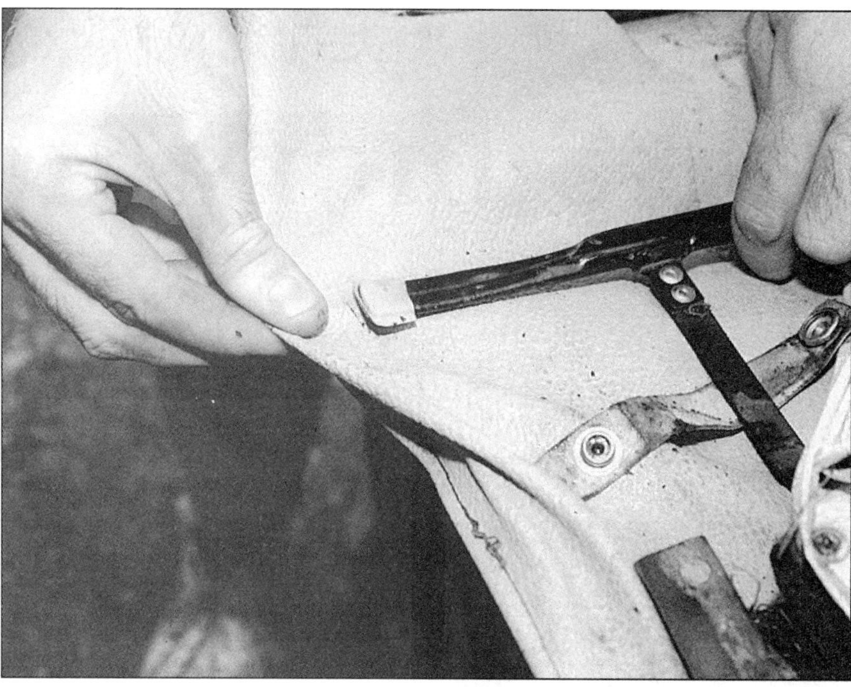

▲ *11.87. The cross-bars supporting the inner lining can now be carefully withdrawn from their slots/pockets in the covering material.*

▲ *11.88. The inner and outer assemblies can now be separated.*

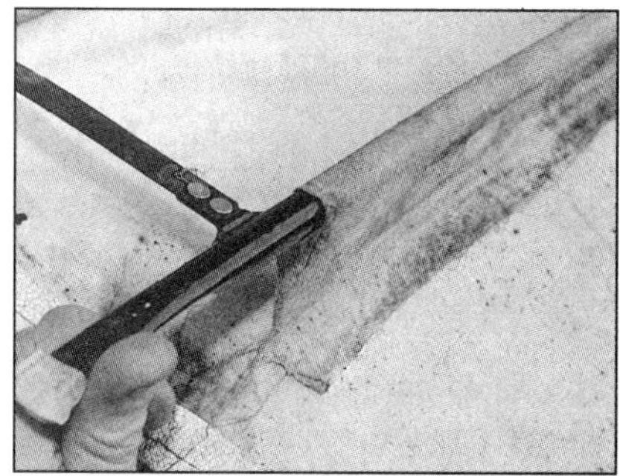

▲ *11.89. The bars supporting the inner lining are attached to it by means of pockets of material – in effect the inner lining hangs from the bars, when the roof is assembled. To remove the bars from the pockets, the rivets securing the bars to the longitudinal members must be drilled out.*

Chapter 12

Sundry items

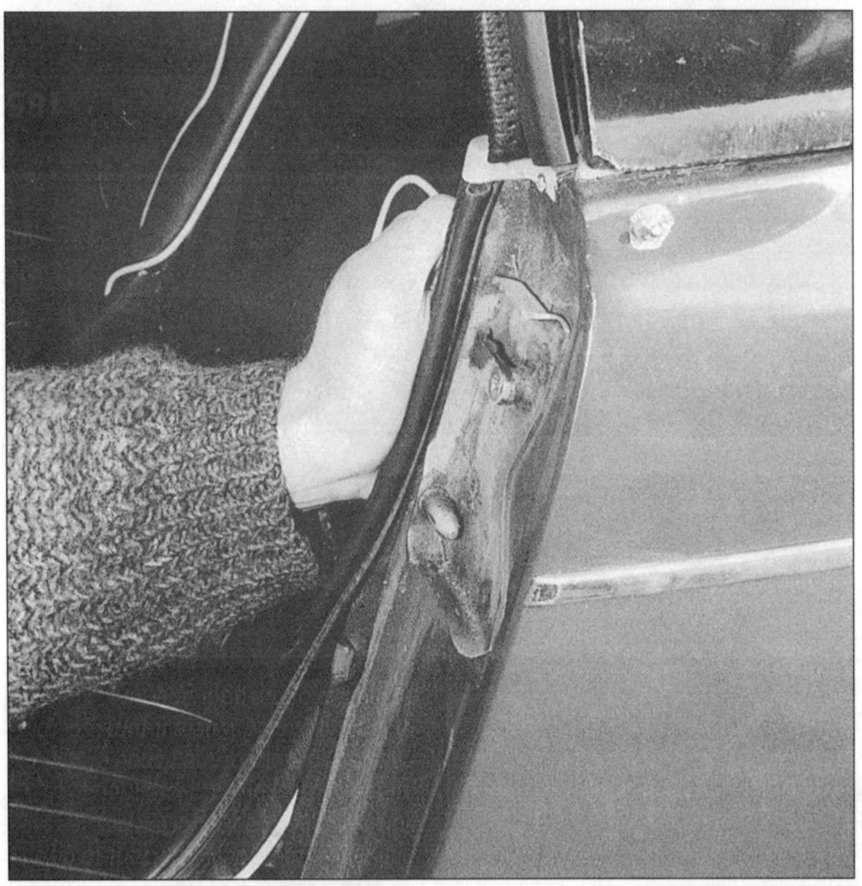

As well as the specific major areas covered by preceding chapters, there are a number of other operations which are important, but which don't fall neatly under any of the main headings. This chapter deals with these operations, many of which are vital to give your car interior that finishing touch which distinguishes a really tidy car from an average example.

DOOR APERTURE TRIMS

Several types of trim/seal can be encountered, depending on the age and type of vehicle. Furflex draught excluder was used on many cars. This consists of a rubber tube, within a fur-like outer covering. It is attached to the vehicle by means of a material flange, which is glued or tacked in position around each door aperture. It is readily available from vehicle trim suppliers. The photographs in this section show Furflex being fitted to a Mark II Jaguar saloon.

Other varieties of aperture trims include U-shaped aluminium snap-on types, covered with woven or fur-like material, with or without an integral rubber sealing tube attached. All are easily obtained, but ensure that what you are buying exactly matches the original in terms of size and method of fitting. Difficulties can arise if it does not! The sequence shows the fitting of a commonly encountered variety, as fitted to an MG Midget. It was also used on a wide range of BMC saloon cars.

In every case, it pays to keep the original trims until the new ones have been installed – the originals can provide useful clues to the length of trim required around each door, and can also give indications regarding where and how the trims negotiate sharp bends, also the starting and finishing points around each aperture – and so on.

Note that in some older cars, 'hidem' banding was used around the door apertures. When dismantling, note the sequence of fitting – the banding is usually fitted after the draught excluder, and serves to hide the cut edges of the headlining and draught excluder.

FITTING FURFLEX

▶ *12.1. Position the draught excluder around the door aperture, starting the trim in the same place as the original. If there is no trace of the original trim, make allowance for sill tread plates, etc. – the ends of the new draught excluder normally tuck under such plates.*

▼ *12.2. To enable the Furflex to negotiate the tight bends which usually feature in the corners of the door apertures, it is necessary to make a series of V-cuts in the material flange. Don't take the cuts too close to the main body of the draught excluder, or they will show.*

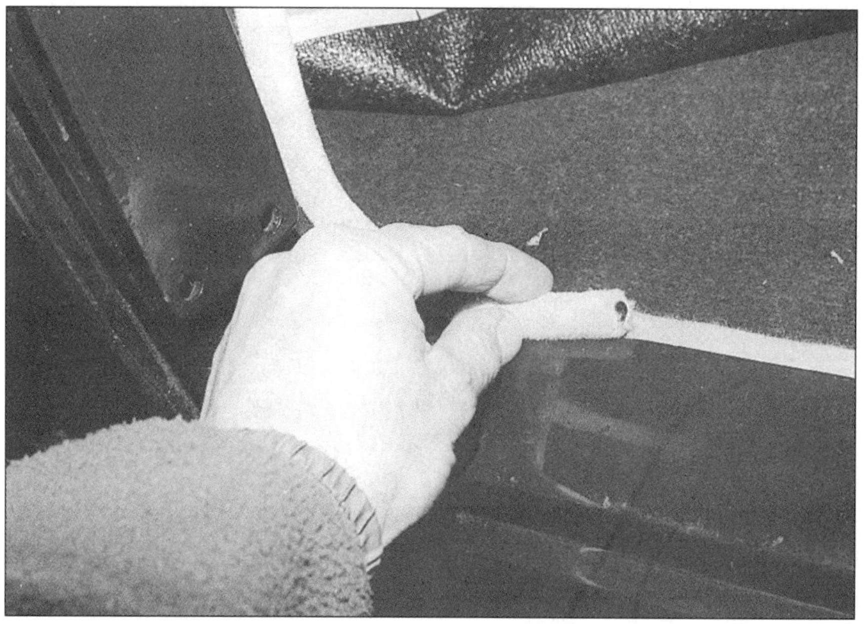

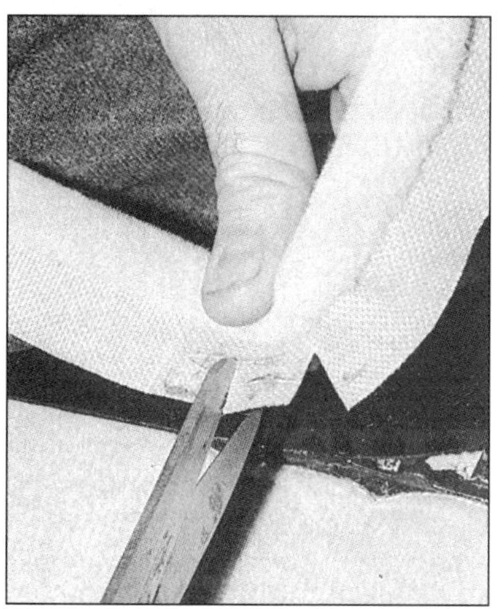

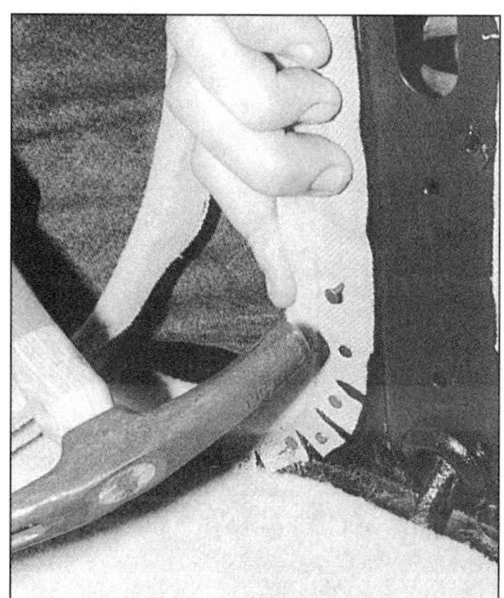

▲ *12.3. Secure the Furflex to the vehicle by tacking the flange to the built-in tacking strip, where fitted.*

◀ *12.4. For sections where there is no tacking strip evident, apply contact adhesive both to the flange of the draught excluder, and to the corresponding part of the vehicle, and allow it to turn tacky. Take great care to ensure that the adhesive does not extend beyond the perimeter of the flange, when fitted.*

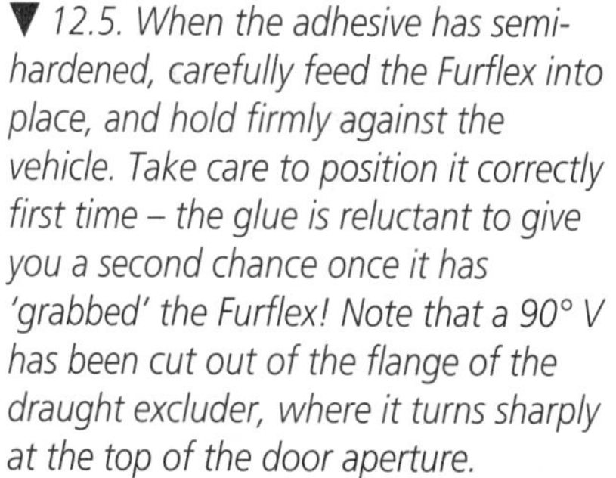

▼ *12.5. When the adhesive has semi-hardened, carefully feed the Furflex into place, and hold firmly against the vehicle. Take care to position it correctly first time – the glue is reluctant to give you a second chance once it has 'grabbed' the Furflex! Note that a 90° V has been cut out of the flange of the draught excluder, where it turns sharply at the top of the door aperture.*

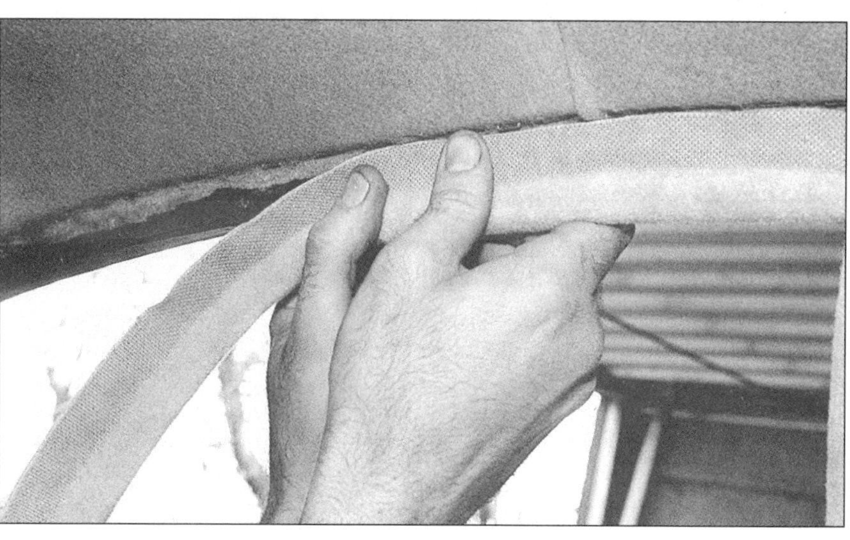

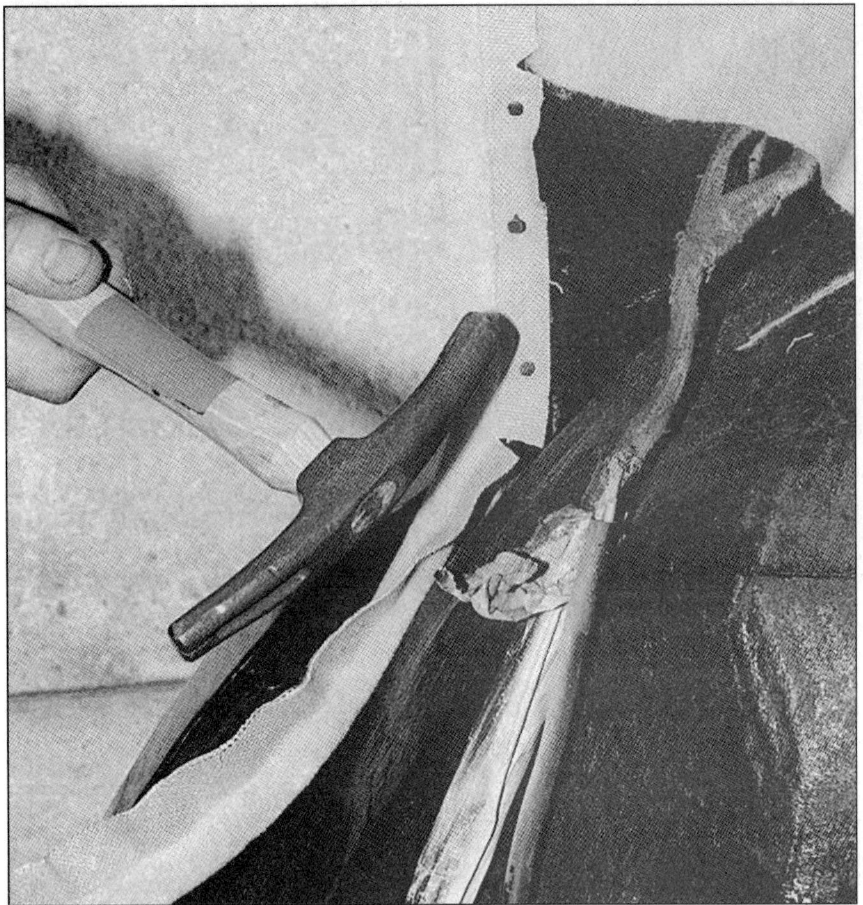

▲ *12.6. The rear door apertures on this Jaguar are multi-curved, so once again it is necessary to make a series of slots and V-cuts when fitting the Furflex around them. Take your time to get it right!*

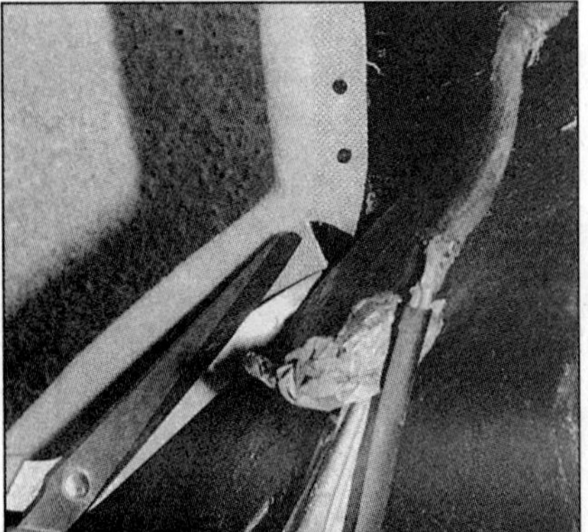

▲ *12.7. The width of the V-cuts required will depend on the angle through which the Furflex needs to be turned. Start by making a fairly narrow cut, and widen if necessary – you can't do it the other way round!*

▼ *12.8. The Furflex, once fitted, should sit neatly all around the aperture. Final smoothing into place is often necessary as fitting progresses.*

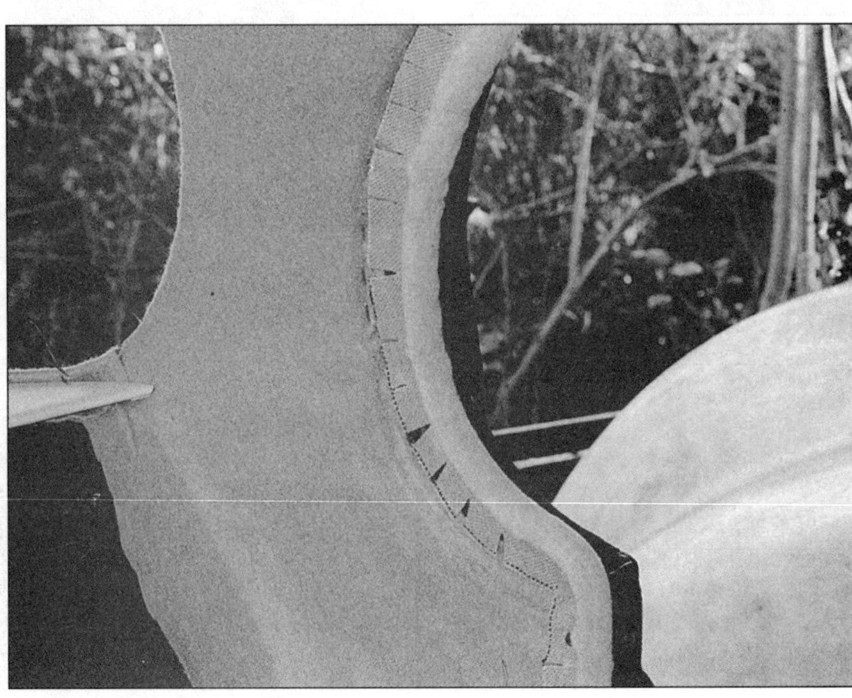

CLIP-ON DOOR APERTURE TRIMS

This sequence shows the fitting of clip-on trim/seal assemblies to a 1964 MG Midget. On this car the trim comprises a U-shaped aluminium channel, covered with fabric and joined to a rubber sealing tube.

The open side of the U-channel pushes over the flange around the door aperture (having barbed retaining clips at intervals around the aperture) and the channel is then squeezed together to hold it in place. The principles of fitting shown here apply to many cars.

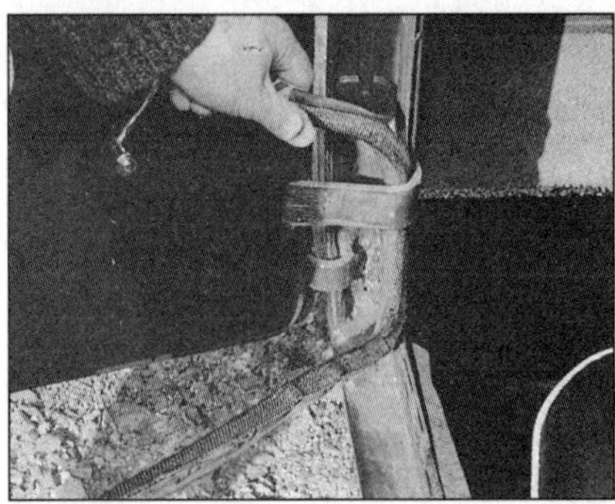

▲ *12.9. First, remove the old trim. This is gently eased away from the door aperture. To start with, you may need to spread apart the open end of the U-shaped channel with an old screwdriver.*

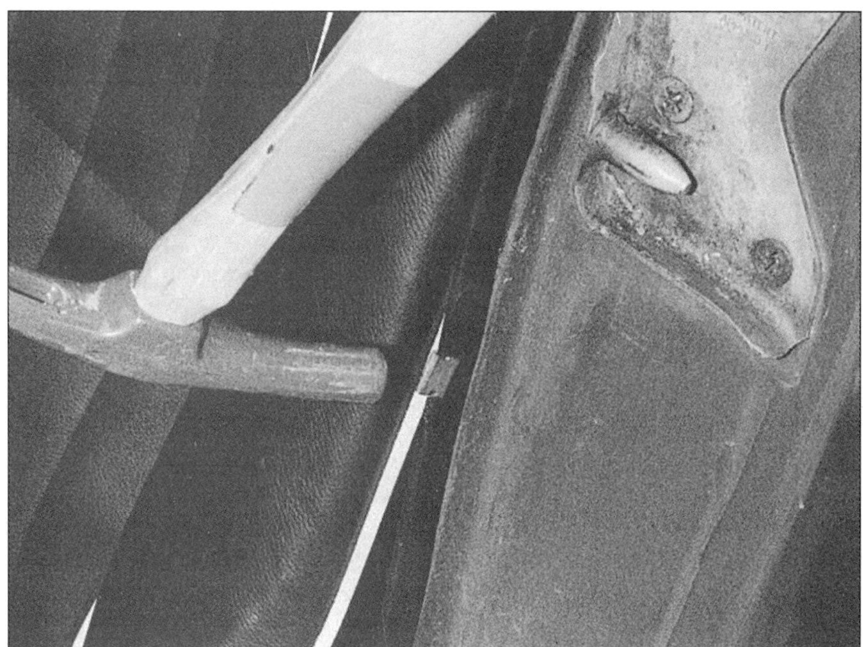

▲12.10. If necessary, clean up, de-rust and paint the aperture lip, and allow to dry. Next, ensure that adequate numbers of barbed retaining clips are fitted at intervals around the door aperture. Buy and fit new (they simply tap into place) if the old ones are broken or missing.

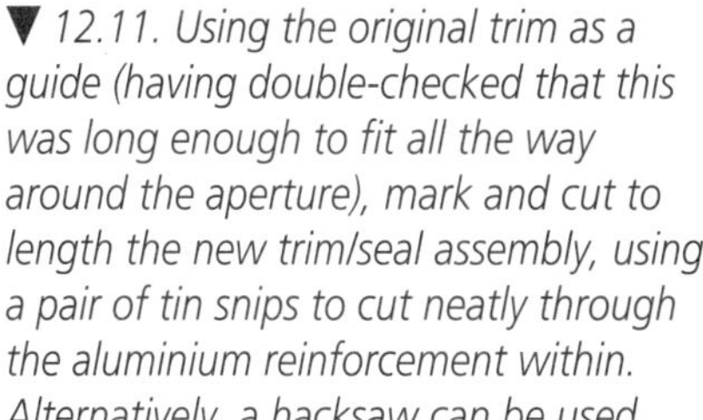

▼ 12.11. Using the original trim as a guide (having double-checked that this was long enough to fit all the way around the aperture), mark and cut to length the new trim/seal assembly, using a pair of tin snips to cut neatly through the aluminium reinforcement within. Alternatively, a hacksaw can be used.

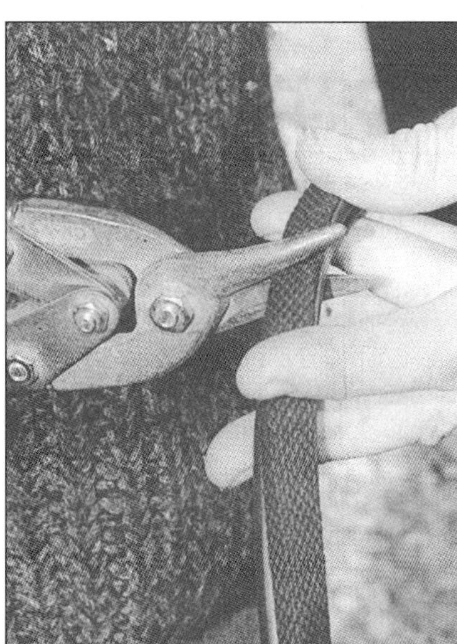

▼ 12.12. Use an old screwdriver to spread apart the U-shaped aluminium channel forming the backbone of the trim assembly. Mind your fingers!

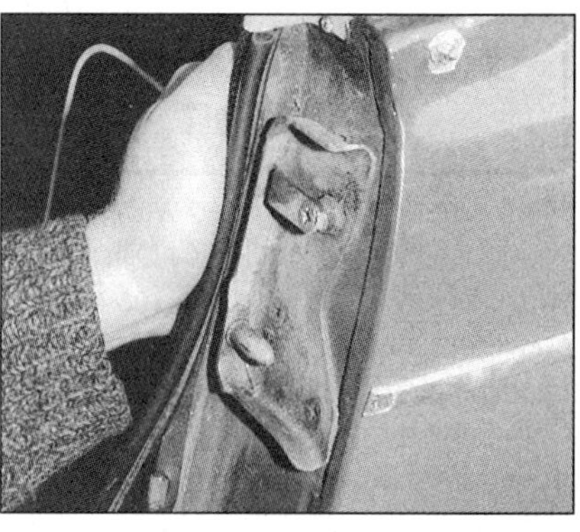

▲ 12.13. Carefully offer up the trim to the vehicle, and use the heel of a hand to push it into place. Start at one end, gradually feeding the trim into position, and taking particular care when negotiating tight corners. Ensure that the open ends of the sealing tubes are correctly positioned under their cappings (where fitted). A self-grip wrench, with the jaws shielded by a soft cloth, can be useful for final squeezing together of the aluminium channel once the trim is in place.

REAR WINDOW BLINDS

Many older cars were fitted with rear window blinds, controlled by pull cords, with the forward end usually mounted above the driver's seat at the side of the headlining. Some types pull upwards, from behind the rear seat, others drop down, from above the rear window.

In every case, it is important to study and note the manner in which the blind and its pull cord(s) are assembled. Ideally, make sketches and/or take photographs or video film to be sure that you will be able to refit the blind in the same way as originally installed.

Take particular care not to damage or lose the small fixing buttons and screw mountings, as replacements can be difficult to find in good condition.

The following abbreviated photograph sequence shows how the rear blind from a pre-war Flying Standard saloon was tackled.

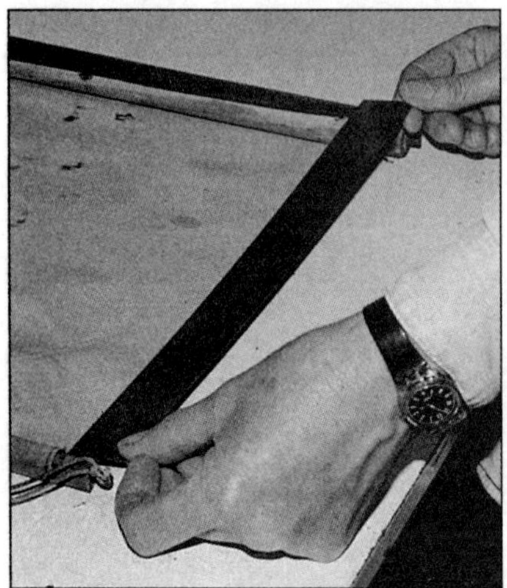

▲ *12.14. The first step, after removing the blind and its pull cord assembly from the vehicle, is to unroll the blind and measure the material, transferring the dimensions onto a sheet of new calico or thinner polycotton fabric. Allow sufficient additional material to provide hems at the sides and bottom of the blind, to match the original. Normally, the lower hem is wider, forming a pocket in which the wooden bar, attached to the pull cord, is placed.*

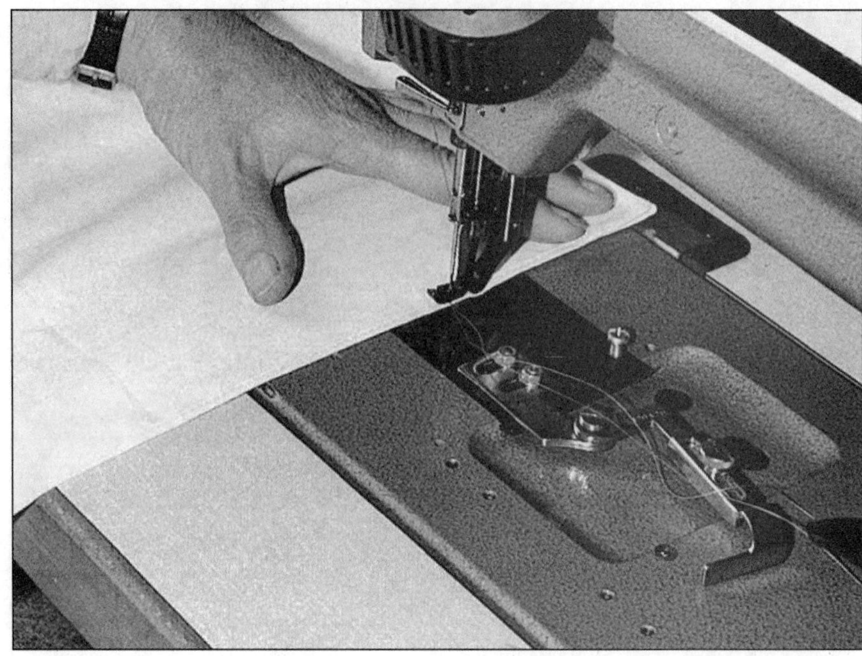

▲ *12.15. Sew the hems neatly in position. A domestic sewing machine can be used for this job, if you don't have an industrial-type machine. There is no need to form a hem at the top, since the material is glued directly to the wooden roller.*

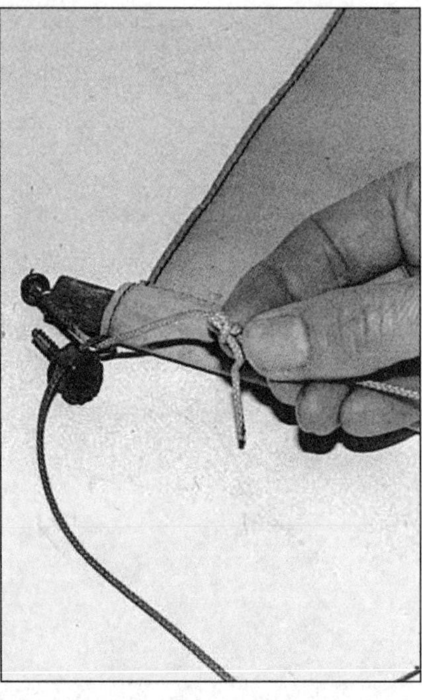

▲ *12.16. Only after making careful note of the positions of the various cord(s) and their knots, detach the cord(s) from one end of the operating bar.*

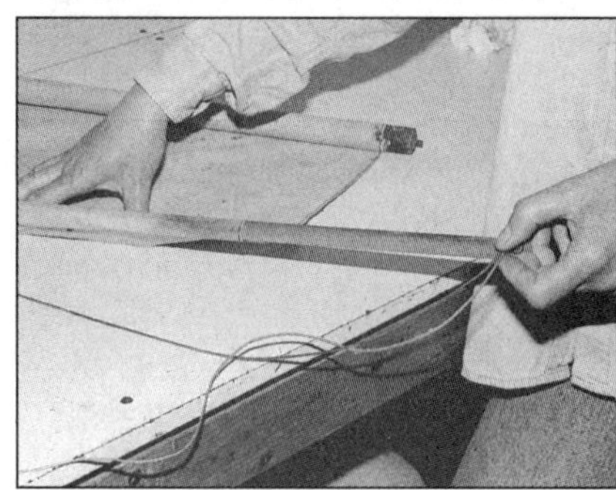

▲ *12.17. Withdraw the wooden bar from the blind. If in good condition, simply transfer the bar to the new blind, replacing the cord if there is any doubt about its condition. Refit the blind to the car, with the fixings in their original positions.*

OTHER ITEMS

Other items encountered can include sun visors, centre consoles, and so on. Such components often require re-covering. The techniques described earlier in the book – particularly those in Chapter 6 and Chapter 8 should enable you to successfully tackle this work. In every case, a close study of the original item is required, followed by making patterns from it, then transferring the profiles to the new covering material, which is then cut out and secured in place – usually by the use of contact adhesive.

Appendix – Useful Addresses

The following lists (which are not exhaustive) are intended to provide a helpful guide to some of the firms and individuals who are able to assist those restoring their car interiors. They concentrate on those who can help with the supply of tools, materials, and the more specialised services, and for space reasons deliberately do not, for example, include all the businesses which carry out only trim renovation work (and which do not, generally, supply materials), since the listing of all of them would, in itself, fill a book!

However, many of these firms are small and locally-based, and can be found listed in 'Yellow Pages' and 'The Thomson Directory' under the heading 'Car Trimmers and Upholsterers'.

In cases where materials are supplied *and* trimming/upholstery services are offered, the trimming/upholstery service is often the main part of the business, and we have, if appropriate, indicated this in brackets, after details of the materials supplied.

In compiling these lists - in purely alphabetical order - we have also endeavoured to include suppliers of 'general' tools, equipment, materials and specialist services to suit a wide range of vehicles. However, it is worth noting that, in addition, upholstery supplies and 'pre-made' trim sets for individual models are sometimes available from suppliers of parts for that specific vehicle. Further information - and, sometimes, recommendations - on these can be obtained by joining the relevant 'one make' club and talking to other owners.

It should be noted that inclusion of a firm or individual in the lists does not imply recommendation, and readers are advised to check personally with regard to the availability, quality and cost of materials and services on offer.

Entries are listed under the headings 'Tools and Equipment', 'Suppliers of Materials, Specialist Services, etc.' and 'Specifically Woodwork', as appropriate.

TOOLS AND EQUIPMENT

Specialist Tools and Equipment:
Frost Auto Restoration Techniques Ltd., Crawford Street, Rochdale, Lancashire, OL16 5NU. Tel. (01706) 658619. Fax. (01706) 860338.
Website: www.frost.co.uk
E-mail: order@frost.co.uk
Varied line-up of special implements and equipment to aid d-i-y restoration of interiors and general vehicle renovation work. Detailed, fully illustrated catalogue available.

Heavy duty sewing machines:
J and B Sewing Machines Co. Ltd., Curlew Close, Queensway Meadows, Newport, South Wales, NP9 0SY. Tel. (01633) 281555. Fax. (01633) 281666.
Website: www.jbsew.co.uk
E-mail: info@jbsew.co.uk
Sales, service, repairs, spares and attachments, also machine hire.

Sewtech, Rail Crossing Yard, Dyehouse Lane, Glastonbury, Somerset, BA6 9LZ. Tel. (01458) 835375. Fax. (01458) 833009.
Website: www.sewtech.co.uk
E-mail: sales@sewtech.co.uk
Heavy duty sewing machines, suitable for leather and other upholstery work, etc., sales, servicing, machine hire, spares, and so on.

SUPPLIERS OF MATERIALS, SPECIALISED SERVICES, ETC.

Aldridge Trimming, Castle House, Drayton Street, Wolverhampton, West Midlands, WV2 4EF. Tel. (01902) 710805 and 710408. Fax. (01902) 427474.
Website: www.aldridge.co.uk
E-mail: mail@aldridge.co.uk
Interior trim, including hoods (established 1931).

All Trim, The Old Works, Dover Street, Maidstone, Kent, ME16 8LE.
Tel. (01622) 721465.
Materials and sundries supplied by mail order (main business - trimming/upholstery services).

Autohides, also **Car Hoods Direct Ltd.**, 16, Maidstone Road, Pembury, Tunbridge Wells, Kent, TN2 4DE. Tel. (08456) 588007. Fax. (08456) 588009.
Website: www.autohides.co.uk and www.carhoodsdirect.co.uk
E-mail: sales@autohides.co.uk and sales@carhoodsdirect.co.uk
Leather hides and other materials supplied for automotive upholstery, also hoods supplied/fitted.

Auto Interiors, 56, Norfolk Street, Liverpool, L1 0BE. Tel. (0151) 708 8881.
Fax. (0151) 708 6002.
'Traditional' quality carpet and jute soundproofing makers.

The Automobile Trimmings Co., Stonebridge Works, Cumberland Road, Stanmore, Middlesex, HA7 1EL. Tel. 020 8204 8242. Fax. 020 8204 0255.
Website: www.automobiletrim.com
E-mail: info@automobiletrim.com
Manufacturers of car carpet, weatherstrip, door seals, edge trims and interior upholstery. Established 1952.

Automotive and Industrial Chemicals Ltd., Unit 9, Hendy Industrial Estate, Hendy, Pontardulais, Swansea, Dyfed, SA4 1XP.
Tel. (01792) 884348.
Manufacturers of Vinylkote and associated preparation substances for restoring/changing the colour of interior soft plastics and leather.

The Automotive Interiors Company, 16A, Beamsley Road, Eastbourne, East Sussex, BN22 7EH. Tel. (01323) 416606.
Fax. (01323) 64783.
Quality fitted carpets made as close as possible to originals.

Kevin Baggs Trimming, Unit 6, Cortry Close, Branksome, Poole, Dorset, BH12 4BQ.
Tel. (01202) 744544.
Trimming/upholstery services, including hoods, carpets, seats, trim panels, etc.
Website: www.kbaggstrimming.co.uk
E-mail: info@kbaggstrimming.co.uk

Paul Beck Vintage Supplies Ltd., Crosswinds, Happisburgh, Norwich, Norfolk, NR12 0RX. Tel. (01692) 650455.
Fax. (01692) 651451.
Wide range of trimming materials and fasteners, etc., for pre-1960 vehicles. Illustrated catalogue available.

Bradleys Plastic Finishers, Old Station Yard, Main Road, Marlesford, Woodbridge, Suffolk, IP13 0AG.
Tel. (01728) 747900.
Stockists of Vinylkote and associated preparation materials for re-colouring trim panels, etc.

Bridge of Weir Leather Company, Baltic Works, Bridge of Weir, Renfrewshire, PA11 3RH. Tel. (01505) 612132.
Fax. (01505) 614964.
Website: www.bowleather.co.uk
E-mail: mail@bowleather.co.uk
Suppliers of leather.

Bristol Upholstery Spring Co. Ltd., 79A, Grove Road, Fishponds, Bristol, BS16 2BP. Tel./Fax. (0117) 958 3995. Suppliers of replacement hand sprung seats and backs.

British Trim Company, 'Brambles', Catsash Road, Christchurch, Newport, Gwent, NPE 1JJ. Tel. (01633) 423976. Trim (including carpet, vinyls and headlining materials) to original specification for Minis.

Car Trims, 2, Brook Yard, Chatsworth Road, Brampton, Chesterfield, S40 2AH. Tel. (01246) 276507. Materials and fasteners for d-i-y trimming (main business - trimming/upholstery services).

Cheshire Coachtrimmers, Howshoots Farm, Knutsford Road, Grappenhall, Warrington, Cheshire, WA4 4SJ. Tel. (01925) 753767. Materials for sale (main business - trimming/upholstery services, leather renovation, etc.).

Classic Steering Wheels, Truro, Cornwall, TR1 1XS. Tel. (01872) 865449. Steering wheels.

Classic Sunroofs, 7, Nightingale Walk, Billingshurst, West Sussex, RH14 9TY. Tel. (01403) 785326. Sun roofs, headlinings, vinyl roofs - etc.

Coach Trimming Specialists, 108A, Station Street East, Coventry. Tel. (01203) 637472. Trimming materials supplied (and coach trimming services).

Coachtrimming Supplies, Unit 6, Saxon Way, off Chelmsley Road, Chelmsley Wood, Birmingham, B37 5AY. Tel. (0121) 694 5664. Fax. (0121) 694 5665. Trimming materials supplied.

The Complete Automobilist, Crosswinds, Happisburgh, Cambs., Norwich, Norfolk, NR12 0RX. Tel. (01692) 650084. Fax. (01692) 651451. Website: www.completeautomobilist.co.uk E-mail: info@completeautomobilist.co.uk Interior (and exterior) fittings, etc. for veteran, vintage and classic cars (mail order service).

Coral Trim, 47, Herbert March Close, Radyr Vale, Cardiff, Wales. Tel. (01222) 552104. Suppliers of trimming materials and accessories for vintage and classic vehicles. Mail order catalogue available.

County Radiators Ltd., 32, Brook Road, Rayleigh, Essex, SS6 7XN. Tel. (01268) 747001. Fax. (01268) 745657. Makers of car mats.

Coverdale Carpets, Coverdale House, Wetheral Close, Hindley Industrial Estate, Hindley, Wigan, Lancashire, WN2 4HS. Tel. (01942) 255535. Fax. (01942) 255524. Website: www.coverdalecarpets.com E-mail: sales@coverdalecarpets.com Manufacturers of original type carpets; several ranges available, also wide variety of trimming materials and hooding (etc.).

Creech Coachtrimming Centre, 45, Anerley Road, Crystal Palace, London, SE19 2AS. Tel. (020) 8659 4135. Fax. (020) 8659 2720. All interior trimming materials and fasteners, etc. supplied (also trimming services available).

D. H. Day, Aldrans, Church Hill, Wroughton, Swindon, Wiltshire, SN4 9JR. Tel. (01793) 812323. Fax. (01793) 845323. Steering wheel re-covering, etc.

The Don Trimming Company Ltd., 2A, Hampton Road, Erdington, Birmingham, B23 7JJ. Tel. (0121) 373 1313. Fax. (0121) 377 7631. Website: www.donhoods.com E-mail: enquiry@donhoods.com Manufacturers of hoods, tonneau covers, carpet sets, seats, trim panels and so on. Hoods available in a wide choice of materials and complete with fixings, etc. Colour leaflet available. Established 1958.

P. J. Donnelly (Rubber) Ltd., 70, Soho Road, Birmingham, B21 9SR. Tel. (0121) 551 6222. Makers of rubber mouldings, extrusions, etc.

Dugdale Vintage Motor Supplies, Vintage House, 2, Lower Polsham Road, Paignton, Devon, TQ3 2AF. Tel. (01803) 665244. Website: www.dugdalevms.co.uk E-mail: enquiries@dugdalesvms.co.uk All interior trim supplies, mouldings, fasteners, etc.

Dunlop Adhesives, Chester Road, Birmingham, B35 7AL. Tel. (0121) 373 8101. Fax (0121) 384 2826. A very wide range of adhesives to suit all aspects of vehicle interior restoration.

Earlwood Motor Products, 7A, Beaufort Road, Birkenhead, Merseyside, L41 1HE. Tel./Fax. (0151) 652 1572. Hoods, underfelt and carpet sets, trim, etc. (also trimming service available) .

The Easirider Company Ltd., S2 and S3 (second floor), Nene Centre, Freehold Street, Northampton, NN2 6EF. Tel. (01604) 714103. Fax. (01604) 714106. Website: www.easirider.co.uk E-mail: seatcovers@easirider.co.uk Makers of seat covers (sheepskin), mats, lambswool 'over rugs', etc.

East Kent Vintage Trim Supplies, Jubilee Road, Worth, near Deal, Kent, CT14 0DT. Tel. (01304) 611681. Fax. (01304) 619936. Website: www.classiccar-trim.com Screen rubbers, window channels, fasteners, etc. supplied (also trim/hood fitting service offered).

Edgware Motor Accessories, Unit 5, Ballards Mews, Edgware, Middlesex, HA8 7BN. Tel. (020) 8952 4789 or 9311. Fax. (020) 8952 4752. Manufacturers and sellers of upholstery materials, rubber seals, etc. for vehicles from 1920s onwards.

Edgware Motor Rubber and Trim, P. O. Box 1067, Bushey, Herts., WD20 4WZ. Tel. (020) 8950 4694. Fax. (020) 8950 6557. Website: www.rubbertrim.co.uk E-mail: info@rubbertrim.co.uk Rubber seals and sheet, extrusions (700 profiles on database), etc. plus vinyl and other upholstery materials supplied. Short runs of rubber mouldings made to order, with short minimum run requirements.

E.T.P. Sales and Agencies, 2, 'Goldcroft', Yeovil, Somerset, BA21 4DQ. Tel. (01935) 433538. Fax. (01935) 706874. Suppliers of fabrics, threads, hook and loop fasteners, zip fasteners, and so on and so on, in small or large quantities. Contact Mr. E.T. Patch.

Fairweather Restorations, Beulah House, High Street, Fincham, nr. King's Lynn, Norfolk, PE33 9EH. Tel. (01366) 347700. Weekend restoration courses in classic car trimming (main business - comprehensive upholstery and trimming services).

Family Repair Service, 2, Beales Close, Andover, Hampshire, SP10 1HT. Tel. (01264) 323144. Website: www.familyrepairservice.co.uk E-mail: info@familyrepairservice.co.uk Upholstery materials supplied (main business - trimming/upholstery services).

Fortés Leather Redressers, 288, Verdant Lane, Catford, London, SE6 1TW. Tel. (020) 8698 1191. Fax. (020) 8695 5950. Specialist leather re-dressers.

Frost Auto Restoration Techniques Ltd., Crawford Street, Rochdale, Lancashire, OL16 5NU. Tel. (01706) 658619. Fax. (01706) 860338. Website: www.frost.co.uk E-mail: order@frost.co.uk Broad range of materials and products to assist with restoring vehicle interiors. Items include repair kits for steering wheels, vinyl, leather and fabric, re-colouring system for interior trim, adhesives, and so on. Detailed, fully illustrated catalogue available.

Gliptone Leathercare U.K., Enterprise House, 250, Halifax Road, Todmorden, West Yorkshire, OL14 5SQ. Tel. (01706) 819365. Fax. (01706) 839962. Website: www.liquidleather.co.uk Leather maintenance/renovation - 'Liquid Leather' products – including dyes, leather food and restoration aids.

Barry Hankinson Ltd., 15, Copse Cross Street, Ross-on-Wye, Herefordshire, HR9 5PD. Tel. (01989) 565789. Fax. (01989) 567983. Interior trim and rubber seals (to original specification) for Jaguars.

Carl Howorth, 7, St. Helens Road, Retford, Notts., DN22 7HA. Tel./Fax. (01777) 705 503. Re-manufactured items of trim and carpets.

Intatrim, Unit 3, Trench Lock Industrial Estate, Sommerfeld Road, Trench Lock, Telford, Shropshire, TF1 4SW. Tel. (01952) 641712 or 506318. Trimming materials supplied (main business - trimming/upholstery services; leather restoration specialists).

Jay Products, P.O. Box 21095, Cleveland, Ohio, United States of America. Mail order supply (only) of complete d-i-y woodgraining kits for facias, door frames and so on.

Kirks, 25, Oxford Street, Swansea, West Glamorgan, SA1 3AO. Tel. (01792) 648806. Leather and vinyl colouring supplies.

Kwik Strip (U.K.) Ltd., P.O. Box 1087, Church Road, Winscombe, Avon, BS25 1BH. Tel. (01934) 843100. Fax. (01934) 844119. Service for removing varnish and paint from metal and wood (branches around Britain).

La Salle, Golygfa, Pontrhydfendigaid, Dyfed, SY25 6BB. Tel. (01974) 831659. Fax. (01974) 831530.0 Land Rover and Range Rover trim panels and headlinings made, also dashboards. Website: http://freespace.virgin.net/lasalle.trim E-mail: lasalle.trim@virgin.net

Latex Cushion Ltd., 830, Kingsbury Road, Erdington, Birmingham, B24 9PU. Tel. (0121) 373 0026. Fax. (0121) 373 4496. Specialists in Dunlopillo cushioning and industrial/tractor seating since 1937.

Leather Renovations, Norcross, Poplar Close, Bransgore, near Christchurch, Dorset, BH23 8JQ. Tel. (01425) 674060. D-I-Y kits supplied for leather and vinyl work (main business - trimming/upholstery services, interior renovation).

Leather Restorations, Tann's Yard, Irthlingborough Road (A6), Finedon, Northants., NN9 5EH. Tel. (01933) 682046. Leather and trimming materials supplied (main business - trimming/upholstery services, interior renovation).

Loctite UK (Henkel Loctite Adhesives Ltd.), Technologies House, Wood Lane End, Hemel Hempstead, Hertfordshire, HP2 4RQ. Tel. (01442) 278100. Fax. (01442) 278293. Website: www.loctite.co.uk E-mail: From within website Producers of many adhesives, including Vinyl Bond, specifically designed to bond vinyl and PVC.

Martrim Ltd., Unit 10, Millbuck Way, Springvall Industrial Estate, Sandbach, Cheshire, CW11 3HT. Tel. (01270) 767771. Fax. (01270) 767774. Website: www.martrim.co.uk E-mail: trim@martrim.co.uk Vast array of trimming materials of all types supplied.

Matco, 138, Walton Road, Liverpool, L4 4AY. Tel./Fax. (0151) 207 2858. Re-colouring materials for vinyl and leather.

D. and M. Middleton and Son, Rawfolds Mill, Cleckheaton, West Yorkshire. Tel. (01274) 871509. Fax. (01274) 869950. Carpets, seat materials, fabrics, vinyls, etc. supplied (carpets also made to order).

A. W. Midgley and Son Ltd., Combe Batch, Wedmore, Somerset, BS28 4DU. Tel. (01934) 712387. Fax. (01934) 713290. Premium leather hides supplied.

Mota-Lita Ltd., Thruxton Racing Circuit, Andover, Hampshire, SP11 8PW. Tel. (01264) 772811. Fax. (01264) 773102. Website: www.mota-lita.com E-mail: www.mota-lita.co.uk Makers of steering wheels.

Motor Upholstery Supplies, 14, Anne Road, Wellingborough, Northants., NN8 2HH. Tel. (01933) 223602 or 227166. Suppliers of materials for interior renovation.

Newton Commercial Ltd., Eastlands Industrial Estate, Leiston, Suffolk, IP16 4LL. Tel. (01728) 832880. Fax. (01728) 832881. Original specification interior trim makers, especially for Minis (traditional and new varieties), Morris Minors, and Triumph Herald, Vitesse and Spitfire models, also MGF, VW Beetle and Karmann-Ghia.

Oxted Trimming Co., Amy Road, Oxted, Surrey, RH8 0PX. Tel. (01883) 712112; Fax. (01883) 717038. Website: www.oxted-trimming.co.uk E-mail: info@oxted-trimming.co.uk Manufacture and repair of frames for hoods and seats (main business - trimming/upholstery services).

Parkstone Auto Trimming, 99, Uppleby Road, Poole, Dorset, BH12 3DD. Tel. (01202) 380907. E-mail: barrie.chappell@ntlworld.com Upholstery materials supplied (main business - trimming/upholstery services; vintage, classic and modern cars).

Pearsall's Ltd, Tancreed Street, Taunton, Somerset, TA1 1RY. Tel. (01823) 274700. Fax. (01823) 336824. Website: www.pearsallsembroidery.com E-mail: info@pearsallsembroidery.com Suppliers of threads.

Pennine Adventure, Royd Works, Hebden Bridge, Halifax, West Yorkshire. Tel./Fax. (01422) 846005. Suppliers of quality nylon/rayon car carpet.

Polyfacto Ltd., Unit 9, Station Road Industrial Estate, Hailsham, East Sussex, BN27 2EL. Tel. (01323) 841399. Fax. (01323) 841715. Trimming materials supplied for do-it-yourself use, also comprehensive interior renovation services offered.

Prestige Autotrim Products Ltd., Prestige House, Oak Tree Place, Rock Ferry, Birkenhead, Wirral, Cheshire, CH42 1 NS. Tel. (0151) 643 9555. Fax. (0151) 643 9634. Website: www.miatatops.com E-mail: sales@prestigecarhoods.com Makers of interior trim, convertible hoods and carpets in a variety of materials (also soundproofing kits supplied).

Bryan Purves, Applegarth, Holtye Road, East Grinstead, Sussex, RH19 3PP. Tel./Fax. (01342) 315065. Woodgraining effect applied to steel dashboards and door cappings, etc., also Austin Seven upholstery supplies (s.a.e. for list, please).

Renovo International Ltd., P.O. Box 404, Haywards Heath, Sussex, RH17 5YN. Tel. (01444) 443277. Fax. (01444) 455135. Website: www.renovointernational.com E-mail: From within website. Care kits and 'revivers' for soft tops.

Frank Rouse Motor Trimmers, Unit 8, Maida Vale Business Centre, Maida Vale Road, Cheltenham, Gloucestershire, GL53 7ER. Tel./Fax. (01242) 513394. Materials and fasteners available for d-i-y enthusiasts (main business - trimming/upholstery services).

SC Ltd., Units 1, 2 and 3, Hill Farm, Radlett, Herts., WD7 7HP. Tel. (01923) 853844/5; Fax. (01923) 853825.
Re-covering service for plastic steering wheels, etc.

Mike Satur Automotive Interior Design, Unit 3E, Goldthorpe Industrial Estate, Commercial Road, Goldthorpe, Rotherham, South Yorkshire, S63 9BL.
Tel. (01709) 890555. Fax. (01709) 890642.
MG interiors and dashboards manufactured, especially MGB/MGF. Interiors for other sports cars also undertaken (including Mazda MX5).

M. Segal (Motor Trimmings) Ltd., Trimcar House, 29, Blackfriars Road, Salford, Manchester, M3 7AQ. Tel. (0161) 834 7994. Fax. (0161) 832 4716.
Suppliers of carpets and all upholstery supplies.

John Skinner Manufacturing Ltd., 82b, Chesterton Lane, Cirencester, Gloucestershire, GL7 1YD.
Tel. (01285) 657410. Fax. (01285) 650013.
Manufacturer of trim for classic cars, especially Jaguars, Triumph TR and Austin Healey models.

Sound Service (Oxford) Ltd., 55, West End, Witney, Oxon, OX8 6NJ.
Tel. (08707) 203093. Fax. (01993) 779569.
Website: www.soundservice.co.uk
E-mail: soundservice@btconnect.com
Vehicle soundproofing materials supplied for d-i-y installation.

Tarot Tops, 129, Trafalgar Street, Gillingham, Kent, ME7 4RP.
Tel. (01634) 853354.
Materials and advice for d-i-y restorers (main business - trimming/upholstery services).

Tregunna Electroplating, 6-8, Hatton Row, Hatton Street, London, NW8 8PP.
Tel. (0207) 7262 5678. Fax. (0171) 724 2354.
Website: www.tregunnachrome.co.uk
E-mail: enquiries@tregunnachrome.co.uk
Makers of hood components, etc.

Trident Racing Supplies, Unit 31, Silverstone Circuit, Silverstone, Northamptonshire, NN12 8TN.
Tel. (01327) 857822. Fax. (01327) 858096.
Website: www.tridentracing.co.uk
E-mail: From within website.
Hood fasteners, etc. supplied.

Vee Bee Plastic Coatings, 70, Springfield Road, Middleton, Manchester, M24 3DL.
Tel. (0161) 643 2191.
Re-coating of steering wheels (in plastic).

Wardle Storeys, Storeys Industrial Products Ltd., Brantham, Manningtree, Essex, CO11 1NJ. Tel. (01206) 392401.
Website: www.wardlestoreys.com
Suppliers of 'Rexine', Ambla and other specialist materials.

Whittle Brothers (Curriers) Ltd., Mersey Tannery, Mersey Street, Warrington, Cheshire, WA1 2BE. Tel. (01925) 30188.
Fax. (01925) 416998.
Wide range of leather supplied for vehicle upholstery work, also colour matching and perforation service.

Woolies (I. and C. Woolstenholmes Ltd.)., Whitley Way, Northfields Industrial Estate, Market Deeping, Peterborough, Cambs., PE6 8AR.
Tel. (01778) 347347. Fax. (01778) 341847.
Website: www.woolies-trim.co.uk
E-mail: info@woolies-trim.co.uk
Comprehensive range of trimming supplies, for vehicles from the veteran and vintage eras up to the 1980s. Fast mail order service. Excellent, illustrated catalogue incorporates useful d-i-y 'hints and tips'.

SPECIFICALLY WOODWORK

B. H. Veneered Dash Facias, Unit 2, Townend Farm, Audley Road, Alsager, Staffordshire, ST7 2QR.
Tel./Fax. (01270) 883933.
Wood veneers supplied (main business - restoration and repair of wood trim, including veneering, lacquering, and polishing, etc., plus making dashboards).

John Boddys Fine Wood and Tool Store Ltd. Riverside Sawmills, Boroughbridge, North Yorkshire, YO5 9LJ.
Tel. (01423) 322370.
Website: www.john-boddy-timber.ltd.uk
E-mail: info@john-boddy-timber.ltd.uk
Timber supplied; catalogue available. Established 1935.

Charltons Timber Centre, Frome Road, Radstock, Bath, BA3 3PT.
Tel. (01761) 436229. Fax. (01761) 433903.
Veneer and wood suppliers.

City Polishers Ltd., The Fine Woodworking Group, 156, Broadgate, Weston Hills, Spalding, Lincs., PE12 6DQ. Tel./Fax. (01406) 380904.
Website: www.nicholas-martin.co.uk
E-mail: nick@nicholas-martin.co.uk
Makers and restorers of wooden dashboards (also veneering, etc.).

J. Crispin and Sons, Unit 12, Bow Industrial Park, Carpenters Road, Stratford, London, E15 2DZ.
Tel. (020) 8525 0300. Fax. (020) 8525 0070.
Website: www.jcrispinandsons.co.uk
E-mail: jcrispin@fsmail.net and capvneer@aol.com
Veneer merchants and importers (established 1900). Very large variety of woods available.

Kwik Strip (U.K.) Ltd., P.O. Box 1087, Church Road, Winscombe, Avon, BS25 1BH.
Tel. (01934) 843100. Fax. (01934) 844119.
Service for removing varnish and paint (branches around Britain).

Menim Motors, Bow Street, Langport, Somerset, TA10 9PL. Tel. (01458) 252157.
Fax. (01458) 253449.
French polishing and interior woodwork services (plus restoration of ash framing, etc.).

Oakwood, Unit 16, Old Yarn Mill, Westbury, Sherborne, Dorset, DT9 3QY.
Tel./Fax. (01935) 817295.
Specialist hardwood suppliers. Very extensive range of woods, including walnut, mahogany, ash, sycamore, oak - and so on, and so on. Helpful advice given. Cutting and planing services.

Robbins Timber, Brookgate, Ashton Vale Trading Estate, Bristol, BS3 2UN.
Tel. (0117) 9633136. Fax. (0117) 963 7927.
Website: www.robbins.co.uk
E-mail: timber@robbins.co.uk
Suppliers of wood and wood veneers.

Ken Sparks Classic Car Restorations, 31, Coppins Close, Sawtry, Hunts., PE17 5UB.
Tel. (01487) 831891 (evenings).
Wood rim steering wheels tackled (also other woodwork and trimming operations).

Henry Stringer, 47, Strings Way, Ilkley, West Yorkshire, LS29 8TE.
Tel. (01943) 602201.
Woodwork supply (and restoration) for pre-War cars, including Austin Sevens.